International and Global Marketing

Concepts and Cases

THE IRWIN/MCGRAW-HILL SERIES IN MARKETING

Levy & Weitz
RETAILING MANAGEMENT, 3/E

Levy & Weitz
ESSENTIALS OF RETAILING, 1/E

Loudon & Della Bitta
CONSUMER BEHAVIOR: CONCEPTS & APPLICATIONS, 4/E

Lovelock & Weinberg
MARKETING CHALLENGES: CASES AND EXERCISES, 3/E

Mason, Mayer & Ezell
RETAILING, 5/E

Mason & Perreault
THE MARKETING GAME!

McDonald
MODERN DIRECT MARKETING, 1/E

Meloan & Graham
INTERNATIONAL AND GLOBAL MARKETING CONCEPTS AND CASES, 2/E

Monroe
PRICING, 2/E

Moore & Pessemier
PRODUCT PLANNING AND MANAGEMENT: DESIGNING AND DELIVERING VALUE, 1/E

Oliver
SATISFACTION: A BEHAVIORAL PERSPECTIVE ON THE CONSUMER, 1/E

Patton
SALES FORCE: A SALES MANAGEMENT SIMULATION GAME, 1/E

Pelton, Strutton & Lumpkin
MARKETING CHANNELS: A RELATIONSHIP MANAGEMENT APPROACH, 1/E

Perreault & McCarthy
BASIC MARKETING: A GLOBAL MANAGERIAL APPROACH, 12/E

Perreault & McCarthy
ESSENTIALS OF MARKETING: A GLOBAL MANAGERIAL APPROACH, 7/E

Peter & Donnelly
A PREFACE TO MARKETING MANAGEMENT, 7/E

Peter & Donnelly
MARKETING MANAGEMENT: KNOWLEDGE AND SKILLS, 5/E

Peter & Olson
CONSUMER BEHAVIOR AND MARKETING STRATEGY, 4/E

Peter & Olson
UNDERSTANDING CONSUMER BEHAVIOR, 1/E

Quelch
CASES IN PRODUCT MANAGEMENT, 1/E

Quelch, Dolan & Kosnik
MARKETING MANAGEMENT: TEXT & CASES, 1/E

Quelch & Farris
CASES IN ADVERTISING AND PROMOTION MANAGEMENT, 4/E

Quelch, Kashani & Vandermerwe
EUROPEAN CASES IN MARKETING MANAGEMENT, 1/E

Rangan
BUSINESS MARKETING STRATEGY: CASES, CONCEPTS & APPLICATIONS, 1/E

Rangan, Shapiro & Moriarty
BUSINESS MARKETING STRATEGY: CONCEPTS & APPLICATIONS, 1/E

Rossiter & Percy
ADVERTISING AND PROMOTION MANAGEMENT, 2/E

Stanton, Spiro & Buskirk
MANAGEMENT OF A SALES FORCE, 10/E

Sudman & Blair
MARKETING RESEARCH: A PROBLEM-SOLVING APPROACH, 1/E

Thompson & Stappenbeck
THE MARKETING STRATEGY GAME, 1/E

Ulrich & Eppinger
PRODUCT DESIGN AND DEVELOPMENT, 1/E

Walker, Boyd & Larreche
MARKETING STRATEGY: PLANNING AND IMPLEMENTATION, 2/E

Weitz, Castleberry & Tanner
SELLING: BUILDING PARTNERSHIPS, 3/E

Zeithaml & Bitner
SERVICES MARKETING, 1/E

SECOND EDITION

International and Global Marketing

Concepts and Cases

Taylor W. Meloan
University of Southern California

John L. Graham
University of California, Irvine

Boston, Massachusetts   Burr Ridge, Illinois   Dubuque, Iowa   Madison, Wisconsin
New York, New York   San Francisco, California   St. Louis, Missouri

Irwin/McGraw-Hill

A Division of The **McGraw·Hill** Companies

INTERNATIONAL AND GLOBAL MARKETING: CONCEPTS AND CASES
International Editions 1998

Exclusive rights by McGraw-Hill Book Co – Singapore for manufacture and export. This book cannot be re-exported from the country to which it is consigned by McGraw-Hill.

2 3 4 5 6 7 8 9 0 KKP UPE 0 9

Library of Congress Cataloging-in-Publication Data

International and global marketing : concepts and cases / [edited by]
    Taylor W. Meloan, John L. Graham. – 2nd ed.
      p.   cm.
   Includes bibliographical references.
   ISBN 0-256-21894-3
   1. Export marketing.   2. Export marketing–Case studies.
I. Meloan, Taylor W.   II. Graham, John L.
HF1416.I54   1997
658.8' 48–dc21   97-5424

http://www.mhcollege.com

When ordering this title, use ISBN 0-07-115800-6

Printed in Singapore

This book is dedicated to the late Richard D. Irwin,
a man of integrity, vision,
and a great love of life.

ABOUT THIS BOOK

This is an impressive and comprehensive compilation of classic and cutting-edge articles on major aspects of international and global marketing. Selected high-quality cases and a global decision simulation are also important supplements to the readings.

I commend this book to academicians and practitioners as a very valuable companion text in undergraduate and graduate courses in international and global marketing.

Roy A. Herberger, Jr.
President and Professor of International
    Marketing
American Graduate School
    of International Management (Thunderbird)
Glendale, Arizona

ABOUT THE EDITORS

Taylor W. Meloan is professor of marketing and the Robert E. Brooker emeritus professor of marketing in the Gordon S. Marshall School of Business at the University of Southern California. He has served as marketing department chair and dean in USC's business school. He has participated as a faculty member at five overseas universities and institutes, most recently at the Madrid Business School in 1993. During the same year, he was a visiting faculty member at the University of Hawaii. He holds degrees from Indiana University, Washington University, and St. Louis University.

He is a member of the Foreign Trade Association of Los Angeles and the International Marketing Association of Orange County. He has served as national publications chair and director and as president of the Southern California chapter of the American Marketing Association. During 1986–90, he served as a member of the National Advertising Review Board. In 1993, he was elected to the board of the World Affairs Council of Orange County. He is a member of the board of the Institute for Shipboard Education, the governing body of the semester at sea program. Author of many research papers and cases, he is co-author or co-editor of seven books. Currently he serves on the editorial boards of three professional publications. In 1997, he was designated a distinguished member of the university faculty by the President of USC.

John L. Graham is professor of marketing in the Graduate School of Management at the University of California, Irvine. He has taught at the University of Southern California (1979–89) and was visiting Professor at the Madrid Business School (1991–92). In 1996–97 he was a visiting scholar at Georgetown University.

He holds a PhD in marketing (with an emphasis in cultural anthropology) from the University of California, Berkeley. He previously worked as a market analyst for a division of Caterpillar Tractor Co. With a number of colleagues, Graham has published more than forty articles and three books dealing primarily with international marketing topics.

His articles on international marketing negotiations have appeared in the *Journal of Marketing, Marketing Science,* the *Journal of Consumer Research,* the *Strategic Management Journal,* the *Journal of International Business Studies,* and the *Harvard Business Review.* Recently, he and his co-authors published a paper in *Management Science* that received a citation of excellence from the Lauder Institute of International Management at the Wharton School.

PREFACE

In planning internationally oriented courses, seminars, and workshops, educators and practitioners today typically look beyond the contents of traditional textbooks. They seek insights and concepts in professional journals, research studies, working papers, and government publications from around the world. Your editors have endeavored to perform this search for you, bringing together an integrated matrix of timely articles and papers on international and global marketing. After reviewing more than 250 global citations, our final selections include recently published papers, timeless classics, cases, and an international negotiations simulation. Each has been written by an authority in his or her field.

We believe that increased coverage should be given in courses and seminars to exporting/importing entrepreneurship. Rather than focusing largely on the marketing opportunities and barriers facing multinationals, greater emphasis should be given to preparing entrepreneurs and the owners/managers of smaller businesses to expand abroad. Along with our careful selection of readings, we believe that this orientation differentiates this book from other anthologies.

We hope sincerely that our selections will add a relevant extra dimension that will enhance lively discussion and debate in courses, seminars, and workshops. The editors acknowledge with appreciation the contributions of the authorities cited herein and their willingness to permit us to reproduce their work. We acknowledge also the encouragement of Craig Beytien, Publisher, Karen Westover, Sponsoring Editor, Andrea Hlavacek, Editorial Coordinator, and Gladys True, Project Manager with Irwin/McGraw-Hill. Harriet Stockanes assisted in securing permissions, and Sue McCullough proofread the manuscript.

Taylor W. Meloan
John L. Graham

x

CONTENTS

AUTHOR AFFILIATIONS

(Affiliations at Date of Article or Case Publication)

ARTICLES

1. Taylor W. Meloan, with the University of Southern California
2. Theodore Levitt, with Harvard University
3. Susan P. Douglas, with New York University
   Yoram Wind, with the University of Pennsylvania
4. William B. Werther, Jr., with the University of Miami
5. Christopher A. Bartlett, with Harvard University
   Sumantra Ghoshal, with INSEAD
6. Edward T. Hall, with Edward T. Hall Associates
7. David A. Ricks, with the American Graduate School of International Management (Thunderbird)
8. John L. Graham, with the University of California, Irvine
9. Gordon Redding, with the University of Hong Kong
10. Johny K. Johansson, with Georgetown University
    Massaki Hirano, with Waseda University, Tokyo
11. Salil S. Pitroda, with Harvard International Review
12. Peggy E. Chaudhry and Michael G. Walsh, both with Villanova University
13. Earl Naumann and Douglas J. Lincoln, both with Boise State University
14. George S. Yip, with the University of California, Los Angeles
15. Carl F. Fey, with the University of Western Ontario
16. Kathryn Rudie Harrigan, with Columbia University
17. Michael R. Czinkota, with Georgetown University
    Masaaki Kotabe, with the University of Texas, Austin
18. Christopher H. Lovelock, with Harvard University
    George S. Yip, with the University of California, Los Angeles
19. Tom Reilly, with Ernst & Young, Inc.
20. Bruce Leeds, with Hughes Aircraft Company

21. Marc Bourgery, with Groups FCA!
    George Guimaraes, with Bloom FCA!
22. Ronald E. Dulek, John S. Fielden, and John S. Hill, all with the University of Alabama, Tuscaloosa
23. John A. Quelch and Lisa R. Klein, both with Harvard University
24. John L. Graham, with the University of California, Irvine
    Shigeru Ichikawa, with Chuyko University, Nagoya
    Yao Apasu, with Florida International University
25. S. Tamer Cavusgil, with Michigan State University
26. John P. Fraedrich, with Southern Illinois University
    Connie Rae Bateman, with the University of North Dakota
27. Myron M. Miller, with Michigan State University
28. Thomas S. Clasen, with the law firm, Foley & Lardner
29. John F. Preble, with the University of Delaware
    Richard C. Hoffman, with Salisbury State University
30. Thomas Donaldson, with the University of Pennsylvania
31. Sheila M. Puffer and Daniel J. McCarthy, both with Northeastern University
32. Mary C. Gilly and John L. Graham, both with the University of California, Irvine

CASES AND DECISION SIMULATION

1. Robert J. Dolen, with Harvard University
2. Andrea Alexander and Johny K. Johansson, both with Georgetown University
3. Susan W. Nye and Barbara Priovolos, both with IMEDE
4. Ilkka A. Ronkainen, with Georgetown University
5. Christopher Gale, with the University of Virginia
6. J. Alex Murray, with Windsor University
   Gregory M. Gazda and Mary J. Molenaar, both with the University of San Diego
7. Tom Delay and Susan Schneider, both with INSEAD
8. W. Kent Moore and Phyllis G. Holland, both with Valdosta State University
9. Robert F. Bruner and Robert Spekman, both with the University of Virginia
10. John L. Graham, with the University of California, Irvine

International and Global Marketing

Concepts and Cases

I INTRODUCTION

The worldwide growth of marketing is one of the most important and far-reaching developments in business over the last quarter of a century. The governments of most nations of the world are committed to the enhancement of international trade. They recognize that trade is the principal vehicle necessary to raise the standards of living of their peoples, thereby contributing to societal harmony. The reduction of trade barriers provides for greater marketing opportunities. It is also a major bulwark in the maintenance of world peace. The introductory section of this book contains five contributions. The first of these, *International and Global Marketing: An Overview,* summarizes export market entry vehicles, risk assessment, and tailoring the marketing mix to meet the needs and expectations of selected international target markets.

The next two contributions explore the dichotomy of international marketing versus global marketing. A leading authority argues that global-minded firms should treat the entire world as a single market and regard regional and national differences as superficial and unimportant. The global firm should do the same things in the same way everywhere. The alternative view, cogently argued, is that marketing globalization is essentially a myth. These authorities hold that one or more elements of the marketing mix must be tailored for successful export of most products or services.

The concluding two papers in this section summarize and interpret social, economic, and managerial trends that are expected to result in increased international competition, enhanced marketing effectiveness, and higher standards of living globally. The author of *Toward Global Convergence* analyzes three self-reinforcing megatrends: homogenization of global youth cultures, freer markets around the world, and the convergence of global economic development, technology, and business. It is a compelling and positive scenario. The authors of *What Is a Global Manager?* argue that there is no such person as a universal global manager. Rather, effective international marketers today link three groups of interactive specialists: business managers, country managers, and functional managers whose work is coordinated and integrated by top managers at corporate headquarters.

INTERNATIONAL AND GLOBAL MARKETING: AN OVERVIEW

Taylor W. Meloan

Competition in a Shrinking World

Increasingly we all live in a shrinking world that has become dramatically more competitive. Five key factors explain this unparalleled competitive environment.

Communications and Logistical Revolution. Remember when the printed words in newspapers and books, supplemented by radio, were the principal vehicles of communications? Today, with worldwide Internet messages, fax transmissions, and satellite reception, instant economic, political, business, and personal communications have become the norm. Major events around the world are common knowledge within minutes. Jet transport has also contributed to a shrinking world. People, products, and components are transported within hours over vast distances, facilitating the production and distribution process.

Financial and Nonmonetary Settlement Systems. The dramatic growth of international business and investment has been facilitated by efficiently functioning modes of payment and the settlement of financial accounts. In recent years, this has been supplemented by increased counter-

trading wherein all or part of the payment is made in goods rather than in currency. The simplest form of countertrading is barter—the exchange of goods of one kind for products of another, whether finished, semifinished, or raw material. Other varieties of countertrading are more complex; part of the payment may be in goods with the balance in currency. Infinite variations have accelerated competition and provided for new marketing opportunities.[1]

Worldwide Dedication to Trade. Most nations of the world are committed to the enhancement of international trade. This dedication has manifested itself in the General Agreement on Trade and Tariffs (GATT), and its successor, the World Trade Organization (WTO). The WTO is an institution for the resolution of trade disputes between member nations who will be expected to provide greater access to their markets and seek to insure a more level playing field.

Dedication to international trade by the major nations of the world has led to the encouragement of exports by their governments and, in many instances, direct or indirect subsidies of exporters' operations. This can lead to exported products being sold in foreign markets at lower prices than identical merchandise offered in the home market. Such "dumping" and export subsidization inevitably lead to efforts by governments to protect themselves and their indigenous industries from injury. All this has resulted in a more competitive and complex environment for marketers.

Role of the Multinationals.   Multinational corporations have contributed to international competition and the shrinking world phenomenon. While there is no commonly accepted definition of a multinational, it is generally perceived as a large firm enjoying a dominant position in one or more industries with subsidiaries in many countries. Typically it manufactures and has R&D facilities in major markets where it competes. Multinationals tend to lose their national identity because of their omnipresence and widespread operations. Because of their economic power, they are often feared and resented by lesser competitors and by the governments of emerging nations in which they operate. Most of the major American oil companies, automotive manufacturers, and international banks, for example, are multinationals.

The Importance of Peace.   The universal desire for peace has been an important contributor to the shrinking world phenomenon. The peoples of all nations yearn for meaningful international arms agreements and arsenal inspections to enhance the likelihood of continued peaceful coexistence. Although the world has experienced periodic localized aggression and a recent rise in terrorism, relative peace and lack of worldwide war have provided a fertile commercial environment in which marketing has played a major role.

Barriers to Exporting

According to the U.S. Department of Commerce, approximately 20,000 American firms could export successfully but currently are not. Five factors explain why. The American market is the largest in the world. Many firms can grow and prosper without exporting. Only when sales and profits plateau domestically do many companies consider marketing abroad. Second, most companies don't know how to go about exporting. They don't know

whether they need to tailor products or services for international markets. They don't know how to price, promote, or select distributors abroad, or how to research such questions. They don't know which area to consider for exporting. Consequently, they procrastinate.[2] Third, Americans tend to be ethnocentric—they lack comprehension of the cultures, business practices, and languages of other peoples. Because English is the major business language of the world, there is little incentive to learn the languages of others. Fourth, foreign aggression and sporadic terrorism reduce American receptivity to export consideration. Assessing foreign political and economic risk is difficult for most Americans to contemplate, let alone do. Finally, protected markets abroad have made many countries difficult to penetrate. Tariff barriers, nontariff barriers (NTBs) including import quotas, burdensome licensing requirements, antitrade product specifications, and bureaucratic red tape all combine to discourage American exporters in many countries.

Export Market Entry Vehicles

Export entry vehicles range from reactive to proactive modes, from simple to complex in nature. The following alternatives begin with simple, weak commitments to international marketing and proceed to dedicated major efforts on a global basis.

Indirect Exporting.   Often this toe-in-the-water approach involves the sale of a manufactured product or line to a domestic intermediary who takes title to the goods, stores, and resells to markets abroad where it has contracts. This mode avoids the need for the producer to research, promote, price, and find distributors in other countries. The export firm takes over these functions. Persuading another manufacturer who is already exporting, with perhaps a complementary line, to act as one's agent abroad is another indirect vehicle. Using an export management company is a third possibility. These small, service-oriented marketing organizations, typically with only a few employees, are usually agents for domestic manufacturers that need exporting expertise. They provide market information and access to prospects in parts of the world where they have developed contacts.

Direct Exporting: Reactive Mode. Many intermediate and smaller firms began exporting in response to unsolicited inquiries and orders from abroad. Based on cursory analyses of such orders, neophyte exporters seek customers abroad with business characteristics similar to those of the inquiries. Gradually a cadre of customers abroad is developed, largely via this mode, with modest proactive solicitation of business.

Direct Exporting: Proactive Mode. This mode requires a commitment to actively explore the feasibility of exporting to selected target markets whose sales and market potentials have been researched. Distributors and/or agents in the target market(s) must be appointed, products or lines may be modified to meet the needs or expectations of foreign buyers, appropriate price levels and margins must be determined, and an appropriate personal selling, advertising and sales promotional mix must be devised to achieve penetration objectives. The international marketer must also become familiar with export procedures and documentation, as well as the vehicles for international payments and settlement of accounts.

Proactive international marketers should develop rosters of prospective distributors and agents from a network of business contacts, including their banks, advertising agencies, competitors, export management companies, trade associations, chambers of commerce, and agencies of the federal government. They may then prune the list by writing to each prospective agent or distributor to ascertain interest in being appointed in the target market area. Letters should be accompanied by catalogs and brochures documenting the scope of the line, elements of superiority, and pricing information. Those who express interest can be researched. Banks with which they have dealt and other firms they have represented are logical sources of input. Choices from the final list should be made only after personal interface with each

candidate in the target countries. While this step may require considerable time and travel expense, there is no substitute for face-to-face exploration of mutual expectations with prospective agents and distributors. At that time the terms, conditions, duration of an appointment, and provisions for possible termination should be reviewed.

Sales Branches and Subsidiaries. As the international phase of business operations expands, sales branches may be established in selected target markets where the potential warrants the cost. Agents and distributors are compensated largely via commissions and markups, but establishing a sales branch requires the commitment of upfront monies to finance office, storage, and/or repair facilities, overhead expenses, and sales force maintenance and supervision. Significantly greater sales volume is required to warrant the upgrade from an agency/distributorship mode to sales branch.

In contrast with sales branches, subsidiaries are separate legal entities that are created to assume responsibilities designated by the home company.[3] Subsidiaries are controlled but not always entirely owned by the parent. A foreign government may require that subsidiary ownership be shared to limit the financial commitment of the parent and to facilitate management participation by foreign nationals.

Sometimes subsidiaries operate in several nations or regions of the world. In other instances, they are smaller in scope, essentially upgraded sales branches. Their relationship to the parent may range from relatively autonomous to highly dependent, depending on the philosophy of the home company.

Licensing. The principal attraction of this international marketing entry vehicle is that it limits investment and commitment, while simultaneously offering the possibility of substantial profitability through licensing fees or royalty payments. The principal costs are those associated with negotiating the licensing agreements and monitoring their implementation. Licensing offers quick access to international business, market share, and cash flow. Typically the licensee is already established in the target market and can finance use of the license. Licensing can also circumvent tariff barriers that limit the quantity or raise the price of imports.[4]

Licensees may receive technical know-how, patent usage, access to production processes, the right to use a trademark, or copyrighted materials from the licensor. Licenses may be granted on an exclusive basis, meaning that other firms will not be given a license in the same geographic area. Or they may be nonexclusive, implying that other licenses are possible in a given region. Delineating the license's field of use can restrict the markets in which technological know-how may be used.[5]

A likely disadvantage of licensing is that licensees may ultimately become competitors. When a licensee acquires technological know-how, management expertise, and market position, it becomes tempting to terminate the license and continue in the field as a competitor. Or the licensee may endeavor to revise the license on more advantageous terms.

While the licensor typically conducts periodic audits and spot checks in an effort to ensure licensee compliance with the parameters of the licensing agreement, these are often not as reassuring as one would like. The licensor's lack of control over the operations of licensees can be a nagging problem. Short of terminating the license (where that can be done for cause), the licensor must rely on persuasion and example to upgrade marginal licensee performance. Finally, licensing can limit the profits of the licensor vis-à-vis doing its own manufacturing and marketing abroad. Balancing this potential disadvantage are the limitation on risk and the modest financial commitment licensing generally requires.[6]

Franchising.   Franchise marketing refers to a contractual arrangement whereby a franchisor who has developed a format and operational procedures for a particular type of business extends to franchisees the right to conduct such a business, provided that they follow the established *modus*

operandi of the franchisor. Franchisees are expected to adhere to the format, management guidelines, and accounting controls of the franchisor. In turn, the franchisees expect to acquire the expertise of the franchisor and receive guidance, training, and continuing support. Franchisees also acquire the name, logo, image, and reputation of the franchisor as part of the franchise package.

Because the franchisor can rely in part on funds provided by franchisees, expansion is facilitated. These monies are in the form of initial franchisee fees, annual renewals, and orders for materials and supplies needed by the franchisees. In international franchising, area franchises are often granted for a specified geographic region or sometimes an entire nation. Such master franchisees have the right to subfranchise to those who operate individual units in the subfranchise chain.

The franchisor has a tailor-made chain of units with reasonably predictable demand, domestic or international, for its product or service. Such a franchisor is not subject to the whims of independent dealers who are completely free to buy where they wish. This interdependence facilitates planning and control of overall operations.

As in corporate chains, franchisors are able to spread their risks among a variety of outlets and parts of the world. Inevitably, certain locations will prove to be superior to others. Obviously, the goal of any chain operator, corporate or franchise, is to have all units, wherever located, stand on their own feet. But the overall health of the organization is not impaired unduly even if a few locations or parts of the world are less satisfactory than anticipated.[7]

Another possible advantage of this mode of international distribution is the expectation that franchisees will be more highly motivated than salaried employees. It is assumed that people who regard themselves as their own boss will do a better than average job. This is especially important in small retail operations that require long, hard physical work. But franchisees who regard themselves as self-employed may not be disposed to accept guidance and direction from a franchisor or to standardize their operations for reasonable uniformity throughout the system. Conversely, franchisors may spend too much time seeking new franchisees around the world, neglecting the development of those they already have. This can result in system tensions.

The attraction of international franchising stems from franchisors' desire to maximize the utilization of their accumulated experience and know-how, expectation of enjoying the dedication and cultural empathy of indigenous franchisees, desire to minimize nationalistic restrictions on foreign ownership and control, and hope of avoiding exposure to lawsuits in another country and expropriation of overseas assets and facilities.

In spite of the potential advantages of international franchising, this mode of distribution tends to limit one's profit possibilities due to the need to share profits with franchisees. Coordinating and controlling a far-flung franchise system is also a likely source of difficulty. Many franchisors find themselves stretched thin as they attempt to motivate and maintain communications with franchisees even in the United States. This problem is compounded with foreign franchisees whose expectations, needs and mind-sets are likely to be different from those of Americans.

Joint Ventures.   When a firm joins with one or more partners to establish a new business abroad, a joint venture is created. These partners may be firms indigenous to the nation in which the joint venture is to be located, or they may be state agencies or governmental enterprises.[8] Such direct investment typically requires the commitment of equity and/or other assets, including physical plant, raw materials, management talent, or intellectual property. The joint venture may or may not involve establishment of a new manufacturing facility. The proportion and value of the investment generally determine the percentage shares held by the joint venture partners. American companies typically wish to have a majority share in order to ensure control, but many nations do not permit foreign firms to have a majority ownership position in a joint venture. This is especially true of developing countries.[9]

Foreign government opposition to direct investment may make a joint venture the only feasible mode of foreign market penetration. But joint ventures are also popular because they limit the American firm's commitment of capital and other resources. They can also combine the management know-how of a foreign partner and his or her understanding of the business environment with that of the host nation. The joint venture partner's personal contact with competitors, channel of distribution members, raw material and component suppliers, government officials, and trade association sources may be invaluable. This is the prime reason why certain companies have gone the joint venture route in Japan even though sole ownership of a new undertaking is open to them. Joint ventures also appeal to firms with little experience in international operations.[10]

A major key to joint venture success is choice of the local partner. Each firm in the partnership should contribute strengths and expertise that synergistically result in a whole greater than the sum of the parts. The parameters of the joint venture must be codified contractually, but communication and trust are of equal importance. When joint ventures fail, it is usually due to problems in these areas.

Joint venture partners acquire the technological, management, and marketing know-how of each other. If the partnership is dissolved for whatever reason, the foreign partners can become competitors of the American firm that perhaps provided much of the initial expertise. There is some risk that successful joint ventures can become targets for expropriation in certain countries where multinationals are suspect.

Contract Manufacturing.   If an internationally oriented firm finds export entry to a given target market blocked by onerous restrictions, contract manufacturing may be feasible. This often requires the transfer of technological and operational assistance to a foreign manufacturer with whom one contracts for local production of a product or line built to the specifications of the contractor. Contract manufacturing requires only a modest level of commitment, allows for easy entry, and sidesteps ownership of foreign manufacturing facilities. It permits an internationally oriented firm to retain control over marketing and product service. It may be tempting to pursue this route when the market potential is too thin to warrant on-site manufacturing of one's own. The key problems associated with contract manufacturing are (1) finding a local manufacturer who has excess capacity and the ability to adhere to specifications, (2) maintaining ongoing quality control, and (3) avoiding having such a producer become a future competitor.

Turnkey Projects.   Multinational firms with planning and construction expertise sometimes contract to build an entire plant or project. The fully equipped plant is turned over to the foreign owners when it is fully operational. This is often done on a fee or cost-plus basis with escalation clauses for unanticipated construction delays. Large manufacturing plants or hydroelectric facilities are illustrative of such turnkey projects.

Management Contracts.   Marketers with management expertise offer their services on a contractual basis to manage or operate a facility for the owners. This is sometimes done as part of a turnkey project to make sure a facility will be operational upon construction completion. Often this is a short-term arrangement until permanent employees can be trained to assume the responsibilities of operation.[11] Hotel corporations operate their own facilities but often manage hotels bearing their name that are owned by others.

The Multinational Firm and the Global Corporation

Major multinational marketers competing on a global basis combine various market entry strategies. In certain markets, they engage in direct investment via joint ventures or sole ownership and management of foreign operations. In other markets, they utilize licensing or direct exporting. The choice of strategies depends largely on their perceived global mission, financial strength, comparative cost analyses, product characteristics, channel of distribution availability, nature and strength of competition, and the environmental and political risks involved.

In contrast with the multinational firm, the global corporation endeavors to treat the entire world as a single entity. It markets "the same things in the same way everywhere." Products and brands are standardized worldwide.[12]

Risk Assessment

When a multinational entity considers alternative market entry strategies, it must do so within the context of risk assessment and acceptable assumption of risk. Two major categories of risk assessment are germane. The first is analysis of the governmental and political environment and stability in the host nation. The economic climate and prognosis in the target market are of equal importance. Included are assessment of possible future nationalization or expropriation of the multinational's assets and facilities, along with the likelihood of unanticipated or discriminatory taxes, strikes, riots, and/or revolutions which could imperil or doom the enterprise.[13]

The second category of risk assessment involves interaction between the host government and other nations, world organizations, or nongovernmental groups or movements. The possibility of retaliatory tariffs or quotas being imposed by the host nation, boycotts, embargoes, deteriorating political relationships, and/or terrorism are all elements of this category.[14]

International Marketing Research and Intelligence

The essence of sound marketing is discerning what customers and prospects need, want, and will buy, then creating a satisfying mix of goods and services from which buyers can select. To ascertain what the public wants, will buy, and at what price, research is needed. International marketing research utilizes the same methodologies and tools as research in the United States. The problem under study must be defined, the sources of information to address the problem ascertained, the germane data from either secondary or primary sources gathered, and the data analyzed and translated into a report of findings.

Secondary source data is available from federal agencies in the United States, from international organizations like the United Nations, the Organization for Economic Cooperation and Development, the European Community, and from host nations where international marketers contemplate competing. Private secondary sources of data include trade associations, international chambers of commerce, international banks, and research organizations that gather data and sell them to clients. International marketers typically subscribe to many ongoing journals, studies, and research reports as part of their continuing international marketing intelligence function. By contrast, garnering secondary data for a specific project is generally regarded as an aspect of marketing research. Gathering and interpreting secondary data from international sources is generally considered more difficult and suspect than doing so in the United States from domestic sources alone. International data are generally more difficult to obtain, may be unreliable or dated, can be subject to translation errors from another language into English, or may be misinterpreted because of cultural bias.

Primary data are obtained via survey research, observation, or controlled experiments. Survey research involves personal interviewing, or data gathering by means of telephone or mail surveys. All are more difficult in an international milieu than in the United States. Consumers may be unwilling to respond to research questions. Companies in many parts of the world are much more secretive than in the United States and disinclined to reveal details of their business operations. Observational research, unless done by skilled researchers with in-depth knowledge of the culture being observed, is subject to possible bias, making controlled experiments difficult to implement. (Such experiments involve holding all variables constant except for the one being researched—for example, the sales effect of a given advertising campaign or price change.[15])

The International Marketing Mix

The four decision variables for which international marketers have responsibility are (1) product scope and mix, (2) promotional strategies, media, and appeals, (3) pricing and discount strategies, and (4) channel of distribution choices. Channel of distribution alternatives are summarized under Export Market Entry Vehicles (p. 4). Each of these variables is interrelated.

Product Scope and Mix.   In product planning, a basic decision is whether to export or produce abroad virtually the same product or line as that in the home market. Certain firms resolved this question long ago; Coca-Cola and Pepsi-Cola are virtually the same around the world. This is also true for many industrial marketers. For other firms, it is a more complex issue. While standardized products have the appeal of simplicity and cost savings, long-run profitability may be better served by tailored products, whether destined for consumer or industrial markets, that meet local needs and cultural expectations. In certain instances, products must be modified because of the need for design changes, metric calibration, alternative voltage systems, or customer demands.[16]

Product and packaging color may also be affected by cultural taboos. In Japan and many other Asian countries, for example, white is associated with death. By contrast, black signifies death to Americans. A red circle on a logo or package is reminiscent of the Japanese flag and it should be avoided in countries with anti-Japanese feelings. Local views about color appropriateness must be researched with sensitivity by the international marketer.

It behooves international marketers to be alert to the possibility of counterfeit and look-alike versions of their products. Counterfeits are goods bearing an unauthorized trademark or products that are identical or highly similar to the goods for which the trademark is registered. Look-alikes are similar to genuine products but do not involve infringements of patents, trademarks, or copyrights. In addition to highly advertised consumer goods, product categories that are frequently counterfeited today include computers and software, drugs, medical devices, military hardware, and automotive parts.[17] International marketers sometimes retain private investigators to unearth infringing merchandise at the source. This is an initial step in stanching the flow of such goods into legitimate trade channels. Anticounterfeiting actions involve high-technology labels and packaging so advanced that duplication is nearly impossible.[18]

Promotional Issues.   Advertising Themes. Many well-known international marketers have launched advertising campaigns that have proved ineffective because of cultural insensitivity. The Marlboro man on horseback with his omnipresent cigarette has been effectively used in America and Europe, but this rugged masculine theme was not well received in urbanized Hong Kong. The ad was remade showing a younger model with a truck. Ford introduced a vehicle abroad under the name "Fiera" only to learn that it means "ugly old woman" in Spanish.[19]

Media Availability. Advertising media are either too scarce or too plentiful, depending upon the country. Government restrictions on commercials limit access to television and sometimes radio in certain nations. In some countries, more advertising is offered than can be accepted in the limited range of available newspapers and magazines. In certain other countries, so many newspapers are available with such modest circulations that coverage of the market in a cost-effective manner is difficult or impossible.[20]

Circulation data are closely related to the issue of media availability. Reliable circulation and mar-

ket coverage information in most parts of the world is difficult to obtain, or may be suspect. Often the figures are exaggerated, but one can never be sure to what extent. As a result, measuring cost per thousand readers, listeners, or viewers and comparing one medium to another become very tenuous.

Personal Selling. For several reasons, including foreign limitations on media availability, personal selling often becomes an important aspect of the promotional mix. Lower wage costs in developing nations can make the use of sales representatives even more attractive.

International salespeople perform one or more of three essential sales functions: (1) to promote the product or line to the trade, i.e., distributors or dealers, (2) to influence end users of the firm's offerings with the expectation that they will order more from distributors or dealers, and (3) to assist in identifying and solving the technical problems of buyers, especially those in industrial or engineering-based firms. Securing trial orders is also part of this process.

Sales Promotion. Aspects of an overall promotional program that are not personal selling or mass communications are typically referred to as sales promotion. Store demonstrations, displays, shows, contests, coupons, product sampling, and premiums are all aspects of sales promotion.

In an international context, trade fairs and shows are an especially important part of sales promotion. Hundreds of such shows are held in countries around the world for a wide variety of products and services. The most common trade fair is one where broad categories of products are shown, with representatives from many firms and nations. The second is restricted to a narrower range of products for a more limited clientele. A third possibility is a trade show devoted to the products of a single firm.[21]

Pricing Decisions. While pricing is a key decision variable in any business enterprise, domestic or international, it is especially complex in international marketing. Strategically, a firm must decide whether to stress nonprice competition in its international operations or to focus on sound value for a competitive price. Nonprice competition emphasizes product quality and features, plus service and repair, all projected via advertising and sales promotion. The alternative approach highlights price and value for the money.[22]

Although a firm may espouse uniform prices in its domestic market, this is typically not feasible when competing in diverse countries around the world. Productive costs, shipping expenses, the character and depth of competition, exchange rate fluctuations, duties and taxes all affect the multinational firm differently from one market to another, thereby mandating a tailored pricing strategy. But this can lead to a charge of dumping if the price abroad is lower than that in the home market without demonstrable justification for the differences.

Summary

Success in international marketing requires commitment, careful research of target markets, tailoring the product or line where appropriate to meet local needs, optimizing modes of market entry, skilled use of promotional and pricing strategies, long-term nurturing, and cultural sensitivity that transcends ethnocentric misperceptions.[23] But one should not be deterred. Mistakes will inevitably be made, but mistakes enhance learning and offer the opportunity to enlarge sales and profits internationally.

References

1. Pompiliu Verzariu, *Countertrade, Barter, Offsets: New Strategies for Profit in International Trade* (Riverside, CA: Global Risk Assessments, 1985).
2. John L. Graham and Taylor W. Meloan, "Preparing the Exporting Entrepreneur," *Journal of Marketing Education,* Spring 1986, pp. 11–20.
3. See Johnny K. Johansson, *Global Marketing* (Burr Ridge, IL: Richard D. Irwin, Inc., 1997), p. 157,

for a review of the similarities and differences between sales subsidiaries and manufacturing subsidiaries.
4. Vincent D. Travaglini, "Foreign Licensing and Joint Venture Arrangements," in *Foreign Business Practices* (Washington, DC: U.S. Department of Commerce, 1981), p. 75.
5. See Noel Capon, "Amicon Corporation," in *Problems in Marketing,* ed. E. Raymond Cory, Christopher Lovelock, and Scott Ward (New York: McGraw-Hill Book Co., 1981), pp. 302–15, for a review of field of use considerations in granting a blood plasma license.
6. Jean Pierre Jeannet and Hubert D. Hennessey, *International Marketing Management* (Boston: Houghton Mifflin Co., 1995), pp. 300–302.
7. Michael R. Czinkota and Ilkka A. Ronkainen, *International Marketing* (Chicago: The Dryden Press, 1995), pp. 312–17.
8. Brian Toyne and Peter G. P. Walters, *Global Marketing Management* (Boston: Allyn and Bacon, 1993), pp. 120–22, for a review of the advantages and disadvantages of joint ventures.
9. See Sak Onkvisit and John J. Shaw, *International Marketing (*New York: Macmillan Publishing Co., 1993), pp. 430–31, for a summary of key C.I.S. joint ventures.
10. Martin C. Schnitzer, Marilyn L. Liebrenz, and Konrad W. Kubin, *International Business* (Cincinnati: Southwestern Publishing Co., 1985), pp. 67–68.
11. Franklin R. Root, *Foreign Market Entry Strategies* (New York: AMACOM, 1982), pp. 127–28.
12. See Theodore Levitt, "The Globalization of Markets," *Harvard Business Review,* May/June 1983, p. 13. See also Philip R. Cateora, *International Marketing* (Burr Ridge, IL: Richard D. Irwin, Inc., 1996), pp. 22–26.
13. See Jerry Rogers (ed.), *Global Risk Assessments: Issues, Concepts and Applications* (Riverside, CA: Global Risk Assessments, Inc., 1983), for a detailed summarization of risk categories.
14. See Yonah Alexander (ed.), *International Terrorism: National, Regional and Global Perspectives* (New York: Praeger Publishers, 1978), for a review of terrorism in the major regions of the world.
15. A. Coskun Samli, Richard Still, and John S. Hill,

International Marketing (New York: Macmillan Publishing Co., 1993), pp. 375–93,

16. Warren J. Keegan, *Global Marketing Management* (Englewood Cliffs, NJ: Prentice Hall, 1995), pp. 476–86.

17. Eileen Hill, "Protecting U.S. Intellectual Property Rights," *Business America* (April 14, 1986), pp. 2–6.

18. *Product Counterfeiting* (Arlington, VA: Council of Better Business Bureaus, 1985), pp. 34–35.

19. David A. Ricks, *Big Business Blunders: Mistakes in Multinational Marketing* (Homewood, IL: Dow Jones-Irwin, 1983), pp. 39, 52.

20. Dennis Chase, "The Impact of Globalization," *Advertising Age* (May 26, 1986), p. 32.

21. L. R. Thomas, "Trade Fairs: Gateways to European Markets," *Business America* (April 20, 1981), pp. 7–9.

22. See Lee D. Dahringer and Hans Muhlbacher, *International Marketing* (Reading, MA: Addison-Wesley Publishing Group, 1991), pp. 518–25, for a review of factors that influence international pricing. See Subhash C. Jain, *Export Strategy* (New York: Quorum Books, 1989), pp. 144–50, for a summary of the bases for export price determination, and Subhash C. Jain, *International Marketing Management* (Belmont, CA: Wadsworth Publishing Co., 1993), pp. 551–53, for a review of the factors influencing transfer pricing among units of a firm and the methods used to set transfer prices.

23. See Vern Terpstra and Ravi Sarathy, *International Marketing* (Fort Worth, TX: The Dryden Press, 1994), pp. 111–19, for a review of the religions of the world and their impact on culture.

THE GLOBALIZATION OF MARKETS

Theodore Levitt

A powerful force drives the world toward a converging commonality, and that force is technology. It has proletarianized communication, transport, and travel. It has made isolated places and impoverished peoples eager for modernity's allurements. Almost everyone everywhere wants all the things they have heard about, seen, or experienced via the new technologies.

The result is a new commercial reality—the emergence of global markets for standardized consumer products on a previously unimagined scale of magnitude. Corporations geared to this new reality benefit from enormous economies of scale in production, distribution, marketing, and management. By translating these benefits into reduced world prices, they can decimate competitors that still live in the disabling grip of old assumptions about how the world works.

Gone are accustomed differences in national or regional preference. Gone are the days when a company could sell last year's models—or lesser versions of advanced products—in the less-developed world. And gone are the days when prices,

margins, and profits abroad were generally higher than at home.

The globalization of markets is at hand. With that, the multinational commercial world nears its end, and so does the multinational corporation.

The multinational and the global corporation are not the same thing. The multinational corporation operates in a number of countries and adjusts its products and practices in each—at high relative costs. The global corporation operates with resolute constancy—at low relative cost—as if the entire world (or major regions of it) were a single entity; it sells the same things in the same way everywhere.

Which strategy is better is not a matter of opinion but of necessity. Worldwide communications carry everywhere the constant drumbeat of modern possibilities to lighten and enhance work, raise living standards, divert, and entertain. The same countries that ask the world to recognize and respect the individuality of their cultures insist on the wholesale transfer to them of modern goods, services, and technologies. Modernity is not just a wish but also a widespread practice among those who cling, with unyielding passion or religious fervor, to ancient attitudes and heritages.

Who can forget the televised scenes during the 1979 Iranian uprisings of young men in fashionable French-cut trousers and silky body shirts thirsting with raised modern weapons for blood in the name of the Islamic fundamentalism?

In Brazil, thousands swarm daily from pre-industrial Bahian darkness into exploding coastal cities, there quickly to install television sets in crowded corrugated huts and, next to battered Volkswagens, make sacrificial offerings of fruit and fresh-killed chickens to Macumban spirits by candlelight.

During Biafra's fratricidal war against the Ibos, daily televised reports showed soldiers carrying bloodstained swords and listening to transistor radios while drinking Coca-Cola.

In the isolated Siberian city of Krasnoyarsk, with no paved streets and censored news, occasional western travelers are stealthily propositioned for cigarettes, digital watches, and even the clothes off their backs.

The organized smuggling of electronic equipment, used automobiles, western clothing, cosmetics, and pirated movies into primitive places exceeds even the thriving underground trade in modern weapons and their military mercenaries.

A thousand suggestive ways attest to the ubiquity of the desire for the most advanced things that the world makes and sells—goods of the best quality and reliability at the lowest price. The world's needs and desires have been irrevocably homogenized. This makes the multinational corporation obsolete and the global corporation absolute.

Living in the Republic of Technology

Daniel J. Boorstin, author of the monumental trilogy *The Americans,* characterized our age as driven by "the Republic of Technology [whose] supreme law . . . is convergence, the tendency for everything to become more like everything else."

In business, this trend has pushed markets toward global commonality. Corporations sell standardized products in the same way everywhere —autos, steel, chemicals, petroleum, cement, agricultural commodities and equipment, industrial and commercial construction, banking and insurance services, computers, semiconductors, transport,

electronic instruments, pharmaceuticals, and telecommunications, to mention some of the obvious.

Nor is the sweeping gale of globalization confined to these raw material or high-tech products where the universal language of customers and users facilitates standardization. The transforming winds whipped up by the proletarianization of communication and travel enter every crevice of life.

Commercially, nothing confirms this as much as the success of McDonald's from the Champs Elysees to the Ginza, of Coca-Cola in Bahrain and Pepsi-Cola in Moscow, and of rock music, Greek salad, Hollywood movies, Revlon cosmetics, Sony televisions, and Levi's jeans everywhere. "Hightouch" products are as ubiquitous as high-tech.

Starting from opposing sides, the high-tech and the high-touch ends of the commercial spectrum gradually consume the undistributed middle in their cosmopolitan orbit. No one is exempt and nothing can stop the process. Everywhere everything gets more and more like everything else as the world's preference structure is relentlessly homogenized.

Consider the cases of Coca-Cola and Pepsi-Cola, which are globally standardized products sold everywhere and welcomed by everyone. Both successfully cross multitudes of national, regional, and ethnic taste buds trained to a variety of deeply ingrained local preferences of taste, flavor, consistency, effervescence, and aftertaste. Everywhere both sell well. Cigarettes, too, especially American-made, make year-to-year global inroads on territories previously held in the firm grip of other, mostly local, blends.

These are not exceptional examples. (Indeed their global reach would be even greater were it not for artificial trade barriers.) They exemplify a general drift toward the homogenization of the world and how companies distribute, finance, and price products.[1] Nothing is exempt. The products and methods of the industrialized world play a single tune for all the world, and all the world eagerly dances to it.

Ancient differences in national tastes or modes of doing business disappear. The commonality of preference leads inescapably to the standardization of products, manufacturing, and the institutions of trade and commerce. Small nation-based markets transmogrify and expand. Success in world competition turns on efficiency in production, distribution, marketing, and management, and inevitably becomes focused on price.

The most effective world competitors incorporate superior quality and reliability into their cost structures. They sell in all national markets the same kind of products sold at home or in their largest export market. They compete on the basis of appropriate value—the best combinations of price, quality, reliability, and delivery for products that are globally identical with respect to design, function, and even fashion.

That, and little else, explains the surging success of Japanese companies dealing worldwide in a vast variety of products—both tangible products like steel, cars, motorcycles, hi-fi equipment, farm machinery, robots, microprocessors, carbon fibers, and now even textiles, and intangibles like banking, shipping, general contracting, and soon computer software. Nor are high-quality and low-cost operations incompatible, as a host of consulting organizations and data engineers argue with vigorous vacuity. The reported data are incomplete, wrongly analyzed, and contradictory. The truth is that low-cost operations are the hallmark of corporate cultures that require and produce quality in all that they do. High quality and low costs are not opposing postures. They are compatible, twin identities of superior practice.[2]

To say that Japan's companies are not global because they export cars with left-side drives to the United States and the European continent, while those in Japan have right-side drives, or because they sell office machines through distributors in the United States but directly at home, or speak Portuguese in Brazil is to mistake a difference for a distinction. The same is true of Safeway and Southland retail chains operating effectively in the Middle East, and to not only native but also imported populations from Korea, the Philippines, Pakistan, India, Thailand, Britain, and the United States. National rules of the road differ, and so do distribution channels and languages. Japan's distinction is its unrelenting push for economy and value enhancement. That translates into a drive for standardization at high-quality levels.

Vindicauon of the Model T

If a company forces costs and prices down and pushes quality and reliability up—while maintaining reasonable concern for suitability—customers will prefer its world-standardized products. The theory holds at this stage in the evolution of globalization, no matter what conventional market research and even common sense may suggest about different national and regional tastes, preferences, needs, and institutions. The Japanese have repeatedly vindicated this theory, as did Henry Ford with the Model T. Most important, so have their imitators, including companies from South Korea (television sets and heavy construction), Malaysia (personal calculators and microcomputers), Brazil (auto parts and tools), Colombia (apparel), Singapore (optical equipment) and, yes, even from the United States (copiers, computers, bicycles, castings), Western Europe (automatic washing machines), Rumania (housewares), Hungary (apparel), Yugoslavia (furniture), and Israel (pagination equipment).

Of course, large companies operating in a single nation or even a single city don't standardize everything they make, sell, or do. They have product lines instead of a single product version, and multiple distribution channels. There are neighborhood, local, regional, ethnic, and institutional differences, even within metropolitan areas. But although companies customize products for particular market segments, they know that success in a world with homogenized demand requires a search for sales opportunities in similar segments across the globe in order to achieve the economies of scale necessary to compete.

Such a search works because a market segment in one country is seldom unique; it has close cousins everywhere precisely because technology has homogenized the globe. Even small local segments have their global equivalents everywhere and become subject to global competition, especially on price.

The global competitor will seek constantly to standardize his offering everywhere. He will digress from this standardization only after exhausting all possibilities to retain it, and he will push for reinstatement of standardization whenever digression and divergence have occurred. He will never assume that the customer is a king who knows his own wishes.

Trouble increasingly stalks companies that lack clarified global focus and remain inattentive to the economics of simplicity and standardization. The most endangered companies in the rapidly evolving world tend to be those that dominate rather small domestic markets with high value-added products for which there are smaller markets elsewhere. With transportation costs proportionately low, distant competitors will enter the now-sheltered markets of those companies with goods produced more cheaply under scale-efficient conditions. Global competition spells the end of domestic territoriality, no matter how diminutive the territory may be.

When the global producer offers his lower cost internationally, his patronage expands exponentially. He not only reaches into distant markets, but also attracts customers who previously held to local preferences and now capitulate to the attractions of lesser prices. The strategy of standardization not only responds to worldwide homogenized markets but also expands those markets with aggressive low pricing. The new technological juggernaut taps an ancient motivation—to make one's money go as far as possible. This is universal—not simply a motivation but actually a need.

The Hedgehog Knows

The difference between the hedgehog and the fox, wrote Sir Isaiah Berlin in distinguishing between Dostoevski and Tolstoy, is that the fox knows a lot about a great many things, but the hedgehog knows everything about one great thing. The multinational corporation knows a lot about a great many countries and congenially adapts to supposed differences. It willingly accepts vestigial national differences, not questioning the possibility of their transformation, not recognizing how the world is ready and eager for the benefit of modernity, especially when the price is right. The multinational corporation's accommodating mode to visible national differences is medieval.

By contrast, the global corporation knows everything about one great thing. It knows about the absolute need to be competitive on a worldwide basis as well as nationally and seeks constantly to drive down prices by standardizing what it sells and how it operates. It treats the world as composed of a few standardized markets rather than many customized markets. It actively seeks and vigorously works toward global convergence. Its mission is modernity and its mode, price competition, even when it sells top-of-the-line, high-end products. It knows about the one great thing all nations and people have in common: scarcity.

Nobody takes scarcity lying down; everyone wants more. This in part explains division of labor and specialization of production. They enable people and nations to optimize their conditions through trade. The medium is usually money.

Experience teaches that money has three special qualities: scarcity, difficulty of acquisition, and transience. People understandably treat it with respect. Everyone in the increasingly homogenized world market wants products and features that everybody else wants. If the price is low enough, they will take highly standardized world products, even if these aren't exactly what mother said was suitable, what immemorial custom decreed was right, or what market-research fabulists asserted was preferred.

The implacable truth of all modern production—whether of tangible or intangible goods—is that large-scale production of standardized items is generally cheaper within a wide range of volume than small-scale production. Some argue that CAD/CAM will allow companies to manufacture customized products on a small scale—but cheaply. But the argument misses the point. If a company treats the world as one or two distinctive product markets, it can serve the world more economically than if it treats it as three, four, or five product markets.

Why Remaining Differences? Different cultural preferences, national tastes and standards, and business institutions are vestiges of the past. Some inheritances die gradually; others prosper and expand into mainstream global preferences. So-called ethnic markets are a good example. Chinese food, pita bread, country and western music, pizza, and jazz are everywhere. They are market segments that exist in worldwide proportions. They don't deny or contradict global homogenization but confirm it.

Many of today's differences among nations as to products and their features actually reflect the respectful accommodation of multinational corporations to what they believe are fixed local preferences. They *believe* preferences are fixed, not because they are but because of rigid habits of thinking about what actually is. Most executives in multinational corporations are thoughtlessly accommodating. They falsely presume that marketing means giving the customer what he says he wants rather than trying to understand exactly what he'd like. So they persist with high-cost, customized multinational products and practices instead of pressing hard and pressing properly for global standardization.

I do not advocate the systematic disregard of local or national differences. But a company's sensitivity to such differences does not require that it ignore the possibilities of doing things differently or better.

There are, for example, enormous differences among Middle Eastern countries. Some are socialist, some monarchies, some republics. Some take their legal heritage from the Napoleonic Code, some from the Ottoman Empire, and some from the British common law; except for Israel, all are influenced by Islam. Doing business means personalizing the business relationship in an obsessively intimate fashion. During the month of Ra-

madan, business discussion can start only after 10 o'clock at night, when people are tired and full of food after a day of fasting. A company must almost certainly have a local partner; a local lawyer is required (as, say, in New York), and irrevocable letters of credit are essential. Yet, as Coca-Cola's Senior Vice President Sam Ayoub noted, "Arabs are much more capable of making distinctions between cultural and religious purposes on the one hand and economic realities on the other than is generally assumed. Islam is compatible with science and modern times."

Barriers to globalization are not confined to the Middle East. The free transfer of technology and data across the boundaries of the European Common Market countries is hampered by legal and financial impediments. And there is resistance to radio and television interference ("pollution") among neighboring European countries.

But the past is a good guide to the future. With persistence and appropriate means, barriers against superior technologies and economics have always fallen. There is no recorded exception where reasonable effort has been made to overcome them. It is very much a matter of time and effort.

A Failure in Global Imagination

Many companies have tried to standardize world practice by exporting domestic products and processes without accommodation or change—and have failed miserably. Their deficiencies have been seized on as evidence of bovine stupidity in the face of abject impossibility. Advocates of global standardization see them as examples of failures in execution.

In fact, poor execution is often an important cause. More important, however, is failure of nerve—failure of imagination.

Consider the case for the introduction of fully automatic home laundry equipment in Western Europe at a time when few homes had even semiautomatic machines. Hoover, Ltd., whose parent company was headquartered in North Canton, Ohio, had a prominent presence in Britain as a producer of vacuum cleaners and washing machines. Due to insufficient demand in the home market and low exports to the European continent, the large washing machine plant in England operated far below capacity. The company needed to sell more of its semiautomatic or automatic machines.

Because it had a "proper" marketing orientation, Hoover conducted consumer preference studies in Britain and each major continental country. The results showed feature preferences clearly enough among several countries (see the exhibit below).

The incremental unit variable costs (in pounds sterling) of customizing to meet just a few of the national preferences were:

	£	s.	d.
Stainless steel vs. enamel drum	1	0	0
Porthole window		10	0
Spin speed of 800 rpm vs. 700 rpm		15	0
Water heater	2	15	0
6 vs. 5 kilos capacity	1	10	0
	£6	10s	0d
$18.20 at the exchange rate of that time.			

Considerable plant investment was needed to meet other preferences.

The lowest retail (in pounds sterling) of leading locally produced brands in the various countries were approximately:

U.K.	£110
France	114
West Germany	113
Sweden	134
Italy	57

Product customization in each country would have put Hoover in a poor competitive position on the basis of price, mostly due to the higher manufacturing costs incurred by short production runs

for separate features. Because Common Market tariff reduction programs were then incomplete, Hoover also paid tariff duties in each continental country.

How to Make a Creative Analysis

In the Hoover case, an imaginative analysis of automatic washing machine sales in each country would have revealed that:

1. Italian automatics, small in capacity and size, low-powered, without built-in heaters, with porcelain enamel tubs, were priced aggressively low and were gaining large market shares in all countries, including West Germany.

2. The best-selling automatics in West Germany were heavily advertised (three times more than the next most promoted brand), were ideally suited to national tastes, and were also by far the highest priced machines available in that country.

3. Italy, with the lowest penetration of washing machines of any kind (manual, semiautomatic, or automatic) was rapidly going directly to automatics, skipping the pattern of first buying hand wringer, manually assisted machines and then semiautomatics.

4. Detergent manufacturers were just beginning to promote the technique of cold-water and tepid-water laundering then used in the United States.

The growing success of small, low-powered, low-speed, low-capacity, low-priced Italian machines, even against the preferred but highly priced and highly promoted brand in West Germany, was significant. It contained a powerful message that was lost on managers confidently wedded to a distorted version of the marketing concept according to which you give the customer what he says he wants. In fact the customers *said* they wanted certain features, but their behavior demonstrated they'd take other features provided the price and the promotion were right.

In this case it was obvious that, under prevailing conditions, people preferred a low-priced automatic over any kind of manual or semiautomatic machine and certainly over high-priced automatics, even though the low-priced automatics failed to fulfill all their expressed preferences. The supposedly meticulous and demanding German consumers violated all expectations by buying the simple, low-priced Italian machines.

It was equally clear that people were profoundly influenced by promotions of automatic washers; in West Germany, the most heavily promoted ideal machine also had the largest market share despite its high price. Two things clearly influenced customers to buy: low price regardless of feature preferences and heavy promotion regardless of price. Both factors helped homemakers get what they most wanted—the superior benefits bestowed by fully automatic machines.

Hoover should have aggressively sold a simple, standardized high-quality machine at a low price (afforded by the 17 percent variable cost reduction that the elimination of £6–10–0 worth of extra features made possible). The suggested retail prices could have been somewhat less than £100. The extra funds "saved" by avoiding unnecessary plant modifications would have supported an extended service network and aggressive media promotions.

Hoover's media message should have been: *this is the machine that you, the homemaker, deserve to have to reduce the repetitive heavy daily household burdens, so that you may have more constructive time to spend with your children and your husband.* The promotion should also have targeted the husband to give him, preferably in the presence of his wife, a sense of obligation to provide an automatic washer for her even before he bought an automobile for himself. An aggressively low price, combined with heavy promotion of this kind, would have overcome previously expressed preferences for particular features.

The Hoover case illustrates how the perverse practice of the marketing concept and the absence of any kind of marketing imagination let multinational attitudes survive when customers actually want the benefits of global standardization. The whole project got off on the wrong foot. It asked people what features they wanted in a washing machine rather than what they wanted out of life. Selling a line of products individually tailored to each nation is thoughtless. Managers who took pride in practicing the marketing concept to the

Features	Great Britain	Italy	West Germany	France	Sweden
Shell dimensions*	34" and narrow	Low and narrow	34" and wide	34" and narrow	34" and wide
Drum material	Enamel	Enamel	Stainless steel	Enamel	Stainless steel
Loading	Top	Front	Front	Front	Front
Front porthole	Yes/no	Yes	Yes	Yes	Yes
Capacity	5 kilos	4 kilos	6 kilos	5 kilos	6 kilos
Spin speed	700 rpm	400 rpm	850 rpm	600 rpm	800 rpm
Water-heating system	No†	Yes	Yes††	Yes	No†
Washing action	Agitator	Tumble	Tumble	Agitator	Tumble
Styling features	Inconspicuous appearance	Brightly colored	Indestructible appearance	Elegant appearance	Strong appearance

* 34-inch height was (in process of being adopted as) a standard work-surface height in Europe.

† Most British and Swedish homes had centrally heated hot water.

†† West Germans preferred to launder at temperatures higher than generally provided centrally.

fullest did not, in fact, practice it at all. Hoover asked the wrong questions, then applied neither thought nor imagination to the answers. Such companies are like the ethnocentricists in the Middle Ages who saw with everyday clarity the sun revolving around the earth and offered it as Truth. With no additional data but a more searching mind, Copernicus, like the hedgehog, interpreted a more compelling and accurate reality. Data do not yield information except with the intervention of the mind. Information does not yield meaning except with the intervention of imagination.

Accepting the Inevitable

The global corporation accepts for better or for worse that technology drives consumers relentlessly toward the same common goals—alleviation of life's burdens and the expansion of discretionary time and spending power. Its role is profoundly different from what it has been for the ordinary corporation during its brief, turbulent, and remarkably protean history. It orchestrates the twin vectors of technology and globalization for the world's benefit. Neither fate, nor nature, nor God but rather the necessity of commerce created this role.

In the United States, two industries became global long before they were consciously aware of it. After over a generation of persistent and acrimonious labor shutdowns, the United Steel Workers of America have not called an industrywide strike since 1959; the United Auto Workers have not shut down General Motors since 1970. Both unions realize that they have become global—shutting down all or most of U.S. manufacturing would not shut out U.S. customers. Overseas suppliers are there to supply the market.

Cracking the Code of Western Markets

Since the theory of the marketing concept emerged a quarter of a century ago, the more managerially advanced corporations have been eager to offer what customers clearly wanted rather than what was merely convenient. They have created marketing departments supported by professional market researchers of awesome and often costly proportions. And they have proliferated extraordinary numbers of operations and product lines—highly tailored products and delivery systems for many different markets, market segments, and nations.

Significantly, Japanese companies operate almost entirely without marketing departments or market research of the kind so prevalent in the West. Yet, in the colorful words of General Electric's chairman John F. Welch, Jr., the Japanese, coming from a small cluster of resource-poor islands, with an entirely alien culture and an almost impenetrably complex language, have cracked the code of Western markets. They have done it not by looking with mechanistic thoroughness at the way markets are different but rather by searching for meaning with a deeper wisdom. They have discovered the one great thing all markets have in common—an overwhelming desire for dependable, world-standard modernity in all things, at aggressively low prices. In response, they deliver irresistible value everywhere, attracting people with products that market-research technocrats described with superficial certainty as being unsuitable and uncompetitive.

The wider a company's global reach, the greater the number of regional and national preferences it will encounter for certain product features, distribution systems, or promotional media. There will always need to be some accommodation to differences. But the widely prevailing and often unthinking belief in the immutability of these differences is generally mistaken. Evidence of business failure because of lack of accommodation is often evidence of other shortcomings.

Take the case of Revlon in Japan. The company unnecessarily alienated retailers and confused customers by selling world-standardized cosmetics only in elite outlets; then it tried to recover with low-priced world-standardized products in broader distribution, followed by a change in the company president and cutbacks in distribution as costs rose faster than sales. The problem was not that Revlon didn't understand the Japanese market; it didn't do the job right, wavered in its programs, and was impatient to boot.

By contrast, the Outboard Marine Corporation, with imagination, push, and persistence, collapsed long-established three-tiered distribution channels in Europe into a more focused and controllable two-step system—and did so despite the vociferous warnings of local trade groups. It also reduced the number and types of retail outlets. The result was greater improvement in credit and product-installation service to customers, major cost reductions, and sales advances.

In its highly successful introduction of Contac 600 (the timed-release decongestant) into Japan, SmithKline Corporation used 35 wholesalers instead of the 1,000-plus that established practice required. Daily contacts with the wholesalers and key retailers, also in violation of established practice, supplemented the plan, and it worked.

Denied access to established distribution institutions in the United States, Komatsu, the Japanese manufacturer of lightweight farm machinery, entered the market through over-the-road construction equipment dealers in rural areas of the Sunbelt, where farms are smaller, the soil sandier and easier to work. Here inexperienced distributors were able to attract customers on the basis of Komatsu's product and price appropriateness.

In cases of successful challenge to prevailing institutions and practices, a combination of product reliability and quality, strong and sustained support systems, aggressively low prices, and sales compensation packages, as well as audacity and implacability, circumvented, shattered, and transformed very different distribution systems. Instead of resentment, there was admiration.

Still, some differences between nations are unyielding, even in a world of microprocessors. In the United States, almost all manufacturers of microprocessors check them for reliability through a so-called parallel system of testing. Japan prefers the totally different sequential testing system. So Teradyne Corporation, the world's largest producer of microprocessor test equipment, makes one line for the United States and one for Japan. That's easy.

What's not so easy for Teradyne is to know how best to organize and manage, in this instance, its marketing effort. Companies can organize by product, region, function, or by using some combination of these. A company can have separate marketing organizations for Japan and for the United States, or it can have separate product groups, one working largely in Japan and the other in the United States. A single manufacturing facility or marketing operation might service both markets, or a company might use separate marketing operations for each.

Questions arise if the company organizes by product. In the case of Teradyne, should the group handling the parallel system, whose major market is the United States, sell in Japan and compete with the group focused on the Japanese market? If the company organizes regionally, how do regional groups divide their efforts between promoting the parallel versus the sequential system? If the company organizes in terms of function, how does it get commitment in marketing, for example, for one line instead of the other?

There is no one reliably right answer—no one formula by which to get it. There isn't even a satisfactory contingent answer.[3] What works well for one company or one place may fail for another in precisely the same place, depending on the capabilities, histories, reputations, resources, and even the cultures of both.

The Earth Is Flat

The differences that persist throughout the world despite its globalization affirm an ancient dictum of economics—that things are driven by what happens at the margin, not at the core. Thus, in ordinary competitive analysis, what's important is not the average price but the marginal price; what happens not in the usual case but at the interface of newly erupting conditions. What counts in commercial affairs is what happens at the cutting edge.

What is most striking today is the underlying similarities of what is happening now to national preferences at the margin. These similarities at the cutting edge cumulatively form an overwhelming predominant commonality everywhere.

To refer to the persistence of economic nationalism (protective and subsidized trade practices, special tax aids, or restrictions for home market producers) as a barrier to the globalization of markets is to make a valid point. Economic nationalism does have a powerful persistence. But, as with the present, almost totally smooth internationalization of investment capital, the past alone does not shape or predict the future.

Reality is not a fixed paradigm, dominated by immemorial customs and derived attitudes, heedless of powerful and abundant new forces. The world is becoming increasingly informed about the liberating and enhancing possibilities of modernity. The persistence of the inherited varieties of national preferences rests uneasily on increasing evidence of, and restlessness regarding, their inefficiency, costliness, and confinement. The historic past and the national differences respecting commerce and industry it spawned and fostered everywhere are now subject to relatively easy transformation.

Cosmopolitanism is no longer the monopoly of the intellectual and leisure classes; it is becoming the established property and defining characteristic of all sectors everywhere in the world. Gradually and irresistibly it breaks down the walls of economic insularity, nationalism, and chauvinism. What we see today as escalating commercial nationalism is simply the last violent death rattle of an obsolete institution.

Companies that adapt to and capitalize on economic convergence can still make distinctions and adjustments in different markets. Persistent differences in the world are consistent with fundamental underlying commonalities; they often complement rather than oppose each other—in business as they do in physics. There is, in physics, simultaneously matter and antimatter working in symbiotic harmony.

The earth is round, but for most purposes it's sensible to treat it as flat. Space is curved, but not much for everyday life here on earth.

Divergence from established practice happens all the time. But the multinational mind, warped into circumspection and timidity by years of stumbles and transnational troubles, now rarely challenges existing overseas practices. More often it considers any departure from inherited domestic routines as mindless, disrespectful, or impossible. It is the mind of a bygone day.

The successful global corporation does not abjure customization or differentiation for the requirements of markets that differ in product preferences, spending patterns, shopping preferences, and institutional or legal arrangements. But the global corporation accepts and adjusts to these differences only reluctantly, only after relentlessly testing their immutability, after trying in various ways to circumvent and reshape them as we saw in the cases of Outboard Marine in Europe, SmithKline in Japan, and Komatsu in the United States.

There is only one significant respect in which a company's activities around the world are important, and this is in what it produces and how it sells. Everything else derives from, and is subsidiary to, these activities.

The purpose of business is to get and keep a customer. Or, to use Peter Drucker's more refined construction, to *create* and keep a customer. A company must be wedded to the ideal of innovation—offering better or more preferred products in such combinations of ways, means, places, and at such prices that prospects *prefer* doing business with the company rather than with others.

Preferences are constantly shaped and reshaped. Within our global commonality enormous variety constantly asserts itself and thrives, as can be seen within the world's single largest domestic market, the United States. But in the process of world homogenization, modern markets expand to reach cost-reducing global proportions. With better and cheaper communication and transport, even small local market segments hitherto protected from distant competitors now feel the pressure of their presence. Nobody is safe from global reach and the irresistible economies of scale.

Two vectors shape the world—technology and globalization. The first helps determine human preferences; the second, economic realities. Regardless of how much preferences evolve and diverge, they also gradually convert and form markets where economies of scale lead to reduction of costs and prices.

The modern global corporation contrasts powerfully with the aging multinational corporation. Instead of adapting to superficial and even entrenched differences within and between nations, it will seek sensibly to force suitably standardized products and practices on the entire globe. They are exactly what the world will take, if they come also with low prices, high quality, and blessed reliability. The global company will operate, in this regard, precisely as Henry Kissinger wrote in *Years of Upheaval* about the continuing Japanese economic success—"voracious in its collection of information, impervious to pressure, and implacable in execution."

Given what is everywhere the purpose of commerce, the global company will shape the vectors of technology and globalization into its great strategic fecundity. It will systematically push these vectors toward their own convergence, offering everyone simultaneously high-quality, more or less standardized products at optimally low prices, thereby achieving for itself vastly expanded markets and profits. Companies that do not adapt to the new global realities will become victims of those that do.

References

1. In a landmark article, Robert D. Buzzell pointed out the rapidity with which barriers to standardization were falling. In all cases, they succumbed to more and cheaper advanced ways of doing things. See "Can You Standardize Multinational Marketing?" *HBR,* November–December 1968, p. 102.
2. There is powerful new evidence for this, even though the opposite has been urged by analysts of PIMS data for nearly a decade. See "Product Quality: Cost Production and Business Performance—A Test of Some Key Hypotheses" by Lynn W. Phillips, Dae Chang, and Robert D. Buzzell, Harvard Business School Working Paper No. 83–13.
3. For a discussion of multinational reorganization, see Christopher A. Bartlett, "MNCs: Get Off the Reorganization Merry-Go-Round," *HBR,* March–April 1983, p. 138.

THE MYTH OF GLOBALIZATION

Susan P. Douglas and Yoram Wind

In recent years, globalization has become a key theme in every discussion of international marketing strategy. Proponents of the philosophy of "global" products and brands, such as professor Theodore Levitt of Harvard, and the highly successful advertising agency, Saatchi and Saatchi, argue that in a world of growing internationalization, the key to success is the development of global products and brands, in other words, a focus on the marketing of standardized products and brands worldwide (Levitt, 1983). Others, however, point to the numerous barriers to standardization, and suggest that greater returns are to be obtained from adapting products and marketing strategies to the specific characteristics of individual markets (Fisher, 1984; Kotler, 1985; Vedder, 1986).

The growing integration of international markets as well as the growth of competition on a worldwide scale implies that adoption of a global perspective has become increasingly imperative in planning marketing strategy. However, to conclude that this mandates the adoption of a strategy of universal standardization appears naive and oversimplistic. In particular, it ignores the inherent complexity of operations in international markets, and the formulation of an effective strategy to pen-

etrate these markets. While global products and brands may be appropriate for certain markets and in targeting certain segments, adopting such an approach as a universal strategy in relation to all markets may not be desirable, and may lead to major strategic blunders. Furthermore, it implies a product orientation and a product-driven strategy, rather than a strategy grounded in a systematic analysis of customer behavior and response patterns and market characteristics.

The purpose of this paper is thus to examine critically the notion that success in international markets necessitates adoption of a strategy of global products and brands. Given the restrictive characteristics of this philosophy, a somewhat broader perspective in developing global strategy is proposed which views standardization as merely one option in the range of possible strategies which may be effective in global markets.

The paper is divided into four parts. First, the traditional perspective on international marketing strategy focusing on the dichotomy between "standardization" and "adaptation" is reviewed. The second part examines the key assumptions underlying a philosophy of global standardization, as well as situations under which this is likely to prove effective. In the third part, the constraints to the implementation of a global standardization strategy are reviewed, including not only external market constraints, but also internal constraints arising from the structure of the firm's current operations. Finally, based on this review, a more general approach is suggested, enabling consideration of a range of alternative strategies incorporating varying degrees of standardization or adaptation.

The Traditional Perspective on International Marketing Strategy

Traditionally, discussion of international business strategy has been polarized around the debate concerning the pursuit of a uniform strategy worldwide versus adaptation to specific local market conditions. On the one hand, it has been argued that adoption of a uniform strategy worldwide enables a company to take advantage of the potential synergies arising from multicountry operations, and constitutes the multinational company's key competitive advantage in international markets. Others however, have argued that adaptation of strategy to idiosyncratic national market characteristics is crucial to success in these markets.

Fayerweather (1969) in his seminal work in international business strategy described the central issue as one of conflict between forces toward unification and those resulting in fragmentation. He pointed out that within a multinational firm, internal forces created pressures toward the integration of strategy across national boundaries. On the other hand, differences in the sociocultural, political and economic characteristics of countries as well as the need for effective relations with the host society constitute fragmenting influences which favor adaptation to the local environment.

This theme has been elaborated further in subsequent discussions of international business strategy. Doz (1980), for example, characterizes the conflict as one between the requirements for economic survival and success (the economic imperative), and the adjustments to strategy made necessary by the demands of host governments (the political imperative). Economic success or profitability in international markets is viewed as contingent on the rationalization of activities across national boundaries.

The political imperative, on the other hand, implies a strategy of "national responsiveness," forgoing potential benefits of global integration and allowing local subsidiaries substantial autonomy to develop their own production policies and strategy. A third alternative, "administrative coordination" is, however, postulated. In this case, each strategic decision is made on its own merits, allowing flexibility either to respond to pressures for national responsiveness or alternatively to move toward worldwide rationalization.

Recent discussion of global competitive strategy (Porter, 1980; 1985) echoes the same theme of the dichotomy between the forces that have triggered the globalization of markets and those that constitute barriers to global competition. Factors such as economies of scale in production, purchasing, faster accumulation of learning from operating worldwide, decrease in transportation and distribution costs, reduced costs of product adaptation, and the emergence of global market segments have encouraged competition on a global scale. However, barriers such as governmental and institutional constraints, tariff barriers and duties, preferential treatment of local firms, transportation costs, differences in customer demand, etc., call for nationalistic or "protected niche" strategies.

Similar arguments have characterized the debate concerning uniformity versus adaptation of marketing and advertising strategies. In this context, greater attention has generally been focused on barriers to standardization (Buzzell, 1968; Elinder, 1964). Differences in customer behavior and response patterns, in local competition, in the nature of the marketing infrastructure, as well as government and trade regulation have all been cited as calling for, and in some cases rendering imperative, the adaptation of products, advertising copy, and other aspects of marketing policy (Miracle, 1968; Dunn, 1966; Donnelly and Ryans, 1969; Ryans, 1969). Yet, some advocates of a uniform or standardized strategy worldwide, especially in relation to advertising copy, have emerged—who point to a growing internationalization of lifestyles, and increasing homogeneity in consumer interests and tastes (Britt, 1974; Fatt, 1967; Boote, 1967; Killough, 1978). They have, for example, noted benefits such as development of a consistent uniform image with customers worldwide, improved planning and control, exploitation of good ideas on a broader geographic scale, as well as potential cost savings.

Compromise solutions such as "pattern standardization" have also been proposed (Peebles, Ryans, and Vernon, 1978). In this case, a global promotional theme or positioning is developed, but execution is adapted to the local market. Similarly, it has been pointed out that even where a standardized product is marketed in a number of countries, its positioning may be adapted in each market (Keegan, 1969). Conversely, the positioning may be uniform across countries, but the product itself adapted or modified.

Although this debate first emerged in the 1960s, it has recently taken on a new vigor with the widely publicized pronouncements or proponents of "global standardization" such as Professor Levitt and Saatchi and Saatchi. Levitt, for example, in his provocative article (1983) stated:

> A powerful force (technology) now drives the world toward a single converging commonality. The result is a new commercial reality—the explosive emergence of global markets for globally standardized products, gigantic world-scale markets of previously unimagined magnitudes.
>
> Corporations geared to this new reality generate enormous economies of scale in production, distribution, marketing, and management. When they translate these into equivalently reduced world prices, they devastate competitors that still live functionally in the disabling grip of old assumptions about how the world now works.

The sweeping and somewhat polemic character of this argument has sparked a number of counterarguments as well as discussion of conditions under which such a strategy may be most appropriate. It has, for example, been pointed out that the

potential for standardization may be greater for certain types of products such as industrial goods or luxury personal items targeted to upscale consumers, or products with similar penetration rates (Huszagh, Fox, and Day, 1985). Opportunities for standardization are also likely to occur more frequently among industrialized nations, and especially the Triad countries, where customer interests as well as market conditions are likely to be more similar than among developing countries (Hill and Still, 1983; Huszagh, Fox, and Day, 1985; Ohmae, 1985).

The role of corporate philosophy and organizational structure in influencing the practicality of implementing a strategy of global standardization has also been recognized (Quelch and Hoff, 1986). Here, it has been noted that few companies pursue the extreme position of complete standardization with regard to all elements of the marketing mix, and business functions such as R & D, manufacturing, and procurement in all countries throughout the world. Rather, some degree of adaptation is likely to occur relative to certain aspects of the firm's operations or in certain geographic areas. In addition, the feasibility of implementing a standardized strategy will depend on the autonomy accorded to local management. If local management has been accustomed to substantial autonomy, considerable opposition may be encountered in attempting to introduce globally standardized strategies.

An examination of such counterarguments suggests that there are a number of dangers in espousing a philosophy of global standardization for all products and services, and in relation to all markets worldwide. Furthermore, there are numerous difficulties and constraints to implementing such a strategy in many markets, stemming from external market conditions (such as government and trade regulation, competition, the marketing infrastructure, etc.), as well as from the current structure and organization of the firm's operations.

The rationale underlying the philosophy of global products and brands is next examined in more detail, together with its inherent limitations.

The Global Standardization Philosophy: The Underlying Assumptions

An examination of the arguments in favor of a strategy of global products and brands reveals three key underlying assumptions:

1. Customer needs and interests are becoming increasingly homogeneous worldwide.
2. People around the world are willing to sacrifice preferences in product features, functions, design and the like for lower prices at high quality.
3. Substantial economies of scale in production and marketing can be achieved through supplying global markets.

(Levitt, 1983)

There are, however, a number of pitfalls associated with each of these assumptions. These are discussed here in more detail.

Homogenization of the World Wants. A key premise of the philosophy of global products is that customers' needs and interest are becoming increasingly homogeneous worldwide. But while global segments with similar interests and response pattern may be identified in some product markets, it is by no means clear that this is a universal trend. Furthermore, there is substantial evidence to suggest an increasing diversity of behavior within countries and the emergence of idiosyncratic country-specific segments.

Lack of Evidence of Homogenization. In a number of product markets ranging from watches, perfume, handbags, to soft drinks and fast foods, companies have successfully identified global customer segments and developed global products and brands targeted to these segments. These include such stars as Rolex, Omega, and Le Baume & Mercier watches, Dior, Patou, or Yves St. Laurent perfume. But while these brands are highly visible and widely publicized, they are often, with a few notable exceptions, such as Classic Coke or

McDonald's, targeted to a relatively restricted upscale international customer segment (Ohmae, 1985).

Numerous other companies, however, adapt lines to idiosyncratic country preferences and develop local brands or product variants targeted to local market segments. The Findus frozen food division of Nestlé, for example, markets fish cakes and fish fingers in the UK, but beef bourguinon and coq au vin in France, and vitello con funghi and braviola in Italy. Their line of pizzas marketed in the UK includes cheese with ham and pineapple topping on a French bread crust. Similarly, Coca-Cola in Japan markets Georgia, cold coffee in a can, and Aquarius, a tonic drink, as well as Classic Coke and Hi-C.

Growth of Intra-Country Segmentation Price Sensitivity. Furthermore, there is a growing body of evidence which suggests substantial heterogeneity within countries. In the U.S., for example, the VALS study has identified nine value segments (Mitchell, 1983), while other studies have identified major differences in behavior between regions and subcultural segments (Kahle, 1986; Garreau, 1981; Wallendorf and Reilly, 1983; Saegert, Moore, & Hilger 1985). Lifestyle approaches such as the Yankelovich Monitor (Beatty, 1985) or the customized AIO approach (Wells, 1975) have also identified different lifestyle segments both generally and relative to specific product markets.

Many other countries are also characterized by substantial regional differences as well as different lifestyles and value segments. The Yankelovich Monitor and AIO approaches have, for example, been applied in a number of countries throughout the world (Broadbent and Segnit, 1973; the RISC Observer No. 1 & 2, 1986). In some cases, this has resulted in the identification of some common segments across countries, but country-specific segments have also emerged (Douglas and Urban, 1977; Boote, 1982/3). Lifestyle segmentation studies conducted by local research organizations in other countries also reveal a variety of lifestyle profiles (Hakuhodo, 1985).

Similarly, in industrial markets, while some global segments, often consisting of firms with international operations, can be identified, there also is considerable diversity within and between countries. Often local businesses constitute an important market segment and, especially in developing countries, may differ significantly in technological sophistication, business, philosophy and strategy, emphasis on product quality, and service and price, from large multinationals (Hill and Still, 1984; Chakrabarti, Feinman, and Fuentivilla, 1982).

The evidence thus suggests that the similarities in customer behavior are restricted to a relatively limited number or target segments, or product markets, while for the most part, there are substantial differences between countries. Proponents of standardization counter that the international marketer should focus on similarities among countries rather than differences. This may, however, imply ignoring a major part of a local market and the potential profits that may be obtained from tapping other market segments.

Universal Preference for Low Price at Acceptable Quality.

Another critical component of the argument for global standardization is that people around the world are willing to sacrifice preferences in product features, functions, design and the like for lower prices assuming equivalent quality. Aggressive low pricing for quality products which meet the common needs of customers in markets around the world is believed to further expand the global markets facing the firm. Although an appealing argument, this has three major problems.

Lack of Evidence of Increases.

Evidence to suggest that customers are universally willing to trade off specific product features for a lower price is largely lacking. While in many product markets there is invariably a price-sensitive segment, there is no indication that this is on the increase. On the contrary, in many product and service markets, ranging from watches, personal computers, household appliances, to banking and insurance, an interest in multiple product features, product quality and service appears to be growing.

For example, findings from the PIMS project overwhelmingly suggest that product quality is the driving force behind successful marketing strategies not only in the U.S., but also in other developed countries (Douglas and Craig, 1983; Gale, Luchs, and Rosenfeld, 1986). In industrial markets, insofar as global market segments consist of multinational corporations, they may be more concerned with the ability to supply and service their operations worldwide than with the price. Similarly, in consumer markets where global market segments consist of upscale affluent customers, they are likely to look for distinctive prestige, high-quality products such as Cartier watches and handbags and Godiva chocolates. Consequently, it is arguable that world customers are less price sensitive than other customers.

Low Price Positioning Is a Highly Vulnerable Strategy.

Also, from a strategic point of view, emphasis on price positioning may be undesirable especially in international markets, since it offers no long-term competitive advantage. A price-positioning strategy is always vulnerable to new technological developments which may lower costs, as well as to attack from competitors with lower overhead and lower operating or labor costs. Government subsidies to local competitors may also undermine the effectiveness of a price-positioning strategy. In addition, price-sensitive customers typically are not brand or source loyal.

Standardized Low Price Can Be Overpriced in Some Countries and Underpriced in Others.

Finally, a strategy based on a combination of a standardized product at a low price, when implemented in countries that vary in their competitive structure, as well as the level of economic development, is likely to result in products that are overdesigned and overpriced for some markets and underdesigned and underpriced for others. There is, for example, substantial evidence to suggest that where markets in developing countries are price sensitive, a strategy of product adaptation and simplification may be the most effective (Hill and Still, 1984). Cost advantages may also be negated by transportation and distribution costs as well as tariff barriers and/or price regulation (Porter, 1980; 1985).

Economies of Scale of Production and Marketing.

The third assumption underlying the philosophy of global standardization is that a key force driving strategy is product technology, and that substantial economies of scale can be achieved by supplying global markets. This does, however, neglect three critical and interrelated points: (*a*) technological developments in flexible factory automation enable economies of scale to be achieved at lower levels of output and do not require production of a single standardized product, (*b*) cost of production is only one and often not the critical component in determining the total cost of the product, and (*c*) strategy should not be solely product-driven but should take into account the other components of a marketing strategy, such as positioning, packaging, brand name, advertising, P.R., consumer and trade promotion and distribution.

Developments in Flexible Factory Automation.

Recent developments in flexible factory automation methods have lowered the minimum efficient scale of operation and have thus enabled companies to supply smaller local markets efficiently, without requiring operations on a global scale. However, diseconomies may result from such operations due to increased transportation and distribution costs, as well as higher administrative overhead and additional communication and coordination costs.

Furthermore, decentralization of production and establishment of local manufacturing operations enable diversification of risk arising from political events, fluctuations in foreign exchange rates, or economic instability. Recent swings in foreign exchange rates, coupled with the growth of offshore sourcing, having underscored the vulnerability of centralizing production in a single loca-

tion. Government regulations relating to local component and/or offset requirements create additional pressures for local manufacturing. Flexible automation not only implies that decentralization of manufacturing and production may be cost-efficient but also makes minor modifications in products of models in the latter stages of production feasible, so that a variety of model versions can be produced without major retooling. Adaptations to product design can thus be made to meet differences in preferences from one country to another without loss of economies of scale.

Production Costs Are Often a Minor Component of Total Cost.

In many consumer and service industries, such as cosmetics, detergents, pharmaceuticals, or financial institutions, production costs are a small fraction of total cost. The key to success in these markets is an understanding of the tastes and purchase behavior of target customers and distribution channels, and tailoring products and strategies to these rather than production efficiency. In the detergent industry, for example, mastery of mass-merchandising techniques and an effective brand management system is typically considered the key element in the success of the giants in this field, such as Procter and Gamble (P&G) or Colgate-Palmolive.

For many products, the establishment of an effective distribution network is often of prime importance in penetrating international markets. This is particularly the case for consumer products in countries where the absence or limited reach of mass-communication channels such as TV or magazines preclude the use of "pull" strategies. Distribution may also be crucial for products such as agricultural machinery, which require extensive after-sales service and maintenance. Furthermore, for some companies such as Avon with their Avon sales ladies network, or direct marketing insurance companies, distribution may constitute the crux of their marketing strategy and be a major component of their costs.

In these cases, the potential for scale economies arising from a standardization of operations may be negligible or nonexistent. In some instances, greater efficiency in operational systems and procedure may result from experience in multiple country market environments, but, as noted previously, there may also be significant scale diseconomies.

The Standardization Philosophy Is Primarily Product-Driven. The focus on product and brand related aspects of strategy in discussions of global standardization is misleading since it ignores the other key marketing strategy variables. Strategy in international markets should also take into consideration other aspects of the marketing mix, and the extent to which these are standardized across country markets rather than adapted to local idiosyncratic characteristics. Thus, not only should the effectiveness of using standardized positioning strategy promotional and advertising campaigns be considered, but a standardized distribution system and uniform pricing should be considered as well. There are, however, often formidable barriers to such a strategy, which will be discussed subsequently.

Requisite Conditions for Global Standardization

The numerous pitfalls in the rationale underlying the global standardization philosophy suggest that such a strategy is far from universally appropriate for all products, brands, or companies. Only under certain conditions is it likely to prove a "winning" strategy in international markets. These include: (*a*) the existence of a global market segment, (*b*) potential synergies from standardization, and (*c*) the availability of a communication and distribution infrastructure to deliver the firm's offering to target customers worldwide.

Existence of Global Market Segments.   As noted previously, global segments may be identified in a number of industrial and consumer markets. In consumer markets, these segments are typically luxury or premium-type products. Global segments are, however, not limited to such product markets, but also exist in other types of markets, such as motorcycle, record, stereo equipment, and computer, where a segment with similar needs and wants can be identified in many countries.

In industrial markets, companies with multinational operations are particularly likely to have similar needs and requirements worldwide. Where the operations are integrated or coordinated across national boundaries, as in the case of banks or other financial institutions, compatibility of operation systems and equipment may be essential. Consequently, they may seek vendors who can supply and service their operations worldwide, in some cases developing global contrasts for such purchases. Similarly, manufacturing companies with worldwide operations may source globally in order to ensure uniformity in quality, service, and price of components and other raw materials throughout their operations.

Marketing of global products and brands to such target segments and global customers enables development of a uniform global image throughout the world. In some markets such as perfume, fashions, etc., association with a specific country of origin or a foreign image in general may carry a prestige connotation. In other cases, for example, Sony electronic equipment, McDonald's hamburgers, Hertz or Avis car rental, IBM computers, or Xerox office equipment, it may help to develop a worldwide reputation for quality and service. Just as multinational corporations may seek uniformity in supply worldwide, some consumers who travel extensively may be interested in finding the same brand of cigarettes and soft drinks, or hotels in foreign countries. This may be particularly relevant in product markets used extensively by international travelers.

While the existence of a potential global segment is a key motivating factor for developing a global product and brand strategy, it is important to note that the desirability of such a strategy depends on the size and economic viability of the segment in question, the strength of the segment's preference for the global brand, as well as the ability to reach the segment effectively and profitably.

Synergies Associated with Global Standardization.

Global standardization may also have a number of synergistic effects. In addition to those associated with a global image noted above, opportunities may exist for the transfer of good ideas for products of promotional strategies from one country to another. For example, a new product or an effective promotional strategy developed in one country (not necessarily the country in which the product or brand originated) may be effectively exploited in other countries. For example, U.S. detergent companies have acquired or developed new, more effective detergent formulas and fabric softeners to cope with harder water conditions in European markets. These have subsequently been introduced into the U.S. home market. Similarly, promotional campaigns such as the Marlboro cowboy may also prove effective in several countries.

Global marketing also generates experience of operating in multiple and diverse environments. Experience gained in one foreign environment may thus be transferred to another country, or may facilitate more rapid adaptation to new environmental conditions, even if these have not been previously experienced. Consequently, the range of experience acquired may result in the introduction of operating efficiencies.

The standardization of strategy and operations across a number of countries may also enable the acquisition or exploitation of specific types of expertise which would not be feasible otherwise. Expertise in assessing country risk or foreign exchange risk, or in identifying and interpreting information relating to multiple country markets, may, for example, be developed.

Such synergies are not, however, unique to a strategy of global standardization, but may also occur wherever operations and strategy are coordinated or integrated across country markets

(Takeuchi and Porter, 1985). In fact, only certain scale economies associated with product and advertising copy standardization and the development of a global image as discussed earlier are unique to global standardization.

Availability of an International Communication and Distribution Infrastructure.

The effectiveness of global standardization also depends to a large extent on the availability of an international infrastructure of communications and distribution. As many corporations have expanded overseas, service organizations have followed their customers abroad to supply their needs worldwide.

Advertising agencies such as Saatchi and Saatchi, McCann Erickson and Young and Rubicam now have an international network of operations throughout the world, while many research agencies can also supply services in major markets worldwide. With the growing integration of financial markets, banks, investment firms, insurance and other financial institutions are also becoming increasingly international in orientation and are expanding the scope of their operations in world markets. The physical distribution network of shippers, freight forwarding, export and import agents-customs clearing, invoicing, and insurance agents is also becoming increasingly integrated to meet demand for international shipment of goods and services.

Improvements in telecommunications and in logistical systems have considerably increased capacity to manage operations on a global scale and hence facilitate adoption of global standardization strategies. The spread of telex and fax systems, as well as satellite linkages and international computer linkages, all contribute to the shrinking of distances and facilitate globalization of operations. Similarly, improvement in transportation systems and physical logistics such as containerization and computerized inventory and handling systems have enabled significant cost savings as well as reducing time required to move goods across major distances.

Operational Constraints to Effective Implementation of a Standardization Strategy

While adoption of a standardized strategy may be desirable under certain conditions, there are a number of constraints that severely restrict the firm's ability to develop and implement a standardized strategy. These include both external or environmental constraints, the nature of the marketing infrastructure, resource market conditions or the type of competition, as well as internal constraints that stem from the firm's current strategy or organization of international operations.

External Constraints to Effective Standardization. The numerous external constraints that impede global standardization are well recognized and have been clearly identified in the classic discussion by Buzzell (1968). Here, four major categories are highlighted, namely: (*a*) governmental and trade restrictions, (*b*) differences in the marketing infrastructure, such as the availability and effectiveness of promotional media, (*c*) the character of resource markets, and differences in the availability and costs of resources, and (*d*) differences in competition from one country to another.

Governmental and Trade Restrictions. Government and trade restrictions, such as tariff and other trade barriers, product, pricing or promotional regulation, frequently hamper standardization of the product line, pricing, or promotion strategy. Tariffs, or quotas on the import of key materials, components, or other resources may, for example, affect production costs and thus hamper uniform pricing or alternatively result in the substitution of other components and modifications in product design. Local content requirements or compensatory export requirements, which specify that products contain a certain proportion of components manufactured locally or that a certain volume of production is exported to offset imports of components or other services, may have a similar impact.

Regulation of business practices may also affect the feasibility of standardization. In Japan, for example, in many product markets such as electronics and food, product design and composition must conform to standards established by the relevant trade body, necessitating adaptation by foreign companies. Similarly, severe advertising regulation in countries such as Germany and Switzerland has restricted the use of many campaigns successful in other countries.

The existence of cartels such as the European steel cartel, or the Swiss chocolate cartel, may also impede or exclude standardized strategies in countries covered by these agreements. In particular, they may affect adoption of a uniform pricing strategy as the cartel sets prices for the industry. Cartel members may also control established distribution channels, thus preventing use of a standardized distribution strategy. Extensive grey markets in countries such as India, Hong Kong, and South America may also affect administered pricing systems and require adjustment of pricing strategies. For example, Wilkinson's attempt to market its line of razor blades in India suffered greatly from price undercutting in the grey market.

The Nature of the Marketing Infrastructure. Differences in the marketing infrastructure from one country to another may hamper use of a standardized strategy. These may, for example, include differences in the availability and reach of various promotional media, in the availability of certain distribution channels or retail institutions, or in the existence and efficiency of the communication and transportation network. Such factors may, therefore, require considerable adaptation of strategy of local market conditions.

The type of media available as well as their reach and effectiveness differ from country to country. For example, TV advertising, while a major medium in the U.S., Japan and Australia, is not permitted in Scandinavian countries. Where TV advertising is permitted, it may reach only a limited number of households due to limited ownership of TVs, as for example in South Africa, Nigeria, or Indonesia. Similarly, in countries with high levels of illiteracy, the effectiveness of print media is severely limited. Conversely, in some countries certain media are particularly effective or unique to the country. These include the circular street advertising to be found in Paris, or the neon advertising common in Japan.

The nature of the distribution system and structure also differs significantly from one country to another. While in the U.S. supermarkets account for the major proportion of food sales, in other countries there are virtually no supermarkets, and Mom and Pop-type stores predominate. This severely limits the effectiveness of a "pull" type strategy and ability to use "in store" promotions or display to stimulate customer interest. Even in industrialized nations such as Japan, Italy, Belgium, Portugal, and Spain, more than 75 percent of retail sales are done through small retailers. Again, discount outlets common in many industrialized nations may not exist in other countries, which may restrict a company's ability to use an aggressive price penetration strategy.

The physical and communications infrastructure also varies from country to country. Inadequate mail service (as, for example, in Brazil or Italy) will limit the effectiveness of direct mail promotion. A poor or ill-maintained road network may necessitate use of alternative modes of transportation, such as rail or air. Inaccessibility of outlying rural areas due to the nature of the physical terrain in countries such as Canada, Australia, and Peru may also require the design of logistical systems specifically adapted to their unique conditions.

Interdependencies with Resource Markets. Yet another constraint to the development of standardized strategies is the nature of resource markets and their operation in different countries throughout the world, as well as the interdependency of these markets with marketing decisions. Availability and cost of raw materials, as well as labor and other resources in different locations, will not only affect decisions regarding sourcing of and hence the location of manufacturing activities but

can also affect marketing strategy decisions such as product design. For example, in the paper industry, availability of cheap local materials such as jute and sugar cane may result in their substitution for wood fiber. Similarly, the relative cost of paper versus plastic materials may affect product packaging decisions. In Europe, use of plastic rather than paper is more common than in the U.S. due to differences in the relative cost of the two materials.

Cost differentials relative to raw materials, labor, management, and other inputs may also influence the trade-off relative to alternative marketing mix strategies. For example, high packaging cost relative to physical distribution may result in use of cheaper packaging with a shorter shelf-life and more frequent shipments. Similarly, low labor costs relative to media may encourage a shift from mass media advertising to labor intensive promotion, such as personal selling and product demonstration.

Availability of capital, technology, and manufacturing capabilities in different locations will also affect decisions about licensing, contract manufacturing, joint ventures, and other "make-buy" types of decisions for different markets, as well as decisions about countertrade, reciprocity, and other long-term relations.

The Nature of the Competitive Structure. Differences in the nature of the competitive situation from one country to another may also suggest the desirability of adaptation strategy. Even in markets characterized by global competition, such as agricultural equipment and motorcycles, the existence of low-cost competition in certain countries may suggest the desirability of marketing stripped-down models or lowering prices to meet such competition. Even where competitors are predominantly other multinationals, preemption of established distribution networks may encourage adoption of innovative distribution methods or direct distribution to short-circuit an entrenched position. Thus, the existence of global competition does not necessarily imply a need for global standardization.

All such aspects thus impose major constraints

on the feasibility and effectiveness of a standardized strategy, and suggest the desirability or need to adapt to specific market conditions.

Internal Constraints to Effective Standardization.

In addition to such external constraints on the feasibility of a global standardization strategy, there are also a number of internal constraints which may need to be considered. These include compatibility with the existing network of operations overseas, as well as opposition or lack of enthusiasm among local management toward a standardized strategy.

Existing International Operations.

Proponents of global standardization typically take the position of a novice company with no operations in international markets, and hence fail to take into consideration the fit of the proposed strategy with current international activities. In practice, however, many companies have a number of existing operations in various countries. In some cases, these are joint ventures or licensing operations or involve some collaboration in purchasing, manufacturing, or distribution with other companies. Even where foreign manufacturing and distribution operations are wholly owned, the establishment of a distribution network will typically entail relationships with other organizations, as for example, an exclusive distributor agreement.

Such commitments may be difficult if not impossible to change in the short run, and may constitute a major impediment to adoption of a standardized strategy. If, for example, a joint venture with a local company has been established to manufacture and market a product line in a specific country or region, resistance from the local partner (or government authorities) may be encountered if the parent company wishes to shift production or import components from another location. Similarly, a licensing contract will impede a firm from supplying the products covered by the agreement from an alternative location for the duration of the contract, even if it becomes more cost-efficient to do so.

Conversely, the establishment of an effective dealer or distribution network in a country or region may constitute an important resource to a company. The addition of new products to the product line currently sold or distributed by this network may therefore provide a more efficient utilization of company resources than expanding to new countries or geographic regions with the existing product line, as this would require substantial investment in the establishment of new distribution networks.

In addition, overseas subsidiaries may currently be marketing not only core products and brands from the company's domestic business, but may also have added or acquired local or regional products and brands in response to local market demand. P&G, for example, acquired Domestos, an established local brand of household cleanser in the UK, and added it to its product line in a number of other European markets. In some cases, therefore, introduction of a global product or brand may be likely to cannibalize sales of local or regional brands.

Advocates of standardization thus need to take into consideration the evolutionary character of international involvement, which may render a universal strategy of global products and brands suboptimal. Somewhat ironically, the longer the history of a multinational corporation's involvement in foreign or international markets and the more diversified and far-flung its operations, the more likely it is that standardization will not lead to optimal results.

Local Management Motivation and Attitudes.

Another internal constraint concerns the motivation and attitudes of local management with regard to standardization. Standardized strategies tend to facilitate or result in centralization in the planning and organization of international activities. In particular, product development and positioning as well as key promotional themes are likely to be developed at corporate headquarters. Especially if input from local management is limited, this may result in a feeling that strategy is "imposed" by corporate headquarters and/or not adequately adapted nor appropriate in view of specific local market characteristics and conditions. Local management is likely to take the view, "it won't work here—things are different," which will reduce their motivation to implement a standardized strategy effectively.

Standardization tends to conflict with the principle of local management responsibility. Emphasis on local management autonomy stems from the advantages traditionally associated with decentralization and a concern with encouraging local entrepreneurship. The establishment of a standardized strategy by corporate headquarters may therefore reduce the overall effectiveness of the firm. It also restricts local management's ability to adapt to local market-competitive conditions, for example, in promotion or distribution decisions, which can result in suboptimal reactions to competition.

A Framework for Classifying Global Strategy Options

This review of the rationale underlying "global standardization" thus suggests that it's appropriate only in relation to certain product markets or market segments under certain market environment conditions, and dependent on company objectives and structure. The adoption of a global perspective should not therefore be viewed as synonymous with a strategy of global products and brands. Rather for most companies, such a perspective implies consideration of a broad range of strategic options of which standardization is merely one.

In essence, a global perspective implies planning strategy relative to markets worldwide rather than on a country-by-country basis. This may result in the identification of opportunities for global products and brands and/or integrating and coordinating strategy across national boundaries to exploit potential synergies of operating on an international scale. Such opportunities should, however, be weighed against the benefits of adaptation to idiosyncratic customer characteristics.

The development of an effective global strategy thus requires a careful examination of all alternative international strategic options in terms of standardization versus adaptation open to the firm. These are, however, vast in number given the range of possible geographic areas, countries, market segments, product variants, and marketing strategies to be considered. It is, therefore, helpful to classify these options based on the degree of standardization. A continuum can thus be identified, ranging from "pure standardization" to "pure differentiation," where most options fall into the intermediate category of mixed or "hybrid" strategies. This is shown in Chart 1.

In the extreme case of pure standardization, all dimensions of marketing strategy are standardized or uniform throughout the world. In practice, as noted previously, not only is such a strategy fraught with problems, but it is rarely likely to be feasible in relation to all elements of the mix. The other extreme is that of totally differentiated strategy, in which each component of the mix is adapted to the specific idiosyncratic customer and environmental characteristics in each country. Management in each country thus develops its own strategy independently, with no coordination across countries nor attempt to identify any commonality from one country to another.

In between these two extremes is a set of mixed or hybrid options including some standardized and some differentiated components. Here, a variety of different patterns may be identified. These include those in which some components of the mix are standardized, while others are adapted to local market factors; those where strategies are standardized across regions or cluster of countries; strategies standardized by market segment; as well as combinations of the above.

For example, as shown in Chart 2, some components of the marketing mix, product, or advertising copy are standardized across countries, but others, such as distribution policy or pricing, are adapted to specific country or environmental characteristics. For example, companies marketing global products or brands may pursue different distribution or pricing policies in each country.

CHART 1

The Standardization–Differentiation Continuum

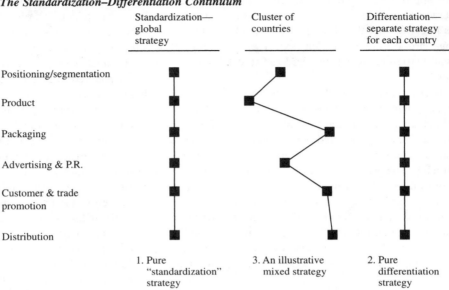

Positioning/segmentation

Product

Packaging

Advertising & P.R.

Customer & trade promotion

Distribution

Standardization—global strategy	Cluster of countries	Differentiation—separate strategy for each country
1. Pure "standardization" strategy	3. An illustrative mixed strategy	2. Pure differentiation strategy

Apple Computers, for example, while selling a standardized product line worldwide, has different positioning, promotional, and distribution strategies in each country.

Another option is to standardize strategy across regions or clusters of countries. Ford, for example, develops different models for its European operations as compared with the U.S. market. The Fiesta, Granada, and Taurus models were all initially developed for the European market, as were the positioning strategy and promotional themes.

Alternatively, strategies might be standardized by customer segments. Revlon, for example, targets its Charlie line to working women worldwide, using the same positioning strategy and advertising copy. Almay cosmetics targets its line to the global segment of women with sensitive or delicate skin throughout the world.

Combinations of these alternatives can also be adopted. For example, a company might market a standardized or uniform product worldwide but adapt its promotional strategy for different coun-

tries or regions. For example, P&G sells its Pampers brand of diapers worldwide, but the promotional strategy is adapted to different geographic regions. Similarly, Kellogg's Corn Flakes is sold worldwide, but in some regions, such as Latin America and the Far East, promotional themes are standardized, while in other areas, such as Europe, promotional themes, packaging, and distribution strategies are specific to each country. Again, Virginia Slims is targeted to "liberated" women throughout the world, but in Japan, the advertising copy is changed from "You've Come a Long Way Baby" to "Oh, So Slim and Sexy" (translation from Japanese).

In addition to such options which all assume a worldwide strategy, companies may also target specific and unique product markets and segments in a given geographic region or country. In the detergent market, for example, a company may market its line of powdered detergents worldwide, its liquid detergents and softeners in industrialized countries, and for the developing countries, de-

CHART 2

Key Dimensions of Global Marketing Strategy

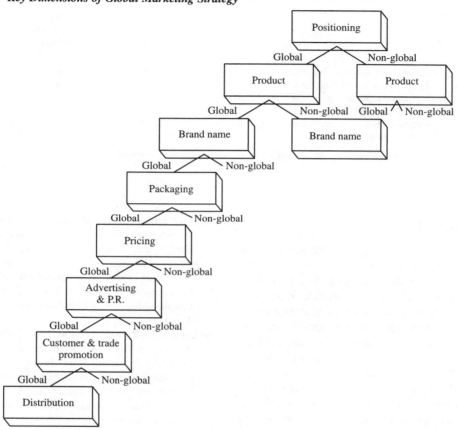

velop a line of synthetic detergents and bar soaps. Similarly in India, a major segment of the tooth cleansing market consists of black and white tooth-cleansing powders. Multinationals such as P&G and Colgate have each developed a brand of white tooth-cleansing powder to tap this market.

A firm's international operations are thus likely to be characterized by a mix of strategies, including not only global products and brands, but also some regional products and brands and some national products and brands. Similarly, some target segments may be global, others regional, and others national. Hybrid strategies of this nature thus enable a company to take advantage of the benefits of standardization and potential synergies from operating on an international scale, while at the same time not losing those afforded by adaptation to specific country characteristics and customer preferences. Guidelines and an approach for developing such a strategy based on a dynamic portfolio perspective have been proposed (Wind and Douglas, 1987). These take into consideration the company's existing network of operations, the current mix of products and brands, and their competitive positioning in each country, in designing an effective global marketing strategy.

EXHIBIT 1   A Standardized Global Strategy Checklist

	YES Continue to Explore	NO Standardization Not Appropriate
1. Is there a global market segment for your product?	Yes	No
2. Are there synergies associated with a global strategy?	Yes	No
3. Are there no **external** constraints or government regulations on ability to implement a global strategy?	Yes	No
4. Are there no **internal** constraints to implementing a global strategy?	Yes	No
If yes to all 4, consider global		

Conclusion

The main thesis of this paper is that the design of an effective global marketing strategy does not necessarily entail the marketing of standardized products and global brands worldwide. While such a strategy may work for some companies and certain product lines, for other companies and other product markets adaptation to local or regional differences may yield better results. The key to success is rather a careful analysis of the forces driving toward globalization as well as the obstacles to this approach, and assessment, based on the company's strengths and weaknesses, of where the most attractive opportunities and the company's differential advantage in exploiting these appear to lie.

References

Boote, Alfred S. (1982/83), "Psychographic Segmentation in Europe," *Journal of Advertising* (December/January).

Britt, Steuart Henderson (1974), "Standardizing Marketing for the International Market," *Columbia Journal of World Business* (Winter), 39–45.

Buzzell, R. (1968), "Can You Standardize Multinational Marketing?" *Harvard Business Review* (November–December), 102–13.

Donnelly, James H., Jr., and John K. Ryans (1969), "Standardized Global Advertising. A Call as Yet Unanswered," *Journal of Marketing,* April, 57–60.

Chakrabarti, Alok K., Stephen Feinman, and William Fuentivilla (1982), "The Cross-National Comparison of Patterns of Industrial Innovations," *Columbia Journal of World Business* (Fall), 33–38.

Douglas, Susan P., and Christine Urban (1977), "Life Analysis to Profile Women in International Markets," *Journal of Marketing,* 41 (July), 46–54.

Douglas, Susan P. and C. Samuel Craig (1983), "Examining the Performance of U.S. Multinationals in Foreign Markets," *Journal of International Business Studies* (Winter), 51–62.

Doz, Yves (1980), "Strategic Management in Multinational Companies." *Sloan Management Review,* 21 (Winter), 27–46.

Dunn, S. Watson (1966), "The Case-Study Approach in Cross-Cultural Research," *Journal of Marketing Research,* February, 26–31.

Elinder, Erik (1965), "How International Can European Advertising Be?" *Journal of Marketing,* April, 7–11.

Fatt, Arthur C. (1967), "The Danger of 'Local' International Advertising," *Journal for Marketing* (January).

Fayerweather, John (1969), *International Business Management: A Conceptual Framework,* New York: McGraw-Hill.

Fisher, Anne B. (1984), "The Ad Viz Gloms onto Capital," *Fortune,* November 12.

Gale, Bradley, Robert Luch, and Joel Rosenfeld (1987), "Who Will Succeed in Europe's Changing Marketplace?" *International Management Development Review* (to appear).

Garreau, J. (1981), *The Nine Nations of North America,* Boston, MA: Houghton Mifflin Co.

Hakuhodo Institute of Life and Living (1983), *Hitonami: Keeping Up With the Satos,* Tokyo: Hill.

Hill, J. S., and R. R. Still (1984), "Adapting Products to LDC Tastes," *Harvard Business Review,* 62 (March/April), 92–101.

Huszagh, Sandra, Richard J. Fox, and Ellen Day, "Global Marketing: An Empirical Investigation," *Columbia Journal of World Business,* Twentieth Anniversary Issue, 1985, 31–43.

Kahle, Lynn R. (1986), "The Nine Nations of North America and the Value Basis of Geographic Segmentation," *Journal of Marketing,* 56 (April), 37–47.

Killough, James (1978), "Improved Payoff from Transnational Advertising," *Harvard Business Review* (July–August), 103.

Kotler, Philip (1985), "Global Standardization—Courting Danger," panel discussion, 23 American Marketing Association Conference, Washington, D.C.

Levitt, T. (1983), "The Globalization of Markets," *Harvard Business Review* (May–June), 92–102.

Miracle, Gordon (1968), "Internationalizing Advertising Principles and Strategies," *MSU Business Topics,* Autumn, 29–36.

Mitchell, A. (1983), *The Nine American Lifestyles,* New York: Macmillan Publishing.

Ohmae, Kenichi (1985), "Becoming a Triad Power: The New Global Corporation," *The McKinsey Quarterly,* Spring, 2–25.

Ohmae, Kenichi (1985), *Triad Power,* New York: The Free Press.

Peebles, Dean M., John K. Ryans, and Ivan R. Vernon (1978), "Coordinating International Advertising," *Journal of Marketing,* 46 (Winter), 27–35.

Porter, Michael (1980), *Competitive Strategy: Techniques for Analyzing Industries and Competitors,* New York: The Free Press.

Porter, Michael (1985), *Competitive Advantage,* New York: The Free Press.

Quelch, Joan A., and Edward J. Hoff (1986), "Customizing Global Marketing," *Harvard Business Review* (May/June).

The RISC Observer, No. 1 and 2 (1986), Paris: RISC (mimeographed).

Ryans, John K. (1969), "Is It Too Soon to Put a Tiger in Every Tank?" *Columbia Journal of World Business* (March), 69–75.

Saegert, Joel, Robert J. Hoover, and Marye Thorp Hilger (1985), "Characteristics of Mexican American Consumers," *Journal of Consumer Research,* 12 (June), 104–9.

Segnit, Susanna, and Simon Broadbent, "Lifestyle Research," *European Research,* 1 (January 1973), 1 (March 1973).

Takeuchi, H., and M. E. Porter (1985), "The Strategic Role of International Marketing: Managing the Nature and Extent of Worldwide Coordination," Michael E. Porter (ed.), Competition in Global Industries, Cambridge, MA: Harvard Graduate School of Business Administration.

TOWARD GLOBAL CONVERGENCE

William B. Werther, Jr.

"In the long run, we are all dead," observed British economist John Maynard Keynes. Although speculation about tomorrow is, at best, problematic, three seemingly unconnected undercurrents are converging with nearly the same certainty as Lord Keynes's morbid prediction. One trend is the "global youth culture"; another is "freed markets." Together these two help shape a third pattern, "competitive convergence." All three "megatrends"—as John Naisbitt might have labeled them—are global in consequence. The result will mean a need to further rethink management and marketing in this fast-growing, billion-plus subculture.

These self-reinforcing trends will not mean the "end of history"—though the result may make war, famine, discrimination, and nation-states as uncommon as modern-day crucifixions. And, admittedly, the full force of these trends remains just out of view, somewhere beyond the short time horizons of this decade and just shy of that distant "long run" Keynes spoke of. Nevertheless, an early glimpse of that future is embodied in the McDonald's Generation.

The McDonald's Generation

No hard and fast date marks the start of the McDonald's Generation. For me, it began in 1969. In that year, while baby-sitting an early rising four-year-old, I was watching Saturday morning cartoons during which a McDonald's commercial appeared. At the time, it seemed odd that a sophisticated company like McDonald's would "waste" its advertising dollars on four-year-olds who lacked the wherewithal to buy a Big Mac. That is, it seemed odd until the following Friday evening, when his mother came home from work asking, "Where are we going for dinner?" Faster than an adult could translate her question into the universal statement of "I'm not cooking," it was answered from the back bedroom by a small voice crying, "McDonald's! McDonald's!" Thus was recorded one birth into the McDonald's Generation. A pixel of the picture fell into place, though the sociological shift it suggested went unnoticed because it was only a sample of one.

My generation (early Baby Boomers) and previous ones would have been far less likely to shout "McDonald's!" (or, in my youth, "Howard Johnson's!") in response to a mother's question about dinner. First, it was unlikely that our mothers would be returning from work at dinnertime; more likely, they would already have been home making

Reprinted by permission of *Business Horizons* (January/February 1996), 3–9.

dinner. Second, eating out was seldom the extemporaneous decision it is today, and was more likely reserved for special occasions. Third, and perhaps more telling, my generation and those before it were more likely to be "seen, not heard." "Children don't speak unless spoken to" was a kindly enforced dictum one rarely risked violating with unsolicited outbursts. Simply put, the plea for "McDonald's!" mirrored the culturally significant exodus of mothers from home to the brave new world of paid work.

Also mirrored in that outburst were even more fundamental changes. Whether motivated by guilt or fatigue or the pressure of "Madison Avenue," the parent-centered family changed its orbit and became a child-centered household. This was not true for all homes, and perhaps not even for most, but it represented a significant beginning. Indeed, a visit to the supermarket on Saturday mornings—then or now, whether in North or South America, Europe or Asia—allows one to eavesdrop on the insistent demands of the grocery-cart set as they are chauffeured down the sugar-coated aisles of today's stores, preprogrammed to "buy" by a ubiquitous electronic media. Or watch their older brothers and sisters in China or Chile as they enjoy the same movies and music in the U.S. and Europe, dress in the same blue jeans, tee shirts, and athletic shoes, stop by the Citibank ATM, and then rush off to Taco Bell, Kentucky Fried Chicken, Pizza Hut, or McDonald's outlets.

A pixel here, a pixel there.

And it is not just the toddlers or teenagers, either. Most professors I know have experienced a student lamenting a low grade with the irrelevant (and seldom true) argument, "But Professor, I was there every day!" Their repetition of that whining mantra suggests that life has taught them to plead long enough and they too can get the grade (or the sugar-coated cereal, or the trip to McDonald's).

From McDonald's to MTV

The 1950s lament "Rock 'n roll will corrupt our youth" has proven to be largely true in the minds of many parents and grandparents. But rock 'n roll has had a much more pervasive impact than even its harshest critics of the 1950s could imagine. Music has served as the battle cry of each post-World War II generation. More impressively, it has become a global language uniting successive generations from Santiago to Miami, Beijing to Moscow, in a common perspective that says: Authority figures are stupid. From parents and police to teachers and time-keepers, they all cling to the outdated and the outmoded.

The "authority figure is wrong" shows up as the central theme of many films aimed at the moviegoing youth of the world. Whether in the cinemas of the world's cities or the bicycle-generator-powered VCRs of remote Africa and Asian villages, the media—the largely English-speaking media—have permeated the globe, molding an increasingly uniform teenage culture. One need only listen to the rock 'n roll of hotel lobbies around the world, watch the satellite movie broadcasts in the room, and then walk out on the streets and observe the Levi's and Nike-clad youth of Los Angeles or Hong Kong, Bombay or Melbourne to see that this is so.

And why not? For most of civilization, cultural values have been transmitted to children by their grandparents, while parents worked in the fields and later in the factories and offices. But with increased urbanization, grandparents play an increasingly trivialized role in the transmission of values. Extended families increasingly give way to nuclear families. This "marginalization" of grandparents and societal values is most noticeable where migration to cities is high, as in the United States and in newly industrialized countries that see migration patterns such as China's 100-million member "floating work force" or Brazil's, Indonesia's, and Nigeria's massive shifts from the countryside to urban slums. Those migration patterns often sever the reinforcing influence of extended families and close-knit communities, replacing them with the anonymity of the city and culture-leveling television.

To some degree, technology has filled the void of grandparents and even mothers as the keeper of the culture. Today, TVs increasingly serve as a combination babysitter and values transmitter. The spread of MTV, videos, and satellite movies around the globe injects previously diverse cultures with a virus of values more common and potent than mere music and dress. It adds a growing uniformity to the values of the "global youth culture." The result? Teenagers today in Seoul and the South Bronx have a commonality of values, tastes, and aspirations that are more similar to each other than to those of their respective grandparents.

Such values and aspirations go beyond the outward symbols of pop music, jeans, Nike shoes, and Big Macs. At a deeper level, one finds a greater demand for personal freedom. The traditional antiauthority message aimed at youth in the developed nations for the past couple of generations has gained near-universal distribution. Where once the expectation of freedom was limited to the developed nations, the media have brought this expectation to the developing countries. Even in the oppressive societies of the planet, we now see youths stand before tanks or pointed rifles—just as their predecessors did in developed countries a generation earlier by erecting barricades in Paris or being shot at Kent State. At the same time, one can witness among the world's young people a growing acceptance of such issues as women's rights and concern for the ecological consequences of technological advancement. Whether the complaint is the destruction of rain forests or French nuclear testing, spontaneous protests spring up in Chile and Japan, Germany, and the United States. There is a greater recognition of Spaceship Earth as our common lifeboat.

The argument here is not that traditional values and aspirations of family, health, and well-being are being discarded. Rather, this era is witnessing the injection of new, widely agreed-upon values of freedom and ecological concern that are permeating the remotest regions of the world and cutting across the most diverse cultures. The pattern is far from universal, but it is moving toward universality.

Such a growing uniformity of culture results from billions of points of contact among young people and the media every day. Though each interaction is insignificant, the pervasiveness of these contacts is like the combined impact of thousands of tiny pixels in a television: A picture begins to emerge of a separate subculture with implications for management and marketing as well as for governance and global unity.

Looking through the Trendline

The still-fuzzy picture painted suggests an unheralded and uncoordinated—but nonetheless real—linkage around the globe, uniting in some peculiar ways today's youth, tomorrow's decision makers. Before these young people attain leadership roles, they will reshape organizations, local and global, small and large, public and private. Consider but a few areas of impact:

- "McDonaldized" youths already expect—even demand—greater participation in decisions that affect them at home, in school, and at work, guiding them toward new leadership strategies and behaviors.
- "Empowerment" is not just an active organizational response to competitive pressures. It is also a reaction to a cultural reality shaped by youth-driven expectations of the more egalitarian participation patterns they have encountered in today's less autocratic families and schools.
- Traditional middle-class values of hard work, patience, earnestness, and striving for future rewards may become secondary concerns when compared with the instant gratification and immense wealth seen every day as a result of lawsuits, lotteries, game shows, sports and entertainment salaries, and the drug deal going down on the corner. Those same middle-class work values don't seem to hold a candle to being "cool" and "accepted." A look at rap music and ghetto-inspired grungy dress, for example, suggests that perhaps for the first time in history, middle-class youths are emulating their lower-class counterparts. Though parallels with the 1960s can be drawn, today's dress code may be more than a fashion statement as it extends across diverse cultures and reaches beyond teenagers to those both younger and older. Such "coolness" and accep-

tance seldom come from a job—at least not those outside sports and entertainment.

• The growing proportion of out-of-wedlock babies born to middle-class girls (and women) in the United States now stands at 30 percent, following the trend set by the lower classes and the disadvantaged groups a generation earlier. Do these trends suggest that fundamental societal changes may reach all the way into core middle-class values, making changes in dress and musical tastes seem superficial? If something as fundamental as mating practices changes in one generation, can the work ethic be far behind?

• A growing uniformity of values along generational lines leads to different attitudes about attendance, loyalty, and responsibility. Unlike the "work-then-play" values of earlier generations, senior supervisors often report that jobs are seen as an interruption of the younger generation's personal plans, especially when overtime is concerned. Is

this merely stereotypical thinking among old-timers? Or has the work ethic already shifted?

These implications go on to suggest even more questions:

• With children having children, who transmits societal values besides the media? Though demands for employer-provided child care will continue to grow in countries where these demands have not already been institutionalized, will employers need to be concerned with values education among employees *and* their children? Is business going to face the *in loco parentis* responsibilities that universities gave up in the 1960s?

• As the youth culture spreads around the "global electronic village" (as some view Spaceship Earth), will today's ethnic, tribal, racial, and religious differences loom as large tomorrow? Will one or two more generations of "global culture" ameliorate these ancient differences as national media and mobility have largely smoothed over the regional diversity between North and South in the United States during the last two generations? Are not intergenerational differences *always* resolved in favor of the younger generation, sooner or later?

• If ideas, dress, music, entertainment, sociosexual mores, and values are converted to digitized pixels that freely roam across the borders of even the most repressive political states, how meaningful are those borders? How well will they contain the next generation, now being force-fed by a steady stream of satellite movies, commercials, and rock videos? Will those billion-plus youths of developing countries follow their fathers and older brothers, tracing those electronic beams back toward their origin in search of some fantasy world—an imaginary electronic world that comes closer to science fiction than the reality most of the planet's teenagers now experience? Does anyone know how many young Mexicans have already done so by moving to the world's second largest Mexican city, Los Angeles? Ditto for young Cubans drifting along the Gulf Stream to Miami, the world's second largest Cuban city? London, Amsterdam, Paris, Lisbon, and other European cities are already swelling with youthful immigrants from former colonies, while Lagos, Rio de Janeiro, Santiago, Beijing, Bombay, and other third-world cities bulge from migration.

With the possible exception of North Korea (where all televisions and radios only receive the two government-controlled channels), there already exists a McDonald's Generation of perhaps a billion pre-teens, teenagers, and young adults, peppered throughout every other country on earth. If that does not constitute a megatrend, move forward 50 years when this cadre embraces those age 70 and under.

The Macro Trend: Freed Markets

Beginning with the demise of the "Articles of Confederation" that preceded the present-day constitution of the United States, the 13 colonies have grown to become 50 integrated and free American markets. In 1993, the European Economic Community, begun in the late 1950s, transformed itself into the European Union (EU). And beginning in 1994, Mexico's approximately 92 million people joined Canada and the United States in eliminating almost all trade barriers to form another continent-spanning market, the North American Free Trade Agreement (NAFTA).

Recent years have also seen free trade agreements signed between Mexico, Columbia, and Venezuela. Brazil and its neighbors are also dismantling trade barriers. More recently the EU voted to add Sweden, Norway, Finland, and Austria to its membership, with the middle European countries standing in line waiting to join. Likewise, Chile and others are seeking membership in NAFTA. Restated, at the global level we see country-sized pixels clustering together into integrated, free-market collections.

The emerging picture suggests that markets, once freed, are lifting nation-states onto a faster-track economic growth. For example, between 1990 and 1993, Chile pulled one million of its 13 million citizens out of poverty. Though a feat not likely to be duplicated, the Chilean government has achieved this little-known success through free-market inspired growth. By pulling down trade barriers, cutting taxes, stabilizing its government, and redesigning its Social Security system, Chile stands as a beacon, attracting imitators in adjoining Argentina, Bolivia, and Peru that want to play by similar, macroeconomic rules.

In Chile's case, it took an economically enlightened (albeit politically repressive) military dictatorship to follow the free-market advice of the "Chicago boys"—youthful economists from the University of Chicago and their protégés. Import tariffs fell from 400 percent to 11 percent. Public businesses and services were privatized, ranging from major utilities to city buses and street sweepers. Even Social Security was converted from the thinly disguised tax and welfare program typical in Europe and North America into a privately administered retirement account. This account allows Chilean workers to send their funds to a choice of for-profit investment firms that report their results to these "micro-capitalist" investors three times a year. Every worker has become an "investor" in Chile's system of developing capitalism, adding to the country's political stability. Ironically, as this Chilean model is exported up the Andes and across the pampas, freed markets find governments giving up economic controls, tariffs, and other impediments to the efficient flow of goods. In other words, governments' involvement in the economies lessens.

As business leaders and entrepreneurs respond, domestically and internationally, to such activity, separate nation-states (usually those nearest) also become increasingly interdependent, lessening the likelihood of war. This story could be repeated using Singapore and its neighbors—Malaysia, Indonesia, and Thailand. Does anyone expect another war among those who comprise the European Union, for example? The resulting prosperity also yields resources to stave off famine. Even in the face of local crop failures, free economies become less dependent upon agriculture as they move up to higher value-added industries and services. Discrimination—within and between countries—lessens, at least to the extent that such discrimination emerges out of poverty and the ignorance it fosters.

In time, the economic interdependencies may overshadow the importance of political units, as has happened with the decline of "states' rights" in the United States and as appears destined to continue among the EU countries. Whether NAFTA and other economic structures evolve into tentative political unions in the long run is uncertain, but ample precedent exists.

Youth, Freed Trade, and Competitive Convergence

The issues of the global youth culture and the expansion of free trade that have brought the world to its present configuration are obvious to see. Less obvious, but perhaps equally powerful, is a third trend—competitive convergence. Here the argument is straightforward: similarities in macroeconomic and political policies affecting competition have given birth to free trade areas (such as

NAFTA), economic union (such as Western Europe), and the General Agreement on Tariffs and Trade (GATT) and its successor, the World Trade Organization. These similarities, combined with a growing uniformity of expectations among the upcoming generation of workers, will lead to a convergence in competitive practices.

Competitive convergence will be driven by competitive necessity. The need to battle stronger and stronger global competitors, which are likely to emerge from larger and larger free markets, will not permit firms to ignore practices that meet a pragmatic test (does it work?). At the same time, fewer trade barriers will mean that those who do not rapidly adopt global best practices will find fewer "safe" or "home" markets in which to continue their less efficient ways. And with growing homogeneity of values among the young, the cultural, political, and economic roadblocks to global best practices will be dismantled by an ever-expanding (and aging) youth culture as it reaches the levers of political and corporate power.

By way of illustration, consider some preliminary examples of best practices that have been adapted across borders and cultures with increasingly less resistance. Management examples first:

• Just-in-time production and inventory techniques developed in Japan have spread to many U.S. and European businesses, as have time-to-market innovations for new product introductions, such as concurrent engineering.

• Downsizing—the forced reduction in company employment—has remained a predominantly U.S. management approach, restricted by tradition among Japan's large employers and by employment laws throughout most of the EU. However, with Japan's often overstaffed white-collar positions and European employer reluctance to hire new workers, the U.S. competitive advantage in costs, flexibility, and speed is causing Nissan and other large Japanese firms to announce work force reductions that are poorly disguised downsizing efforts. Likewise, EU ministers—in the name of "labor law equalization"—are discussing the politically sensitive revision of restrictive employment laws.

• Continuous quality improvement efforts, largely pioneered by U.S. statisticians before and during World War II, gave Japan a competitive edge that led to adoption by U.S. and European producers. This is evidenced by a look at the U.S. Malcolm Baldrige Award and the EU's ISO 9000 standards.

• Flexible manufacturing systems, long used in the Japanese automobile industry to balance production flows with market demand and accelerate model changeover times, are gaining popularity in American factories.

Global best practices extend to marketing and distribution:

• MTV (and its imitators), specializing in English-language rock 'n roll, can be seen even in the jungles of Africa, Asia, and South America, advertising a largely identical parade of products, sometimes even using the original English language ads found in the United States.

• With parents in tow by their four-year-olds, one of the largest McDonald's restaurants can be found in Beijing's Tiananmen Square (ironically located only a few hundred yards from China's major tourist attraction—Mao's crypt).

• Coke and Pepsi battle for the youth market from Shanghai to Chicago, touting to investors the growth potential of the third world.

• Sonae Investments—Portugal's largest group of private companies—proudly counts among its holdings the Pizza Hut franchise for the country.

• Jeans, running shoes, and printed tee shirts are the global youth culture's uniform everywhere, implying a standard dress (and product) configuration for one globalwide demographic segment.

If there has been one growth industry that accelerated through the global recession of the early 1990s, it is the worldwide explosion of MBA programs—particularly in developing countries. Though not necessarily a "global best practice," similarity of curricula and training in business disciplines seems likely to hasten further the spread of (past and future) competitive best practices.

Admittedly, a handful of anecdotal illustrations do not prove competitive convergence. Nor is the argument being made for some future universality of business practices. German and Japanese business leaders are likely to retain longer planning horizons than their U.S. counterparts; Asian nations are more likely to subordinate personal freedoms to the good of the group; and long-term employment stability is more likely in Japan or Europe than in the United States for the foreseeable future. Nevertheless, evidence for a convergence of global best practices seems strong. Other trends—from computer networking to proliferating international alliances—make competitive convergence appear to be the not-so-invisible hand and sword of competition.

From here on into the future, the evidence for trends is replaced, of necessity, by speculation. Certainly, extending the past 25 years of cultural dispersion, movements toward freed trade, and competitive convergence is—like any extrapolation—dangerous, because it assumes that current conditions will hold in the distant future. Paradoxically, such an assumption is both unlikely *and* the most reasonable basis from which to proceed.

So we plunge into a future where, current conditions suggest, in less than 15 years trade barriers in North America will effectively be gone—probably along with those between Central America, the Caribbean, northern South America, and the Andes countries. The Southern Cone of Argentina (which has already pegged its currency to the dollar), Brazil (which is trying to), Uruguay, and Paraguay will be even further advanced in eliminating their intra-regional barriers. Perhaps with greater stability in Brazil, these Southern Cone members will already have joined their neighbor, Chile, in affiliation with the descendants of NAFTA—forming a truly hemispheric free trade area of more than half a billion people.

Of approximately equal size, one might imagine a European Union early in the next century that (in various stages of social and economic integration) reaches from Ireland to the Urals, becoming truly pan-European. Assuming some form of Asian free trade area, one might also imagine three billion people stretching from Pakistan through India and Southeast Asia to Indonesia, the Philippines, China, Japan, Korea, and eastern Siberia.

Faced with the prospects of a three-billion member free trade area, it takes only a little more imagination to see a European-oriented North and South America achieving some form of economic free trade (though not necessarily political) arrangement with an enlarged European Union. In fact, geopolitical economic realities may demand the formation of a billion-member free trade area stretching east from the beaches of Hawaii to North America and Europe to the Ural mountains deep in Russia. This Eurocentric trade area may well be needed to offset the staggering possibility of 21st century Japanese technology combining with Chinese entrepreneurship, industriousness, and markets.

At this stage—perhaps within a generation from now and well within the lifetimes of even Baby Boomers—a free trade agreement between the West and the East may become a prudent reality to ensure peace and economic stability for a world of investors and micro-capitalists. Then the economies of the Middle East, Africa, and Oceania (not already affiliated with one or more trading areas) could be folded into a truly global, free trade environment. Presumably, higher standards of living for the then 10 billion or so inhabitants of Spaceship Earth would create additional political freedoms.

Remember, too, the youth trend. Today's teenagers a quarter of a century from now will be the middle-aged business and government leaders who will negotiate these ever-expanding agreements. They, more than any generation in history, will have been nurtured on a world-oriented culture and are more likely to see similarities where their grandparents saw differences. Being less focused on regional or ethnocentric differences, they are likely to view international differences in politics, culture, and economics as unimportant impediments to a more culturally and economically unified planet.

Of course, this scenario and its assumptions are far from certain. Just as mass production gave rise to the affluence that allowed "mass customiza-

tion," the backlash to an increasingly uniform, global culture will undoubtedly be the need to reassert individual, even group, differences. One need only think of the war in the former Yugoslavia or the French separatist movement in Québec to see centuries-old cross-currents vigorously resisting the forces of convergence. Freedom of choice to those not used to it may be a burden to be resisted more than a joy to be embraced. Likewise, when rising expectations are blunted by a stagnant reality that offers little improvement for some and reverses for many, counterrevolutions may arise to reattain some idealized, if not ideal, past. Certainly there are many in the former Soviet Union who would prefer a return to the past over their turbulent adventure into the future. And deeply embedded cultural and religious beliefs will still be communicated by family and community, continuing to resist the modern forces of economic and social convergence well beyond the foreseeable future.

Nor does such an optimistic scenario suggest 10 billion people uniformly marching to an identical drum beat. Instead, what is proposed here is that as the drum grows louder, more people will march to its unifying beat. Ten billion pixels will not suddenly snap into focus. Instead they will slowly emerge to reveal a world increasingly devoid of war, famine, bigotry, and oppression—because none of these conditions are particularly favorable for free trade and a world of voters turned micro-capitalists.

The result will not be Utopia. Poverty will exist, even if hunger does not. Social tensions from mass migrations and immigrations will still strain relations between "different peoples," even though these differences will erode under the bombardment of satellite-based TV, telephone, and computer communications. It won't quite be one planet, one people, one culture—one world. But a growing number of people will hold MBAs, not guns. And in this not-so-long run, many of us will defy Keynes' dictum and still be alive to enjoy the fruits of this new millennium—fresh fruits undoubtedly provided by Chilean businesses during the Northern hemisphere's long winters.

WHAT IS A GLOBAL MANAGER?

Christopher A. Bartlett and Sumantra Ghoshal

In the early stages of its drive overseas, Corning Glass hired an American ex-ambassador to head up its international division. He had excellent contacts in the governments of many nations and could converse in several languages, but he was less familiar with Corning and its businesses. In contrast, ITT decided to set up a massive educational program to "globalize" all managers responsible for its worldwide telecommunications business—in essence, to replace its national specialists with global generalists.

Corning and ITT eventually realized they had taken wrong turns. Like many other companies organizing for worldwide operations in recent years, they found that an elite group of jet-setters was often difficult to integrate into the corporate mainstream; nor did they need an international team of big-picture overseers to the exclusion of focused experts.

Success in today's international climate—a far cry from only a decade ago—demands highly specialized yet closely linked groups of global business managers, country or regional managers, and

worldwide functional managers. This kind of organization characterizes a *transnational* rather than an old-line multinational, international, or global company. Transnationals integrate assets, resources, and diverse people in operating units around the world. Through a flexible management process, in which business, country, and functional managers form a triad of different perspectives that balance one another, transnational companies can build three strategic capabilities:

- Global-scale efficiency and competitiveness.
- National-level responsiveness and flexibility; and
- Cross-market capacity to leverage learning on a worldwide basis.

While traditional organizations, structured along product or geographic lines, can hone one or another of these capabilities, they cannot cope with the challenge of all three at once. But an emerging group of transnational companies has begun to transform the classic hierarchy of headquarters–subsidiary relationships into an integrated network of specialized yet interdependent units. For many, the greatest constraint in creating such an organization is a severe shortage of executives with the skills, knowledge, and sophistication to operate in a more tightly linked and less classically hierarchical network.

In fact, in the volatile world of transnational corporations, there is no such thing as a universal global manager. Rather, there are three groups of specialists: business managers, country managers, and functional managers. And there are the top executives at corporate headquarters, the leaders who manage the complex interactions between the three—and can identify and develop the talented executives a successful transnational requires.

To build such talent, top management must understand the strategic importance of each specialist. The careers of Leif Johansson of Electrolux, Howard Gottlieb of NEC, and Wahib Zaki of Proctor & Gamble vividly exemplify the specialized yet interdependent roles the three types of global managers play.

The Business Manager: Strategist + Architect + Coordinator

Global business or product-division managers have one overriding responsibility: to further the company's global-scale efficiency and competitiveness. This task requires not only the perspective to recognize opportunities and risks across national and functional boundaries but also the skill to coordinate activities and link capabilities across those barriers. The global business manager's overall goal is to capture the full benefit of integrated worldwide operations.

To be effective, the three roles at the core of a business manager's job are to serve as the strategist for his or her organization, the architect of its worldwide asset and resource configuration, and the coordinator of transactions across national borders. Leif Johansson, now president of Electrolux, the Swedish-based company, played all three roles successfully in his earlier position as head of the household appliance division.

In 1983, when 32-year-old Johansson assumed responsibility for the division, he took over a business that had been built up through more than 100 acquisitions over the previous eight years. By the late 1980s, Electrolux's portfolio included more than 20 brands sold in some 40 countries, with acquisitions continuing throughout the decade. Zanussi, for example, the big Italian manufacturer acquired by Electrolux in 1984, had built a strong market presence based on its reputation for innovation in household and commercial appliances. In addition, Arthur Martin in France and Zoppas in Norway had strong local brand positions but limited innovative capability.

As a result of these acquisitions, Electrolux had accumulated a patchwork quilt of companies, each with a different product portfolio, market position, and competitive situation. Johansson soon recognized the need for an overall strategy to coordinate and integrate his dispersed operations.

Talks with national marketing managers quickly convinced him that dropping local brands and standardizing around a few high-volume regional and global products would be unwise. He agreed with the local managers that their national brands were vital to maintaining consumer loyalty, distribution leverage, and competitive flexibility in markets that they saw fragmenting into more and more segments. But Johansson also understood the views of his division staff members, who pointed to the many similarities in product characteristics and consumer needs in the various markets. The division staff was certain Electrolux could use this advantage to cut across markets and increase competitiveness.

Johansson led a strategy review with a task force of product-division staff and national marketing managers. While the task force confirmed the marketing managers' notion of growing segmentation, its broader perspective enabled Johansson to see a convergence of segments across national markets. Their closer analysis also refined management's understanding of local market needs, concluding that consumers perceived "localness" mainly in terms of how a product was sold (distribution through local channels, promotion in local media, use of local brand names) instead of how it was designed or what features it offered.

From this analysis, Johansson fashioned a product-market strategy that identified two full-line regional brands to be promoted and supported in all European markets. He positioned the Electrolux brand to respond to the cross-market segment for high prestige (customers characterized as "conservatives"), while the Zanussi brand would fill the segment where innovative products were key (for "trendsetters").

The local brands were clustered in the other two market segments pinpointed in the analysis: "yuppies" ("young and aggressive" urban professionals) and "environmentalists" ("warm and friendly" people interested in basic-value products). The new strategy provided Electrolux with localized brands that responded to the needs of these consumer groups. At the same time, the company captured the efficiencies possible by standardizing the basic chassis and components of these local-brand products, turning them out in high volume in specialized regional plants.

So, by tracking product and market trends across borders, Leif Johansson captured valuable global-scale efficiencies while reaping the benefits of a flexible response to national market fragmentation. What's more, though he took on the leadership role as a strategist, Johansson never assumed he alone had the understanding or the ability to form a global appliance strategy; he relied heavily on both corporate and local managers. Indeed, Johansson continued to solicit guidance on strategy through a council of country managers called *the 1992 Group* and through a set of product councils made up of functional managers.

In fact, the global business manager's responsibility for the distribution of crucial assets and resources is closely tied to shaping an integrated strategy. While he or she often relies on the input of regional and functional heads, the business manager is still the architect who usually initiates and leads the debate on where major plants, technical centers, and sales offices should be located—and which facilities should be closed.

The obvious political delicacy of such debates is not the only factor that makes simple economic analysis inadequate. Within every operating unit there exists a pool of skills and capabilities that may have taken a lot of time and investment to build up. The global business manager has to achieve the most efficient distribution of assets and resources while protecting and leveraging the competence at hand. Electrolux's household appliance division had more than 200 plants and a bewildering array of technical centers and development groups in many countries. It was clear to Johansson that he had to rationalize this infrastructure.

He began by setting a policy for the household appliance division that would avoid concentration of facilities in one country or region, even in its Scandinavian home base. At the same time, Johansson wanted to specialize the division's development and manufacturing infrastructure on a "one product, one facility" basis. He was determined to allocate important development and manufacturing tasks to each of the company's major markets. In trying to optimize robustness and flexibility in the long term rather than minimize short-term costs, Johansson recognized that a specialized yet dispersed system would be less vulnerable to exchange-rate fluctuations and political uncertainties. This setup also tapped local managerial and technical resources, thereby reducing dependence on the small pool of skilled labor and management in Sweden.

Instead of closing old plants, Johansson insisted on upgrading and tailoring existing facilities, whenever possible. In addition to averting political fallout and organizational trauma, Electrolux would then retain valuable know-how and bypass the start-up problems of building from scratch. An outstanding example of this approach it Zanussi's Porcia plant in Italy, which Electrolux turned into the world's largest washing machine plant. After a massive $150 million investment, the Porcia plant now produces 1.5 million units a year.

Although acquisition-fueled growth often leads to redundancy and overcapacity, it can also bring new resources and strengths. Instead of wiping out the division's diversity through homogenization or centralization, Johansson decided to leverage it by matching each unit's responsibilities with its particular competence. Because of the Scandinavian flair for modular design, he assigned the integrated kitchen-system business to Electrolux's Swedish and Finnish units. He acknowledged Porcia's experience in component production by consolidating design and production of compressors there. Johansson's reshaping of assets and resources not only enhanced scale economies and operational flexibility but also boosted morale by giving operating units the opportunity to leverage their distinctive competences beyond their local markets.

Newly developed business strategies obviously need coordination. In practice, the specialization of assets and resources swells the flow of products and components among national units, requiring a firm hand to synchronize and control that flow. For organizations whose operations have become more dispersed and specialized at the same time that their strategies have become more connected and integrated, coordination across borders is a tough challenge. Business managers must fashion a repertoire of approaches and tools, from simple centralized control to management of exceptions identified through formal policies to indirect management via informal communication channels.

Leif Johansson coordinated product flow—across his 35 national sales units and 29 regional sourcing facilities—by establishing broad sourcing policies and transfer-pricing ranges that set limits but left negotiations to internal suppliers and customers. For instance, each sales unit could negotiate a transfer price with its internal source for a certain product in a set range that was usually valid for a year. If the negotiations moved outside that range, the companies had to check with headquarters. As a coordinator, Johansson led the deliberations that defined the logic and philosophy of the parameters; but he stepped back and let individual unit managers run their own organizations, except when a matter went beyond policy limits.

In contrast, coordination of business strategy in Johansson's division was managed through teams that cut across the formal hierarchy. Instead of

centralizing, he relied on managers to share the responsibility for monitoring implementation and resolving problems through teams. To protect the image and positioning of his regional brands—Electrolux and Zanussi—he set up a brand-coordination group for each. Group members came from the sales companies in key countries, and the chairperson was a corporate marketing executive. Both groups were responsible for building a coherent, pan-European strategy for the brand they represented.

To rationalize the various product strategies across Europe, Johansson created product-line boards to oversee these strategies and to exploit any synergies. Each product line had its own board made up of the corporate product-line manager, who was chair, and his or her product managers. The Quattro 500 refrigerator-freezer, which was designed in Italy, built in Finland, and marketed in Sweden, was one example of how these boards could successfully integrate product strategy.

In addition, the 1992 Group periodically reviewed the division's overall results, kept an eye on its manufacturing and marketing infrastructure, and supervised major development programs and investment projects. Capturing the symbolic value of 1992 in its name, the group was chaired by Johansson himself and included business managers from Italy, the United Kingdom, Spain, the United States, France, Switzerland, and Sweden.

Indeed, coordination probably takes up more of the global business manager's time than any other aspect of the job. This role requires that a manager have great administrative and interpersonal skills to ensure that coordination and integration don't deteriorate into heavy-handed control.

Many traditional multinational companies have made the mistake of automatically anointing their home country product-division managers with the title of global business manager. Sophisticated transnational companies, however, have long since separated the notions of coordination and centralization, looking for business leadership from their best units, wherever they may be located. For example, Asea Brown Boveri, the Swiss-headquartered electrical engineering corporation, has tried to leverage the strengths of its operating companies and exploit their location in critical markets by putting its business managers wherever strategic and organizational dimensions coincide. In Asea Brown Boveri's power-transmission business, the manager for switch gear is located in Sweden, the manager for power transformers is in Germany, the manager for distribution transformers is in Norway, and the manager for electric metering is in the United States.

Even well-established multinationals with a tradition of tight central control are changing their tack. The head of IBM's telecommunications business recently moved her division headquarters to London, not only to situate the command center closer to the booming European market for computer networking but also "to give us a different perspective on all our markets."

The Country Manager: Sensor + Builder + Contributor

The building blocks for most worldwide companies are their national subsidiaries. If the global business manager's main objective is to achieve global-scale efficiency and competitiveness, the national subsidiary manager's is to be sensitive and responsive to the local market. Country managers play the pivotal role not only in meeting local customer needs but also in satisfying the host government's requirements and defending their company's market positions against local and external competitors.

The need for local flexibility often puts the country manager in conflict with the global business manager. But in a successful transnational like Electrolux, negotiation can resolve these differences. In this era of intense competition around the world, companies cannot afford to permit a subsidiary manager to defend parochial interests as "king of the country."

Nor should headquarters allow national subsidiaries to become the battleground for corporate holy wars fought in the name of globalization. In many companies, their national subsidiaries are hothouses of entrepreneurship and innovation—homes for valuable resources and capabilities that must be nurtured, not constrained or cut off. The subsidiaries of Philips, for one, have consistently led product development: in television, the company's first color TV was developed in Canada, the first stereo model in Australia, and the first teletext in the United Kingdom. Unilever's national subsidiaries have also been innovative in product-marketing strategy: Germany created the campaign for Snuggle (a fabric softener); Finland developed Timotei (an herbal shampoo); and South Africa launched Impulse (a body perfume).

In fact, effective country managers play three vital roles: the sensor and interpreter of local opportunities and threats, the builder of local resources and capabilities, and the contributor to and active participant in global strategy. Howard Gottlieb's experience as general manager of NEC's switching-systems subsidiary in the United States illustrates the importance of all three tasks.

As a sensor, the country manager must be good at gathering and sifting information, interpreting the implications, and predicting a range of feasible outcomes. More important, this manager has the difficult task of conveying the importance of such intelligence to people higher up, especially those whose perceptions may be dimmed by distance or even ethnocentric bias. Today, when information gathered locally increasingly applies to other regions or even globally, communicating effectively is crucial. Consumer trends in one country often spread to another; technologies developed in a leading-edge environment can have global significance; a competitor's local market testing may signal a wider strategy; and national legislative initiatives in areas like deregulation and environmental protection tend to spill across borders.

Gottlieb's contribution to NEC's understanding of changes in the telecommunications market demonstrates how a good sensor can connect local intelligence with global strategy. In the late 1980s, Gottlieb was assigned to build the U.S. market for NEAX 61, a widely acclaimed digital telecom switch designed by the parent company in Japan. Although it was technologically sophisticated, early sales didn't meet expectations.

His local-market background and contacts led Gottlieb to a quick diagnosis of the problem. NEC had designed the switch to meet the needs of NTT, the Japanese telephone monopoly, and it lacked many features U.S. customers wanted. For one thing, its software didn't incorporate the protocol conversions necessary for distributing revenues among the many U.S. companies that might handle a single long-distance phone call. Nor could the switch handle revenue-enhancing features like "call waiting" and "call forwarding," which were vital high-margin items in the competitive, deregulated American market.

In translating the needs of his U.S. division to the parent company NEC, Gottlieb had a formidable task. To convince his superiors in Japan that redesigning NEAX 61 was necessary, he had to bridge two cultures and penetrate the subtleties of the parent company's Japanese-dominated management processes. And he had to instill a sense of urgency in several corporate management groups, varying his pitches to appeal to the interests of each. For instance, Gottlieb convinced the engineering department that the NEAX 61 switch had been underdesigned for the U.S. market and the marketing department that time was short because the Bell operating companies were calling for quotes.

A transnational's greater access to the scarcest of all corporate resources, human capability, is a definite advantage when compared with strictly local companies—or old-line multinationals, for that matter. Scores of companies like IBM, Merc, and Procter & Gamble have recognized the value of harvesting advanced (and often less expensive) scientific expertise by upgrading local development labs into global centers of technical excellence.

Other companies have built up and leveraged their overseas human resources in different ways. Cummins Engine, for example, has set up its highly skilled but surprisingly low-cost Indian engineering group as a worldwide drafting resource; American Airlines's Barbados operation does much of the corporate clerical work; and Becton Dickinson, a large hospital supply company, has given its Belgian subsidiary pan-European responsibility for managing distribution and logistics.

Indeed, the burden of identifying, developing, and leveraging such national resources and capabilities falls on country managers. Howard Gottlieb, after convincing Tokyo that the United States would be an important market for NEC's global digital-switch design, persuaded headquarters to permit his new engineering group to take part early on in the product development of the next generation switch—the NEAX 61 E. He sent teams of engineers to Japan to work with the original designers; and, to verify his engineers' judgments, Gottlieb invited the designers to visit his customers in the United States. These exchanges not only raised the sensitivity of NEC's Japan-based engineers to U.S. market needs but also significantly increased their respect for their American colleagues. Equally important, the U.S. unit's morale rose.

As a builder, Gottlieb used this mutual confidence as the foundation for creating a software-development capability that would become a big corporate asset. Skilled software engineers, very scarce in Japan, were widely available in the United States. Gottlieb's first move was to put together a small software team to support local projects. Though its resources were limited, the group turned out a number of innovations, including a remote software-patching capability that later became part of the 61 E switch design. The credibility he won at headquarters allowed Gottlieb to expand his design engineering group from 10 to more than 50 people within two years, supporting developments not only in North America but also eventually in Asia.

In many transnationals, access to strategically important information—and control over strategically important assets—has catapulted country managers into a much more central role. As links to local markets, they are no longer mere implementers of programs and policies shaped at headquarters; many have gained some influence over the way their organizations make important strategic and operational decisions. In most of today's truly transnational companies, country managers and their chief local subordinates often participate in new-product-development committees, product-marketing task forces, and global-strategy conferences. Even at the once impenetrable annual top management meetings, national subsidiary managers may present their views and defend their interests before senior corporate and domestic executives—a scenario that would have been unthinkable even a decade ago.

Of course, the historic position of most national units of worldwide companies has been that of the implementer of strategy from headquarters. Because the parent company's accepted objectives are the outcome of discussion and negotiation involving numerous units, divisions, and national subsidiaries, sometimes a country manager must carry out a strategy that directly conflicts with what he or she has lobbied for in vain.

But a diverse and dispersed worldwide organization, with subsidiaries that control many of the vital development, production, and marketing resources, can no longer allow the time-honored "king of the country" to decide how, when, and even whether his or her national unit will implement a particular strategic initiative. The decision made by the North American subsidiary of Philips to outsource its VCRs from a Japanese competitor rather than the parent company is one of the most notorious instances of how a local "king" can undermine global strategy.

At NEC, Howard Gottlieb spent about 60 percent of his time on customer relations and probing the market and about 30 percent managing the Tokyo interface. His ability to understand and interpret the global strategic implications of U.S. market needs—and the software-development group he built from scratch—allowed him to take part in NEC's ongoing strategy debate. As a result, Gottlieb changed his division's role from implementer of corporate strategy to active contributor in designing that strategy.

The Functional Manager: Scanner + Cross-Pollinator + Champion

While global business managers and country managers have come into their own, functional specialists have yet to gain the recognition due them in many traditional multinational companies. Relegated to support-staff roles, excluded from important meetings, and even dismissed as unnecessary overhead, functional managers are often given little chance to participate in, let alone contribute to, the corporate mainstream's global activity. In some cases, top management has allowed staff functions to become a warehouse for corporate misfits or a graveyard for managerial has-beens. Yet at a time when information, knowledge, and expertise have become more specialized, an organization can gain huge benefits by linking its technical, manufacturing, marketing, human resources, and financial experts worldwide.

Given that today's transnationals face the strategic challenge of resolving the conflicts implicit in achieving global competitiveness, national responsiveness, and worldwide learning, business and country managers must take primary responsibility for the first two capabilities. But the third is the functional manager's province.

Building an organization that can use learning to create and spread innovations requires the skill to transfer specialized knowledge while also connecting scarce resources and capabilities across national borders. To achieve this important objective, functional managers must scan for specialized information worldwide, "cross-pollinate" leading-edge knowledge and best practice, and champion innovations that may offer transnational opportunities and applications.

Most innovation starts, of course, when managers perceive a particular opportunity or market threat, such as an emerging consumer trend, a revolutionary technological development, a bold competitive move, or a pending government regulation. When any of these flags pops up around the world, it may seem unimportant to corporate headquarters if viewed in isolation. But when a functional manager acts as a scanner, with the expertise and perspective to detect trends and move knowledge across boundaries, he or she can transform piecemeal information into strategic intelligence.

In sophisticated transnationals, senior functional executives serve as linchpins, connecting their areas of specialization throughout the organization. Using informal networks, they create channels for communicating specialized information and repositories for proprietary knowledge. Through such links, Electrolux marketing managers first identified the emergence of cross-market segments, and NEC's technical managers were alerted to the shift from analog to digital switching technology.

In the same manner, Wahib Zaki of Procter & Gamble's European operations disapproved of P&G's high-walled organizational structures, which isolated and insulated the technical development carried out in each subsidiary's lab. When Zaki became head of R&D in Europe, he decided to break down some walls. In his new job, he was ideally placed to become a scanner and cross-pollinator. He formed European technical teams and ran a series of conferences in which like-minded experts from various countries could exchange information and build informal communication networks.

Still, Zaki needed more ammunition to combat the isolation, defensiveness, and "not invented here" attitude in each research center. He distributed staff among the European technical center in Brussels and the development groups of P&G's subsidiaries. He used his staff teams to help clarify the particular role of each national technical manager and to specialize activities that had been duplicated on a country-by-country basis with little transfer of accumulated knowledge.

In response to competitive threats from rivals Unilever, Henkel, and Colgate-Palmolive—and to

a perceived consumer trend—P&G's European headquarters asked the Brussels-based research center to develop a new liquid laundry detergent. By that time, Zaki had on hand a technical team that had built up relationships among its members so that it formed a close-knit network of intelligence and product expertise.

The team drew the product profile necessary for healthy sales in multiple markets with diverse needs. In several European markets, powdered detergents contained enzymes to break down protein-based stains, and the new liquid detergent would have to accomplish the same thing. In some markets, a bleach substitute was important; in others, hard water presented the toughest challenge; while in several countries, environmental concerns limited the use of phosphates. Moreover, the new detergent had to be effective in large-capacity, top-loading machines, as well as in the small, front-loading machines common in Europe.

Zaki's team developed a method that made enzymes stable in liquid form (a new technique that was later patented), a bleach substitute effective at low temperatures, a fatty acid that yielded good water-softening performance without phosphates, and a suds-suppressant that worked in front-loading machines (so bubbles wouldn't ooze out the door). By integrating resources and expertise, Zaki cross-pollinated best practice for a new product.

The R&D group was so successful that the European headquarters adopted the use of teams for its management of the new brand launch. P&G's first European brand team pooled the knowledge and expertise of brand managers from seven subsidiaries to draft a launch program and marketing strategy for the new liquid detergent Vizir, which ensured its triumphant rollout in seven countries in six months. P&G's homework enabled it to come up with a product that responded to European needs, while Colgate-Palmolive was forced to withdraw its liquid detergent brand, Axion— which had been designed in the United States and wasn't tailored for Europe—after an 18-month market test.

As a reward for his performance in Europe,

Wahib Zaki was transferred to Procter & Gamble's Cincinnati corporate headquarters as a senior vice president of R&D. He found that researchers there were working on improved builders (the ingredients that break down dirt) for a new liquid laundry detergent to be launched in the United States. In addition, the international technology-coordination group was working the P&G's Japanese subsidiary to formulate a liquid detergent surfactant (the ingredient that removes greasy stains) that would be effective in the cold-water washes common in Japanese households, where laundry is often done in used bath water. Neither group had shared its findings or new ideas with the other, and neither had incorporated the numerous breakthroughs represented by Vizir—despite the evidence that consumer needs, market trends, competitive challenges, and regulatory requirements were all spreading across national borders.

Playing the role of champion, Zaki decided to use this development process to demonstrate the benefits of coordinating P&G's sensitivity and responsiveness to diverse consumer needs around the world. He formed a team drawn from three technical groups (one in Brussels and two in the United States) to turn out a world liquid laundry detergent. The team analyzed the trends, generated product specifications, and brought together dispersed technical knowledge and expertise, which culminated in one of Procter & Gamble's most successful product launches ever. Sold as Liquid Tide in the United States, Liquid Cheer in Japan, and Liquid Ariel in Europe, the product was P&G's first rollout on such a global scale.

As Zaki continued to strengthen cross-border technology links through other projects, Procter & Gamble gradually converted its far-flung sensing and response resources into an integrated learning organization. By scanning for new developments, cross-pollinating best practice, and championing innovations with transnational applications, Wahib Zaki, a superlative functional manager, helped create an organization that could both develop demonstrably better new products and roll them out at a rapid pace around the world.

The Corporate Manager: Leader + Talent Scout + Developer

Clearly, there is no single model for the global manager. Neither the old-line international specialist nor the most recent global generalist can cope with the complexities of cross-border strategies. Indeed, the dynamism of today's marketplace calls for managers with diverse skills. Responsibility for worldwide operations belongs to senior business, country, and functional executives who focus on the intense interchanges and subtle negotiations required. In contrast, those in middle management and front-line jobs need well-defined responsibilities, a clear understanding of their organization's transnational mission, and a sense of accountability—but few of the distractions senior negotiators must shoulder.

Meanwhile, corporate managers integrate these many levels of responsibility, playing perhaps the most vital role in transnational management. The corporate manager not only leads in the broadest sense; he or she also identifies and develops talented business, country, and functional managers—and balances the negotiations among the three. It's up to corporate managers to promote strong managerial specialists like Johansson, Gottlieb, and Zaki, those individuals who can translate company strategy into effective operations around the world.

Successful corporate managers like Floris Maljers, co-chairman of Unilever, have made the recruitment, training, and development of promising executives a top priority. By the 1980s, with Maljers as chairman, Unilever had a clear policy of rotating managers through various jobs and moving them around the world, especially early in their careers. Unilever was one of the first transnationals to have a strong pool of specialized yet interdependent senior managers, drawn from throughout its diverse organization.

But while most companies require only a few truly transnational managers to implement cross-border strategies, the particular qualities necessary for such positions remain in short supply. According to Maljers, it is this limitation in human resources—*not* unreliable or inadequate sources of capital—that has become the biggest constraint in most globalization efforts.

Locating such individuals is difficult under any circumstances, but corporate managers greatly improve the odds when their search broadens from a focus on home-country managers to incorporate the worldwide pool of executives in their organization. Because transnationals operate in many countries, they have access to a wide range of managerial talent. Yet such access—like information on local market trends or consumer needs that should cross organizational boundaries—is often an underexploited asset.

As a first step, senior executives can identify those in the organization with the potential for developing the skills and perspectives demanded of global managers. Such individuals must have a broad, nonparochial view of the company and its operations yet a deep understanding of their own business, country, or functional tasks. Obviously even many otherwise talented managers in an organization aren't capable of such a combination of flexibility and commitment to specific interests, especially when it comes to cross-border coordination and integration. Top management may have to track the careers of promising executives over a number of years before deciding whether to give them senior responsibilities. At Unilever, for example, the company maintains four development lists that indicate both the level of each manager and his or her potential. The progress of managers on the top "A1" list is tracked by Unilever's Special Committee, which includes the two chairmen.

Once corporate managers identify the talent, they have the duty to develop it. They must provide opportunities for achievement that allow business, country, and functional managers to handle negotiations in a worldwide context. A company's ability to identify individuals with potential, legitimize their diversity, and integrate them into the organization's corporate decisions is the single clearest indicator that the corporate leader is a true global manager—and that the company itself is a true transnational.

II THE ENVIRONMENT OF INTERNATIONAL AND GLOBAL MARKETING

THE CULTURAL AND ECONOMIC ENVIRONMENT

Readers will discover in this section a rich selection of contributions examining major world cultures that marketers must understand and appreciate if they are to maximize the likelihood of success in the international marketplace. "Culture is everything that people have, think and do as members of a society."[1] Culture is the summation of customs, skills, arts, values, attitudes, sociopolitical beliefs, religious roots, language, education, and productive systems of people that order their lives and are passed on to succeeding generations. Understanding cultural differences from one market to another is one of the most daunting issues facing international marketers today.

The selections begin with a venerable paper on cross-cultural communications—the silent language that often baffles international marketers in their efforts to influence overseas buyers. It is followed by a companion classic on avoiding business blunders abroad, especially those relating to product positioning, promotional programs, brand names, and packaging.

There are three other insightful papers in this section on the cultural and economic aspects of international operations. *The Importance of Culture in International Business Negotiations* documents the cultural understanding and skills needed for successful international negotiations. These insights are based on analysis of hundreds of business people in international negotiation simulations throughout the world. In the next selection, the multidimensional aspects of capitalism around the world are explored—the individualistic North American version, the communitarian European model, the Japanese version, the Korean approach, and the Chinese family business. It is a revealing analysis.

In the 1990s, Japan has suffered from a major, persistent, and structurally rooted recession that is often referred to as the post-bubble era. In the concluding selection, the adaptive post-bubble marketing strategies of Japanese firms are analyzed. It is a timely update on an important trading partner.

---

[1] Gary P. Ferraro, The Cultural Dimension of International Business (Englewood Cliffs, NJ: Prentice Hall, 1990), p. 18.

THE SILENT LANGUAGE IN OVERSEAS BUSINESS

Edward T. Hall

With few exceptions, Americans are relative newcomers on the international business scene. Today, as in Mark Twain's time, we are all too often "innocents abroad," in an era when naïveté and blundering in foreign business dealings may have serious political repercussions.

When the American executive travels abroad to do business, he is frequently shocked to discover to what extent the many variables of foreign behavior and custom complicate his efforts. Although the American has recognized, certainly, that even the man next door has many minor traits that make him somewhat peculiar, for some reason he has failed to appreciate how different foreign businessmen and their practices will seem to him.

He should understand that the various peoples around the world have worked out and integrated into their subconscious literally thousands of behavior patterns that they take for granted in each other.* Then, when the stranger enters, and behaves differently from the local norm, he often quite unintentionally insults, annoys, or amuses the native with whom he is attempting to do business. For example:

In the United States, a corporation executive knows what is meant when a client lets a month go by before replying to a business proposal. On the other hand, he senses an eagerness to do business if he is immediately ushered into the client's office. In both instances, he is reacting to subtle cues in the timing of interaction, cues that he depends on to chart his course of action.

Abroad, however, all this changes. The American executive learns that the Latin Americans are casual about time and that if he waits an hour in the outer office before seeing the Deputy Minister of Finance, it does not necessarily mean he is not getting anywhere. There people are so important that nobody can bear to tear himself away; because of the resultant interruptions and conversational detours, everybody is constantly getting behind. What the American does not know is the point at which the waiting becomes significant.

In another instance, after traveling 7,000 miles an American walks into the office of a highly recommended Arab businessman on whom he will have to depend completely. What he sees does not breed confidence. The office is reached by walking through a suspicious-looking coffeehouse in an old, dilapidated building situated in a

Reprinted and excerpted by permission of *Harvard Business Review,* "The Silent Language in Overseas Business," by Edward T. Hall, May–June 1960, pp. 87–96. Copyright 1960 by the President and Fellows of Harvard College; all rights reserved.
* For details see my book, *The Silent Language* (New York: Doubleday & Co., 1959).

crowded non-European section of town. The elevator, rising from dark, smelly corridors, is rickety and equally foul. When he gets to the office itself, he is shocked to find it small, crowded, and confused. Papers are stacked all over the desk and table tops—even scattered on the floor in irregular piles.

The Arab merchant he has come to see had met him at the airport the night before and sent his driver to the hotel this morning to pick him up. But now, after the American's rush, the Arab is tied up with something else. Even when they finally start talking business, there are constant interruptions. If the American is at all sensitive to his environment, everything around him signals, "What am I getting into?"

Before leaving home he was told that things would be different, but how different? The hotel is modern enough. The shops in the new part of town have many more American and European trade goods than he had anticipated. His first impression was that doing business in the Middle East would not present any new problems. Now he is beginning to have doubts. One minute everything looks familiar and he is on firm ground; the next, familiar landmarks are gone. His greatest problem is that so much assails his senses all at once that he does not know where to start looking for something that will tell him where he stands. He needs a frame of reference—a way of sorting out what is significant and relevant.

That is why it is so important for American businessmen to have a real understanding of the various social, cultural, and economic differences they will face when they attempt to do business in foreign countries. To help give some frame of reference, this article will map out a few areas of human activity that have largely been unstudied.

The topics I will discuss are certainly not presented as the last word on the subject, but they have proved to be highly reliable points at which to begin to gain an understanding of foreign cultures. While additional research will undoubtedly turn up other items just as relevant, at present I think the businessman can do well to begin by ap-

preciating cultural differences in matters concerning the language of time, of space, of material possessions, of friendship patterns, and of agreements.

Language of Time

Everywhere in the world people use time to communicate with each other. There are different languages of time just as there are different spoken languages. The unspoken languages are informal; yet the rules governing their interpretation are surprisingly *ironbound*. In the United States, a delay in answering a communication can result from a large volume of business causing the request to be postponed until the backlog is cleared away, from poor organization, or possibly from technical complexity requiring deep analysis. But if the person awaiting the answer or decision rules out these reasons, then the delay means to him that the matter has low priority on the part of the other person—lack of interest. On the other hand, a similar delay in a foreign country may mean something altogether different. Thus:

In Ethiopia, the time required for a decision is directly proportional to its importance. This is so much the case that low-level bureaucrats there have a way of trying to elevate the prestige of their work by taking a long time to make up their minds. (Americans in that part of the world are innocently prone to downgrade their work in the local people's eyes by trying to speed things up.)

In the Arab East, time does not generally include schedules as Americans know and use them. The time required to get something accomplished depends on the relationship. More important people get fast service from less important people, and conversely. Close relatives take absolute priority; nonrelatives are kept waiting.

In the United States, giving a person a deadline is a way of indicating the degree of urgency or relative importance of the work. But in the Middle East, the American runs into a cultural trap the minute he opens his mouth. "Mr. Aziz will have to make up his mind in a hurry because my board meets next week and I have to have an answer by then," is taken as indicating the American is overly demanding and is exerting undue pressure. "I am going to Damascus tomorrow morning and will have to have my car tonight," is a sure way to get the mechanic to stop work, because to give another person a deadline in this part of the world is to be rude, pushy, and demanding.

An Arab's evasiveness as to when something is going to happen does not mean he does not want to do business; it only means he is avoiding unpleasantness and is sidestepping possible commitments which he takes more seriously than we do. For example:

The Arabs themselves at times find it impossible to communicate even to each other that some processes cannot be hurried, and are controlled by built-in schedules. This is obvious enough to the Westerner but not to the Arab. A highly placed official in Baghdad precipitated a bitter family dispute because his nephew, a biochemist, could not speed up the complete analysis of the uncle's blood. He accused the nephew of putting other less important people before him and of not caring. Nothing could sway the uncle, who could not grasp the fact that there is such a thing as an *inherent* schedule.

With us, the more important an event is, the further ahead we schedule it, which is why we find it insulting to be asked to a party at the last minute. In planning future events with Arabs, it pays to hold the lead time to a week or less because other factors may intervene or take precedence.

Again, time spent waiting in an American's outer office is a sure indicator of what one person thinks of another or how important he feels the other's business to be. This is so much the case that most Americans cannot help getting angry after waiting 30 minutes; one may even feel such a delay is an insult and will walk out. In Latin America, on the other hand, one learns that it does not mean anything to wait in an outer office. An American businessman with years of experience in Mexico once told me, "You know, I have spent two hours cooling my heels in an executive's outer office. It took me a long time to learn to keep my

blood pressure down. Even now, I find it hard to convince myself they are still interested when they keep me waiting."

The Japanese handle time in ways that are most inexplicable to the Western European and particularly the American. A delay of years with them does not mean that they have lost interest. It only means that they are building up to something. They have learned that Americans are vulnerable to long waits. One of them expressed it, "You Americans have one terrible weakness. If we make you wait long enough, you will agree to anything."

Indians of South Asia have an elastic view of time as compared to our own. Delays do not, therefore, have the same meaning to them. Nor does indefiniteness in pinpointing appointments mean that they are evasive. Two Americans meeting will say, "We should get together sometime," thereby setting a low priority on the meeting. The Indian who says, "Come over and see me; see me anytime," means just that.

Americans make a place at the table that may or may not mean a place made in the heart. But when the Indian makes a place in his time, it is yours to fill in every sense of the word if you realize that by so doing you have crossed a boundary and are now friends with him. The point of all this is that time communicates just as surely as do words and that the vocabulary of time is different around the world. The principle to be remembered is that time has different meanings in each country.

Language of Space

Like time, the language of space is different wherever one goes. The American businessman, familiar with the pattern of American corporate life, has no difficulty in appraising the relative importance of someone else, simply by noting the size of his office in relation to other offices around him:

Our pattern calls for the president or the chairman of the board to have the biggest office. The executive vice president will have the next largest, and so on down the line until you end up in the "bull pen." More important offices are usually located at the corners of and on the upper floors. Executive suites will be on the top floor. The relative rank of vice presidents will be reflected in where they are placed along "executive row." The French, on the other hand, are much more likely to lay out space as a network of connecting points of influence, activity, or interest. The French supervisor will ordinarily be found in the middle of his subordinates where he can control them.

Americans who are crowded will often feel that their status in the organization is suffering. As one would expect in the Arab world, the location of an office and its size constitute a poor index of the importance of the man who occupies it. What we experience as crowded, the Arab will often regard as spacious. The same is true in Spanish cultures. A Latin American official illustrated the Spanish view of this point while showing me around a plant. Opening the door to an 18-by-20-foot office in which 17 clerks and their desks were placed, he said, "See, we have nice, spacious offices. Lots of space for everyone."

The American will look at a Japanese room and remark how bare it is. Similarly, the Japanese look at our rooms and comment, "How bare!" Furniture in the American home tends to be placed along the walls (around the edge). Japanese have their charcoal pit where the family gathers in the *middle* of the room. The top floor of Japanese department stores is not reserved for the chief executive—it is the bargain roof!

In the Middle East and Latin America, the businessman is likely to feel left out in time and overcrowded in space. People get too close to him, lay their hands on him, and generally crowd his physical being. In Scandinavia and Germany, he feels more at home, but at the same time the people are a little cold and distant. It is space itself that conveys this feeling.

In the United States, because of our tendency to zone activities, nearness carries rights of familiarity so that the neighbor can borrow material possessions and invade time. This is not true in England. Propinquity entitles you to nothing. American Air Force personnel stationed there

complain because they have to make an appointment for their children to play with the neighbor's child next door.

Conversation distance between two people is learned early in life by copying elders. Its controlling patterns operate almost totally unconsciously. In the United States, in contrast to many foreign countries, men avoid excessive touching. Regular business is conducted at distances such as 5 feet to 8 feet; highly personal business, 18 inches to 3 feet—not 2 or 3 inches.

In the United States, it is perfectly possible for an experienced executive to schedule the steps of negotiation in time and space so that most people feel comfortable about what is happening. Business transactions progress in stages from across the desk to beside the desk, to the coffee table, then on to the conference table, the luncheon table, or the golf course, or even into the home—all according to a complex set of hidden rules that we obey instinctively.

Even in the United States, however, an executive may slip when he moves into new and unfamiliar realms, when dealing with a new group, doing business with a new company, or moving to a new place in the industrial hierarchy. In a new country, the danger is magnified. For example, in India it is considered improper to discuss business in the home on social occasions. One never invites a business acquaintance to the home for the purpose of furthering business aims. That would be a violation of sacred hospitality rules.

Language of Things

Americans are often contrasted with the rest of the world in terms of material possessions. We are accused of being materialistic, gadget crazy. And, as a matter of fact, we have developed material things for some very interesting reasons. Lacking a fixed class system and having an extremely mobile population, Americans have become highly sensitive to how others make use of material possessions. We use everything from clothes to houses as a highly evolved and complex means of ascertaining each other's status. Ours is a rapidly shifting system in which both styles and people move up or down. For example:

The Cadillac ad men feel that not only is it natural but quite insightful of them to show a picture of a Cadillac and a well-turned-out gentleman in his early fifties opening the door. The caption underneath reads, "You already know a great deal about this man."

Following this same pattern, the head of a big union spends in excess of $100,000 furnishing his office so that the president of United States Steel cannot look down on him. Good materials, large space, and the proper surroundings signify that the people who occupy the premises are solid citizens, that they are dependable and successful.

The French, English, and the Germans have entirely different ways of using their material possessions. What stands for the height of dependability and respectability with the English would be old-fashioned and backward to us. The Japanese take pride in often inexpensive but tasteful arrangements that are used to produce the proper emotional setting.

Middle East businessmen look for something else—family, connections, friendship. They do not use the furnishings of their office as part of their status system; nor do they expect to impress a client by these means or to fool a banker into lending more money than he should. They like good things, too, but feel that they, as persons, should be known and not judged solely by what the public sees.

One of the most common criticisms of American relations abroad, both commercial and governmental, is that we usually think in terms of material things. "Money talks," says the American, who goes on talking the language of money abroad, in the belief that money talks the *same* language all over the world. A common practice in the United States is to try to buy loyalty with high salaries. In foreign countries, this maneuver almost never works, for money and material possessions stand for something different there than they do in America.

Language of Friendship

The American finds his friends next door and among those with whom he works. It has been noted that we take people up quickly and drop them just as quickly. Occasionally a friendship formed during schooldays will persist, but this is rare. For us, there are few well-defined rules governing the obligations of friendship. It is difficult to say at which point our friendship gives way to business opportunism or pressure from above. In this we differ from many other people in the world. As a general rule, in foreign countries friendships are not formed as quickly as in the United States but go much deeper, last longer, and involve real obligations. For example:

It is important to stress that in the Middle East and Latin America your "friends" will not let you down. The fact that they personally are feeling the pinch is never an excuse for failing their friends. They are supposed to look out for your interests.

Friends and family around the world represent a sort of social insurance that would be difficult to find in the United States. We do not use our friends to help us out in disaster as much as we do as a means of getting ahead—or, at least, of getting the job done. The United States systems work by means of a series of closely tabulated favors and obligations carefully doled out where they will do the most good. And the least that we expect in exchange for a favor is gratitude.

The opposite is the case in India, where the friend's role is to "sense" a person's need and do something about it. The idea of reciprocity as we know it is unheard of. An American in India will have difficulty if he attempts to follow American friendship patterns. He gains nothing by extending himself in behalf of others, least of all gratitude, because the Indian assumes that what he does for others he does for the good of his own psyche. He will find it impossible to make friends quickly and is unlikely to allow sufficient time for friendships to ripen. He will also note that as he gets to know people better they may become more critical of him, a fact that he finds hard to take. What he does not know is that one sign of friendship is speaking one's mind.

Language of Agreements

While it is important for American businessmen abroad to understand the symbolic meanings of friendship rules, time, space, and material possessions, it is just as important for executives to know the rules for negotiating agreements in various countries. Even if they cannot be expected to know the details of each nation's commercial legal practices, just the awareness of and the expectation of the existence of differences will eliminate much complication.

Actually, no society can exist on a high commercial level without a highly developed working base on which agreements can rest. This base may be one or a combination of three types:

1. Rules that are spelled out technically as law or regulation.
2. Moral practices mutually agreed on and taught to the young as a set of principles.
3. Informal customs to which everyone conforms without being able to state the exact rules.

Some societies favor one, some another. Ours, particularly in the business world, lays heavy emphasis on the first variety. Few Americans will conduct any business nowadays without some written agreement or contract.

Varying from culture to culture will be the circumstances under which such rules apply. Americans consider that negotiations have more or less ceased when the contract is signed. With the Greeks, on the other hand, the contract is seen as a sort of way station on the route to negotiation that will cease only when the work is completed. The contract is nothing more than a charter for serious negotiations. In the Arab world, once a man's word is given in a particular kind of way, it is just as binding, if not more so, than most of our written contracts. The written contract, therefore, violates the Moslem's sensitivities and reflects on his honor. Unfortunately, the situation is now so hopelessly confused that neither system can be counted on to prevail consistently.

Informal patterns and unstated agreements often lead to untold difficulty in the cross-cultural situation. Take the case of the before-and-after patterns where there is a wide discrepancy between the American's expectations and those of the Arab:

In the United States, when you engage a specialist such as a lawyer or a doctor, require any standard service, or even take a taxi, you make several assumptions: (*a*) the charge will be fair; (*b*) it will be in proportion to the services rendered; and (*c*) it will bear a close relationship to the "going rate."

You wait until after the services are performed before asking what the tab will be. If the charge is too high in light of the above assumptions, you feel you have been cheated. You can complain, or can say nothing, pay up, and take your business elsewhere the next time.

As one would expect in the Middle East, basic differences emerge that lead to difficulty if not understood. For instance, when taking a cab in Beirut it is well to know the going rate as a point around which to bargain and for settling the charge, which must be fixed before engaging the cab.

If you have not fixed the rate *in advance,* there is a complete change and an entirely different set of rules will apply. According to these rules, the going rate plays no part whatsoever. The whole relationship is altered. The sky is the limit, and the customer has no kick coming. I have seen taxi drivers shouting at the top of their lungs, waving their arms, following a red-faced American with his head pulled down between his shoulders, demanding for a two-pound ride 10 Lebanese pounds, which the American eventually had to pay.

It is difficult for the American to accommodate his frame of reference to the fact that what constitutes one thing to him, namely, a taxi ride, is to the Arab two very different operations involving two different sets of relationships and two sets of rules. The crucial factor is whether the bargaining is done at the beginning or end of the ride! As a matter of fact, you cannot bargain at the end. What the driver asks for he is entitled to!

One of the greatest difficulties Americans have abroad stems from the fact that we often think we have a commitment when we do not. The second complication on the same topic is the other side of the coin, that is when others think we have agreed to things that we have not. Our own failure to recognize binding obligations, plus our custom of setting organizational goals ahead of everything else, has put us in hot water far too often.

People sometimes do not keep agreements with us because we do not keep agreements with them. As a general rule, the American treats the agreement as something he may eventually have to break. Here are two examples:

Once while I was visiting an American post in Latin America, the Ambassador sent the Spanish version of a trade treaty down to his language officer with instructions to write in some "weasel words." To his dismay, he was told, "There are no weasel words in Spanish."

A personnel officer of a large corporation in Iran made an agreement with local employees that American employees would not receive preferential treatment. When the first American employee arrived, it was learned quickly that in the United States he had been covered by a variety of health plans that were not available to Iranians. And this led to immediate protests from the Iranians which were never satisfied. The personnel officer never really grasped the fact that he had violated an iron-bound contract.

Certainly, this is the most important generaliza-tion to be drawn by American businessmen from this discussion of agreements: there are many times when we are vulnerable *even when judged by our own standards*. Many instances of actual sharp practices by American companies are well known abroad and are giving American business a bad name. The cure of such questionable behavior is simple. The companies concerned usually have it within their power to discharge offenders and to foster within their organization an atmosphere in which only honesty and fairness can thrive.

But the cure for ignorance of the social and legal rules that underlie business agreements is not so easy. This is because:

The subject is complex.

Little research has been conducted to determine the culturally different concepts of what is an agreement.

The people of each country think that their own code is the only one, and that everything else is dishonest.

Each code is different from our own; and the farther away one is traveling from Western Europe, the greater the difference is.

But the little that has already been learned about this subject indicates that as a problem it is not insoluble and will yield to research. Since it is probably one of the more relevant and immediately applicable areas of interest to modern business, it would certainly be advisable for companies with large foreign operations to sponsor some serious research in this vital field.

HOW TO AVOID BUSINESS BLUNDERS ABROAD

David A. Ricks

A major fast-food company planned to open an outlet in Munich, West Germany. To ensure a successful location, the company carefully counted the number of people passing by several prospective sites. A highly trafficked location was then selected, but sales proved unexpectedly poor. Why? Investigation revealed that the activity level in the area was due to a nearby bordello—the individuals walking by had more than hamburgers on their minds!

This is just one example of the unexpected problems that occur in international business ventures. Overseas marketing can be extremely tricky. Even though a company may employ sophisticated management techniques, it still runs a real risk of blundering if any detail is overlooked. However, many of the problems that have been encountered by companies operating in foreign territory can be avoided.

For example, merely asking the right question can prevent a giant blunder. In one reported case, a firm neglected to inspect some wooded land for sale in Sicily prior to its purchase. Only after the company had bought the land, built a plant, and hired a labor force did it realize that the trees avail-

able were only knee high and were not usable for making paper. The result? They imported logs!

Another company encountered a somewhat similar experience when it built a pineapple cannery near the delta of a Mexican river. The pineapple plantation was established upriver, and barges were purchased to float the crop down to the cannery. It was not discovered until the fruit was ripe that the river current was too strong to allow the barges to be tugged back upriver from the cannery to the fields. As a result, the plant was useless in that location and was sold for a mere 5 percent of its cost. These errors are regrettable, but we can learn from them. There is no need to repeat the mistakes others have made.

Picking the Package

Numerous problems result from the failure to correctly adapt packaging for local environments. Occasionally, only the color of the package needs to be altered to enhance a product's sales. White, for instance, symbolizes death in Japan and much of Asia; green represents danger or disease in Malaysia. Consequently, the use of these colors in certain countries can produce negative reactions to products.

A lesser known variable worthy of consideration is the use of numbers. Packages that prominently display a specific number increase the risk of consumer avoidance. For example the number *four* is an evil number in Japan, where it represents death. Even the number of products pictured on a label can prove troublesome.

Sometimes it is not the number displayed on the package or the color that creates a problem, but rather the picture on the label. A baby food manufacturer discovered this important lesson the hard way. It tried to sell jars of baby food in an African country using labels that depicted a happy baby. Unfortunately, most of the prospective customers were illiterate and could only determine the contents of a container by looking at the label. The picture of a baby indicated to them that the jar literally contained bottled babies.

A simple test market experiment, a brief survey, a few interviews with potential buyers, or a discussion with knowledgeable local residents would have uncovered many of the problems just described at an early stage.

Changing the Product

In many instances the product itself requires alteration. Food, beverages, and tobacco products often need to be modified in order to accommodate the tastes of local consumers. Cigarette manufacturers learned long ago that American brands sell well overseas if the tobacco is carefully blended to suit local preferences. Market tests can help determine the appropriate blends.

Not only can the taste of a product hinder sales, but occasionally its consistency or texture creates difficulties. After correctly determining the flavors considered desirable by the British, Jell-O tried to sell its products in powdered form (just as in the United States). But the British avoided the products because they normally purchase this type of food in jelled form. After discovering this, Jell-O successfully marketed its products in a ready-to-consume form.

Campbell Soup Company encountered a similar experience. The Campbell's cans originally marketed in Great Britain were the same size as those available in the United States. Instructions carefully stated that water should be added—the normal procedure for most American soups. The British, however, were accustomed to purchasing diluted soup. Since buyers never bothered to read the fine print on the label, Campbell's condensed soups appeared more expensive because consumers received less volume for their money. Sales were low until Campbell's discovered the problem and began marketing a diluted soup in larger cans. Because consumer expectations play a vital role in sales and acceptance, companies must always examine potential competitive products and how they are marketed.

Sometimes significant product modification is required to market products abroad. A dishwasher built to U.S. norms may need an electric motor that requires 220 voltage rather than 110 voltage, may need to tolerate different water pressures than those available in the United States, or may need to accommodate local dishes and utensils of different shapes. Products that are not modified to meet local needs may fail.

The Language Barrier

A close examination of foreign markets and language differences is necessary and should be required before a product's domestically successful name is introduced abroad. Unfortunately, this step is sometimes neglected in a company's enthusiasm to plunge into overseas marketing operations.

Sometimes, the company or product name may require alteration because it conveys the wrong message in a second language. Large and small firms alike have discovered this. For example, when the Coca-Cola Company was planning its marketing strategy for China in the 1920s, it wanted to introduce its product with the English pronunciation of "Coca-Cola." A translator used a group of Chinese characters that, when pronounced, sounded like the product name. These characters were placed on the cola bottles and marketed. Was it any wonder sales levels were low?

The characters actually translated to mean "a wax-flattened mare" or "bite the wax tadpole." Since the product was new, sound was unimportant to the consumers; meaning was vital. Today Coca-Cola is again marketing its cola in China. The new characters used on the bottle translate to "happiness in the mouth." From its first marketing attempts, Coca-Cola learned a valuable lesson in international marketing.

General Motors was faced with a similar problem. It was troubled by a lack of enthusiasm among Puerto Rican auto dealers for its recently introduced Chevrolet "Nova" about 10 years ago. The name "Nova" means star when literally translated. However, when spoken it sounded like "no va" which, in Spanish, means "it doesn't go." This obviously did little to increase consumer confidence in the vehicle. To remedy the situation, General Motors changed the automobile name to "Caribe" and sales increased.

Comparable situations have also been experienced by other car manufacturers. In fact, problems with the names used in international automobile promotions seem to crop up frequently. For example, the American car name "Randan" was interpreted by the Japanese to mean "idiot." The American Motors Corporation's car "Matador" might conjure up images of virility and strength in America, but in Puerto Rico it means "killer"—not a favorable connotation in a place with a high traffic fatality rate.

A U.S. company was taken by surprise when it introduced its product in Latin America and learned that the name meant "jackass oil" in Spanish. Another well-intentioned firm sold shampoo in Brazil under the name "Evitol." Little did it realize that it was claiming to be selling a "dandruff contraceptive." One manufacturing company sold its machines in the Soviet Union under the name "Bardak"—a word that signifies a brothel in Russian. The name of an American product that failed to capture the Swedish market translated to "enema," which the product was not!

Of course, foreign firms can make mistakes, too. A Finnish brewery introduced two new beverages in the United States—"Koff" beer and "Siff" beer. Is it any wonder that sales were sluggish? Another name Americans found unappealing was on packages of a delicious chocolate and fruit product sold in German and other European delicatessens. The chocolate concoction had the undesirable English name "Zit!"

Many times the required name change is a rather simple one. Wrigley, for example, merely altered the spelling of its "Spearmint" chewing gum to "Speermint" to aid in the German pronunciation of the flavor. "Maxwell House" proved slightly more difficult: the name was changed to "Maxwell Kaffee" in Germany, to "Legal" in France, and to "Monky" in Spain.

Product names are not the only ones that can generate company blunders. If a firm's name is misinterpreted or incorrectly translated, it, too, can have the same humorous, obscene, offensive, or unexpected connotations.

For example, a private Egyptian airline, Misair, proved to be rather unpopular with the French nationals. Could the fact that the name, when pronounced, meant "misery" in French have contributed to the airline's plight? Another airline trying to gain acceptance in Australia only complicated matters when it chose the firm name "EMU." The emu is an Australian bird incapable of flying. When Esso realized that its name phonetically meant "stalled car," it understood why it had had difficulties in the Japanese market.

As final illustration, consider the trade magazine that promoted giftware and launched a worldwide circulation effort. The magazine used the word "gift" in its title and part of its name. When it was later revealed that "gift" is the German word for "poison," a red-faced publishing executive supposedly retorted that the Germans should simply find a new word for poison!

Of course, some company names have traveled quite well. Kodak may be the most famous example. A research team deliberately developed this name after carefully searching for a word that was pronounceable everywhere but had no specific meaning anywhere. Exxon is another name that was reportedly accepted only after a lengthy and expensive computer-assisted search.

Multinational corporations have experienced many unexpected troubles concerning company or product names, and even attempts to alter names have led to blunders. It should be evident that careful planning and study of the potential market is necessary because name adaptation can be every bit as important as product or package modification.

Respecting Nationalism

Many avoidable problems occur because managers are insensitive to the nationalistic feeling of the people of the host country. Except at the retail level, it is usually best for companies to maintain a low profile. Seldom does a firm need to turn an overseas manufacturing plant into a "Little America." Companies that have tried to do this have met stiff resistance from both employees and local customers. One U.S. firm, for example, acquired a Spanish manufacturing plant and promptly announced that it would be bringing in superior U.S. technology. The company changed the prestigious Spanish name and even raised the U.S. flag. Naturally employee morale and sales were hurt.

Foreign manufacturers in the United States learned long ago to keep a low profile. About 2 percent of the American labor force is now working for foreign-owned firms, but many of the workers are unaware of this. This is considered desirable for the foreign owners because it reduced the likelihood of problems.

Management should avoid any unnecessary comparisons that might reflect the home country management's belief that the host country is inferior. It is often possible—sometimes even desirable—to compare products, but it is not wise to publicly compare governments, management practices, labor, or technology.

One way to maintain a low profile is to hire most, if not all, top-level managers of the overseas subsidiary from the available host country management pool. Not only will these individuals pro-

ject a local image, but they usually understand local problems well and can often help the company avoid blunders.

If an expatriate is to be hired, extra care must be taken. To be effective, an expatriate manager must possess special abilities and traits if he or she is to avoid blundering. Among the most important characteristics are the following:

- An ability to get along well with people.
- An awareness of cultural differences.
- Open-mindedness.
- Tolerance of foreign cultures.
- Adaptability to new cultures, ideas, and challenges.
- An ability to adjust quickly to new conditions.
- An interest in facts, not blind assumptions.
- Previous business experience.
- Previous experience with foreign cultures.
- An ability to learn foreign languages.

Problems with Promotions

Many companies have run into serious troubles trying to coordinate their sales and promotional efforts. For example, one firm authorized a large promotional drive to introduce a new product in Latin America. The promotion ran smoothly, but someone forgot to coordinate product delivery—the home office was totally unaware of the sales push and had no plans to ship the product. Consumers were confused and money was wasted when the promoted product was not available.

All plans should be in writing, and someone should be responsible for central coordination. Hence, risks are lessened and opportunities to save money may arise. Coca-Cola, for instance, requires that all overseas marketing plans be submitted to the central office well in advance. This gives the company a chance to examine the concepts. Previous experiences with similar plans can be reviewed and necessary changes can be suggested. Sometimes central company managers find that similar plans for overseas ventures have failed in the past. Minor improvements tried overseas with success should also be reported. There is no need to reinvent the wheel. Coordination not only reduces the chance of errors, it also provides opportunities to learn improved methods.

With so many details to consider, it is rather easy to understand how so many firms have blundered. Nevertheless, their errors illustrate the importance of paying attention to detail. The McDonnell Douglas Corporation, for example, experienced unexpected difficulties when it produced an aircraft brochure for distribution to potential customers in India. The promotional material depicted turbaned men, but the photos were not well received. The company had used old *National Geographic* pictures and had overlooked the fact that the turbans were being worn by Pakistani men—not by Indians!

If a theme works exceedingly well in one country, it becomes very tempting for a firm to use it elsewhere. The risks involved in doing this are high, however, because good themes are often culturally oriented. Consider the popular and successful Marlboro advertisements. The Marlboro man projects a strong masculine image in America and in Europe. But the promotion was unsuccessful in Hong Kong, where the totally urban people did not identify at all with horseback riding in the countryside. So Phillip Morris quickly changed its ad to reflect a Hong Kong-style Marlboro man. The Hong Kong version is still a virile cowboy, but he is younger, better dressed, and owns a truck and land.

Local weather conditions can also foul up a multinational corporation's promotional campaign. One firm, for example, tried to use a typical U.S. radio advertisement to promote its swimsuits in Latin America. The ad boasted that one could wear the swimsuit all day in the sun and it would not fade. To local Latins, however, this point meant little because the weather is always too hot to stay in the sun for very long.

In many cases, the language of the promotional effort is correct but its physical presentation is not effective. As a classic illustration, consider the company that rented space on a wall beside the main road leading from the airport into Buenos Aires. The following message was placed on the wall: "With (brand name) you'd be there already." Just one slight problem—the message was written on a cemetery wall!

Symbols or logos have also caused troubles. A U.S. firm marketing in Brazil was a bit embarrassed when it used a large deer as a sign for masculinity. The word "deer" is a Brazilian street name for homosexual. Another company blundered in India when it used an owl in its promotional efforts. To an Indian, the owl is a symbol for bad luck!

One laundry detergent company certainly wishes that it had contacted a few residents before it initiated a promotional campaign in the Middle East. All of the company's advertisements pictured soiled clothes on the left, its box of soap in the middle, and the clean clothes on the right. But because in that area of the world people generally read from right to left, many potential customers interpreted the message to mean that the soap actually soiled the clothes.

Another U.S. company had problems in Britain. In a U.S. promotion, the firm had effectively used the phrase, "You can use no finer napkin at your dinner table" and decided to use the same commercials in England. After all, the British do speak English. To the British, however, the word "napkin" or "nappy" actually means "diaper." The American firm was unknowingly advertising that "You could use no finer diaper at your dinner table." The ad could hardly be expected to boost sales.

One fairly common American practice is to utilize the same promotional strategy for all domestic subsidiaries, with promotional budgets based on a fixed percentage of sales. This strategy may work well with domestic ventures, but usually proves foolish when it is attempted for overseas subsidiaries. Those U.S. companies that try to force such standardization are sometimes asking their foreign managers to do the impossible.

For one thing, some types of media are not legally available. In many countries, no television advertisements are permitted, and this alone makes a U.S.-style promotional budget infeasible. A second problem is one of scale. The use of a standard percentage of sales may be appropriate for large, domestic subsidiaries, but for small foreign subsidiaries 10 percent of sales may not support a single promotional campaign. Each market offers different opportunities and challenges at different cost structures. A better strategy is to standardize the methods used to analyze opportunities and then develop local promotional budgets. The subsidiaries can be urged to follow the established methods.

This does not mean, however, that each country is totally unique and must *always* be treated independently. One company, for example, sold a popular detergent in Austria and Germany under two different brand names. The people in both countries speak German, and they heard and read ads that originated in both countries. Consequently, they thought there were two products that were in competition. The company could have consolidated its promotional effort to cover both countries.

Observing Local Customs

A lack of awareness of cultural differences or insensitivity to local customs can create problems. There are norms for each country; sometimes they are very strict. Several manufacturing plants have encountered serious troubles in England because of the famed British tea break. American managers have tried—usually to no avail—to persuade their British employees to drop their tea-break habit. It is now considered wiser to accept such local traditions.

This also applies to local holidays. The host country may seem to have many holidays, but generally there is little that can be done to change the situation. A company usually must either pay overtime, close on the holiday, or face high levels of employee absenteeism, turnover, and unrest.

And consider the public display of affection between members of the opposite sexes. In many countries, such as Thailand, this is unacceptable and offensive. A firm trying to introduce its mouthwash there, however, was not aware of this taboo and promoted its products with an ad that displayed a young couple holding hands. But when the advertisement was changed to feature two women, the commercials were no longer offensive to the Thais.

The Asian Indians found a BiNoca Talc ad disturbing even though the woman in the advertisement was wearing a body stocking. The promotion, which appeared in many of the major local newspapers featured an attractive but apparently nude young woman lavishly powdering herself with BiNoca's talcum. Strategic portions of her body were carefully covered with the slogan "Don't go wild—just enough is all you need of BiNoca talc." The public, however, found the ads indecent.

The display of certain parts of the body generally thought innocuous can be offensive to certain groups. For example, Mountain Bell experienced a problem in the Middle and Far East when one of its promotional photos depicted an executive talking on the telephone with his feet propped up on his desk. The photos were considered by local residents to be in poor taste. To them the display of the sole of the foot or shoe is one of the worst possible insults. Exposure of the foot is also considered an insult in Southeast Asia.

Since social norms vary so greatly from country to country, it is extremely difficult for any outsider to be knowledgeable of them all. Therefore, local input is vital in avoiding blunders. Many promotional errors could have been averted had this warning been heeded.

One of the best-known promotional blunders occurred in Quebec. There, a manufacturer of canned fish ran advertisements in the local newspapers that depicted a woman in shorts playing golf with a man. The caption explained that a woman could go golfing with her husband in the afternoon and still get home in time to serve a great dinner of canned fish that same evening. The entire promotional effort was off target. In Quebec, women did not wear shorts on local golf courses and were usually not permitted to golf with men. Furthermore, regardless of how much preparation time is available, women in Quebec would not consider serving canned fish for dinner, especially as the major course. The company neglected to consider local customers and, obviously, the product failed.

Pepsodent reportedly tried to sell its toothpaste in regions of Southeast Asia with a promotion that stressed that the toothpaste helped enhance white teeth. However, in this area, some local people deliberately chew betel nut in order to achieve the social prestige of darkly stained teeth, so the ad was understandably less than effective. The slogan "Wonder where the yellow went," was also viewed by many as a racial slur.

A marketer of eyeglasses promoted his spectacles in Thailand with commercials featuring animals wearing glasses. It was an unfortunate decision, however, because in Thailand, animals are considered a low form of life and it is beneath humans to wear anything worn by an animal.

The failure to consider specialized aspects of local religions has led to a number of problems. Companies have many times tried to incorporate a picture of a Buddha in their Asian promotions. Religious ties are strong in this area and the use of local religious symbols in advertising is resented—especially when words are deliberately or even accidentally printed across the picture of Buddha.

A refrigerator manufacturer made a similar blunder in the Middle East. The typical refrigerator advertisement often features a refrigerator full of delicious food, and because these photos are difficult to take, they are often used in as many places as possible. This company used its stock photo, depicting a prominently placed chunk of ham, in one place too many, though—because Muslims do not eat ham. Local residents considered the ad to be insensitive and unappealing.

Be Sure It Translates

Many international advertising errors are due to faulty translations. The translation should embody the general theme and concept rather than be an exact or precise duplication of the original slogan. This point hit home when Pepsi reportedly learned that its ad "Come alive with Pepsi" literally translated into German to mean "Come alive out of the grave with Pepsi." And in Asia, it was translated as "Bring your ancestors back from the dead."

Other companies have translated "stepping stone" to "stumbling block," have changed the words "car wash" into "car enema," and have said that a battery is "over rated" when the phrase should have been "highly rated."

Hunt Wesson Foods can attest to the risk of translation. The company planned to market its "beans in tomato sauce" product in Quebec, Canada, under the name "Grose Jos." Just before the product was to be released, a local employee advised the company to reassess this name because it could be translated colloquially as "big breasts."

Translators must be attuned to the local language and possible double meanings. An ink pen manufacturer, for example, ran an ad campaign in Latin America. The ad was mistakenly translated to imply that the ink pen would help avoid unwanted pregnancies—the ad copy stated that the ink pen would help avoid embarrassment, but "embarrassment" there implies pregnancy.

General Motors encountered problems in Belgium when "Body by Fisher" was translated into Flemish as "Corpse by Fisher." Obviously, literal translations can prove deadly!

Another U.S. company may have actually been the victim of translation sabotage. The firm tried to sell its products in the Soviet Union with the help of a Russian translator. The company innocently displayed a translated poster in Moscow which, it soon discovered, said that the company's oil well equipment was good for improving a person's sex life.

What Can Be Done.   There are several ways to avert potential translation disasters.

A brilliant translator may have an extraordinary gift for the language or may have studied in the country, but certain idiomatic expressions and slang may be unfamiliar. It is often wise to also hire a second translator who is familiar with the local slang and unusual idioms to *backtranslate*.

Backtranslation is one of the best techniques available to reduce translation errors. This method requires that one individual translate the message into the desired foreign language and that a second person translate the foreign version back to the original language. This allows a company to determine if the intended message is the one actually being presented. An Australian soft drink company discovered the value of backtranslation during the planning stages of its Hong Kong market entry. The company wanted to introduce its successful slogan, "Baby, it's cold outside," but first had it translated back into English. This proved to be a wise decision. The message backtranslated to "Small mosquito, on the outside it is very cold." Even though "small mosquito" was a local colloquial expression for a small child, the phrase simply did not convey the same thing as the friendly English slang word "baby." The intended message was lost.

Backtranslation reveals many translation errors, but it can prove frustrating if done by mediocre translators. Naturally, the better the translator, the fewer the problems and delays. The difficulty, therefore, lies in being able to determine the ability of a potential translator. Firms should thoroughly investigate the translator's qualifications. The following points should be covered in an interview:

• Does the translator maintain or have access to a library or reference books dealing with the appropriate subject and industry?

• Does the translator understand the required technical terms? Does he or she know of the foreign words for these specialized terms? If not, how does he or she intend to learn them?

• Does the translator have a staff or access to experts in various fields (such as law)?

• Will someone check the work? If so, what are the credentials of the assistant? (It is often advisable to request references and copies of material translated for other clients.)

• How recently has the translator visited the foreign country? Sometimes it is necessary to determine just how current the translator's knowledge is, because languages do change. It is not enough to have someone familiar with the foreign language and culture. Even a native tends to lose track of slang and idioms after being away from home for a few years. Experience that is 10 years old may be too old.

Once a translator has been chosen, there are several things that a company can do to simplify his or her job. For instance, when the company has spent several months developing good promotional materials, a translator should not be asked to translate the material overnight. Simple literal translation is not generally appropriate, so a translator needs time to be creative.

This is not to say that the translator should not be given a deadline—the person should be given a reasonable time frame and the expected promotion schedule. And be sure to tell the translator what season the ad will appear in.

Also, the translator should understand the type of media to be used and the general characteristics of the audience. This allows him or her to determine the proper level of formality and the correct tone. A translator must be given the freedom to modify original wording to avoid disastrous literal translations.

If possible, firms should avoid overly technical terms and industry jargon. It is also advisable to limit the use of large numbers. Any number over 10,000 may be easily mistranslated. The number "billion," for example, numerically contains 9 zeros in the United States, but contains 12 zeros in Europe.

Also, humor can be impossible to translate, so

it is best to avoid jokes in advertising. What is deemed funny by some is often not funny to others.

And because the translated version of a message may require more words than the original, don't limit the translator to a particular amount of time or space. Doing so may seriously jeopardize the effectiveness of the message.

Finally, the translator should be informed of the message's objectives and theme. If the translator is allowed to examine previous company translations as well as translated slogans of competing companies, he or she not only can assure that any key phrase associated with the company is included but also can avoid accidentally using a competitor's phrases.

Sometimes companies have found that the best solution to the translation problem is simply not to translate the material. In countries experiencing high levels of illiteracy, visual methods of communication can be used. Libby, for instance, has successfully promoted its products through inexpensive commercials featuring a clown enjoying Libby products. In these ads, no words are spoken.

Using English in Non-English-speaking Countries.   If the local residents can understand some English or if they really don't need to comprehend the spoken message, then it may be safe for a firm to stick with the English copy. To reduce the problems that may occur when English is used in such situations:

- Keep the entire message short and simple, including the words and sentences.
- Avoid jargon or slang.
- Avoid idioms.
- Avoid humor, if possible.
- Use appropriate currencies and measurements.
- Cite examples, if feasible.
- Repeat important points.

If a company decides to go ahead with an English message through a verbal advertisement directed to an audience whose native language is not English, the speaker should speak slowly and carefully, pronounce all words, and pause between sentences.

Research Can Help

Proper market research can reduce or eliminate most international business blunders. Market researchers can uncover adaptation needs, potential name problems, promotional requirements, and proper market strategies. Even many translation blunders can be avoided if good research techniques are used.

A number of mistakes have occurred because firms tried to use the same product, name, promotional material, or strategy overseas that they used at home. But even though standardization promotes certain efficiencies and cost reductions, in many instances it is not a worthwhile strategy to pursue abroad. Limitations do exist, and it is important for firms to recognize and understand these barriers.

The use of market research enables a firm to determine its limits of standardization. It serves two major functions: the research can help a company identify what it can hope to accomplish and realize what it should not do. Neither dimension should be overlooked.

Few question the value of marketing research as part of international business planning. Unfortunately, market research is an extremely difficult and complex undertaking. Specific data requirements depend on the firm, its products, and the type of decisions being made. Different sets of data are needed for a company to determine whether or not to go abroad, which countries to enter, how to enter the foreign markets, and what the best marketing strategies are. Research methods must be tailored to the particular situation. There is no short, simple list of variables all firms should always research.

Market tests can be tricky to initiate and conduct. It is difficult indeed to "cover all the angles," and one of the hardest tasks is to identify the proper testing location. Firms normally identify sample areas as representative of a country or region. Some companies use an area of France for their West European test market, and others use Belgium. Each firm, however, must determine the region most appropriate for its product. This is no easy task. In fact, a combination of locations may be necessary. Wherever these places are, though, they must be found because market testing is essential.

We can learn from our mistakes. Blunders have been made, but they need not be repeated by others. Awareness of differences, consultation with local people, and concern for host-country feelings will reduce problems and will save money. Many companies—especially those that blundered—have already learned this and are doing much better. But there is still room for improvement.

THE IMPORTANCE OF CULTURE IN INTERNATIONAL BUSINESS NEGOTIATIONS

John L. Graham

NEW JERSEY.   A few years ago I attended a conference on international business alliances sponsored by the Rutgers and Wharton Business Schools. Now you New Yorkers probably see a Jersey joke coming (culture in New Jersey?), but the keynote speaker at the conference started out a bit differently.

"You've all heard the story about the invention of copper wire—two Dutchmen got a hold of a penny." This bit of anecdotage was served up during a dinner speech by the American president of a joint venture owned by AT&T and Philips. At one level the story is a friendly gibe, although the professor from the Netherlands sitting at our table didn't appreciate the American's remarks in general or the ethnic joke in particular. Indeed, at another level the story is stereotyping of the worst sort.

However, at an even deeper level there is an important lesson here for all managers of international commercial relationships. Culture can get in the way. The American president was in his "humorous" way attributing part of the friction between him and his Dutch associates to differences in cultural values. He might have blamed personality differences or clashing "corporate" cultures, but instead he identified national cultural barriers to be a major difficulty in managing his joint venture. And although I also did not appreciate his humor, I certainly agree that cultural differences between business partners can cause divisive, even decisive problems.

Kathryn Harrigan at Columbia University suggests that a crucial aspect of international commercial relationships is the negotiation of the original agreement. The seeds of success or failure are often sown at the negotiation table, *vis-à-vis* (face-to-face), where not only are financial and legal details agreed to, but perhaps more important, the ambiance of cooperation is established. Indeed, as Harrigan indicates, the legal details and the structure of international business ventures are almost always modified over time, and usually through negotiations. But the atmosphere of cooperation established initially face-to-face at the negotiation table persists or the venture fails.

Most Americans, **by nature,** have a difficult time in international negotiations. Certainly there are some Americans who are quite successful in foreign environments. However, our huge home market and previous economic dominance have often led to an unhealthy combination of ethnocentricity, xenophobia, and poor language skills which, in turn, causes us big problems when we

From *International Business Communications,* J. D. Usunier and P. H. Ghauri (Editors). Reprinted by permission of Elsevier Science Ltd., 1996.

are sitting across the table from our foreign business partners or clients.

Although at this point it may seem so, this article is not about American bashing. You don't need me for that. There are more objective sources. I ran across this quote in *Expansion,* a Spanish business newspaper: *"Los mejores negociadores son los japoneses, capaces de pasarse dias intentando conocer a su oponente. Los peores, los norteamericanos, que peinsan que las cosas funcionan igual que en su pais en todas partes"* (November 29, 1991, p. 41). Roughly translated, this says, "The best negotiators are the Japanese because they will spend days trying to get to know their opponents. The worst are Americans because they think everything works in foreign countries as it does in the USA." Part of the reason I've included this quote is it balances out the aforementioned "penny stretching crack." That is, Samfrits Le Poole, the quoted author of *How to Negotiate with Success,* is Dutch. And I always listen to the Dutch guys. As a national group they have the best international skills. It seems they all speak about five languages and have lived in as many countries.

As mentioned, there are some Americans who are very effective in international business negotiations. And in some circumstances, the best prescription might be something we call an American approach. However, in the pages to follow I must be critical at times, because a secondary purpose of this article is to get you to change your behavior. But usually meaningful changes in behavior take both time and many contacts with your foreign counterparts. In fact, the best way to learn to behave appropriately in a foreign country is by letting yourself unconsciously imitate those with whom you interact frequently. And a penchant for careful observation is also crucial. Hopefully, this article will help you sharpen your observation skills.

The **primary** purpose of this article is to make you aware of the multiple ways cultural differences in values and communication styles can cause serious misunderstandings between otherwise positively disposed business partners. And

many of these problems manifest themselves in face-to-face meetings at the international negotiation table. For example, a silent Japanese doesn't necessarily mean reticence and a Spaniard's frequent interruptions shouldn't communicate rudeness to you. And what does it mean to be kissed by your Russian businesspartner?

I cannot answer all of these questions here. Clearly, after you have finished the article, you'll still have more work to do. It will be your responsibility to deepen your understanding of cultural differences by asking your clients and partners directly about the strange things they do that weren't mentioned in Graham's article. Such informal interaction in a friendly place and in a friendly way will in the long run be far more important than any article, book, or course on this subject, including mine!

Negotiation Styles in Other Countries

During the last 15 years, a group of colleagues[1] and I have systematically studied the negotiation styles of businesspeople in 16 countries (18 cultures)—Japan, Korea, Taiwan, China (northern and southern), Hong Kong, the Philippines, Russia, the Czech Republic, Germany, France, the United Kingdom, Spain, Brazil, Mexico, Canada (Anglophones and Francophones), and the United States. More than 1,000 businesspeople have participated in our research. I chose these countries because they comprise America's most important present and future trading partners. I'd very much like to study negotiation styles in Tahiti, but, at the moment, we don't do much business there.

I have learned two important lessons by looking broadly across the several cultures. The first, I no longer generalize about regions. Had you asked me 10 years ago, "Do Koreans and Japanese negotiate in the same way?" I would have responded, "I suppose so; they're both Oriental cultures." Anyone who has negotiated in both places knows the folly in that naiveté. Indeed, the Japanese and Korean styles are quite similar in some ways, but, in other ways, they couldn't be more different. So now I talk about one country at a time, and even then the locals will always advocate within-country regional differences. For example, the Spaniards at my last seminar in Madrid told me the best negotiators in Spain are from Valencia, because of the persistent mercantile influence of the ancient Phoenicians. Now that's a stretch! But the point is, they see a difference between behaviors typical in Madrid and Valencia.

The second lesson from the list of countries is that Japan is a strange place. I don't mean that in a negative way. It's just that on almost every dimension of negotiation style we consider, the Japanese are on or near the end of the scale. Sometimes, we Americans are on the other end. Recall Le Poole's earlier comment. But, actually, most of the time

we Americans are somewhere in the middle. You'll see this evinced in the data we present later in the article. The Japanese approach, however, is most distinct, even *sui generis*.

The methods of our studies include a combination of (1) interviews with experienced executives from both sides of the table, (2) field observations of business negotiations in most of the countries listed, and (3) behavioral science laboratory simulations (please see Box 1 for details regarding the simulations). The integration of these approaches allows a "triangulation" of our findings—that is, we can compare results across research methods. Indeed, we have found mostly consistency across methods, but we have also discovered discrepancies. For example, when we interviewed Americans who had negotiated with Japanese, their com-

---

Box 1

Behavioral Science Laboratory Simulation

The participants in the study included businesspeople from 18 cultures. There were at least 40 in each group. All have been members of executive education programs or graduate business classes, and all have at least two years' business experience in their respective countries. The average age of the 1,066 participants was 35.2 years, and the average work experience was 11.2 years.

We asked participants to play the role of either a buyer or a seller in a negotiation simulation. In the case of the Japanese and Americans, three kinds of interactions were staged: Japanese/Japanese, American/American, and American/Japanese. In the other countries, only intracultural negotiations (that is, Koreans with Koreans, Brazilians with Brazilians, etc.) were conducted. The negotiation game involved bargaining over the prices of three commodities. The game was simple enough to be learned quickly, but complex enough to provide usually one-half hour of face-to-face interaction (Kelley, 1966).

Following the simulation, results were recorded

and each participant was asked to fill out a questionnaire that included questions about each player's performance and strategies and his/her opponent's strategies. The profits attained by individuals in the negotiation exercise constituted the principal performance measure. We used a variety of statistical techniques to compose the results of the several kinds of interactions.

Finally, we videotape-recorded some of the exercises for further analysis. Several trained observers then documented the persuasive tactics negotiators used, as well as a number of nonverbal behaviors (facial expressions, gaze direction, silent periods, etc.). Each of the Japanese and American participants was also asked to observe his/her own interaction and to interpret events and outcomes from his/her own point of view. Each participant's comments were tape-recorded and transcribed to form retrospective protocols of the interaction. Here, also, we employed a variety of statistical techniques in the analysis, as well as a more inductive, interpretive approach.

ments were consistent with those of Van Zandt (1970), "Negotiations take much longer." And, when in the behavioral science laboratory we match American negotiators with Japanese, the negotiations take longer (an average of about 25 minutes for Americans with Americans, 35 minutes for Americans with Japanese). So, in this respect, our findings are consistent for both interviews and laboratory observations. When we talk with Americans who have negotiated with Japanese, universally they describe them as being "poker-faced," or as displaying no facial expressions. However, in the laboratory simulations, we focused a camera on each person's face and recorded all facial expressions. We then counted them, finding no difference in the number of facial expressions (smiles and frowns). Apparently, Americans are unable to "read" Japanese expressions, and they wrongly describe Japanese as expressionless. Thus, discrepancies demonstrate the value of balancing and comparing research methods and results.

A Hierarchy of Problems

We find that cultural differences cause four kinds of problems in international business negotiations:

1. Language.
2. Nonverbal behaviors.
3. Values.
4. Thinking and decision-making processes.

The order is important. As you go down the list, the problems are more serious because they are more subtle. Both negotiators notice immediately if one is speaking Japanese and the other German. The solution to the problem may be as simple as hiring an interpreter or talking in a common third language, or it may be as difficult as learning a language. But the problem is obvious.

Alternatively, cultural differences in nonverbal behaviors are almost always hidden below our awareness. That is, in a face-to-face negotiation, we nonverbally give off and take in a great deal of information, and some argue that such information

is the more important exchanged. Almost all this signaling goes on below our levels of consciousness, and when the nonverbal signals from our foreign partners are different, we are most apt to misinterpret them without even being conscious of the mistake. When that French client consistently interrupts, we tend to feel uncomfortable without noticing exactly why. In this manner, interpersonal friction often colors business relationships and goes on undetected and, consequently, uncorrected. Differences in values and thinking processes are hidden even deeper and therefore are even harder to cure.

Problems at the Level of Language

I finally found a country worse at foreign languages than the United States. At a seminar in Melbourne, the Australian managers all agreed that they were worse. Being "so far" from everyone else, foreign languages were given little attention in their educational system. But even if we're not worse than the Aussies, we're clearly down at the bottom of the languages list along with them. I must add that recently American undergrads have begun to see the light and are flocking to language classes. Unfortunately, we don't have the teaching resources to satisfy the demand, so we'll stay behind for some time to come.

It's also fascinating to learn that the Czechs are now throwing away a hard-earned competitive advantage. Young Czechs won't take Russian anymore. It's easy to understand why, but the result will be a generation of Czechs who can't leverage their geographic advantage because they won't be able to speak to their neighbors to the East. However, even more appalling is my own university's contemplated elimination of the Russian language program. This is short-sightedness at its worst.

The most common complaint I hear from American managers regards foreign clients and partners breaking into side conversations in their native languages. Americans hate it. At best, we see it as impolite, and, quite naturally, we are likely to attribute something sinister to the content of the foreign talk—they're plotting or telling secrets or . . .

This is our mistake. We've videotaped and translated many such conversations, and their usual purpose is to straighten out a translation problem. For instance, one Korean may lean over to another and ask, "What'd he say?" Or the side conversation can regard a disagreement among the foreign team. Both circumstances should be seen as positive signs by Americans, because getting translations straight enhances the efficiency of the interactions, and concessions often follow internal disagreements. But because most Americans speak only one language, we can't appreciate either circumstance. By the way, I always advise foreigners to give Americans a brief explanation of the content of their first few side conversations to assuage the sinister attributions.

Data from our simulated negotiations are also informative. Using the approach detailed in Graham (1985), we studied the verbal behaviors of negotiators in 14 of the cultures (6 negotiators in each of the 14 groups were videotaped). The numbers in the body of Exhibit 1 are the percentages of statements that were classified into each category. That is, 7 percent of the statements made by Japanese negotiators were promises, 4 percent were threats, 20 percent were questions, and so on. The verbal bargaining behaviors used by the negotiators during the simulations proved to be surprisingly similar across cultures. Negotiations in all 14 cultures studied were comprised primarily of information-exchange tactics—questions and self-disclosures. However, it should be noted that once again the Japanese appear on the end of the continuum of self-disclosures. Their 34 percent (along with the Spaniards and the Anglophone Canadians) was the lowest across all 14 groups, suggesting that they are the most reticent about giving information.

Consider for a moment the complexity of this part of our work. Six businesspeople in each culture played the same negotiation game in their na-

tive languages, we videotaped each negotiation, transcribed, translated, and classified each statement made into one of 12 categories, calculated percentages and averaged across the six negotiators. And look how similar are the verbal tactics used across the cultural groups!

Nonverbal Behaviors

Reported in Exhibit 2 are the analyses of some linguistic aspects and nonverbal behaviors for the 14 videotaped groups, as in Graham (1985). While our efforts here merely scratch the surface of these kinds of behavioral analyses, they still provide indications of substantial cultural differences. Note that, once again, the Japanese are at or next to the end of almost every dimension of the behaviors listed in Exhibit 2. Their facial gazing and touching are the least among the 14 groups. Only the northern Chinese used the words "no" less frequently, and only the Russians used more silent periods than did the Japanese.

A broader examination of the data in Exhibits 1 and 2 reveals a more meaningful conclusion. That is, the variation across cultures is greater when comparing linguistic aspects of language and nonverbal behaviors than when the verbal content of negotiations is considered. For example, notice the great differences between Japanese and Brazilians in Exhibit 1 vis-à-vis Exhibit 2.

Summary Descriptions Based on the Videotapes

Following are further descriptions of the distinctive aspects of each of the 14 cultural groups we have videotaped. Certainly, we cannot draw conclusions about the individual cultures from an analysis of only six businesspeople in each, but the *suggested* cultural differences are worthwhile to consider briefly:

Japan. Consistent with most descriptions of Japanese negotiation behavior in the literature, the

EXHIBIT 1 Verbal Negotiation Tactics
(The "What" of Communications)

Bargaining Behaviors and Definitions (Anglemar and Stern, 1978)	Cultures (in each group, n = 6)													
	JPN	KOR	TWN	CHN[a]	RUSS	GRM	UK	FRN	SPN	BRZ	MEX	FCAN	ECAN	USA
Promise. A statement in which the source indicated his intention to provide the target with a reinforcing consequence which source anticipates target will evaluate as pleasant, positive, or rewarding.	7*	4	9	6	5	7	11	5	11	3	7	8	6	8
Threat. Same as promise, except that the reinforcing consequences are thought to be noxious, unpleasant, or punishing.	4	2	2	1	3	3	3	5	2	2	1	3	0	4
Recommendation. A statement in which the source predicts that a pleasant environmental consequence will occur to the target. Its occurrence is not under source's control.	7	1	5	2	4	5	6	3	4	5	8	5	4	4
Warning. Same as recommendation, except that the consequences are thought to be unpleasant.	2	0	3	1	0	1	1	3	1	1	2	5	0	1
Reward. A statement by the source that is thought to create pleasant consequences for the target.	1	3	2	1	3	4	5	3	3	2	1	1	3	2
Punishment. Same as reward, except that the consequences are thought to be unpleasant.	1	5	1	0	1	2	0	3	2	3	0	2	1	3
Positive normative appeal. A statement in which the source indicates that the target's past, present, or future behavior was or will be in conformity with social norms.	1	1	0	1	0	0	0	0	0	0	0	1	0	1
Negative normative appeal. Same as positive normative appeal except that the target's behavior is in violation of social norms.	3	2	1	0	0	1	1	0	1	1	1	2	1	1
Commitment. A statement by the source to the effect that its future bids will not go below or above a certain level.	15	13	9	10	11	9	13	10	9	8	9	8	14	13
Self-disclosure. A statement in which the source reveals information about itself.	34	36	42	36	40	47	39	42	34	39	38	42	34	36
Question. A statement in which the source asks the target to reveal information about itself.	20	21	14	34	27	11	15	18	17	22	27	19	26	20
Command. A statement in which the source suggests that the target perform a certain behavior.	8	13	11	7	7	12	9	9	17	14	5	5	10	6

* Read "7% of the statements made by Japanese negotiators were promises."
[a] Northern China (Tianjin and environs).

EXHIBIT 2 Structural Aspects of Language and Nonverbal Behaviors
("How" Things Are Said)

Bargaining Behaviors (per 30 minutes)	Cultures (in each group, n = 6)													
	JPN	KOR	TWN	CHN[a]	RUSS	GRM	UK	FRN	SPN	BRZ	MEX	FCAN	ECAN	USA
Structural Aspects														
"No's." The number of times the word "no" was used by each negotiator.	1.9	7.4	5.9	1.5	2.3	6.7	5.4	11.3	23.2	41.9	4.5	7.0	10.1	4.5
"You's." The number of times the word "you" was used by each negotiator.	31.5	34.2	36.6	26.8	23.6	39.7	54.8	70.2	73.3	90.4	56.3	72.4	64.4	54.1
Nonverbal Behaviors														
Silent Periods. The number of conversational gaps of 10 seconds or longer.	2.5	0	0	2.3	3.7	0	2.5	1.0	0	0	1.1	0.2	2.9	1.7
Conversational Overlaps. Number of interruptions.	6.2	22.0	12.3	17.1	13.3	20.8	5.3	20.7	28.0	14.3	10.6	24.0	17.0	5.1
Facial Gazing. Number of minutes negotiators spent looking at opponent's face.	3.9	9.9	19.7	11.1	8.7	10.2	9.0	16.0	13.7	15.6	14.7	18.8	10.4	10.0
Touching. Incidents of bargainers touching one another (not including handshaking).	0	0	0	0	0	0	0	0.1	0	4.7	0	0	0	0

[a] Northern China (Tianjin and environs).

results of this analysis suggest their style of inter-action is among the least aggressive (or most po-lite). Threats, commands, and warnings appear to be de-emphasized in favor of the more positive promises, recommendations, and commitments. Particularly indicative of their polite conversa-tional style was their infrequent use of "no" and "you" and facial grazing, as well as more frequent silent periods.

Korea. Perhaps one of the more interesting as-pects of this study is the contrast of the Asian styles of negotiations. Non-Asians often general-ize about the Orient. Our findings demonstrate that this is a mistake. Korean negotiators used consid-erably more punishments and commands than did the Japanese. Koreans used the word "no" and in-terrupted more than three times as frequently as the Japanese. Moreover, no silent periods occurred between Korean negotiators.

China (northern). The behaviors of the nego-tiators from northern China (i.e., in and around Tianjin) are most remarkable in the emphasis on asking questions at 34 percent. Indeed, 70 percent of the statements made by the Chinese negotiators were classified as information exchange tactics. Other aspects of their behavior were quite similar to the Japanese—the use of "no" and "you" and silent periods.

Taiwan. The behavior of the businesspeople in Taiwan was quite different from that in China and Japan but similar to that in Korea. The Chinese on Taiwan were exceptional in the time of facing gaz-ing, on the average almost 20 out of 30 minutes. They asked fewer questions and provided more in-formation (self-disclosures) than did any of the other Asian groups.

Russia. The Russians' style was quite different from that of any other European group, and, in-deed, was quite similar in many respects to the style of the Japanese. They used "no" and "you"

infrequently and used the most silent periods of any group. Only the Japanese did less facial gaz-ing, and only the Chinese asked a greater percent-age of questions.

Germany. The behaviors of the western Ger-mans are difficult to characterize because they fell toward the center of almost all the continua. How-ever, the Germans were exceptional in the high percentage of self-disclosures at 47 percent and the low percentage of questions at 11 percent.

United Kingdom. The behaviors of the British negotiators are remarkably similar to those of the Americans in all respects.

Spain. *"Diga"* is perhaps a good metaphor for the Spanish approach to negotiations evinced in our data. When you make a phone call in Madrid, the usual greeting on the other end is not *"hola"* (hello) but is, instead, *"diga"* (speak). The Spaniards in our negotiations likewise used the highest percentage of commands (17 percent) of any of the groups and gave comparatively little in-formation (self-disclosures, 34 percent). More-over, they interrupted one another more frequently than any other group, and they used the terms "no" and "you" very frequently.

France. The style of the French negotiators is perhaps the most aggressive of all the groups. In particular, they used the highest percentage of threats and warnings (together, 8 percent). They also used interruptions, facial gazing, and "no" and "you" very frequently compared to the other groups, and one of the French negotiators touched his partner on the arm during the simulation.

Brazil. The Brazilian businesspeople, like the French and Spanish, were quite aggressive. They used the highest percentage of commands of all the groups. On average, the Brazilians said the word "no" 42 times, "you" 90 times, and touched one another on the arm about five times during 30 min-utes of negotiation. Facial gazing was also high.

Mexico. The patterns of Mexican behavior in our negotiations are good reminders of the dangers of regional or language-group generalizations. Both verbal and nonverbal behaviors are quite different than those of their Latin American (Brazilian) or continental (Spanish) cousins. Indeed, Mexicans answer the telephone with the much less demanding *"bueno."* In many respects, the Mexican behavior is very similar to that of the negotiators from the United States.

Francophone Canada. The French-speaking Canadians in our study behaved quite similarly to their continental cousins. Like the negotiators from France, they, too, used high percentages of threats and warnings, and even more interruptions and eye contact. Such an aggressive interaction style would not mix well with some of the more low-key styles of some of the Asian groups or with English speakers, including Anglophone Canadians.

Anglophone Canada. The Canadians in our study who speak English as their first language used the lowest percentage of aggressive persuasive tactics (that is, threats, warnings and punishments totaled only 1 percent) of all 13 groups. Perhaps, as communications researchers suggest, such stylistic differences are the seeds of interethnic discord as witnessed in Canada over the years. With respect to international negotiations, the Anglophone Canadians used noticeably more interruptions and "no's" than negotiators from either of Canada's major trading partners, the United States and Japan.

United States. Like the Germans and the British, the Americans fell in the middle of most continua. They did interrupt one another less frequently than all the others, but that was their sole distinction.

These differences across the cultures are quite complex. Specifically, you should not use this material *by itself* to predict the behaviors of your foreign counterparts. Please be very careful of the stereotypes. Rather, the key here is to be aware of *these kinds of differences* so you don't misinterpret the Japanese silence, the Brazilian "no, no, no . . . ," or the French threat.

Differences in Values

It's true what Le Poole said earlier about us Americans presuming that everyone else in the world shares our values. After all, how could anyone **not** see the sense in objectivity, competitiveness, equality, and punctuality?

Objectivity. We Americans make decisions based upon the bottom line and on cold, hard facts. We don't play favorites. Economics and performance count, not people. Business is business.

Roger Fisher and William Ury have written the single most important book on the topic of negotiation, *Getting to Yes.* I highly recommend it to both American and foreign readers. The latter will learn not only about negotiations but, perhaps more important, about how Americans think about negotiations. Fisher and Ury are quite emphatic about "separating the people from the problem," and they state, "Every negotiator has two kinds of interests: in the substance and in the relationship" (p. 20). This advice is probably quite worthwhile in the United States or perhaps in Germany, but in most places in the world, their advice is nonsense. **In most places in the world, personalities and substance are not separate issues and can't be made so.**

For example, look at how important nepotism is in Chinese or Hispanic cultures. John Kao (1993) tells us that businesses don't grow beyond the bounds and bonds of tight family control in the burgeoning "Chinese Commonwealth." Things work the same way in Spain, Mexico, and the Philippines **by nature.** And, just as naturally, negotiators from such countries not only will take things personally but will be personally affected by negotiation outcomes. What happens to them at the negotiation table will affect the business relationship regardless of the economics involved.

Competitiveness and Equality.   Our simulated negotiations can be viewed as a kind of experimental economics wherein the values of each cultural group are roughly reflected in the economic outcomes. The simple simulation we use well represents the essence of commercial negotiations—it has both competitive and cooperative aspects. That is, the "negotiation pie" can be made larger through cooperation before it is divided between the buyer and seller.

Our results are summarized in Figure 1. The Japanese are the champions at making the pie big. Their joint profits in the simulation were the highest (at $9,590) among the 18 cultural groups. The American pie was more average-sized (at $9,030), but at least it was divided relatively equally (51.8 percent of the profits went to the buyers). Alternatively, the Japanese (and others) split their pies in strange ways, with buyers making higher percentages of the profits (53.8 percent). The implications

of our experimental economics are completely consistent with our own field work, the comments of other authors, and the adage that in Japan the buyer is "kinger." By nature, Americans have little understanding of the Japanese practice of giving complete deference to the needs and wishes of buyers. That's not the way things work in America. American sellers tend to treat American buyers more as equals. And the egalitarian values of American society support this behavior. Moreover, most Americans will, by nature, treat Japanese buyers more frequently as equals. Likewise, as suggested by Nakane (1970) and Graham (1981), American buyers will generally not "take care of" American sellers or Japanese sellers.

The American emphasis on competition and individualism represented in our findings is, in different ways, consistent with the work of both Geert Hofstede, the guru of international management, and J. Scott Armstrong of the Wharton

FIGURE 1

*Cultural differences in competitiveness and equality**

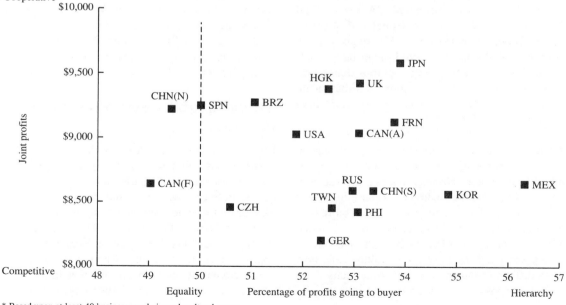

* Based upon at least 40 businesspeople in each cultural group.

School. Hofstede reports that Americans scored the highest among 40 other cultural groups on his individualism (versus collectivism) scale. Armstrong reports that "competition-oriented" objectives can have negative effects on profits. Of course, Adam Smith argued that competition ultimately serves society. However, in the context of the little society of our negotiation simulation, Smith's ideas don't appear to hold up. Perhaps the reason we hear so much about "win-win" negotiations here in the United States is because we really haven't learned the lesson well enough yet.

Finally, when we run the numbers on the Japanese and American results, not only do Japanese buyers achieve higher results than Americans do, but Japanese sellers ($4,430), compared to American sellers ($4,350), also get more of the commercial pie, as well. Interestingly, when I show these numbers to Americans in my executive seminars, the majority still prefer the American seller's role. That is, even though the American sellers make lower profits than the Japanese, the American managers prefer lower profits if those profits are yielded from an equal split of the joint profits. Such an emphasis on equality is also echoed in a survey of American managers: "A recent Wall Street poll revealed this potentially destructive side of economic nationalism. Eighty-six percent of those polled said they would rather have a policy of slower growth in both countries than a policy of faster growth in both countries if that meant allowing Japan to take the lead" (*The Wall Street Journal,* July 2, 1990, p. 1).

Time. "Just make them wait." Everyone else in the world knows no negotiation tactic is more useful with Americans. Nobody places more value on time. Nobody has less patience when things slow down. Nobody looks at their wristwatch more than Americans. Edward T. Hall (1960) in his seminal writing is best at explaining how the passage of time is viewed differently across cultures and how these differences most often hurt Americans.

But it is possible to put time to our own uses. In the mid-1970s, my former company, Solar Turbines International (a division of Caterpillar), sold $34 million worth of industrial gas turbines and compressors to the Soviet Union for a natural gas pipeline application. It was agreed that final negotiations would be held in a neutral location, the south of France. In previous negotiations, the Soviets had been tough, but reasonable. But in Nice, the Soviets weren't nice. They became tougher and, in fact, completely unreasonable.

It took a couple of discouraging days before our people diagnosed the problem, but once they did, a crucial call was made back to headquarters in California. Why had the Soviet attitude turned so cold? Because they were enjoying the warm weather in Nice and weren't interested in making a quick deal and heading back to Moscow. The call to California was the key event in this negotiation. Our people in San Diego were sophisticated enough to allow our negotiators to take their time.

The routine of the negotiations changed to brief, 45-minute meetings in the mornings, with afternoons at the golf course, beach, or hotel, making calls and doing paperwork. Finally, during week four, the Soviets began to make concessions and to ask for longer meetings. Why? They couldn't go back to Moscow after four weeks on the Mediterranean **without a signed contract.** This strategic reversal of the time pressure yielded a wonderful contract for Solar.

Thinking and Decision-Making Processes

When faced with a complex negotiation task, most Westerners (I will generalize here) divide the large task up into a series of smaller tasks. Issues such as prices, delivery, warranty, and service contracts may be settled one issue at a time, with the final agreement being the sum of the sequence of smaller agreements. However, in Asia, a different approach is more often taken wherein all the issues are discussed at once, in no apparent order, and concessions are made on all issues at the end of the discussion. The Western sequential approach and the Eastern holistic approach do not mix well.

For example, American managers report great difficulties in measuring progress in Japan. After all, in America, you're half done when half the issues are settled. But in Japan, nothing seems to get settled. Then, surprise, you're done. Often, Americans make unnecessary concessions right before agreements are announced by the Japanese. For example, we know of an American retail goods buyer traveling to Japan to buy six different consumer products for a large chain of discount department stores. He told us that negotiations for his first purchase took an entire week. In the United States, such a purchase would be consummated in an afternoon. So, by his calculations, he expected to have to spend six weeks in Japan to complete his purchases. He considered raising his purchase prices to try to move things along faster. But before he was able to make such a concession, the Japanese quickly agreed on the other five products in just three days. This particular businessman was, by his own admission, lucky in his first encounter with Japanese bargainers.

This American businessman's near blunder reflects more than just a difference in decision-making style. To Americans, a business negotiation is a problem-solving activity, the best deal for both parties being the solution. To a Japanese businessperson, a business negotiation is a time to develop a business relationship with the goal of long-term mutual benefit. The economic issues are the **context,** not the **content,** of the talks. Thus, settling any one issue really isn't important. Such details will take care of themselves once a viable, harmonious business relationship is established. And, as happened in the case of our retail goods buyer, once the relationship was established—signaled by the first agreement—the other "details" were settled quickly.

American bargainers should anticipate such a holistic approach and be prepared to discuss all issues simultaneously and in an apparently haphazard order. Progress in the talks should not be mea-

sured by how many issues have been settled. Rather, Americans must try to gauge the quality of the business relationship. Important signals of progress will be:

- Higher-level foreigners being included in the discussions;
- Their questions beginning to focus on specific areas of the deal;
- A softening of their attitudes and position on some of the issues—"Let us take some time to study this issue";
- At the negotiation table, increased talk among themselves in their own language, which may often mean they're trying to decide something; and
- Increased bargaining and use of the lower level, informal, and other channels of communication.

Implications for Managers

Having read what I've written so far, it's a wonder that any international business gets done at all. Obviously, the economic imperatives of global trade make much of it happen despite the potential pitfalls. But an appreciation of cultural differences can lead to even better international commercial transactions—it is not just business deals but highly profitable business relationships that are the goal here.

Another reason for our global business successes is the large numbers of skillful international negotiators. These are the managers who have lived in foreign countries and speak foreign languages. In many cases, they are immigrants to the United States or have been immersed in foreign cultures in other capacities. (Peace Corps volunteers and Mormon missionaries are common examples.) The Thunderbird School in Phoenix has long been a supplier of managers with international competencies. Thankfully, at more of our other business schools we are beginning to reemphasize language training and visits abroad. Indeed, it is interesting to note that the original Harvard Business School catalogue of 1908–09 listed German, French, and Spanish correspondence within its curriculum.

While I was teaching at the Madrid Business School in 1992, I was most encouraged to see as the February 10th cover story of *Business Week,* "Ford and Mazda: The Partnership That Works." Although the article didn't credit directly the training program I helped design,[2] the interviews with Ford people throughout reflected lessons learned in their Executive Development Center programs on Japan. Ford does more business with Japanese companies than any other firm. They own 33 percent of Mazda, they build a successful minivan with Nissan, and they buy and sell component parts and completed cars from and to Japanese companies. But perhaps the best measure of Ford's Japanese business is the 8,000 or so U.S.-Japan round-trip tickets the company buys annually!

Ford has made a large investment in training its managers with Japanese responsibilities. More than 1,500 of their executives have attended a three-day program on Japanese history and culture and the company's Japanese business strategies. More than 700 of their managers who work *vis-à-vis* with Japanese have attended a three-day program, "Managing Negotiations: Japan" (they call it MNJ), designed using many of the ideas in Yoshi Sano's and my book, *Smart Bargaining, Doing Business with the Japanese* (see Box 2 for testimony regarding the latter program's effectiveness). The program includes negotiation simulations with videotape feedback, lectures with cultural differences demonstrated via videotapes of Japanese/American interactions developed in our research, and rehearsals of upcoming negotiations. The company also conducts similar programs on Korea and the Peoples Republic of China.

Despite my own pride in MNJ, I have to credit the broader Japan training efforts at Ford for their successes. Certainly, we see MNJ alumni exercising influence across and up the ranks regarding Japanese relationships. But the organizational awareness of the cultural dimensions of the Japan-

---

Box 2

Proactive and direct is the approach Ford uses to develop competence in employees who interact with the Japanese. This occurs through a variety of practices, including programs that help Ford personnel better understand the Japanese culture and negotiating practices and by encouraging the study of the spoken language. By designing training that highlights both the pitfalls and the opportunities in negotiations, we increase the chance to "expand the negotiation pie."

Back in 1988, the key personnel on our minivan team attended one of the first sessions of the Managing Negotiations: Japan Program at the Ford Executive Development Center. Our negotiations with the Nissan team improved immediately. But perhaps the best measure of the usefulness of the MNJ Program is the success of the Nissan joint-venture product itself. Reflected in the Villager/Quest are countless hours of effective face-to-face meetings with our Japanese partners.

Not everyone negotiating outside the U.S. has the advantages of in-house training. However, many sources of information are available—books (particularly, on Japan), periodicals, and colleagues with firsthand experience. To succeed, I believe negotiators have to be truly interested in and challenged by the international negotiating environment. Structuring negotiations to achieve win-win results AND building a long-term relationship takes thoughtful attention and commitment.

Joe Gilmore is the Ford executive in charge of the minivan project with Nissan (marketed as the Mercury Villager and the Nissan Quest).

ese business system was quickly raised by their broader three-day program.

Please recall my story about the Soviets in Nice. There were two critical events. First, our negotiators diagnosed the problem. Second, and equally important, their California superiors appreciated the problem and approved the investments in time and money to outwait the Russians. So it is that the Ford programs have targeted not only the negotiators working directly with the Japanese but **also** their managers who spend most of their time in Detroit. Negotiators need information specific to the cultures in which they work. Their managers back in the United States need a basic awareness and appreciation for the importance of culture in international business so that they will be more apt to listen to the "odd" recommendations coming from their people in Moscow, Rio, or Tokyo.

Conclusions

In the almost 20 years I've been working in this area, things are getting better. The "innocents abroad" or cowboy stereotypes of American managers are becoming less accurate (see Graham and Herberger, 1983). Likewise, we hope it is obvious that the stereotypes of the reticent Japanese or the pushy Brazilian evinced in our research may no longer hold so true. Experience levels are going up worldwide, and individual personalities are important. So you can find talkative Japanese, quiet Brazilians, **and** effective American negotiators. But culture still does, and always will, count. Hopefully, it is fast becoming the **natural** behavior of American managers to take it into account.

Notes

1. Over the past 15 years, a group of colleagues and I have been gathering data for this research. The following institutions and people have provided crucial support for the research for this article: U.S. Department of Education; Toyota Motor Sales USA, Inc.; Solar Turbines, International (a division of Caterpillar Tractors Co.); the Faculty Research and Innovation Fund and the International Business Educational Research (IBEAR) Program at the University of Southern California; Ford Motor Company; The Marketing Science Institute; Madrid Business School; and Professors Nancy J. Adler (McGill University), Nigel Campbell (Manchester Business School), A. Gabriel Esteban (University of Houston—Victoria), Leonid I. Evenko (Russian Academy of the National Economy), Richard H. Holton (University of California, Berkeley), Alain Jolibert (Universite de Sciences de Grenoble), Dong Ki Kim (Korea University), C. Y. Lin (National Sun-Yat Sen University), Hans-Gunther Meissner (Dortmund University), Alena Ockova (Czech Management Center), Sara Tang (Mass Transit Railway Corporation, Hong Kong), and Theodore Schwarz (Monterrey Institute of Technology).

2. G. Richard Hartshorn, Antigone Kiriacopoulou, and Bruce Gibb were the other original design team members.

References

Anglemar, R., and Stern, L. W. (1978). "Development of a content analytic system for analysis of bargaining communication in marketing." *Journal of Marketing Research* (February): 93–102.

Graham, J. L. (1981). "A hidden cause of America's trade deficit with Japan." *Columbia Journal of World Business* (Fall): 5–15.

Graham, J. L., and Herberger, Roy A. Jr. (1983). "Negotiators abroad—Don't shoot from the hip." *Harvard Business Review* (July–August): 160–68.

Hall, E. T. (1960). "The silent language in oversees business." *Harvard Business Review* (May–June); 87–96

Kao, J. (1993). "The worldwide web of Chinese business." *Harvard Business Review* (March–April): 24–96.

Kelley, H. H. (1966). "A classroom study of the dilemmas in interpersonal negotiations." *Strategic interaction and conflict,* edited by K. Archibald. Berkeley Institute of International Studies, University of California.

Nakane, C. (1970). *Japanese society.* Berkeley, CA: University of California Press.

THE IMPLICATIONS OF OTHER FORMS OF CAPITALISM*

Gordon Redding

There are, in simple terms, five successful forms of capitalism at present: Western capitalism divides into two: the individualistic North American type and the communitarian European model. In Asia there are three; the Japanese led by the Keiretsu; the Korean, led by the Chaebol; and the Chinese family business. This is the first division of world business—the premier league.

But with one hidden proviso: each one is playing a different game. Imagine two sets of people who decide to play a game together with a small hard ball and bats, two competing sides, a scoring system, 10 or so players each, and an umpire. They arrive on the same field and try to make progress. They do not know that one is playing baseball and the other cricket. You can imagine the confusion:

The Americans saying:

"This limey wants to put sticks in the ground."

"They got *two* guys with bats."

"Silly mid-off, deep fine leg, extra cover, lbw, what the hell is this?"

and on the other hand, the Brits:

"I say, old chap, wouldn't you like a wider bat."

"I'm terribly sorry but only fielders can throw it that way."

"But we simply must break for tea."

As one familiar with and deeply fond of the United States since bumming around as a student in 1957, and in 1995 still not knowing what an RBI is, I am sensitive to the meaning of the phrase "it's a different ball game around here." In Hong Kong as an observer for 23 years of western multinationals coming to terms with Asia, the same metaphor has, to me, expanded in relevance and significance.

In that context I would propose for your consideration three points:

1. There is no reason why one formula for putting together a successful system of capitalism should have a world monopoly, and every reason to see capitalisms in the plural as embedded in their own distinct cultures and histories.

2. Some of the alternative capitalist systems may be more efficient in future world market competition than systems dominant earlier.

---

* Luncheon presentation at the eighth annual Asia/Pacific Business Outlook Conference, co-sponsored by the International Business Education and Research (IBEAR) Program of the University of Southern California and the U.S. & Foreign Commercial Services of the U.S. Department of Commerce, Los Angeles, March 13–15, 1995.

3. The firm attempting to globalize to a point where it can take on indigenous capitalisms on their own terms and in their own territories has not yet been invented. In my view it may never be, because the cost of integration will destroy its competitiveness.

Let me expand briefly on those three points.

Firstly, the embeddedness of systems of economic coordination and control, otherwise known as *firms*. What is the matrix in which they are embedded? A simple answer is culture, but I would qualify that by saying "at least culture," because it is not the only thing in the explanation. There are also political philosophy, technical borrowing, the accidents of timing historically, world economic conditions, and, in some instances, personality.

But culture provides the rules for designing organizations. It does so by providing a particular society's answers to the three core dilemmas in persuading human beings to get organized. These dilemmas are: How do I know whom to trust? Why should I accept a particular kind of authority as legitimate? And what are my primary allegiances in this society? Trust, authority, allegiance. Organizations have to be built around these three requirements. They determine the standard formulas in a society for handling the structures and systems of vertical and horizontal cooperation which organizations and economies are.

The extent to which a culture is clear and strong may be measured by the clarity with which it deals with these issues. So, for instance, in American culture, in simple terms you trust anyone as long as there is legal protection underpinning the exchange. Authority is legitimized by demonstrated competence. And allegiance, in a highly individualistic society, is primarily to the self. America's real national anthem is Frank Sinatra singing *My Way*. These values are morally based and historically robust. They are just as visible in the pages of de Tocqueville as they are in the pages of *Vanity Fair* or the TV show the Simpsons (either version). More particularly, the classic U.S. divisionalized corporation and the ideal behaviors inside it celebrated in the textbooks of the world's business school libraries are practical celebrations of the power of such moral forces to shape human social behaviors.

In Chinese culture, on the other hand, or at least that form of it that can express itself freely in places like Hong Kong, Taiwan, and in the ethnic Chinese communities of the Pacific Asian Diaspora, the ground rules are different. The moral norms are even older and come from a quite different historical and philosophical base.

Trust for the Chinese cannot be handled legally. It is an interpersonal matter. The ethics behind it are about mutual obligations, and in consequence you only trust those people you have built a bond with. This, in turn, defines the structures for exchange in the sphere of business, and hence the crucial networks that give the economy its efficiency.

Authority for the Chinese stems from ownership, and so too does status. "It's better to be the head of a chicken than the backside of an ox." Being an employee makes you second grade. Ownership is where it's at, even if it's just a noodle stall. This obsession is visible in the title of a new book on business structures in Taiwan Boss Island. If you are an owner you then have the right to behave as a Confucian father-figure, and by the judicious exercise of paternalism, seek what Lucian Pye once described (of East Asian organizations) as "the efficiency of benevolence."

In Chinese society the primary focus of allegiance is the family, and all firms for the Chinese overseas, are family firms—even the largest. The Chinese culture legitimizes that as the recent story in the *South China Morning Post* recently illustrates:

All in the Family

The folks at a distinguished local bank are not going to win any marks for imagination when it comes to board appointments, though. Two of the three directors appointed earlier this week are related to David Chan Kwok-po, the chief executive. That brings to seven the number of Mr. Chan's family members on the 15-strong board, and that does not include more tenuous links by marriage. The chairman is venerable banker, Chan Fook-wo, David's uncle. David's father, Chan Fook-shu, is also on the board. Alan Chan Fook-sum, who owned the legendary racehorse Gilgit, is a cousin and director. Professor Arthur Chan Kwok-cheung, appointed to the board this week, is David's brother. Simon Chan Fook-sean, the famous legal chap, is an uncle, while Aubrey Chan Kwok-sing, the broker, is the son of Chan Fook-wo.

The odd thing is that the Chan family is not a major shareholder. It has a few million shares tucked away, but that is nothing compared with the 734 million in issue. Well, every company has the right to appoint its own directors, but it was a bit much for the company to announce that it "welcomed the new directors and congratulated them on their appointment." After all, the introductions are not going to take long at their first board meeting.

It would be possible to cite similar contrasts from Japan or Korea to illustrate a core point and it is this: Each society works out its own formula for handling trust, authority, and allegiance, and there is no reason why they should all come up with the same answers. Their historical experiences and their core philosophies will inevitably be different, and so too their present-day beliefs about appropriate conduct. But what is not sufficiently realized is how deeply and invisibly such ideas penetrate organizational life.

This is visible if you consider varieties of organizations in terms of a simple fundamental question nobody asks because they assume they know the answer. The question is why does the organization exist? Or what is it there for? And of course the universal answer is long-term survival. But this is simplistic. If you ask more probing questions about its less-explicit central purposes, you will need to acknowledge that the latent purposes visible in action itself, separate out intriguingly, culture by culture.

A classic large American corporation is there firstly and essentially to satisfy public demand for return on capital. Nor can it survive without secondly meeting societal expectations about its behavior in markets, environments, and employment.

Thirdly, it is also designed to compete on regulated, level playing fields. It is, in other words, a creature of its context, an adapted species.

In Asia, the contexts are very different and so too are the games. Three powerful teams dominate the arena, each playing a subtly different game. They are set up to do different things. They are for different purposes. The Japanese Keiretsu, the Korean Chaebol and the Chinese family business are not playing an American game.

In Japan, large corporations are driven to survive by mechanisms distinct to their context. Firstly, they exist primarily to keep a loyal workforce in employment. Secondly, their behavior competitively is driven by league table competition within what Rodney Clark called "clubs of industry." Thirdly, there is a deep sense of their representing Japanese efficiency which affects their wider work. Note the absence of stockholder power.

The Chinese family business exists firstly to serve the interests of a family, as an instrument for the accumulation of family wealth and status. It is a totally different main rationale from that of the U.S. or Japanese corporation. Its other main purposes are secondly the protection of a set of employees treated as family, and thirdly, the finding and taking of opportunities using carefully acquired knowledge not available to others.

These reasons for the organization's existence cannot but inform the organization's behavior, at both the operating and the strategic levels. Contrast U.S. "downsizing" with the Chinese family business as an "iron rice bowl." Contrast the speed of response to an opportunity of a Chinese family business entrepreneur with any other contender worldwide, and you will see he is in an Olympic category of his own. Contrast the quarterly results-driven U.S. chief executive with any of his Asian counterparts with their luxuriously long views, and you might even be inspired to sympathize with his plight (until of course you see his pay packet).

Contrast the Japanese, standing on the edge of China, and not really going in, biting their nails with anxiety because they can't indulge their national passion for the awesomely patient accumulation of reliable information. Or the Americans, in full pursuit of an apparently seductive "China maiden" with whom the U.S. has had a 200-year-long love affair (suffering like most love affairs from periods of disenchantment), only to discover that the energy expended seems unrelated to the satisfaction.

In China, contrast that with the behavior of Chinese family entrepreneurs, described graphically by someone as a "feeding frenzy," home at last, seeking both the crevices and the crevasses in a decidedly unlevel playing field, and opportunity-seeking, as if the property speculators nirvana of Hong Kong had just been expanded a thousandfold—which of course it has. Anyway, they have committed at least $100 billion in the pursuit of the family dreams of collective absentee landlordship. If you want rentier capitalism—nobody does it better.

The business environments of Asia outside Japan are jungles. You cannot see the terrain. The surrounding threats are multiple and invisible. You need local knowledge to cope. You also need guides. The Asian business jungles of China, Vietnam, Indonesia, Malaysia, Philippines, Thailand, Korea, and Taiwan require guerrilla tactics, not regiments trained for parade ground drill.

Local adaptations in the behavior of organizations include the co-opting of local political support, the use of rare, reliable information as a currency for barter in the market for relationships, and the cultivating of a very high speed of response. If you can't perform this way, then you'll be lucky to survive. The rules of jungle warfare have their own special manual. Let me give you examples of those adaptations.

Co-opting Local Political Support.

An American friend of mine who was investing several hundred million dollars in a major plant in the country was being helped by an ethnic Chinese local banker. On asking about an impending change of government and the support of the next Finance Minister, the local banker said "Don't worry, I can deliver anybody who might be Finance Minister."

Information.   In a recent *Fortune* article on the Overseas Chinese, a major entrepreneur said, "I don't tell anyone, not even some of my family members, the names of my contacts in China."

Speed of Response.   An American friend of mine, advising an Overseas Chinese on a possible chemical plant investment, asked if he should proceed to a detailed feasibility study after a tour of the site. "Don't bother," said the Chinese. "Just find me a manager; I bought the plant over lunch."

I said at the beginning that such alternative forms of capitalism as this are successful in world markets. The data on national success make this manifest. The foreign reserves of Taiwan, Hong Kong, and Singapore are now probably at $200 billion. I pay my secretary in Hong Kong more than I was offered for a senior professorship of management studies in the UK recently. At least four Asian capitals are now trying to build the world's tallest building. As Jim Abegglen says, there is a "Sea Change" as the world's businesses come to terms with what the World Bank calls the East Asian miracle.

But what does "coming to terms with" mean for an American corporation? It can obviously enter the arena in a physical sense, but can it play the same game? If it can't or won't, can it create a change of rules?

These are the dilemmas of globalizations now being struggled with and they are visible in the agonizing reappraisal of American organizational efficiency of the past decade. They are more visible in the advice which leads such rethinking.

- Work at Wharton on the 21st century enterprise;
- Work at Harvard by Bartlett on new forms of management;
- The whole reengineering revolution;
- Peter Senke's work at MIT on learning organizations;

- The Michigan studies on organizational capability;
- And of course work here at USC on operationalizing excellence.

These research works universally attempt to breathe fresh life into bureaucracies—to get elephants to dance. They also all advocate "global competence." In real terms huge progress has been made. The revival has been a form of elongated revolution.

But is the truly global firm visible? I think not. The core character of a firm is so central to its survival, the cement that holds it together, that to diffuse it is like robbing an individual of personality. Nobody knows what it stands for below the surface of the official pronouncements.

That is because firms are cultural artifacts, and, as I have proposed, are embedded in societal value systems. They are none the worse for that, but let us not fool ourselves into thinking that they can be built to take on all comers if the game is played with the all comers, playing at home, on their own grounds, in the plural.

I am not saying it is impossible. I am saying nobody has worked out yet how to do it in a sustained way. Certainly there are successful experiments, but the costs of integration, once differentiation has proceeded to the extent necessary, are frightening to contemplate.

We all hope the laboratory produces an answer. In the meantime, let us not be deluded by slogans. The globalization of a firm in a true sense will stretch human skills in coordination beyond any point so far reached. And then people have to be persuaded to keep doing it.

What it means is a team able to win the World Series and the Super Bowl and perform respectably in a test match, the FA Cup final, the pelota in Macau, badminton in Jakarta, and sumo wrestling in Japan. Then they have to take on the real competition of the Overseas Chinese, whose own special team game is making money.

JAPANESE MARKETING IN THE POST-BUBBLE ERA

Johny K. Johansson and Masaaki Hirano

Introduction

A number of forces combined to change the Japanese marketing landscape in the early 1990s. In Japan, the bursting of the bubble with its accompanying fall in real estate and stock market prices led to illiquid consumers and squeezed corporate profits. With no overtime pay, and with banks unable to lend, consumers reduced spending. Faced with overcapacity, companies curtailed new investment. As markets contracted, price emerged as a prime determinant of buyer choice (*The Japan Times,* 1994e).

Overseas, despite the successes of the GATT/WTO and NAFTA accords, Japanese market successes were at risk. Increased competitiveness of Western companies and vigilante trade negotiators combined to put pressure on Japanese market shares in the United States and in Europe (*The New York Times,* 1994b). Asian markets seemed more promising, with China booming and India reopening; but even here the Japanese companies faced strong competition from other Asian countries and the reawakened West.

In Japan, the SII (Structural Impediments Initiative) and related efforts by Western powers to pry open the Japanese distribution system had won some victories, including the easing of the limiting large-store law, putting additional pressure on entrenched domestic marketers (see, for example, *The Japan Times,* 1994h). Beginning in 1993, the yen started to rise against the dollar, gaining over 20 percent in less than a year, further crimping the Japanese companies' efforts overseas. Although a company such as Honda with strong overseas manufacturing could keep its new model prices down, many Japanese companies relying on exports saw their margins shrink considerably (*Business Week,* 1994).

This article attempts to identify some of the marketing consequences of these developments. As the distribution system opens up, imports made cheaper by the rising yen should pose a strong competitive threat to domestic companies in Japan. Faced also by lower revenues in yen from overseas sales, Japanese companies might have to change their marketing strategies, with implications for their strength in foreign markets. In the Japanese home market, as prices and costs become important to buyers, and the insistence on Japanese suppliers and high quality weakens, new opportunities are likely to emerge for Western companies, newcomers as well as those experienced with Japan. This article attempts to assess to what extent these likely changes are taking place.

From *The International Executive,* Vol. 38(1) 33–51
(January/February 1996) © 1996 John Wiley & Sons, Inc.

Data Sources

The study draws on a variety of data sources. First, there are published data that track the changes in some of the economic indicators. Japan's Economic Planning Agency, MITI, and Jetro track prices in selected consumer markets, company investment plans, company hiring and firing, and overseas investment activity. Of more direct relevance for the present study, Nikkei (short for *Nihon Keizai Shimbun,* Japan's leading financial newspaper) and other newspapers publish data and stories concerning sales and profitability records, market entries by foreign companies, and new strategic alliances and other tie-ups.

While these data paint the broad picture of the economy and show newsworthy incidents in new products and market entries, it is much harder to gain a complete picture of the developments in marketing specifically. Profitability for individual products is rarely available outside the company, systematic records of new product entries have to be built company by company, advertising spending for new entries is often kept confidential, and the effects of new distribution arrangements are not manifested or at least recorded until some time has passed. Given this situation, the approach used here was to identify "key informants" who could be expected to be knowledgeable about changes in the Japanese markets and the responses by Japanese corporations.

The key informants selected included Japanese management professors, a Japan-based strategic planner for a Western multinational advertising agency, and a manager in marketing for one of the largest Japanese firms in consumer packaged goods. They were selected because of their expertise in their respective areas, and because they had all been active in discussions and seminars concerning marketing in Japan. The informal interviews were structured around changes in seven topic areas: marketing philosophy, marketing research, market segmentation, and product positioning, pricing, distribution, and promotion. The informants were given a one-page sheet with ex-amples of questions under each topic. The audio-taped interviews were all carried out by the first author and lasted on average one hour.

In addition to these interviews, Western and Japanese-language publications (trade reports and newspaper and magazine articles) and more informal discussions with executives and academicians were combined to produce the picture of the marketing changes taking place presented here.

Changing Consumers

Perhaps the greatest change in the opportunities faced by Western companies in Japan has to do with recent shifts in buyer behavior:

Increased Price Sensitivity. Not surprisingly, there is general agreement between various commentators and our key informants that the price sensitivity on the part of the Japanese consumer has increased considerably in the last two years. Whereas earlier the Japanese consumers were often said to pay attention to quality and not worry about price, they have now become more price conscious. As a lowered cash flow and uncertain bonuses have curtailed spending, more consumers are paying attention to the price tags of the products they contemplate buying.

For example, "open price" goods (those without a recommended retail price), introduced in electronics and home appliances a few years ago, have been gaining hold, especially in the past year. In the past, consumers disliked open pricing because they were used to judging the value of the products against the recommended retail price. Retailers disliked them as well because they could not "show off" the depth of discount from the recommended price on their price tags. But now the lure of lower prices outweighs the inconveniences.

But reduced or more uncertain incomes are not the only reason for the attention to prices. Lower-priced imports are now more generally available in the gradually opening distribution channels, and they have put price pressure on domestic retail prices. Some of these imports are private-label brands of retailers. Accordingly, the consumer is faced with lower-priced alternatives, not only in new discount outlets, but also in established retail stores. The Japanese consumer today benefits from strong interbrand price competition, and exposure to overseas markets and prices has taught that lower prices do not always mean lower quality.

Furthermore, while traditional retail outlets try to sustain premium brand prices, discount outlets have also begun to sell brand name products at reduced prices. Manufacturers cannot stop shipments to those outlets because of the antimonopoly legislation patterned after the United States and now being enforced. In addition, a good deal of the brand name products are direct imports from overseas. This practice has been going on for some time in consumer durables, such as autos, cameras, and stereos, and has now spread to food products, packaged goods, and apparel. For example, Kirin beer imported from the United States can now be bought in Shinjuku at 20 percent under the domestic price, and men's suits, a mainstay of department stores, are heavily discounted in new low-price outlets such as Aoki's and Aoyama's. Accordingly, while uniform prices made intrabrand search uneconomical in the past, because of parallel imports there is now also a good deal of price competition within brands. Even not-so-poor consumers get price sensitive when there are large savings to be gained.

The parallel imports have not lowered prices as much as one would perhaps have expected. For example, a BMW 700-series model is still about $40,000–50,000 more expensive than in the United States, and there is no adaptation (and only minor preparation) of it for the Japanese market. The company estimates that about 15–20 percent of its sales are from direct imports. The figure for Mercedes is closer to 25 percent, and for Volvo less than 10 percent. These companies are trying to make sure that these figures stay low, although the antimonopoly laws prohibit direct action.

Suburban Shopping.   Although distribution is still key in the densely populated Japan, it is no

longer so important to offer the company's product at many points of purchase. The Japanese are finally finding it worthwhile to get in the family car, drive to the large supermarket or out to the suburbs, and do their shopping once a week. For soft drinks, cigarettes, and snacks, the convenience stores are still used and they thrive on proximity and easy reach. But improved storage conditions in the home with efficient refrigerators and freezers make it possible to buy in larger quantities.

Packaging innovations, such as condensed detergents and vacuum packs, alleviate the still-severe space problems. Furthermore, as Jeeps and four-wheel-drive off-road vehicles become ever more popular, the family today has a car that can carry the purchases comfortably. And high real estate prices mean that families live in even more cramped apartments, making the weekend excursion seem a blessing. The Japanese are becoming more similar to Westerners in their leisure and shopping behavior, if not in their work habits.

Lower Brand Consciousness.   When the Japanese consumers' disposable incomes were growing, there was a considerable amount of status-oriented consumption. Well-known global brand names fetched high price premiums, especially in the luxury product categories. There was an emphasis on newness in products and brands, and a number of minifads developed around new foreign and domestic offerings. Of course, the latest Western and domestic fashions in dress and cosmetics were eagerly absorbed and seemingly as quickly abandoned. The marriage of Miss Owada and the crown prince generated a fad for long hairstyles and muted colors among young women, while teenagers came to school with Gucci bags, and businessmen without the obligatory daily organizer from Filofax felt deprived, etc., etc.

Although there are still signs of this behavior, things have now changed. Less secure financially, consumers take time to evaluate products, shifting the emphasis from brand and status toward functionality on the preference spectrum. They have become what one informant calls "value-conscious," and do not necessarily demand the very latest products (although for some product categories and for some consumers this is not uniformly true). Rather than focusing on brand and all the latest features, many consumers are learning to make trade-offs between what they really need to have and what the price is.

Quality: "Still Going Strong." According to the interviewees, this does not mean lesser quality is accepted. Quality, according to them, does not reside in the features of a product. For the Japanese it is not an attribute defining the product. Quality simply means that the product performs the promised function without fault. The many new features desired before the present slowdown were all to come with zero-defect quality, which they largely did, thanks to the vaunted Japanese manufacturing skills. When today the Japanese consumer trades off features and prices, she still claims to make no compromise on quality.

This insistence on quality means that there are still a number of imported products that are specially prepared and refinished by the Japanese importer before being placed on the market. Similarly, it is true that the Japanese companies have read the trend toward more value, and are producing product lines with simpler versions of their upscale product lines. These simpler versions keep only the main features of the higher-end products and are sold at lower prices. However, they are still of the functional quality associated with Japanese companies and carry their brand names.

Segment Differentiation. With the new emphasis on price and value, the Japanese market has become more differentiated than previously. For each product category, there are upscale segments, middle of the roaders who buy the tried and true, and those buying on price, looking for imports and private labels. In this way, the Japanese market has become more similar to the American. For example, in certain product categories, many consumer packaged goods, such as private labels, are becoming very important, prices matter, and

whether one buys from traditional outlets, a new discount store, or even over the telephone or via catalogs matters little. This can even affect big-ticket categories, such as stereos, television, and personal computers. As for purchases in the gift-giving season, younger people in Japan are more willing to buy from discount stores than from the expensive department stores favored by traditionalists.

Not all has been sacrificed on the altar of frugality. Now and then the consumers in Japan still have a need for something more than just functionality, just as they became used to in the 1980s bubble (see, for example, *The Japan Times,* 1994f, and the *New York Times,* 1994a). Consumers find occasion to indulge themselves, spending extra in special situations, including weddings, funerals, births, vacations, and graduations, and also on their own creature comforts.

Overall, however, while the Japanese customers were always demanding in terms of quality, service, and up-to-date technology and design, they have now had to reconcile these demands with a lower spending budget. The trade-off seems to have been made in favor of quality while sacrificing service and fashionable but inessential features. Bargain is no longer a dirty word. And, as one interviewee put it, while customer satisfaction scores for discount and convenience stores are low, consumers flock to them. The new situation spells opportunity for Western companies, perhaps particularly the Americans, who are used to operating in markets where customers face wide price ranges and consequently become very price sensitive.

Changes in Competition

Because of the downturn and the need to cut costs through low-price imported parts and supplies, the ties between domestic firms have also been affected by the downturn. The traditional entry barriers in *keiretsu* linkages and the closed access to distribution are being eroded, opening doors for Western competitors.

Keiretsus under Pressure. So far the price competition at the retail level has not affected the manufacturers as much as the retailers. A company such as Kao is still able to charge relatively high prices to retailers for its household products. The retailers, faced by increased competition, have reduced prices and are the ones footing the bill. But presumably not for long. The stores need Kao's leading brands to attract buyers, and then the stores convert the customers to their own private label. But as sales of Kao's brands come down because of the new competition, one would expect the company to start lowering prices. There is yet no case similar to the Marlboro price cut in Japan; but if present trends continue, one would expect to see it before long.

In preparation for such reduction of prices, many manufacturers are shifting sources to lower cost locations abroad, especially Asia. The move is combined with a stress on reengineering, considered the corporate fad of 1994 by the interviewees. Needless to say, such sourcing strategies are putting the established keiretsu suppliers under stress. Longstanding obligations between suppliers and manufacturers are being reevaluated, if not entirely given up. It affects especially the vertical keiretsus, where suppliers have close links with a certain large firm; the Toyota system is a typical example. While in the past a major supplier such as Nippon Denso, a manufacturer of electrical components for Toyota, would be limited to Toyota sales, these ties have now weakened. On the one hand, Toyota wants to source for cheaper parts where possible. On the other hand, Nippon Denso does not want to be so dependent on the fortunes of one company, and can grow faster by selling to other car manufacturers as well.

This breakup can also be seen in retailing. In late spring 1994, the most prestigious of the old-time department stores, Mitsukoshi, started direct buying abroad to shore up its apparel business, bypassing its existing keiretsu suppliers. Furthermore, in the following summer, Mitsukoshi started experimenting with a self-service food and grocery department similar to those in supermarkets.

Other department stores are expected to follow suit to also cut costs.

No doubt some of the suffering keiretsu players will come up with survival strategies that will make their contribution more valuable. The trading companies, for example, are trying to become much more world players, offering various financial and technical services in addition to the typical transactions of raw materials and supplies (Blustein, 1995). The tiered levels through which the vertical keiretsus operate have so far allowed the primary suppliers to pass on the cost pressures to lower levels and smaller suppliers. Also, innovations in collaborations such as Honda's "design-in" concept give the suppliers a greater role in new product development and unloads costs from the manufacturer. On the opposite side, there is also some evidence of more arm's-length market-based relationships, allowing suppliers to diversify their customer base. As one interviewee cautioned, however, when the suppliers are chosen on a strict bidding basis, it leaves little room for innovation and joint creativity; and the Japanese companies seem to recognize this.

Foreign Entrants. The cost of doing business in Japan, always high, has been exacerbated by the high yen rate. Failing to turn a profit, over the last few years several Western firms have closed out their Japanese operations, only to attempt comebacks later. Merrill Lynch, Honeywell, and Cadbury's are only three of the more visible examples. At the same time, in some industries where profits at the top are still high, there is a tendency to change from the typical joint venture or licensing operations with a Japanese partner to wholly owned subsidiaries. In autos, for example, BMW, Volvo, and Mercedes operate subsidiaries; and BMW's operation is the most profitable among the company's international markets (H. Hohgi, pers. comm., 1994).

If the high yen has made Japan less attractive as a manufacturing site, it has also made it more profitable as a market. This has not been lost on non-manufacturing entrants from abroad, in particular, retailers. The Toys "R" Us successful entry, ardently fought by domestic toy retailers, continues ablaze. The 7–Eleven stores, now wholly owned by its Japanese licensee, Ito–Yokado, are more vigorous than ever. McDonald's, Kentucky Fried Chicken, and Coca-Cola are other continuing success stories (Hirano, 1994). Personal computer companies such as Dell and Compaq are now exporting units with prices that ruin the profit margins of market leaders NEC and Toshiba (*Asahi Evening News,* 1994).

Japanese Licensees.   The traditional way for foreigners to sell in Japan is to appoint exclusive distributors and licensees who serve as importers, and then distribute the products through the infamously complex traditional networks. Most foreign products in the stores arrive through such traditional channels, with highly inflated prices. Past rises in the value of yen have been slow to materialize at the consumer level because they are siphoned off as windfall profits through the layers in the distribution chain.

The periodic surveys from Jetro and Ministry of Finance show some price decline at the consumer level, even though at an average of approximately 4 percent, it is less than the 20 plus percentage yen rises in the last 18 months (as reported in *The Japan Times,* 1994a). Prices are of course naturally sticky because an opposite change in the yen rate might soon come, and purchase contracts are often signed for some months into the future. Furthermore, the numerous Japanese middlemen do not give up their gains voluntarily. Nevertheless, it is clear that the development of parallel trade has had a downward effect on prices at the retail level.

In fact, according to the interviews, one of the most visible consequences of the consumers' increased price sensitivity, as well as a cause of it, is the increased availability of branded products at heavily discounted prices in alternative channels. As noted above, in product categories such as men's suits and apparel in general, beer, and consumer electronics, the traditional retailers have

been hit hard by direct imports, even of Japanese brand-name products. Added to this is the rise of private labels from Korea, Taiwan, and even the United States and Europe, initiated by large discounters such as Daiei and Ito–Yokado. Not surprisingly, the traditional channels such as department stores are now busy trying to develop their own direct sourcing abroad.

Overall, competition in the Japanese marketplace has shifted to price and value. Foreign producers and suppliers are no longer at a disadvantage because their continued presence in Tokyo is questioned. The Japanese companies are learning to buy directly from overseas sources, and the gate-keeping roles of a few trading companies and exclusive distributors have been undercut by parallel channels with overseas connections. And the recession coupled with the high yen is forcing Japanese companies to take a hard look at their cost structures, where they are now uncompetitive with many Western firms.

Japanese Firms' Strategies

When considering the strategic responses by Japanese firms to the changes in the marketplace, it is useful to remember that companies are not passively reactive but their actions also help drive the changes among consumers and competitors. This is important to recognize when marketing in Japan. It means that staying close to the customers and offering quality products and service is not sufficient for success in Japan. The company also needs to monitor its competitors closely, because they tend to guide and lead market preferences with their new products.

Product Policies.   The typical Japanese approach to product line policies is, by and large, still followed. Although there are differences among companies, most of the large competitors follow each others' policies closely. New products are quickly imitated, the me-too versions offer some new features, and quality is consistently high. Relatively innovative companies such as Sony and

Honda have to keep churning out new models and product improvements as competitors follow on their heels. The basic source of differential advantage lies less in the technology or design, than in the relative newness and styling of the brand and product. As we have seen above, growing incomes allowed the Japanese to change to new products quickly. Buying a slightly used product, such as a VCR or auto, was not only uncommon because of traditional social norms, but was also uncommon because they were likely to be functionally out of date.

In the latter half of the 1980s, the clamor for newness led to a supply of fashionably designed products, even in product categories such as consumer durables, with new Walkmen, new notebook computers, new car models, and new home appliances launched throughout the year. The Japanese consumer was virtually assaulted by a new product avalanche that has only recently started to abate. Even today one is struck by the new format "bazooka" TVs, the flat screen video camcorders, the number of new beer brands, and the onslaught of new soft drinks (see, for example, *The Japan Times* 1994b–d). The new investments in productive capacity undertaken in the euphoria of the 1980s are now on-stream, and the markets are in mid-1995 still flooded by new products in established, mature markets.

But according to the interviews, since about 1992 there has also been a discernible counter-tendency. Quite a few firms have been pruning their product lines to reduce and keep costs down. This is happening not only in industrial goods, but also in consumer goods (see also *Business Week,* 1994). Some packaged goods companies, such as Kao, concentrate on maintaining the top one or two brands in each category, getting rid of small share brands. This is because retailers, forced to sell at low prices, are willing to make little or no money on the leading brands, allowing the manufacturer to still make profits. Kao estimates that in the competitive household detergent category, Procter & Gamble and Unilever may not be making any money at the moment.

In a related strategic move, manufacturers have designed "simpler" products that offer fewer and more basic features, and are priced lower than the "full-feature" state of the art. Video camcorders are a case in point. Matsushita was one of the earliest to offer a small-scale, stripped down, easy-to-operate version of their camcorder. Ostensibly the target was women–housewife users, who had time and opportunity to record their children's progress (while the husband worked his long hours at the company). These simpler versions have not yet been offered overseas, so as not to undercut the strong sales of the full-feature units to fathers who spend time with their small children. But in Japan, with other companies soon following suit, the camcorders have been a big hit, and Matsushita has extended the policy to other electronic products (*The Japan Times,* 1994g). Similar efforts are underway in automobiles and home appliances. As became usual in the 1980s, these simpler products are often manufactured overseas in low-wage countries, shifting successively to cheaper labor pools as factory investments are made. For example, a Sharp calculator model designed in Japan and made in Taiwan two years ago is now produced in a Thai factory.

These lower-end products are still marketed under the company brand names, providing stiff competition for private label imports from lower-wage countries such as Korea and Taiwan. It is in fact quite remarkable that Korean products, benefiting from their currency ties to the dollar, have not succeeded better in the current market in Japan. The interviewers alluded generally to an underlying negative country of origin effect that still haunts Korean products in Japan, and makes Korean producers opt for an original equipment manufacturing (OEM) supplier relationship to Japanese private labelers (see also Nagai, 1993, 1994).

Pricing Policy. Apart from the general tendency toward lower prices already dealt with at length above, in terms of manufacturer pricing policies, one is struck by the apparent disparity between producers and retailers. The efforts by the producers so far seem mainly to be rearguard actions, attempting to save the comfortably high price levels of the past, while letting the retailers suffer from new discounting competitors. No doubt the vaunted lifetime employment system is partly to blame: the manufacturers cannot cut costs by eliminating manpower (although the big companies have drastically curtailed new hirings, especially of women, and are expanding the use of early retirement schemes).

According to the interviews, one major hurdle against cost-cutting is the effect it has on the innovative capabilities of the organizations. As the Japanese companies came to global prominence in the 1980s, many of the companies tried to develop internal cultures that rewarded creativity and risk taking. Japanese business leaders perceived an opportunity to become leaders and not only followers of the West. This new corporate culture gradually emerged only to find the 1990s presenting a completely different challenge. The most pressing top management problem today seems to be the balancing between the economic necessities of cutting costs and the desire to maintain some innovative capability within the organizations.

Thus, the big manufacturers in Japan are looking for alternative ways of maintaining the pricing umbrella and not be caught in cutthroat price competition. One solution that has emerged is the creation of what can be called "horizontal" combinations or alliances between independent firms. In these alliances, one partner focuses on innovation and high-end products, while the other partner is responsible for the low-cost, low-price, target markets. For example, rather than expanding its product line, Honda has established an alliance with Isuzu to produce vans for Honda (the "Odyssey"), while Honda allows Isuzu to offer some of its autos under the Isuzu marque. Discussions about similar alliances are underway in other industries as well. Sony uses its alliance with Aiwa to expand its product line downward, for example.

Another type of alignment that helps manufac-

turers offer low prices without jeopardizing their clout in regular channels is represented by the various tie-ups arranged by 7–Eleven. Companies such as Philip Morris, Hershey, and Haagen–Dazs will make specially designed products available for sale in 7–Eleven stores only. For example, under one arrangement, the Kraft division of Philip Morris will sell smaller-sized cheesecakes through the convenience store chain. Although reflective of the power of 7–Eleven in Japan, the alliances are also illustrative of how Western manufacturers seem more able to cope with the new distribution outlets in Japan than their domestic counterparts.

Promotional Policies.   In the new environment, not surprisingly, companies have curtailed advertising spending; and revenues for a giant such as Dentsu fell about 10 percent between April 1993 and April 1994, although it has since recovered somewhat. The recession induced companies to cut spending, and advertising has always been an easy target because of its intangibility and uncertain payoffs. As consumers cut spending and turned toward low-price, no-frills alternatives, the role of advertising diminished correspondingly. The rise of direct marketing and catalog sales left the agencies out, the major players being retailers and manufacturers. Although the major agencies have some expertise to offer in direct marketing, their traditional roles of controlling media and of focusing on the creative work have combined to make them slow movers in direct marketing.

With the emergence of low-service discounters, one might have expected advertising to take on a more hard-hitting, price-and-value type of message than before. There is evidence of this in the stores and the newspapers, but the TV advertising is still surprisingly Japanese, offering the usual fare of good feelings and image. The point-of-purchase advertising and in-store promotions have taken on greater roles, however, with sale and bargain signs supported by displays and fact-giving visuals. One way the low-price outlets have kept a lid on contact costs is to let the sales clerks package their sales pitches of products, using in-store displays with photos and handwritten explanations.

There are also striking promotional innovations that capitalize on the growth of new distribution channels. The largest video chain in Japan, CCC (Cultural Convenience Club) keeps close track of its 12 million card members and their video habits. Realizing that these data can be used to target prospects and potential customers, Kawasaki, the motorbike manufacturer, produced a "safe rider" video, distributed it among the CCC outlets, traced the borrowers of the tapes, and presented them with further promotional material. Such practices can, of course, compromise member privacy rights, but the Japanese are seemingly far less militant about this.

Distribution Policies.   There is perhaps no need to repeat that the emergence of alternative, low-price channels and the pressures on the vertical distribution keiretsus mean that most producers question their existing channel strategies. In many product categories, market shares in Japan have traditionally been linked to a strong distribution network, dominated by the manufacturer. For companies as diverse as Matsushita, Kao, Shiseido, and Toyota, distribution has often been cited as a key success factor (see, for example, the review by Munns, 1994). On the negative side, for Sony, Honda, Mazda, and of course most foreign entrants, weak distribution has similarly been identified as a major culprit.

This is no longer true. In May 1994, Shiseido announced a complete overhaul of its store network and the highly commended, but expensive to manage, Shiseido membership club of customers (Munns, 1994). Matsushita complains about its dealers tying them down and making it impossible to cut costs. The many small, traditional outlets served the manufacturer well when store proximity was valued and a salesman's recommendation and after-sales support was the only sales argument. In today's cutthroat competition, the dealer

network needs to be rationalized and many small stores consolidated. This has proved a difficult task with many small but independent-minded shop owners reluctant to change their ways. On a larger scale, this same structural change in distribution is going on in the distribution system as a whole. The small Mom and Pop operations are overrun by franchised operations with large-scale advantages and more professional practices. The franchisors in many cases are the very Moms and Pops who did business in the location before. Cashing in on their real-estate locational advantage, the family has been able to raise enough equity to finance a conversion to a modern-day franchised operation. Needless to say, many of the older Moms and Pops have not been able to make this conversion work for them, and have retired upstairs, while a younger son or daughter is trying to make the business work.

The established businesses are naturally interested in diversifying their pressured traditional operations and want to participate in this structural change. Some of the financing for the new franchised chain operations comes from established retailers and manufacturers. Department stores such as Isetan, for example, have started discount branches, offer catalog sales, and buy directly from abroad. But the traditional channel members often do not have the required know-how and the managerial skills to manage such operations. In a typical switch, Toys "R" Us combined with McDonald's when entering Japan, not with an established retailer.

Much of the management and financing of the new discounters come from alliances between trading companies and individual entrepreneurs, sometimes foreigners. Trading companies such as Itohchu and Marubeni can use their existing networks to advantage, but consumer products need more in-depth market understanding than trading companies traditionally possess. Company-affiliated traders such as Sony Trading, on the other hand, excel in exactly the kind of products and markets required; and these companies are prime movers behind the new distribution outlets. Similarly, the many franchised convenience store chains, such as Lawson's, am-pm, Monte–Yamazaki, and others, bank on the entrepreneurship of a few individuals with experience and perhaps education in the West and the financial backing of trading companies and company-related importers. The typical discount store or franchised operation involves only a few central managers, usually drop-outs from a big corporation, who see the opportunity, develop the idea, and raise the necessary money. These are self-made men in the American tradition (Munns, 1994).

Marketing Rethinking. In the big picture, the actions taken so far by the vaunted Japanese marketers at home have been tentative and without strong convictions. Where the actions have been decisive, the strategies are patterned after Western models. The horizontal tie-ups are one example. In the future, the Japanese companies can of course be expected to invent their own solutions to the new challenges, and create their own wrinkles on the Western strategies.

The hesitation no doubt reflects a hope that the difficulties are cyclical and simply due to the recession. But it is also based on a recognition that the new Japanese consumer is only imperfectly understood by the Japanese companies. For example, Matsushita's market forecasts for new products in the Japanese market used to be quite accurate. In recent cases, however, their forecasts have been very wrong. For one product, a forecast of 15,000 first-year units turned into actual sales of approximately 2,500. In another, a forecast of 2,000–3,000 units translated into orders for close to 50,000 units, a volume the company could not supply.

The old wisdom is being challenged on several fronts. Even though quality is said to still be important, the shift to more of a value orientation among consumers suggests there are opportunities even for "imperfect" foreign products. The Japanese companies' insistence that they know what their customers want is partly based on their common cultural heritage. As economic realities gain the upper hand, culture might "be damned," and longstanding keiretsu and customer loyalty ties given up in favor of a lower price. Even the hint of this tendency that has surfaced so far has affected marketing in Japan profoundly, and is likely to be even stronger in the future.

The cost-cutting necessities that all indicators point to also affect the old marketing wisdom. Reengineering is difficult when channel members are used to face-to-face communications rather than phone or fax. Reluctance to lay off people makes it difficult, and unnecessary, to invest in new office information technology to raise white-collar productivity. Teleshopping, with menu-driven services and computerized sales records, might not lead to great customer satisfaction scores, but it offers what one interviewee called the "essential" service of convenience. Some Japanese companies are catching onto this trend, and even department stores are trying to get in on the action; but in the main the Japanese distribution channels are technological latecomers compared to the Americans (Munns, 1994). If Japanese companies fall farther behind in the use of computerization of the office and of customer links, more technologically advanced low-price foreign entrants are likely to find the Japanese market much easier to penetrate.

Japanese Competitiveness Abroad

It is common to attribute at least part of the Japanese marketing prowess overseas to their honing of products and skills against the demanding customers in the home market. Furthermore, there is the oft-quoted practice of the Japanese to use the home market as a cash-generating base for ventures overseas. Because of these connections, one would expect that as conditions at home change, marketing practices overseas will be affected.

As the yen rises in value, prices might of course have to be raised. So far there have been selective price increases of Japanese products to account for some of the exchange rate losses (see, for example, Blustein, 1995). A fair amount of the recent success of U.S. automobiles is due to higher prices on Japanese cars. The same is true for sales of consumer electronics, where Koreans and others are making inroads, and where some of the new Japanese products have yet to be introduced overseas (*The Wall Street Journal,* 1995).

To handle the pricing problem, the Japanese have stepped up their direct investment in overseas facilities, trying to ensure that the Japanese products can be marketed competitively abroad regardless of exchange rates. Thus, on the overseas markets, a good deal of the impact is being absorbed by a hollowing out of the Japanese manufacturing base. In fact, the aim of many Japanese manufacturers today is to become local manufacturers in the major markets. This decoupling of domestic and overseas markets is already underway (see, for example, *Business Week,* 1994).

How will this affect marketing practices? For some companies it looks as if past marketing practices will continue and perhaps be further fine-tuned. A company such as Honda, for example, is giving its North American operation much more independence, and aims to eliminate exports from Japan to the United States entirely. Honda is admittedly ahead of other Japanese companies in its reliance on overseas production, but this model is clearly attractive to other companies as well. And it is important to recognize that local marketing in a country can be managed well even if manufacturing is done elsewhere.

But it is clear that if the lower-end products in Japan cannot be accommodated through the horizontal combinations with other companies, the big Japanese exporter will not be able to focus on the higher-end, advanced technology products at home. This may not be important in developing markets, including China and some other Japanese neighbors in Asia; but it is likely to cramp their overseas effort in mature Western markets, with weaker product lines than at present. This is one of the reasons the Japanese are reluctant to get on

with the cost cutting suggested by reengineering. Without the innovation and the creativity that comes with the higher-end, state-of-the-art products, the Japanese companies will not have such attractive offerings from the home market. And while their R&D efforts overseas are increasing, the companies there face the same conditions that Western companies face. It seems unavoidable that the slump in the Japanese marketplace will adversely affect the competitive strength of the Japanese abroad.

References

Asahi Evening News (1994) "A success story for U.S. PC firms," July 6, 7.

Blustein, Paul (1995) "Giant Trading Companies Battle to Preserve Japan Inc.'s Edge," *Washington Post,* April 12, A18, A19.

Business Week (1994) "Trying to Rev Up: Can Japan's Carmakers Regain Lost Ground?" January 24, 32, 34.

Hirano, Masaaki (1994) "Performance of Foreign Firms in Japan: Is Japanese Management Any Good?" Working Paper, Institute for Systems Science, Waseda University, Tokyo.

Munns, Peter J. S. (1994) *Marketing and Distribution in Japan Today,* Master's Thesis, Graduate School of Management, International University of Japan.

Nagai, Takeshi (1993) "Understanding the Japanese Business Market: What the Purchasers Want," Manufacturing Roundtable, Boston University.

Nagai, Takeshi (1994) "A Positioning Approach to the Japanese Market from the Aspect of *Opinion Disleaders,*" Working Paper, Waseda Business School, Tokyo.

New York Times (1994a) "Japanese Taking to Wide-Screen TV," September 15, D1, D3.

New York Times (1994b) "Now It's Japan's Turn to Play Catchup," November 21, D1, D6.

The Japan Times (1994a) "Minicar Specs Spark Maker Debate," May 3, 11.

The Japan Times (1994b) "Automakers Promoting Recreational Vehicles," May 13, 12.

The Japan Times (1994c) "Camcorders Send Pictures by Phone," May 13, 12.

The Japan Times (1994d) "Toshiba to Market New Dynabook and Extra Bright LEDs," May 13, 12.

The Japan Times (1994e) "Gas Station Opens in Protest," May 19, 12.

The Japan Times (1994f) "Matsushita Rejects Cut-Price Brands," June 4, 7.

The Japan Times (1994g) "Panel Urges Good to Suit Buyer Needs," June 4, 8.

The Japan Times (1994h) "Farmers Protest U.S. Apple Imports," July 8, 10.

The Wall Street Journal (1995) "Koreans Move to Grab Memory-Chip Market from the Japanese," March 14, 1, 5.

THE LEGAL AND POLITICAL ENVIRONMENT

The citations in this section contribute to the understanding of the legal and political environments impacting the implementation of international marketing strategies. The evolving legal environment facilitates trade liberation and the resolution of trade disputes. Simultaneously governments can encourage trade within their borders or inhibit or even ban trading practices. Understanding international legal agreements and governmental policies is essential for international marketing success.

The first selection in this section traces the evolution of the loosely structured General Agreement on Tariffs and Trade (GATT) to the promise of the World Trade Organization (WTO), an institution with the legal and political authority to resolve international trade disputes involving goods, services, and intellectual property.

The protection of intellectual property rights has been recognized in the United States since its inception as a nation in Article 1 of the Constitution. The second paper in this section documents the protection of such rights under the General Agreement on Tariffs and Trade (GATT), the European Union (EU), and the North American Free Trade Agreement (NAFTA). The authors focus on patent piracy in the pharmaceutical industry as a major problem. The final paper documents the nature and importance of 20 key nontariff barriers imposed by governments that adversely affect firms seeking to penetrate foreign markets. Entry strategies to be considered by small business owner/managers are included in this contribution.

FROM GATT TO WTO

The Institutionalization of World Trade

Salil S. Pitroda

Over the past few decades, a system of relatively open exchange, particularly in merchandise trade, has prevailed in the world under the auspices of the General Agreement on Tariffs and Trade (GATT). Today, most economists acknowledge this trading system as one of the greatest contributors to the world's rapid recovery from the desolation of the second World War, and to the phenomenal growth in world output thereafter. Through all of those years, however, GATT has served its member countries through a loose and informal structure, with all the inevitable problems that accompany a weak and ill-defined authority. With the passage of the Uruguay Round of trade talks, this trading system is poised to take on a new shape in a permanent institution known as the World Trade Organization (WTO). Although much skepticism and controversy have surrounded the birth of WTO, it is the hope of all free-traders that the new WTO will be able to amend what went amiss with GATT.

From *Harvard International Review,* Spring 1995, pp. 46–47, 66–67. © 1995 by the Harvard International Relations Council. Reprinted by permission.

A Brief History of Trade

At the beginning of the nineteenth century, economists began to make advances in interpreting why human beings had always engaged in economic exchange. The theory of comparative advantage posited that countries specialize in those goods and services that they can produce more efficiently relative to other countries. When nations concentrate their production on commodities in which they have a comparative advantage, consumers as a whole benefit from lower prices and a greater range of consumption possibilities. Because each good is produced by the country that is best at producing it, scarce world resources are allocated efficiently. Like all economic activities, the distribution of the benefits of trade is not uniform; yet in general and in the long run, trade leads to a more optimal economic outcome with greater competition and greater productivity—a rising tide on which all boats float.

In 1947, such a view of the benefits of international cooperation inspired a group of visionaries gathered in Bretton Woods, New Hampshire, to erect a new economic world order from the ravages of the second World War. The Bretton Woods Accords, which celebrated their fiftieth anniversary last year, established the World Bank and the International Monetary Fund and led to the creation of GATT. These structures, albeit not always true to the visionary spirit in which they were founded, have formed the underpinnings of world economic development for the past half century.

GATT has become the framework for international trade in our time. The body was formed as an interim secretariat for trade negotiations after the United States, bowing to protectionist sentiment, refused to ratify the charter of the stillborn International Trade Organization, a full-fledged institution of the stature of the World Bank and the IMF. Based in Geneva and currently encompassing over 120 member nations, GATT has acted as a conduit for multilateral negotiations on a variety of international trade issues, including tariff and quota policy and trading practices. It has sponsored several rounds of protracted, though eventually fruitful, trade talks where members gathered to hammer out the details of the set of rules governing economic exchange. GATT panels make recommendations on changes in trade regulations and review complaints against member countries.

Despite GATT's success in coordinating international trade policy, it must be remembered that GATT is only an interim body without a fully defined institutional structure and with little legal enforcement power. For instance, many loopholes exist in the mechanism dealing with disputes regarding unfair trade practices. If a country complains of unfair trading practices on the part of another country and a GATT panel concurs with the complaint, the accused country can dissent from the finding, effectively vetoing it and preventing the complaining country from retaliation within the GATT framework. Another increasingly popular way of doing business in an extra-GATT environment is through the creation of regional trade blocs, such as the European Union (EU), the North American Free Trade Agreement (NAFTA) and the impending Association of Southeast Asian Nations (ASEAN) free trade agreement. These regional agreements, in effect, set their own rules

of trade, encouraging cooperative exchange within a bloc but hinting of protectionism against countries outside the region. Nontariff trade barriers (NTBs), such as a German requirement that, for health reasons, beer sold in Germany be made with German water, are also another device for bending GATT rules. Another way of eschewing GATT policy through these regional trading arrangements is to manipulate the rules of origin stipulation. By raising the requirement of local content value, aspiring profiteers and vested interests can turn an ostensible reduction in a tariff into an actual increase by subjecting formerly tariff-exempt goods to duties, thus circumventing the GATT guideline that for any free trade agreement, the new common external tariff be no higher than the average tariff of the constituent states before the accord. Without any institutional framework or legal authority, the most that GATT can do, when confronted with such adroit legerdemain with its regulations, is to urge and exhort a spirit of cooperation among member states, each of whom has an individual incentive to cater to local interests by eschewing a rule here and raising a protectionist wall there.

Seeking to address some of these problems, the Uruguay Round of negotiations was launched nearly nine years ago. Under the leadership of GATT Director-General Peter Sutherland, this latest round of trade talks has arrived at a consensus on implementing changes to the international framework that will encourage greater openness and trade integration among the world's nations. First and foremost, the Uruguay Round promises a lowering of trade barriers and a slashing of tariffs by an average of one-third. It broadens the scope of liberalization to include traditionally protected industries such as textiles and apparel. Reflecting the changing nature of world trade, the Uruguay Round will open up exchange in the previously closed but rapidly emerging areas of agriculture, services, and intellectual property. It imposes a new discipline on NTBs and government procurement and offers clarification on subsidies, dumping regulations, quota restrictions, and voluntary export restraints. It also lays the foundation for further talks dealing with important trade issues including the treatment of foreign direct investment, labor, and environmental concerns, and capital and currency market fluctuations. Most importantly, the Uruguay Round of accords has boldly moved the world a step closer to global free trade by calling for the establishment of the WTO to succeed the GATT secretariat.

The Birth of WTO

The WTO will be a new international institution, on par with the World Bank and the IMF, that will outline a framework for all areas of international trade and will have the legal authority to settle trade disputes. In legal terms, it represents the maturation of the GATT secretariat into a full-fledged, permanent international entity. The supreme decision-making body will be a biannual ministerial meeting, affording the organization more political clout and a higher international profile. This WTO council will then have subsidiary working bodies that specialize in areas of trade including goods, services, and intellectual property. Unlike GATT, the WTO will have a clearly defined dispute settlement mechanism. Independent panel reports will automatically be adopted by the WTO council unless there is a clear consensus to reject them. Countries who are accused of engaging in unfair trade practices can appeal to a permanent appellate body, but the verdict of this body will be ultimately binding. If an offending nation fails to comply with WTO panel recommendations, its trading partners will be guaranteed the right to compensation as determined by the panel or, as a final resort, be given the right to impose countervailing sanctions. All members of the WTO will have legal access to these multilateral dispute settlement mechanisms, and all stages of WTO deliberation will be time-limited, ensuring efficiency in dispute settlement. The World Trade Organization will be akin to an International Court of Justice for world trade, with the institutional strength and legal mandate to ensure fair trade and global economic integration.

Who will be the pioneering leader of this newly constructed international organization? The ideal candidate must possess a strategic global vision of world trade while being comfortable with technical complexity. He or she must combine the finesse of a diplomat, the organizational acumen of an experienced administrator, and the leadership qualities of a seasoned statesman.

Since Peter Sutherland, the incumbent Director-General of GATT, has indicated his wish to step down in favor of fresh leadership, the competition to be the head of the WTO has been opened up to three dynamic candidates. Renato Ruggiero, the favored candidate of the EU, is a former trade minister of Italy and has also been suggested in the past as a possible president of the European Commission. He has emphasized his experience as a capable administrator with international experience in Brussels, the GATT, and world economic summits. Carlos Salinas de Gortari, who during his tenure as the President of Mexico defined the paradigm of economic liberalization in developing countries, is the candidate favored by the Americas. His international stature as a head of state and his commitment to free trade—as evinced by his personal crusade for NAFTA—are Salinas's most important assets. The South Korean trade minister, Kim Chul-Su, has proven international experience and is naturally supported by countries in Asia and Australia, the fastest-growing region in the world. In the end, politics will most likely decide who heads the WTO. Similar leadership positions are opening up at the Organization for Economic Cooperation and Development (OECD) and other international organizations, with political horse-trading sure to play an integral role in determining the new leaders of these organizations.

There are various other strategic issues relating to the establishment of the WTO. At least for the initial transition stage, the new organization is expected to grow by expanding on the existing GATT structure. The WTO will most probably be situated in the existing GATT building in Geneva and will require an increase in GATT's present budget and staff. Yet even with this augmentation in resources, the WTO will still remain far smaller in size than either the World Bank or the IMF.

Aside from such logistical matters, however, the precise nature of the transition between GATT and WTO remains more nebulous. Some countries, such as the United States, have already announced that they will terminate their GATT membership within 60 days of joining the WTO. Such a strict view of WTO's successor status to GATT raises interesting questions about U.S. obligations to GATT members who have yet to ratify their entry into WTO.

Other countries envision the two organizations operating in tandem for a period of two years, with GATT still binding, to ease the transition to the WTO. There is also the question of new memberships. Will Slovenia and Croatia, for instance, who have just applied for GATT membership, be granted direct membership in the WTO? If the WTO does not completely supersede GATT immediately, where does that leave a country like the Sudan, which is not a GATT member, but has applied directly for WTO membership?

Of course, there is also the thorny problem of China, which has just been denied the opportunity of being a founding member of WTO, and Taiwan, whose competing applications will surely pose more dilemmas of politics and protocol. Certainly, careful deliberation will be needed to work out the multitude of implementational, organizational, and transitional issues.

The Foundation of the New Order

Given these birth pangs, what are the fundamental qualities upon which the WTO must lay its foundation? As Carlos Salinas de Gortari has outlined in a recent article in *The Financial Times,* the WTO must be representative, reliable, and responsive. It must embrace all countries, regardless of their level of economic development, and ensure

their prompt and satisfactory integration into a multilateral trading system. Reliability is a much tougher criterion to satisfy. The WTO must clarify GATT rules, broaden its mandate, and improve its dispute settlement mechanisms to demonstrate to all member nations that they have a stake in abiding by a rules-based trade regime. Finally, flexibility and responsiveness to the evolving changes of the international economy will ensure that the WTO retains the political support necessary to carrying out its work.

As an organization that has ambitions of leading the global economy into the next millennium, the WTO needs to legitimize its standing in the eyes of politicians and economists wearied by decades of trade negotiations by confronting some concrete and difficult problems. One of the first tasks it might have to face is deciding whether or not it should extend the rules regulating conduct in international trade to cover national competition policies. Ideally, countries should have roughly comparable standards on antitrust legislation so that greater competition from all-comers, whether domestic or foreign, can be welcomed. But by treading on such sensitive territories, the WTO may stray too far from the trade-related issues at the core of its mandate. The animosities that it incurs in those confrontations may permanently impair its ability to unite its membership on other, arguably even more important, issues in the long run.

One of the most crucial tasks of the WTO will be presiding over the economic and political integration of the former socialist economies. It must provide stable and expanding outlets for these countries' products to encourage the liberalization of their economies and to help them attract much-needed foreign direct investment. In fact, all the newly open economies in Latin America, Africa, and Asia must be nurtured by a transparent, rules-based and mutually beneficial trading system. In particular, the WTO must encourage the reversal of the growing lethargy in North-South cooperation, especially with regard to Sub-Saharan African countries, which desperately need open international markets for their growth. The organization also has a special responsibility to bring the nearly two billion citizens of China and India, 40 percent of the planet's population, into the world trading regime as full and active members.

On a more macroscopic level, the WTO must effectively coordinate regional free trade agreements to ensure that they do not conflict in goals or create islands of protectionism, but are instead regional building blocks toward the eventual realization of global free trade which almost every economic theory praises as the ideal for future world economic relations. Pursuant to this objective of regional coordination, the institution must stiffen its regulations and their enforcement so that less and less protectionism can be veiled behind devices such as NTBs, rules of origins requirements, and other technical loopholes. It must convince member nations that their greatest economic interest is to cooperate with the other nations of the world and not bow to vested interests by taking short-sighted unilateral action. The best means for guaranteeing this end is a vigorous and binding dispute settlement mechanism. In planning for the future, the organization must also proactively embrace the changing nature of the global economy from trade in manufactured goods to trade in information-intensive services and intellectual property. The technical complexity of those issues and the administrative difficulty that will inevitably accompany any rules governing them will be a challenge to WTO's energy, resourcefulness, and resolve.

Finally, and very importantly, the WTO must acknowledge and deal with some of the local pains that uncompetitive industries in member nations will feel. In order to avoid the image of an elitist other-worldliness to which so many other well-intentioned international organizations have fallen prey, the WTO must ensure that the gains from trade are trickled down to the populace. Without at least some semblance of equity to compensate for the sacrifices that the working poor will be asked to make in any transition, it will be difficult for WTO to maintain the political and moral support

that it needs to push through its vision of worldwide free trade. Ideally, some sort of structural adjustment fund and a common program for retraining displaced workers should be a pillar of the WTO, so that humanity and compassion, as well as hard-nosed efficiency, may be integrated into the organization's founding philosophy. There are undoubtedly a host of other important issues the new WTO should consider, but careful deliberation on the fundamentals outlined here will be a major step toward solidifying and validating a global free trade system.

Positive Sums from Cooperation

The bottom line of the emergence of the new WTO from GATT is that world trade will be institutionalized in the formal legal structure of an international organization. The more formal status of the WTO will allow it to give more focus and publicity to efforts that attempt to create greater global cooperation in international trade. The institutionalization of trade through the WTO will give some bite to the bark of a well-articulated set of trading rules and policies. With its creation, there will exist an independent political entity that can view the world trading system from a holistic perspective and to check and balance competing interests that seek to bend the trading rules in their national or sectoral favor. By paying judicious attention to the fundamental issues in international trade, the WTO has the potential of becoming a visionary organization that outlines a bold path for international trade and leads the world into a new economic renaissance.

Recent studies have released estimates of the global economic effects of the ratification of the GATT Uruguay Round and the creation of the World Trade Organization. A GATT report released in November 1994 prognosticated that implementation of the Uruguay Round will spur an increase of $510 billion a year in world income by the year 2005. This figure is a vast underestimate, for it does not account for the impact of strengthened procedures and rules in the services trade or better dispute settlement mechanisms. Breaking up the gains by region, the report predicted that by 2005 the annual income gain will be $122 billion for the United States, $164 billion for the European Union, $27 billion for Japan, and $116 billion for the developing and transitional socialist economies as a group. Figures estimating the increase in volume in the goods trade range from 9 to 24 percent once the liberalization of the Uruguay Round comes into effect. In 1992 dollars, this gain represents an increase in trade flows of upwards of $670 billion. The report also suggests that Uruguay Round provisions for developing and transition economies will have the intended result of encouraging rapid growth, as exports and imports from this group are likely to be 50 percent over and beyond the increase for the rest of the world as a whole. The economic impact of a well-structured and credible institutionalization of international trade is likely to be enormous.

What remains to be done is the actual construction of this economic structure. Nowhere has the debate over GATT and the WTO been more pronounced than in the world's economic leader, the United States. As is to be expected before embarking on any bold new initiative, those who stand to suffer short-term losses are trying to stand in the way of long-term progress. Protectionist concerns and irresponsible exaggeration have been vociferously fed to the press and the deliberative bodies of the government. One example of such red herrings is a concern about a loss of U.S. sovereignty

in becoming a member of the WTO. In truth, any changes in the law of the United States or any other nation will have to be ratified by proper legislative bodies in that country, and so the practical encroachment on national sovereignty is little more than negligible. Of course, there is a germ of truth in this argument, for when any nation enters into an international treaty, it must lose some "sovereignty" to the extent that it agrees to abide by the terms of the agreement. Some kind of consensus, such as the sensitive balance that needs to be achieved by the WTO, must be reached to preserve a predictable and liberal international trade regime. To carp at the WTO for having the potential to compromise national sovereignty is little different from saying that national sovereignty is compromised because a country has to abide by any international treaty.

All nations, the U.S. in particular, must realize that partnerships are more advantageous than going it alone, and that economic cooperation is not a zero-sum game. Free trade makes each and every nation more prosperous because it makes the entire world more prosperous. Government leaders around the world would do well to hearken to the words of Rufus Yerxa, Deputy U.S. Trade Representative and Ambassador to GATT: "International cooperation will bring about the economic growth of the future. We cannot survive as an island in a sea of change. If we don't embrace this change, it will be our enemy rather than our friend. Cooperation is in our own self-interest."

INTELLECTUAL PROPERTY RIGHTS

Changing Levels of Protection under GATT, NAFTA, and the EU

Peggy E. Chaudhry and Michael G. Walsh

The importance of protecting intellectual property rights has been recognized in the United States since its inception. Article I, Section 8, of the Constitution of the United States expressly grants to Congress the right to protect rights in intellectual property. By the mid-nineteenth century, other nations had recognized the need for international agreements on intellectual property rights. This led to the Paris Convention for the Protection of Industrial Property Rights and the Berne Convention for the Protection of Literary and Artistic Works.

In recent decades, challenges to the existing international scheme of regulation of intellectual property have emerged. In some countries, patent and copyright infringements are routine. Many countries have failed to implement and enforce adequate measures to prevent the importation of infringing goods. Some developing nations have questioned the appropriateness of intellectual property protection.[1]

The lack of global protection of intellectual property rights has harmed several industries. Finding that pirates have diversified their offerings of counterfeit goods, Harvey and Ronkainen reported that the counterfeit marketplace has ex-

panded from "traditional counterfeit goods," such as Christian Dior apparel, Gucci handbags, and Rolex watches, to include "nontraditional counterfeit goods," such as pacemakers, Johnson's baby shampoo and Ovulen-21 birth control pills.[2] Indeed, *Business Week* reported that patent pirates took their heaviest toll on U.S. pharmaceuticals, software, movies, sound recordings, and books. Of these industries, the article estimated that in 1991 the U.S. software and pharmaceutical industry lost sales of $9 billion and $4 billion, respectively, to international pirates.[3]

In this paper, we provide a succinct review of the multilateral trade framework that governs intellectual property rights through such agreements as the recent completion of the Uruguay Round in the General Agreement of Tariffs and Trade (GATT), the North American Free Trade Agreement (NAFTA), and the European Union (EU). After briefly describing the various intellectual property rights that are subject to protection throughout the international community, we will examine the intellectual property issues that are most relevant to the pharmaceutical industry. We selected the pharmaceutical industry as the case study for our analysis since drugs are fairly simple to steal using patent data or chemical analysis. In addition, *Business Week* estimates that "of all the major American sectors plagued by piracy, the pharmaceutical

With permission from *The Columbia Journal of World Business,* Summer 1995, 80–92.

industry is the largest and most multinational."[4] Likewise, the World Health Organization estimates that counterfeit drugs now account for about 5 percent of world pharmaceutical trade and that 70 percent of drugs used in developing countries are fake. In the past three years, more than 400 deaths in Argentina, Bangladesh, India, and Nigeria have been associated with the consumption of medicines containing diethylene glycol antifreeze wrongly labeled as propylene glycol.[5]

Next, we will discuss the controversy surrounding the arguments against the recognition of pharmaceutical patents. For example, we will examine disputes from the developing countries, such as the view that research in pharmaceutical products should be considered part of the public domain, freely available to indigent countries as a social welfare concern.[6] Likewise, we will discuss the changing attitude regarding "nurturing" the pharmaceutical industry in the mostly developed countries, such as France, Germany, Italy, the United Kingdom, and the United States.[7]

The Protection of Intellectual Property Rights in the GATT

Seeking to enforce rights in the international arena, governments have turned to the GATT. The Uruguay Round of trade negotiations, begun in Punta del Este, Uruguay, in December 1986, concluded with an agreement on Trade-Related Aspects of Intellectual Property Rights (TRIPs). The Paris Convention is still the basic international agreement on patent protection, but TRIPs extends the term of protection to 20 years from the date of filing for all inventions in almost all fields of technology. Prior to the Uruguay Round, GATT addressed intellectual property only in recognizing an exception that permits measures "necessary to secure compliance with laws or regulations . . . including those relating to . . . the protection of patents, trademarks and copyrights and the prevention of deceptive practices."[8]

GATT (Article 3) addresses the concept of "national treatment" or "reciprocity" by requiring each Member to accord to the nationals of other Members treatment no less favorable than it grants to its own nationals with respect to the protection of intellectual property. For example, the reciprocity requirement will require signatory countries of the GATT to provide the same market access for a foreign pharmaceutical firm as an indigenous pharmaceutical company to foster a "level playing field" for the industry.

Another provision of the GATT (Article 4) deals with the philosophy of "most-favored-nation" treatment. Thus, any intellectual property advantage, favor, privilege, or immunity granted by a member to the nationals of any other country must be accorded, with a few exceptions, immediately and unconditionally to the nationals of all other Members. Therefore, through the GATT clause of most-favored-nation in the TRIPs agreement, the pharmaceutical industry should overcome tariff and nontariff barriers to trade on both their imports and exports of pharmaceuticals since signatory countries will be required to grant each other the most favorable treatment they concede to another trading partner.

Trademarks.   The TRIPs accord (Article 15) makes eligible for registration any "trademark," defined as "[a]ny sign, or any combination of signs, capable of distinguishing the goods or services of one undertaking from those of other undertakings." Members may make a mark's registrability dependent on distinctiveness acquired through use. They may require, as a condition of registration, that signs be "visually perceptible."

Rights conferred.   The owner of a registered trademark is given the exclusive right to prevent all others not having proper permission from using identical or similar signs for goods and services when such use would result in a likelihood of confusion. This principle recognizes that a crude, obvious imitation of a trademark poses little or no threat to consumers, who will not be confused by the counterfeit. On the other hand, if the symbol is seemingly identical or very similar to the protected mark, consumers are likely to be confused by the similarity. This poses the greatest threat to them and to the owner of the mark, especially in the case of pharmaceuticals where the consumer would not be able to differentiate between a genuine or counterfeit Zantac (Glaxo's anti-ulcer drug).

An example of the "confusingly similar" dilemma recently occurred in the retail industry when the U.S. Customs Service seized a shipment of Liz Claiborne purses found in the drawers of a furniture shipment from Asia. The U.S. Customs officials were not certain whether these goods were counterfeit or gray-market merchandise. Therefore, the U.S. Customs Service sent samples of this shipment to the Liz Claiborne manufacturer under the premise that the purses were "confusingly similar" to the genuine purses. However, the manufacturer was unable to discern whether the products were counterfeit, gray market, or simply samples of an outdated line of merchandise. This anecdote discredits the cliché that counterfeit goods are obviously inferior goods and the consumer can tell the difference between the authentic versus fake merchandise. Indeed, some manufacturers have been known simply to hire their counterfeit rivals in foreign countries as future suppliers of their own merchandise.[9]

Licensing and assignment.   Members have the right to determine conditions on the licensing and assignment of trademarks by the owner of a mark to others. The owner of a trademark cannot be forced to permit someone else to use the mark, with or without the payment of a fee. The owner must be granted the right to assign the trademark, with or without the transfer of the business to which it belongs. For example, a pharmaceutical manufacturer can permit another company to use its trademark on a particular drug without giving up any control of its business. In general, compulsory licensing cannot be permitted. This policy is a benefit to the pharmaceutical industry, since several countries used compulsory licensing to discriminate against foreign competitors. For instance, in 1993, Canada ceased requiring that pharmaceutical manufacturers license a generic version of a drug after 7 to 10 years of patent pro-

tection. This change lured C$676 million (or about $540 million) of investment into new Canadian facilities from foreign drug manufacturers in 1992.[10]

Patents.   Members must make patents available for "any inventions, whether products or processes, in all fields of technology, provided that they are new, involve an inventive step and are capable of industrial application." Patents must be available, and patent rights must be enjoyable, without discrimination regarding the place of invention, the field of technology, and whether products are imported or locally produced.

Rights conferred.   A patent confers on its owner the exclusive right:

• In the case of a product, to make, use, offer for sale, sell, or import the product; and

• In the case of a process, to prevent third parties from using the process without consent, or using, offering for sale, selling, or importing the product obtained directly by that process.

Large multinational pharmaceutical firms were strong advocates of the TRIPs agreement in the GATT. Patents reward these firms' exorbitant costs of innovation. Several pharmaceutical firms have argued that without such protection, cures for AIDS or Alzheimer's disease may never be developed. Thus, the protection of pharmaceutical patents, considered one of the most difficult issues in the negotiations, is covered by a clause requiring developing countries to accept the filing of pharmaceutical applications from the beginning of the transition period. (One year for developed countries; 5 years for developing countries; and 11 years for the least-developed countries.) Although the patent does not have to be granted until the end of this period, the drug is protected from the date of filing. If market authorization is obtained during the transitional period, the developing country involved must offer an exclusive marketing right for the pharmaceutical or other product for five years or until a product patent is granted, whichever period is shorter.

Exclusions. Members have the right to deny patents to inventions to protect the public or morality, including the protection of human, animal, plant life, or health, or to avoid serious prejudice to the environment. This exclusion can also be found in the EC treaty and NAFTA. In our opinion, this exclusion provides member countries of the GATT, EU, and NAFTA with a large "loophole" to maintain their national barriers to trade, especially in the pharmaceutical industry, which faces onerous regulation in most countries. National governments can operate under the guise of a "social policy," that is, to protect the public health, to prohibit the free flow of goods in this industry. On January 1, 1995, the European Agency for the Evaluation of Medicinal Products began to provide regulatory approval for ethical drugs in this marketplace. Therefore, it will be interesting to see how this regulatory body for the EU and its major counterpart, the United States Food and Drug Administration, will be affected (if at all) by the TRIPs agreement.

Undisclosed Information.

The TRIPs agreement speaks not of trade secrets but of "undisclosed information." Both natural and legal persons may prevent information lawfully within their control from being "disclosed to, acquired by, or used others without their consent in a manner contrary to honest commercial practices" if such information:

- Is secret, that is, not generally known among or readily accessible to persons who normally deal with this kind of information;
- Has commercial value because of its secrecy; and
- Has been subject to reasonable steps under the circumstances, by the person who legally controls the information, to keep it secret.

Members may require, as a condition to approving the marketing of pharmaceutical products that use new chemical entities, the submission of secret test or other data that resulted from consid-

erable effort. If they do, the members must protect the data from unfair commercial use. This is a major concern for the pharmaceutical industry, as manufacturers must submit drug dossiers to a multitude of regulatory authorities. Harvey and Ronkainen expressed this concern for the disclosure of company information in this way:

> The U.S. Freedom of Information Act [FOIA] of 1966 is often mentioned as a source of problems, aiding and abetting the piracy of products and technologies. Pfizer Inc., for example, estimated that more than four-fifths of the 34,000 FOIA requests for the release of information were commercially motivated.[11]

Overall, the pharmaceutical industry is faced with several pragmatic questions regarding the protection of "undisclosed information" in the GATT. For example, will this section of the TRIPs agreement overrule nation legislation, such as the FOIA in the United States?

Enforcement Procedures. The current battle to protect a firm's intellectual property rights through legal recourse on an international scale has been an ordeal for several industries, including the pharmaceutical sector. Some firms use a prosecution strategy to deter pirates. However, this is an expensive strategy, and many firms find legal recourse an ineffective approach to discourage counterfeiters and prefer out-of-court settlements. For example, Sterling Drug recently won a case to halt production of one of its trademarked products by a local Venezuelan pharmaceutical firm only to discover that the maximum penalties on infringement of patent and trademark rights include fines of Bs50 to Bs2,000 (approximately $0.30 to $12.00 using the June 15, 1994, exchange rate of Bs164.80/$ quoted in *The Wall Street Journal*) and prison terms of 1 to 12 months.[12] Glaxo used a warning strategy to deter pirates and placed holograms on the packaging of their anti-ulcer drug, Zantac, three years ago.[13]

The TRIPs agreement requires that members make certain that enforcement procedures are available under their national laws to permit effective actions against any act of infringement of intellectual property rights covered by the agreement. As of January 1995, under the Uruguay Round agreement, the World Trade Organization (WTO) supersedes the GATT and has stronger powers to enforce the new trade arrangements, which include intellectual property rights.[14]

The major implications of the TRIPs accord in the GATT agreement are summarized in Exhibit 1.

Protection of Intellectual Property Rights in the EU

The EC Treaty devotes considerable attention to intellectual property rights. Coopers & Lybrand summarize the current EU policy toward the protection of intellectual property rights as follows:

> The European Community's policy for intellectual property is twofold: on the one hand, it wants to ensure that "products" are adequately protected both internally and externally, while on the other, it seeks to harmonize national legislation on intellectual

property rights so as to remove any trade restrictions between Member States. In particular, the Community seeks to establish greater protection of intellectual property rights . . . and efficient control over illegal and counterfeit goods.[15]

In general, the Treaty (Article 30) seeks to insure the free movement of goods among the Member States by eliminating customs duties and other barriers. Court interpretations of Article 30 have sharply limited the right of a manufacturer to control the distribution of its product once it has been introduced in one Member State within the EU. However, the Treaty (Article 36) contains certain exceptions to this free-movement policy. Some of these exceptions are relevant to intellectual property rights. For example, prohibitions and restrictions on imports or exports of goods are justified to protect industrial and commercial property, a term that includes intellectual property rights. The prohibitions or restrictions, however, cannot constitute a means of arbitrary discrimination or a disguised restriction on trade between Member States.

EXHIBIT 1 Synopsis of Intellectual Property Rights Protection in the GATT

Main Provisions for TRIPs in the GATT	Major Implications
Article 3	Grants all intellectual privileges that exist for nationals to foreign Members—the concept of national treatment or reciprocity.
Article 4	Applies the concept of "most-favored-nation" to the area of intellectual property rights.
Article 7	States the goal that intellectual property rights "should contribute to the promotion of technological innovation."
Article 8	Prevents discrimination in the international transfer of technology.
Trademarks Article 15	Governs the registration of a trademark. Initial registration and renewals of a trademark must be for a term of no less than seven years. The trademark must be renewable indefinitely.
Patents	Requires all members to grant patents for any inventions, whether a product or a process, as long as the innovation is an "inventive step" and is capable of "industrial application." The term of patent protection is 20 years from the filing date.
Undisclosed Information	Gives the right to keep information within the control of the firm. For example, the test data for creating a new chemical entity in the pharmaceutical sector can now be protected from unfair commercial use.
Enforcement	Requires that the signatory countries make "fair and equitable" enforcement procedures under their national laws.

"Exhaustion of Rights" Doctrine. The rights of an owner of an intellectual property right are sharply limited by what has become known as the "exhaustion of rights" doctrine, established in the 1974 decision of the European Court of Justice (ECJ) in *Centrafarm B.V.* v. *Sterling Drug Inc.* This doctrine provides that, once the owner of the intellectual property right markets its product in a second Member State, it is presumed to have recovered its "innovation reward" and cannot control the subsequent distribution of the product. In *Centrafarm,* the ECJ reasoned that allowing the holder of a patent on a pharmaceutical product to restrict the distribution of the product in a second Member State would permit it to partition the national markets and restrain trade between the Member States in direct violation of Article 30 of the Treaty.[16]

Cases decided by the ECJ in the two decades since *Centrafarm* have affirmed and expanded the doctrine. For instance, in *Merck & Co.* v. *Stephar B.V.,* the ECJ held that the "exhaustion of rights" doctrine applied even when the second Member State (in this case, Italy) in which the drug was marketed did not provide patent protection for the drug, thus reducing the return on the investment of the patent holder because of the decreased monopoly value in Italy.[17] Thus, if a manufacturer or its agent chooses to market its product in a Member State where the law does not provide intellectual property protection, it must accept the consequences of its choice with respect to the circulation of the product within the EU.

Patents. The "exhaustion of rights" doctrine first arose in connection with patent rights in a pharmaceutical product. The shadow cast by this doctrine should not obscure the fact that a patent, which is intended to reward the creative effort of the inventor, grants to the inventor the exclusive right to use the invention with a view to manufacturing a product and putting the product into circulation for the first time, either directly or through the use of licenses granted to third persons, and to oppose infringements.[18]

Trademarks. A trademark can be used to prevent the importation of products marketed under another trademark that causes confusion in connection with the first mark, if both were acquired by different, independent proprietors under different national laws, so long as there are no agreements restricting competition or legal or economic ties between them. Therefore, the owner of a trademark cannot prevent the marketing of goods in one Member State that were lawfully marketed in another Member State under an identical trademark with the same origin.

Pharmaceutical Cases. Although the "exhaustion of rights" doctrine applies to trademarks as well as to patents, cases involving the marketing of pharmaceutical products in the EU have established certain exceptions to the doctrine in trademark cases. For example, in *Centrafarm B.V.* v. *American Home Products Corp.,* the ECJ ruled that the proprietor of a trademark protected in one Member State can legally prevent (under Article 36) a product displaying that trademark from being marketed by a third party in another Member State.[19] This is true even if the third party affixes the trademark to the original product. The essential function of the trademark—to guarantee the identity of the origin of the trademarked product to the consumer or ultimate user—would be jeopardized, the court reasoned, if a third party were permitted to use the mark. The court made it clear, however, that a proprietor of different trademarks for the same product cannot use the marks to artificially partition the markets for the drug, which would amount to a disguised restriction on trade between Member States in violation of Article 30.

Subsequent ECJ trademark cases have predominantly addressed the issue of parallel trade of ethical drugs between Member States as opposed to counterfeit drugs.[20] As stated above, a pharmaceutical firm is not allowed to partition the markets of the EU by means of different trademarks (brand names) of their ethical drug since this would constitute a "disguised restriction on trade." However, a recent study discovered that several pharmaceutical firms engage this "multiple-brand name strategy" to deter parallel traders. The study concluded:

> Parallel traders believe strongly that different names are deliberately used by manufacturers in order to obstruct parallel trade. Manufacturers reply that their general policy is to have only one brand name across Europe. They claim that standard marketing practice encourages the promotion of one brand name rather than several. Where different brand names are used, this is because the brand name of first choice was rejected on some ground by the registration authority or seemed unsuitable in the local language.[21]

According to this study, a few cases of counterfeit drugs have been reported within this trade block. Thus, the threat of pirated drugs entering the EU marketplace is negligible. However, in 1993 the *Observer* reported that cases of counterfeit drugs produced in non-EU countries and bearing fake trademarks were seized entering the British marketplace. Indeed, the drug pirates were linked to the narcotics trade and funded terrorist groups, such as the IRA.[22]

Know-How. The Treaty never specifically addresses trade secrets, a concept found in the GATT, United States law, and NAFTA. However, it does address the topic of "know-how." Effective on April 1, 1989, EC Regulation 556/89 establishes a block exemption for know-how licensing agreements. These are agreements whereby the licensor transmits the licensee's nonpatented technical information, or know-how. The regulation, which applies Article 85(3) to certain categories of know-how licensing agreements, is to remain in force until December 31, 1999.[23]

We have summarized the major implications of the EC treaty for the protection of intellectual property rights in Exhibit 2.

EXHIBIT 2   Synopsis of Intellectual Property Rights Protection in the EU

Main Provisions for IPRs in the EC Treaty	*Major Implications*
Article 30	Seeks to insure the free movement of goods among the Member States and has sharply limited the right of the firm to control the distribution of its product once it has been introduced in one Member State.
Article 36	Can preclude Article 30 of the treaty to protect industrial and commercial property. However, this Article may not be used as a means of arbitrary discrimination or disguised restriction of trade between Member States.
Patents	Makes owner's patent rights subject to "exhaustion of rights" doctrine (below).
Trademarks	Guarantees to the owner that it has the exclusive right to use the mark for the purpose of putting the product into circulation for the first time.
Know-How	Protects from disclosure any body of technical information that is secret, substantial, and identified in any appropriate form.
Exhaustion of Rights Doctrine	States that a firm cannot control the distribution or marketing of a product once it markets the product in a second EU Member State.
Merck & Co. v. *Stephar B.V.*	Held that, once the product is marketed in a EU Member State, the good can be sold in a second Member State that does not provide patent protection for the drug.
Centrafarm B.V. v. *American Home Products Corp*	Upholds the right of the trademark holder to provide a guarantee of origin to the consumer. Hence, a company can legally restrict the sale of a product from being marketed in a third country.

Protection of Intellectual Property Rights in NAFTA

The NAFTA sets forth numerous provisions that ensure and provide for the protection and enforcement of intellectual property rights. This agreement contains provisions relating to the enforcement of intellectual property rights in general. For example, Article 1714 requires each party to the treaty to ensure that its domestic law makes available enforcement procedures that permit "effective action" to be taken against any act of infringement of intellectual property rights. In addition, each party must make certain that its procedures for the enforcement of intellectual property rights are fair, equitable, expeditious, and not unnecessarily complicated or costly.

Patents.   This trade accord requires (in Article 1709) each party to the treaty to make patents available for "any inventions, whether products or processes, in all fields of technology," so long as the inventions are (1) new, (2) the result of an "inventive step" (i.e., are nonobvious), and (3) "capable of industrial application" (i.e., are useful). Like Article 36 of the EC treaty and an exclusion in the TRIPs accord, a party is entitled to exclude any invention from patentability if necessary to protect the public or morality, including the protection of "human, animal or plant life or health or to avoid serious prejudice to nature or the environment." In addition, a party may exclude from patentability "diagnostic, therapeutic and surgical methods for the treatment of humans or animals," "plants and animals other than microorganisms," and "essentially biological processes for the production of plants or animals." As previously discussed, this clause can provide national governments with effective "loopholes" to circumvent this agreement.

Pharmaceuticals.   If a party fails to make available product patent protection for pharmaceuticals as generally required under the patent provisions of NAFTA, the party must provide to the inventor of any pharmaceutical product protection for that product for the unexpired term of the patent for the product granted in another country that is party to the treaty. This presumes that the product has not been marketed in the party providing protection and the person seeking protection makes a timely request.

Scope of Patent Protection.   The scope of patent protection found under NAFTA depends on whether the subject matter of the patent is a product or a process. In the case of a product, each party to the treaty must provide that the patent confers on the patent owner "the right to prevent other persons from making, using, or selling" the patented product without the patent owner's consent. In the case of a process, the party must provide that the patent confers on the patent owner the right to prevent other persons from "using, selling, or importing at least the product obtained directly by that process" without the patent owner's consent.

Trademarks.   The treaty (Article 1708) permits a party to require, as a condition for registration, that a sign be "visually perceptible." Each party must give the owner of a registered trademark the right to prevent anyone from using, without the owner's consent, an identical or similar sign for goods or services, if this use would result in a "likelihood of confusion."

Trade Secrets.   Each party is required to provide the legal means for anyone to prevent trade secrets from being disclosed to, acquired by, or used by others without the consent of the person lawfully in control of the information in violation of "honest commercial practices." To qualify for this protection, the information must indeed be secret. That is, it cannot be generally known among or readily accessible to persons who normally deal with this kind of information, it must have commercial value because of its secrecy, and the person lawfully in control of the information must have taken reasonable steps to keep it secret.

If a party requires the manufacturer of pharmaceutical products using new chemical entities to submit undisclosed test or other data necessary to determine whether such products are safe and effective, it must protect against the disclosure of the data, when the origination of the data involves considerable effort, unless disclosure is necessary to protect the public. In addition, test results and data are protected from "me too" (generic drug) applicants. The U.S. Department of Commerce reports:

> No "me too" applicant may rely on previously submitted test results and data to obtain marketing approval for a generic product for at least five years after the submission of the original data. This process protects pharmaceutical producers from bearing huge costs for testing that their competitors avoid by filing applications that rely on previously submitted test data.[24]

We have summarized the major implications of NAFTA for the protection of intellectual property rights in Exhibit 3.

North-South Controversy

Developing countries have argued that technological innovation is a public rather than a private capital good. They point out that these medical innovations can provide lifesaving cures. For example, Indira Ghandi stated in her address to the World Health Assembly in May 1982: "The idea of a better-ordered world is one in which medical discoveries will be free of all patents and there will be no profiteering from life and death."[25] Other arguments made by the developing countries center on the issue of price and the protection of indigenous industry. Basically, a common fear is that patent protection will result in exorbitant pharmaceutical prices. This viewpoint was expressed as follows:

> Government officials and industrialists in many developing countries argue that they have every right to copy existing products. "Who is robbing who?" asks Jose Fernando Magalhaes, a director of Sintofarms, a Brazilian company that makes one of the local copies

---

EXHIBIT 3   Synopsis of Intellectual Property Rights Protection in NAFTA

Main Provisions for IPRs in NAFTA	Major Implications
Article 1714	Requires each country to establish expeditious procedures for the enforcement of intellectual property rights.
Article 1709 Patents	Requires each country to provide patent for products and processes in all fields of technology.
Scope of Patent Protection	Establishes the term of patent protection as 20 years from date of filing in Canada and Mexico, and 17 years from issuance in the United States.
Nondiscrimination Provisions	Requires patents to be available regardless of the field of technology, the territory of the party where the invention was made, and whether products are imported or locally produced.
Article 1708 Trademarks	Provides that only marks that are "visually perceptible" can be registered; permits the owner of the mark to prevent the use of a similar mark creating a "likelihood of confusion."
Term of Registration	Mandates that initial registration of a trademark shall be for a term of at least 10 years and renewable indefinitely.
Compulsory Licensing	Prohibits each party from requiring compulsory licensing of trademarks. The owner of the trademark has the right to assign the trademark with or without the transfer of the business to which the trademark belongs.
Country of Origin	Establishes that each party can refuse to register, or invalidate the registration of, a trademark containing or consisting of a geographical territory, region, or locality if this use would mislead the public regarding the origin of the good.
Article 1711 Trade Secrets	Prohibits the disclosure by any government of test data submitted by pharmaceutical firms regarding the safety and effectiveness of their products.

of [Pfizer's] Feldene. "Are we robbing from the patient? I don't think so." Like other Brazilian drugmakers, he calls for compulsory licensing of patented drugs to local producers. "Patients in any country must have the option of buying a drug at the best possible price," he says.[26]

In addition, some developing countries claim that several of their local producers of pharmaceuticals will go out of business if patents are recognized. However, others argue that there should be increased investment in the countries that strengthen their patent protection. Pearson et al. support this increased foreign direct investment by stating:

> The actions to make the world safer for intellectual property will spur investments by U.S. companies to export more patented and copyrighted products and also step up production abroad. . . . In Argentina, where legislators are expected to act by midyear [1992] to strengthen patent protection, Pfizer has doubled its sales force and is "spending money like mad to introduce new products," says Brower A. Meriam, executive vice-president at Pfizer International. In Canada, Johnson & Johnson has expanded its research 50 percent as a result of earlier steps by Ottawa to strengthen patent protection.[27]

In contrast, *The Economist* refutes the idea that increased protection through the TRIPs accord will stimulate investment. *The Economist* recently claimed that Merck, a giant U.S. pharmaceutical firm, invested heavily in countries such as Italy, Spain, and Mexico, prior to effective patent protection because of other foreign direct investment incentives, which include national laws on ownership, market size, and the state of the domestic industry.[28]

The "South" controversy surrounding the protection of intellectual property rights may no longer be feasible under the TRIPs accord in the recent negotiations of the GATT. For example, adversaries in Latin America mention invoking Article 30 of the TRIPs agreement, which grants limited exclusion to patent rights. However, this developing-country debate is unreasonable given the unlikelihood of any signatory country of the

GATT relinquishing its rights under this multilateral trade accord.

Changing Perspectives in the Developed Countries

The regulatory pressures on the pharmaceutical industry in both the United States and Europe have escalated in recent years. The Member States of the EU have initiated further measures for reducing health-care costs—the primary target is spending on drugs. For example, recent changes include:

- The British government's move to lower ceilings on drug company profits;
- The French government's proposal of a 10 percent across-the-board cut in drug advertising;
- The German government's assessment of penalties for doctors who exceed the government's fixed budget for drug spending and endorsement of a 5 percent decline in government payments to drug companies on about one-third of all ethical drugs; and
- The Italian government's increase in the amount of a patient's co-payment for the drug and reduction of government reimbursement on drugs by approximately 4.5 percent.[29]

The pharmaceutical industry recently came under attack by both the Clinton administration and consumer advocates. The Clinton administration proposed a National Health Review Board to monitor a suggested compulsory discount of 17 percent (or around $2.5 billion) on all drugs purchased by Medicare.[30] Consumer advocates who recently studied pharmaceutical prices in the United States concluded that: (1) pharmaceutical profits in the 1980s were abnormally high due to continual price increases, not from growth in sales, (2) pharmaceutical prices are still rising faster than inflation for those consumers who pay for drugs out-of-pocket, (3) pharmaceutical consumers are subsidizing much of the world's pharmaceutical industry since the United States is the only industrialized country that (currently) makes no effort to regulate drug prices, and (4) pharmaceutical consumers also subsidize the industry through their tax dollars spent on biomedical research funded by the National Institutes of Health by awarding private pharmaceutical firms exclusive rights to commercialize what amounts to hundreds of millions of dollars of free research.[31]

The health-reform implications of this study and the recent government pressure in some of the high-income countries have effectively communicated the changing perspective of "nurturing" this innovative industry.

Managerial Implications

The trend toward greater protection of intellectual property rights is an encouraging development for managers concerned with enforcement of their patents, trademarks, and trade secrets in the international environment. Whether it will produce the changes desired by global managers, at least in the more developed countries, remains to be seen. Unfortunately, each of the agreements discussed in this article contains one or more provisions that may create a dilemma for the company seeking to enforce its intellectual property rights outside its nation's borders. As mentioned previously, under the EU, GATT, and NAFTA, an individual nation may deny protection to the intellectual property rights of a foreign business in the interest of protecting the health and safety of its citizens. As noted above, such efforts in the EU have been closely monitored by the European Court of Justice and rejected when they seem motivated by a desire on the part of a business to partition the European market in violation of Article 30 of the EC treaty. It is too soon to tell whether the courts will be as vigilant in enforcing the provisions of GATT and NAFTA that protect intellectual property rights when those provisions are sought to be evaded on grounds of public health or safety. For example, under both GATT and NAFTA, member

nations have the right to deny patents to inventions so as to protect the public health or morality; protect human, animal, or plant life; or avoid serious prejudice to the environment. It seems safe to assume that domestic businesses opposing enforcement of foreign patents or other intellectual property rights will lobby their own governments vigorously to deny protection to a foreign competitor.

Pharmaceutical manufacturers are likely to discover that the intellectual property protections found in GATT and NAFTA will come under attack by individual nations seeking to deny these protections ostensibly to protect their citizens' health and safety. No such trade controversy can yet be found in the pharmaceutical industry. However, the European Union, Japan, and Canada have published reports that these governments will address unfair trade barriers in WTO tribunals in the areas of food labeling laws, the Nuclear Non-Proliferation Act, drug-testing laws, state recycling laws, and even electrical-shaving safety requirements.[32] A current dispute between Canadian health officials and United States tobacco companies offers a glimpse into future disputes of these regional and multilateral trade agreements.

In order to decrease cigarette consumption, especially among Canadian youths, the Canadian government would like to enforce plain packaging for cigarettes using either a white or yellow background with black lettering. The cigarette package would include the brand name but not the logo, such as RJR's infamous camel.[33] The Canadian government launched this social policy despite warnings from the Canadian Bar Association and the Patent and Trademark Institute of Canada that this would violate domestic and international trademark laws under the 1925 Paris Convention, GATT and NAFTA.[34] This government intervention has prompted RJR Reynolds Holdings Corporation and Philip Morris to hire two former U.S. trade negotiators, Carla Hills and Jules Katz, to debate this infringement of the manufacturers' trademarks. Mr. Katz summarized the situation as follows:

You [Canada] have an unquestioned right to regulate the product. What you do not have a right to do, under international agreements to which Canada is a party, is to use the impairment of trademarks as a way of indirectly affecting the consumption of a product.[35]

Currently, research studies are being conducted by the University of Toronto and Health Canada to discern whether generic packaging will discourage cigarette consumption. Some advocates of the cigarette industry claim that this governmental social strategy will result simply in a resurgence of cigarette smuggling and could backfire by making smoking more attractive.[36] Other special-interest groups, such as the Canadian printing industry, claim that 1,200 printing industry jobs will be lost in the southern Ontario region if the Canadian government forces the removal of trademarks and distinctive coloring from the cigarette packages.[37] William Webb, president of Philip Morris International, forewarned government officials that this trademark infringement, in addition to prompting the cigarette industry to seek millions of dollars in compensation claims from the Canadian government, would have significant repercussions on the company's future investment decisions.[38]

This type of trade conflict is likely to surface repeatedly in the cases of GATT and NAFTA. Thus, the enforcement of intellectual property rights across international boundaries is likely to involve considerable litigation and remain cloudy for the foreseeable future. Overall, we support *The Economist's* conclusion that current trade wars between the United States and Canada are a direct result of either the Canadian Free Trade Agreement or NAFTA to preclude the use of impenetrable domestic trade laws to reconcile international disputes.[39]

Conclusion

The current government and social pressure on the pharmaceutical industry places even greater emphasis on the future protection of this industry's intellectual property rights on a global basis. The industry is faced with a paradox. On the one hand, there is mounting pressure to further regulate this industry in some of the developed countries. On the other hand, the recent TRIPs accord in the GATT and regional integration in the EU and NAFTA have further strengthened this industry's ability to secure future profits under the protection of their trademarks, patents, and trade secrets. In addition, these regional trade blocks will expand their membership in the near future.

The developing-country debate regarding the protection of pharmaceutical patents should diminish, since several of these countries are members of the GATT and will have to support the recent TRIPs accord. Indeed, even after complete ratification of this multilateral trade accord, future studies will have to address the actual enforcement of these intellectual property agreements by member countries. As mentioned previously, will these regional and multilateral agreements supersede national legislation, such as the Freedom of Information Act in the United States, or will the agreements incite an endless debate on the issue of sovereignty? We can only hope that the WTO will have stronger "teeth" than the GATT in applying enforcement procedures. Likewise, future research should address whether countries frequently use the major "loopholes" of these trade agreements under the facade of a "social policy," such as to protect the public-health interests of their citizens from the consumption of certain pharmaceuticals. The recent trade dispute between the Canadian government and cigarette manufacturers is indicative of future debates of sovereignty regarding the protection of intellectual property rights.

Trade disputes seem certain to arise in the future, especially when a nation refuses to recognize the intellectual property rights of a foreign company in the name of protecting the health and safety of that nation's citizens. Hence, the trade issue for managers to follow in the future is whether these trade agreements will supersede national laws. These trade treaties signify the commencement of a more consistent scheme of global protection of intellectual property rights, a step in the right direction, but managers must realize that these agreements are initiating a period of transition that is replete with uncertainty.

Notes

1. Joseph Greenwald and Charles Levy, *International Economic Law Documents* (1989).
2. Michael Harvey and Ilkka Ronkainen, "International Counterfeiters: Marketing Success Without the Cost and the Risk," *Columbia Journal of World Business* (Fall 1985).
3. John Pearson, Geri Smith, Joseph Weber, and Mark Maremont, "The Patent Pirates Are Finally Walking the Plank," *Business Week* (February 17, 1992).
4. *Ibid.*
5. "U.K.: Billion-Pound Drugs Fraud Hits U.K., *Observer* (March 14, 1993).
6. W. Siebeck, R. Evenson, W. Lesser, and C. Primo Braga, *Strengthening Protection of Intellectual Property in Developing Countries.* World Bank Discussion Paper No. 112, The World Bank, Washington, D.C. (1990).
7. "Drugmakers Start Reaching for the Painkillers," *Business Week* (August 30, 1993).
8. Document IV; *Protection of Intellectual Property Rights BNA's Patent, Trademark & Copyright Journal* 47 PTCJ 222, Issue No. 1162 (January 1994).
9. "International Counterfeiters," *Columbia Journal of World Business.*
10. *NAFTA Opportunities: Pharmaceuticals.* U.S. Department of Commerce, International Trade Administration, Washington, D.C. (1994).
11. "International Counterfeiters," *Columbia Journal of World Business.*
12. "Protection of Intellectual Property," *Economist Intelligence Unit Investing Licensing & Trading,* Lexis-Nexis database (September 1, 1993).
13. "U.K: Billion-Pound Drugs Fraud Hits U.K.," *Observer* (March 14, 1993).
14. "Talks on Trade Not Complete," *The Financial Times* (June 14, 1994).
15. *Intellectual Property.* A report on EC commentaries by Coopers & Lybrand. Lexis-Nexis database (1994).
16. *Centrafarm B.V. v. Sterling Drug, Inc.,* E.C.R. 1147, 2 C.M.L.R. 480 (1974).
17. *Merck & Co. v. Stephar B. V.,* E.C.R. 2063, 3 C.M.L.R. 463 (1981).
18. *Intellectual Property* (1994).
19. *Centrafarm B.V. v. American Home Products Corp.,* E.C.R. 1823, 1 C.M.L.R. 326 (1979).
20. See: *Hoffman-La Roche & Co. AG v. Centrafarm Vertriebsgesellschaft Pharmazeutischer Erzeugnisse mbH,* E.C.R. 1139, 3 C.M.L.R. 217 (1978); and *Regina v. Pharmaceutical Society of Great Britain,* E.C.R. 2 C.M.L.R. 751 (1989).
21. *Impediments to Parallel Trade in Pharmaceuticals Within the European Community.* A final report prepared by Remit Consultants for DG IV of the Commission of the European Communities, Luxembourg: Office for Official Publications of the European Communities (1992).
22. "U.K.: Billion-Pound Drugs Fraud Hits U.K., *Observer* (March 14, 1993).
23. *Intellectual Property* (1994).
24. *NAFTA Opportunities: Pharmaceuticals* (1994).
25. *Strengthening Protection of Intellectual Property in Developing Countries* (1990).
26. "The Patent Pirates Are Finally Walking the Plank," *Business Week.*
27. "The Patent Pirates Are Finally Walking the Plank," *Business Week.*
28. "Intellectual Property . . . Is Theft," *The Economist* (January 22, 1994).
29. G. Schares, C. Hoots, J. Weber, and J. Flynn, "Drugmakers Start Reaching for the Painkillers," *Business Week* (August 30, 1993).
30. "American Drug Firms: Kicking the Habit," *The Economist* (January 7, 1994).
31. "The High Cost of Prescriptions," *Consumer Reports* (October 1993).
32. "Justice and Trade Treaty Would Chip Away at Limits on Multinationals," *The Times Union,* Lexis-Nexis database (July 24, 1994).
33. "Tobacco Firms Fume Over Plans for Plain Packs," *South China Morning Post,* Lexis-Nexis database (June 12,1994).
34. "Ottawa Warned on Plain Packs," *The Financial Post,* Lexis-Nexis database (October 5, 1994).
35. "The Squabbles Start," *Latin American Regional Reports: Mexico and Central America,* Lexis-Nexis database (June 16, 1994).
36. "Some MPs Ready to Butt Out On Plain Cigarette

Packages. Move Won't Cut Tobacco Sales, Say Panel Members," *The Toronto Star* (June 13, 1994).

37. "Plain-pack Smokes Scheme Postponed," *The Toronto Star* (June 14, 1994).

38. "Fuming Over Cigarette Packs; U.S. Tobacco Industry Warns Canada Against Plain Packaging Law," *The Toronto Star* (May 17, 1994).

39. "NAFTA's Progress: Northern Rumblings," *The Economist* (January 15, 1995).

Non-Tariff Barriers and Entry Strategy Alternatives: Strategic Marketing Implications

Earl Naumann and Douglas J. Lincoln

Currently, the U.S. export market is dominated by large companies and multinational corporations. Kathawaba, Judd, Montipallil, and Weinrich (1989) state that only 10 percent of the total U.S. export business is conducted by small business despite the fact that foreign markets may offer the smaller firm solid opportunities for long-term growth and profitability. Furthermore, involvement in international business is not typically a formal objective flowing from the strategic thought processes of most U.S. small businesses. Instead, initial attempts to export are often stimulated by an inquiry from a potential customer located in a specific foreign country (Suzman and Wortzel, 1984; Piercy, 1981). Graham and Meloan (1986) found that 86 percent of the firms in their study initiated exporting as a result of these foreign inquiries and only 17 percent of the firms indicated that any significant research was completed before exporting began. Johnston and Czinkota (1985) had similar findings in their study of three industries. Only 38 percent, 50 percent, and 53 percent of the firms in each industry actively sought their first foreign order; conversely, between 47 percent

and 62 percent of these firms received their first order on an unsolicited basis. Thus, despite the potential for sales growth and the existence of numerous government and private sector support programs, it appears that the majority of American small businesses begin exporting because someone overseas seeks them and/or their product, not because of a planned marketing strategy to enter a foreign market. Ironically, very few small businesses attempting to compete domestically would admit that they can be successful by waiting for customer to come to them. It may be just as illogical to expect high levels of international marketing success by taking this reactive approach.

Although small businesses can seemingly achieve some success in exporting by waiting for foreign customers to contact them on an unsolicited basis, the more successful exporters probably pursue a focused, planned approach that clearly identifies foreign target markets and adapts their current domestic strategy when and where necessary (Dawson, 1985; Kaynak et al., 1987; Namiki, 1988). While a well-organized, planned entrance into international markets will enhance the probability of success as well as the level of success (e.g., sales or profit volumes), many obstacles and challenges are likely to be encountered.

Reprinted from the *Journal of Small Business Management*, April 1991, pp. 60–70.

These obstacles originate from sources both internal and external to the firm.

Non-tariff barriers (NTBs) constitute a complex set of constraints that can frustrate and thwart the small business's international efforts. Recent literature has suggested that NTBs may now be the major obstacle faced by firms attempting to enter foreign markets (Czinkota, Rivoli, and Ronkainen, 1989; Jeannet and Hennessey, 1988).

The purpose of this article is to provide an analysis of the NTBs most likely to be encountered by small businesses and to suggest strategies that can be used to overcome these constraints to international trade. NTBs are thus viewed as "restraints" to the small business international marketing efforts that can require business strategy changes in order to adapt to market differences.

Non-Tariff Barriers

Non-tariff barriers did not seriously affect trade flows until the mid-1960s (Baldwin, 1970). Prior to that time, tariffs (e.g., financial surcharges) were the dominant means of distorting world trade flows to the benefit of a particular host country. However, the success of the General Agreement on Tariffs and Trade (GATT) rounds has resulted in relatively low tariff levels (averaging between 4 and 7 percent) among industrialized countries. As tariff protection has diminished, non-tariff protection has emerged as a difficult, challenging constraint and may now be the most significant trade distorting mechanism (Ray and Marvel, 1984). While a free, unconstrained flow of world trade is a theoretical economic ideal, political realities make protectionism a persistent fact of life. Thus, small businesses entering international trade markets must be familiar with the pervasiveness of NTBs. Any encounter with NTBs can spell instant failure for the small business not cognizant of the implications. Simply stated, NTBs provide a challenge not typically encountered in the smaller firm's domestic markets.

NTBs may be defined as "government laws, regulations, policies, or practices that either pro-tect domestic producers from foreign competition or artificially stimulate exports of particular domestic products" (*Foreign Trade Barriers,* 1987). For all practical purposes, this definition is normally broadened to include private-sector business practices, such as monopolistic or oligopolistic industrial structures (e.g., closed distribution systems) that effectively preclude foreign access to domestic markets or restrain competition with domestic organizations. This broader definition is used here, and includes both public- and private-sector practices that distort trade flows.

Types of Non-Tariff Barriers

While NTBs are acknowledged to be important trade distorting mechanisms, few studies have addressed their strategic implications for either large or small businesses. Several studies have categorized NTBs in some manner (Cao, 1980; Onkvisit and Shaw, 1988; Ray, 1981; Ray and Marvel, 1984). Other studies have provided comprehensive lists of possible NTBs (Organization for Economic Cooperation and Development, 1985, United Nations Conference on Trade and Development, 1983). Moreover, other studies have provided insight into the NTBs that may influence a particular product (Monke and Taylor, 1985) or a particular industry (Food and Agriculture Organization, 1986). However, these studies generally focus on international trade policy issues and neglect the strategic implications for businesses.

The remainder of this section will provide a brief discussion of each of the 20 NTBs presented in Exhibit 1. These 20, based on our review of the literature, appear to be those most likely to be encountered by U.S. small businesses that are initiating international trade efforts. It is important to note that NTBs are not applied uniformly from country to country or even among different industries in a given country. Hence, the following discussion is intended to be *illustrative* of the most common types of NTBs; in specific situations, other NTBs not addressed here could be quite important.

EXHIBIT 1   20 Common NTBs

---

1. Import quotas	11. Packaging and labeling requirements
2. Minimum import pricing	12. Low-cost government financing and subsidies
3. Marketing or advertising restrictions	13. Local content regulations
4. Restrictive transportation requirements	14. Rebate of domestic taxes to exporters
5. Port of entry taxes or levies	15. Discriminatory government procurement contracts
6. Import licensing requirements	16. Required countertrade
7. Complex customs procedures	17. Voluntary export restraints
8. Product quality or technical standards	18. Domestic monetary restrictions
9. Arbitrary product classification	19. Volatile exchange rates
10. Safety and health requirements	20. Lack of access to suitable market channels

---

Import quotas are fairly straightforward quantitative restrictions on imports and may be expressed as individual units imported or as a total value of imports. Since quotas are commonly imposed on an annual basis, this type of NTB has the effect of forcing imports into the first part of the year as foreign competitors rush to capture domestic share before the quota is reached and all imports cease. This NTB has implications for inventory levels (i.e., stock buildup), timing of promotional efforts (i.e., early in the year), and financing and credit strategies (arranging inventory financing).

Minimum import pricing is intended to provide a pricing floor that is pegged in some manner to the domestic price structure. Depending on the required price level, this can effectively increase the domestic firm's gross profit margin and shift its marketing strategy emphasis to nonprice elements. This may be a significant strategic barrier for small business with generic or commodity products where product differentiation is difficult or impossible to achieve.

Marketing or advertising restrictions are placed on the types of products that can be advertised, the types of advertising claims allowed, and ads that name competing products (i.e., comparative advertising). Small businesses whose domestic promotional strategies rely on such approaches may find creating customer awareness very difficult in foreign markets.

Restrictive transportation requirements may include pallet size, container size, and material-handling limitations. Also, many less-developed countries (LDCs) simply lack a reliable domestic transportation infrastructure. China offers an excellent example of this NTB.

Port-of-entry taxes or levies are sometimes placed on imports flowing through a country's ports of entry. The original purpose of this NTB was to generate a user-based tax to help defray infrastructure development costs for airports as well as port facilities. However, these taxes often endure well past the time necessary to offset the original capital cost and are often higher than operating costs would indicate. These NTBs may vary from port of entry to port of entry in the same country. As with many other NTBs, a small business looking into foreign markets must assess the impact of these taxes on their anticipated margins, price competitiveness, and overall financing goals.

Import licensing requirements can take one of two forms. First, the right to import certain types of products can be limited through the allocation of import licenses, restricting the number of foreign competitors in a given industry. Thus, a late market entrant would be excluded from that country. Second, import licenses may be unlimited, but the process of obtaining the license is difficult. Due to bureaucratic delays. it may take a year or more to obtain the right to import products. Thus, a strategic window could close before a firm would be able to respond to a market opportunity. Without a foreign agent or partner who "knows the system," a small business may be excluded from such markets.

Custom procedures, while uniformly applied, may be an NTB through sheer complexity. Without the help of foreign-based expertise, the American small business may experience great difficulty in overcoming this NTB.

Product quality or technical standard for determining a product's quality level are not uniform from country to country and product testing performed in one country may be of little or no value in another country. Thus, the product testing for many products must be done in those foreign countries due to the unacceptability of foreign data. Also, product adaptation may be necessary to meet unique technical requirements.

Arbitrary product classification refers to the sometimes unpredictable manner in which a foreign country classifies the small business's product(s). A given product's classification, which can be highly subjective, affects its duty status. In some cases, the small business may be able to change its classification to a more advantageous position by altering its packaging or other informational programs.

Safety and health requirements can be an obstacle, as many countries have unique product content requirements not found elsewhere. Again, product changes for the small business represent one of the costliest changes and may therefore suggest a "no-go" entry decision.

Packaging and labeling are typically unique for each country. This NTB requires that inventory be maintained separately for each destination country and carries with it significantly increased finished product inventory levels.

Low-cost government financing or direct government subsidies to domestic firms indicates the relationship between government and business in many foreign countries is much closer and more symbiotic than in the U.S. This often results in the government, either directly or indirectly, providing loans at very favorable rates to its domestic businesses. This pattern is particularly prevalent in the "planned" economies of the Pacific Rim.

Local content regulations are typically expressed as a minimum percentage of a product's total value added that must be produced in a host country to avoid high tariffs. This can be satisfied through acquisition of component parts, product assembly, or finish work and is intended to provide a degree of domestic employment.

Rebates of domestic taxes to exporters are often found in countries with a heavy export reliance. Commonly, a portion of value-added taxes are rebated or credited to domestic producers based on the total value of exports. This has the effect of reducing the marginal cost associated with the level of production that is exported. Another commonly rebated tax is the import duty on items such as component parts intended for further re-export. Somewhat less common is the rebating of tariffs on imported equipment and machinery, if the equipment or machinery is used to support an export-directed product. The small firm that exports to such a country may actually pay the import tax while the domestic firm receives the rebate.

Discriminatory government procurement contracts are one of the oldest and most common NTBs. This NTB reflects the desire to spend public funds in the domestic economy. Examples of this NTB can be found in almost every country (e.g., U.S. Government purchases), and the large volume of public expenditures in the industrialized economies make the economic impact of this NTB significant. Bidding deadlines are also often sufficiently short to make it difficult for foreign small businesses to effectively respond.

Required countertrade is an NTB found primarily in developing countries and less-developed countries. The intent is to boost domestic exports while maintaining an even balance of trade. A small business will have to carefully assess whether or not it can use and/or effectively market products that it would receive as part of a countertrade arrangement.

Voluntary export restraints (VER), sometimes referred to or "orderly market arrangements," are "gentlemen's agreements" among countries that limit the level of product flows in international trade. The internal allocation of exports is typically fixed on a base year, and market share becomes fixed at that level. This implies that "growing" countries or firms are at a disadvantage while the industry leader is at a distinct advantage. Looking from the opposite side, small businesses "late" into a market would be precluded from exporting to a country enforcing a VER.

Domestic monetary restrictions, particularly those in the less developed or newly industrialized countries, impose limitations on the expatriation (removal) of profits from their country. This effectively forces profits to be reinvested domestically. Tight controls on cash transactions are also imposed in many countries, thus dictating cash management strategy.

Exchange rates between industrialized countries are often allowed to float within targeted ranges while exchange rates in less-developed countries are more volatile. Large differences in relative exchange rates may result in a competitive delivered cost position in one country and a prohibitively high delivered cost in another country. The small business manager must anticipate exchange fluctuations and deal with this NTB just as larger organizations do.

Lack of access to suitable marketing channels occurs in many of the Pacific Rim countries that are "planned" economies requiring close coordination between government and industry. The frequent result of this coordination is the development of industries that are controlled by relatively few firms. If a U.S. small business attempts to export to such a situation, it must deal with one of the dominant firms or be shut out of the desired market.

NTB Summary

The NTBs discussed above appear to be the more important ones that may occur in many foreign markets. However, there are numerous other NTBs that can be significant obstacles in specific situa-

tions. Additionally, NTBs are rarely applied individually. Rather, they are often used in combination so that the effective level of protectionism can be quite high. In some cases, the quantity and severity of a foreign country's NTBs may be such that the small business's entry into the market is not economically viable. However, in other cases, the costs are not as large, and knowledge of NTBs suggests to the small business *why* and *how* their current (domestic) business/marketing strategy should be altered to achieve international success.

Entry Strategies

Once small business owners/managers decide to engage in international trade, they must decide how they are going to enter foreign markets. The alternative approaches are referred to as entry strategies. It has been noted that closed markets (i.e., those with a high level of tariffs and/or NTBs) are the biggest challenge to firms entering international trade (Jeannet and Hennessey, 1988). However, the level of protectionism encountered may be influenced by a firm's choice of entry strategies. The entry strategies of direct and indirect exporting usually face more barriers than other strategies such as joint ventures, foreign licensing, or direct investment. Since exporting countries or firms gain more benefits (profits, wages, employment, etc.) than importing countries or firms (lower prices, increased variety), many countries may discriminate against imports. Those same countries may be very encouraging for joint ventures or licensing agreements, however. Therefore, the selection of an entry strategy should be directly related to the level and nature of protectionism likely to be encountered. Thus, the choice of an entry strategy should "flow" from knowledge about specific NTBs that will be encountered. The following sections will review the various entry strategies that a small business might pursue in relation to obstacles presented by the NTBs discussed previously.

Indirect exporting involves using a middleman to handle exporting activities. The most common types of middlemen are export brokers and manufacturing export agents who develop expertise in particular countries. These individuals develop a network of contacts in a given country and gain experience in penetrating foreign markets. Thus, they become quite familiar with the various NTBs in a country and are often knowledgeable about whether or not one can circumvent trade constraints, and if so, how. By operating on a commission basis, these middlemen represent only variable costs for the exporter. Unfortunately the use of indirect exporters typically results in the small business gaining very little direct knowledge about how NTBs affect its success. Thus, a small business that shifts from an indirect to direct marketing exporting approach to seek more profits often does so without the aid of this significant experience. A small business that finds success in indirect exporting may only learn that foreign demand for its products exists in a given country. However, it may never be fully cognizant of how or why certain NTBs affect its strategy and related success or failure.

Direct exporting typically requires that the small business assume responsibility for all the activities necessary to deliver its product(s) to a foreign market. Such a business might hire specialized firms to assist in fulfilling various tasks, but the ultimate responsibility rests with the exporter. Due to the higher level of involvement, small businesses gain experience in international trade very quickly. A working, first-hand knowledge of NTBs is a major benefit of direct exporting. However, much international trade experience is unique to a given country. Therefore, specific NTB knowledge may not be transferable to other foreign markets. One study of small business exporters indicated that each exporter was exporting to an average of nine countries (Kedia and Chhokar, 1985). If this is typical of all small business exporters, much managerial commitment and many resources will be necessary to become familiar with the unique environment in each country.

Licensing allows a foreign firm to produce and/or market product(s) in return for an initial fee and a royalty on each unit sold. License agreements may include patents, copyrights, production and technical expertise, etc. The license agreement normally specifies geographical and time horizon agreements. This entry strategy requires little initial cash investment by the domestic small business, but it does require careful research in identifying the possible foreign firms(s) to license. Foreign licensing can provide additional cash flow to defray product development costs and effectively extend product life cycles. A possible limitation of foreign licensing is the emergence of the foreign licensee as a competitor in other markets. Also, countries with currency restrictions make the repatriation of royalty earnings difficult. The small business may also have to buy products for export in the host country, import the products to the United States, and sell the product to realize the royalty earnings (that is, it may have to countertrade).

Franchising is essentially an advanced form of licensing that results in a much higher level of control by the franchisor. The franchisor typically provides marketing programs, training, managerial support, and operations policies and guidelines. As with licensing, franchising usually requires a foreign firm to pay an initial franchise fee and subsequent royalties with little direct foreign investment required by the franchisor. The problems of franchise selection, product adaptation, and repatriation of royalty fees are the primary constraints.

Joint ventures typically involve equity infusions from both the host country small business firm and the foreign firm. To be successful, both partners must have goal congruity and clearly defined responsibility. Often the host country partner will maintain operating control. Joint ventures often are intended to circumvent protectionistic barriers due to import restraints or restrictions on foreign business ownership. The problems with cultural differences, divergent goals, and disputes over control and responsibility are the major difficulties in joint venture relationships. These relationships, to be successful, require a substantial amount of research and information seeking. Many small businesses lack the resources and commitment to fully develop meaningful joint ventures.

Wholly owned subsidiaries usually involve larger multinational corporations pursuing a direct investment strategy. A more recent type of international strategy (strategic alliances) occurs when two firms agree to share resources and expertise. While both of these strategies are common among larger firms, they are typically beyond the resources of most small businesses. Therefore, smaller firms are unlikely to use these strategies.

Implications

The selection of an entry strategy is a result of both internal and external analysis. The internal analysis focuses on resources that a small business has at its disposal and management's willingness to commit resources to international marketing efforts. If a firm has a limited resource base, it may lack the ability to make a long-term investment to penetrate a foreign market through internal efforts. In this situation, pursuing indirect exporting through the use of export agents or brokers may be the most appropriate entry strategy. Similarly, a small business that has excess productive capacity may be looking for a short-term market to reduce inventory. This situation would also favor the indirect exporting strategy. Conversely, if a firm anticipates significant potential in foreign markets, possesses sufficient resources, and is committed to a strategic focus on international markets, a direct exporting or joint venture entry strategy may be more appropriate. However, such a strategy may take years to implement and require significant managerial commitment and financial resources. Thus, the longer term a firm's commitment to international marketing is, the more appropriate the more complex entry strategies.

The external analysis consists of identifying market potential, evaluating the competitive situation, and assessing the environment for international trade. The focus of this article was on the environmental constraints of diverse protectionistic measures exemplified by non-tariff barriers

(NTBs), but the foreign competitors also influence the international trade decision and are quite important. The small business considering international trade must gather considerable data to make effective "go/no-go" and "how to" decisions.

Assuming that a small business decides to conduct research on the international trade opportunities and obstacles prior to developing an entry strategy, the first step must be information acquisition. Sources of information are diverse and variable from state to state and from country to country. Exhibit 2 presents a summary of sources commonly available. Due to the geographical diversity, these types of organizations may not exist in all states, or they may be supplemented by other organizations in some states. However, the sources will provide the starting point for information acquisition.

Many of the foreign organizations fulfill a somewhat different role than their U.S. equivalents. For example, banks play a more active trade development role in many foreign countries than in the U.S. Accounting firms provide a diverse array of services overseas, much broader than found in the U.S. Thus, businesspeople seeking information should not be restricted by their perceptions of what services will be available. The original role of the Japanese External Trade Organization (JETRO) was to encourage and facilitate Japanese exports. However, the current primary role of JETRO is to facilitate imports into Japan. Therefore, JETRO now provides extensive databases on market potential in Japan.

When evaluating the array of entry strategies, it is essential for a small business to take a long-term perspective. Some marketing mix variables, such as pricing and promotion, can be changed very quickly, but other mix variables, such as product features and channels of distribution, are much more costly to change. Since selection of an entry strategy is, at least, an implicit selection of a distribution channel, a small business must carefully consider its long-term international business goals. If the long-term goal is to establish a permanent presence in foreign markets, then investing the

EXHIBIT 2   Sources of Information on Non-Tariff Barriers

State or Local
Other small business exporters (international business
   directories)
Commercial banks (international divisions)
State department of commerce
Export development councils
Export management companies
Export trading companies
Colleges and universities (center for international business)

Federal Government
U.S. Department of Commerce
U.S. International Trade Administration
U.S. Small Business Administration
U.S. Department of State
Export–Import Bank
Office of U.S. Trade Representative

Other U.S. Sources
World Trade Center
Industry trade associations
Foreign Credit Insurance Association
Foreign embassies or consulates

Overseas Sources
State trade development offices
U.S. Foreign Commercial Service
U.S. embassies or consulates
U.S. Chamber of Commerce
Importers' associations
Foreign banks
Consulting firm (marketing, accounting, management, etc.)
Trade fairs
Foreign government agencies (i.e., JETRO in Japan, Hong
   Kong Trade Development Council in Hong Kong)
Import brokers, agents
Foreign trading companies

time and money to pursue direct exporting would probably be justified. Due to a greater level of managerial control, direct exporting also holds more sales and profit potential over the long term. Conversely, if a small business is simply experimenting with exporting to reduce inventory or to determine if foreign demand exists, then an indirect exporting strategy, which requires less commitment, may be more appropriate. Knowledge of NTBs should dramatically aid the small business in assessing this risk/return tradeoff.

Conclusion

International trade is often viewed as a complex, high-risk activity for small businesses. It is interesting (but not surprising) to note that small businesses involved in exporting have consistently more favorable attitudes toward exporting than firms not engaged in exporting (Kedia and Chhokar, 1985; Johnston and Czinkota, 1985; Cavusgil and Nevin, 1981). Thus negative perceptions of exporting may be a significant deterrent to initiating export efforts.

If closed markets are the biggest challenge to international trade, as suggested by Jeannet and Hennessey (1988), then studying the level of protectionism must be a major part of market analysis. With the decreasing level of tariffs and increased use of NTBs instead as trade distorting measures, the study of NTBs in a particular country of interest seems to be a critical starting point for the small business contemplating business in foreign markets.

A major determinant of success in international business is managerial commitment to international activities (Cavusgil and Nevin, 1981). To overcome the array of important NTBs found in foreign markets, a small business must be strongly committed to international trade. This is likely to be reflected in an aggressive, opportunistic approach to international efforts and will clearly require a long-term commitment and a well-designed strategy. Specifically, overcoming NTBs requires a well-organized effort that extends over a period of several years. Furthermore, the choice of entry strategies (exporting, foreign direct investment, joint ventures, acquisition, mergers, etc.)

must reflect the relative importance of NTBs as an environmental constraint in a given country. Overlooking the importance of this environmental constraint can lead to failure of a small business's attempt to enter international markets.

References

Baldwin, Robert E. (1970), "Non-Tariff Distortions of International Trade," Washington, D.C.: The Brookings Institute.

Cao, A.D. (1980), "Non-Tariff Barriers to U.S. Manufactured Exports," *Columbia Journal of World Business* (Summer), 93–102.

Cavusgil, Tamer, and J. R. Nevin (1981), "International Determinants of Export Marketing Behavior: An Empirical Investigation," *Journal of Marketing Research* 18 (1), 114–19.

Czinkota, Michael R., Pietra Rivoli, and Ilkka A. Ronkainen (1989), *International Business.* New York: Dryden Press.

Dawson, Leslie M. (1985), "Marketing to Less Developed Countries," *Journal of Small Business Management* 23 (4), 13–19.

Food and Agriculture Organization (1986), "Trade in Forest Products: A Study of the Barriers Faced by Developing Countries," Rome.

Foreign Trade Barriers (1987), Office of the United States Trade Representative, United States Department of Commerce.

Graham, John L., and Taylor W. Meloan (1986), "Preparing the Exporting Entrepreneur," *Journal of Marketing Education* (Spring), 11–20.

Jeannet, Jean-Pierre, and Hubert D. Hennessy (1988), *International Marketing Management Strategies and Cases,* Boston: Houghton Mifflin, 54–58.

Johnston, Wesley, and Michael R. Czinkota (1985), "Export Attitudes of Industrial Manufacturers," *Industrial Marketing Management* 14, 123–32.

Kathawaba, Y., R. Judd, M. Montipallil, and M. Weinrich (1989), "Exporting Practices and Problems of Illinois Firms," *Journal of Small Business Management* 27 (1), 53–59.

Kaynak, Erdener, Pervez N. Ghauri, Torbjorn Olofsson-Brendenlow (1987), "Export Behavior of Small Swedish Firms," *Journal of Small Business Management* 25 (2), 26–32.

Kedia, Ben L., and Jagdeep Chhokar (1985), "The Impact of Managerial Attitudes on Export Behavior," *American Journal of Small Business* (Fall), 7–16.

Monke, Eric A., and Lester D. Taylor (1985), "International Trade Constraints and Commodity Market Models: An Application to the Cotton Market," *The Review of Economics and Statistics* 67 (3), 98–107.

Namiki, Nobuaki (1988), "Export Strategy for Small Business," *Journal of Small Business Management* 26 (2), 32–37.

Onkvisit, Sak, and John Shaw (1988), "Marketing Barriers in International Trade," *Business Horizons* (May–June) 64–72.

Organization for Economic Development (1985), "Costs and Benefits of Protectionism," Paris: OECD, 9–24.

Piercy, Nigel (1981), "British Export Market Selection and Pricing," *Industrial Marketing Management* 10, 287–97.

Ray, Edward J. (1981), "The Determinants of Tariff and Non-Tariff Barriers to Trade in the United States and Abroad," *The Review of Economics and Statistics* 63 (May), 161–68.

Ray, Edward J., and Howard P. Marvel (1984), "The Pattern of Protection in the Industrialized World," *Review of Economics and Statistics* (August), 452–58.

Suzman, C. L., and L. H. Wortzel (1984), "Technology Profiles and Export Marketing Strategies," *Journal of Business Research* 12, 183–94.

United Nations Conference on Trade and Development (1983), "Protectionism, Trade Relations, and Structural Adjustment," UNCTAD-274 (January).

PART

III INTERNATIONAL AND GLOBAL MARKETING STRATEGIES

In the first article in this section, the author describes the successes of Japanese firms in terms of their globally integrated marketing strategies. He contrasts Japanese strategies with American, and explains that the "unusual" Japanese home culture causes them to be more careful in adapting some aspects of marketing in foreign countries. However, at the same time, a central theme in Japanese international marketing is a strong emphasis on global branding.

One of the most frequently recommended strategies for foreign market entry is a joint venture—the next two pieces are on that topic. The author of the first asserts that the factors that lead to joint venture success in Russia are carefully choosing partners, developing trust at the start, profit-sharing systems, and backward integration. The last is a necessity in countries like Russia because an infrastructure of competent suppliers often does not exist. McDonald's success in Russia is presented as an exemplary implementation formula. The second article is a classic on the topic and addresses more broadly a variety of forms of international strategic alliances, their formation, and their management. The author argues that the seeds of success or failure are often sown in the initial negotiations between international partners.

GLOBAL STRATEGY AS A FACTOR IN JAPANESE SUCCESS

George S. Yip

Although Japan is undergoing post-bubble reconstruction of its economy, its multinational companies (MNCs) continue to be highly successful in international competition. Many explanations have been advanced for this success. These explanations include the Confucian work ethic and national culture (Yoshino, 1968), business–government collaboration ("Japan, Inc."), unfair trade practices (Prestowitz, 1988), managerial culture (Theory Z of Ouchi, 1981; Pascale and Athos, 1981), competitive dedication (Abegglen and Stalk, 1985), long-term orientation and lesser concern for profitability (Clark, 1979: 221; Kagono et al., 1984; Kono, 1984; Picken, 1987), and intercompany connections (the *keiretsus*). All of these explanations have some validity in what is undoubtedly a multicausal phenomenon. But many of the causes cannot be readily replicated by companies in other nations, being rooted in the culture and institutions of Japan. This article proposes an additional factor that can be copied by non-Japanese companies, and that may be particularly easy for U.S. companies to adopt. *This additional explanation lies in Japanese companies' greater use of globally integrated strategy.* Conceptual arguments, case histories, and the results of a comparative study of 36 American and Japanese worldwide businesses are provided in support of this thesis. In addition, it will be argued that any lessened international competitiveness on the part of Japanese companies today partly arises from Japan's straying from its earlier dedication to globally integrated strategy and from the MNCs of other countries catching up in the use of global strategy.

Stages of a Total Global Strategy

As argued by Yip (1992), globally integrated strategy is not synonymous with international strategy, but is one of three components that make up a "total global strategy." Figure 1 illustrates the three stages of global strategy—developing the core strategy, internationalizing the strategy, and globalizing the strategy. Japanese companies have been particularly successful in either moving quickly through all three stages or even implementing the three simultaneously, while their Western rivals have lingered too long in the first two stages.

The typical pattern of international expansion for American (and European) MNCs has been to develop, first, a successful core strategy for its home market, although, more recently, such initial

The International Executive, Vol. 38(1) 145–167 (January/February 1996) © 1996 John Wiley & Sons, Inc.

FIGURE 1

Components of a total global strategy

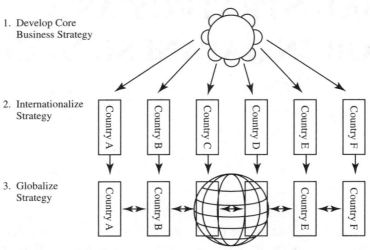

1. Develop Core
   Business Strategy

2. Internationalize
   Strategy

3. Globalize
   Strategy

strategies may be developed in multiple "home" bases (Rugman and D'Cruz, 1993; Rugman and Verbeke, 1993). Next, companies typically internationalize the core strategy by adapting it as they enter different foreign markets. (Even a core strategy developed in a number of base countries needs to be adapted when expanding to the rest of the world.) This approach follows the accepted wisdom in international business of adaptation for local markets. But Western MNCs have increasingly found a drawback with this approach: the internationalization process gradually pulls the core strategy in many directions until the business winds up with a fragmented multilocal strategy that fails to achieve any global scale or synergy benefits. A core strategy that has been developed in a number of markets is even more susceptible to such fragmentation.

This problem has become increasingly acute with falling trade barriers and the global convergence, in many industries, of customer needs and tastes. Philips developed one of the most fragmented international strategies. For example, in the television receiver business, Philips found itself by the early 1970s with dozens of factories around the world, some within short distances of each other on either side of disappearing frontiers,

producing dozens of product variants adapted for local markets. But then came Japanese competitors with high-quality globally standardized products manufactured in centralized factories that enjoyed high levels of scale economies. Not surprisingly, the Japanese challengers were able to defeat Philips in country after country (Aguilar and Yoshino, 1987). This pattern was repeated in other product categories. So over the last decade, Philips has been striving, at great cost, to achieve global integration in the third stage of total global strategy—globalizing the strategy.

While Philips overlocalized, many other Western MNCs stuck too much to the domestic core formula and failed to adapt sufficiently for local markets, a typical failing of American companies overfocused on the huge U.S. market. Even sophisticated marketers like Procter & Gamble have repeatedly stumbled in efforts to penetrate foreign markets because of a lack of adaptation, as evidenced by their mistakes in laundry detergent and disposable diapers in Japan. In contrast, Japanese companies have generally made more use of the third stage of a globalized strategy. This greater use may partly arise from Japan's relative lateness in entering international markets. First, most Japanese companies have not had as much time in the internationalization stage to build up country-by-country businesses. Second, Japanese international expansion has occurred in a period of lower barriers and differences and faster communication between countries. So, by necessity and circumstance, Japanese companies have tended to spend little time or effort in the second, internationalization stage of global expansion, and much more time in the third, globalization stage. As late entrants into international competition, Japanese companies had to focus and get it right. Furthermore, just as Japan turned its disadvantages of scarce resources and limited space into an advantage by creating efficient, space-saving products (from automobiles to the Sony Walkman), Japanese companies turned their international latecomer disadvantage into an advantage.

Industry Drivers of Global Strategy

Global strategy yields competitive advantage in industries where globalization forces minimize intercountry barriers to strategic activities (Porter, 1986). Four groups of industry globalization drivers—market, cost, government, and competitiveness—represent the industry conditions that determine the potential and need for competing with a global strategy (Yip, Loewe, and Yoshino, 1988). Japanese successes have tended to come in the very industries that have high potential for global strategy (as well as other characteristics, particularly skilled-labor intensity, that favor Japan's national strengths). For example, the automobile, computer and office equipment, consumer electronics, and steel industries have many characteristics favoring global integration: common customer needs, low culture embeddedness, global customers, high economies of scale, low transportation cost, and high product development cost.

In contrast, Japanese companies have not succeeded internationally in industries with very strong needs for the local adaptation of products and marketing strategy, in particular, the very large sector of consumer packaged goods that ranges from household cleaners to personal care to food. Potential for global strategy is necessary, but not

sufficient, for an industry to have favored Japanese success. Other characteristics, particularly the intense use of skilled labor and complex manufacturing processes, matching Japan's national strengths, also need to apply. In the absence of these other characteristics, the Japanese have yet to overcome their latecomer disadvantages in other industries with high potential for global strategy. Both the chemical and pharmaceutical industries have many aspects favoring global strategy (including common customer needs and high economies of scale in production for chemicals and in R&D for pharmaceuticals), but they also pose significant barriers to latecomers (in-place production capacity in the chemical industry and patent protection in the pharmaceutical industry). Indeed, as of 1993, Western companies held a 25 percent share of Japan's domestic market for pharmaceuticals, and 45 percent if licensed products are included, while Japanese companies still hold negligible shares of overseas markets in this industry.

Also, there is likely to be a very different pattern of globalization drivers facing Japanese and American companies. This is easiest to see in terms of government drivers. Japanese and American companies come from very different home countries in terms of trade barriers, and also face different trade barriers in major market areas such as the European community. Cost drivers are also likely to differ perceptually, because the home country costs will differ. Market drivers may not be so different, but looking at the world from Japan rather than the United States may change the subjective reality. In particular, the relatively wide global diffusion of many aspects of American culture, contrasted with almost no diffusion to date of Japanese culture, may make customer tastes seem more globally homogenous to American eyes than to Japanese ones. Similarly, the same may hold for perceptions of the transferability and viability of global marketing (e.g., global brand names and global advertising). Competitive drivers may seem different, because Japanese companies are much more focused on their compatriots. There is the oft-mentioned tendency of the Japanese companies to pattern their strategies on their Japanese competitors (e.g.,

Kotler, Fahey, and Jatusripitak, 1985). This means not necessarily a direct imitation, but rather that they pay close attention to the strategies employed by competition, and develop strategies that partly depend on the competitors' actual and anticipated moves. Sony and Matsushita's rivalry is well-known, as is that among the four major automobile manufacturers. American companies, by contrast, tend to differentiate themselves more from competition, striving for a competitive advantage that makes them unique in the eyes of their customers (e.g., Ghemawat, 1991).

Japanese Use of Globalized Strategy

Globalization strategy involves the use of five major substrategies—global market participation, global products and services, global location of activities, global marketing, and global competitive moves—as well as appropriately supportive organization and management approaches. Use of global strategy can achieve one or more of four major categories of potential globalization benefits: cost reductions, improved quality of products and programs, enhanced customer preference, and increased competitive leverage (Yip, 1989). This section will elaborate how Japanese companies have used global strategy and what benefits they have gained. These benefits are summarized in Exhibit 1.

Global Market Participation. In a multilocal participation strategy, countries are selected on the basis of their stand-alone potential in terms of revenues and profits. In a global market participation strategy, countries need to be selected in terms of their potential contribution to globalization benefits. This may mean entering a market that is unattractive in its own right, but has global strategic

---

EXHIBIT 1   Summary of Japanese Benefits from Use of Global Strategy

Global Market Participation
Careful sequencing of market entry increased success rate by gaining experience before taking on tough competitors.
Focus on globally strategic markets increased global competitive leverage.
Denial of Japanese market to foreign rivals prevented them from gaining equivalent benefits.

Global Products
Focus on small number of global products provided economies of scale in development and manufacture, and increased investments available for each product.
Global products provided way of avoiding proliferation needed to match Western rivals.

Global Location of Activities
Concentration of manufacturing at home and in satellite countries reduced costs by avoiding duplication and by maximizing economies of scale.
Local buildup of strong downstream activities, such as distribution, selling, and service, increased competitive strength in national markets.

Global Marketing
Concentration on globally uniform corporate brand names built worldwide customer awareness and provided umbrella for launching multiple products.
Localization of selling and distribution efforts reduced disadvantages of distance and unfamiliarity.

Global Competitive Moves
Playing of global rather than country-by-country chess game gave more options in attack and defense.
Willingness to cross-subsidize among country businesses magnified competitive leverage.
Advance planning of country moves minimized competitive resistance.

significance, such as the home market of a global competitor. Or it may mean concentrating resources on building share in a limited number of key markets rather than more widespread coverage. A pattern of a major share in major markets is advocated in Ohmae's (1985) concept of the United States–Europe–Japan "triad." In contrast, under a multilocal strategy, no particular pattern of participation is required—the pattern accrues from the pursuit of local advantage. The same considerations also apply to determining the level at which to participate, primarily the target market share, and to determining the nature of participation—building a plant, setting up a joint venture, and so on. Managers may, of course, often make market selection decisions from a mixture of motives, and many multinational companies have grown that way. The key is to recognize that there is a difference in the two motivations and in their potential consequences.

To have a global level of market participation requires significant global market share, a reasonable balance between the business's geographic spread and the market's spread, and presence in globally strategic country markets. Perhaps the most important difference between market participation for the sake of internationalization and that for the sake of globalization is the role of globally strategic countries. Such countries are important beyond their stand-alone attractiveness. There are several ways in which a country can be globally strategic as a market:

- Large source of revenues or profits;
- Home market of global customers;
- Home market of global competitors;
- Significant market of global competitors; and
- Major source of industry innovation.

The relative lateness in foreign entry of Japanese companies has encouraged them to bypass strategically irrelevant countries and focus on strategically important ones, except when these other countries are stepping stones in a planned sequence of moves.

Heineken's first international markets. The internationalization history of Heineken, the Dutch brewer, provides a classic example of choices made on the basis of stand-alone attractiveness. Heineken's first international markets were Egypt, Ceylon, Singapore, Indonesia, the West Indies, and the Congo. What did these six countries have in common? Heineken chose the first five countries because they were either former Dutch colonies or on shipping routes to them. These factors made these markets very attractive to Heineken, even though each country had little effect on Heineken's global position. The last country on the list, the Congo, came about because a Belgian brewer that also had business in the Congo had been sold to a Belgian bank, who then asked Heineken to take care of the company. Most other multinational companies can tell a similar story of one-by-one decisions based on country-by-country stand-alone attractiveness and happenstance. As the world's most global beer company (in terms of international revenues), Heineken now recognizes the global strategic importance of major markets like North America. The company has a major target of building up its business in the United States and Canada, which in 1990 accounted for less than 10 percent of sales.

Japanese companies' expansion paths. In contrast to Heineken's experience, the internationalization of Japanese companies provides many examples of a global strategy approach to market selection. They have used global market participation by selecting markets for entry on the basis of global strategic importance as well as stand-alone attractiveness, and have invested accordingly. According to Kotler et al. (1985), there have been three typical paths of expansion, each exhibiting a clear global plan. The most common has been to move from Japan to developing countries to developed countries. This occurred in steel, automobiles, petrochemicals, consumer electronics, home appliances, watches, and cameras. In this path, the Japanese companies built up experience and capacity in the smaller and easier developing countries. Typically, the United States was then the first developed country to be penetrated, because of its large size, its relative closeness to Japan, and the lower level of tariff, cultural, and language barriers than in Europe. The second expansion path—going straight to developed countries, particularly the United States—occurred in high-technology industries such as computers and semiconductors. In this expansion mode, the Japanese also sometimes used countries similar to the United States as trial markets. Fujitsu used Australia this way in computers. A third expansion path was to start directly with developed countries. This happened with products where the Japanese home market was still not developed or too small— videotape recorders, color televisions, and sewing machines.

James (1984) provides a similar story in the automobile industry. In Europe, Japanese automobile manufacturers entered Finland and Switzerland in the early 1960s. Neither of these countries had a domestic automobile industry to protect. So the Japanese faced little governmental or consumer resistance based on trade conflicts. Once experience was gained in these two countries, the Japanese entered Scandinavia, the United Kingdom, and the Benelux countries in the late 1960s. Last, the competitively toughest markets of West Germany and France were entered only in the 1970s, after the Japanese had built a solid base of demand and experience in the other markets.

On the other hand, Pascale (1984) and others have argued that Japanese companies do not plan their strategies very much, but rely instead on quick and strong response to opportunities as they emerge. But whatever the source of opportunities, planned or accidental, it is notable that Japanese companies have generally chosen to respond to opportunities in a fashion that results in a strategically optimal sequence of market entry.

Global Products. In a multilocal product strategy, the products and services offered in each country are tailored to local needs. In a global product strategy, the ideal is a standardized core product that requires a minimum of local adaptation. Cost reduction is usually the most important

benefit of product standardization. Levitt (1983) has made the most extreme case for product standardization. Others stress the need for a broad product portfolio, with many product varieties in order to share technologies and distribution channels (Hamel and Prahalad, 1985), or stress the need for flexibility (Kogut, 1985). In practice, some multinationals have pursued global product standardization to a greater or lesser extent some of the time (Walters, 1986).

Globally standardized products or global products are, perhaps, the one feature most commonly identified with global strategy. But the idea of a fully standardized global product that is identical all over the world is a near myth that has caused great confusion. Such products are very rare and hard to attain. Standardization occurs, of course, along a continuum. The benefits of global products (or services) can be achieved by standardizing the core product or large parts of it, while customizing peripheral or other parts of the product. For example, most of Sony's consumer electronic products are primarily standardized except for the parts that meet national electrical standards. Indeed, Japanese companies have often been masters at getting customers around the world to accept their globally standardized products (e.g., Honda cars, Canon photocopiers, Panasonic VCRs).

Japanese companies' relative lateness to international markets has probably required them to make greater use of global product standardization, rather than developing large numbers of national products. The passenger automobile industry provides an excellent example of the wide range of global standardization, both between companies and between model lines within a company. The industry also highlights American–Japanese differences in globalization. At one end, Honda, for example, sells products that are highly standardized globally. At the other end, General Motors has had little in common between its North American and European product offerings, although that is now changing. The Japanese focus and concentration on a relatively small number of products is one of the reasons for the Japanese success in automobiles. Toyota markets a far smaller number of models around the world than does General Motors, even allowing for its unit sales being half that of General Motors. Toyota has concentrated on improving its few models while General Motors has fragmented its development funds. For example, the Toyota Camry is the U.S. version of a basic worldwide model, and is the successor to a long line of development efforts. The Camry is consistently rated as the best in the class of medium-sized cars. Conventional wisdom in international business would argue that General Motors was adapting to foreign markets. The argument here is that GM and Ford overadapted locally, to the detriment of their global business systems. Ford has now recognized this error. In 1993, the company finally launched a genuine world car, the Mondeo, and in 1994 merged its previously separate North American and European divisions to help integrate its global strategy. In contrast, Ford's previous attempt in 1981 at a world car produced the Escort, that, because of rivalries between the North American and European divisions, ended up as two very different models, sharing nothing more than one part—a tiny water pump seal.

Faster new product development methods coupled with flexible manufacturing have also allowed manufacturers to develop and produce many more models than before, making it more possible to customize for local markets while enjoying global scale economies. So, for example, Toyota, which used to field fewer passenger-car models than its American rivals, now offers more models than Ford (59 versus 44). But Toyota developed and makes these 59 models from just 22 basic designs. So the company still benefits from focus on a relatively small number of core products. Improvement in design and development methods, particularly in the use of overlapping rather than consecutive stages of development, has allowed Toyota and other Japanese manufacturers to drastically shorten the time from drawing board to market (Stalk and Hout, 1990). Flexible manufacturing, including the use of just-in-time inven-

tory management, has then allowed Toyota to efficiently produce the large number of models put out by the development process. In summary, Toyota now seems to be able to benefit from both the global benefits of product and production focus and the local benefits of product proliferation.

Some Japanese companies have been particularly successful at getting countries to accept their standardized version of the product. This was a case of necessity because, when they first entered international markets, Japanese companies simply could not afford to offer different models to each country, or even a broad product line within the same country. Where they succeeded was in identifying those core product features that customers truly wanted, then providing that basic product at a price low enough and at a quality high enough that customers would give up the frills. American manufacturers' position of being able to afford many versions of a product turned out to be an Achilles' heel. This was particularly the case in automobiles, where domestic manufacturers were wedded to the multioption approach, most of which options were superficial to the basic function of an automobile. Furthermore, American automobile manufacturers made no attempt until very recently to market globally common products around the world. They had trained the U.S. consumer to want a product that was very different from what the rest of the world could afford.

One statistical study supports the argument that companies benefit from using globally standardized products. Kotabe and Omura (1989) found that the market share and profit performance of 71 European and Japanese firms serving the U.S. market was *negatively* related to the extent to which products were adapted for the U.S. market, i.e., businesses with global products performed better.

Ironically, the Japanese automotive companies strayed in the late 1980s from their earlier strategy of focus on a small number of products and options. Nissan proliferated options on Japan-only models, such as the Nissan Laurel, escalating to 87 different steering wheel sizes, colors, and other variations. Toyota offered at one time 84 versions of its Camry Vista in Japan. In post-bubble reconstruction, these companies have drastically pruned back such proliferation *(Business Week,* 1992).

Global Activity Location. In a multilocal strategy, all or most of the value chain is reproduced in every country. In another type of international strategy, exporting, most of the value chain is kept in one country. In a global strategy, the value chain is broken up and each activity may be conducted in a different country. The major benefits lie in cost reduction. One type of value chain strategy is partial concentration and partial duplication. The key feature of a global position on this strategy dimension is the systematic placement of the value chain around the globe.

Traditionally, MNCs have faced two choices in activity location. On the one hand they can duplicate an activity in multiple foreign locations. The classic multinational strategy has been to reproduce activities in many countries, particularly the production function by setting up factories and other manufacturing assets. On the other hand, MNCs can keep activities concentrated in the home country. The classic export-based strategy has been to locate as much of the value chain as possible back home, while locating overseas only downstream activities, such as selling, distribution, and service, that have to be performed close to the end customer. But a global strategy for activity location involves a third approach: locating each individual activity in the one (or a few) countries most appropriate for that activity. So a business pursuing a global activity strategy might locate research in the United Kingdom, development in Germany, raw material processing in Mexico, subassembly in the United States, final assembly in Ireland, and so on. Japanese companies have often managed the global location of their value chains to maximize economic leverage, typically starting in Japan, then gradually shifting production to other Asian countries and now to Europe and the United States. Again, their lateness, plus their initial export-based strategy, has led Japanese companies to build globally integrated value chains. Al-though American companies have attempted the same kind of strategy, they have been hindered in having a high-cost country as the home base.

A global approach to the location of activities requires both some geographic dispersion and some central coordination of the activity network. On the one hand, Japanese companies mostly have a less-extensive global manufacturing network, given their export-based strategy. Only in the last decade or so have Japanese companies begun to make significant foreign direct investment (Burton and Saelens, 1987; Yoshida, 1987). In contrast, many major American MNCs have been securely established overseas in manufacturing at least since World War II. On the other hand, Japanese companies usually have a tighter coordination of their worldwide activities, following their well-known tendency for central control. It is only recently that Japanese MNCs have started to give more autonomy to overseas subsidiaries (Sugiura, 1986, 1990; Seto, 1989; Turner, 1989).

Global Marketing. In a global marketing strategy, a uniform marketing approach is applied around the world, although not all elements of the marketing mix need be identical. Every element of the marketing mix—product design, product and brand positioning, brand name, packaging, pricing, advertising strategy, advertising execution, promotion, and distribution—is a candidate for globalization. As with other global strategy levers, the use of global marketing can be flexible. A business can make some elements of the marketing mix more global and others less so. Within each element, some parts can be globally uniform and others not. For example, a global pack design may have a common logo and illustration in all countries, but a different back-ground color in some countries. So both marketing as a whole and each individual marketing element can be global to a greater or lesser extent in its *content.*

For a number of reasons, Japanese companies have made less use than American companies of some elements of globally uniform marketing. First, their cultural uniqueness has made them less confident that they can devise globally acceptable marketing approaches. So they placed greater reliance on local experts to develop marketing campaigns. Paradoxically, Japanese companies have probably benefitted from the great differences between Japanese and Western cultures: Japanese executives easily recognized that they had to learn local cultures and adapt to them in marketing efforts. In contrast, the ubiquity and popularity of American culture (e.g., movies, music, food, and clothing) has probably deluded many American companies into making insufficient adaptation for local tastes. Second, Japanese companies have usually placed great stress on getting very close to local markets, particularly in terms of developing distribution relationships with local partners (Kotler et al., 1985). Third, their drive for market share has typically led to aggressive marketing tactics, such as low prices, rapid product line extensions, and high expenditures on advertising, promotion, and dealer incentives (Furstenberg, 1974; Suzuki, 1980; Doyle, Saunders, and Wong, 1986). Such aggressiveness has resulted in greater local tailoring of marketing efforts.

But their lateness to international markets has made Japanese companies more globally uniform in strategically the most important marketing element—branding. Japanese companies have a great deal invested in building global brand names. Initially uneuphonic to western ears, brands like Sony and Hitachi have become globally recognized symbols of quality. These global brand names have provided a platform on which to build their worldwide competitive strategies. It is notable that Japanese companies achieved four of the top 13 positions in a recent survey to identify global brands. A 1990 study found only 19 truly global brands in the sense of high worldwide awareness and esteem (Landor Associates, 1990). The ranking of these brands was as follows: (1) Coca-Cola, (2) *Sony,* (3) Mercedes–Benz, (4) Kodak, (5) Disney, (6) Nestlé, (7) *Toyota,* (8) McDonald's, (9) IBM, (10) Pepsi-Cola, (11) Rolls–Royce, (12) *Honda,* (13) *Panasonic,* (14) Levi's, (15) Kleenex, (16) Ford, (17) Volkswagen, (18) Kellogg's, and

(19) Porsche. This Japanese achievement should be viewed in the context of the much shorter time period in which they have marketed internationally—about 30 years as opposed to 60 years or more for the American and European brands.

Perhaps the biggest mistake in failing to use a global brand name comes, interestingly, from a Japanese company, Nissan. When Nissan first exported its automobiles it used the name Datsun. After many years of establishing the name in the United States and elsewhere outside Japan, Nissan dropped the Datsun name in the early 1980s and went to the company name. The goal of the worldwide name change, as stated by the Nissan Management Council, was to create a unified international image for the company. Before the change, Nissan had been the largest Japanese automobile importer into the United States. It now lags both Toyota and Honda in share of the U.S. market. In 1981, Nissan was the world's fourth-largest manufacturer, with a 7.3 percent worldwide share. By 1986, it had fallen to fifth, with a 5.7 percent share, and continues at that rank. While a string of relatively weak Nissan products bears the brunt of the blame, the name change must also have played a major role in the decline. It is no coincidence that Nissan is not on the list of truly global brands.

Toyota has moved to using globally standardized advertising. In the launch of their new Camry model in 1993, the company used a television commercial that was identical around the world (from the United States to the Middle East, Hong Kong, Poland, and many other countries), save for the voiceover. Not surprisingly, this commercial was created by one of the advocates of global advertising, the Saatchi & Saatchi agency.

Global Competitive Moves.   In a multilocal competitive strategy, an MNC fights its competitors one country at a time in separate contests, even though it may face other MNCs in many of the same countries. In a global competitive strategy, competitive moves are integrated across countries. The same type of move is made in different countries at the same time or in some systematic sequence, or a competitor is attacked in one country in order to drain its resources for another country, or a competitive attack in one country is countered in a different country. Perhaps the best example is the counterattack in a competitor's home market as a parry to an attack on one's own home market.

Globally integrated competitive moves require both strong global coordination and the ability to take a longer-term view, because of the need for some country subsidiaries to sacrifice their interests for the benefit of other sister subsidiaries or of the company as a whole. Given the collective responsibility typical in Japanese management, Japanese companies have been particularly able to execute global competitive moves that involve coordination and cross-subsidization. Kotler et al. (1985) described how Japanese companies typically take a coordinated approach in sequencing the markets that they enter. Smothers (1990) has described the Japanese ability to combine sequences of strategic moves. Another critical aspect of being able to make globally integrated competitive moves is to have a good understanding of competitors. Montgomery (1991) provides some examples of how Japanese companies go to great lengths to study and assess their competitors. He cites the example of Matsushita having tens of people focusing on competitor analysis in the United States alone, and of Komatsu keeping a representative in Peoria, Illinois, whose assignment is to notify headquarters in Osaka of events at Caterpillar. The camera and VCR industries also provide case histories of differing American and Japanese approaches to global competitive moves.

Kodak's mistakes and recovery in Japan. In the 1980s, Eastman Kodak lost its share in the U.S. and European markets for photographic film that it had long dominated. These losses resulted from a fierce global onslaught by a newly internationalized competitor, Japan's Fuji Photo Film. Kodak's response, which included drastic attempts to cut costs and prices, cost it dearly in margins and profitability. Kodak had seemed impregnable with a strong basis for competitive advantage—its high quality, worldwide name recognition and distribution system—and had also globalized this strategy successfully. Kodak had widespread global market participation, a globally standardized product line, an efficient and concentrated activity chain, and memorable global marketing, including its highly distinctive and recognizable global packaging. But Kodak's global strategy had a number of potentially serious flaws. First, although its global market participation was widespread, it had neglected a globally strategic country. This country, Japan, was globally strategic as the home of a strong potential global competitor, and as the market for some of the world's most demanding customers. In this omission, Kodak was making the same mistake that many other Western companies had done, avoiding Japan as unattractive on a stand-alone basis, while not seeing its global strategic importance. So Kodak made little investment in Japan and relied on a Japanese trading company to act as its local distributor. As part of this neglect, Kodak did not adapt its core strategy sufficiently to meet Japanese needs, such as printing Japanese on its packaging (not until 1984) or offering the right kind of products. Ignoring the Japanese market allowed Fuji to grow little challenged until it was powerful enough to take on Kodak outside Japan.

By the early 1980s, Fuji held 70 percent of a very large Japanese market, while Kodak held only a few percentage points. Then Kodak made a second mistake in terms of globally integrated competitive moves. Kodak defended against Fuji's challenge in the same countries in which it was attacked. With its larger sales base, any price cuts and special promotions that Kodak made wound up hurting itself more than Fuji. Eventually, around 1984, Kodak realized that it needed to use the fifth global strategy element, the counterparry as part of globally integrated competitive moves, in conjunction with the first global strategy element, increasing market participation in Japan. Kodak decided to counterattack its rival's home market. Kodak invested an estimated $500 million to revamp its distribution system (taking control by setting up a joint venture with its distributor), to take equity stakes in its suppliers, and to spend heavily on promotion. This counterstrategy worked, squeezing Fuji's domestic margins, forcing it to recall some of its best executives from abroad, and generally weakening its global competitive capabilities. By 1990, Kodak had multiplied its share of the Japanese amateur photographer market to 15 percent and had started to turn back a severe global challenge.

Sony and Matsushita's successes in VCRs. In the videocassette recorder industry, Japanese manufacturers like Sony and Matsushita combined rapid coverage of all key markets, offering the first global products, and an efficient production network based in the Far East, to secure adequate volume and a strong competitive position, including in the U.S. market. American competitors such as RCA, Zenith, or General Electric never had a chance to put up a fight, let alone take the battle to Japan. By the time these companies had set up their activity network with production and component purchasing in the Far East, the Japanese products were established and competing no longer on price, but on recognized quality (Henzler and Rall, 1986).

Empirical Evidence on Use of Global Strategy

The arguments of this study on the greater use of global strategy by Japanese companies are supported by data from a study comparing 36 worldwide businesses in major American and major Japanese MNCs. These businesses were all leading participants in a cross section of industries, including automotive, chemicals, computers, consumer electronics, consumer toiletries, electrical goods, food and beverages, industrial controls, and office equipment. Through personal interviews, data were collected for each business on the measures of industry globalization drivers and elements of global strategy discussed in this article. The methodology and sample have been detailed in Yip (1994) and Johansson and Yip (1994). Of particular relevance to this article (and reported here only) are the findings comparing the American and Japanese businesses on the overall use of global strategy and on a key organizational reason for the greater Japanese use of global strategy. Exhibit 2 describes the measures used.

EXHIBIT 2   Definition of Measures in Empirical Study

Industry Globalization Drivers[a]

Overall market drivers: overall strength of market factors favoring globalization in the industry category today
Overall cost drivers: overall strength of cost factors favoring globalization in the industry category today
Overall government drivers: overall strength of government factors favoring globalization in the industry category today
Overall competitive drivers: overall strength of competitive factors favoring globalization in the industry category today

Global Strategy[b]

Actual overall global strategy: how global the overall strategy is today
Optimal overall global strategy: how global the overall strategy should be today

Organization & Management

Global staff heads: yes/no measure on whether there is a single head with staff (coordination) responsibility for each function
     measured—research, purchasing, raw material processing, subassembly, final assembly, marketing, and selling

---

All items are on a five-point scale unless otherwise indicated.

[a] Questions were asked only after previous questions on the individual drivers in each category (e.g., common customer needs as an individual market globalization driver).

[b] These two questions were asked only after previous questions on the individual elements of global strategy: market participation, standardized products, activity location, marketing uniformity, and integrated competitive moves.

Regressions on Use of Global Strategy.

Exhibit 3 reports on multivariate regression analysis of actual overall global strategy and optimal overall global strategy on measures of four overall categories of globalization drivers (market, cost, government, and competitive) and on a dummy variable representing nationality (0 if American, 1 if Japanese). While this is only a simple analysis, the results confirm that when controlling for industry globalization drivers, the Japanese businesses do seem to make greater overall use of global strategy (regression 1): the dummy for Japan has a positive standardized coefficient of 0.65 that is significant at the 0.01 level. This coefficient value implies quite a large difference, compared with a mean of 3.35 for the dependent variable. Similarly, the same effect applies, although to a lesser extent, for how global the overall strategy should be now (regression 2), with a positive coefficient for the Japan dummy of 0.28, significant at the 0.10 level.

Comparison of Global Coordination.

A key way in which the Japanese businesses in this study achieved greater global integration came from their much greater use of global staff heads to coordinate their worldwide activities. As shown in Exhibit 4, a higher proportion of the Japanese businesses had global staff heads for every function than did the American businesses.

Caveat.

This study relies on self-reported data on a cross-national basis. Hence, biases may arise from both these aspects. Nevertheless, these data reinforce the arguments made in the body of this article, and should be viewed in this supporting role.

Links to Other Explanations of Japanese Success

The arguments above have referred to many of the distinctive aspects of Japan cited as sources of Japanese success in international business, and have linked these aspects to Japanese companies' ability to formulate and implement global strategy. This last section summarizes some of the key linkages between Japanese success factors and Japanese use of global strategy.

Centralized Management.

Many observers have noted the high degree to which Japanese companies maintain tight centralized control of their international operations. This central control has accompanied great success, thus posing a paradox to Western management theory that has increasingly found disfavor with the notion of centralization. The paradox can partly be resolved by considering that this centralization brought the benefits of globally integrated strategy. These benefits presumably more than offset the disadvantages of centralization (which are probably less

EXHIBIT 3   REGRESSIONS ON USE OF GLOBAL STRATEGY

	Global Strategy	
	Actual	*Optimal*
Intercept	0.33	1.23[b]
	(0.68)	(0.50)
Overall		
Market driver	0.63[c]	0.55[a]
	(0.12)	(0.09)
Cost drivers	0.04	0.06
	(0.10)	(0.07)
Government drivers	0.18	0.04
	(0.13)	(0.10)
Competitive drivers	−0.10	0.11
	(0.10)	(0.07)
Nationality (Japan)	0.65[c]	0.28[a]
	(0.25)	(0.15)
R^2	0.57	0.69
Adjusted R^2	0.50	0.64
F	8.06[c]	13.42[c]

$n = 36$. Values are coefficients with SE in parentheses.

[a] Significance at 0.10 level.

[b] Significance at 0.05 level.

[c] Significance at 0.01 level.

EXHIBIT 4   **USE OF GLOBAL STAFF HEADS**

	American Businesses (%)	Japanese Businesses (%)	Significance of Difference
Research	17	33	NS
Development	17	28	NS
Purchasing	11	39	0.05
Raw material processing	6	33	0.05
Subassembly/intermediate production	6	39	0.05
Final assembly/final production	6	39	0.05
Marketing	22	39	NS
Selling	11	28	NS
General management	8	56	0.01

NS, nonsignificant. n = 36.

anyway for the Japanese given their lesser cultural preference for individual autonomy).

Cooperative Managerial Culture.   Cooperation between managers in different countries is an essential requirement for the successful implementation of global strategy. The group-oriented Japanese managerial culture has greatly helped Japanese MNCs achieve the necessary global cooperation.

Focus on Competitors.   Global strategy requires a clear understanding of each major competitor's worldwide strengths and weaknesses, and the ability to collect and process competitive intelligence centrally. The relentless Japanese focus on competitors has helped them develop and execute successful sequences of global competitive moves.

Unfair Trade Practices.   The global market participation leg of global strategy requires companies to build a pattern of market participation that is stronger than that achievable by their rivals. Japan's successful shielding of its home market in many industries (e.g., automobiles and electronics) has greatly limited the ability of foreign companies to build a fully global market presence and

has also denied them participation in a globally strategic market.

Less Concern for Profit.   Last, the complex sequence of moves and investments needed to implement a global strategy often hurt short-term profitability. Japanese companies usually have, or at least report, significantly lower profitability on average than do American companies (e.g., Haar, 1989; Odagiri, 1990). This lesser concern of Japanese companies for short-term profitability has helped them significantly in all aspects of global strategy.

Conclusion

Japanese companies' use of global strategy is not by any means the sole explanation of their international success. But a global strategy perspective does provide an integrating theme for many explanations of Japanese prowess. Furthermore, this perspective reveals some specific mechanisms by which general Japanese traits have been converted into worldwide competitive advantage. Furthermore, in post-bubble reconstruction, Japanese companies may need to return to the strategies that helped them so well previously.

References

Abegglen, James C. and Stalk, George Jr. (1985) *The Japanese Corporation,* New York: Basic Books Inc.

Aguilar, Francis J. and Yoshino, Michael Y. (1987) "The Philips Group: 1987," Case No. 9-388-050, Harvard Business School, Boston.

Business Week (1992) "Overhaul in Japan," December 21, 80–86.

Burton, F. N. and Saelens, F. H. (1987) "Japanese Strategies for Serving Overseas Markets: The Case of Electronics," *Management International Review,* 27(4), 13–18.

Clark, Rodney (1979) *The Japanese Company,* New Haven, CT: Yale University Press.

Doyle, P., Saunders, J., and Wong, V. (1986) "Japanese Marketing Strategies in the UK: A Comparative Study," *Journal of International Business Studies,* 17, 27–46.

Furstenberg, F. (1974) *Why the Japanese Have Been So Successful in Business,* London: Leviathan House.

Ghemawat, Pankaj (1991) *Commitment: The Dynamic of Strategy,* Boston: Harvard Business School Press.

Haar, Jerry (1989) "A Comparative Analysis of the Profitability Performance of the Largest U.S., European and Japanese Multinational Enterprises," *Management International Review,* 29(3), 5–18.

Hamel, Gary and Prahalad, C. K. (1985) "Do You Really Have a Global Strategy?" *Harvard Business Review,* Vol. 63(4), 139–48.

Henzler, Herbert and Rall, Wilhelm (1986) "Facing Up to the Globalization Challenge," *The McKinsey Quarterly,* Winter, 52–68.

James, B. G. (1984) *Business Wargames,* New York: Viking Penguin.

Johansson, Johny K. and Yip, George S. (1994) "Exploiting Globalization Potential: U.S. and Japanese Strategies," *Strategic Management Journal,* 15, 579–601.

Kagono, Tadao, Nonaka, Ikujiro, Okumura, Akohiro, Sakakibara, Kiyonri, Komatsu, Yoichi, and Sakashita, Akinobu (1984) "Mechanistic vs. Organic Management Systems: A Comparative Study of Adaptive Patterns of Americans and Japanese Firms," in Kazuo Sato and Yasuko Hoshino (Eds.), *The Anatomy of Japanese Business,* New York: M. E. Sharpe, 27–69.

Kogut, Bruce (1985) "Designing Global Strategies: Profiting from Operational Flexibility," *Sloan Management Review,* Fall, 27–38.

Kono, Toyohiro (1984) *Strategy and Structure of the Japanese Enterprises,* New York: M. E. Sharpe.

Kotabe, Masaaki and Omura, Glenn S. (1989) "Sourcing Strategies of European and Japanese Multinationals: A Comparison," *Journal of International Business Studies,* 20, 113–30.

Kotler, Philip, Fahey, Liam, and Jatusripitak, S. (1985) *The New Competition,* Englewood Cliffs, NJ: Prentice-Hall, 1985.

Landor Associates (1990) "The World's Most Powerful Brands," San Francisco.

Levitt, Theodore (1983) "The Globalization of Markets," *Harvard Business Review,* 61(3), 92–102.

Montgomery, David B. (1991) "Understanding the Japanese as Customers, Competitors and Collaborators," *Japan and the World Economy,* 3, 61–91.

Odagiri, Hiroyuki (1990) "Unravelling the Mystery of Low Japanese Profit Rates," *Business Strategy Review* (London Business School), Spring, 25–36.

Ohmae, Kenichi (1985) *Triad Power: The Coming Shape of Global Competition,* New York: Free Press.

Ouchi, William G. (1981) *Theory Z: How American Business Can Meet the Japanese Challenge,* Reading, MA: Addison-Wesley.

Pascale, Richard Tanner (1984) "Perspectives on Strategy: The Real Story Behind Honda's Success," *California Management Review,* 16(3).

Pascale, Richard Tanner and Athos, Anthony G. (1981) *The Art of Japanese Management: Applications for American Executives,* New York, Simon & Schuster.

Picken, Stuart D. B. (1987) "Values and Value Related Strategies in Japanese Corporate Culture," *Journal of Business Ethics,* 6, 137–43.

Porter, Michael E. (1986) "Changing Patterns of International Competition," *California Management Review,* 28(2), 9–40.

Prestowitz, Clyde V. (1988) *Trading Places,* New York: Basic Books.

Rugman, Alan M. and D'Cruz, Joseph (1993) "How to Operationalize Porter's Diamond of International Competitiveness," *The International Executive,* 35, 283–99.

Rugman, Alan M. and Verbeke, Alain (1993) "Foreign

Subsidiaries and Multinational Strategic Management: An Extension and Correction of Porter's Single Diamond Framework," *Management International Review,* 33(2), 71–84.

Seto, Reiji (1989) "Patterns of Internationalisation of Japanese Firms: New Developments and Managerial Issues," *Management Japan,* 22(2), 14–19.

Smothers, Norman P. (1990) "Patterns of Japanese Strategy: Strategic Combinations of Strategies," *Strategic Management Journal,* 11, 521–33.

Stalk, George Jr. and Hout, Thomas M. (1990) *Competing Against Time,* New York: Free Press.

Sugiura, Hideo (1986) "Internationalisation and Localisation," *International Journal of Technology Management,* 1, 319–26.

Sugiura, Hideo (1990) "How Honda Localizes Its Global Strategy," *Sloan Management Review,* 32, 77–82.

Suzuki, N. (1980) "The Changing Pattern of Advertising Strategy by Japanese Business Firms in the U.S. Market: Content Analysis," *Journal of International Business Studies,* Winter, 63–72.

Turner, Ian D. (1989) "How Japanese Companies Approach Globalization," *Journal of General Management,* 14(4), 1–8.

Walters, Peter G. P. (1986) "International Marketing Policy: A Discussion of the Standardization Construct and Its Relevance for Corporate Policy," *Journal of International Business Studies,* Summer, 55–69.

Yip, George S. (1989) "Global Strategy . . . In a World of Nations?" *Sloan Management Review,* 31, 29–41.

Yip, George S. (1992) *Total Global Strategy: Managing for Worldwide Competitive Advantage,* Englewood Cliffs, NJ: Prentice-Hall; and *Japanese Edition* (1995), Tokyo: The Japan Times.

Yip, George S. (1994) "Industry Drivers of Global Strategy and Organization," *The International Executive,* 36, 529–56.

Yip, George S., Loewe, Pierre M., and Yoshino, Michael Y. (1988) "How To Take Your Company to the Global Market," *Columbia Journal of World Business,* Winter, 37–48.

Yoshida, Mamoru (1987) "Macro-Micro Analyses of Japanese Manufacturing Investments in the United States," *Management International Review,* 27(4), 19–31.

Yoshino, Michael Y. (1968) *Japan's Managerial System, Tradition and Innovation,* Cambridge, MA: MIT Press.

SUCCESS STRATEGIES FOR RUSSIAN-FOREIGN JOINT VENTURES

Carl F. Fey

There is no question that starting a joint venture in Russia is not for the faint of heart. International joint ventures, or IJVs, in Russia must deal with a weak infrastructure, an unstable environment, constantly changing legislation, corruption, and bureaucracy. However, with more than 148 million people, a well-educated labor supply, and excellent natural resources, Russia presents great opportunities for skillfully designed joint ventures. Investing in Russia can be a bargain, but it is becoming more expensive every day. Firms considering starting Russian-foreign joint ventures can substantially improve their chances of success learning from the experience of JVs already operating in Russia.

International joint ventures are not a new phenomenon in Russia. In the 1920s, foreign companies, including those from Western countries, were allowed to start joint ventures with the USSR as part of Lenin's New Economic Policy. However, in the early 1930s, Stalin ended most joint venture activity in Russia. Between 1930 and 1987, joint ventures were allowed only between Russia and Eastern European countries through the Council for Mutual Economic Assistance, or CMEA.

In January 1987, a new wave of joint venture activity began when the USSR Council of Ministers passed a decree, "The Establishment and Operation, on the Territory of the USSR, of Joint Ventures with Participation of Soviet Organizations and Firms from Capitalist and Developing Countries." This decree opened the door for all foreign firms to open joint ventures with Russia.

Foreign investors are now allowed to start wholly foreign-owned firms in Russia, and IJVs no longer receive preferential treatment over other forms of business. In most cases, however, IJVs still represent the optimal method of foreign direct investment in Russia. From the foreign partners' perspective, several key factors make a joint venture desirable:

• Russian partners can provide country-specific knowledge and valuable help in navigating through Russian bureaucracy.

• Joint ventures often receive lower prices for services than wholly owned foreign firms.

• The risk of starting to do business in Russia can be shared between two or more firms.

• Russian partners can often provide access to prime real estate.

From the Russian partners' perspective, IJVs help them to:

• Obtain needed starting capital;

With permission from *Business Horizons,* November–December 1995, pp. 49–54.

- Learn Western management practices;
- Develop leading-edge technology; and
- Gain assistance in marketing products in the West.

Russia is too important a market and has too many attractive resources to be ignored by foreign investors. In addition to its population of more than 148 million, it is the largest country in the world, occupying one-eighth of the world's land. It has an inexpensive and highly educated work force; the average Russian, in fact, has more education than the average American. Russia is also rich in natural resources. For example, the country is the world's largest producer of oil and second-largest steel producer.

Even with these resources, some investors worry. Since the Nationalists received 25 percent of the votes in the elections of 1994, many Western investors have expressed concern that Russia may turn away from capitalism. This vote, however, should not be interpreted as a vote against capitalism. Most Russians are quick to point out that it was, rather, simply a vote against the shock therapy method of transition to capitalism chosen by the Yeltsin government.

Again, it is important to keep in mind that operating an IJV in Russia poses many unique challenges. Therefore, it is necessary to try to understand thoroughly how Russian businesses work before being able to make useful recommendations to them. The optimal way to run a business in the West is not necessarily optimal in Russia. Unfortunately, far too many foreigners have forgotten this point in the past. The common Western opinion that all Russian management practices are inferior to Western management practices is simply wrong.

More than 10,000 IJVs have been registered in Russia since 1987, when they first became legal. Experts such as Rosten (1991), however, estimate that only about 20 percent of them have actually begun operation. Understandably, this figure, combined with some of the well-publicized difficulties of operating a business in Russia, causes concern

among foreign investors. Potential investors, though, can learn much from the experience of joint ventures already operating there.

This study aims to facilitate such learning by suggesting strategies for Russian-foreign JVs that will enable them to have a greater chance for success. Recommendations are based on interviews conducted in 1993 with general managers of 20 randomly selected Russian-foreign JVs, and on follow-up interviews in 1994. These were all large North American-Russian joint ventures that had to have been started by January 1, 1991, be located in Moscow or St. Petersburg, and employ at least 20 people. Interviews lasted between one and three hours, and averaged about 85 minutes. Eight additional joint ventures were also added to the study in 1994. Executives of one or both parent firms, as well as the general manager and sometimes other managers, were interviewed for each IJV. Between 5 and 35 hours of interviews were conducted for each joint venture.

Following Yin (1984), the case-study methodology was selected because of the exploratory nature of the study and to enable the richness of the situations to be captured. The longitudinal nature of the study offered more thorough understanding of the joint ventures by observing them over time.

What follows are 11 success strategies for Russian-foreign IJVs to heed if they are to have a greater chance at success. The first six strategies involve issues of design, and the last five revolve around partner relations.

1. Backward Integrate

One of the greatest difficulties in starting a joint venture in Russia is the lack of infrastructure. Obtaining needed input products is often very difficult—especially getting products on time, and of acceptable quality. As a result, many of the most successful Russian joint ventures have backward integrated to extremes.

Moscow McDonald's, a Russian-Canadian JV, is without question one of the most successful Russian-foreign joint ventures ever. Three restaurants are now operating in Moscow, with the Pushkin Square restaurant having the distinction of being the busiest McDonald's in the world. On a monthly basis, Moscow McDonald's serves 687,607 orders of french fries and 436,583 Big Mac sandwiches. It has served more than 73 million customers since it opened its first restaurant in January 1990. All three of the McDonald's restaurants in Moscow provide service that is the envy of most McDonald's organizations in other countries.

Kjamzat Khasbulatov, deputy general manager, credits much of this success to McDonald's recognition of the need to backward integrate in Russia because obtaining quality inputs on a timely basis is so difficult. As a result, McDonald's started a farm to raise cows for beef and grow potatoes for french fries. The corporation also invested $45 million to build McComplex, a state-of-the-art food processing plant located in the Solntsevo region of Moscow. The food processing plant provides most of the food products for Moscow McDonald's, with a meat production line, potato processing plant, garnish line, bakery, pie line, liquid products line, quality control laboratory, and distribution center. Khasbulatov explains that McDonald's normally does not deal with food processing because it considers its core business to be operating restaurants. The company realized, however, that to be successful in Russia, becoming involved in food processing was necessary.

2. Ensure a Good Horizontal Flow of Information

Traditionally, Russian companies have been very good with vertical information flow, yet the horizontal flow of information from one department to a parallel department without first going through a common manager has traditionally been difficult. Technopark is a Russian-Italian JV that has benefited from developing good horizontal information flow in its organization. The IJV helps Russians who have good high-tech ideas to develop them into viable businesses by providing office space,

financing, marketing assistance, and aid in planning the business, among other services. After about two years of assistance, the new corporations set off on their own. In return, Technopark receives a share of future profits.

In struggling to allow this IJV to have good horizontal information flow, Boris Antoniuk, the general manager of Technopark, reported that he spent much effort in making division heads break with Russian tradition and allow free communication between workers of different divisions. Some of the division heads viewed such changes as giving up some of the control over their division, and they remained strongly against the idea. Antoniuk finally had no choice but to replace them if Technopark was going to obtain the horizontal flow of information it needed to be successful.

An IJV must explicitly empower and encourage its workers to communicate so that they may learn specific solutions to problems from their colleagues in other departments. Empowering workers to have good horizontal communication is also essential for effective cross-department teams, which discuss companywide problems and matters common to each department. Cross-department teams are often used in the West, and are recommended for Russian-foreign IJVs as well.

3. Implement a Profit-Sharing Program

Implementing a profit-sharing program with IJV workers is an advantageous move. In addition to their base salary, workers would receive a portion of the firm's overall profit, thus giving them a greater incentive to help the firm be successful. The Russian-American restaurant JV Tren-Mos has benefited from this strategy.

Tren-Mos owns and operates two trendy restaurants and a bar featuring traditional American cuisine such as steak and apple pie. Jeff Zeiger, the company's general manager, credits the excellent service customers receive at Tren-Mos as one of the keys to its success. One of the ways Zeiger has encouraged his employees to provide such excellent service is by instituting a profit-sharing program with them. This gives them a real incentive to ensure that the customers are satisfied. Zeiger has made sure all employees are fully aware that satisfying customers means *more* customers and, hence, more profit for the joint venture—which, of course, means more money for all workers because of the profit-sharing program. The Russian-foreign joint ventures with profit-sharing systems were among the most successful in the study. Given the proper training and incentives, Russians—like most employees anywhere—can be excellent workers who produce quality products and provide quality service.

4. Take Advantage of Inflation

Although inflation is a great evil on the demand side of the economy, it can provide significant opportunities on the supply side. In environments with high inflation, significant gains can often be made by purchasing products when their price is low and either reselling them or using them later when the price has risen.

Perestroika is a real estate joint venture that has enjoyed great success because of wisely realizing what high inflation and other changes in Russia would mean for the real estate market. Earl Worsham, an Atlanta real-estate developer, and Andrei Stroyev, president of Mosinzhstroi, the Moscow City Council's construction company, started Perestroika in 1988 with $60,000 from Worsham's firm, "The Worsham Group." This money was used to purchase computers, which were then sold at a healthy margin to generate 1.2 million rubles in starting capital. Five years later, Perestroika owned and operated more than nine office buildings in Moscow, which it was able to acquire and renovate without incurring any debt. This was accomplished primarily by obtaining advance payment of a year's rent by future tenants. Perestroika's assets today are valued at well over $100 million.

5. Develop a Clear Strategic Business Plan

Developing a strategic business plan for the IJV is of critical importance to its success. The feasibility study required of all IJVs by the Ministry of Finance is not an acceptable substitute. The goals of the IJV and the means for implementing them need to be clearly outlined in the strategic plan. Boris Antoniuk, general manager of Technopark, the IJV that helps people with good scientific ideas go into business, believes that one of the main reasons his JV has been so successful in Russia's unstable environment is that its managers put a great deal of energy into strategic contingency planning.

Strategic planning is even more important in Russia than in most countries because Russia's environment is changing so radically. Nevertheless, very few Russian IJVs do much, if any, strategic planning. The reason normally given for this is that IJV general managers claim they have no time to plan strategically because they are using all of their time simply to keep the venture alive. But this study demonstrates that strategic planning itself can actually help IJVs stay alive; in an environment as unpredictable as Russia's, in fact, IJVs are likely to fail without it.

Contingency planning is a particularly important part of a strategic business plan for any Russian-foreign IJV because of this unpredictable environment. One especially important type of contingency planning that needs to be considered is alternative sourcing of input materials; the availability of all materials is sporadic in Russia.

6. Provide Quality Service

Russian firms are beginning to realize the importance of producing a quality product. However, most of them, including Russian-foreign JVs, have a long way to go in understanding the importance of quality *service*. For example, many foreign businesspeople are surprised that business moves so slowly in Russia. It is very common to leave a telephone message for someone and not have the call returned for three or four days—if at all. In the West, this situation would simply be unacceptable. Further, much time and effort are required to obtain information.

Additionally, if customers experience a problem with a product just purchased, they must often solve the problem themselves. Doing business in such a way may have worked for an IJV initially because most likely it was the only firm that sold that particular product or provided that particular service. However, as more IJVs enter the Russian market, providing good service will be essential in attracting and maintaining customers. As Vladimir Elokhin of V.A. Instruments, a joint venture that produces elemental analysis equipment in St. Petersburg, says, "Our IJV is successful primarily because we provide the best service in the industry for our customers."

7. Develop Trust

In this first strategy of dealing with partner relations, it is extremely important that a high level of trust be developed between all parents and the IJV itself. The firm Dialogue offers an excellent example of a JV that has been very successful in part because of the high degree of trust that has been developed between the partners. Dialogue was started in 1987 by Joe Ritchie, a highly successful commodities trader from Chicago. The joint venture is run by a husband-and-wife team—Tatyana and Pytor Zrelova. Tatyana Zrelova, deputy general director of Dialogue, recalls her surprise when she and her husband met with Joe Ritchie so that he could read and sign all of the foundation documents they had prepared for the joint venture. Ritchie asked the Zrelovas if they had written the documents themselves. The Zrelovas said yes, and Ritchie signed the documents without reading them. Ritchie later explained to the Zrelovas that he believed if a partner really wanted to cheat him, no document would save him. That is probably true, but from Zrelova's point of view, the most

important result of this initial unilateral display of trust on the part of Ritchie was that it set the tone for their relationship. Such trust has been reciprocated time and time again by both the Zrelovas and Ritchie.

8. Spend Time Selecting a Partner

Choosing a partner is the most important decision a company will ever make regarding an IJV. If the wrong partner is chosen, the venture is simply doomed to fail. For example, choosing a JV partner merely because it is the first one the firm can find generally spells failure. Also, IJVs that select a partner that is only needed initially often don't make it in the long run once that partner is no longer needed. It is very important that all partners in the IJV are truly necessary and that they will continue to be needed in the future. Of course, it is also very important that firms select partners they can trust, and that they clearly understand each other's goals for the IJV and determine whether both sets of goals are mutually obtainable.

In the interviews conducted for this study, the most common cause of IJV failure was a basic misunderstanding about the roles or goals of the partners. In most cases, these differences existed from the very beginning, but the companies were not aware of them because they did not spend enough time initially learning about each other's goals and ideas. In-depth discussions during the formation stage could have alerted them to most of these differences so that they might have been resolved early. Or it could have been determined that the differences could not be resolved and thus concluded that the firms should search for other partners. Of course, everyone is eager to finalize the negotiation phase and get on with the work of the joint venture. Nevertheless, data show that spending extra time in the negotiation phase to understand the other partner more thoroughly is a wise investment.

Some joint ventures experienced trouble because of disagreements over the role of the foreign parent. The Russians, for instance, thought the foreign firm was supposed to find customers for the IJV, which did not happen. In a similar disagreement, common in several IJVs, the Russian partner wanted to conduct some research and development, but the foreign firm was interested in the venture only as a sales representative. A clear understanding of the partner's views on such issues should be determined while selecting the appropriate partners.

9. Develop Good and Regular Communication Among All Parties

Reliable and frequent communication between the different partners is essential for maintaining valuable input and guidance. The use of electronic mail, in addition to the more conventional methods of communication (fax, phone, telex, express mail, visit), is very useful for Russian-foreign IJVs. Fax transmission quality is far from desirable when normal Russian telephone lines are used, and usually results in wasted time and unnecessary expense and delays. As a result, many IJVs find that purchasing a special international fax line from an international phone carrier is well worth the initial expense because it eases communication greatly. When workers' time and efficiency are included in cost calculations, having an international fax line generally results in decreased costs.

DAR is a successful U.S.–Russian joint venture that provides consulting and marketing assistance primarily for foreign firms in Russia. It has an impressive list of clients that include Westinghouse, Bell Helicopter, and Motorola. Alexander Kulakov, the young, hard-working managing director, feels that regular communication with DAR's American and Russian parents has been extremely helpful. He says, "Without the help of our parents there would be no DAR." Kulakov urges other people starting a joint venture to use their parents' resources and maintain good communication with them.

10. Have Both Russian and Foreign Personnel Work in the IJV

An IJV has a greater chance of success if some foreign personnel are permanently stationed there. As an example, Polaroid started a joint venture with Russian parents that has grown beyond anyone's wildest expectations to create one of the corporation's major markets. This limited liability partnership, Svetozor Ltd. (Svetozor is roughly translated as "shining light"), distributes Polaroid products in Russia as well as produces a number of electronic components for Polaroid products sold around the world. Having both Russian and American personnel working at Svetozor has helped immeasurably in its success.

Foreign personnel perform a number of functions. They can teach Russian managers about Western management styles and often provide additional technical expertise. It is essential, however, that foreign managers realize there are large differences between the optimal way to run a Russian-foreign IJV and the traditional method by which most Western firms are operated. These differences exist because Russian workers are used to a centrally planned management system that differs radically from those used in the West. In addition, Russia has special environmental problems not present in other countries. As a result, by observing Russian managers, foreign personnel can also learn the optimal means for managing a joint venture in Russia.

Thus, an added benefit of having foreign personnel permanently on site at an IJV is that in learning about Russian management practices, they will likely discover that the common notion of the inferiority of Russian methods to Western ones is simply incorrect. The expatriate employees can then explain these differences to the foreign parent, enabling the parent to develop a better understanding of Russia and hence a better opportunity to make the joint venture work.

11. Decide Whether to Reinvest or Repatriate Before Starting the Joint Venture

The question of whether to reinvest or repatriate IJV profits is often the cause of heated discussion between the partners. Russian partners prefer to reinvest money in IJV because this will hopefully facilitate future profit. Meanwhile, they are content to be compensated in the short term with managerial salaries that are high by Russian standards, but still quite modest by Western standards. The foreign partner, on the other hand, often favors repatriating profits because that is the only way it can see any financial benefits from the IJV. Such a conflict is one of the main reasons George Ermolenko, general manager of the Moscow-based joint venture TISSA-R, gives for the failure of that IJV.

How the partners will decide exactly what to do with profits must be determined during the initial negotiation. Deciding on an acceptable ratio of payout to reinvestment during the formation phase is one way of solving this problem and can be more than helpful in preventing later disagreements.

Starting a Russian-foreign joint venture defi-nitely entails risk. Russia, however, presents attractive opportunities for foreign companies experienced in conducting international business to form skillfully designed joint ventures. Further, foreign investors can greatly increase their chances of success by learning from the experience of joint ventures already operating in Russia. Such learning can be facilitated by following the success strategies presented in this article to increase an IJV's chance of success.

References

"Commercial Overview of Russia," information sheet, BISNIS, Washington, DC, 1994.

Kari Liuhto, "A Comparison of Foreign Nepmen and Contemporary Joint Ventures in Russia" working paper, Turku School of Economics and Business Administration, Turku, Finland, 1994.

Tatyana Popova, "Joint Ventures on the Map of Russia," *Business and Investment in the CIS,* No. 7 1993, p. 1.

Keith Rosten, "Soviet–U.S. Joint Ventures: Pioneers on a New Frontier," *California Management Review,* Winter 1991, pp. 88–106.

Robert Yin, *Case Study Research* (Beverly Hills, CA: Sage Publications, 1984).

WHY JOINT VENTURES FAIL

Kathryn Rudie Harrigan

Joint ventures are in fashion again, and many firms throughout the world are rushing to find partners. Even skeptical managers are being swept up by the contagious belief that joint ventures and other forms of corporate marriage will solve their firms' problems with a handshake and the stroke of a pen. Managers hope that by teaming up with partners that offer strengths that their own firms lack, the result will be a stronger competitive posture in the markets they hope to serve.

Strategic alliances are, in fact, as difficult to sustain and nurture as marriages. The difficulties of making joint ventures succeed cause many managers to throw up their hands in despair. Yet the benefits provided by joint ventures and other forms of cooperative strategy frequently make them well worth the extra effort of learning how to

Reprinted from the *Euro-Asia Business Review,* July 1987. Used with permission from the Euro-Asia Centre, Boulevard de Constance, 77309 Fontainebleau Cedex, France. This article is based on materials contained in K. R. Harrigan, *Strategies for Joint Ventures.* Lexington, MA: Lexington Books, 1985, and K. R. Harrigan, *Managing for Joint Venture Success.* Lexington, MA: Lexington Books, 1986. Permission to use this material is gratefully acknowledged. Research support from the Strategy Research Center, Columbia University, and suggestions from its Chairman, William H. Newman, are also gratefully acknowledged.

cope with the complexities of shared ownership and shared decision-making.

Joint Ventures Defined

"Joint ventures" are owned by two or more sponsoring firms that share resources and skills to create new entities. Examples include International Himont (Montedison and Hercules), NUMMI (General Motors and Toyota), and General Numeric (Siemens and Fujitsu). In such ventures, owners contribute resources, personnel, technology, and market access; they share in the returns from their venture's operations through equity ownership; and share decision-making responsibility for their venture's day-to-day operations as well. (Note that minority investments involve shared equity, but they do not have the shared decision-making feature of strategic alliances— whether such alliances involve equity ownership of the venture or not—that are the focus of this article.)

Firms also cooperate through non-equity ventures, including cooperative agreements, research and development partnerships, cross-production, cross-licensing and cross-marketing agreements, and joint bidding activities. Although they may not create a separate organizational entity, many of the problems I have seen that prevent managers from effectively exploiting the advantages of strategic alliances apply to non-equity forms of venture as well as to joint ventures.

Joint ventures have been a commonplace way of doing business for decades in industries like offshore oil and gas exploration, petrochemicals, mining, metals processing, and electronic components. Cooperative strategies have often been required in strategic industries (like aerospace) or as the price of admission into some countries' markets.

Now joint ventures (and other forms of strategic alliance) have become popular as a strategy option in a wide variety of troubled industries, such as communications services, pharmaceuticals and medical products, steel, precision controls and robotics, financial services, entertainment programming, and programming packaging, among others, where cooperation has less of a track record.

The Cooperative Strategy Option.   More firms are embracing strategic alliances in their home markets now because the requirements for successful competition have become more demanding. As Exhibit 1 suggests, domestic joint ventures are becoming more widespread now due to: (1) economic deregulation, (2) increasingly rapid rates of technological change (hence shorter product lives), (3) larger capital requirements (to undertake risky new projects and develop new processes), (4) entry by new firms (that are supported by their respective governments), (5) industry and economic maturation in the United States, Europe, and Japan, (6) improved communications and computational power, and (7) globalization in industries where competition was previously constrained by geographic boundaries.

Joint ventures will become particularly important in markets where industry boundaries are blurring between formerly disparate activities. For example, when the capabilities of information processing and data transmission technologies link old activities in new ways and products are redefined to encompass a wider scope of activity, firms may seek partners to supplement the skills they lack in-house, especially if they fear being left behind as a promising marketplace develops.

Joint Venture Dynamics.   Terms of the formal (and informal) agreements creating joint ventures may change over time, as Exhibit 2 indicates, due to (1) changes in the venture's industry (and success requirements therein) and the effectiveness of the venture's strategy for serving its industry, (2) changes in the sponsoring firm's needs for joint activity with its current partner under the agreement's current terms, and (3) changes in the pattern of autonomous activity or close owner-venture coordination needed for the venture's competitive success. Although the terms of a joint venture agreement are modified (or the venture is terminated) when the arrangement has fulfilled its purpose, many such ventures are ended before completing their task due to problems among sponsoring firms, managerial problems within the venture itself, or problems in the relationship between owners and their ventures.

My insights concerning why strategic alliances never fulfilled their promise were obtained from interviews in the United States with a variety of experienced managers. (See Appendix 1 for details of the study.)

Managers suggested that joint ventures are most likely to fail because:

1. The market for the venture's product disappears,
2. What is thought to be good technology from one partner (or whatever the contribution is to be) does not prove to be as good as is expected,
3. Partners cannot get along,
4. Partners simply renege on promises to deliver on their part of the agreement,
5. Venture managers from disparate partners cannot work together,
6. Managers within the venture cannot work with managers within sponsoring firms,
7. Owners that are to contribute information or resources to their venture cannot get their personnel down the line to deliver what has been promised, or
8. Other reasons destroy partners' cooperative spirits.

EXHIBIT 1   Motivations for Joint Venture Formation

A. Internal Uses
1. Cost and risk sharing (uncertainty reduction).
2. Obtain resources where there is no market.
3. Obtain financing to supplement firm's debt capacity.
4. Share output of large minimum efficient scale plants.
   a. Avoid wasteful duplication of facilities.
   b. Utilize by-products, processes.
   c. Shared brands, distribution channels, wide product lines, and so forth.
5. Intelligence: obtain window on new technologies and customers.
   a. Superior information exchange.
   b. Technological personnel interactions.
6. Innovative managerial practices.
   a. Superior management systems.
   b. Improved communications among strategic business units.
7. Retain entrepreneurial employees.

B. Competitive Uses (Strengthen Current Strategic Positions)
1. Influence industry structure's evolution.
   a. Pioneer development of new industries.
   b. Reduce competitive volatility.
   c. Rationalize mature industries.
2. Preempt competitors ("first-mover" advantages).
   a. Gain rapid access to better customers.
   b. Capacity expansion or vertical integration.
   c. Acquisition of advantageous terms, resources.
   d. Coalition with best partners.
3. Defensive response to blurring industry boundaries and globalization.
   a. Ease political tensions (overcome trade barriers).
   b. Gain access to global networks.
4. Creation of more effective competitors.
   a. Hybrid's possessing owners' strengths.
   b. Fewer, more efficient firms.
   c. Buffer dissimilar partners.

C. Strategic Use (Augment Strategic Position)
1. Creation and exploration of synergies.
2. Technology (or other skills) transfer.
   a. Toehold entry into new markets, products, or skills.
   b. Rationalization (or divestiture) or investment.
   c. Leverage-related owners' skills for new uses.

These same managers also offered some hope for the future use of strategic alliances because many of them believed that there is an experience curve in using joint ventures in the sense that as managers better understand what works, they are more eager to replicate their successes and they become more skillful at doing so.

Joint Ventures and Competitive Success Requirements

Competitive stakes increased in the 1980s as many firms tried to assimilate information-processing, telecommunications and other competitive skills. Because no firm could develop the many technolo-

---

EXHIBIT 2   Joint Venture Change Forces

The stability of a joint venture agreement (and timing of changes in its terms) depends upon:

1. Changes in the venture's industry (and success requirements therein).
2. Effectiveness of joint venture's competitive strategy.
3. Changes in partners' relative bargaining power vis-à-vis each other.
4. Changes in owners' strategic missions.
5. Changes in importance of the joint venture to owners.
6. Changes in venture's need for autonomous activities.
7. Changes in patterns of owner–venture coordination needed for competitive success.

---

gies they needed in-house or afford to fund all of the projects needed to remain competitive on several fronts, they looked to joint ventures as a means to cope with their industries' changing success requirements.

Many firms in the 26 industries I examined did obtain easier access to expertise and to distribution outlets through joint ventures, and results suggest that few firms could have moved as quickly in securing market share if they had to develop the assets enjoyed by their joint ventures on their own. By pooling facilities, firms are able to keep their costs low until their internally generated sales volumes reach the critical mass that justifies having their own plant, equipment, sales force, and other facilities.

But results also suggest that there are limits to the widespread efficacy of joint ventures, and firms must adjust their cooperative strategies to the special problems of particular competitive environments. In particular, learning to work together in joint ventures can slow down the speed with which firms move into promising markets or respond to competitors' manoeuvres. Cumbersome agreements can be deadly in volatile competitive environments because some market opportunities evaporate within months if they are not exploited quickly. High technology products, in particular, often need rapid market penetration in order to place them into distribution channels and into consumers' hands before products become obsolete or can be copied by others.

Embryonic Industries.   In embryonic industries, for example, where great uncertainty looms concerning which marketing approaches will prove most successful or which technological standards customers will embrace, successful firms form more liaisons—each of shorter duration—than in better-established industries. Astute managers adopt less binding partnership terms in order to avoid entanglements that might prove to be wrong later. Moreover, experienced firms do not work through ventures exclusively with any particular partner for long in environments of high uncertainty.

Some managers have even concluded that ventures in embryonic industries should not be bound by arrangements involving shared equity. Instead, their firms create non-equity entities on a project-by-project basis in highly changeable environments. They do so because when partners' interest change, their joint ventures must end in a non-disruptive fashion as firms move on to their next dancing partners. To facilitate easy transitions, agreements are formed for only a few months at a time, and proceed on a handshake rather than a voluminous legal document.

Shorter Product Lives.   It becomes especially important to have access to international market linkages within industries where technology (or product design) changes rapidly, yet must be compatible with devices in operation throughout the globe. Firms find it increasingly expensive to reach key markets within global industries quickly when the half-life of a technology is very short because firms can scarcely recoup their development costs by going it alone.

This expense explains, in part, why so many joint ventures, cross-marketing contracts, cooperative agreements, and minority investments were made in the pharmaceutical industry in the early 1980s; firms sought products to enter new therapeutic categories and market access to reach more customers with existing products before their source of competitive advantage had expired.

Stable Industry Environments.   Joint ventures are more likely to result when partners join forces in the early stages of industry maturity, when technology changes less rapidly and when product standards have at last been established. As demand uncertainty lessens, concerning the nature of customer tastes, price sensitivities, product features, and other market traits, and as firms become more concerned with how to forge effective strategies to satisfy demand, they begin to seek the talents of accomplished partners and form joint ventures of greater scope and longevity.

Much of the criticism that is leveled against joint venture strategies fails to recognize that different cooperative strategies—of differing durations and involving different types of progeny—are best used in industries of different ages and infrastructure stability. Where there is still great uncertainty concerning the efficacy of technologies, customers' tastes and other structural traits that can affect profit-making opportunities within an industry, effective managers keep their firms' joint activities informal and brief. When their industries mature, as more competitors enter and technological standards are better accepted, managers forge fewer joint ventures per firm, and each venture encompasses a larger-sized investment or broader market scope, as in the petrochemical, communications equipment, and home video entertainment industries. Thus, managers are more likely to be disappointed in their ventures if they try to make them overly formal or inflexible too early in an industry's development.

Solving Technological Problems.   Although few firms engage in partnerships in basic R&D or other areas that are highly sensitive to their strategic postures, ventures to exploit knowledge in new applications or markets thrive in mature economies.

Technological prowess is the key to attaining competitive advantage when technologies (1) change frequently, (2) are highly risky, and (3) require extremely high creativity in design or precision in manufacturing. Joint ventures permit firms to hedge their bets concerning competing standards and keep abreast of other innovations while sharing in development costs.

Cooperation is a fundamental structural trait of many high technology industries, yet licenses and informal agreements are more commonplace than shared-equity joint ventures. Difficulties in managing owner-venture relationships and, in particular, transferring knowledge and skills, explain part of the shortfall in joint venture activity in high-technology industries. Their inability to collaborate effectively with partners' personnel also explains, in part, why joint ventures seldom realize their promise in solving technological problems.

A Spider's Web of Ventures.   Success within industries requires firms to forge many, parallel ventures in a pattern like a spider's web (with themselves at the hub). When firms must move quickly to exploit a transitory advantage, partners are needed that offer attractive solutions for particular customer problems. Few stand-alone ventures result from these marriages, and like the musical chairs pairing of the electronic components industry, no firm is expected to solve all problems alone.

A willingness to dance with several partners allows firms to move faster in responding to charges in market demands than exclusive arrangements of longer durations. Part of their flexibility in using a spider's web of agreements arises from the informality of these alliances. (A caution: this very practice comes back to haunt firms that engage in spider's webs of ventures without telling their existing Japanese partners, since it is interpreted as a loss of confidence in the existing partner's abilities.)

Loose alliances—personal service contracts, OEM vendor agreements, or other arm's length arrangements—are preferred by managers when dealing with highly dissimilar partners, entrepreneurs, and other situations where managers feel uncomfortable about forming joint ventures. Examples where this approach is preferred include creative people who want an equity participation but do not want a salary nor to be part of a corporate monolith. Results suggest that the national origins of partners matter less to venture success than whether partners are of similar asset size and venturing experience. Most importantly, successful partnerships agree on the venture's priorities—they share similar values—regardless of their national origins.

Managing Partnerships

Good partners should be prized because managers will return to them with increasing frequency to create new ventures in the future. Yet despite their apparent worth, opportunities to create advantageous joint ventures are often missed because (1) managers are unwilling to pay deference to differences in corporate cultures, and (2) firms will not be open with potential partners during the negotiating process.

If managers cannot discuss cooperation in an open and flexible way, the strain that an inarticulate and narrow negotiating team places on any venture that results can reduce severely the joint venture's chances of realizing its full promise. Although the venture's management team may overcome this false start and find a way to work together, sponsoring firms will always be uneasy if they started their relationship awkwardly and cannot provide adequately for their true expectations concerning the venture when they negotiate its terms.

Negotiating an Agreement.   Individuals with hidden agendas make joint ventures fail. It is more important for potential partners to talk through

everything of importance to them—even if it means that the ultimate agreement is very different from the original venture concept—than it is to become bogged down in financial details. If care is taken in finding good partners and letting the proposed arrangement work its way through both firms' organizations, the deal can eventually be done with great enthusiasm on both sides.

Experience pays.   The results of my U.S.-based research indicate that successful and experienced venture sponsors prefer to work with equally experienced partners. Their objective in choosing a joint venture partner is to find one that complements their firm's strengths. The more experienced the partner, the more realistic his expectations about joint ventures, and the more willing he is for a little give and take to occur in hammering out a satisfactory joint venture compromise.

Move cautiously.   Unsatisfied managers suggested, in retrospect, that poor matches are made when negotiating teams devote too much attention to questions of who will control the venture's technology and what the financial arrangements will be, while too little attention is devoted to questions of how partners' relationships will be managed. This is not to suggest that attention should not be directed also to details concerning financial arrangements, technology, transfer, or other issues concerning sponsoring firms' assets. But rather, it cautions managers not to confine their negotiating teams to lawyers who will not have bottom line responsibility for making the venture work.

Build on success.   Managers who take a cautious approach—a little project, then another one if the first experience is a good one—are more satisfied with the use of joint ventures than those who move too fast or not carefully enough in forming alliances. The incremental approach to negotiations enables managers to keep adding to the complexity or breadth of things that they trust a partner to do on the basis of previous experience. The incremental approach also keeps their expectations for a particular partner lower and enables managers to be more analytical in assessing why a particular venture did not work out.

Assessing Partners. The promised advantages of cooperation are not always realized, though this is rarely acknowledged. If stock prices enjoy speculative gains when joint ventures are announced (especially those concerning technology transfers), valuation errors are never admitted to outsiders later. If there are start-up problems or partners' contributions are not as promised, these realities are often masked by the apparent delight of investors that small firms are betting their technological positions (by allying with big firms) or that big firms that were doing nothing impressive in a particular line of research have found a promising way to catch up.

Do your homework. Therefore, it is necessary for managers to be well-informed on the value of technologies before discussing joint ventures because it is easy to become perplexed in discussions of risky and unproven technological approaches. The most successful technological joint ventures are formed by firms that have each done considerable R&D work on the problem prior to their collaboration. With such preparations, managers know whether a joint venture is technically appropriate and commercially viable.

Test potential partners. If managers are uneasy with their counterparts, they can learn more about potential partners in many ways. Cautious managers favor a step-by-step relationship when forming a joint venture with new partners. They suggest giving potential partners a proposal and some issues to study. If the firm's managers return for negotiations with suggestions and can articulate their firm's concerns on the critical points of the venture, a small project is warranted. If that cooperation works out, another joint venture is formed.

Build consensus. The managers of one successful firm with several joint ventures to its credit take a very deliberate approach toward the formation of their firm's joint ventures. They identify the

need for a partnership. They search methodically throughout the globe for the best possible partners, by interviewing the customers they hope their joint venture will serve, by interviewing research institutes and any other experts with knowledge concerning where the technologies they seek might be obtained.

Managers develop a list of potential partners and screen them. They approach several partners simultaneously to discuss the venture and judge which candidate will be the best partner for the venture in question. Managers insist on a long engagement period where executives and operating managers on both sides move slowly to consensus on how to operate their venture. When the marriage is finally consummated, the venture receives everything needed to run as a stand-alone entity. Subsequent interventions by sponsoring firms in their venture's operating decisions are minimal because the resulting management team closely reflects the values of its owners.

Partner disharmony. Partners must understand their venture's activities and trust its management team well enough to avoid becoming a source of irritation to the joint venture relationship. Schisms occurred frequently in partnerships where managers from sponsoring firms doubted (or did not like) what they were told but did not understand the venture well enough to alleviate their doubts. Although it is difficult to avoid friction between owners and overly enthusiastic venture managers, care is needed in negotiating the venture to ensure that partners obtain adequate information to evaluate its performance.

Managing Jointly Owned Ventures

Managers within sponsoring firms sometimes believe erroneously that they can set up joint ventures and let them run themselves. They overlook the importance of their choices concerning which managers to place in charge of the venture's operations, how to evaluate the venture's performance, and how to transfer knowledge between owner and venture. The venture's management team must possess both diplomatic skills and entrepreneurial aggressiveness in order to balance the need to represent each owner's viewpoint fairly to its partners against the need to make the venture an economic success. Results suggest that if managers want the venture to succeed badly enough, they find a way to work together—regardless of their origins.

Joint Venture Management Style. Joint ventures can fail if the wrong executives are chosen to lead them. Sponsoring firms cannot tap their managers' entrepreneurial tendencies if joint ventures become personnel dumping grounds or if supervising managers drive out risk-taking zeal through their control system demands. In one disastrous venture, high-performing managers were removed from joint venture assignments soon after the first honeymoon was over. In this company, burnt-out, low potential, or politically embarrassing managers were sent to joint ventures, and the venture's requests for assistance were treated accordingly. Rather than make joint ventures a convenient parking place for senior executives awaiting retirement, firms can make them a reward for enterprising managers, if they want the venture to succeed.

Joint venture managers must be skilled in diplomacy in order to capture the support of the managers within sponsoring firms, but they should also be detached from loyalties to any particular owner in decision-making. To combat the problem of split loyalties in their venture's managers, some firms close the "revolving door" back to their organizations and hire outsiders—with loyalties to no owner—to lead the venture and staff critical jobs. Managers representing each owner are still placed in the venture to coordinate the venture's activities with those of its owners, but they need not have line responsibility.

The Changeling. Sponsoring firms must be prepared for their venture's success. That means funding must be provided to exploit opportunities that may develop for the joint venture, and if own-

ers cannot provide the cash needed for new opportunities, their venture must approach the capital markets in its own right to obtain funding. Withholding the means for success will sap the venture managers' spirits. Moreover, managers within sponsoring firms must recognize that the interests of the venture may diverge from their own.

In many cases, the venture is an underdog. Its rag-tag managers receive little respect because they are the "black sheep" of their respective firms. The pressures venture managers feel from their respective owners often drive them together in their efforts to make the venture succeed, especially if there is no possibility of returning to their previous corporate positions. Venture managers will become champions for their organization and will expect the venture to be rewarded for its successes like any other business unit. If the venture's team becomes so successful at working together that the venture outperforms wholly owned units and competes for their resources, managerial jealousies within sponsoring firms may result and these animosities must be diffused.

Managing Owner-Venture Relationships

The preceding section has raised the problems created by overly zealous venture managers who want more autonomy than managers within sponsoring firms are willing to sanction. Boisterous managers are less of a problem if they can be given control over the resources needed for their competitive success and allowed to operate autonomously. Problems arise, however, in managing owner-venture relationships effectively when close coordination between them is needed. Industry differences can suggest how quickly ventures should evolve from loose cooperation to partnerships to stand-alone entities (if at all). Some relationships retrogress, as in the example of Xerox pulling Rank-Xerox more closely under its control as competition intensified and profit margins thinned, while others allowed the venture more autonomy over time.

Joint ventures offer a unique management problem due to their shared-ownership nature: decision-making is cumbersome within a joint venture. This problem becomes especially germane when sponsoring firms hope to create synergies through their joint ventures because resource-sharing requires close coordination in order to be successful. Yet managers within sponsoring firms often become frustrated when negotiations with other owners are needed to change output allocations, for example.

Managers often take out their frustrations with the joint venture form of cooperation on the venture's management team. Unfortunately, their resentment can draw the venture closer when its managers need greater autonomy to compete effectively, or their anger may cut off the venture's managers when greater coordination between owner and venture is needed. If the linkages owners employ to monitor and influence their venture's activities are inappropriate, they can destroy the opportunities to realize synergies or transfer knowledge for which the venture was created.

Creating Synergies.

If synergies are to be created through joint ventures, they will accrue from vertical relationships or from sharing resources. But these relationships may require managers to evaluate joint venture performance differently than they would evaluate that of wholly owned, stand-alone business units. For example, a joint venture need not have any downstream facilities, provided it is not penalized for its failure to sell outputs that are not consumed by its owners.

If owners rely too heavily on the products, services, and innovations supplied by their joint venture, they cut themselves off from a way of evaluating whether their venture is obsolete. If joint ventures are restricted from dealing with outsiders—by right-of-first-refusal arrangements or outright prohibition—they may become overly reliant on their owners when they should instead be providing them with intelligence about competitive conditions. An appropriate balance must be found.

Sharing Knowledge.

One of the side benefits of working together in joint ventures is the cross-pollination process whereby ideas are shared among research, manufacturing, or marketing personnel and transferred to owners' organizations. Some firms consciously try to encourage technological bleedthrough. Bleedthrough is knowledge (not covered by formal agreements) that is gained by working with partners on joint ventures. Successful sponsors of joint ventures develop a system for managing relationships between owner and venture to ensure that knowledge of work methods, managerial practices, and technology is returned to them and readily accepted by their in-house research organizations. Some sponsoring firms run parallel research experiments in their wholly owned laboratories or move scientists and the other technical people through the joint venture and back to their wholly owned laboratories to disseminate information.

Other firms ensure that the knowledge gained through exposure to partners in joint ventures is diffused back to owner laboratories through meticulous programs of repatriation. At the group level, for example, firms hold annual technical meetings where engineering managers and leading R&D scientists gather divisional engineering and R&D personnel for an interchange of information and ideas.

At the corporate level, top technical officers coordinate the use of technology developed in-house in joint ventures with other divisions or with outsiders, as well as technology that is received from others—through licenses or joint ventures—that might be useful in some other part of the company. Some firms use an integrated sales force and marketing organization that sells products from all divisions, regardless of their ownership status.

Evaluating Joint Ventures

Joint venture termination need not suggest that a venture has failed. Even well-informed and well-managed joint ventures must end some day because the necessity that once spurred a venture's creation will not exist forever in evolving competitive markets. Moreover, the tensions of shared decision-making encourage one partner to buy out the others. Finally, human resource development policies that rotate managers to differing assignments can accelerate a joint venture's demise if the sponsoring firms' management teams change so dramatically that the new personnel can no longer recall the logic that once stimulated the venture's creation. Consequently, these managers are more likely to terminate joint ventures that they do not understand rather than nurture them.

From the examples and discussion above, it is evident that joint ventures go awry because they are far more complex to manage than many firms have recognized. They can go awry when partners forget their purpose, when owners become inflexible concerning how they use their ventures, when venture managers forget their role in sponsoring firms' strategies, or when other factors upset their delicate balance. Joint ventures have a high mortality rate and do not last long in most industries. But their short life cycles do not suggest that joint ventures cannot be effective in attaining their objectives.

The outlook and skills needed to master joint ventures are still alien to most managers, and many executives deny their firms' needs for cooperative strategies because they do not believe that the benefits of joint ventures justify the efforts needed to run them effectively. But the success rate for joint venture in mature economies is improving as more firms apply creative solutions to their old ideas concerning what joint ventures can do, how long ventures must last, who must be in charge, and what each partner should bring to the party.

A balanced assessment of the value of cooperative strategies should suggest that these skills are well worth learning, particularly if joint ventures will become increasingly important as a means of keeping abreast of competition. Joint ventures are a way to manage transitions; they are an intermediate step on the way to something else. Joint ventures should always offer greater opportunities for profitability because there are greater scale economies, integration economies, and other cost savings from pooled resources that can reduce the total cost of doing business. From a wealth-creating owner's perspective, the well-managed joint venture should always offer an opportunity to improve upon what firms can do alone.

Joint ventures (and other forms of cooperation) are an important change in the way that firms do business. They require a different approach to management by virtue of their complexity. If managed skillfully, joint ventures can offer sponsoring firms wider range of strategic flexibility than they can hope to develop by going it alone.

Appendix I

Research Methodology for Studying Joint Ventures

Target firms were selected from announcements of joint ventures and non-equity cooperative agreements contained in *Mergers & Acquisitions* and from a special compilation of joint ventures contained in the *Funk & Scott Index of Corporate Change*. Questionnaires requesting details of these announcements were mailed to 2,094 sponsoring firms, yielding 884 usable responses, of which 492 (or 55 percent) concerned joint ventures.

Information concerning competitive conditions at the time of the joint venture's announcement (and thereafter) was gathered from archival sources that included annual reports, other financial disclosure documents, trade journals and trade association publications, and government documents.

Background papers were prepared for 26 industries, and experienced executives within them were interviewed. Information concerning joint venture formation, operation, and termination was refined through 444 field interviews and telephone conversations. Results were corroborated through additional interviews, follow-up letters, and revisions to the background papers and interview transcripts. Data were gathered for statistical analyses from 197 of the 492 respondents with experience in using joint ventures.

IV INTERNATIONAL AND GLOBAL MARKETING OPERATIONS

PRODUCTS AND SERVICES

In *Product Development the Japanese Way,* the authors note that the Japanese utilize an incrementalist view of product development that emphasizes continuous technology-rooted improvements in order to make successful products even better for customers. Japanese firms use the marketplace as an R&D laboratory to gain insights from customers about how to enhance products and services on an ongoing basis.

For the United States, the growth of international sales of services will continue to outpace the growth in merchandise sales well into the next century. Currently, tourism, transportation, and financial services are important. The huge new opportunities for American firms in the global marketplace will be in franchising, health care, and information systems engineering and consulting. The second article in this section regards developing global strategies for such service businesses.

National and international standards are a key issue for the development and marketing of products and services. The third article in the section addresses the dynamic changes occurring because of European Union integration. Quality standards have been and are being adopted for some 400 million consumers in the European Union. This includes a new, mutual recognition of safety and performance testing across the member countries. Threats for companies from countries outside the Union are standards written to favor European firms. Alternatively, huge economies of scale can be appreciated by all, even American firms, competing in the new, *integrating* European market.

The article on marketing of satellites internationally addresses an aspect of industrial marketing which has heretofore been neglected in the literature. It covers the commercial, political, economic, and counter-trade characteristics of the international outreach of American technology.

PRODUCT DEVELOPMENT THE JAPANESE WAY

Michael R. Czinkota and Masaaki Kotabe

The decade of the 1980s saw a great surge in the global market success of Japan. Increasingly, there has been talk about the beginning of the Japanese century and the emergence of an overpowering Japanese economy.

Policymakers have responded to these visions by expressing concern about the trade competitiveness of the United States and taking actions designed to break down real or perceived trade barriers. Competitiveness, however, is driven and maintained to a large degree by individual firms and their marketing efforts. A quick review of the successes and inroads achieved by Japanese products confirms this perspective.

Japanese firms have been successful in established industries in which U.S. firms were once thought invincible, as well as in newly developing industries. They have been able not only to capture third-country market share from the U.S. competition but also to obtain major footholds in the U.S. domestic market. They supplied almost 20 percent of U.S. imports in 1989 and achieved their surplus in trade in manufactured goods on the basis of both high-technology and nonhigh-technology products.

Reprinted from *The Journal of Business Strategy* (November–December 1990). Permission granted by Faulkner & Gray, 11 Penn Plaza, New York, NY 10001.

As a result, U.S. producers' domestic market share for color televisions has dropped from 90 percent in 1970 to less than 10 percent today, and the domestic share of semiconductor production has declined from 89 percent to 60 percent. Even more startling are the developments in the newly emerging high-definition television (HDTV) technology, which harbors the promise of a new electronic age. Several Japanese electronics giants have developed HDTV technology commercially. U.S. producers, which previously balked at the idea of such technology because they did not see a ready market for it, are now seeking shelter behind standard-setting rules by the U.S. Government.

In spite of the expenditure of vast funds on research and development (R&D), a number of U.S. products do not seem to be able to perform sufficiently well in the marketplace. Yankee ingenuity once referred to the ability of U.S. firms to successfully imitate and improve on foreign technology.

For example, the British discovered and developed penicillin, but it was a small U.S. company, Pfizer, that improved on the fermentation process and became the world's foremost manufacturer of penicillin. The Germans developed the first jet engine, but it was two American companies, Boeing and Douglas, that improved on the technology and eventually dominated the jet airplane market.

177

Yankee ingenuity seems to have vanished and reemerged in the form of Japanese marketing techniques, which appear to see what many others do not recognize and often are right on target in identifying market needs. Perhaps it is time that U.S. firms rediscover their former talents in order to compete with renewed vigor in the global market.

Incrementalism versus the Giant Leap

Technology researchers argue that the natural sequence of industrial developments comprises imitation (manufacturing process learning), followed by more innovations. In other words, continual improvements in manufacturing processes enable a firm not only to maintain product innovation-based competitiveness but also to improve its innovative abilities in the future. Failed innovators, in turn, lack the continual improvement of their products subject to a market-oriented focus.

During the postwar period, Japanese firms relied heavily on licensed U.S. and European technology for product development. Product quality was improved through heavy investment in manufacturing processes with the goal of garnering differential advantage over foreign competitors. Continued major investment in R&D earmarked for product innovation heralded the technological maturation within Japanese firms, where the quality and productivity levels began to match or even surpass those of the original licensor.

U.S.-style product innovation has placed major emphasis on pure research, which would allegedly result in "giant leap" product innovations as the source of competitive advantage. By comparison, incremental improvements in products and marketing processes were neglected and relegated to applied research. As Peter Drucker has argued, however, research success may very well require the end of the nineteenth-century demarcation between pure and applied research. Increasingly, a minor change in machining may require pure research into the structure of matter, while creating a

totally new product may involve only careful reevaluation of a problem so that already well-known concepts can be applied to its solution.

By contrast, the Japanese incrementalist view of product development emphasizes continual technological improvement aimed at making an already successful product even better for customers. Take the case of Japanese very-large-scale integration (VLSI) technology. The origin of VLSI technology was the transistor. Recognizing consumers' unsatisfied need to tune in their favorite music anywhere at any time, Sony introduced small portable transistor radios in 1955. Other Japanese companies quickly followed suit. There was quick market acceptance of the product worldwide.

Mass production made it possible to lower the cost and improve the quality of the product. In a short time, Japan reached a technological level at par with, and soon surpassing, that of the United States in transistor technology. As the age of integrated circuits (ICs) began, compact electronic calculators using this emerging technology boosted the growth of Japan's IC industry. The IC evolved into the large-scale integration (LSI) and now into VLSI.

These emerging technologies are used in consumer products, including personal computers, Japanese-language word processors, videocassette recorders (VCRs), compact disk players, and HDTVs. Many electronics products have sold in extremely large volumes, a fact that has subsequently made ongoing investment in production possible, as well as further technological development. Incremental improvements in IC technology have made it possible for Japanese firms to improve continually on a variety of products. In the end, emerging products such as HDTV are truly different from what they used to be both in form and concept.

This incremental technological improvement is not limited to high-tech industries. Steel making is considered a mature or declining industry in most developed countries. However, Japanese steel makers are still moving toward higher levels of technological sophistication, for example by developing a vibration-damping steel sheet (i.e., two steel sheets sandwiching a very thin plastic film).

It is a small technological improvement that has a wide range of possible applications. Due to the growing popularity of quiet washing machines in Japan, this steel sheet has been used successfully as the outer panel of washing machines and is increasingly finding its way into other noise-reducing applications, such as roofing, flooring, and automotive parts.

The Marketplace as R&D Lab

Due to the incrementalist product-development approach, Japanese firms have also been able to increase the speed of new product introductions, meet the competitive demands of a rapidly changing marketplace, and capture market share. Japanese firms adopt emerging technologies first in existing products to satisfy customer needs better than their competitors. This affords an opportunity to gain experience, debug technological glitches, reduce costs, boost performance, and adapt designs to customer use.

In other words, the marketplace becomes a virtual R&D laboratory for Japanese firms to gain production and marketing experience as well as to perfect technology. This requires close contact with customers, whose inputs help Japanese firms improve their products on an ongoing basis.

In the process, they introduce newer products one after another. Year after year, Japanese firms unveil not-entirely new products that keep getting better, more reliable, and less expensive. For example, Philips marketed the first practical VCR in 1972, three years before Japanese competitors did. However, Philips took seven years to replace the first-generation VCR with the all-new V2000, while late-coming Japanese manufacturers launched an onslaught of no fewer than three generations of improved VCRs in this five-year period.

The continuous introduction of "newer" products also brings greater likelihood of market success. Ideal products often require a giant leap in technology and product development and are subject to a higher risk of consumer rejection. Not only does the Japanese approach of incrementalism allow for continual improvement and a stream of new products, but it also permits quicker consumer adoption. Consumers are likely to accept improved products more rapidly than they accept very different products, since the former are more compatible with the existing patterns of product use and lifestyle.

Japanese firms also display a willingness to take the progress achieved through incrementalism and develop a new market approach around it. An excellent example is provided by the strategies used by different Japanese automobile manufacturers. After decades of honing refinements in their products, these firms, within a short period of time, developed the Infiniti, Lexus, and Acura brands, which were substantially different in the consumer's mind from existing cars.

Each of these new brands was introduced to the market through an entirely new distribution system. Even though pundits had argued that in the automotive sector the time for new brands was over, let alone the likelihood of success for new channels, the approach chosen seems to be crowned by greater success than the more traditional acquisition route taken by Ford (Jaguar) or General Motors (Saab).

Market research is a key ingredient for successful ongoing development of newer products. The goal is to provide customers with more "value" in the products they purchase. Product value is determined by cost and quality factors. In the United States, cost reduction and quality improvements are too often thought to be contradictory objectives, particularly when quality is perceived to be measured mainly by choice of materials or engineering tolerances.

Japanese firms, by contrast, see cost reduction and quality improvement as parallel objectives that go in tandem. The word *Keihakutansho* epitomizes the efforts of Japanese firms to create value by simultaneously lowering cost and increasing quality. *Keihakutansho* literally means "lighter, slimmer, shorter, and smaller" and thus implies less expensive and more useful products that are economical in purchase, use, and maintenance.

Furthermore, Japanese perceptions consider quality in a product to be generated as well by the contextual usage of the product. If a product "fits" better for a given usage or usage condition, it delivers better quality. That is why Japanese firms always try to emphasize both the "high tech" and the "high touch" dimension in their product innovations.

The recent market success of Sony's black-and-white TV set illustrates this point. Conventional market research failed to show that a market existed for such products in the United States. However, by studying the contextual usage of TV sets, Sony found that in addition to a family's main color TV set, Americans wanted a small portable TV to use in their backyards or to take away with them on weekends.

How Does Japanese Market Research Differ?

U.S. market researchers, after developing an insulated staff function of their own, have grown enamored of hard data. By processing information from many people and applying sophisticated data manipulations, statistical significance is sought and, more often than not, found.

Toru Nishikawa,[1] marketing manager at Hitachi, summarizes the general Japanese attitude toward such so-called scientific market research. He provides five reasons against relying too much on a general survey of consumers for new-product development:

1. **Indifference.** Careless random sampling causes mistaken judgment, since some people are indifferent toward the product in question.

2. **Absence of responsibility.** The consumer is most sincere when spending, but not when talking.

3. **Conservative attitudes.** Ordinary consumers are conservative and tend to react negatively to a new product.

4. **Vanity.** It is human nature to exaggerate and put on a good appearance.

5. **Insufficient information.** The research results depend on the information about product characteristics given to survey participants.

Japanese firms prefer more "down to earth" methods of information gathering. Johansson and Nonaka[2] illustrate the benefit of using context-specific market information based on a mix of soft data (e.g., brand and product managers' visits to dealers and other members of the distribution channels) and hard data (e.g., shipments, inventory levels, and retail sales). Such context-specific market information is directly relevant to consumer attitudes about the product or to the manner in which buyers have used or will use specific products.

Several things stand out in Japanese new-product development (or in their continual product improvements). First Japanese new-product development involves context-specific market research as well as ongoing sales research. Second, some of the widely observed idiosyncrasies of the Japanese distribution system serve as major research input factors. For example, when a manufacturer dispatches his own sales personnel to leading department stores, not only are business relationships strengthened, but a direct mechanism for observation and feedback is developed as well.

Third, significant effort is expended on developing data, be it through point-of-sale computer scanners or the issuance of discount cards to customers, which also carry electronically embedded consumer profiles. Fourth, engineers and product designers carry out much of the context-specific research.

Toyota recently sent a group of its engineers and designers to southern California to nonchalantly "observe" how women get into and operate their cars. They found that women with long fingernails have trouble operating the door and operating various knobs on the dashboard. Toyota engineers and designers were able to "understand" the women's plight and redraw some of their automobile exterior and interior designs.

City, another highly acclaimed small Honda car, was conceived in a similar manner. Honda dispatched several engineers and designers on the City project team to Europe to "look around" for a suitable product concept for City. Based on the Mini-Cooper, a small British car developed decades ago, the Honda project team designed a "short and tall" car, which defied the prevailing idea that a car should be long and low.

Yet, hands-on market research by the very people who design and engineer a prototype model is not necessarily unique to Japanese firms. Successful U.S. companies also have a similar history. For example, the Boeing 737 was introduced about twenty years ago to compete with McDonnell-Douglas's DC-9. However, DC-9s were a somewhat superior plane; they had been introduced three years before the Boeing 737 and were faster.

Witnessing a growing market potential in Third World countries, Boeing sent a group of engineers to those countries to "observe" the idiosyncrasies of Third World aviation. These engineers found that many runways were too short to accommodate jet planes. Boeing subsequently redesigned the wings, added low-pressure tires to prevent bouncing on shorter landings, and redesigned the engines for quicker takeoff. As a result of these changes, the Boeing 737 has become the best-selling commercial jet in history.

Hands-on market research does not negate the importance of conventional market research, emphasizing quantity of data and statistical significance. In developing the ProMavica professional still video system, which, unlike conventional 35mm still cameras, records images on a two-inch-square floppy disk, Sony did extensive market research involving a mail survey, personal and telephone interviews, and on-site tests to elicit user response to the product during its development. What was unique was that the ProMavica task

force included both engineers and sales/marketing representatives from Sony's medical systems and broadcast units. Sony's engineers gained insights from talking with prospects as much as did their marketing peers, and they incorporated user comments into product modifications.

It is clear that engineers and designers, people who are usually detached from market research, *can* and *should* also engage in context-specific market research side by side with professional market researchers. After all, these engineers and designers are the ones who convert market information into products.

Some Recommendations

Clearly, U.S. new-product development and market research are sophisticated and successful. Yet, in order to improve competitiveness further, several aspects of Japanese activities could be considered by U.S. firms.

First, the incrementalist approach to product development appears to offer advantages in the areas of costs, speed, learning, and consumer acceptance. Second, such an approach requires a continuous understanding of current and changing customer needs and of the shortcomings of one's own products and those of the competition. In order to achieve such understanding, market research is essential.

In order for such research to be successful, the contextual usage and usage conditions of products need to be investigated and, once found, acted upon. While extremely useful in their own right, hard data alone are not the answer. This type of information often provides only limited insights into these contextual conditions.

It is therefore important to include soft information based on down-to-earth market observation. Since the ability to recognize dimensions of context is not uniquely confined to market researchers, it is important to fully include product managers, designers, and engineers in the research process.

Marketing research should not be a "staff"

function performed only by professional market researchers, but rather a "line" function executed by all participants in the product development process. Not only will such an approach permit the discovery of more knowledge, but it will also immediately achieve the transformation of gleaned market data into information that is disseminated and applied throughout the entire organization.

References

1. Nishikawa, "New Product Planning at Hitachi," 22 *Long Range Planning,* 20–24 (1989).
2. Johansson and Nonaka, "Marketing Research the Japanese Way," 65 *Harvard Business Review,* 16–22 (1987).

DEVELOPING GLOBAL STRATEGIES FOR SERVICE BUSINESSES

Christopher H. Lovelock and George S. Yip

How do the distinctive characteristics of service businesses affect globalization and the use of global strategy? This is a crucial question for managers in numerous industries. Not only are services continuing to grow rapidly in domestic economies, but international trade in services is increasing, too. The United States, like some other developed countries, has a trade surplus in services that helps offset the deficit in merchandise trade. In contrast, Japan has been much less successful in internationalizing its service businesses.[1] So it is essential to national competitiveness that governments, as well as companies, achieve a better understanding of how to develop effective global strategies for different types of service businesses.

Most research to date has focused either on why and how service firms internationalize or on different modes of internationalization.[2] In contrast, we examine how globalization drivers and the use of global strategy might apply to various types of services, and what differences might exist relative to manufacturing businesses. In doing so, we combine two different frameworks, one developed to analyze global strategy[3] and one for service businesses.[4]

Overview

A major theme in international business is the increasing use of global strategies. These involve the worldwide integration of strategy formulation and implementation, in contrast to a multidomestic (or multilocal) approach that provides for independent development and implementation of strategies by country or regional units.[5] One key theme is that globalization potential depends on industry characteristics,[6] and on specific industry globalization drivers—market, cost, government, and competitive.[7] A second key theme is that the use of global strategy should differ by dimension of strategy and for different elements of the value-adding chain.[8] The linkage between industry globalization drivers and global strategy—as well as the relationship of these drivers to organization structure and management processes and to consequent effects on performance—have been empirically tested for manufacturing businesses in major American and Japanese multinational corporations (MNCs).[9] But research into global strategy for service businesses is still in an evolutionary stage.[10]

Defining Globalization. The terms "global" and "globalization" are often used rather loosely. Many writers use them interchangeably with words such as international (and internationaliza-

From *California Management Review,* Winter 1996.

tion), transnational,[11] and multinational. We believe that some clarification is in order. Strictly speaking, any service firm doing business across national frontiers can claim to be international. When passengers ride a scheduled bus line from Buffalo, New York, to Toronto, Ontario, they are using an international transportation service. A retail chain that operates in both the United Kingdom and Ireland can claim to be an international business. Moving up a notch, a bank with offices in several European countries could even claim to be multinational. None of these services, however, is global in scope. Nor, for that matter, is an insurance company doing business throughout Europe and North America.

In our view, a truly global company is one that not only does business in both the eastern and western hemispheres, but also in both the northern and southern ones. In the process, geographic distances and time-zone variations are maximized. With the rise of non-Japan Asia, Latin America, and Eastern Europe, operating in just the "Triad" of North America, Western Europe, and Japan is no longer sufficient. Other differences also tend to be sharpened, such as the variety of languages, currencies, cultures, legal and political systems, government policies and regulations, educational backgrounds of managers and employees, levels of national economic development, and climates. In this article, we will emphasize companies that meet our criterion of being truly global, although not all our examples will do so. Furthermore, we shall stress that simply operating globally does not mean that a company possesses a global strategy.

Defining Service Businesses.   We will examine the ways in which global strategy for service businesses, given their distinctive characteristics, should be significantly different from manufacturing businesses. Furthermore, a fundamental premise underlying our analysis is that not all services are the same. So we will use three "lenses" with which to examine the global strategies of service-based businesses:

- A set of characteristics by which service-based businesses differ from goods-based businesses.
- A categorization of three fundamental types of service businesses.
- A set of eight supplementary services surrounding the core product or offering.

An Overall Global Strategy Framework for Service Businesses.   Our overall global strategy framework is illustrated in Figure 1. In this framework, industry globalization drivers give rise to industry globalization potential, but this effect is filtered by the special characteristics of service businesses. In turn, industry globalization potential should result in four types of global strategy response: in terms of market participation, the service offering, the location and configuration of the value-adding chain, and in the nature of the marketing strategy. Here, the global strategy response is filtered by the three distinct types of service businesses. Lastly, supplementary services, which augment the core product like petals around the center of a flower, play a direct role in the makeup of each aspect of global strategy.

Understanding the Nature of Services

"Services versus Goods" Distinctions. Early research into services sought to differentiate them from goods, focusing particularly on four generic differences—intangibility, heterogeneity (variability), perishability of output, and simultaneity of production and consumption.[12] Although these characteristics are still commonly cited, they have been criticized as too generic,[13] and there is growing recognition that they are not universally applicable to all services. A better sense of the processes underlying service delivery is provided in an alternative set of eight characteristics.[14] These characteristics begin with the nature of the output—a performance rather than an object—and also include customer involvement in production,

FIGURE 1

Globalization framework for service businesses

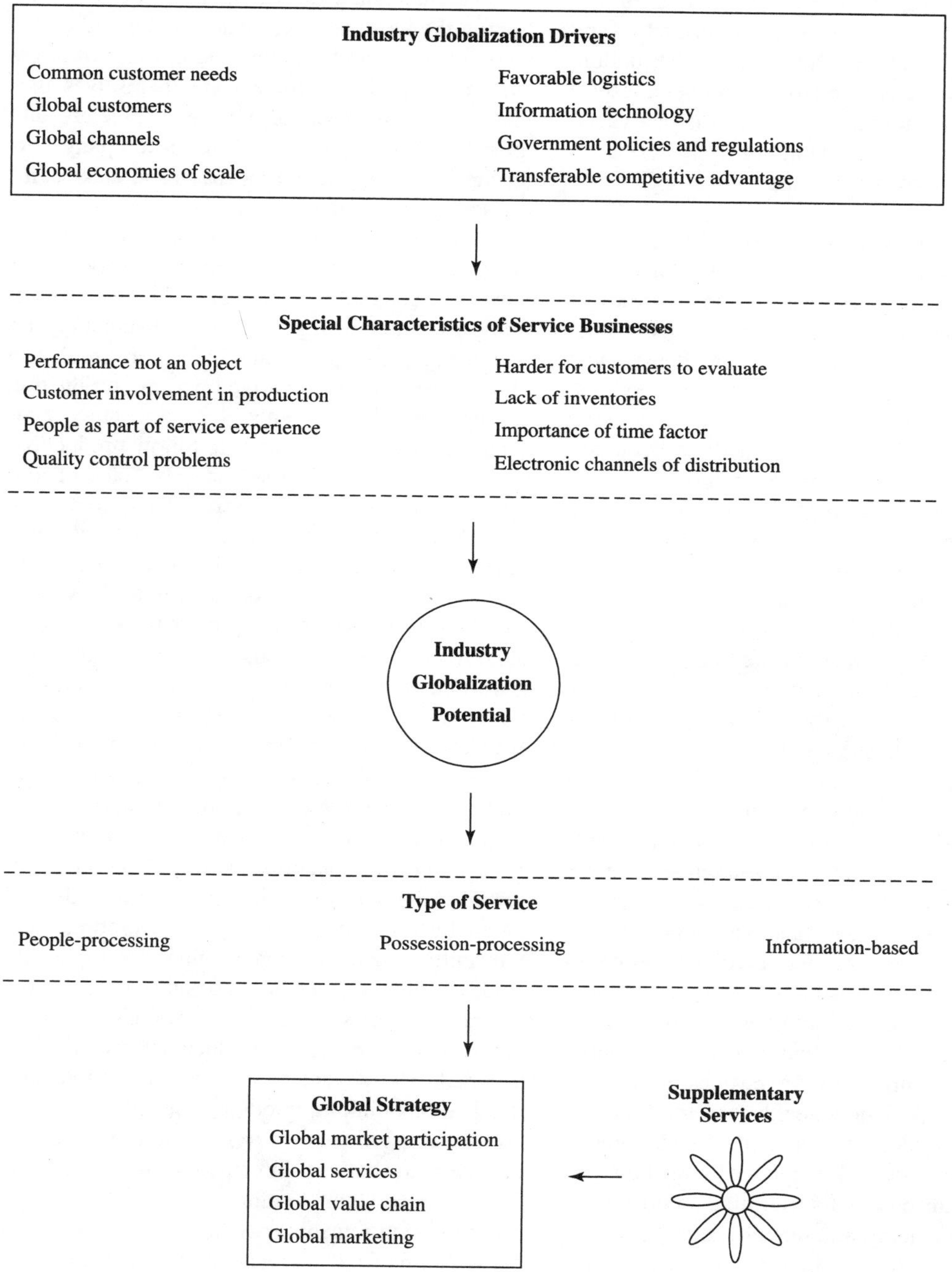

Industry Globalization Drivers

Common customer needs	Favorable logistics
Global customers	Information technology
Global channels	Government policies and regulations
Global economies of scale	Transferable competitive advantage

↓

Special Characteristics of Service Businesses

Performance not an object	Harder for customers to evaluate
Customer involvement in production	Lack of inventories
People as part of service experience	Importance of time factor
Quality control problems	Electronic channels of distribution

↓

**Industry
Globalization
Potential**

↓

Type of Service

People-processing   Possession-processing   Information-based

---

↓

Global Strategy
Global market participation
Global services
Global value chain
Global marketing

←

**Supplementary
Services**

people as part of the service experience, greater likelihood of quality control problems, harder for customers to evaluate, lack of inventories for services, greater importance of the time factor, and availability of electronic channels of distribution. Although these characteristics provide a useful starting point for thinking about the distinctive aspects of service management, not every service is equally affected by all of them.

Three Categories of Services. The previous list helps distinguish service-based businesses from goods-based ones. But service businesses also differ from each other. All products—both goods and services—consist of a core element that is surrounded by a variety of sometimes optional supplementary elements. Whether one is looking at service strategy locally or globally, it is unwise to talk in broad brush terms about the service sector or service industries as though all organizations faced more or less the same strategic problems. At the same time, it is also a mistake to fall into the trap of examining services only on an industry-by-industry basis. Probably the most useful and relevant classification concerns differences and commonalities in operational processes, since the way in which inputs are transformed into outputs has a significant effect on strategy.[15]

By looking at core services from an operational perspective, we can assign them to one of three broad categories, depending on the nature of the process (whether it is primarily tangible or intangible) and the extent to which customers need to be physically present during service production.

People-processing services involve tangible actions to customers in person. These services require that customers themselves become part of the production process, which tends to be simultaneous with consumption. In businesses such as passenger transportation, health care, food service, and lodging services, the customer needs to enter the "service factory" (although we know it by such names as an airliner and air terminal, a hospital, a restaurant, or a hotel) and remain there during service delivery. Either customers must travel to the factory or service providers and equipment must come to the customer. In both instances, the firm needs to maintain a local geographic presence, stationing the necessary personnel, buildings, equipment, vehicles, and supplies within reach of target customers. If the customers are themselves mobile—as in the case of business travelers and tourists—then they may patronize a company's offerings in many different locations and make comparisons between them.

Possession-processing services involve tangible actions to physical objects to improve their value to customers. Examples include freight transport, warehousing, equipment installation and maintenance, car repair, laundry, and disposal. The object needs to be involved in the production process, but the customer does not, since consumption of the output tends to follow production. Again, the service "factory" may be fixed or mobile. A local geographic presence is required when the supplier needs to provide service to physical objects in a specific location on a repeated basis. In the case of smaller, transportable items, the vendor can provide remote service centers for servicing—although transportation costs, customs duties, and government regulations may constrain shipment across large distances or national frontiers. Modern technology now allows a few service processes to be administered from a distance, using electronic diagnostics to pinpoint the problem.

Information-based services are, perhaps, the most interesting category from the standpoint of global strategy development because they depend on collecting, manipulating, interpreting, and transmitting data to create value. Examples include accounting, banking, consulting, education, insurance, legal services, and news. Customer involvement in production of such services is often minimal. The advent of modern global telecommunications, linking intelligent machines to powerful databases, makes it possible to use electronic channels to deliver information-based services from a single "hub" to almost any location. Local presence requirements may be limited to a terminal—ranging from a telephone or fax machine to a computer or more specialized equipment like a bank ATM—connected to a reliable telecommunications infrastructure. If the latter is inadequate, then use of mobile or satellite communications may solve the problem in some instances.

Service production and delivery systems can be divided into "back office" and "front office," the latter being the portion of the "service factory" encountered by customers.[16] People-processing services necessarily involve a high degree of contact with service personnel and facilities; possession-processing and information-based services, by contrast, have the potential to be much lower contact in nature. Retail banking, for instance, can take place either through traditional branch banks or through such channels as mail, telephone, and Internet.

The Role of Supplementary Services.   The core service product—a bed for the night, restoring a defective computer to good working order, or a bank account—is typically accompanied by a variety of supplementary elements. Most businesses, whether they are classified in government statistics as manufacturing or service, offer their customers a package that includes a variety of service-related activities, too. Increasingly, these supplementary elements not only add value, but also provide the differentiation that separates successful firms from the also-rans; they also offer opportunities for firms to develop effective globalization strategies. Writers and managers alike often use the terms "augmented product,"[17] "extended product," or "product package" to describe the supplementary elements that add value to the core product.[18]

There are potentially dozens of different supplementary services, although they can be grouped into eight categories (information, consultation, order-taking, hospitality, caretaking, exceptions, billing, and payment) encircling the core product like a corona of petals: collectively, they comprise "the flower of service" (Figure 2 and Exhibit 1).[19] Many of these petals are based on informational processes that can be located in one part of the world and delivered electronically to another. Not

every core product—whether a good or a service—is surrounded by supplementary elements from all eight clusters. In practice, the nature of the product, customer requirements, and competitive practices help managers to determine which supplementary service must be offered and which might usefully be added to enhance value and make it easy to do business with the organization.

One determinant of what supplementary services to include is the market positioning strategy that management has selected. A strategy of adding benefits to gain a competitive edge will probably require more supplementary services (and also a higher level of performance on all such elements). In developing a global strategy, management must decide which, if any, supplementary elements should be consistent across all markets and which might be tailored to meet local needs, expectations, and competitive dynamics. This is the essence of standardization and customization, but services offer much more flexibility in this respect than do physical goods, lending themselves in many contexts to what is known as "mass customization."[20]

Industry Globalization Drivers

What drives globalization of service businesses? Many types of drivers have been suggested for the analysis of manufacturing firms.[21] We identify here the eight most relevant ones (listed in Figure 1) for service businesses, then systematically evaluate how the characteristics of different types of services might strengthen or weaken the effects of these drivers. We will also examine how these effects differ among the three categories of service business—people-processing, possession-processing, and information-based services.

Common Customer Needs.   Industries with customer needs and tastes that are common across countries offer more potential for globalization. Product categories such as consumer electronic devices, cigarettes, soft drinks, and computer hard-

FIGURE 2

Supplementary services surrounding the core product

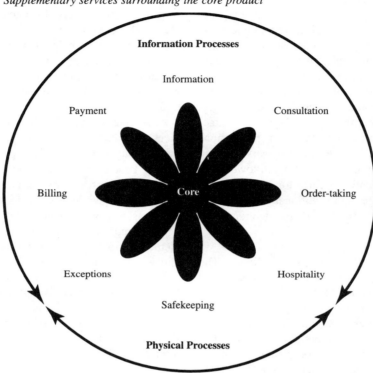

ware provide many instances of successful global standardization. (The simultaneous presence of successful local strategies in these categories in no way undermines the global opportunity for multinational companies. Similarly, less than total standardization, as in Coca-Cola's local adaptation of its syrup, does not void the benefits of pursuing global standardization as much possible in the appropriate industries and categories.) The service characteristic of "customer involvement in production" reduces the degree to which many services can be standardized and still meet the needs of a broad cross section of customers around the world. In general, the less the involvement, whether physical or psychological, the better the opportunity for a global approach. So we are more likely to see global standardization in fast food and

airlines, where customer involvement is tightly controlled, than in medical care or education, where customer involvement is both stronger and more prolonged. Note that our observations apply to the broad "middle market" rather than to the relatively small market segment composed of affluent, highly educated, cosmopolitan customers.

The service characteristic of "people as part of the service experience" also limits the potential commonality of customer needs and tastes. Differences can arise even within the same industry. In banking, the service provided by human tellers is far less standardized and standardizable than that provided by automated teller machines. Accounting services depend heavily on people. The higher status of accountants in Britain than in the United States means that British accountants pro-

EXHIBIT 1   Eight Categories of Supplementary Services

Information

To obtain full value from any good or service, customers need relevant information about it, ranging from schedules to operating instructions, and from user warnings to prices. Globalization affects the nature of that information (including the languages and format in which it is provided). New customers and prospects are especially information hungry and may need training in how to use an unfamiliar service.

Consultation and Advice

Consultation and advice involve a dialogue to probe customer requirements and then develop a tailored solution. Customers' need for advice may vary widely around the world, reflecting such factors as level of economic development, nature of the local infrastructure, topography and climate, technical standards, and educational levels.

Order-Taking

Once customers are ready to buy, suppliers need to make it easy for them to place orders or reservations in the language of their choice, through telecommunications and other channels, at times and in locations that are convenient to them.

Hospitality: Taking Care of the Customer

Well-managed businesses try, at least in small ways, to treat customers as guests when they have to visit the supplier's facilities (especially when, as is true for many people-processing operations, the period extends over several hours or more). Cultural definitions of appropriate hospitality may differ widely from one country to another, such as the tolerable length of waiting time (much longer in Brazil than in Germany) and the degree of personal service expected (not much in Scandinavia but lavish in Indonesia).

Safekeeping: Looking After the Customer's Possessions

When visiting a service site, customers often want assistance with their personal possessions, ranging from car parking to packaging and delivery of new purchases. Expectations may vary by country, reflecting culture and levels of affluence.

Exceptions

Exceptions fall outside the routine of normal service delivery. They include special requests, problem solving, handling of complaints/suggestions/compliments, and restitution (compensating customers for performance failures). Special requests are particularly common in people-processing services, as in the travel and lodging industries, and may be complicated by differing cultural norms. International airlines, for example, find it necessary to respond to an array of medical and dietary needs, sometimes reflecting religious and cultural values. Problem solving is often more difficult for people who are traveling overseas than it would be in the familiar environment of their native country.

Billing

Customers need clear, timely bills that explain how charges are computed. With abolition of currency exchange restrictions in many countries, bills can be converted to the customer's home currency. Hence, currencies and conversion rates need to be clarified on billing statements. In some instances, prices may be displayed in several currencies, even though this policy may require frequent adjustments in the light of currency fluctuations.

Payment

Ease and convenience of payment (including credit) are increasingly expected by customers when purchasing a broad array of services. Major credit cards and traveler's checks solve the problem of paying in foreign funds for many retail purchases, but corporate purchasers may prefer to use electronic fund transfers in the currency of their choice.

vide more general business advice than do their American counterparts. And U.S.-style psychotherapy is unlikely to yield a global "McShrink" franchise.

One of the greatest dilemmas in global strategy for manufacturing businesses is the need to balance global standardization with local customization. Designing, then manufacturing, a global product with a degree of local customization requires major tradeoffs. In contrast, the nature of service delivery—at the point of consumption in many cases—makes both standardization and customization equally feasible. Local elements (e.g., Balinese dancing in Indonesia) can be easily added to a global formula (Club Med vacations); using local nationals as service providers may overcome the foreignness of a standardized service (e.g., use of local cabin crews by international airlines). The practice of augmenting a core service with many supplementary elements makes it relatively easy to provide a globally standardized core service augmented (and differentiated) by nationally customized supplementary service elements. This tends to be easier than for manufacturing businesses.[22]

Global Customers.   As large corporate customers become global, they often seek to standardize and simplify the array of services they consume. For instance, firms may seek to minimize the number of auditors they use around the world, using "Big Six" accounting firms that can apply a consistent worldwide approach (within the context of national rules within each country of operation). Global management of telecommunications is provided by the "Concert" service offered by British Telecom and its American partner MCI, allowing a multinational company to outsource all responsibility for management of its purchase and use of telecommunications. Corporate banking, insurance, business logistics, and management consulting are further examples. Individuals act as global customers when they purchase goods and services on their travels. The service characteristics of "a performance rather than

an object" and "greater importance of the time factor" create special opportunities for travel-related services, a very large and growing segment that starts with transportation but extends to credit, communication, and emergency support.

Global customers for possession-processing services prefer common procedures and standards. For example, airlines absolutely depend on their aircraft being maintained in the same way everywhere—and, increasingly, so do customers of factory and machinery maintenance services. Global customers for people-processing services may care particularly about ubiquity, especially when traveling. The New Zealander who breaks her leg in Pamplona needs medical treatment on the spot. Global customers for information-based services may have a more diffuse set of needs, but these certainly include comprehensiveness, accuracy, and accessibility. The American executive who has lost his traveler's checks in Shanghai needs reimbursement there, now, not back home in Indiana, later.

Global Channels.   Distributors of physical goods have globalized relatively slowly. Few distributors in any category have adequate worldwide coverage. National giants like Wal-Mart and Toys R Us from the United States, Carrefour and IKEA from Europe, and Watson's and Dairy Farm from Asia, are beginning to establish regional networks, but all are far from being able to distribute worldwide. In contrast, the "availability of electronic channels of distribution" for services provides nearly total global coverage for more and more service offerings—notably travel services, banking, customer support services, entertainment, and most forms of information products themselves. Furthermore, these electronic global channels support not just information-based services but augment people-processing (e.g., health care) and possession-processing (e.g., delivery of time-sensitive materials) services. The latest electronic channel, the World Wide Web, now offers global outreach to even the smallest of companies. The Web can help sell any type of core product through information-based supplementary services and can actually deliver many information-based services directly to customers.

Global Economies of Scale. Global scale economies apply when single-country markets are not large enough to allow competitors to achieve optimum scale. Scale can then be increased through participation in multiple markets, combined with product standardization and/or concentration of selected value activities. But "lack of inventories," "customer involvement in production," and "people as part of the service experience" all work against being able to concentrate production to achieve scale. So service companies typically have to find global scale economies by standardizing production processes rather than through physical concentration, as well as by concentrating the upstream, rather than the downstream, stages of the value chain.

The effect of cost globalization drivers, like global scale economies, varies sharply according to the level of fixed costs required to enter an industry (although equipment leasing schemes, or awarding franchises to local investors, provides a way to minimize such entry barriers). So cost globalization drivers may be less favorable for services that are primarily people-based and face lesser scale economies and flatter experience curves. One common solution for the would-be global company is to do as McDonald's does—substitute equipment for labor in order to achieve lower costs and better performance than local companies using traditional business systems.

Favorable Logistics. Low transportation costs allows concentration of production for physical goods. For services, "customer involvement in production" raises the logistical stakes in globalization. In most people-processing services, the need for convenience prevents concentration. But in some possession-processing services, customers are willing to transport their possessions to another location for better service. Thus, many airlines bring their aircraft to Singapore. Some people-pro-

cessing services have achieved similar success in having customers come to them. London hospitals maintain a flourishing business among wealthy Middle Eastern patients, as do Miami hospitals for patients from Latin America.

Companies have to balance the tradeoffs between logistics and appeal. Disney favored logistics over appeal in selecting northern France rather than southern Spain for the location of Euro Disney. More people can get more easily to the Euro Disney site outside Paris, but once there they often face cold weather and colder service. Service businesses can also create their own favorable logistics. Club Med organizes charter flights from urban centers to its off-the-beaten-path locations. British Airways and Air France provide limousine ground transport to and from their Concorde flights.

Lastly, logistics is seldom a barrier to globalization for information-based services. Using electronic channels to deliver such services allows providers to concentrate production in locations that have specific expertise and to offer cost savings or other meaningful advantages. For instance, banks in the Cayman Islands are not conveniently located from a purely geographic standpoint, but money can be shipped there electronically to take advantage of the tax benefits conferred by offshore funds status.

Information Technology. For information-based services, the growing availability of broadband telecommunication channels, capable of moving vast amounts of data at great speed, is playing a major role in opening up new markets. Access to the Internet or World Wide Web is accelerating around the world. But there may be no need to duplicate all informational elements in each new location. Significant economies may be gained by centralizing "information hubs" on a global basis, as Federal Express does in Memphis. For all three types of services, the use of information technology may allow companies to benefit from favorable labor costs or exchange rates by consolidating operations of supplementary services (such as reservations) or back office functions (such as accounting) in just one or a few countries. While a globalization driver in its own right, information technology also interacts with all of the other drivers.

Government Policies and Regulations. Host governments affect globalization potential through import tariffs and quotas, nontariff barriers, export subsidies, local content requirements, currency and capital flow restrictions, technical and other standards, ownership restrictions, and requirements on technology transfer. Governments' exercise of these policies and regulations can make it difficult for companies to globalize. For services, "customer involvement in production" may mitigate many government barriers to global strategy. Government drivers are often favorable for people-processing and possession-processing services that require a significant local presence, since they create local employment opportunities. On the other hand, governments often impose regulations to protect home carriers in the case of mobile services, such as passenger and freight transportation. For instance, restricting foreign airlines' landing rights or ability to pick up passengers at an intermediate stop ("third freedom" rights) provides a way to protect home-based airlines on international routes.

Nations may perceive both an economic and a cultural threat in unrestricted imports of information-based services through electronic channels. Government regulations range from controls on international banking to bans on private ownership of satellite dishes (as in countries such as China, Singapore, and Saudi Arabia). Some nations are now trying to manage citizen access to the World Wide Web.

For people-processing services, government barriers to global strategy include country differences in social policies (e.g., health) affecting labor costs, the role of women in front line jobs, and the hours or days on which work can be performed. For possession-processing services, tax laws, environmental regulations, and technical

standards may decrease/increase costs and encourage/discourage certain types of activity. For information-based services, special policies on education, censorship, public ownership of communications, and infrastructure quality may apply; technical standards may vary; and government policies may distort pricing.

Transferable Competitive Advantage. The single most important competitive globalization driver arises from transferability of competitive advantage. If one industry participant can leverage its competitive position in one country to build an advantage in other countries, all its competitors need to develop a global strategy too.[23] For services, "customer involvement in production," and "lack of inventories" limit the leverage of competitive advantage based on foreign factors of production such as labor productivity (e.g., no "Toyota" exports), although advantage in management systems can be a basis for globalization (e.g., Hilton). So Hong Kong hotel chains, such as Mandarin, Peninsula, and Regent, that have set world class standards for service, find such excellence far harder to reproduce as they expand overseas. Similarly, Disney has suffered from not being able to transfer to Paris Disneyland the highly motivated and pliant staff of its U.S. parks.

Overall Assessment of Drivers. As we look at the three categories of services identified earlier, it seems that most industry globalization drivers do apply to services, but their impact varies by service type and even by industry. For example, government drivers (expressed in terms of economic policy, regulation, and protectionism) are often industry specific (as evidenced by the recent Uruguay Round of negotiations on GATT and bilateral British-American negotiations on commercial air travel). This conclusion highlights the importance of conducting a systematic evaluation of globalization drivers for individual industries, rather than taking generalized views that service businesses can be more (or less) easily globalized than can manufacturing businesses.

Service Effects in Global Strategy

To complete our analysis, we now present a more detailed view of how each dimension of global strategy might differ for service businesses. We use four dimensions ("global strategy levers") that determine whether international strategy is more multilocal or more global.[24] The global end of each dimension consists of the following:

- *Global Market Participation*—countries are selected not just on the basis of stand-alone attractiveness, but also in terms of their potential contribution to globalization benefits.
- *Global Products and Services*—a standardized core product or service that requires a minimum of local adaptation.
- *Global Location of Value-Adding Activities*—the value chain is broken up; each activity may be conducted in a different country, rather than many activities being duplicated around the world.
- *Global Marketing*—a uniform marketing approach is applied around the world, although not all elements of the marketing mix need be identical.

Services and Global Market Participation.

A global strategy approach to market participation involves building significant share in globally strategic markets. Such countries are important beyond their stand-alone attractiveness and may be a source of volume to meet economies of scale, the home or significant market of global customers or global competitors, or a major source of industry innovation. Failure to participate in strategic markets can undermine global competitiveness. Many American and European manufacturing companies have suffered from not building significant positions in Japan, thereby limiting their potential economies of scale in manufacturing, lacking exposure to the innovation and high customer standards in Japan, and being unable to create a hostage for good behavior on the part of Japanese rivals.

A few Western service companies have built successful businesses in Japan, either because their Western orientation (such as American-style fast food) appealed to Japanese consumers or because they were creating an international network that could not afford to be absent from such a major market. For network firms, such as airlines, financial services, and logistics firms, highly specific geographic locations may be seen as essential. No financial service firm with global ambitions, for instance, can afford not to have a presence in New York, London, and Tokyo. With the exception of such network organizations, it is hard to see how presence or absence in Japan (or any other individual country) significantly affects a service firm's global strategic position, other than contributing revenues and profits.

Travel-related services pose an exception. Inherently, wider global market participation makes a brand of service more valuable to a customer. Thus, American Express traveler's checks and credit cards are useful precisely because they are widely accepted in most countries. Similarly, international airlines enhance their appeal as they fly to more destinations.

Designing and Delivering Globally Standardized Services.

Globally standardized products or "global products" are, perhaps, the one feature most commonly identified with global strategy. As mentioned earlier, the fact that services comprise a bundle of core and supplementary services makes them particularly easy to both globalize and localize. In perhaps the most extreme example, McDonald's now plans to open restaurants in India that, in deference to Hindu reverence for cows, will not serve hamburgers at all. Were McDonald's a goods-based business, that would be equivalent to selling a car without an engine. But as a service-based business, the other core and supplementary elements can make up for the lack of beef. McDonald's also adds items, such as Veggie Burgers, to menus to meet local tastes.

In Britain, McDonald's includes both tea and coffee in its menus, while in France and Germany it also serves beer. Interestingly, these local variations are in the food itself, the product element, rather than in the service elements.

Hewlett-Packard is a global leader in computer-based customer support services for its customers. It maintains a globally standardized set of services that range from site design to systems integration and remote diagnostics. This global standardization includes seamless service at any hour of the day or night from anywhere in the world.

Professional service firms vary in their ability to provide a globally standardized service. Some firms, such as those in the accounting industry, face significant international differences in technical standards, making uniformity more difficult. But it is also a matter of strategy. Arthur Andersen has chosen to lead in offering globally standardized services. Its competitors now have to play catch-up. Similarly, advertising agencies face international differences in culture and consumer behavior, but some have chosen to overcome these differences.

Global Location of Value-Adding Service Activities.   Where to locate a business's activities and how to coordinate them constitute critical choices in global strategy. Every functional or value-adding activity—from research to manufacturing to customer service—is a candidate for globalization.[25] Traditionally, multinational companies (MNCs) have faced two choices in activity location. The classic MNC strategy has been to reproduce activities in many countries. Alternatively, an MNC can concentrate activities in its home country.

The trend in global strategy is to concentrate each activity as much as possible, although not necessarily all activities in the same country.[26] As discussed earlier, many service businesses need local presence for their downstream activities. But at the same time, they can take advantage of differences in national comparative advantage to build more efficient and effective value chains. Some

service-based businesses conduct key activities that can be conducted in a different country from their customers. For example, some U.S. banks and insurance companies now send checks and claims to be processed in East Asia or in Ireland. McKinsey & Company, the management consulting firm, now sends some of its work for clients from high-cost countries to its offices in low-cost countries like India.

To provide its global customer support service, Hewlett-Packard maintains a global chain of activity locations—its more than 30 Response Centers around the world are integrated into a global network headed by four major centers: Bracknell (United Kingdom), Atlanta (Georgia) and Mountain View (California) in the United States, and Melbourne (Australia). Each center is staffed during extended daytime hours, 7 days a week, by between 12 and 200 engineers. Problems that cannot be resolved in a smaller center may be transferred to one of the major centers. Because of time-zone differentials, at least one of the major centers is always in full operation at any time.

Citibank, one of the world's largest banks, has positioned itself as a "uniquely global consumer bank."[27] The company's objective is to allow its customers to do their banking "any way, any where, any time." To provide this service, it has expanded its Citicard Banking Centers with their automated teller machines to 28 countries. These centers are globally linked, allowing 24-hour 7-days-a-week access. And, of course, noncash transactions can be conducted by phone.

Global Marketing of Services.   A worldwide business uses global marketing when it takes the same or similar approach or content for one or more elements of the marketing mix, i.e., the same or similar brand names, advertising, and other marketing elements in different countries. The uncertainty engendered by intangibility requires strong branding to offset it. So the primary task of the brand name or trademark for a service is to offer recognition and reassurance, rather than performing other functions such as positioning or local adaptation. McDonald's, for instance, has to be the same name around the world, so that both locals and travelers know that they will get the genuine McDonald's experience. (We doubt, however, that the Spago and Planet Saigon restaurants in Ho Chi Minh City will provide the same experiences as the Hollywood originals after which they are named.) Travel-related services virtually require the same name globally. What use would an American Express Card be if the brand were Russian Express in Moscow? One solution is to be both global and local. Federal Express combines global and local brand names. In France the company uses partly localized names like FedEx Priorité, FedEx Rapide, and FedEx Fret.

Global positioning is also important. McDonald's has a globally consistent positioning and image, but this is not a globally neutral image. It is clearly American, so it stands for "us" in the United States, and "them" elsewhere. Similarly, Chili's, a U.S.-based restaurant chain offering Mexican food, has its largest store in Monterrey, Mexico. But customers there go for an "American experience," not a Mexican one. In contrast, Benetton, both a goods-based (clothes) and a service-based (stores) company, strives for a universalistic, non-national image.

Global advertising works equally for goods-based and service-based businesses. Whether to use it depends on such industry globalization drivers as common customer needs and the salience of global customers or global channels. Travel-related services can obviously benefit from global advertising, although the communications task may vary by country. A solution is the dual campaign, one for global themes and one for local messages. For many years, British Airways has used a succession of dramatic global advertising campaigns to establish its position as "The World's Favourite Airline" (backed up by significant improvements in service quality since privatization). At the same time, British Airways provides a smaller budget for local campaigns that focus on schedules, prices, and promotion of special tour packages. Singapore Airlines has achieved significant advertising impact with its temporally and globally consistent theme of the "Singapore Girl," a highly successful way of personalizing and differentiating a commodity service.

While most services are not physically packaged, staff uniforms and the layout and decor of facilities can be considered part of the package. Global consistency can bring significant benefits. Singapore Airlines has maintained the same uniform for its stewardesses for over 25 years. The "sarong kebaya," designed by Paris couturier, Pierre Balmain, makes the Singapore Airlines stewardess globally recognizable, unlike those of most other airlines. And like McDonald's, Citibank designs its new retail branches to look and operate in the same way around the world.

In contrast, "lack of inventories" in many service businesses means that such firms need worry less about using global pricing. Manufacturing businesses increasingly need to charge globally uniform prices to provide consistency with global customers and distribution channels, and to avoid "gray market" parallel importing or "trans-shipment." It is relatively difficult to buy a service in one country and resell it in another.

McDonald's prices certainly vary, so much so that *The Economist* magazine uses a "McDonald's Big Mac Price Index" to compare the cost of living in major business cities around the world. In the case of multinational customers as opposed to individuals, however, even service businesses need to avoid charging different prices in different countries to the same customer without good justification. Increasingly, multinational companies are beginning to behave as global rather than multilocal customers. Hewlett-Packard, for example, now provides worldwide contracts to its major global accounts for both products and services.

Implications for Types of Service Businesses.   While there are always exceptions, some overall conclusions can be made about the three types of service business and how easily they can use each of the four dimensions of global strategy.

Global market participation. Some types of service business seem very easy to spread around the world, and others very difficult. In the easy category fall simple service concepts that are easily replicable (and therefore franchisable). All three types of services have such simple examples (e.g., fast food in the people-processing category, package delivery in the possession-processing category, and English-language news in the information-based category). In contrast, some "essential" services—such as banking, telecommunications, hospitals, and airlines—operate in heavily regulated environments, making it difficult to get rapid penetration of foreign markets.

Historically, businesses that rely on trust and the reputation of their personnel—such as law firms and other professional service providers—have found it difficult to demonstrate quality to potential foreign customers and to adopt a professional style that fits the local culture. Ways to overcome such hurdles include extensive advertising and public relations as well as hiring host country nationals who have obtained education and work experience in other countries.

Globally standardized service. Possession-processing businesses can probably provide the most globally standardized offerings. These services need not cope with cultural and taste differences, only with those technical specifications that vary geographically, such as differences in electrical voltages or measurement systems. For people-processing services, some deviation from standardization is almost always needed. For information-based services, such deviation will vary widely, from none at all (e.g., information on international flight schedules) to near total (e.g., local weather forecasts or tax advice).

Global location of value chain. By their "virtual" nature, most information-based services should find it the easiest to locate globally. In many cases, such as pure information services, no local physical presence may be needed at all. In other cases, information services that also have a

physical component (e.g., the provision of currency or traveler's checks) or require specialized delivery equipment (e.g., pay-per-view entertainment) will need some local physical presence, provided by the company itself or by local partners. The ease of global value chain location for people-processing and possession-processing services will depend on the extent of local presence needed. In general, more local sites will be needed for people processing, making that type of service probably the most difficult to operate globally.

Globally uniform marketing. All three types of services should be able to make use of globally uniform marketing, although the extent will differ for each element of the marketing mix. Uniform pricing will be least possible for people-processing services, given the wide international variations in both costs and per capita income. Conversely, people-processing services probably have the most to gain from uniform branding as a way to build recognition with both local and foreign (visiting) customers. Possession-processing services often attract multinational customers (e.g., aircraft maintenance and package delivery), making it necessary to coordinate global marketing strategy and offer uniform terms of service.

Discussion: Implications for Theory and Practice

What are the implications of our framework for both theory building and management practice? A key point is that making broad generalizations about "services" cannot be expected to provide useful insights into opportunities for globalization. Instead, researchers and managers alike have to understand the components of a service and the processes by which its different elements are created and delivered. First, they need to distinguish between the core product (which may be either a service or a physical object) and supplementary service elements. Second, they must recognize that there are three broad categories of core product, reflecting differences in the underlying processes, degree of customer involvement, and potential for delivery through electronic channels. Third, the Flower of Service model offers both researchers and practitioners a means of understanding and disaggregating the package of "supplementary services" that augments and adds value to the core product.

Locating the Service Facility.   In the future, we shall see a greater distinction between services that require an on-site "factory" in each country and those that require only a delivery system. By definition, all people-processing services that do not require customers to travel outside their home country for service delivery will require on-site operations in each country. The same will be true of any possession-processing service that cannot readily transport the object in question to another location for servicing. In these instances, managers may find that the best way to achieve global consistency in the core products is to create easily replicable service concepts, backed by clear standards, that allow for either franchises or country managers to clone the original core product in a new setting.

Information-based services offer management greater flexibility to split the back office and front office, with opportunities to centralize the former on a global or regional basis. Production can thus take place in one location (or just a few), yielding economies of scale and access to global expertise, while delivery remains local. Banking, insurance, and other financial service products lend themselves well to delivery through electronic channels. Many forms of news, information, and entertainment can also be delivered worldwide through public or private networks. Key issues in globalization include the constraints imposed by language, culture, and government regulations.

Customizing Global Services through Supplementary Service Elements.   Increasingly, core service products that are sold globally are more likely to be standardized than customized (McDonald's Veggie Burgers should be seen as an exception rather than a trend). Managers should, however, be looking for supplementary service elements that can be customized in other ways that tailor the overall service package to meet local requirements. Each of the eight petals in the Flower of Service lends itself to adaptation on three dimensions: the level of service provided can be adapted to reflect local preferences and ability to pay; the style of delivery can be adapted to cultural norms; and information transfers can be adapted to local idioms and offered in local languages.

Global Location of Value Chain.   Different service elements can be sourced from different locations. The physical supplies needed for certain types of service delivery (such as food for hotels, fuel for transport vehicles, or spare parts for repair jobs) are often shipped from one country for consumption in another. The same is sometimes true for imported labor. But some companies, like McDonald's, are choosing to build up a network of local suppliers and to train host country nationals for local jobs as quickly as possible.[28]

As noted earlier, information-based services can be produced in one part of the world and delivered through electronic channels for consumption elsewhere. Indeed, information technology is emerging as a key globalization driver for such services. In mutual funds, for instance, offerings are now being pieced together from elements created in many different countries. Unlike physical goods, the logistics of service "assembly" and delivery tend to be much simpler once the necessary infrastructure and network are in place. Further, as shown in Exhibit 1 earlier, a majority of the petals of the Flowers of Service are information-dependent and can potentially be delivered from remote locations. In theory, a global company could centralize its billing on a global basis, using postal or telecommunication distribution channels to deliver the bills to customers, suitably converted to the relevant currency.

Similarly, information, consultation, order-taking/reservations, and many aspects of problem solving and payment could all be handled through telecommunications channels, ranging from voice telephone to the World Wide Web. So long as service personnel speaking the appropriate languages are available, many such service elements could be delivered from almost anywhere. Recent patterns of immigration in a country may create a comparative advantage in multilingual capabilities. By contrast, hospitality and safekeeping will always have to be provided locally because they are responsive to the physical presence of customers and their possessions.

Like manufacturers, service firms should be looking for opportunities to exploit differences in national comparative advantages as they seek to build more efficient value chains. Significant economies may be gained by centralizing "information hubs" on a global basis, as Federal Express does in Memphis. Through outsourcing, firms can also reduce the need for large fixed-cost investments. Taking advantage of favorable labor costs and exchange rates, a growing number of service-based businesses have identified key back-office activities that can be conducted more cheaply but without loss of quality in a different country from where their customers are located. This is happening with front-office elements, too, as companies build global reservation and customer service systems that are networked around the world.

Global Marketing of Services.   Difficulties in evaluating services lead to uncertainty, but this problem can be offset by strong branding and a globally consistent use of corporate design elements. Hence, the primary task of the brand name or trademark for a service may be to offer recognition and reassurance, rather than performing other functions such as positioning or local adaptation. Global branding should be supported by global advertising and globally consistent corporate design, featuring recognizable color schemes (yellow for Hertz, bright green for BP service stations), an easily identified logo and trademark, and even consistency in retail office design. One of the challenges when creating global campaigns is to create visual themes that will travel well across different cul-

tures (it is relatively simple to add voice-overs in the local language). This requirement may pose a need to retain a global advertising agency.

In contrast, simultaneity of production and consumption in many service businesses means that firms have less need to worry about globally consistent pricing. Except for those information-based services that can be captured in printed or electronic hard copies, it is still relatively difficult to buy a service created in one country for resale in another. On the other hand, there are sometimes wide disparities between prices for international telephone calls, depending on the country in which it originates. For instance, a call from Rome to New York is far more expensive than from New York to Rome. (This anomaly has been exploited by companies such as AT&T, which offers customers traveling abroad the opportunity to dial a local number to place the call and charge it at American rates to the customer's home account.) In the case of multinational customers, service businesses need to consider the use of global account management as a means of achieving coordination and consistency.[29]

Conclusion

More and more service businesses are now operating across national borders. Globalization and global strategy concepts developed for manufacturing businesses can also be applied to service businesses. Some significant differences may exist, particularly among people-processing, possession-processing, and information-based services. Companies can develop effective global strategies by systematically analyzing the specific globalization drivers affecting their industries and the distinctive characteristics of their service businesses.

Notes

1. Johny K. Johansson, "Japanese Service Industries and their Overseas Potential," *The Service Industries Journal,* 10/1 (January 1990): 85–109.
2. See John H. Dunning, "Transnational Corporations

and the Growth of Services: Some Conceptual and Theoretical Issues," *United Nations Centre on Transnational Corporations,* Series A, No. 9 (March 1989); Hervé Mathe and Cynthia Perras, "Successful Global Strategies for Service Companies," *Long Range Planning,* 7/1 (1994): 36–49; Sandra Vandermerwe and Michael Chadwick, "The Internationalization of Services," *The Services Industry Journal* (January 1989), pp. 79–93.

3. George S. Yip, *Total Global Strategy: Managing for Worldwide Competitive Advantage* (Englewood Cliffs, NJ: Prentice Hall, 1992).

4. Christopher H. Lovelock, *Services Marketing* (Englewood Cliffs, NJ: Prentice Hall, 1991); Christopher H. Lovelock, *Product Plus: How Product + Service = Competitive Advantage* (New York, NY: McGraw-Hill, 1994).

5. See Thomas Hout, Michael E. Porter, and Eileen Rudden, "How Global Companies Win Out," *Harvard Business Review* (September/October 1982), pp. 98–108; C. K. Prahalad and Yves L. Doz, *The Multinational Mission: Balancing Local Demands and Global Vision* (New York, NY: Free Press, 1987); George S. Yip, "Global Strategy . . . In a World of Nations?" *Sloan Management Review,* 31/1 (Fall 1989): 29–41.

6. Michael E. Porter, "Changing Patterns of International Competition," *California Management Review,* 28/2 (Winter 1986): 9–40.

7. Yip (1989), op. cit.; Yip (1992), op. cit.

8. See, for example, Bruce Kogut, "Designing Global Strategies: Comparative and Competitive Value-Added Chains," *Sloan Management Review* (Summer 1985), pp. 27–38; Prahalad and Doz, op. cit.

9. Johny K. Johansson and George S. Yip, "Exploiting Globalization Potential: U.S. and Japanese Strategies," *Strategic Management Journal* (October 1994), pp. 579–601.

10. See Suzan Segal-Horn, "Strategic Issues in the Globalization of Service Industries: A Discussion Paper," in P. Jones, ed., *The Management of Service Industries* (London: Pittman, 1988/89); Ram Kesavan and Eric Panitz, "Standardizing Services for Global Competitiveness: Literature Review and Hypotheses Generation," in Ben L. Kedia and Lars Larson, eds., *U.S. Competitiveness in the Global Marketplace: A Special Focus on the Service Sector,* Conference Proceedings, CIBER, Memphis State University, Memphis, TN, 1991; Alexandra Campbell and Alain Verbeke, "The Globalization of Service Multinationals," *Long Range Planning,* 2 (1994): 95–102; and Mathe and Perras, op. cit.

11. Christopher A. Bartlett and Sumantra Ghoshal, *Managing Across Borders: The Transnational Solution* (Boston, MA: Harvard Business School Press, 1989).

12. W. Earl Sasser, R. Paul Olsen, and D. Daryl Wyckoff, *Management of Service Operations: Text, Cases, and Readings* (Boston, MA: Allyn & Bacon, 1978).

13. Christopher H. Lovelock, "Think Before You Leap in Services Marketing," in L. L. Berry, G. Lynn Shostack, and G. D. Upah, Proceedings of Conference on *Emerging Perspectives in Services Marketing,* American Marketing Association, Chicago, 1983, pp. 115–19.

14. Lovelock (1991), op. cit.

15. Christopher J. Lovelock, "Classifying Services to Gain Strategic Marketing Insights," *Journal of Marketing,* 47 (Summer 1983): 9–20; Lovelock (1991), op. cit.; Lovelock (1994), op. cit.

16. Richard B. Chase, "Where Does the Customer Fit in a Service Operation?" *Harvard Business Review* (November/December 1978), pp. 137–42.

17. See Theodore Levitt, *Marketing for Business Growth* (New York, NY: McGraw-Hill, 1974), p. 47.

18. Several theorists have attempted to develop frameworks for understanding the structure of service products. G. Lynn Shostack, "Breaking Free from Product Marketing" *Journal of Marketing,* 41 (April 1977): 73–80, developed a molecular model, applicable to either goods or services, to help marketers visualize and manage what she termed a "total market entity." At the centre is the core benefit, addressing the basic customer need, which is then linked to a series of other service elements. She argues that, as in chemical formulations, a change in one element may completely alter the nature of the entity. Surrounding the molecules are a series of bands representing price, distribution, and market positioning (communication messages).

19. Lovelock (1994), op. cit.

20. B. Joseph Pine, *Mass Customization: A New*

Frontier in Business Competition (Boston, MA: ABS Press, 1993).

21. See review in Yip (1989), op. cit.; Yip (1992), op. cit.
22. Kesavan and Panitz (1991), op. cit.
23. Gary Hamel and C. K. Prahalad. "Do You Really Have a Global Strategy?" *Harvard Business Review* (July/August 1985), pp. 139–48.
24. Yip (1992), op. cit.
25. For an in-depth discussion of the role of value-adding activities in competitive strategy, see

Michael E. Porter, *Competitive Advantage* (New York, NY: The Free Press, 1985).
26. Johansson and Yip (1994), op. cit.
27. Pei-yuan Chia, "Citibanking the World," *Bank Management* (July/August 1995).
28. Andrew E. Serwer, "McDonald's Conquers the World," *Fortune,* October 17, 1994, pp. 103–16.
29. See George S. Yip and Tammy L. Madsen, "Global Account Management: The New Frontier in Relationship Marketing," *International Marketing Review* (Forthcoming 1996).

THE HARMONIZATION OF STANDARDS IN THE EUROPEAN UNION AND THE IMPACT ON U.S. BUSINESS

Tom Reilly

The goal of the European Union is to strengthen Europe's economy by creating an internal free market among the community's 15 member nations with common external trade barriers to the rest of the world. This internal market is based on the removal of barriers to allow for the free movement of products, labor, and capital. The 15 nations include: Belgium, France, Italy, Luxembourg, Netherlands, and Germany (as established by the 1957 Treaties of Rome); Denmark, Ireland, and the United Kingdom (added in 1973); Greece (1981); Spain and Portugal (1986); and Austria, Finland, and Sweden (1995).

The success of the single European market depends on three major developments: the elimination of internal customs barriers and immigration restrictions; the reduction of fiscal barriers and the possible creation of a single European currency; and the harmonization of product standards among the 15 member nations. And although all of these developments are sure to have a profound impact on European firms, the creation of pan-European product standards is likely to have the most far-

reaching effects on U.S. companies. To predict the consequences of European standardization on American firms, an understanding of the EU's standard-setting process is needed.

European Standardization

Although the term *standard* is used in various ways throughout the European Union (EU), a broad definition refers to a commonly accepted set of principles, practices, or requirements that goods or services must meet to be marketed within a particular jurisdiction. Standards may be voluntary or mandatory, and may be set by a governmental or private standard-setting body. They may define necessary product features or mandatory elements of a production process.

There are several motivating factors behind the harmonization of standards within the European Union. First, uniform standards are designed to promote minimum health and safety requirements for workers and consumers across the community. Nations have traditionally set minimum qualifications on a wide variety of products and work-related situations, ranging from motor vehicle passenger protection to meat production procedures. Health and safety standards often translate into

From *Business Horizons,* March/April 1995, pp. 28-34. © 1995 by the Foundation for the School of Business at Indiana University. Reprinted by permission.

technical specifications, such as requiring a lawn mower to have specific guards (safety standard) and maximum noise level (health standard). Manufacturers may be forced to make major design changes to conform with a particular health or safety standard imposed in a nation or trading area. Recent EU product liability laws have intensified the need for manufacturers to meet health and safety standards.

Harmonized standards are also a means of eliminating trade barriers disguised as national standards. Because standards dictate the requirements a product must meet to be marketed in a particular area, they are often viewed as nontariff barriers (NTBs) to trade. Problems may arise when governments set standards in such a way that a national industry is protected from competition. Some examples of standards as NTBs include the French standard that all tractors must be equipped with automobile-style headlights, whether they travel on roads or not; this favors French manufacturers who traditionally designed equipment in this way. The Belgium standard stating that margarine must be packed in cubes favors local producers. International agreements such as the General Agreement on Tariffs and Trade (GATT), to which the U.S. and EU are signatories, have also striven to eliminate unnecessary national standards. GATT, which operates by granting Most Favored Nation (MFN) status to members, bars the use of unnecessary national standards when the standard results in a restraint of trade. GATT also outlines many situations in which standards are necessary, such as in cases involving health and safety.

As part of the completion of the internal market, the EU has done much to prevent its member states from banning imports on the basis of nonconformance to local regulations. The EU, however, has made a major exception and left member states with control of local regulations in health and safety standards. This gap creates problems for companies in industries such as pharmaceuticals, engineering, foodstuffs, and precision medical equipment, and adds cost to industries such as motor vehicles.

Uniform standards facilitate cooperation among firms by promoting compatibility of product specifications. They serve to ensure that a part built in one plant will be compatible with parts in another plant, and that the product will be able to be used in various parts of the world. Standardization simplifies the coordination of firms, which can avoid costly mistakes by specifying that all products must be *"produced to EU standards."* German companies, for example, have traditionally noted "Specification According to DIN" (*Deutshes Institut fur Normung,* or German Institute for Standardization) with no additional explanation necessary. This simplifies transactions, ensures that parts from different suppliers will be compatible, and helps avoid costly misunderstandings. The compatibility of parts allows for economies of scale. In the past, lack of cooperation has resulted in varying operating environments in areas as fundamental as electrical equipment, weights and measures, and automotive regulations. Currently, for example, the electrical systems in Europe have widely varying voltages, quality, and plugs and fixtures. And though most European countries converted weights and measures to a decimal system in the second half of the twentieth century, many still use more than one measurement system, such as in measuring temperature. Creation of a single set of European standards will allow producers to take advantage of economies of scale in production and distribute a single product on a European-wide basis.

Although the importance of uniform product standards is generally acknowledged throughout the European Union, nations remain divided over such basics as sizes of clothing, electrical plugs, and units of measurement. Fundamental differences in culture and custom are still widespread in Europe. And there are nine different languages in common use in the EU's product packaging and labeling.

History of European Standardization.
Traditionally, many European countries had centralized national standard systems and standard-setting organizations. In Germany, the DIN has ex-

isted for more than 70 years and has created more than 20,000 standards. Similar standard-setting bodies, such as the British Standards Institute (BSI) and the *Association Française de Normalisation* (AFNOR), have been in place throughout Europe and have developed national guidelines ranging from testing nuclear reactors to the standard height of automotive headlights. European national standards systems normally dictate regulations and minimum requirements in the form of mandatory codes. Although individual nations have had centralized national standards, companies wishing to sell products across Europe historically have had to meet as many as 19 sets of varying standards.

The diversity of European standards seems relatively mild compared to the standard-setting system in the United States, which is highly decentralized with more than 400 organizations producing standards. The U.S. relies on voluntary standards developed and enforced by private organizations rather than a uniform national policy. Most U.S. standards are coordinated through the American National Standards Institute (ANSI), which is a private, industry-supported organization. ANSI has become actively involved in the European standard-setting process and has recently opened an office in Brussels.

Attempts at the harmonization of European standards can be traced to the April 1951 signing of the Treaty of Paris and the inception of the European Coal and Steel Community. After the signing of the 1957 Treaties of Rome, the current standard-setting institutions of the EU were established. The European Commission, in its 1985 White Paper, condemned varying national standards as creating additional costs, hampering cooperation between nations, and hindering the common European market. A European Court ruling known as the "Casis de Dijon" did much to establish the idea that EU members should not ban certain imports on the basis of a product's nonconformance to local regulations. Again, this ruling provided latitude in the case of local health and safety standards.

Originally, the task of harmonization was to be conducted by a central standard-setting body that would draft detailed descriptions of minimum requirements to be accepted throughout Europe. It was estimated that the EU would have to harmonize standards in more than 10,000 product categories simply to meet the 1992 deadline set by the Single European Act. The size and scope of European standardization proved easier said than done, however, and some negotiations promised to take years to settle. To speed the process, the EU implemented a *new approach* that focused on 1,500 of the most vital product categories that had to be completed for 1992.

The "New Approach."   The EU's new approach put into place a system of mutual recognition of member states' standards in some areas while setting new Europeanwide minimum standards in a number of other areas. Theoretically, a producer that is allowed to sell products in one country cannot be prevented from selling the same product in another member country; a product will only have to meet one European standard, not a dozen different ones. Instead of preparing individual directives aimed at removing trade-related problems (as in the old approach), the EU will prepare broad technical directives to cover such areas as health, safety, and environmental protection. Specific directives will be made only in areas where serious conflict exists between member nations. If a serious conflict exists and a specific Europewide standard cannot be agreed upon, the standard-setting bodies will prepare a *harmonization document,* which specifies essential requirements that must be met and outlines customized local versions for each member.

The caveat to this new approach is that every EU member is obliged to acknowledge that products meeting the guidelines of this system are suitable for sale and use in the local market. Overall, conforming to a local standard, whether or not a specific EU directive applies, should ensure acceptance throughout the EU. A single set of Europeanwide essential requirements has already been

FIGURE 1

Areas in which Europeanwide essential requirements have been set

- Building products.
- Gas appliances.
- Lifting and loading equipment.
- Machine safety.
- Medical devices.
- Mobile machines.
- Earth movers.
- Personal protection equipment.
- Rollover protection equipment.
- Simple pressure vessels.
- Light industrial trucks.
- Telecommunications equipment.
- Toys.

agreed upon in some areas (see Figure 1), while proposals to cover other areas are in the works.

Administration of Standards. The task of harmonizing standards for the EU falls upon the European Commission, which works closely with international standard-setting bodies. The implementation of new EU standards is conducted by a common European decisionmaking body, which is

consulted by various government and nongovernment standardization committees. Within the standard-setting bodies, there is fierce debate among committees trying to influence the final version of the standard.

Several committees have been charged with the development of standards in specific areas. The organization that handles product standards in general is the CEN (*Comité Européen de Normalisation,* or European Committee for Standardization), which is made up of subcommittees from various parts of the EU. The CEN is organized into three major segments: a *supervisory* segment, a *technical standardization* segment, and a *certification* segment. An outline of its structure is presented in Figure 2.

The supervisory work of the CEN is conducted by its general assembly, which is made up of delegates from each EU member nation, and the administrative board, comprising the directors of participating national standards organizations. All proposed standards and requirements must be approved first by the administrative board and finally by the general assembly. The technical office, relying on consultation from program committees or

FIGURE 2

Organization of CEN

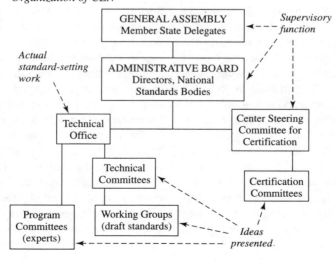

technical committees, does the actual standard-setting work. Program committees are made up of experts who supply necessary advice for specific standardization issues. Technical committees are made up of working groups that propose drafts of standards. It is important for outsiders to monitor the work going on in the technical committees, since this is where various countries and industries present concerns and lobby to have their version of a standard adopted for all of Europe. By the time the proposed standards leave the technical office for submission to the administrative board, almost all of the major issues have been resolved.

The standard-setting process, as illustrated in Figure 3, is conducted by the CEN and experts from interested countries. Before a standard can be formally accepted, it must pass the CEN general assembly's voting process. Each of the member nations receives a number of votes proportionate to its relative size in the European market. The criteria for passing the voting process are that a majority must accept the proposed standard, there must not be more than 22 "No" votes, and there must not be more than three countries voting "No." The process typically involves eight months or more of intense negotiation.

The desired result of the process is a European-wide standard that is the same in all member countries. When members decide that a single European standard will be impractical, unnecessary, or too difficult to agree upon, a harmonization document is created.

Mutual Recognition and Testing. The *Global Approach to Certification and Testing* was initiated in 1989 to promote confidence in product safety, manufacturers, testing laboratories, and certification bodies. This approach is designed to measure a product's conformity to an EU directive and attach a recognizable certification mark on satisfactory products. The mark for products on which a European standard has been agreed upon is the "CE" mark shown in Figure 4. Each member must allow all certified products to be marketed as complying to local standards, regardless of the product's origin. An example of the conditions a product must meet to earn a "CE" mark is shown in Figure 5.

Producers in non-EU nations must follow the same certification procedures and have products pass the same requirements as producers within the EU. In accordance with the principles covering technical barriers to trade set forth in GATT, non-EU products have the same rights to certification systems and to bear the "CE" mark as native EU products.

FIGURE 3

CEN standard-setting process

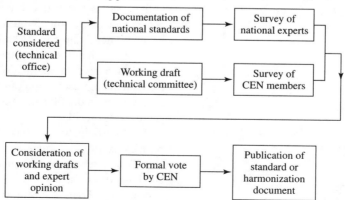

Quality.   Product quality is probably the broadest aspect covered by European standardization. This is because of its wide application in business and its importance in the area of product liability. In 1985, the EU issued a *Product Liability Directive* stating that a producer will be liable, regardless of fault or negligence, if a person is harmed or an object damaged by a faulty product. Because EU law places the burden of proof on the producer (in other words, guilty until proven innocent), a firm will have to prove that its products are free from defects and deficiencies to avoid liability. When defending a product liability claim, a producer must demonstrate that a certified quality assurance program was in use during production.

Current EU quality standards are guided by the International Standards Organization (ISO). They are based on the ISO 9000 series standards, and are appropriately named EN9000. (In the U.S. they are known as the Q90 series.) Many European firms require suppliers and subcontractors to meet European-quality standards or have quality systems audited through third-party certification. Contracts may be written or bids awarded on the grounds that design, development, installation, and servicing meet ISO criteria.

Current trends suggest an increasing role of quality standards in Europe. Some proposed regulations may require producers and importers to permanently monitor the safety of a product throughout its useful life. European firms already require that quality standards be met in about 50 percent of its contracts.

Effects of European Standardization on American Firms

The unification of European standards presents both enormous opportunities and threats to U.S. producers. American companies may soon be able to market a single product to 368 million EU consumers, or they may be shut out by protectionist European policies. The stakes are high for companies planning on entering this market as well as for those with an established European presence.

U.S. Role in International Standardization.

Many American firms had little problem operating in Europe's old regulatory environment. After all, the American standardization system had nearly as many regional variations. At home, U.S. firms were used to meeting varying, often conflicting standards, set by organizations as diverse as the American National Standards Institute (ANSI), the Department of Defense, the Food and Drug Administration, or the Environmental Protection Agency. As mentioned earlier, the U.S. system of standardization is based on a combination of mandatory government regulation and voluntary standards put in place by various public and private standard-setting bodies.

American firms now need to become involved in international standard harmonization, both as a tool to combat regional protectionism and to promote possible economies of scale and scope. The United States has actively worked to further the acceptance of worldwide product standards by entering bilateral agreements and participating in institutions such as the ISO. American firms can also maintain a role in international standard-setting through the representation of ANSI, which is heavily involved in the ISO and has even had a delegate serve as its president.

U.S. participation in the EU's standardization process is limited, since outside nations do not have formal representation in standard-setting proceedings (with the exception of the remaining European Free Trade Association, or EFTA, nations

FIGURE 4

European Union certification symbol

FIGURE 5

Examples of conditions of earning a CE mark

Directive 88/378/EEC on the Safety of Toys		
Producer chooses to conform to:	*Procedure for assessment:*	*CE Mark affixed by:*
Harmonized standard	Producer provides declaration; must make information dossier available for inspection by EC	Producer

OR

Essential requirments of directive	Examination of sample product by EC approval body	Producer, after certification

that participate in the standardization process). American influence can be asserted, informally, through the European subsidiaries of U.S. companies and in the form of passive participation and commentary during EU talks. Often, European standards unintentionally favor European products, since the process is heavily influenced by European designs and preferences.

U.S.–EU Agreements.   In 1989, the U.S. and the EU entered into an agreement to make it easier for U.S. companies to receive advance notice of planned standards and make comments to EU regulatory bodies. This agreement actually gave U.S. companies the right to sit in on EU standardization negotiations and is often cited as an illustration of the EU's genuine concern for the removal of technical barriers to trade.

Efforts have also been made to adopt international standards that transcend both the United States and Europe. In 1991, the two governmental bodies agreed to remove conflicting U.S. and EU standards when consensus international standards were developed. Cooperation between the United States and the EU is conducted by ANSI, the

American Society for Testing and Materials, the European Committee for Norms, the European Telecommunications Standards Institute, and the ISO. Currently, unplanned technical barriers still exist between the two trading regions in such basic areas as voltages for electrical items and sizes of industrial fasteners, such as nuts and bolts.

Potential Threats to U.S. Companies in Europe.   One of the biggest fears among American producers is that the protectionist politics of the EU will result in standards that are created in favor of European products. These fears are compounded by events such as a recent EU ban on U.S. pork and beef, which was condemned because of "substandard" slaughterhouse practices. Whether or not the meat ban was appropriate, at least one U.S. official took offense and stated, "We would not welcome any additional restraints on U.S. exports to Europe."

Some EU members have been accused of stalling standardization talks in an effort to retain the last bits of control over foreign imports. Italy, France, and Spain have been consistently disagreeable when talks focus on automotive safety standards that would allow cars to be sold freely throughout Europe. Blatant attempts to use standards to block competition help enforce the stereotype of "Fortress Europe," in which American products are not welcome.

Many European standards, notably in health and safety, are criticized for being overambitious with no foreseeable benefits. Some products have had to undergo expensive design changes that do not improve—and may even hinder—product performance. The price of making major changes that have not been demanded by customers may be so high that producers will be discouraged from the European market.

Potential Opportunities and Benefits.

Even with the problems, though, U.S. firms face tremendous gains from the harmonization of European standards. The sheer size of the unified European market holds great promise for producers who seek economies of scale or broad marketing reach. The potential of meeting a single standard for 368 million Europeans provides incentive for products that previously did not find the fragmented Europe attractive.

European standardization has also helped pave the way for what may some day be truly worldwide product standards. Global standards are becoming a reality in many areas, allowing U.S. firms to conduct business freely with companies throughout the world. At the very least, the harmonization of standards among regional trading blocks has called attention to the benefits of early cooperation among nations.

Another potential benefit for the United States may arise from the need to implement strict quality control practices for products marketed in Europe. American companies that have not properly implemented comprehensive quality systems will now be forced to do so to compete in Europe. Higher quality is sure to benefit U.S. consumers and producers, who will be able to reap the rewards of better products.

Considering the size and scope of the standards to be harmonized, it is safe to assume that a com-

pletely harmonized set of European standards is still far in the future. The process is painstakingly slow because of the wide variety of factors that must be considered. The size of the European market—368 million people with a combined GDP of almost $6 trillion—will surely mean that standards set there will affect global product and process norms.

Unfortunately, it is quite difficult for outside interests to exert as much influence as EU members during the harmonization process. European standard-setting bodies are naturally influenced by European process designs and products. American firms, on the other hand, must work through representatives of European subsidies and standard-setting bodies.

In the short run, EU standards could hurt the ability of some U.S. firms to compete in Europe. Standards are apt to mean expensive product design changes and the loss of varying degrees of competitiveness to native European firms. Non-European companies may also run into difficulty and expense when trying to meet certification criteria for health, safety, and quality standards. During the early stages of harmonization, many firms may continue to experience unplanned complications in their European operations.

Over the longer term, however, the harmonization of standards could be a boon to U.S. companies by reducing the multiplicity of standards in Europe. American firms and consumers may also benefit from the focus on product quality. Ultimately, after the costs of meeting standards are paid, the cost of operating in Europe could be drastically reduced.

Since the EU has granted the U.S. the right to receive advance notice of standardization and to comment on proposed standards, U.S. concerns have a unique chance of influencing the standards that will affect all of Europe. The benefits to be reaped by those who get involved early and stay on top of the work being done are substantial. Influence may be gained by focusing on the work of standard-setting committees through passive participation or local subsidiaries. Companies that monitor the progress of harmonization can gain valuable insight that will allow them to take active steps in areas that will affect their operations.

U.S. firms should also make an effort to influence the setting of worldwide standards through ANSI representation to global standard-setting bodies. This is especially important since the U.S. and the EU have agreed to allow international standards to supersede conflicting local standards.

Overall, the United States should become ag-gressively involved in European and interregional standardization. This will allow American companies to learn of anticipated changes and possibly help shape future standards.

References

"EC Calls U.S. Meat Unsanitary," *The Wall Street Journal,* October 26, 1990, p. A12.

THE ROLLER COASTER RIDE TO GLOBAL SATELLITE MARKETING

Lessons from Hughes

Bruce Leeds

The use of satellites for communications was in an emergent stage in the 1970s. Back in those days, the manufacturing cost to build a satellite was very high. That didn't include the costs of launch, research, etc.

Hughes Aircraft Company developed the first successful communications satellite and was an early player in this lucrative—but expensive—business. How could we reduce costs? The marketing strategy we developed was to build satellites using the same methods General Motors uses to build Chevrolets. Instead of custom-making individual satellites for each customer, Hughes decided to manufacture a series of satellites that shared common hardware. By modifying some of the electronics and antennas, we could sell them to a variety of customers. We named them our HS 376 line.

Our first customer was Telsat Canada which wanted to purchase two satellites. However, there was a major condition attached to the contract. Hughes had to spend approximately 40 percent of the contract price purchasing Canadian goods and services in return. This would amount to tens of millions of dollars. There's only so much of that

_____

From _Business Forum,_ Winter/Spring 1995, pp. 5–8.

offset that you can achieve by flying on Air Canada and staying at Canadian hotels. Therefore, we launched a drive to identify products the Canadians could manufacture for us. Canada had an existing electronics and aerospace industry, but had limited experience building satellite parts. Hughes assisted the Canadians in learning how to build components for the Hughes satellites. Every time we sold a 376 satellite, we returned to the Canadian suppliers for additional parts.

Paying Duty

Purchasing parts from Canada required paying duty charges, especially in the pre-North American Free Trade Agreement days. This was not a simple matter. The U.S. Customs Service tariff schedule is contained in a large book that lists thousands of items. At that time, the tariff on Canadian imports was the same as for items purchased in Japan or West Germany. Although tariff regulations have a classification for parts of satellites, customs regulations state that if an item you're importing is listed under more than one classification, you must use the most specific one. For example, let's say we were importing automobile parts—a fender, windshield, and a carburetor. Only the fender is listed under "parts of motor vehicles." The windshield is listed under "laminated glass for automobiles" (which requires a higher tariff), and the carburetor can be found under "parts for internal combustion engines."

Now, let's consider duty on satellite parts. There is a key component called a traveling wave tube (TWT), which is produced in Europe and imported. TWTs are microwave electronic tubes that amplify radio signals. Are they duty-free because they are "parts of satellites"? Sorry. Another listing in the customs tariff schedule attaches a 4.2 percent duty to "electronic tubes." TWTs are about one foot long and one and one-half inches around. The cost can range from $100,000 to as much as $250,000. Our satellites require as many as 45 aboard one spacecraft. A TWT may be imported with a power supply attached. In that configuration, it is a TWTA. What does customs do with that? There is another duty category—"parts of radio transmission and reception apparatus"—which applies a 5.9 percent duty on the TWTA. If the TWTA is installed on what's called an electronic shelf in the heart of the spacecraft, and the shelf is imported, the shelf assembly may be classified duty-free as a part of a satellite. Are you still with me?

We made other satellites in the 376 series for Western Union (Westar) and Indonesia (Palpa), sent them to Florida, and launched them from a NASA space shuttle flying 200 miles above earth. After the satellites were far enough from the shuttle, the rocket motors were fired to send them 23,000 miles further. However, the motors failed to ignite, or they ignited improperly, and the satellites were stuck in useless orbits. Now what?

Because both were insured by Lloyds of London, Western Union and the Indonesian government collected on their policies. Lloyds of London, therefore, owned two satellites in useless orbit. Now, enter customs again. Customs has a program dating back to 1789 called "drawback." The idea is that if you import an item and pay duty on it, but then use it to manufacture something else that you export, you can seek a refund for the amount of the original duty. The objective is to en-

courage exports. In the case of satellites, there is an old, still-honored ruling that considers the launch of a satellite an export for drawback purposes. In the case of Westar and Palpa, the two drawback claims amounted to about $300,000.

Retrieval Red Tape

One year later, Lloyds of London contracted with NASA to try to retrieve the satellites. The mission, which was broadcast around the world on television, was a spectacular success. There on the screen were astronauts floating around in their space suits, capturing the satellites, and locking them in the cargo bay. Watching all this was the customs employee who had handled the drawback claims. He telephoned me to ask, "Aren't those the same satellites you filed drawback claims on?" "Yes," I admitted, to which he replied, "Tell you what. On one of them, I know we've already sent you a check, so we expect you to return the money. As for the other one, because we are still processing the refund, we will stop payment." I composed a three-page letter, citing legal precedents about ships sinking at sea, and such, as legal precedents for why they should honor our claim. I pointed out that, regarding merchandise, the owner of the goods is responsible for entry and duty payment. In this instance, the owner was Lloyds of London. I provided the name and address of their agent in the United States, and said: "Collect from them, and give us our refund." The customs official retired the very next month, neglected to stop payment on the second check, and customs never did ask us to repay the original refund.

Once the two satellites were back on Earth, Lloyds of London took possession of them. What could they do with them? They decided to give Hughes a contract to refurbish them. So now we had the satellites and a contract to refurbish them—but for whom? The Palpa satellite was eventually sold back to the Indonesians, and the Westar was sold to a consortium, based in Hong Kong, called AsiaSat.

In the satellite industry, a customer normally

will contract with a company like Hughes or Loral to build the spacecraft and select another firm to build the launch vehicle. When NASA gave up the commercial launch business, other companies filled the void. In the United States, the major builders are Martin-Marietta, McDonnell Douglas, and General Dynamics. The Europeans have a consortium, which builds and launches the Ariane rocket, called Arianespace. The Soviets build the Proton rocket, and the Chinese have the Long March.

AsiaSat chose the Chinese Long March rocket as the launch vehicle. The Long March design originated in Russia as an Intercontinental Ballistic Missile, and the Chinese modified it into a launch vehicle. It was a very good rocket with a high success rate and few launch failures. It was extremely effective in putting Chinese satellites into orbit, but no one except the Chinese had ever used it for that purpose. Because this decision occurred at the time the Reagan administration was enjoying improved relations with China, the administration hinted to Hughes that if it applied for an export license to send the satellite to China for the launch, the authorities might approve the application. So, in the late 1980s, Hughes applied for an export license and subsequently received it.

Plans Continue

When we began our initial preparations to send the satellite to China for the launch, the Tien-an-men Square massacre occurred. That put a stop to everything. The U.S. government suspended all export licenses to China, and our relations with China were in jeopardy. However, our Washington, D.C., office was told by the White House to continue with the plan to launch the satellite. Eventually, we received the go-ahead to ship the satellite to China for launch.

Shipping a satellite and its accompanying test and handling equipment is always a challenge. Although we had shipped satellites to French Guyana for launch on the Ariane, neither we nor anyone else had ever shipped a satellite to China.

Hughes technicians assemble a satellite similar to that launched from China

Shipping the satellite to China required chartering a 747 freighter at considerable expense. However, some of our shipment couldn't be placed on the plane because the airlines wouldn't accept some of the explosives and the highly toxic hydrazine fuel. These would have to be transported by ocean freighter. We were limited to selecting a U.S. flag carrier because of government security requirements. We selected Federal Express. The site selected for the satellite's arrival was a Chinese military air base where no 747 had ever landed. Federal Express insisted on safety assurances. The carrier requested details about the radar and air traffic control systems at the airport, and the width, length, and composition of the runway. When we relayed the request to the Chinese, they simply answered, "Tell them they can land here; we'll take care of everything." Federal Express said, "Sorry, no deal, if you can't give us details about the landing site." This was not only an important project for Hughes, but also quite prestigious for the Chinese, who were very anxious for the project to go forward. For them, it was a matter of national honor to have a foreign satellite launched on their rocket. We relayed Federal Express' answer that they wouldn't fly to China without the airport details. I remember subsequently receiving a seven-page fax from China containing everything you'd ever want to know about that airport.

Several export licenses and extensive documentation are required for a project of this magnitude. We continued to map plans for the project even though we had no export licenses because we were continually told, ". . . not to worry; the licenses would be coming." Christmas 1989 approached, and still we had no licenses. The ocean freighter, carrying explosives and fuel, was set to sail the first week of January 1990. The date for the 747 charter flight was set for mid-February. One week before the ship departed, the licenses arrived. Permission had come directly from the White House. Approving the licenses could be politically sensitive, and it should be noted that the final approval to use the licenses occurred while Congress was in

recess for the holidays. By the time Congress was back in sessions, the ship had already sailed, and we were preparing for the 747 charter.

More Government Dealings

One week before the charter was scheduled to depart, I received a call from the U.S. Department of Commerce in Washington. The Department of State grants export licenses—or did in those days—for such items as satellites and rocket motors. The Department of Commerce issues licenses for such items as test equipment. We had obtained a State Department license to cover everything being sent to China. Department of Commerce officials objected, contending that they might have license jurisdiction over some of the items in this high-visibility project. We had obtained a license for one x-ray machine from the Department of Commerce, but officials believed that this was not enough. I was called to Washington on 24 hours' notice to explain to the department what we had done—five days before the charter was scheduled to depart. We quickly applied for five Department of Commerce licenses which were approved in only three days. They arrived the day before charter left for China.

The ship with the hydrazine, alcohol, and other hazardous cargo sailed from Long Beach, California, to Guangzhou (earlier known as Canton). The destination of the airplane that carried the satellite and other items was Xichang, a town in rural China that was 30 kilometers (about 19 miles) from the launch site. It was at least 1,000 miles from Guangzhou or any major port. To get the chemicals from Guangzhou to the launch site, we requested assistance from the Chinese. They replied that they would ship the goods by rail—a three-week trip.

Then, more problems arose as we researched the process of transporting the cargo. First is the issue of unloading the cargo from the side door of the 747 freighter. That door is two stories off the ground. We needed to use a special K-loader, which is similar to a scissors jack, to safely transfer the satellite out of the plane and onto the back of a truck. The only K-loaders in China were at the Beijing airport, so the Chinese had one transported by railroad to Xichang. Second, the satellite needed to be hauled by a truck equipped with air suspension. There was only one air suspension truck in all of China. The Chinese guaranteed that it would be there to meet the airplane, and it was. Along the road to the launch site was a bridge that was too low to allow the truck with its tall cargo to pass. The Chinese army dynamited the bridge.

About two weeks before the air freighter departed, we learned that still more hazardous materials needed to be shipped to China. These included items such as fuse lines, solvents, and a battery-powered forklift. The U.S. Department of Transportation would not allow these items to be carried aboard a 747 freighter. Fortunately, there were numerous air service cargo planes that flew to Tokyo. The problem became how to move the goods from Tokyo to Beijing. Japan Airlines listed only one trip per month for air freight to Beijing, and the schedule listed its departure "as required." Fortunately, it was scheduled to depart the following week. It arrived in Beijing on the first day of the Chinese New Year.

Holiday Delay

The entire nation of China shuts down for a whole week to celebrate the Chinese New Year. That event posed new problems. Under the terms of our security arrangements for the project, the shipment had to be accompanied by a U.S. national at all times. Where could we store the goods in China under U.S. surveillance 24-hours-a-day for one week? We checked with our parent company, General Motors, which has an office in Beijing, but that office is staffed by Chinese nationals. So much for that idea. The U.S. Embassy came to our rescue and accepted the entire shipment. The explosive bolts, fuses, solvents, and forklift sat there under Marine guard for an entire week. After the Chinese New Year celebration ended, everything was shipped to Xichang.

The Federal Express 747 freighter landed in Beijing for customs clearance and to allow a Chinese navigator to board the aircraft for the flight to Xichang. China has no modern air traffic control system in that part of the country, and airplanes are flown largely by sight. With his charts and maps, the navigator was stationed in the cabin to help direct the plane. Prior arrangements for customs clearance worked to our advantage. Even though we arrived in the middle of the night, a Chinese customs officer boarded the plane, signed the perfunctory paperwork, and left. Under the terms of the U.S.–China agreement, he was not permitted to see the cargo.

Xichang is a town in rural China where Americans had been seldom seen. The citizens certainly had never seen anything like a 747 aircraft. The mood was that of a national holiday when we arrived. The 30-kilometer route from the airport to the launch site was completely lined with curious onlookers. When they saw the trucks coming down the road, they knew it was the biggest event that had happened there in a very long time. They treated us like celebrities, and people followed us as we walked around town. After awhile, the citizens became more accustomed to the Americans, but initially, it was a unique situation.

Food was a problem in that part of China. Culinary and sanitary standards were not the same as in the United States. The Chinese had promised that a chef from one of the largest hotels in Hong Kong would cook for us. What arrived was a cook from the local hotel in Xichang. He was replaced after three days, and the replacement cook left after three more days. Eventually, a cook was brought in from the provincial capital in Chengdu. The Hughes employees showed him how to cook for American tastes. The first time he prepared a pork chop correctly, the Americans gave him a standing ovation. Making subsequent food shipments to China was also challenging. Fashioned after the Berlin Airlift, we had the Xichang Airlift. We arranged for food shipments that included frozen steaks, ice cream, six packs of Coors beer, and a host of other items. Sometimes the shipments had to be re-iced en route to keep the food from spoiling.

The spacecraft launch was almost anticlimactic, considering everything else we'd been through. Our technicians said it was one of the most successful launches they had ever seen. The Chinese rocket performed flawlessly.

Bringing the Equipment Home

Next it was time to test what I call Newton's Law of Export/Import—whatever goes out, comes back. In this case, it was all of the support equipment. One staff member had the assignment of documenting every item sent to, and received back from, China, including the crew's personal effects. This precaution was necessary because customs agents were more concerned about the personal items than any others. We had to charter another 747 for the return trip.

One would think that everything that was imported into, and then exported from, the U.S. would return duty-free because duty had been previously paid. We had test equipment made in Japan, Switzerland, and Taiwan. We had a Japanese VCR and television set plus other items of foreign origin. The rules required that we pay duty again on all foreign-made items. Along with the equipment was one 20-foot container that held 20 Chinese bicycles and three rickshaws. (We had discovered very high-quality bicycles in Xichang for $50 each.) Although the satellite equipment cargo cleared customs in one day, the bicycles and rickshaws required three weeks.

More Launches

We subsequently built two satellites for Australia, and they were both launched in China last year. The first experienced rocket motor shutdown on the launch pad. It was successfully relaunched six months later. The second launch was initially successful, but the satellite separated from the rocket 48 seconds after liftoff. The burning satellite fell to Earth and scattered debris over the Chinese countryside. Hughes paid Chinese farmers 39 cents a pound to gather the remains. They filled a 20-foot container with satellite debris, and it was returned to the U.S. for inspection.

When we were ready to return the scrap satellite debris for failure analysis, new questions arose. What value do you place on it? What tariff does satellite debris take? We declared that it was aluminum, which is duty free. When we sent the satellite to China for the launch, we received a $300,000 duty refund. Normally, if the satellite returned, we'd be required to pay back the refund. However, because of an interpretation of the customs laws, we were not importing a satellite—we were importing scrap aluminum, which is free of duty. We were then able to keep our money on export and didn't have to pay anything on import.

The history of the China launches is fascinating. There are valuable lessons to be learned, the most important that one must plan . . . and also improvise.

PROMOTIONAL STRATEGIES

The authors of the initial article in this section, *Global Ads Say It with Pictures,* believe that marketers of virtually all products and services can create effective advertisements based on universal concepts communicated via strong visual images. Marketers need to visualize concepts for products—not the products themselves—that can be globally presented.

A companion piece summarizes key oral and written communication principles for the international marketer contemplating expansion in nations with high-context and low-context cultures. Adherence to suggested principles should increase the effectiveness of U.S. marketing efforts, especially in the high-context cultures of Latin America, the Middle East, and Asia.

Evolving with super speed and impact are global information technologies. Riding along on this huge wave of innovation are international marketers. The third article in the section well captures current events in global marketing on the internet and makes recommendations for international marketing managers seeking to catch the wave.

Effective promotion of quality products and services is required for commercial success in both the United States and Japan. For many companies, particularly those selling business and industrial products and services, personal selling is the key aspect of promotion. So, proper management of the sales force is crucial in both countries. The last contribution in this section explores similarities and differences of salesperson motivation and management in these two major markets. An examination of sales force recruitment, training, compensation, and retention within both countries is included.

GLOBAL ADS SAY IT WITH PICTURES

Marc Bourgery and George Guimaraes

In 1984, the advertising world was galvanized when Harvard professor and marketing guru Ted Levitt announced that global marketing was here—and here to stay. Leaps in technology and communications, he argued, had made this the time to market products on a global plane. Advertising agencies, he said, would need to align themselves globally, like their clients, to sell a "one sight—one sound" message. After all, he said, if Marlboro and Coca-Cola could do it, why not every product and service? Human emotion was the same the world over, he reasoned, and could be appealed to cross-culturally in the pursuit of marketing efficiency.

Almost 10 years later, there's a lot of evidence to suggest Levitt is right. Mass media are spanning the globe: MTV has crossed borders successfully, communicating strong fashion, music, and design messages. Cable News Network (CNN) is *the* worldwide news vehicle, and *The Price Is Right* seems to play as well in Trentino, Italy, as it does in Peoria, Illinois. Brands like Chivas scotch, Dove soap, and IBM have made a global mark. And just as competitors like Japanese Sony, American AT&T, and Dutch Phillips are now teaming

up across borders to develop the latest technologies, ad agencies have attempted to follow suit by achieving global mass through mergers and global, integrated approaches to communication.

Why then, is there still so much controversy brewing about global advertising? The controversy stems from a lack of understanding of the true essence of communication. Marketers need to focus on how to determine whether concepts for products—not the products themselves—will cross borders. Because the world has evolved into a visual culture, marketers must become as skillful in influencing people's attitudes, feelings, and behavior through the right visual imagery as they have been through language.

Visual imagery is one of the most efficient ways of transcending all language barriers, whether these barriers lie between different languages or "intralingually"—between different interpretations of meaning within the same language. Basing your ads on a strong visual image can also help you keep your messages consistent globally. No one, for instance, would advise McDonald's to advertise as fast food in Europe and the United States, and then to advertise in Russia as luxurious dining.

Advertising agencies today are trying to create a "visual esperanto": a universal language that will make global advertising possible for virtually any

Reprinted from the *Journal of European Business,* May/June 1993. Permission granted by Faulkner & Gray, 11 Penn Plaza, New York, NY 10001.

217

**Cool, calm, and collected is
the visual image in L'Oreal's
pan-European PHAS
campaign, by Bloom FCA!.
You don't need to speak
French in order to
understand what the ad is
saying.**

product or service. The new visual esperanto is based on the idea that visual imagery is more powerful and precise than verbal description (which leaves too much room for personal interpretation). Moreover, all people can comprehend the messages of visual imagery.

Advertising professionals no longer need to be traditional market researchers—corporate marketing professionals are sophisticated enough. Instead, the ad agency's role is to find solutions to communications problems that extend beyond language. This means acting out the message using all available marketing and communications channels.

Smooth as Silk

Consider an ad by Bloom FCA! for Silk Cut cigarettes. The print ad, which appears on billboards and in publications throughout Europe, features a pair of scissors cutting through silk. Because the image describes the cigarette's name, it reinforces name recognition—if you remember the image, you'll probably remember the name when you go

to the store. The image also avoids the problems many current cigarette ads have faced: The ad doesn't depict a person, so antismoking advocates cannot blame the producers for targeting a specific age, sex, or race. It also does not depict a lifestyle—as do cigarette ads that imply smokers will be sexier, healthier, or more active if they puff on the particular brand. The ad doesn't depend on any words, and the visual image—silk—is understood by people everywhere as smooth and elegant—and those are the qualities, the ad implies, of Silk Cut cigarettes.

Portrait Planning

To create the appropriate visual image for your ad, start thinking in pictures as soon as possible. Instead of writing a statement of brand identity, visualize it. Then draw, photograph, or videotape what you've visualized. In other words, create a visual portrait of the personality of a brand. This portrait goes well beyond the typical written brand personality statement. It also keeps a brand's advertising consistent across countries.

Consider an ad, shown here, that used a visual portrait to market PHAS, a line of L'Oreal cosmetics. The visual image in the ad—that of a confident, independent, modern woman on the move—captures the product's personality, or brand identity. The text opposite the photo is almost irrelevant—it is the visual image that sells the product.

Through PHAS' personality portrait, L'Oreal has been able to build brand extensions with similar mood, tone, and image. The portrait also allowed PHAS to go beyond the one-product-equals-one-brand idea of marketing. PHAS has been so successful, in fact, that new product development, launches, advertising, promotions, public relations efforts, and direct marketing efforts have been closely tied to the PHAS personality and image. The advertising concept drives all marketing efforts for the brand. Without varying the message, the PHAS image appears in more than eight countries. The campaign has had a strong, positive impact on L'Oreal's bottom line.

Hitting a Moving Target

Settling on the right visual image for your ad is a little like trying to hit a moving target. As times change, words conjure up different visual images, and images convey different meanings.

Before you settle on a visual image, brainstorm about what messages that image sends to you and how the media have used that image recently. This is what Bloom FCA! calls "the context analysis," a nontraditional research method that allows you to predict emerging consumer influences by evaluating the editorial messages (print, television, movies) reaching consumers over a certain time period and across a spectrum of Western cultures. Context analysis acknowledges and builds on the fact that the media are the predominant forces influencing how consumers think, feel, and react to the world.

For example, take the word "exotic," a strong descriptor frequently used in advertising strategies. Analyzing the context reveals that the visual images associated with this single word have changed in a very short period of time—and so has its meaning.

"Exotic," a few years ago, was often portrayed in images of desolate, white, beautiful beaches—the Western consumer's dream destination. Today, however, when articles and ads refer to the exotic, they show a close-up of a tribal villager from Africa or the inside of a hut in the Andes mountains. This reflects the consumer of the 1990s' desire for firsthand experience of the unexploited world.

Take another example, "ecological." This is an important marketing concept today. Unfortunately, too many companies continue to send ecological messages akin to "save the planet," an idea that has worn itself thin. Marketers, instead, should depict ecology as a sound economic and industrial issue.

Context analysis is merely sensing the kinds of changes that shape the consumer experience. The marketer, however, has the ongoing task of fitting any concept into the consumer's life or "conceptual world." It is vital to depict brand identity visually instead of in writing so that both marketer and advertiser agree on it. This makes sure that "exotic" says "exotic" to the creative director in the same way it will convey the idea to the brand manager and the consumer.

Skipping Breakfast

In a recent interview, *The Wall Street Journal* asked Ted Levitt about how to advertise orange juice. Although orange juice is a universal product, its marketers could not, in its global advertising, depict a family quaffing juice for breakfast because "the French don't drink it for breakfast." Levitt's response was, "Maybe a happy family at breakfast isn't the right metaphor."

In fact, while juice at breakfast may not work well in France, elsewhere it might not work at all—some cultures don't even have breakfast at all. Marketers should think of juice in terms of its main benefits: it quenches your thirst and it's

Worth a Thousand Words in Any Language

Here are a few ads American companies have recently launched successfully in Europe. Each of them depends on strong visual images.

This Apple Computer TV ad entitled "Powerbook Duo" shows a pair of hands closing up Apple's Powerbook, a laptop computer, to fit neatly inside a Macintosh. "The ad is very simple, yet powerful. The camera is always on the computers and keeps the audience aware at all times of the inventiveness of this product," says Kurt Haiman, president of the Art Director's Club of New York.

Jeans are an all-American product, so Lee Jeans looked for a well-known American symbol to associate with its jeans. Lee found what it was looking for in the twin towers of the World Trade Center, which, in "The Jeans That Built America" commercial, fill the two legs of a giant pair of Lee Jeans. "With all the miniaturization and special effects, this ad was a major production, but worth every penny of every detail the concept portrays," says Kurt Haiman.

Ford's "Beauty with Inner Strength" TV ad for its new European car Mondeo uses special effects to highlight the car's distinctive elements both inside and outside. It features a skeleton car, specially built to represent the "inner strength" of Mondeo, merging with a specially built "metal-shell" car, which represents Mondeo's "beauty." Special effects fuse the car's two components. The commercial was launched in 13 European countries in March. Initial reaction to Mondeo has been outstanding throughout Europe, particularly in the U.K. where it has been awarded the 1993 What a Car! Car of the Year Award.

Part of American Express' "Portraits" campaign, a series of celebrity photographs by Annie Leibovitz, "John Cleese in a Red Dress" won a Gold Award at the International Advertising Film Festival in Cannes in June 1992. Is it that people everywhere find a man dressed as a woman funny, or is it that they like to see the British let their hair down?

healthy—especially when compared to most carbonated beverages. As most Western consumers are becoming more and more health-conscious, using a health-related image to advertise orange juice might be more appropriate than using a family at breakfast.

Levitt's point is that global advertising is indeed possible; it just takes the right approach to communicate an idea that's consistent and relevant.

By uncovering and visualizing meaningful concepts common from country to country and culture to culture, marketers can execute global campaigns for virtually any product or service. This in-cludes food, beverages, travel—any of the categories traditionally labeled as too dependent on cultural sensitivities to be advertised globally using one concept.

Marketers and advertising agencies are constantly trying to discover new ways of reaching the consumer through message and media. The trick is discovering how people assimilate information and how they feel—not how they think. That means generating excitement and action through visual communications so that consumers, no matter where they are, understand your product and buy it.

INTERNATIONAL COMMUNICATION: AN EXECUTIVE PRIMER

Ronald E. Dulek, John S. Fielden, and John S. Hill

Euphoria frequently turns to paranoia when domestic executives face their first overseas assignment. Disturbing memories come pressing to the fore:

• A college anthropology professor gleefully pointing out that thousands of languages (and even more thousands of dialects) exist in the world;

• A semester or two of a foreign language that was hated, never mastered, and is now well forgotten;

• A once-hilarious book documenting the communications blunders American businesspeople apparently make every time they set foot on foreign soil (Ricks, 1983).

These and a variety of other doleful thoughts cause now-wary executives to wonder how they—or anyone—could even begin to cope with thousands of different cultures and languages involved in international business. And there is ample evidence that coping with those cultures and languages is necessary.

Fact 1: By the year 2000, experts have predicted that multinational corporations will control

Reprinted from *Business Horizons,* January–February 1991, pp. 20–25. Copyright © 1991 by the Foundation for the School of Business at Indiana University. Used with permission.

approximately half the world's assets. So even if you are not now working for one of these companies, the odds are high that you will be—or that you will be interacting and communicating with other people who work for "foreign" companies.

Fact 2: Today English dominates the international business scene. But it is blind provincialism to believe that English will continue to be used everywhere for all occasions. Even today an ever-increasing number of foreign countries are demanding that contracts be drawn and negotiations be conducted only in the language of that area.

Fact 3: Sad but true, U.S. businesspeople have the lowest foreign language proficiency of any major trading nation. Despite accreditation association pressure, U.S. business schools do not emphasize foreign languages, and students traditionally avoid them.

Fortunately, some generalizations will help U.S. businesspeople communicate more effectively internationally. These generalizations derive from a seemingly simple division of cultures into two polar types, which Edward T. Hall (1976) named high- and low-context societies.

Cultures (see Figure 1) were divided by Hall into those in which:

1. The social context surrounding a negotiation counts as nothing; all that count are the actual writ-

FIGURE 1

Arrangement of high- and low-context cultures

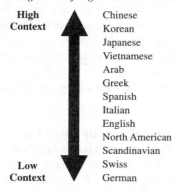

High Context	Chinese
	Korean
	Japanese
	Vietnamese
	Arab
	Greek
	Spanish
	Italian
	English
	North American
	Scandinavian
Low Context	Swiss
	German

Source: Edward T. Hall, *Beyond Culture* (Garden City, NY: Anchor Press/Doubleday, 1976), and "How Cultures Collide," *Psychology Today,* July 1976, pp. 67–74.

ten agreements. These cultures he called *low-context;* and

2. The social context that surrounds a formal, written document is far more important than the written, legal documentation. These he called *high-context cultures.*

Low-Context Cultures.   In low-context cultures (from the German to the North American), what counts is primarily what has been written in contractual form and sanctified by lawyers on both sides. The social context in which the agreement has been forged has no legal standing and, hence, does not count.

High-Context Cultures.   Just the reverse is true about very high-context cultures (from the Chinese to the Arab). These cultures are historically oral cultures; what a person says in writing is held to be much less important than who that person is, his or her status (or rank) in society, and his or her general reputation. The social context in which an agreement has been made counts for at least as much as, and usually far more than, the written agreement. Therefore, in high-context cultures, the process of forging a business relation-

ship is as important as, if not more important than, the written details of the actual deal.

Applying Context to International Communications

Knowledge of where a particular culture falls in the high- and low-context spectrum gives businesspeople valuable clues about how to communicate with people from different cultures. In this article, these clues have been put in the form of three sets of specific "dos" and "don'ts" for businesspeople to remember when they engage in international communication:

1. Conversational principles—those that should be remembered in all aspects of communication, ranging from informal luncheon chats to boardroom meetings.

2. Presentation principles—those applicable when making oral presentations to a foreign group.

3. Writing principles—those to remember when exchanging written information internationally.

Conversational Principle #1: Recognize that many high-context cultures need to know as much as possible about you and the company you represent.   Always remember when you are in Latin America, Asia, and parts of Western Europe that even the most seemingly casual, insignificant conversations have a level of significance far beyond that dictated by the content being discussed. Conversations about your family, your company, or current events are used to "warm up relationships," just as one might warm a car engine on a cold day. You should also give your hosts insights into you as a person and recognize their need to find out what makes you "tick." Americans are not used to talking openly about personal or family intimacies; yet overseas, once the trust "bond" has been established, there are in many cases few things foreigners will not talk about.

The best approach to high-context negotiation,

then, is to acknowledge that you and your company are under close scrutiny. You should take pains to provide your prospective Japanese or Arab client with as much information as possible about you and the company you represent. It is often best to provide information before you visit or entertain visitors from high-context cultures. Americans, it is said, like "to meet and get to know you." Persons from high-context societies often prefer "to get to know about you first and then meet you." Copies of your résumé as well as those of other people who hold important positions in your organization, documents, pamphlets, or annual reports that provide details about your company's history, other pieces of information detailing you and your colleagues' personal interests—all can be forwarded to associates in high-context cultures before your visit begins.

Conversational Principle #2: Speak slowly, clearly, and simply. Avoid jargon, slang, clichés, and idiomatic usage.   When foreigners learn English, they learn a "correct" version of formal English. When they listen to Americans (or Britons or Australians) lapsing into slang or idiom, they become confused. We must realize that even an everyday expression such as "Let's get rolling" or "I'm all ears" can be perplexing if the foreigner tries to translate it literally. Imagine foreigners having to translate a simple English idiom such as "So long" into their language. Also, sayings such as "first among equals" and "last but not least" are often untranslatable because, even when translated correctly, they appear illogical and contradictory.

Conversational Principle #3: Sprinkle your conversation with at least some words and phrases in the language of your listeners.   It is regarded as "good manners" to make at least an attempt to learn a few phrases in your host's language. This shows that you have made a good faith effort to learn something about the other person's language—and, by implication, his or her culture and background.

All of us have seen how statesmen regularly make use of their partial knowledge of another country's language when they visit that country. If the President of the United States visits Mexico and says in Spanish, *"¡Hola! ¡Me gusta estar aquí!"* the audience cheers wildly. We have all seen the care Popes have taken to deliver at least part of their sermons in the native language of the country visited.

Conversational Principle #4: Be careful about what your body language and your tone of voice communicate.   When listeners cannot follow what is being said, they will pay far greater attention to body language. And if they do understand English, they will look for contradictions between what is said and how it is said. If the words carry a message that is not reinforced by concomitant bodily expressions, either confusion results or the listener may conclude that the speaker is not being sincere. When people say to foreigners, "I'm very pleased to meet you," but say so in a bland monotone and an expressionless face, this contradiction between words and action may convince the listeners that the speakers are not at all pleased to meet them. They may immediately wonder how much of what else is said will be truly sincere.

Many of our hackneyed expressions can actually undermine our credibility. In the U.S., someone asks us, "How are you doing?" Regardless of how we actually are doing, we usually answer something on the order of, "Fine, fine." However, when a question like this is asked abroad, Americans should fully expect to receive a sincere answer that may include detailed reasons as to why the respondent is feeling either great or terrible. If after inviting this response we register impatience, foreigners have every right to believe that they have been deliberately made to look foolish, although they may not really understand what was foolish about it.

Tone of voice also plays an important role when communicating internationally. There are vast cultural differences at play here: notice, for example, how softly people from most Asian cultures speak.

Americans often seem loud and aggressive in negotiations and vigorous in arguments. And negotiations in Latin American, Greek, Italian, and Central European countries are far louder, often including heated, arm-waving exchanges of opinion that rarely mean anything personal.

Loud oral communications in Asia or the Middle East, however, are socially unacceptable. There is a Japanese saying that "The nail that sticks out will always be beaten." Disruptive elements such as loud or argumentative voices, waving of arms, and exaggerated hand gestures are all frowned upon.

Presentation Principle #1: Respect many foreign audiences' desire for greater formality of presentation. Different cultures have varying ideas about what constitutes an effective oral presentation. Americans generally like presentations that seem natural and spontaneous, not "canned" or overly rehearsed. Most other countries, both high- and low-context cultures, expect more formality. "Natural" presentations, it is thought, give the impression that the speaker has not respected the audience sufficiently. Speakers who write on blackboards or on transparencies inadvertently give the impression that the presentation is not important enough for them to have prepared proper sets of visual aids prior to the actual presentation.

Also, efforts to customize what you present, as opposed to giving an off-the-shelf generalized presentation, will be appreciated.

Presentation Principle #2: Allow for differences in behavior of foreign audiences. U.S. presenters must not be "thrown off" by seemingly odd behavior of an overseas audience. Japanese audiences, for example, usually sit and nod their heads (which means they understand, not that they agree) and say nothing. However, on some occasions, they may start frenzied talking among themselves. Or, in open discussions, they may suddenly become evasive. What this usually means is that something that has been said is disturbing to them. At this point, presenters should take heed; get off

that topic and go on to something else until they can find out, either directly from the audience or through a go-between, what the problem is.

To Americans, "looking people in the eye" is a sign that mutual respect has been established. U.S. businesspeople traveling overseas are often disappointed by their inability to establish eye contact. This is true especially in superior/subordinate relationships, but is also true in presentations to members of cultures where staring is considered "brash and insolent." Hence, in such countries, audiences will not seem attentive because they will spend most of the time staring down at the floor. It is hard for Americans to realize that this usually means the audience is showing respect, not inattention.

Presentation Principle #3: Have patience; design your presentation's length, completeness, and "interruptability" with the audience's culture in mind. Americans are impatient and are used to fast-paced, efficient presentations. Most foreigners, with the probable exceptions of Germans and the Swiss, prefer slower, more deliberate efforts. In situations where interpreters are used, the pace is automatically slowed. When the presentation is in English and there is no interpreter, a speaker must go very slowly. Be patient also in allowing those who raise questions to have time to search for the precise English word they need. Signs of impatience will be unfavorably received, and the presenter will be downgraded for not showing proper respect and courtesy.

Audiences in high-context cultures, such as Japanese, Latin American, and Arabic audiences, expect a presentation to be in short, separate segments that allow time for questions and digestion of what has been presented. This is wise because many high-context people communicate in what is referred to as "loops"; they will mix circuitous, irrelevant (by American standards) conversations with short dashes of information that go directly to the point. Because they are not as time- or efficiency-oriented, Arabs, for example, prefer presentations that allow frequent deviations from the major business topic. This allows them to relax for a while, after which they will be ready to loop back and listen intently to further discussions. These interruptions can prove wearing even to those who are experienced in international dealings. Yet companies whose presenters are the most patient, tolerant and, in their audience's eyes, "mature," will get the contracts. Impatience in these circumstances is interpreted as childish; the prevailing attitude is, "Who wants to do business with children when there are adults around?"

Presentation Principle #4: Match rank and age of presenter to rank and age of important members of foreign audiences. In many American companies, meritocracy is dominant and fairly young executives rise rapidly to powerful positions early in their career. In high-context cultures, however, age (or seniority) is a major indicator of status. Therefore, sending young executives, regardless of their rank, to negotiate important contracts with businesspeople in high-context cultures can be a disaster. In those cultures, wisdom is associated with age, a throwback to the days when wisdom was assured through years of experience, when knowledge was passed on by elders, not by books or data sets. Hence, a young presenter is unlikely to command the same respect as would an older, more seasoned executive. Sending a young hotshot may even invite interpretation that the American company does not take the foreign venture seriously enough to send in its "first team."

Writing Principle #1: Only in low-context cultures where communication efficiency is highly prized should you organize your communication so that its central point is directly and immediately stated. The higher the context of a culture is, the more we should question whether we should write terse, concise, "bottom-line" communications to persons in that culture. In cultures where language is used not so much to document as to reveal the personal qualities of the individuals and their companies, written communications

may need at times to be longer, more elaborate, more personally revealing, and less focused on getting the job at hand completed with dispatch.

But, oddly enough, just the reverse is frequently true. People from high-context cultures may settle for written business agreements that are extremely short and bottomlined, in some cases merely stating the bare bones of the agreement. The reason for such brevity is that the parties to the agreement have already spent a great amount of time circuitously finding out about each other's integrity. Thus, when both parties are assured of each other's trustworthiness, a brief written statement for the record may be all that is required for this transaction and perhaps those that follow.

U.S. executives should also realize that if a formal, American-style contract is drawn up, the high-context partners will not read it in detail. They will assume that no one would be so crass as to conceal anything in the fine print. While this knowledge might tempt unscrupulous companies to slip in provisions favorable to themselves, one can be sure that succumbing to such a temptation will guarantee that their company will never again do business, not only with the company that was cheated, but probably not even with any other companies in that country.

There is another factor influencing whether communications should be bottom-lined. In international writing, hierarchial power differences between readers and writers affect the organization of messages even more than they do in the U.S. In Malaysia, for example, government bureaucrats bottom-line almost everything they write "down" to the citizenry (analogous to the imperial or bureaucratic "command"). But a businessperson writing "up," asking governmental permission for some action, is expected to be circuitous to the greatest possible extent. The longer the letter, the more "respect" it shows. Moreover, the businessperson is expected to include many long paragraphs praising the bureaucrat (or more subtly, the bureaucrat's administration) in the most lavish terms. This "respect" is necessary because high-context cultures usually have definite social divisions, and there are appropriate sets of verbal behavior depending on whether one is speaking to another who is higher or lower in the social order.

But remember, not all cultures are high-context. Low-context cultures such as German, North American, Swiss, and Scandinavian prefer business messages to be very direct, even to the point of being terse.

Writing Principle #2: Adapt your style of writing to the preferences of the culture to which your readers belong. The culture in which a piece of writing takes place clearly affects the style in which messages are expected to be written. In high-context cultures, there is a marked emphasis on politeness and decorum. Even communications going down in an organization will be phrased in polite and respectful ways and will appear to have less force attached to them. There will be differences in how instructions are given. Where there are close business relations between sender and receiver, great care is taken to observe social writing etiquette that to Americans seems vague and obscure. Underlings are asked to "consider" doing certain things and completion of a task may be "requested, if at all possible." These give the appearance that the recipient of the request has at least the option of refusing to do what is asked (although in reality, there is no such option). As result, what is to be avoided are forceful imperatives such as "Do this!" or "Do that!" A much greater reliance should be placed on a more passive, subtle style.

There are cultural differences and expectations about how formally one should write. In high-context countries, much informal written communication takes place. Information is often exchanged through informal personal notes written at the bottom of documents. In high-context cultures, there is far less need for subordinates to file CYA memos for the record (a person who does so will be thought of as insecure and as calling unnecessary attention to his or her activities). In such cultures, writers do not have to document everything formally because they will not be held personally responsible if something goes wrong. Responsibility will be taken by the top of the organization. The subordinate need not fear being the "fall guy" for a mishap. If mistakes are made in the Middle East, Asia, or some parts of Europe, the person at the top will resign, regardless of whether he or she had anything personally to do with the blunder. In the U.S., responsibility flows all too often to the lowest organizational levels.

Not all cultures prize our flat, objective, "Business English" style of writing. Some cultures exhibit styles of writing that are quite colorful compared with English. Arabic, for example, is a poetic language filled with exaggerations, colorful adjectives, and metaphors. Arabs do not react, as English readers might, with shock or surprise at such colorful writing. Such language is just their normal way of expressing ideas. Compared with English, the Latin languages also delight in colorful verbal turns of phrase. Hence when Americans write in English to members of these cultures, they need not be so hidebound in their expression as they are in standard English.

But many low-context cultures prefer just the reverse. Germans, for example, avoid colorful exaggeration and hyperbole in their writing, believing that people from other cultures (even Americans) exaggerate, abuse superlatives such as "most," "best," and "newest," and demonstrate egocentrism by overusing the personal pronouns "I" and "my." A passive, impersonal style is therefore best in communications with low-context cultures.

Writing Principle #3: Don't count on nonnative readers being able to understand English in all its subtleties and technicalities. Therefore, whenever possible enclose a translation in the recipient's language. If writers are unsure about a foreign reader's ability to understand English, even when it is written as simply and unidiomatically as possible, then they should include a translation. Doing so will often better guarantee a response. Readers with limited command of English may simply not respond because (*a*) they do not know whether the unreadable communication is worth the cost of hiring a translator or (*b*) they may not want to admit publicly that they really don't understand English. Enclosing a translation into the reader's language will not be taken as an insult; instead it will be regarded as helpful and a diplomatic courtesy.

This primer will not make Armand Hammers out of ordinary domestic-variety executives. What it can do, however, is increase U.S. managerial effectiveness, especially in the high-context cultures of Latin American, the Middle East, and Asia. By avoiding cultural *faux pas* and by being sensitive to the needs of other cultures, participants in international business meetings and negotiations can better focus on the real issues in a more relaxed atmosphere. This should enhance the probabilities of successful outcomes and plant the seeds from which international business relationships can be successful both at the corporate and the all-important personal level.

References

Culturegram Series, Brigham Young University, David M. Kennedy Center for International Studies.

Ronald E. Dulek and John S. Fielden, *Principles of Business Communication* (New York: Macmillan, 1990).

John S. Fielden and Ronald E. Dulek, "How to Use Bottom-Line Writing in Corporate Communications," *Business Horizons,* July–August 1984, pp. 24–30.

Edward T. Hall, *Beyond Culture* (Garden City, N.Y.: Anchor Press/Doubleday, 1976).

Edward T. Hall, "How Cultures Collide," *Psychology Today,* July 1976, pp. 67–74.

David A. Ricks, *Big Business Blunders: Mistakes in Multinational Marketing* (Homewood, Ill.: Dow Jones-Irwin, 1983).

The Internet and International Marketing

John A. Quelch and Lisa R. Klein

The Internet promises to revolutionize the dynamics of international commerce and, like the telephone and fax machine, may be a major force in the democratization of capitalism. Small companies will be able to compete more easily in the global marketplace, and consumers in emerging markets, in particular, will benefit from the expanded range of products, services, and information to which the Internet will give them access. As a recent Forrester industry report explains, the Internet removes many barriers to communication with customers and employees by eliminating the obstacles created by geography, time zones, and location, creating a "frictionless" business environment.[1] Much of the current expansion in Internet use, accelerated by the emergence of the World Wide Web (WWW), is driven by marketing initiatives—providing products and product information to potential customers. However, in the future, many companies, especially those operating globally, will realize a much broader range of benefits from this medium's potential as both a communication and a transaction vehicle.

Currently, the Internet is mainly a U.S. phenomenon, due to the later start and historically slower growth of Internet access in other countries. More than half the Internet's nearly 7 million

From *Sloan Management Review,* Spring 1996, pp. 60–75.

host computers are located in the United States, with the remainder spread across 100 other countries.[2] In 1995, 22 countries came on-line.[3] In 1994, there was wide variation in the number of Internet hosts per 1,000 people, ranging from more than 14 in Finland to fewer than 0.5 in South Korea (see Exhibit 1).

With fewer non-U.S. businesses on-line, fewer access nodes, higher telecommunications rates, and lower rates of personal computer ownership, consumer use of the Internet internationally is currently much lower than in the United States, where commercial on-line services like CompuServe and America Online (AOL) have also facilitated Internet use. But CompuServe and AOL have only recently begun to aggressively market their services in other countries. CompuServe first began global expansion in 1987 with entry into Japan through collaboration with Japanese partners. The on-line service now boasts 500,000 subscribers outside the United States. AOL's attempts to establish Europe Online were delayed until late 1995 due to disagreements with its European-based partners. Although these commercial providers are now positioned for aggressive growth abroad, their slower-than-expected expansion has delayed consumer education about and adoption of the Internet.

Internet access in overseas markets now promises to grow rapidly as the on-line services expand and as regional and national governments and telecommunication companies become more interested (see Exhibit 1). For example, China recently launched ChinaWeb, a Web site whose stated purpose is "To help China in her rapid transformation to an information society, and to promote business and commerce with China through the bridge of Internet."[4] As an emerging bellwether market, China's response to the Internet augurs well for its worldwide expansion. Some predict that the European market will fully open only

---

Exhibit 1   International Growth of the Internet

	Number of Hosts (January 1995)	Hosts per 1,000 People	1995 Growth in Hosts (Annual Percentage)
Finland	71,372	14.0	103%
United States	2,044,716	12.4	100
Australia	161,166	9.0	50
New Zealand	31,215	9.0	441
Sweden	77,594	8.8	83
Switzerland	51,512	7.8	40
Norway	49,725	7.7	57
Canada	186,722	7.0	96
Holland	89,227	6.0	98
Denmark	25,935	5.5	181
United Kingdom	241,191	4.0	112
Austria	29,705	3.8	92
Israel	13,251	3.0	96
Germany	207,717	2.5	77
Hong Kong	12,437	2.2	52
Belgium	18,699	2.0	125
France	93,041	1.8	68
Czech Republic	11,580	1.5	153
Japan	96,632	1.0	86
South Africa	27,040	<1.0	147
Spain	28,446	<1.0	141
Taiwan	14,618	<1.0	83
Italy	30,697	<1.0	80
South Korea	18,049	<1.0	101
Poland	11,477	<1.0	121

Source: C. Anderson, "The Accidental Superhighway," *The Economist,* 1 July 1995, p. S3. Survey by M. Lottor, Network Wizards, as summarized by The Internet Society, obtained from <http//www.isoc.org>

---

when the telecommunications industry is deregulated in 1998, reducing phone charges for Internet usage and allowing the number of users to reach the critical mass necessary to spur the growth of European commercial Web sites.[5] However, these transitions will not occur overnight. Some national governments will doubtless try to limit their populations' access to the Internet, fearing the free flow of ideas and the importation of products purchased over the Internet at the expense of local sales taxes and custom duties.

Many international users of the Internet are similar to U.S. users. An on-line survey of more than 13,000 Internet users conducted by Georgia Tech's Graphics, Visualization, and Usability Center (GVU), from April through May 1995, counted 2,500 responses from other countries, primarily from English-speaking users. A comparison of the demographic profiles of foreign and domestic users uncovered few differences, with both audiences skewed toward college-educated white males in their early thirties, earning higher-than-average incomes and employed in the computer, education, and other professional fields.[6]

The long-term international growth of the Internet raises the opportunity for cross-border information flows and transactions. In 1995, transaction volume over the Web was estimated at more than $400 million, up from less than $20 million in 1994—more than 80 percent of which went to U.S. companies. Of the total sales, exports accounted for approximately 43 percent.[7] An informal poll of a dozen Web sites reveals that the internationally based audience comprises, on average, 20 percent of total traffic and transaction volume (see Exhibit 2).

Current estimates predict that global transaction volume will reach more than $1 billion in 1996. However, transactions are concentrated in a limited number of product categories, even within the United States, due to: (1) the distinctive demgraphic profile of current Internet users; (2) the type of product information most easily presented electronically, given limitations in bandwidth; (3) trade regulations; and (4) transaction security concerns.

EXHIBIT 2   International Audiences

Company	Industry	Primary Audience	Secondary Audience	International Business	
				Percentage of Traffic	Percentage of Transactions
Software net	Software	End customers	Suppliers	20%	30%
Wordsworth Books	Books	End customers	Publishers	25	25
CD Now	Music	End customers		20	20
Underground Music Archive	Music	End customers	Musicians	N/A	30
Zima	Liquor	End customers		6	N/A
CatalogSite	Catalogs	End customers	Catalog distributors	15	N/A
Individual Inc.	News service	Customers and subscribers	Advertisers, press, employees	25	25
3M	Diverse business products	Business market end customers and distributors	Consumer market end customers	20	N/A
OnSale	Action house	Buyers and sellers		20	20
Consulting, Inc.	Consulting	Clients and job seekers	Partners and employees	20	N/A
American Venture Capital Exchange	Venture capital	Entrepreneurs and investors		5	3
Building Industry Exchange	Information	Buyers and suppliers		30	N/A

Source: Personal interviews and e-mail correspondence with webmasters at each site conducted from December 1995 to January 1996. Based on sample week hit and transaction counts.

For example, products with generally low prices sell better. A recent survey of Internet shoppers reported that 64 percent of purchases were for software, books, music, hardware, and magazines.[8] The GVU survey revealed that on-line purchasers were much more likely to buy hardware and software priced at under $50 than over $50, with more than 60 percent citing transaction security concerns as the major deterrent. In addition, legal restrictions limit cross-border transactions; many software products cannot be sold internationally for security reasons due to their inclusion of encryption technologies. Likewise, exports of liquor are restricted. But these constraints will likely be overcome as Internet use diffuses and adopter profiles become more heterogeneous, as bandwidth and software capabilities expand, and as data security issues are resolved.

The purpose of this article is to explore how the Internet may change the rules of international marketing. Is the Internet potentially revolutionary or just another marketing channel like home shopping or direct mail? The answer depends on how much added value there is in Internet communications and transactions compared to existing alternatives. The value-added will vary across country markets and according to company type. Because distribution channels tend to be less developed, less direct, or less efficient in emerging markets than in the United States, the Internet may offer special opportunities in these markets. In addition, the differences in speed of, control over, and access to communication and distribution channels between the Internet and traditional media and distribution channels internationally will offer different mixes of opportunities and challenges to large multinational companies (MNCs) and to small businesses.

Types of Web Sites

A company's choice of evolutionary path depends on whether it is an established MNC or a start-up company created to do business solely on the Internet (see Figure 1). (Any company that establishes a site on the Internet automatically becomes a multinational company.) Existing MNCs tend

FIGURE 1

Evolutionary paths of a web site
MNCs

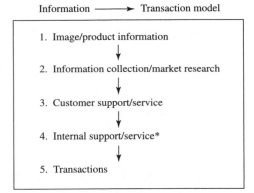

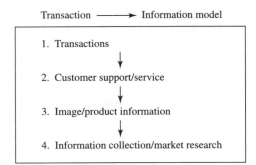

* Recently, the rapid growth in awareness of, and software and support for, such internal information networks or intranets makes it likely that this could be among the first stages for companies establishing a Web site in the future.

to adopt the information-to-transaction model, whereas startup companies tend to use the transaction-to-information model.

The MNC starts by offering information to address the needs of its existing customers. Federal Express's initial site, launched in November 1994, was a relatively small 12-page site focusing on the package-tracking service previously available only to businesses with corporate accounts. Customer response to the service was much greater than expected, causing the company to expand its server capacity and the site itself to include information on the range of delivery options and downloadable desktop software to prepare packages for shipping and keeping records.[9] However, neither FedEx nor its competitor UPS yet offer on-line transactions so customers can arrange for package pick-up, delivery, or billing directly on the Web site.

3M's Web site gives information on a growing number of its nearly 60,000 products, news of innovations in its product markets, and directories of its worldwide operations, but has only recently begun offering items for sale. Currently, it offers a $15 mouse pad—and only within the United States.

Rockport, the shoe company, plans to launch a Web site in spring 1996, which will initially focus on giving existing and potential customers information on foot care and on its product line. The company plans to expand the site to provide links to its local retail outlets and eventually to collect and analyze individual purchase histories to help customers select future purchases. Only with this detailed amount of customer information and involvement does the company see on-line transactions as worthwhile.

On the other hand, simple economics require Internet start-ups to begin with transactions and then continue to use the medium to build a brand image, provide product support, and win repeat purchases. Companies such as Software.net and CD Now have followed this model. Software.net, an on-line software retailer, allows customers to purchase and download software directly from its Web site. This type of on-line distribution was the first of its kind; the company has since added a database of links to product reviews and software manufacturers and created product discussion bulletin boards to help customers choose software. CD Now is an on-line music store. Recent additions to this transactions-driven business include lengthy album and artist reviews, concert calendars, and new release notification.

Whichever of the two business models a company pursues, the specific functions embodied in a Web site, whether targeted to internal or external users, need to generate revenue or reduce costs (see Figure 2). As an MNC or start-up develops its site to incorporate a broader range of functions, it needs to assess how the functions influence the global business model. For example, transaction capabilities can have both revenue-generation and cost-reduction potential, depending on whether the company is attracting new customers and sales or transferring existing sales to a more profitable medium. Similarly, providing information to internal and external audiences can increase revenues by facilitating incremental sales or increased margins. The dissemination of information via the Internet can also reduce costs by replacing communications through less cost-efficient channels.

Many companies are conducting international commerce on the Internet with this range of business models supporting several different types of Web sites. (For a simple framework categorizing these sites, see Figure 3.)

FIGURE 2

Drivers of internet business models

Primary Business Impact

	Cost reduction	Revenue generation
Internal	Technical, legal, and administrative support Database management Internal research **Company Information**	**Marketing and Sales Support/Information**
Customer Focus		
External	Customer service **Transactions**	**Product Information** Promotions Database development Market research **Transactions**

Quadrant 1.   Quadrant 1 (in Figure 3) includes companies using the Web primarily as a communication tool to engage in one-way and two-way communications with a range of outside audiences, such as end users, intermediaries (e.g., dealerships, retail outlets), and suppliers (e.g., software developers). These companies provide customer services to the U.S. market and just happen to attract international traffic as well. The benefit to international consumers is merely the opportunity to access information and support faster, more cheaply, and more directly than existing communication systems like telephone, fax, mail, and direct mail can. For example, the Apple Computer Web site offers up-to-date detailed technical information, software updates, product specifications, and press releases to Macintosh users and developers. International customers can obtain information and product support that is often superior to or more timely than that available from channels in their domestic markets.

Moreover, Apple saves money by providing customer support through this medium. According to a recent Dataquest report, Americans will make an estimated 200 million calls to help desks in 1996, up from 120 million four years ago, with the average length of a call now 13 minutes instead of 8. At an estimated cost of $1.50 a minute to the company, calls to help desks cost the personal computer industry $3.9 billion annually.[10] International service per capita is higher due to the higher costs of mail and fax services. Because marginal costs to access via the Web are minimal, once the site is built to handle the volume, a company such as Apple can reap savings by providing such software support electronically around the globe. Finally, the availability of such Web site services can differentiate Apple and enhance its image among customers and developers.

Quadrant 2.   The companies in Quadrant 2 have a similar domestic focus as those in Quadrant 1 but also offer transactions on-line (or immediately via phone or fax). Internationally, the potential of such transactions enables a company to

FIGURE 3

Categories of Web sites

Audience Focus	Web Site Content: Information Support/service only	Web Site Content: Transactions
Domestic	1 Apple Computer Saturn Reebok CatalogSite	2 Software.net Wordsworth Books Mr. Upgrade CD Now Godiva Chocolates LIGHTNING Instrumentation Yvonne's Weinkabinett
Global	3 Building Industry Exchange Federal Express Sun Microsystems ChinaWeb Gateway to New Zealand Digital Equipment Corp. Eli Lilly & Co. British Airways Consulting Inc.	4 TRADE'ex Underground Music Archive American Venture Capital Exchange Online BookStore CapEx

Site Description	*Location*	*Industry*
3M	United States	Diverse business products
American Venture Capital Exchange	United States	Venture capital
Apple Computer	United States	Computer hardware, software
British Airways	United Kingdom	Airline
Building Industry Exchange	United States	Construction
CapEx	Germany	Venture capital
CatalogSite	United States	Mail-order catalogs
CD Now	United States	Music
ChinaWeb	China	Information
Consulting Inc.	United States	Information
Digital Equipment Corp.	United States	Computer hardware
Eli Lilly & Co.	United States	Pharmaceuticals
Federal Express	United States	Package delivery
Gateway to New Zealand	New Zealand	Information
Godiva Chocolates	United States	Food
LIGHTNING Instrumentation	Switzerland	Networking equipment
Mr. Upgrade	United States	Computer repair
Online BookStore	United States	Books
Reebok	United States	Footwear
Saturn	United States	Automobiles
Software.net	United States	Computer software
Sun Microsystems	United States	Computer hardware, software
TRADE'ex	United States	Computer equipment
Underground Music Archive	United States	Music
Wordsworth Books	United States	Books
Yvonne's Weinkabinett	Germany	Wine

reach consumers who may be inaccessible via other media, due to the company's small size or the limitations of local distribution systems. For example, CD Now is able to offer worldwide customers recordings that, even after shipping and handling costs, are priced lower than at foreign retail outlets. LIGHTNING Instrumentation SA, a Swiss networking equipment manufacturer, experienced a 20 percent increase in sales after establishing a Web site, almost all from outside its domestic market.[11]

A site like Mr. Upgrade, an Arizona computer parts distributor, will secure half its 1995 international sales through orders placed on its Web site, despite the site's simple design and the buyers' inability to conduct their transactions directly on-line for security reasons. (Customers must call an 800 number to place an order.) Of its 12 international accounts (with combined orders of $700,000), half came via the Internet.[12]

Quadrant 3.   This quadrant includes those businesses whose primary motivation for the Web site is attracting an international audience. Moreover, international customers explicitly add value; i.e., the service is more valuable to all users because of the international scope of operations. For example, Sun Microsystems provides global product support, software updates, and hardware service to its worldwide network of internal and external hardware users and software developers. An owner of a Sun system with offices worldwide will benefit from Sun's "one stop" service center where Sun can design solutions for the customer's problems worldwide and distribute them directly via the Internet. Thus, even without transactions, the capability to provide service worldwide instantaneously makes this a valuable medium.

Federal Express's tracking service also adds value in this way by enabling customers to track packages and estimate delivery times anywhere in the world. In addition, this service alone will save Federal Express almost $2 million annually, as the Web site takes the place of more expensive human operators.[13] The Building Industry Exchange is a

new information resource that serves as a global directory for the fragmented construction industry. Consulting Inc.'s corporate site provides links to resources for expatriates, business travelers, and international publications. The site also contains a directory of more than 400 e-mail addresses for users to contact offices and industry groups around the world directly.

Quadrant 4.   Quadrant 4 companies expand on the capabilities of those in Quadrant 3 by offering transactions to customers worldwide. However, as opposed to Quadrant 2, because these transactions tend to involve the matching of buyers and sellers, both reap direct benefits from the global scope of the site. For example, DYNABIT U.S.A.'s new TRADE'ex service creates an exchange for commercial buyers and resellers of computer equipment around the globe. CapEx is a German company that matches entrepreneurs and investors for a range of start-up investment opportunities. Both companies serve as "market makers" by enabling communication between small parties who would not have found each other without this medium. These companies make their profits by taking a commission on consummated transactions and charging registration fees to buyers or sellers.

Another example is Underground Music Archive (UMA), for which international sales represent 30 percent of its business. The added value of this music collection is its "inventory" of 800 artists from more than twenty countries who provide downloadable samples of their music unavailable through traditional channels.

Global value-added can occur whether companies are targeting existing customers and providing service (Sun) or are attracting new customers (TRADE'ex or UMA). The business models represented by Quadrants 3 and 4 are built on the advantages of network externalities, through which benefits multiply exponentially as the network expands. In the computer world, this is often referred to as "Metcalf's Law," which states, "The value of a network—defined as its utility to a population— is roughly proportional to the number of users squared."[14] The scope and depth of the markets served thus influence the value of the services provided.

The Impact on Markets: Effects on Efficiency

Standard Pricing.   Advances in Web browsers and servers will facilitate rapid, frequent price changes and levels of price differentiation to a much finer degree than are currently achieved in alternative media like magazines and direct mail. Prices can be customized, not only by country market, but at the level of the individual user.[15] When a user accesses a Web site, the page she receives when she clicks on a link can be made dependent on her IP address, which is embedded in the commands sent from her browser to the server. This means instant customization of information and prices across borders (as in airline computer reservation systems), furthering the potential for more efficient markets.

While pricing may therefore become both less standardized and more volatile, users will quickly become aware of such price discrimination and may not tolerate it. MNCs with overseas distributors charging different prices in different country markets face especially difficult obstacles. Bob MacPherson, the webmaster for Laboratory Equipment Exchange, an information resource for the sale of used scientific equipment, explains:

> *The companies that advertise through my service . . . have to recognize that there are international consequences to their promotions. For example, if a company were to offer a 20 percent discount on some products to my readers, readers all over the world would see this deal. But in some countries where you have distributors or don't need to discount to get business, the special offer is a problem. So my information network is not attracting MNCs but rather small and medium-sized businesses. The big MNCs are really sitting on the Internet fence waiting to see what happens.[16]*

In addition, smart agents, software programs that can search the Internet for products meeting prespecified criteria, may further combat attempts at price discrimination by uncovering different prices. Taken together, these factors suggest that the Internet will lead to increased standardization of prices across borders or, at least, narrower price spreads across country markets.

Changing Role of Intermediaries.   The Internet can connect end users with producers directly and thereby reduce the importance of (and value extraction by) intermediaries. The ubiquitous availability of the Web enables buyers, particularly in emerging markets, to access a broader range of product choices, bypass local intermediaries, and purchase their goods on the world market at lower prices. A hospital in Saudi Arabia, for example, can put out a request for proposal for equipment over the Internet, secure bids, select a supplier without going through local brokers and distributors, and have the products delivered directly by DHL or Federal Express. Few buffer inventories will be needed in the worldwide distribution system and less working capital will therefore be tied up in inventory.

However, if intermediaries can perform a different mix of services, made necessary by the Internet, they will continue to play critical roles and extract value.[17] While the Internet makes direct contact between end users and producers more feasible, this may also be less efficient over the long term and across a broad range of products. The potential for "information overload" is enormous. An intermediary's value-added may no longer be principally in the physical distribution of goods, but in the collection, collation, interpretation, and dissemination of vast amounts of information. For example, the hospital in Saudi Arabia needs to purchase a broad range of products, probably in differing quantities and at different times. Although it can contact each supplier directly, it would be more efficient to use a single distributor to collect the pricing and product information required, acting more like the robotic software search agents we described above.

The critical resource for such a distributor

would then be information, not inventory. In the international context, the value of such timely, accurate information may be even higher. A logistics company like DHL can handle the physical distribution of goods. When the intermediary roles can be separated, we may see a simultaneous growth and fragmentation at this level of the distribution chain. Since economies of scale for the marketer would then be reduced, smaller companies would be able to compete more effectively in international markets using the Internet.

Making Markets.   There are new opportunities for businesses to serve primarily as market makers, assisting buyers and sellers in locating one another, in negotiating terms of trade, and in executing secure transactions. The two principal market-making vehicles are auctions and exchanges.

Electronic auctions are usually continuous, and the bidders are physically separated. At a site such as OnSale, which auctions off new, but discontinued or outdated, computer equipment, buyers place their bids electronically and are notified continually of their status. Japan's experience with electronic car auctions supports the auctions' potential for expansion to consumer goods on a wide scale. (The average selling price increased in national versus local auctions due to the increased number of bidders.)[18]

Exchanges prescreen buyers and sellers, introduce them to one another, and assist in the transaction process, but do not help them agree on a price. United Computer Exchange offers market-making services for consumers interested in buying and selling used computer equipment. Although the company was established as a phone service, it moved onto the Web to increase its market scope, since both buyers and sellers can participate without making costly, time-dependent phone calls during the bidding process. Exchanges are examples of businesses in which there is true value-added from the international scope of the operations. While most current Internet exchanges are in the computer field, possible product categories include all forms of specialized equipment and consumer durables on a global scale.

Efficient Capital Flows.   The efficiency of international capital flows and foreign direct investment may also increase. American Venture Capital Exchange (AVCE) advertises investment opportunities on the Internet to prospective investors. AVCE accepts only investors who have submitted an application and passed a screening process. The company takes a fee on any deals that are finalized as a result of bringing investors and investment opportunities together. Recently, about 15 of their nearly 200 listings were companies based outside the United States—11 were in Russia. CapEx offers a similar matching service, in both German and English, for potential entrepreneurs and investors. Many start-up companies benefiting from this increased access to capital and investment opportunities are small and located in emerging markets. Improved access to capital will be another factor in leveling the playing field between large and small businesses competing internationally.

Internal Implications: The Intranet

While the early audiences for most Web sites have been external customers, the potential for serving internal customers may be equally as great. Creating internal networks to facilitate communications and transactions among employees, suppliers, independent contractors, and distributors may be the Internet's principal value for MNCs. A 1995 Forrester report defined an intranet as "Internal corporate TCP/IP [transmission control protocol/Internet protocol] networks that carry Internet-developed applications like the Web—and its future cousins." Based on interviews with 50 large corporations, Forrester reported that 22 percent had internal Web servers, and 40 percent were seriously investigating installation. A recent article on intranets revealed that sales of intranet server software had surpassed sales of Internet servers by the end of 1995, as companies recognized broader uses from intranet applications.[19] Internal Web servers have a number of advantages over classic client-server solutions. They are cheaper, faster, and easier to set up than client-server network systems, given the existing use of TCP/IP for outside communications; vendors are quickly developing new products specifically for this market; the architecture is already established and built into PCs; and the platform offers room for growth and flexibility.[20] Web-based internal networks can also offer sufficient security based on encryption technologies and allow companies to adjust levels of access based on a user's status. For example, business partners (e.g., suppliers or developers) can be given more limited access to the internal system than employees, who may themselves be assigned differential access based on their department and position within the company.

We briefly examine the potential value of an intranet as an internal communications vehicle by reviewing the types of communication that it facilitates.[21] First, companies can use the traditional "one to many" or broadcast model to communicate corporate policies and product or market news to worldwide divisions. Similarly, companies can provide employees worldwide with immediate and up-to-date access to company databases, phone directories, and reports. Second, in the "many to one" model, MNCs can use the internal system to ask questions or collect information from divisions and individual employees. Third, in the "many to many" model, perhaps the model with the greatest potential impact, MNCs can use the network to enable real-time, synchronous discussion *among* operating units.

Several intranet applications of these communication models are in use, often aimed at expediting relatively simple but costly and time-consuming tasks like information distribution. Xerox plans to connect its 90,000 employees via its intranet and has begun testing the network with 15,000 employees in 120 offices, primarily to distribute customer support information to salespeople.[22] Digital Equipment's intranet, residing on 400 internal servers, currently connects the company's 61,000

employees and offers a biweekly corporate newsletter, a proprietary search engine, restricted information to corporate partners, and support for sales and service staff.[23]

More complicated two-way communications take fuller advantage of the new technologies. Companywide bulletin boards permit multiparty dialogue on specific problems. As expertise on intranet usage spreads from the MIS department to marketing to other functions, companies can bring together functional departments located at sites around the globe to learn, share, and solve problems. They can also use these real-time forums as training vehicles for selected employees worldwide. Sun Microsystems broadcasts its corporate executives' speeches to its employees and archives them for later access. At Lawrence Livermore National Laboratory in California, employees take safety orientation classes and exams using an internal Web server equipped with audio and video capabilities.[24] Eli Lilly & Co. is using its intranet to manage clinical trials and drug approval processes in more than 120 countries. The network enables employees worldwide to access databases detailing the complex requirements for drug testing and approval in each country, facilitating the process of moving drugs through trials.[25]

In addition, companies are testing intranets as tools for internal transactions. AT&T recently introduced digital transaction technology across divisions that buy and sell goods from one another, so it can test, in a safe and friendly environment, whether it can facilitate internal money transfers before expanding to external transactions.[26]

External Implications: Global Product Reach

The global expansion of the Internet will facilitate both finding markets for new products and developing products for new markets.

• **New Product Diffusion.** New product announcements on the Internet will spawn immediate demand. To respond and to avoid competitive preemption, manufacturers will have to be prepared to distribute and service new products overnight. Slow test-as-you-go rollouts of new products from one country market to another will be less common. At the same time, using sophisticated technologies, companies may find it easier to test multiple new product variations simultaneously if they can control the information flow between test markets. When able to discriminate by a visitor's Internet address, companies can target variations of new products at different groups and get instant feedback on the value of specific features and appeal of various prices. For example, Digital Equipment allows potential customers to obtain demonstrations of its hardware on-line and can offer product variations on the Internet as beta tests for new products.

• **Local Adaptation and Customization.** Marketers are finding it easier to adapt their products inexpensively to local or national preferences, due to factory and marketing customization. The Internet's new communication capabilities may speed this trend. However, if the global community is able to communicate more openly, the global mass-market concept will thrive as consumers retain their desire to share in the latest trends around the world. For example, Asia's imitation of European and American fashion trends will be that much more rapid, due to the instant dissemination of fashion news and widespread availability of direct purchase from U.S. manufacturers via the Internet.

Online BookStore, a U.S.-based book publisher uploads chapters of its forthcoming books in multiple languages for visitors worldwide to "sample." The samples often include feedback links to authors and links to other relevant materials on the Internet as the company aims to customize publishing. Its unique marketing strategy has spawned both new distribution channels and translation of materials into local languages as site visitors from around the world demand the books after sampling the content. This customization is unique because it is driven by end-consumer demand for titles, not by foreign distributor interest as is customary in this industry.[27]

• **Niche Products.** Small companies offering specialized niche products should be able to find the critical mass of customers necessary to succeed through the worldwide reach of the Internet. The Internet's low-cost communications permits firms with limited capital to become global marketers at the early stages of their development.[28] Indeed, the risk that entrepreneurs in other parts of the world will preempt their unique ideas demands that they do so.

Manufacturers of specialized equipment, such as medical and scientific equipment, are beginning to find markets through exchanges such as the Laboratory Equipment Exchange. As Bob MacPherson, the webmaster, explains:

People seeking limited production parts or very specialized hardware can try to locate what they are seeking through my service. An American might not find what he or she is looking for in the United States for two reasons: (1) it is an old piece of hardware and parts are hard to find; or (2) the OEM may have been an offshore company that once thrived in the United States, but has since closed its North American operations.

• **Overcoming Import Restrictions.** Many Internet retailers (selling, for example, CDs, books, or clothing) are finding that they can offer products to consumers directly via their Web sites for a delivered cost significantly lower than most international consumers find in their local retail outlets. However, with the Internet stimulating cross-border product flows, government import regulations may become stiffer.

Information flows have come under similar scrutiny. For example, CompuServe recently bowed to the German government's disapproval of a number of Internet news groups' pornographic content. Due to limitations in its technology, CompuServe was forced to limit all subscriber access worldwide to more than 200 news groups. This, in turn, spawned customers' opposition in countries where such access is legal; they felt their freedoms had been violated. Although the issue was resolved when CompuServe acquired the technology to enable differential screening, defining the boundaries in international law and the carrier's level of responsibility for such information is still being debated among commercial service providers, content providers, and governments.

Understanding Global Consumers

The Internet promises to be an efficient new medium for conducting worldwide market research. Marketers can test both new product concepts and advertising copy over the Internet for instant feedback. They can also test varying levels of customer support to help managers define country market priorities and adapt the marketing mix. Marketers can also establish worldwide consumer panels to test proposed marketing programs across national, regional, or cross-cultural samples. Tracking individual customer behavior and preferences will become easier over time. Requesting customers' consent to monitor such data may prove superior to existing methods of gathering or buying customer information, since the site visitors who voluntarily provide information are likely to be high-potential customers. Moreover, the Internet permits new types of measurement tools that will expand the data available to marketers, including:

• On-line Surveys. Marketers can post surveys on sites and offer incentives for participation. Internet surveys are more powerful than mail surveys because of the medium's "branching" capabilities (asking different questions based on previous answers) and are cheaper than either mail or phone surveys.
• Bulletin Boards. On-line bulletin boards are much like the traditional cork board, except that the software enables "threading" messages, so readers can follow a conversation and easily check responses to each posting. Companies can monitor and participate in such group discussions in many countries simultaneously.
• Web Visitor Tracking. Servers automatically

collect data on the paths that visitors travel while in the site, including time spent at each page. Marketers can assess the value of the information and correlate the observed traffic patterns with purchase behavior.
• Advertising Measurement. Since servers automatically record the link through which each Web visitor enters a site, marketers can accurately assess the traffic, as well as sales, generated by links placed on other Web sites.
• Customer Identification Systems. Both business-to-business and consumer marketers are installing registration procedures that enable them to identify individuals and track purchases over time, creating a "virtual panel."
• E-mail Marketing Lists. Many sites ask customers to sign up voluntarily on a mailing list for company news. The audience generated appears very different from that garnered through traditional direct marketing. Internationally, information can be disseminated quickly to the audiences on these lists at minimal cost.

Challenges for International Marketers

The growth of the Internet as a facilitator of international commerce presents different challenges and opportunities to small Internet start-up companies and to MNCs. Some of the obstacles are unique to each company, while others confront all marketers striving to succeed globally on the Internet.

MNCs usually already do business internationally but may have to revise their operations, strategies, and business models if they want to exploit the opportunities offered by the Internet. The start-up doing business primarily through the Internet must be prepared to operate globally from the outset, which can strain its resources. The company must have (1) twenty-four-hour order taking and customer service response capability, (2) regulatory and customs-handling expertise to ship internationally, and (3) in-depth understanding of foreign marketing environments to assess the relative advantages of its own products and services. Successful start-ups need sufficient staff with multilingual skills and access to information on local laws and trends.

Global Branding. A major challenge for MNCs is the management of global brands and corporate name or logo identification. Consumers may be confused if a company and its subsidiaries have several Web sites, each communicating a different format, image, message, and content. 3M, which has one site for its entire product line, has a focused corporate identity and firm control over the marketing actions of its divisions and subsidiaries. However, many MNCs with one brand name have allowed local entities to develop sites ad hoc and now have several sites around the globe that require tighter coordination. For example, Coopers & Lybrand offices around the world each have their own Web sites using different servers. The Saab USA home page differs greatly in both tone and content from the Saab home page in Sweden. In addition, both sites offer links to a number of individual dealers' Web sites and unofficial sites of Saab enthusiasts. Tupperware, Avon, and Mary Kay have no main company sites, but independent sales representatives from around the world offer their wares directly over the Internet in a range of formats.

On the other hand, developing one site for each brand—while costly and limiting to cross-selling—is preferable when the brands have distinct markets and images. Kraft has already applied for 134 domain names, and Procter & Gamble has reserved 110, although they are currently using only a small number of them.[29] Guinness PLC has separate sites for its beer and single malt Scotch whiskeys.

New Internet users tend to explore the sites of familiar brands first. Trust is a critical factor in stimulating purchases over the Internet, especially at this early stage of commercial development; as a result, sites with known brand names enhance the credibility of the site sponsor, as well as the medium. Recognizing the importance of brand names, many MNCs are establishing single Web sites for each brand.

New Competition. The Web will reduce the competitive advantage of scale economies in many industries and make it easier for small marketers to compete worldwide. First, advertising as a barrier to entry will be reduced as the Web makes it possible to reach a global audience more cheaply. Paying to place links on pages with audiences that mirror or include a company's target customers is less expensive than traditional media. In addition, "free" advertising on other sites can often be exchanged for mutual links. Postings on Internet discussion groups on topics relevant for specific products or markets is another way for small marketers to attract visitors to their sites.

Second, increased advertising efficiency will be available to more marketers. While current Internet usage is skewed heavily toward young, relatively affluent, educated males, further growth will result in a user population that more closely mirrors the broad population. C/Net, a Web computer news service, will soon be able to alter the advertisements to its site visitors, depending on the registered user's reported purchase behavior. Large index and directory sites like Yahoo can selectively show advertisements, depending on visitor characteristics such as hardware platform, domain name, or search topics selected during the visit.

Third, as the role of intermediaries evolves, gaining visibility and distribution will become easier for small companies. In the new Web malls, like the German Electronic Mall Bodensee and the U.S. Internet Shopping Network, small entrepreneurs can reach vast audiences. The traditional networks of international distributors and subsidiaries that MNCs set up are less effective barriers to the entry of smaller competitors than they used to be—except perhaps in the case of products that require significant aftersales service. These existing networks may even impede MNCs' effective, timely response. MacPherson remarked:

Some small companies will grow at the expense of big companies. And some of my small business sponsors are seeing their business opportunities quadruple . . . because of the exposure that my site is giving them. These opportunities are at the expense of the MNC.

However, providing on-site after-sales service will be difficult for manufacturers of products sold directly via the Internet. Local distributors currently fulfill this role but will be unlikely to take it on without profiting from the accompanying sale. MNCs must develop policies for providing such service without disrupting the existing channel arrangements.

Competitive Advantage. For companies marketing on the Internet, technology is a more important source of competitive advantage than size. For example, TRADE'ex has proprietary software that enables direct communication and simplified, secure transactions among its member businesses. The company is now considering licensing its software system to companies in other industries. Another example is Agents Inc., a music company that has patented preference-mapping software. Members, who register on entering the site, describe their music preferences to "teach" the system what music they like. As members continue to rate recommended music, the system becomes smarter in predicting preferences and suggesting new music. A small company like this can quickly become a big player internationally by leveraging technology in ways that respond to customer needs. Virtual Vineyards, an Internet-based wine merchant, has developed a proprietary wine-rating system. Visitors to the site can compare ratings of each wine on-line and, in the future, to their personal taste profile stored by the system.

What does this mean for large MNCs? The advantages of size will erode. As a result, many will need to proactively invent new ways of using the Internet to address customer needs and also to connect their worldwide operations. The current defensive stance that many large MNCs have

adopted, which involves merely establishing "banner" presences on the Internet and hoping that they do not develop into a transactional medium, may well prove unsustainable.

Organizational Challenges. The Internet presents especially serious organizational challenges for MNCs attempting to convert their global businesses to the new medium because its speed and worldwide presence make its audiences intolerant of inconsistencies and slow response. The services that an MNC offers on the Internet should be available to buyers in all countries to prevent confusion and dissatisfaction. For example, although Federal Express's home page currently offers the ability to track a package worldwide, information on delivery options, pricing, and schedules are available only in the United States. FedEx has long been planning worldwide expansion of its service but is hesitant to act too quickly. Robert Hamilton, FedEx's Internet/Online services manager, explained:

> *One thing FedEx is facing is the fact that we have a global brand. A huge percentage of our hits are non-U.S. One of the challenges . . . is how to establish local relevance, yet at the same time put this out to serve a global medium. Once you get a new service, or set of services, you want to be able to speak to those [local] issues. For example, certain [services] that are available to Canadian customers aren't relevant elsewhere.*[30]

An MNC must set up a worldwide task force of executives to coordinate the presentation of its corporate identity on multiple, interconnected Web sites. It might appoint a particular office or operating unit that has been a leader in using the Internet as the center for home page development. It also must have a system for regular updating of Web site information, especially if prices change or inventories go out of stock. Managers of Internet task forces must keep informed about developments around the globe. In addition, an MNC must establish policies for allocating credit for sales orders placed via the home page to foreign subsidiaries, lest the performance measures of the subsidiaries be disrupted.

A specialized customer service staff may be needed to deal with Internet traffic. Internet users have high expectations for timely, efficient response, due to their knowledge of the company's expanded capabilities. For example, if the home page offers a visitor a way to give customer feedback or send questions to the company, customer service reps must answer quickly and monitor customers' e-mail for changes in content, tone, and origin. A company's Internet center should also analyze the server data that tracks customer site access and transactions.

Some sales may be consummated via the Internet, but the Web will probably not become the primary advertising and distribution vehicle for most products and services—except for financial and information services that can be completely delivered on the Web. Marketers will need to integrate their marketing communications and distribution for Internet customers with their existing strategies.

Disseminating Information.   News of product quality problems and cross-border differences in quality, price, and availability will be hard to contain. Critical reviews of Intel's Pentium chip and Microsoft's Windows 95 software spread quickly across the Internet. News of bugs in Netscape's security system reached around the world in hours. There will inevitably be a need for a worldwide approach to crisis management; controversies, especially those surrounding global brands, will be impossible to contain at the national level.

There are other implications of the rapid information flow. Third-party "search agents" can collect pricing information through robots from various sources around the world, so consumers can compare prices and products. This is especially important in emerging markets where such sources of information (like *Consumer Reports*) are not widely available. For example, Andersen Consulting's "Smart Store" seeks the lowest prices on any certificate of deposit that a user requests.[31] In response, many sites are building software codes into their servers to block the robots so that they can continue to vary prices and product offerings by market.

Maintaining Web Sites.   The creation of a Web site is not a one-time effort. A 1995 Forrester report shows that annual costs for site maintenance are two to four times the initial launch cost.[32] The current speed of technological innovation in Web site design and the increasing competitiveness of the medium require global marketers to continually assess their Internet sites' perceived value among target groups across countries. Sites must offer valuable, changing content that will not only attract new customers from many countries but also encourage them to return. Given that individuals around the world will have different product information needs, levels of brand familiarity, and bandwidth capacity, fulfilling such diverse needs on a single site will be challenging.

Currently, most company Web pages are merely online brochures, with added links to related information. Increased sophistication of server software will facilitate more complex content and more customized paths tailored to each visitor through a site. However, many Internet users outside the United States, at least in the short run, will have lower bandwidth and be paying higher prices for access, and therefore will not be able to access complicated graphics quickly and inexpensively. Site sponsors will need to recognize that the users' capabilities in hardware, software, and computer expertise will vary significantly across borders.

Most sites are organized as hierarchical layers of documents, with the rule of thumb that users should not have to delve more than three layers before they access valued information. However, new technologies will permit sophisticated matching of pages to user needs. For example, Software.net delivers Web pages dependent on the user's platform, identified by the server software. Macintosh users see Macintosh offers, while PC users see Windows software. Rockport plans to give its Web site visitors the option of classifying themselves as "rugged," "relaxed," or "refined." Based on each visitor's choice, he or she will see very different sites with specific navigation options. Federal Express recently announced plans to implement new software with different services, advertisements, and interfaces based on the user's country of origin, business type, and bandwidth.[33]

However, with new technologies and the proliferation of Web design and management companies, the temptation to customize content will have to be weighed against the value of maintaining a consistent worldwide image. In addition, companies will have to choose how to maintain, grow, and manage their sites. Should they outsource? Or should they strive to create proprietary content and software?

Language and Culture Barriers.   The Web promises to reinforce the trend toward English as the lingua franca of commerce. There are significant obstacles in translating Chinese and Japanese to the computer, especially the large number of local dialects. In addition, the importance of vocal intonations in these spoken languages may further impede the transfer of business dialogue from voice to text.

Very few MNCs offer translations of their Web site content into local languages. Several translation services have opened on the Internet. In addition, exposure itself raises opportunities. For example, a Japanese company recently approached CatalogSite, an Internet-based mall of catalogs to translate many of its catalogs into Japanese. One enterprising European on-line service based in Sardinia, Video On Line, is quickly expanding its user base by focusing on local content in local languages. The company overcomes the prohibitive costs of telephone use for Europeans by providing direct access through three high-speed dedicated lines between Sardinia, Stockholm, and the United States. Owner Nicola Grauso plans to expand from Sardinia and Italy to 30 countries in four continents, offering local language content in each, including more than a dozen African dialects.[34]

However, cultural barriers remain. When setting up a traditional business operation in a foreign country, managers usually have numerous conversations with local partners and visit the country several times. With a virtual business, the need for such contacts is minimized, and cultural differences may not be as apparent. To avoid cultural pitfalls, many small entrepreneurs without broad contacts use Internet discussion groups to become familiar with local customs, trends, and laws.

Government Influence and Involvement

Foreign government support and cooperation will be critical in determining how the international Internet business environment will evolve. Will foreign governments allow the free flow of trade and ideas? Will they be able to agree on issues such as data security, taxation on transactions, and pornography? Who will lead in developing the infrastructure, educating users, and providing access to the Internet for businesses and consumers?

Early initiatives by some governments, trade associations, and telecommunication companies bode well for future expansion. For example:

• More than 40 organizations in 10 eastern European nations provide Internet services to an estimated 350,000 local consumers and businesses, an increase from only 5,000 in 1992.[35]

• In Thailand, the National Electronics and Computer Technology Center, in cooperation with the state-owned telecommunications industry, is investing $10 million to develop the Internet infrastructure.

• In Russia, where only 500,000 computers were sold last year, the number of subscribers to on-line services is only 10 percent that in the United States, but increasing at 5 percent per month.[36]

• Israel has recently established a local search engine where inquirers can search for Israeli-based Internet resources.[37]

• Europe Online, the counterpart of America

Online, attempts to bring together resources from around Europe, concentrating on entertainment, news, and travel.

• New Zealand focuses its national site, Gateway to New Zealand, on providing visitors with information on travel, commerce, education, weather, and recreation and on giving links to a range of local businesses that offer information and transactions on-line.

• In Latin America, there are more than 15,000 Internet connections, half established within the last year. Many Latin American sites are at universities or on servers in the United States.

• The National Telephone Company in Nicaragua has leased a satellite link to Florida to offer local Internet access to consumers and businesses.

• The Chilean National University Network gives commercial access to private businesses to fund its own growth and further Internet usage in the country.[38]

Some governments in Asia have aggressively led in development of the Internet infrastructure in their countries to further economic growth and to retain control over external access and internal usage. ChinaWeb actively promotes cross-border marketing by Chinese companies, highlighting how conducting business on the Internet can reduce costs and help companies reach specialized market segments in diverse geographical locations. ChinaWeb also offers links to the Shanghai Stock Exchange, with daily updated stock quotes; the Pudong Investment Center, with information on Pudong's special economic zone; Air China, with on-line booking for its flights; a travel agency that offers additional travel arrangements within China; a career directory; and an e-mail database of exporters. The government of the People's Republic of China actively solicits corporate sponsorships by luring companies with the possibility of reaching Chinese people in the United States. However, ChinaWeb does not offer similar opportunities to foreign marketers seeking access to Chinese consumers.

The United Nations has established a "Global Trade Point Network" that assists small and medium-size companies eager to expand globally by linking interested entrepreneurs with information resources on trade regulations, trade associations, and local markets. Similarly, the Hong Kong Trade Development Council has established a computerized "Trade Enquiry Service" that matches overseas buyers with Hong Kong manufacturers and traders in a range of industries. The current database includes more than 320,000 importers, 140,000 Chinese businesses, and 70,000 Hong Kong manufacturers, classified by name, country, and product.[39]

Such government-sponsored "megasites" are more common in Europe and Asia than in the United States and reflect the countries' emphasis on government-led economic development. In Europe, small businesses are likely to establish an on-line presence through regional cooperatives and state organizations that promote local business. In the United States, individual small businesses have rapidly exploited the new opportunities on their own. While joint development efforts reduce costs and risks, they also limit an individual company's freedom to innovate and invest in aggressive marketing on the Web.[40]

Several countries have not yet signed the Bern Convention, which governs copyrights, or enforced the 1994 GATT policies on intellectual property. China and Thailand limit internal use of the Internet to research and academic projects. Quite recently, China has been reevaluating its internal access policies. The government is currently exploring the use of software that will enable it to screen the Internet information flows into, out of, and within the country, creating its own national intranet.[41] In addition, many countries in central and eastern Europe resist the Internet because it threatens to open the culture and people to outside influences too broadly and rapidly.[42] The Internet Society Summit established an Internet Law Task Force in spring 1995 to explore solutions to problems such as privacy, warning labels, copyright and trademark protection, and taxation and to persuade reluctant governments to open Internet access.[43] Nonetheless, numerous issues remain to be resolved:

• Defining the scope of import tariffs and export controls.

• Delineating the boundaries of intellectual copyrights.

• Standardizing regulations on the use and sale of personal information.

• Defining the roles of national governments in limiting the inflow of ideas.

• Creating cross-national laws for regulated industries such as gambling, financial services, and liquor.

An equally daunting obstacle is the poor state of the current infrastructure and the regulation of the telecommunications industry abroad. For example, the Czech Republic's phone company cannot yet provide leased lines with adequate transmission speeds outside Prague. There are currently only 1.7 phones per 100 people in Africa, and little impetus and funds for state-owned monopoly telecommunication companies to invest.[44] In Mexico, consumers often have to wait more than a year for phone service installation. Similar situations prevail throughout developing countries in eastern Europe, Asia, Latin America, and Africa and highly regulated countries in western Europe. These countries need to invest in better telecommunications infrastructures and to promote internal competition before they can take full advantage of the opportunities the Internet offers for global commerce.

Conclusion

While the Internet offers many benefits to both existing MNCs and start-up companies—and, perhaps, to their customers—the challenges of an inadequate technological infrastructure, concerned public policymakers, and, especially for MNCs, existing distribution and organization structures all seem formidable. Any company eager to take advantage of the Internet on a global scale must select a business model for its Internet venture and define how information and transactions delivered through this new medium will influence its existing model. The company must also assess who its diverse Web audiences are, what specific customer needs the medium will satisfy, and how its Internet presence will respond to a changing customer base, evolving customer needs, competitor actions, and technological developments. For international marketers, achieving a balance between the new medium's ability to be customized and the desire to retain coherence, control, and consistency as they go to market worldwide will be a major challenge.

References

1. G. F. Colony, H. W. Deutsch, and T. B. Rhinelander, "Network Strategy Service: CIO Meets the Internet," *The Forrester Report,* volume 12 (Cambridge, Massachusetts: Forrester Consulting, May 1995).

2. As of July 1995, according to an Internet domain survey by Network Wizards, obtained from <http://www.nw.com>. Host computers are those connected directly to Internet gateways. A host computer can serve anywhere from one to hundreds of users, depending on the network setup.

3. B. Bournellis, "Internet's Phenomenal Growth Is Mirrored in Startling Statistics," *Internet World,* volume 6, November 1995.

4. See <http://www.comnex.com>.

5. B. Giussani, "Why Europe Lags on the Web," *Inc.,* 15 November 1995, p. 23.

6. S. Gupta and J. Pitkow, "Consumer Survey of WWW Users: Preliminary Results from 4th Survey," December 1995, obtained from <http://www.umich.edu/~sgupta/hermes/>.

7. These figures, for the World Wide Web alone, were calculated from "Trends in the WorldWide Marketplace," Activmedia, at <http://www.activmedia.com>, 1996. Current estimates of transaction volume, especially predictions of future volume, vary widely based on the source of the data and the types of media included. For example, Forrester Research, in a May 1995 report, estimated 1996 transaction volume from all interactive retail (Internet, WWW, CD-ROMs, and commercial on-line services) at only $500 million.

8. Results reported from a Rochester Institute of Technology survey of 378 Internet shoppers conducted between February and May of 1995, obtained from <http://www.rit.edu>.

9. S. Butterbaugh, "More Than a Pretty Face: FedEx Gears up for a Brand-Intensive 1996," Interactive Monitor, Media Central, obtained from <http://mediacentral.com>, December 1995.

10. S. Lohr, "When Pointing and Clicking Fails to Click: More and More Questions, and Employees, at Computer Help Services, *New York Times,* 1 January 1996, p. 45.

11. T. Seiderman, "Making Net Export Profits," *International Business,* August 1995, pp. 47–50.

12. Giussani (1995).

13. A. Cortese, "Here Comes the Intranet," *Business Week,* 26 February 1996, p. 76.

14. C. Anderson, "The Accidental Superhighway," *The Economist,* 1 July 1995, pp. S1–S26.

15. Currently, there are some intricacies that may complicate this. Due to the international use of both domain (.edu, .com, .gov, .net) and country codes, it is sometimes difficult to identify the visitor's country if he or she is using a domain code. However, more comprehensive databases of hosts, more sophisticated server matching schemes, and user registration procedures can overcome this.

16. Quoted from personal interview with MacPherson via e-mail, January 1996.

17. See M. B. Sarkar, B. Butler, and C. Steinfeld, "Intermediaries and Cybermediaries: A Continuing Role for Mediating Players in the Electronic Marketplace," in R. R. Dholakia and D. R. Fortin, eds., *Proceedings from Conference on Telecommunications and Information Markets,* October 1995, pp. 82–92.

18. See A. Warbelow, J. Kokuryo, and B. Konsynski, "AUCNET" (Boston: Harvard Business School, Case # 9-190–001, July 1989).

19. For examples of the range of Intranet applications in use, see: Cortese (1996), pp. 76–84.

20. P. D. Callahan, D. Goodtree, A. E. Trenkle, and D. F. Cho, "Network Strategy Service: The Intranet," *The Forrester Report,* volume 10 (Cambridge, Massachusetts: Forrester Consulting, December 1995).

21. For a review and application of these models to the new media, see:

D. Hoffman and T. Novak, "Marketing in Hypermedia Computer-Mediated Environments: Conceptual Foundations" (Nashville, Tennessee: Vanderbilt University, Owen Graduate School of Management, Working Paper No. 1, July 1995).

22. J. E. Frook, "Intranets' Grab Mind Share," *Communications Week,* 20 November 1995, p. 1.

23. J. Carl, "Digital's Intranet Comes Together," *Web Week,* volume 2, January 1996, p. 25.

24. K. Murphy, "Web Proves Useful as Training Platform," *Web Week,* volume 2, January 1996.

25. N. Gross, "Here Comes the Intranet," *Business Week,* 26 February 1996, p. 82.

26. E. Booker, "AT&T Using Internal Web to Test Digital Payments," *Web Week,* volume 1, December 1995.

27. See <http://www.obs-us.com/obs/>.

28. M. W. Rennie, "Global Competitiveness: Born Global," *McKinsey Quarterly,* 22 September 1993, pp. 45–52.

29. The policies of domain registration have created a frenzy to register brand names and trademarks since current trademark laws do not cover the registration of domain names. The company responsible for the allocation of the domain names, InterNIC, allocates names on a first-come, first-served basis with the agreement by domain holders that InterNIC will not be held liable for trademark infringements. For further information, see:

"InterNIC Security," *Wired,* 4.01, January 1996, p. 74.

30. Butterbaugh (1995).

31. See <http://bf2.cstar.ac.com/smartstore/>.

32. J. Bernoff and A. Ott, "People and Technology: What Web Sites Cost," *The Forrester Report,* volume 2 (Cambridge, Massachusetts: Forrester Consulting, December 1995).

33. Butterbaugh (1995).

34. L. Marshall, "The Berlusconi of the Net," *Wired,* 4.01, January 1996, pp. 78–85.

35. D. Rocks, N. Ingelbrecht, R. Castillo, and D. Peachey, "Developing World Seeks Highway On-Ramp," *Communications Week,* 2 October 1995, p. 39.

36. J. Zander, "Russia Makes Net Progress," *TechWeb,* obtained from <http://techweb.cmp.com/ia/0108 issue/0108issue.html>.

37. See <http://www.xpert.com/search/>.

38. Rocks et al. (1995).

39. See <http://www.tdc.org.hk/main/main.html>.

40. Guissani (1995).

41. J. Kahn, K. Chen, and M. W. Brauchli, "Chinese Firewall," *The Wall Street Journal,* 31 January 1996, p. A1.

42. C. Grycz, "The International Aspects of Internetting" (Boston: Fall Internet World 1995 on CD-ROM, 1995).

43. C. Mendler, "Stop! Or I'll Yell Stop Again!" *Communications Week,* 2 October 1995, p. 28.

44. Rocks et al. (1995).

MANAGING YOUR SALES FORCE IN JAPAN AND THE U.S.

John L. Graham, Shigeru Ichikawa, and Yao Apasu

Globalization of Competition

The globalization of competition is perhaps the most fundamental challenge facing multinational firms in the 1990s. The strength of firms specializing in domestic markets is being eroded as participation in the two largest markets in the world, Japan and the United States, becomes a competitive necessity. Increasingly domestic success and worldwide success are determined by penetration of these two key markets.

And it is no longer just enough to produce competitive products for these two markets. Efficient and effective *promotion* of quality products often makes the difference between success and disaster in both markets, and for most companies personal selling is the key. Thus, sales force management is a crucial task in both countries.

What are the similarities and differences between managing salespeople in Japan and the United States? A recent survey of salespeople and their managers in America and Japan explored this question. Both the U.S. and Japanese firms were large multinationals producing primarily elec-

tronic products, and more than 150 salespeople were included in each sample.

Unanticipated Similarities

The popular view of management in Japan and the United States holds that careful consideration must be given to the substantial differences in motives of employees in each country. Even the Japanese government has suggested that Japanese workers value economic well-being far more than their American or European counterparts.[1] Our study of the values of salespeople in each country proved the opposite.

When asked to rate the importance of 18 different life goals, both the Japanese and the American sales representatives rated "family security" as their number one priority and "happiness" as number two. Moreover, there was no meaningful difference in their ratings of "freedom": the Americans rated it as number three and the Japanese number five.

The similarities were even more striking when it came to job-related rewards (see Exhibit 1). Both the Japanese and American sales representatives valued a merit increase in pay most highly. The only real difference related to social recognition: the Americans considered sales club awards, etc., to be substantially less important than their Japanese counterparts.

Euro-Asia Business Review, January 1987. Reprinted with permission from The Euro-Asia Centre, Boulevard de Constance, 77309 Fontainebleu Cedex, France.

EXHIBIT 1   The Salespeople Were Asked to: "Distribute 100 points among the Rewards in Terms of Their Importance to You."

Rewards	Relative Importance (mean)	
	Japanese	*Americans*
Job security	18.5	17.6
Promotion	13.7	14.9
Merit increase in pay	24.7	26.2
Feeling of worthwhile accomplishment	18.5	18.2
Social recognition (sales club awards)	8.1	5.2
Personal growth and development	16.6	17.8

The values and goals of sales representatives do not appear to differ much from one side of the Pacific to the other. This suggests that the tools used to motivate sales performance should also be similar. However, most companies selling in the two markets have adopted sales management practices tailored to the external business environment rather than the internal motivations of individual sales representatives in each country.

Employment Practices

The lifetime employment practices of the major Japanese firms are well known. Of equal renown is the high employee turnover common in America. These disparate approaches to firm/employee relations are deeply ingrained into individual values and company policies in each country. And this basic difference in the two business systems translates into significant differences in sales force management practices.

Recruiting.   In the United States, new employees come from two main sources. Many American firms recruit sales representatives straight out of school (universities and colleges), and provide training in sales techniques. Many other firms "buy" experienced sales representatives from other companies—often competitors or customers. Additionally, hiring practices of individual American firms often vary over time; that is, college recruits may be emphasized one year and "buying experience" may be emphasized the next. The expected tenure of a new college sales recruit ranges between two and three years in the United States.

In Japan, college graduates join large companies for life and job-hopping, while not unheard of, is not at all common. Employers use a wide variety of tactics to keep employees, including browbeating, begging, and even appealing to families and neighbors. Moreover, employees are afraid of the stigma attached to switching jobs. So Japanese employers' college recruiting practices are incredibly intense, and far more resources (both money and time) are spent on them than is the case in the United States. The pressure on the recruits is tremendous—they are obliged to make a lifetime decision at age 21!

These differences are reflected in our data. Sixty-four percent of the American sales representatives had previous sales experience; in contrast, only 18 percent of the Japanese reported working for another company. Hiring experienced people in Japan is thus not impossible, but much more difficult than in the United States.

Training and Organizational Culture.   Because hiring experienced people is less common than in Japan, managers must invest more in training their sales representatives. Since employees are wedded to their companies, managers are almost certain to reap the rewards of such investments. Indeed, during the last 15 years, Japanese firms have sent more than 10,000 employees through American MBA programmes—an investment of approximately US$50,000 per person (two years expenses and lost productivity).

Japanese firms have achieved great rewards through this investment—huge market shares in the U.S. market. American companies have done nothing comparable. And now companies in Tai-

EXHIBIT 2   The Sample of Sales Representatives and Managers

Demographic Characteristics		Japanese (N = 175)	Americans (N = 153)
Age	Under 20	—	—
	20–29	26%	21%
	30–39	72%	38%
	40–49	2%	14%
	50 or older	—	27%
Education	High school graduate	46%	2%
	Some college	1%	34%
	College graduate	53%	40%
	Some postgraduate	—	17%
	Graduate degree	—	7%
Income	Under $20,000	9%	2%
	$20,000–$29,000	41%	40%
	$30,000–$39,000	39%	42%
	$40,000–$49,000	9%	10%
	$50,000 and over	2%	6%
Tenure with company (mean)		9.0 years	8.7 years
Percent with previous sales experience		18%	64%
Number of representatives supervised (mean)		5.5	7.9

wan and Korea are following the Japanese example, sending their employees to study the American market in American business schools.

Organizational culture and commitment is strongly promoted in Japanese firms, an approach that American companies have recently begun to imitate. However, examples of successful implementation of this approach are few and far between in the States.

Our study suggested an explanation: the value systems of American sales representatives and their managers displayed a much greater variance than those of the Japanese. The value systems of the Japanese were more homogeneous, and consequently the corporate culture is stronger than amongst Americans.

Compensation.   Another important difference in sales management practices has to do with compensation and monetary incentives. Most American firms use some combination of salary and commission to motivate sales representatives. The

ratio between the two components often varies from year to year, depending on management policy and environmental changes. In contrast, straight salary is much more frequently the practice in Japanese firms.

Both Japanese and American firms also include bonuses as part of compensation packages; however, the bonuses are determined in different ways. For American sales representatives they are based primarily on *individual* performance—meeting quotas, etc.; for Japanese sales representatives they are based on *company* performance. Typically, the labour union negotiates with the management of the company for a yearly bonus (a percentage of salary or wages) to be paid semiannually. The sales representatives of the Japanese firm all receive an identical semiannual percentage bonus to their salaries, regardless of individual performance.

It should be noted that some large Japanese companies, often subsidiaries of American companies, do provide compensation schemes with high

---

Research Method

American Group

Data was collected from a survey conducted in a division of a large American multinational electronics firm. The firm's products are highly technical and are often designed to meet consumer specifications. Its 153 salespeople are required to be flexible and sensitive to customer needs. They are problem solvers and likely to experience conflicting demands from their customers and their firm.

The questionnaires were sent through the company's mailing system with a cover letter indicating the purpose of the study and who was conducting it. The salespeople were assured of the complete anonymity of their responses. They were asked not to sign their names and were to send their responses directly to the investigators.

Japanese Group

The Japanese firm, like the American firm, is a large multinational manufacturing organization selling a diverse line of electronic products. A sample of 175 was drawn consisting of experienced sales representatives attending a corporate training programme. The researcher administered the questionnaire during a scheduled session of the programme. The sales managers of the 175 representatives were mailed the sales manager questionnaire.

---

commission components. Indeed, National Cash Register has pioneered commission selling in Japan, and IBM and some other Japanese firms have followed their example. However, this is the exception, not the rule in Japan.

Employee Satisfaction and Retention.

Given the strong organizational culture in Japanese firms, one would expect Japanese sales representatives to be more satisfied with their jobs than their American counterparts. Surprisingly this is not the case. Indeed, the American sales representatives in our study were more satisfied with pay, opportunities for promotion, everyday duties, fellow workers, and customers than were the Japanese sales representatives. Further, the Japanese salespeople reported greater propensities to leave the firm.

In the United States, employees who are extremely dissatisfied with their jobs leave the company. In Japan, they stay, for all the reasons stated earlier. So Japanese managers must deal with a small cohort of extremely dissatisfied workers, whereas their American counterparts have no such problem.

Management Implications

Guidelines for Successful Sales-Force Management.   Foreign firms trying to enter the Japanese market face substantial barriers to establishing a high-quality sales force. The major, well-established firms have an insurmountable advantage in recruiting the better college graduates. And once they go to work for the established firms, they simply don't leave. So, firms new to the Japanese market are best advised to consider a joint venture or some sort of distribution agreement to obtain the requisite sales force.

In Japan, once a sales force has been established, firms can expect to invest more in training and organizational culture-building activities than in the United States. Because of the loyalty of Japanese employees, sales managers can expect to reap the long-term rewards associated with such investments.

Although notable exceptions exist, the primary means of motivating Japanese sales representatives will be by encouraging their commitment to the firm.

Japanese representatives are subject to closer

supervision than Americans. The mean number of representatives supervised by managers was less than six in Japan and almost eight in the United States.

Individual financial incentives apparently can work in Japan, but this is not common practice, whereas financial compensation is the key factor in sales-force management in the United States. A new firm in the United States can establish a sales force with relative ease, given the ability to buy experienced sales representatives from competitors, customers, or other associate firms. And once the experienced sales force has been established, individual incentive programmes and compensation packages can be designed to efficiently control the activities of sales representatives. This generally allows for looser supervision than in Japan.

Finally, managers of Japanese sales forces must contend with motivating a small contingent of dissatisfied and unproductive representatives. In the United States, such employees would either quit or be fired. This puts pressure on management to work at retaining their staff.

Reference

1. "Youth See Life," *Focus Japan* (December 1978), p. 9.

PRICING ISSUES

It is difficult to generalize about export pricing. Consequently, little has been written to assist decision makers. The author of the first paper in this section has posited six key variables that must be considered in setting prices for exported products and services: the nature of the offering and industry, the locus of production, the system of distribution, the locale and environment of the target market, home country laws and regulations, and the attitudes of the firm's managers about pricing. The paper includes a nine-step decision framework for export pricing.

One of the important advantages of marketing and operating globally is the financial flexibility associated with the complexity of international legal and financial regulations. This can be an equally important disadvantage. One way for executives of multinational companies to manage this complexity is through transfer pricing mechanisms. The authors of the second article in this section provide a guide for decision makers faced with the opportunities and risks of transfer pricing.

Unraveling the Mystique of Export Pricing

S. Tanner Cavusgil

In recent years, hundreds of U.S. companies have become involved in international business. The initial foreign activity is typically exporting. Perhaps the most puzzling part of international business for these firms is making pricing decisions.

What role should pricing play in the exporting company's marketing efforts? Can pricing be used as an effective marketing tool? Or would that practice expose the firm to unnecessary risks? What considerations affect the choice between incremental and full-cost pricing strategies? What approach should management take when setting export prices? How can the firm cope with escalation in international prices? What strategies are appropriate when a strong currency impairs overseas competitiveness? These are only a few of the many questions international marketing managers must answer.

Export pricing is a complex issue, and simple decision rules are often inadequate. The complexity lies in the large number of variables that affect international pricing decisions and the uncertainty surrounding them. These variables can be classified as either internal or external to the organization. The internal group includes corporate goals,

desire for control over prices, approach to costing, and degree of company internationalization. The external group includes competitive pressures, demand levels, legal and government regulations, general economic conditions, and exchange rates.

Despite export pricing's importance and complexity, very little empirical research has been conducted that might give managers norms to follow.[1] This article attempts to illuminate this important area of international marketing management. The overall purpose is to provide a better understanding of export pricing issues and to identify propositions that can be tested by more definitive, large-scale surveys, as well as to generate findings and implications useful to export managers.

Personal interviews, two to three hours in length, were conducted with one or more executives at each of 24 firms. Most of the firms studied were exporters of industrial or specialized products. The typical firm employed about 500 persons. Background information about each firm was collected with the use of a structured questionnaire either prior to or during the interview. All firms were located in the Midwestern United States.

Pricing Literature

Price is the only marketing variable that generates revenue. Top marketing executives call pricing the

255

most critical pressure point of the 1980s.[2] Recently, with accelerating technological advances, shorter product life cycles, and increasing input costs, price changes have become more common. Despite these developments, academic research on pricing has been modest at best.[3]

The neglect of international pricing is even more serious.[4] Intracorporate (transfer) pricing issues received attention during the 1970s, when study of multinational corporations (MNCs) was intense, but other pricing topics remain relatively unexplored.[5]

Other studies have focused on pricing practices under floating exchange rates,[6] location of pricing authority within MNCs,[7] price leadership of MNCs,[8] multinational pricing in developing countries,[9] and uniform pricing.[10] Several studies have had a regional/industry focus. One found a relatively high degree of export price discrimination among industrial firms in Northern England.[11] Another compared the pricing practices of chemical and construction industries in South Africa.[12] A third, on the other hand, studied price-setting processes among industrial firms in the French market.[13]

This last study is particularly important, because it represents an effort to systematically describe and compare the processes used by firms to set prices. Through in-depth analyses of price decisions made by companies, the authors were able to develop flowcharts as well as indices of similarity, participation, and activity. They contend that decision-process methodology can help people gain insights into the dynamic activities of firms. The decision-making model for export pricing discussed in this article employs a similar approach.

The discussion here focuses on three major issues. First, those factors which have a bearing on export pricing are examined, and each factor's relevance is illustrated with company examples. The next section reveals that companies appear to follow one of three export pricing strategies. Finally, a decision framework for export pricing is offered.

Factors in Export Pricing

Export pricing is not a topic that lends itself easily to generalization. As with domestic pricing, any consideration of policies for setting export prices must first address the unique nature of the individual firm. Company philosophy, corporate culture, product offerings, and operating environment all have a significant impact on the creation of pricing policy. In addition, export marketers face unique constraints in each market destination.

The interaction of the internal and external environments gives rise to distinct—yet predictable—pricing constraints in different markets. These to a large extent determine export price strategy. For example, negotiation is normally required in the Middle East, so Regal Ware, a producer of kitchen appliances and cookware, uses a higher list price in such markets to leave a margin for discretion. But D. W. Witter, a manufacturer of grain storage and handling equipment, doesn't make price concessions in the Middle East. Witter is convinced that once a price becomes negotiable, the Middle Eastern buyer will expect and demand future concessions, making future negotiations interminable.

In Algeria, the interest rate is limited by the government. To counter this one company, a manufacturer of mining and construction equipment builds the additional cost of capital into the price.

Six variables have important influences on export pricing. They are:

1. Nature of the product/industry;

2. Location of the production facility;

3. Chosen system of distribution;

4. Location and environment of the foreign market;

5. U.S. government regulations; and

6. Attitude of the firm's management.

A brief discussion of each factor follows.

Nature of the Product/Industry.

A specialized product, or one with a technological edge, gives the firm flexibility. There are few competitors in such cases. In many markets there is no local production of the product, government-imposed import barriers are minimal, and importing firms all face similar price-escalation factors. Under such circumstances, firms are able to remain competitive with little adjustment in price strategy. Firms with a technological edge, such as the Burdick Corporation (hospital equipment) and Nicolet Instruments (scientific instruments), enjoy similar advantages, but both experience greater service requirements and longer production and sales lead times.

A relatively low level of price competition usually leads to administered prices and a static role for pricing in the export marketing mix. Over the years, however, as price competition evolves and technological advantages shrink, specialized and highly technical firms must make more market-based exceptions to their uniform export pricing strategies.

Many firms' export pricing strategies are also influenced by industry-specific factors, such as drastic fluctuations in the price of raw materials and predatory pricing practices by foreign competitors (most notably the Japanese). The presence of such factors demands greater flexibility in export pricing at some companies: Ray-O-Vac adjusts export prices frequently according to current silver prices. Other companies negotiate fixed-price agreements with suppliers prior to making a contract bid.

Location of Production Facility.

Many U.S. companies produce exported products only in the United States. These U.S. exporters are unable to shift manufacturing to locations that make economic sense. Purely domestic companies are tied to conditions prevailing in the home market, in this case in the U.S.

Those companies with production or assembly facilities abroad, often closer to foreign customers, have additional flexibility in overseas markets. These companies find it easier to respond to fluctuations in foreign exchange. Cummins Engine, for example, supplies Latin American customers with U.S. production when the U.S. dollar is weak. When the dollar is relatively strong, U.K. plants assume greater importance.

A number of factors may have impeded the global competitiveness of U.S. manufacturers in recent years. These include lagging productivity in many sectors of the economy and, until recently, reluctance to seek global sources of supply for materials, parts, and components. Also, strong unions and a high standard of living in the U.S. have contributed to higher labor costs. Naturally, these comparative disadvantages are reflected in the quotations submitted to overseas buyers.

Chosen System of Distribution.

The channels of export distribution a company uses dictate much in export pricing. For example, subsidiary relationships offer greater control over final prices, first-hand knowledge of market conditions, and the ability to adjust prices rapidly. With independent distributors, control usually extends only to the landed price received by the exporter. As one might expect, many of the executives interviewed spoke of the difficulty of maintaining price levels. These firms report that distributors may mark up prices substantially—up to 200 percent in some cases.

When a firm initiates exporting through independent distributors, many new pricing considerations arise. Significant administrative costs stem from the selection of foreign distributors and the maintenance of harmonious relationships. Discount policies for intermediaries must be established. Also, the costs of exporting (promotion, freight service, and so forth) must be assigned to either the intermediaries or the manufacturer. To minimize the administrative, research, and travel expenses involved in switching to direct exporting, most firms use a relatively uniform export pricing strategy across different markets. Gross margins are then increased to account for additional levels of distribution. In other cases, companies establish prices on a case-by-case basis.

The use of manufacturers' representatives offers greater price control to the exporter, but this method is used less frequently. Finally, sales to end users may involve negotiation or, in the case of selling to governmental agencies, protracted purchasing decisions. List prices are not used in these circumstances.

Firms often attempt to establish more direct channels of distribution to reach their customers in overseas markets. By reducing the number of intermediaries between the manufacturer and the customer, they offset the adverse effects of *international price escalation*. Excessive escalation of prices is a problem encountered by most exporters. Aside from shorter distribution channels, the firms studied had developed other strategies to cope with price escalation. These alternatives are listed in Exhibit 1.

Location and Environment of the Foreign Market. The climate conditions of a market may necessitate product modification. For exam-

ple, a producer of soft-drink equipment must treat its products against rust corrosion in tropical markets. Another company, an agribusiness concern, must take into account climate, soil conditions, and the country's infrastructure before making any bid. Economic factors, such as inflation, exchange-rate fluctuations, and price controls, may hinder market entry and effectiveness.[14] These factors, especially the value of U.S. currency in foreign markets, are a major concern to most of the firms interviewed. Consequently, several companies have introduced temporary compensating adjustments as part of their pricing strategies. The unusually strong value of the U.S. dollar during the first half of the 1980s was a significant factor in pricing strategy.

Since currency fluctuations are cyclical, exporters who find themselves blessed with a price advantage when their currency is undervalued must carry an extra burden when their currency is overvalued. Committed exporters must be creative, pursuing different strategies during different periods. Appropriate strategies practiced by the firms studied are outlined in Exhibit 2.

EXHIBIT 1   Strategic Options to Deal with Price Escalation

- Shortening channels of distribution by reducing number of intermediaries or engaging in company-sponsored distribution. Fewer intermediaries would also have the effect of minimizing value-added taxes.

- Reducing cost to overseas customers by eliminating costly features from the product, lowering overall product quality, or offering a stripped-down model.

- Shipping and assembling components in foreign markets. Popularity of the Free Trade Zones in Hong Kong, Panama or the Caribbean Basin is due to companies' desire to minimize price escalation.

- Modifying the product to bring it into a different, lower-tariff classification. The Microbattery division of Ray-O-Vac Corporation, for example, ships bulk to foreign marketing companies who then repackage. Another company, through consultations with local distributors, places products in "proper" import classifications. Proper wording is used for initial import registration to qualify for lower duties.

- Lowering the new price (landed price) to reduce tariffs and other charges by the importing country. This can be accomplished through the application of marginal cost pricing or by allowing discounts to distributors. Nicolet Instruments, a producer of scientific instruments, for example, compensates its distributors for the cost of installation and service. Western Publishing Company compensates its distributors for the differences in import duties between book and nonbook exports.

- Going into overseas production and sourcing in order to remain competitive in the foreign markets. Dairy Equipment Company located in Wisconsin, for example, supplies the European market with bulk coolers made at its Danish plant as a way of reducing freight costs.

EXHIBIT 2 **Exporter Strategies under Varying Currency Conditions**

When Domestic Currency Is WEAK	*When Domestic Currency Is STRONG . . . .*
• Stress price benefits.	• Engage in nonprice competition by improving quality, delivery, and aftersale service.
• Expand product line and add more costly features.	• Improve productivity and engage in vigorous cost reduction.
• Shift sourcing and manufacturing to domestic market.	• Shift sourcing and manufacturing overseas.
• Exploit export opportunities in all markets.	• Give priority to exports to relatively strong currency countries.
• Conduct conventional cash-for-goods trade.	• Deal in countertrade with weak-currency countries.
• Use full-costing approach, but use marginal-cost pricing to penetrate new/competitive markets.	• Trim profit margins and use marginal-cost pricing.
• Speed repatriation of foreign-earned income and collections.	• Keep the foreign-earned income in host country, slow collections.
• Minimize expenditures in local, host country currency.	• Maximize expenditures in local, host country currency.
• Buy needed services (advertising, insurance, transportation, etc.) in domestic market.	• Buy needed services abroad and pay for them in local currencies.
• Minimize local borrowing.	• Borrow money needed for expansion in local market.
• Bill foreign customers in domestic currency.	• Bill foreign customers in their own currency.

It must be noted that, while exporters can implement some of these strategies quickly, others require a long-term response. For example, the decision to manufacture overseas is often a part of a deliberate and long-term plan for most companies. And while some strategies can be used by any exporter, others, such as countertrade and speculative currency trading, are limited to use by the larger, more experienced exporters. In fact, most managers interviewed said that high-risk propositions such as countertrade deals should be used only by multinational companies.

The cultural environment and business practices of the foreign market also play a large role in export pricing. Some countries abhor negotiation; others expect it. As previously noted, D. W. Witter has successfully overcome the expectation of price negotiation in the Middle East market. In some markets, a subtle barrier to foreign imports is erected in the form of procurement practices which favor domestic companies.

U.S. Government Regulations. Government policy also affects export pricing strategy. While the majority of the firms interviewed are not directly affected by U.S. pricing regulations, they feel that U.S. regulations such as the Foreign Corrupt Practices Act put them at a significant competitive disadvantage. One company often receives "requests" by overseas customers to add over $100,000 to the contract price and make appropriate arrangements to transfer the money to private accounts abroad. Interestingly, such requests are sometimes openly made. Submission to demands for "grease payments" appears to be the only option if businesses want to compete in certain countries.

Attitude of the Firm's Management. Many U.S. firms still view exporting as an extension of the domestic sales effort, and export pricing policy is established accordingly. Smaller companies whose top management concerns itself mostly with domestic matters have major problems setting export prices. Price determination of export sales is often based on a full-costing approach. The preference for cost-based pricing over market-oriented pricing reflects the relative importance given to profits and market share. This is particularly notable with firms that are unconcerned with market share and require that every quote meet their profit expectations. Other companies are more concerned with selling one product line at any price, even below cost, and reap longer-term benefits from the sale of follow-up consumables and spare parts. Producers of expensive industrial equipment, scientific instruments, and medical equipment fall into this category.

Alternative Approaches to Pricing

Firms typically choose one of three approaches to pricing. These can be called the rigid cost-plus, flexible cost-plus, and dynamic incremental pricing strategies.

Rigid Cost-Plus Strategy.   The complexity of export pricing has caused many managers to cling to a rigid cost-plus pricing strategy in an effort to secure profitability. This strategy establishes the foreign list price by adding international customer costs and a gross margin to domestic manufacturing costs. The final cost to the customer includes administrative and R&D overhead costs, transportation, insurance, packaging, marketing, documentation, and customs charges, as well as the profit margins for both the distributor and the manufacturer. Although this type of pricing ensures margins, the final price may be so high that it keeps the firm from being competitive in major foreign markets.

Nevertheless, cost-plus pricing appears to be the most dominant strategy among American firms. Approximately 70 percent of the sampled firms used this strategy. Over half of the firms using a cost-plus strategy adhered to it rigidly, with no exceptions. This approach may be typical of

other exporting firms in the U.S. The following company examples illustrate the popularity of the rigid cost-plus pricing approach.

Autotrol is a Wisconsin manufacturer of water treatment and control equipment. The firm employs about 80 people, and exports account for about 60 percent of its estimated $14 million annual sales. Principal markets include Western Europe, Japan, Australia, New Zealand, and Venezuela. Autotrol sets export prices 3 percent to 4 percent higher than domestic prices to cover the additional costs. Such costs include foreign advertising, foreign travel, and all costs incurred when shipping the product from the factory to the foreign distributor. The firm has successfully exported for the past 15 years by using a rigid cost-plus strategy.

Chillicothe Metal Co. is a solely owned manufacturer of generator sets, pump packages, engine enclosures, controls, and spare parts. The firm has recently lost a significant portion of its foreign business. Sales dropped from $5 million in 1982 to $3 million in 1984, and the current employment of 40 is down from its 1982 high of 100. The company had successfully exported for more than 15 years, but current exports are down 40 percent from the 1982 level. Principal foreign markets are the Middle East, North Africa, and the Far East. The company adheres to a rigid cost-plus pricing strategy that includes a built-in margin ranging from 5 percent to 15 percent. However, the president has recently taken efforts to control costs, extend credit, and reduce margins for cash-in advance customers in an attempt to counter the effects of the slow business cycle.

Dairy Equipment Co. produces milk machines, bulk coolers, and other high-quality equipment for the dairy industry. The company's annual sales are about $40 million, with current employment at 400. Although the company has exported continuously over the past decade, export earnings have become negligible. This has been caused by a significant drop in sales in the company's primary foreign market—West Germany. Gross profit has remained the company's primary export goal, but the rigid cost-plus pricing strategy has not yet proved to be effective. The company has always sought equal profitability from foreign sales, although fierce competition in some markets has forced it to consider lower profit margins. The company's export pricing policy remains a static element of the marketing mix.

These examples demonstrate that a rigid cost-plus pricing strategy may or may not be effective. They also imply that just because a strategy has been successful in the past, there is no guarantee that it will be successful in the future. Competitive pressures often force firms to reevaluate their pricing decisions and consider new alternatives.

Flexible Cost-Plus Strategy. One such alternative is a flexible cost-plus strategy. This is also the most logical strategy for companies that are in the process of moving away from their traditionally rigid pricing policies.

Flexible cost-plus price strategy is identical to the rigid strategy in establishing list prices. Flexible strategy, however, allows for price variations in special circumstances. For example, discounts may be granted, depending on the customer, the size of the order, or the intensity of competition. Although discounts occasionally are granted on a case-by-case basis, the primary objective of flexible cost-plus pricing is profit. Thus, pricing is still a static element of the marketing mix. The following cases are good examples of companies that use a flexible cost-plus pricing strategy.

Baughman, a division of Fuqua Industries, manufactures steel grain-storage silos and related equipment. The company currently employs about 125 people, and annual sales are around $6 million. The company has traditionally exported about 30 percent of its sales over the past 10 years, but recently exports have grown to over 50 percent of annual sales. Baughman's products are of high quality, and pricing has not often been an active element in the marketing mix. The firm's export sales terms consist of an irrevocable confirmed letter of credit in U.S. currency with no provisions for fluctuating exchange rages. Export and domestic prices are identical before exporting costs are

added. However, Baughman will make concessions to this policy to secure strategically important sales.

Nicolet Instrument Corporation designs, manufactures, and markets electronic instruments that are used in science, medicine, industry, and engineering. The firm employs more than 500 people and has annual sales of over $85 million. Exports account for about 42 percent of total sales, and the firm has been exporting for the past 10 years. Major foreign markets include Japan, West Germany, France, Canada, England, Mexico, Sweden, and the Netherlands. Foreign and domestic prices are calculated according to full cost. Since Nicolet has held a technological edge, it has not been affected by competition in foreign markets. However, the competitive gap has been slowly closing, and the company now varies from administered prices more frequently.

Badger Meter manufactures and sells industrial liquid meters. The company employs 700 people, and its annual sales are estimated at $60 million. The company has sold internationally for more than 50 years, but export sales only account for 9 percent of total sales. Major markets include Europe, Canada, Taiwan, and the Philippines. The company owns a production facility in Mexico and has licenses in Ecuador and Peru. Cost-based list prices are used for both domestic and foreign markets. Although prices usually remain fixed, the company has, at times, offered special discounts to regain market share or to offset unfavorable exchange rates.

Flexible pricing strategies are useful to counter competitive pressures or exchange rate fluctuations. They help firms stay competitive in certain markets without disrupting the entire pricing strategy. However, if competitive pressures persist and technology gaps continue to close, the company could face losing its export market. This is when a company may consider the third alternative.

Dynamic Incremental Strategy. The dynamic incremental pricing strategy was used by approximately 30 percent of the firms studied.

Most firms using this strategy had sales well over $50 million with exports ranging from 20 to 65 percent of total sales. In the dynamic incremental strategy, prices are set by subtracting fixed costs for plants, R&D, and domestic overhead from cost-plus figures. In addition, domestic marketing and promotion costs are also disregarded.

This strategy is based on the assumption that fixed and variable domestic costs are incurred regardless of export sales. Therefore, only variable and international customer costs need to be recovered on exported products. This makes it possible for a company to maintain profit margins while selling its exported products at prices below U.S. list. It is also assumed that unused production capacity exists and that the exported products could not be otherwise sold at full cost. Companies can thus lower their prices and be competitive in markets that may otherwise be prohibitive to enter or penetrate. The following examples illustrate their strategy.

Flo-Con Systems, a subsidiary of Masco Inc., manufacturers high-quality and sophisticated flow-control valves for molten-steel-pouring applications. The company employs 500 people and has sales between $50 and $60 million, of which 25 percent result from exports. A plant located in Canada produces final products, and an additional plant in Mexico is being considered. Flo-Con finds the nature of its markets very competitive. The firm's export prices are based on competitive prices in the local market. Management is often forced to temporarily overlook costs and margins to remain competitive and secure orders.

Ray-O-Vac, a producer of batteries and other consumer goods, has been exporting successfully for over 30 years. Its Micro Power Division employs 250 and has estimated annual sales of $100 million. The major products in this division include batteries for hearing aids and watches. Exports account for 20 percent of total business, and major markets include Europe, Far East, and Japan. These markets are entered through wholly owned subsidiaries strategically located around the world. Each subsidiary may be treated as a cost

or profit center depending upon the market circumstances. Competitive pressures demand flexible pricing, and discounts are often granted to gain market share or secure OEM business. Branch managers may adjust prices on a day-to-day basis to counter exchange-rate fluctuations. Export pricing is a very active ingredient in the firm's marketing mix.

Econ-O-Cloth is an independent manufacturer of optical polishing cloths and a wholesaler of related goods. Although the company has traditionally exported around 25 percent of its sales volume, this figure has slipped to around 5 percent over the past 5 years. Major markets include Canada, Mexico, and Western Europe. Econ-O-Cloth reduced export margins to compensate for the strong dollar in the early 1980s, and it considers pricing an active instrument for achieving marketing objectives. The firm continually monitors the foreign environment and at times modifies its prices and products to blend with foreign consumer demands. Econ-O-Cloth has been squeezed hard by competition, and it is still waiting for its dynamic pricing strategy to pay off.

The above examples demonstrate that pricing strategies are complex and that no single strategy suits a firm at all times. There is no guarantee that pricing strategies that work successfully today will continue to do so in the future. Many traditionally successful exporters have recently experienced sales downturns in their foreign markets. One can only speculate on whether a change of pricing strategies could have prevented these downturns. Also, it is not known to what extent other factors (poor market intelligence, weak distribution networks, no product modifications when they were needed, slow delivery, or poor image) were responsible.

The uncertainties of international business make it difficult for executives to select the pricing strategy that is best for their firm. As a result, most firms use the rigid cost-plus strategy until external pressures force them to reconsider. This strategy makes managers feel secure, and it is frequently used when a firm enters the export market. As competition and other external variables grow more intense, however, the firm typically makes exceptions to its pricing policy, moving from rigid to flexible cost-plus pricing. Few firms have attempted to price their export products according to the dynamic conditions of the marketplace. For these firms the dynamic incremental strategy is usually required, and prices may change frequently in response to competition, the prevailing exchange rate, and other variables.

Most exporting firms appear to establish their pricing policies reactively, changing only when external pressures force the issue. In working this way, however, these firms lose valuable sales and market share during the transition period. Although this strategy may be defensible, three types of lags may result in irreversible damage. The recognition lag is the amount of time between an actual change in the environment and a company's recognition of that change. Reaction lag is the amount of time between the company's recognition of the problem and its decision to react to it. Finally, effectiveness lag is the amount of time needed to implement the decision.

One might conclude that if executives were proactive in their pricing strategy, they might avoid many of the headaches associated with exporting. But how can executives be sure which pricing policy is best for their firms? Considering all the variables that affect price, it is reasonable to assume that different pricing policies should exist for different markets. Furthermore, considering the volatility of foreign markets, one would suspect that these policies should be continuously reviewed and updated. It is not surprising, then, that most executives resort to setting their pricing policies reactively.

A Decision Framework for Export Pricing.
Most companies lack a systematic procedure for setting and revising export prices. The absence of a formal decision-making procedure that incorporates and weighs relevant variables has led to the development of the framework described here. It is not intended to replace management judgment,

since the business executive is usually in the best position to assess the suitability of various strategies and policies, but simply to provide a systematic framework for arriving at export pricing decisions.

Figure 1 illustrates the steps involved in a formal export price determination process. A brief description of each step is presented below.

Verification of Market Potential.   The first step in the analysis gives firm information on the market potential in specific countries. The company can identify market potential for its products by using both formal and informal sources. Formal sources include market-research firms, the U.S. Department of Commerce, banks, and other agencies that provide information on foreign countries. Informal sources include trade shows, local distributors, international trade journals, and business contacts.[15] During this process, those countries that do not demonstrate adequate market potential are dropped from the list of possible markets.

Estimating Target Price Range.   Once it is determined that a market has sufficient potential, the firm observes the price ranges of substitute or competitive products in the local market to find its target price range. This consists of three prices:

- The floor price, that price at which the firm breaks even;
- The ceiling price, the highest price the market is likely to bear for the product; and
- The expected price, the price at which the firm would most likely be competitive.

Estimating Sales Potential.   Assuming that a high enough level of sales potential exists to warrant market entry, management then identifies the size and concentration of customer segments, projected consumption patterns, competitive pressures, and the expectations of local distributors and agents. The landed cost and the cost of local distribution are estimated. The potential sales

FIGURE 1

Decision process for export price determination

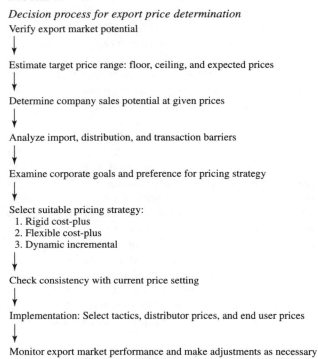

Verify export market potential

↓

Estimate target price range: floor, ceiling, and expected prices

↓

Determine company sales potential at given prices

↓

Analyze import, distribution, and transaction barriers

↓

Examine corporate goals and preference for pricing strategy

↓

Select suitable pricing strategy:
  1. Rigid cost-plus
  2. Flexible cost-plus
  3. Dynamic incremental

↓

Check consistency with current price setting

↓

Implementation: Select tactics, distributor prices, and end user prices

↓

Monitor export market performance and make adjustments as necessary

volume is assessed for each of the three price levels, taking into account the price elasticity of demand.

Analyze Special Import, Distribution, or Transaction Barriers. If adequate sales potential exists, management then assesses any special import barriers not accounted for in its earlier efforts. These barriers include quotas, tariffs and other taxes, anti-dumping, price-maintenance, currency-exchange, and other governmental regulations that affect the cost of doing business in that country. In addition, internal distribution barriers must also be assessed. Lengthy distribution channels, high margins, and inadequate dealer commitment may present difficulties for the exporter. Finally, currency supply, payment terms, and financing availability should be reviewed. Is it customary for prices to be negotiable? Do customers expect certain credit or payment terms? Once again, sales potential, market share, and profitability should be analyzed in light of the above information in order to confirm the desirability of market entry.

Corporate Goals and Preference for Pricing. After deciding on a target market, some companies may not wish to consider anything but full-cost pricing (either rigid or flexible cost-plus). If desired margins can be achieved, this pricing policy can be implemented. If, however, the desired margins cannot be achieved, the firm can either abort market entry or resort to some form of marginal costing approach. If the firm's management is willing consider pricing strategies that focus on market rather than profit objectives, it may continue the analysis with a systematic identification of the optimal pricing strategy.

Systematic Selection of Appropriate Pricing Strategy. The company needs to arrive at a strategy choice by systematically considering all relevant variables. Management faces a basic choice between a dynamic incremental pricing strategy and a cost-plus pricing strategy (either rigid or flexible). Dynamic incremental pricing implies a marginal costing approach, while cost-plus pricing implies full costing.

Exhibit 3 identifies 16 criteria that help management make choices between the two pricing strategies. Some criteria are derived from the general environment of the firm, while others are unique to the specific export opportunity being considered. Management may choose to weigh each group, as well as individual criteria, in arriving at a choice. Exhibit 3 spells out the conditions that call for incremental pricing.

Checking Consistency with Current Pricing. If a firm is already in the targeted market, the recommended pricing strategy should be compared to the strategy currently in place. If deviations exist, they should be explained and justified. If they cannot be justified, the firm should seriously consider adopting the recommended pricing strategy in order to achieve marketing goals more effectively. It is also important to check for consistency of export pricing policies across export markets to minimize any conflicts (such as inter-market shipping by competing middlemen).

Implementation. The exporter will determine specific prices for distributors and end users, in accordance with the recommended pricing strategy, and decide on specific pricing tactics. A strategy may fail in a specific market if execution is not

---

EXHIBIT 3   Criteria Relevant to the Choice between Full and Marginal Costing

Conditions Favoring Marginal Costing/ Aggressive Pricing	Criteria	Conditions Favoring Full Costing/ Passive Pricing
A. Firm-Specific Criteria		
Low	Extent of product differentiation	High
Committed	Corporate stance toward exporting	Half-hearted
Long term	Management desire for recovering export overhead	Short term
Sufficient	Company financial resources to sustain initial losses	Insufficient
Wide	Domestic gross margins	Narrow
High	Need for long-term capacity utilization	Low
High	Opportunity to benefit from economies of scale	Low
B. Situation-Specific Criteria		
Substantial	Growth potential of export market	Negligible
High	Potential for follow-up sales	Low
Continuous	Nature of export opportunity	One-time
High	End-user price sensitivity	Low
High	Competitive intensity	Low
Likely	Opportunity to drive out competition	Unlikely
Favorable	Terms of sale and financing	Unfavorable
Low	Exchange rate risk	High
Low	Cost of internal distribution, service and promotion	High

effective or if reaction to change is slow. For example, distributors may vary their margins as a response to price changes. Similarly, distributors may hold a large inventory of products at the old price, creating a lag before the new pricing policy actually becomes effective.

Monitoring.   Exchange rates can be one of the more volatile variables in international business, especially in developing countries. These rates should be monitored continuously, and the effect of their changes on pricing policy should be evaluated. Variables such as competition, regulations, and price sensitivity can be monitored periodically. As these variables change, the firm can adjust its pricing strategy appropriately. The proposed decision process, therefore, provides a proactive means of establishing pricing policies.

A major implication of this analysis is that no export pricing strategy will fit all of a company's products and markets. International pricing issues are extremely complex, and pricing decisions are fueled by many variables. It is important that the company establish a systematic and periodic approach in selecting a pricing policy. The approach should account for both internal and external variables affecting the firm's export efforts. This framework for export pricing is one such approach. Executives may wish to modify the model in order to better blend it with their firms' perspectives.

A second implication is that many U.S. firms may be overlooking lucrative foreign markets because of their strict adherence to the full-cost pricing approach. Furthermore, this rigid practice may hinder effective market penetration in existing foreign markets. A complete reassessment of the firm's market-share objectives may be needed. Committed exporters will allocate the resources needed to accomplish this task if it becomes necessary.

Finally, there is no guarantee that those pricing policies that are suitable today will work in the future. Changing business trends, exchange rates, consumer preferences, and competition are only a few of the variables that have caught successful exporters off guard. Therefore, a method for monitoring changes in the pricing policy variables should be established. The most volatile variables, such as exchange rates and competitive transaction prices, should be monitored more frequently. Once again, committed exporters will recognize the need for this and allocate the appropriate resources to establish an adequate monitoring system.

Although no best pricing strategy exists, most American firms have adhered to a full-cost approach, often disregarding conditions that are particular to their targeted foreign market. Many companies have abandoned lucrative foreign markets because of seemingly unattractive potentials. Other firms have relinquished sales and market share to local or more aggressive foreign competitors. The full-cost approach is a major deterrent to improving the exports of American businesses.

The establishment of international pricing policies is a dynamic process. Success with one strategy does not guarantee that the same strategy will continue to work. Many companies react passively when global changes make their traditional pricing policies obsolete. Such companies are usually forced to either abandon the market or adapt their pricing strategy to the new conditions. The lag times associated with recognition, reaction, and effectiveness can cause an irreversible deterioration in a company's sales, profits, and market share in the foreign country.

A proactive stance on establishing pricing strategy can often reduce or eliminate these lags, enhancing the firm's flexibility and responsiveness to changing business conditions. To develop a proactive stance, businesses need to establish systematic methods to monitor and evaluate the variables associated with an international pricing policy. Firms that are committed to international business will quickly recognize this and allocate resources accordingly.

The guidelines and decision process discussed in this article have been derived from the experience of exporting firms. Such an empirically based approach to developing managerial guidelines is appropriate, given the current dearth of export pricing literature. Insights obtained from the field can rip away the shroud of mystery that surrounds export pricing decisions. At the same time, it should be noted that the managerial guidelines offered here are appropriate for a given set of conditions. The seasoned executive will realize that these recommendations are not substitutes for good business judgment. The proposed strategies may need minor modifications to better reflect a company's perspectives and constraints on international pricing.

References

1. Vern Terpstra, "Suggestions for Research Themes and Publications," *Journal of International Business Studies,* Spring/Summer 1983, pp. 9–10.
2. "Pricing Competition Is Shaping Up as 84's Top Marketing Pressure Point," *Marketing News,* November 11, 1983, p. 1.
3. Vithala R. Rao, "Pricing Research in Marketing: The State of the Art," *Journal of Business,* January 1984, pp. 539–59.
4. See: James C. Baker and John K. Ryans, Jr., "Some Aspects of International Pricing: A Neglected Area of Management Policy," *Management Decision,* Summer 1973, pp. 177–82; S. Tamer Cavusgil and John R. Nevin, "State-of-the-Art in International Marketing: An Assessment," in B. M. Enis and K. J. Roering, eds., *Review of Marketing 1981* (Chicago: American Marketing Association), pp. 195–216; and Terpstra (see note 1).
5. See: Jeffrey S. Arpan, "Multinational Firm Pricing in International Markets," *Sloan Management Review,* Winter 1973, pp. 1–9; M. Edgar Barrett, "Case of the Tangled Transfer Price," *Harvard Business Review,* May–June 1977, p. 21; Seung H. Kim and Stephen W. Miller, "Constituents of the International Transfer Pricing Decision," *Columbia Journal of World Business,* Spring 1979, pp. 69–77.
6. Llewellyn Clague and Rena Grossfield, "Exporting Pricing in a Floating Rate World," *Columbia Journal of World Business,* Winter 1974, pp. 17–22.
7. Baker and Ryans (see note 4).
8. Donald J. Lecraw, "Pricing Strategies of Transnational Corporations," *Asia Pacific Journal of Management,* January 1984, pp. 112–19.
9. Nathaniel H. Left, "Multinational Corporate Pricing Strategy in Developing Countries," *Journal of International Business Studies,* Fall 1975, pp. 55–64.
10. Peter R. Kressler, "Is Uniform Pricing Desirable in Multinational Markets?" *Akron Business and Economic Review,* Winter 1971.
11. Nigel Piercy, "British Export Market Selection and Pricing," *Industrial Marketing Management,* October 1981, pp. 287–97.
12. Russell Abratt and Leyland F. Pitt, "Pricing Practices in Two Industries," *Industrial Marketing Management,* 14:301–6.
13. John U. Farley, James M. Hulbert, and David Weistein, "Price Setting and Volume Planning by Two European Industrial Companies: A Study and Comparison of Decision Processes," *Journal of Marketing,* Winter 1980, pp. 46–54.
14. Victor H. Frank, Jr., "Living with Price Controls Abroad," *Harvard Business Review,* March–April 1984, pp. 137–42.
15. S. Tamer Cavusgil, "Guidelines for Export Market Research," *Business Horizons,* November–December 1985, pp. 27–33.

Transfer Pricing by Multinational Marketers: Risky Business

John P. Fraedrich and Connie Rae Bateman

Transfer pricing decisions are made every day in multinational corporations. When a department within an MNC transfers its tangible or intangible output to another department or a subsidiary, it regards this transfer as a sale. The price that is placed on such products, services, and know-how is generally regarded as the transfer price, or TP. MNCs regularly use TP policies as strategic tools to increase subsidiary profits when the subsidiary is in a foreign country with a lower tax rate. The subsidiary, in turn, creates value that can yield more profits in the country of entry and minimize effective tax rates.

Depending upon foreign country tax rates, the parent will choose either a low or high TP. When the tax rate is low relative to the United States, American-owned, foreign-based subsidiaries should buy low and sell high, accruing the majority of the profits in the low tax rate country. This cuts the effective tax rate to the parent. When the foreign tax rate is high, the goal is to buy high and sell low (that is, at a minimum profit), accruing the majority of the profits in the low tax rate country. Depending on country-of-entry tax rates relative to the home country and the level of unrelated competition, the TP strategy will affect the risk of an audit.

From *Business Horizons,* January/February 1996, pp. 17–22.

Past practice has set the TP arbitrarily by using a method of cost-plus and a "percentage for contingencies," which has not always been considered carefully. TP policies can sometimes reflect market and competitive dynamics (those set by default or in line with competition), cost and profit objectives (using a TP that promotes efficiency of the seller), or resource allocation decisions (extra human resources needed on the value-added end of production). Setting a TP usually occurs within a legislative vacuum, which can cause inefficiencies.

The "Basic Arm's Length Standard" (BALS) criterion championed by the U.S. has now been accepted worldwide as the preferred standard by which transfer prices should be set. To determine the BALS, the tax authority looks to comparable selling prices set by independent buyers and sellers in similar selling environments. This price level then becomes the "benchmark" by which the BALS is set.

MNC managers must gain as full an understanding as possible of the complex legal foundations of transfer pricing as well as its effects on their business. In this review, the MNC manager is shown how each of the basic TP strategies derived from the BALS affects sales, audit risks, government-assessed penalties, and position in the marketplace.

Transfer Pricing Today

In the past several years, corporate actions have caused U.S. authorities to strengthen their focus on transfer price issues. The policies and procedures implemented by U.S. authorities have resulted in a loss of taxpayer incentives to multiple profits and an increase in the penalties for manipulating profits. Moreover, U.S. officials have become more effective in the development and processing of TP cases and have established a Competent Authority (CA) to resolve disputes. Any manager unaware of these recent events is at an extreme disadvantage.

In making the transfer pricing decision, managers must consider both tax and nontax related criteria. If all relevant criteria are not assessed properly, the MNC will suffer losses that go unnoticed; and if respective tax authorities disagree as to the appropriate calculation of the TP, double taxation can occur. This happens when the same income is taxed in the jurisdiction of the transferor (seller) and also in the jurisdiction of the transferee (buyer). Once a decision is made, the TP policy should be formally defined, clearly communicated to all countries of interest, be based on the BALs, and show no currency or profit manipulation.

In reality, the TP system is often illegally used for tax evasion purposes, shortchanging the U.S. government billions of dollars annually. And the problem is not only with foreign-controlled corporations, but with U.S.-controlled companies and their overseas operations as well. Any MNC that illegally uses TP policies to reduce its overall tax rate effectively puts itself at risk of a TP audit. Section 482 of the IRS Code sets broad rules for evaluating the BALS characteristic of a TP. If the TP is set outside the boundaries of the BALS, the IRS or foreign tax authority may conduct a TP audit and allocate or reallocate profits, deductions, or other income items to determine the true taxable income. Many countries are aggressively dealing with MNCs that use TP as a strategic tool to minimize tax liabilities. In addition, an MNC can be ordered by the tax authority to pay any due taxes and

assessed penalties. As a consequence, it can experience negative press and lose consumer and supplier confidence.

If the MNC decides that a tax authority's decision is unjust, it can appeal the decision and request a Competent Authority (CA) to render a judgment. Ultimately the case can be brought before the Tax Court. Upon hearing the positions in the case, the court in some cases has ruled against the IRS audit findings. For example, in 1981 and 1982, the IRS increased Bausch & Lomb, Inc. consolidated taxable recorded income by allocating income from B&L Ireland to its U.S. parent. In this case, the IRS had recalculated the BALS price using a method not previously used by B&L. The tax court agreed with B&L's position and ruled that the IRS recalculation was an "unreasonable" adjustment, thus supporting B&L's claim that the adjustment was too liberal.

New regulations and additional litigation involving the use or transfer of intangible assets covered by Section 482 are anticipated. Thus, compliance will become a bigger challenge for the MNC. The IRS's new focus on TP issues, the broadening scope of cases heard by the Tax Court, and market-based effects all call for a reevaluation by MNC taxpayers as to what their TP methods will be and how they will defend their position in an audit.

To understand the extent of the challenge involved in developing a TP strategy, managers must recognize that no one strategy is appropriate for all transactions or markets. MNCs face the challenge of balancing differences in foreign tax systems, exchange controls, and competition with the need to allocate economic, human, and financial resources.

Can Compliance with Government Regulation Be That Difficult?
A corporation's TP objective is to price intercompany sales as close as possible to the standard set by the BALS. When the TP approximates the price that would have been charged between an independent seller and buyer, the BALS is met. Failure of the arm's-length method to correctly attribute income to the

taxing jurisdiction, however, is a major problem in U.S. tax policy. The IRS alleges that foreign companies overcharge their American subsidiaries and have avoided paying up to $8 billion in taxes annually.

Regulations across countries can be fundamentally different, adding to TP difficulties. For example, the same good or service transferred between parent and subsidiaries is often priced at different transfer levels using different methods. Each country's tax authority can identify different TP methods, and any deviation from the preferred one increases the risk of an audit. As a result, countries have accepted the BALS as the international standard for assessing TP.

In countries where there is unrelated competition, tax authorities may have difficulty determining a benchmark, which helps the MNC in justifying its TP level. In countries where the level of unrelated competition is reasonable, the tax authority is usually able to identify a more concrete benchmark. For example, Germany and the U.K. have both intensified their scrutiny of MNC transfer prices. When problems occur in Germany, firms rely on the U.K.-German Income Tax Treaty, which contains voluntary arbitration mechanisms available when competent authorities cannot agree. The U.K. government uses MNC objectives to determine TP policy as well.

Japan is also aggressively scrutinizing TPs by including in its tax code a general taxation of foreign corporations, a capital gains tax, specific TP rules, and an antitax avoidance provision. The Republic of Korea's Office of National Tax Administration (ONTA) has enlarged its scope of TP reporting requirements as well. For example, Kee and Jeong (1991) found that (*a*) the transactions subject to transfer pricing rules are the sale and purchase of inventory assets, the provision of services, and the lease of assets and loans; and (*b*) the BALS price can be set by either the comparable/uncontrolled price method, the resale price method, the cost-plus method, or functional analysis (which looks at each party's contribution to income production). ONTA authorities have begun

to recalculate income and secure information regarding TPs between a U.S. parent and Korean subsidiaries.

In intercompany transactions over the U.S.–Canadian border, the governing bodies have relatively similar substantive laws, but increasingly dissimilar compliance and reporting rules. The method for determining a BALS price is company-specific to some degree, so there is a push by tax authorities for advance pricing agreements (APAs). Canadian oil import parent firms have kept subsidiary TPs at significantly less than an arm's-length price (below market) and priced transport costs above market. The effect has been to reduce the taxable income attributable to property in Canada and reduce the overall effective tax rate (Canadian tax rates are higher than those in the United States). Other Canadian corporations have attempted to sidestep U.S. TP regulations by restructuring value-added operations in the U.S. and shifting more of their taxable income to the U.S, which can be illegal in the determination of a TP strategy.

The European Union (EU) is also primed for TP issues. The EU market has had an excess supply of certain products, so price competition has increased. EU fiscal policy response has been to protect parents that have subsidiaries within or between EU states from double taxation. MNCs are encouraged to reach an a priori agreement with authorities on how direct taxes will be handled. In addition, EU policy calls for the establishment of TP adjustment arbitration procedures and provisions.

There is a worldwide move toward more TP regulations, the effects of which are many. The U.S. is stepping up its scrutiny not only of U.S.-controlled companies but of foreign-controlled ones as well, including foreign manufacturers that operate in the U.S. through subsidiaries. The brunt of these effects will be felt by the foreign firms and their governments as they wrestle with double taxation, U.S.-assessed penalties, and other TP issues.

Businesses can take active steps to avoid risking exposure to a transfer pricing audit and any subsequent penalties. One suggestion is to follow the requirements set by the IRS in information reporting, record retention, agency designation, monetary penalties, and determining rules. An APA or an established and acceptable cost-sharing arrangement can also forestall or minimize audit controversies. If an audit does occur, an organization has several options: an administrative or judicial forum, a cooperative versus adversarial approach, or settlement strategies.

Transfer Pricing Methods

To assess whether your current TP meets BALS criterion, your company can calculate a BALS price using one of three methods identified by Section 482 of the IRS Code: comparable/uncontrollable price, resale price, or cost-plus. These are based on the separate entity theory, which compares a given TP to a comparable price on the open market. Many companies prefer the comparable/uncontrollable price method and apply it first. The resale price method is preferred next, followed by cost-plus. Each method will be described below.

The IRS allows the MNC discretion in choosing which TP method it will use, but it will closely evaluate whichever method is chosen. If the MNC opts to use another method, the burden of proof falls on the corporation to show that the BALS has been met. Or it may contact the IRS and form an APA with it that defines an acceptable TP calculation method before implementation. When this occurs, the APA frees the MNC from any TP audit for the time period specified in the contract, usually three to four years.

Comparable/Uncontrollable Price Method.

The comparable/uncontrollable price method most accurately approximates an arm's-length price and has been used in most Section 482 pricing cases. It forces the parent to compare the TP of its controlled subsidiary to the selling price charged by an independent seller to an independent buyer for similar goods. Comparing actual profits of one company to the profitability of a number of unre-

lated companies with similar activities establishes a comparable profit interval. Comparable sales occur when physical property and circumstances of the controlled sales are almost identical to those of uncontrolled sales.

Use of this method is thought to best focus on overall operating profits as they relate to similarly situated firms rather than on similar transactions involving unrelated firms. If comparisons are not possible, then sales of other resellers in the same market could be used. This allows management to evaluate international subsidiaries as it would any other distributor.

Resale Price Method.

The resale price, or market, method places the transferor in direct competition with outside suppliers. It is the strategy used most often for setting a TP for international transfers. In this scenario, the BALS TP is determined by subtracting the gross margin percentage used by comparable independent buyers from the final third-party sales price. It is typically used when the value added by the subsidiary is not substantial.

Cost-Plus Method.

The cost-plus method is computed by adding the gross profit markup (on a percentage basis) earned by comparable companies performing similar functions to the production costs of the controlled manufacturer or seller. (An amount equal to cost times an appropriate gross profit percentage is the gross profit percentage, expressed as a percent of cost, earned by the seller or another party on the uncontrolled sales, to cover some or all of the fixed costs.) An arm's-length price is considered the best approximation of the price that would be charged if companies involved in the sales transactions did not have common ownership.

Other Methods.

Two common TP methods used by MNCs but not recommended by Section 482 are the no-charge method and the cost method. Neither considers a reference to comparable sellers or buyers, and both usually violate BALS criteria, thus jeopardizing the MNC's TP status. When reference to comparable/uncontrolled prices is not available or not considered, the Tax Court applies the unitary entity theory to the MNC's international pricing structure. A relative profit-split strategy is commonly used to assess the appropriateness of the TP. The assumption is that overall profits should be shared in proportion to relative assets employed, functions performed, and risks assumed. Tax courts have not revealed the exact rationale used in splitting profits, so MNCs are responsible for documenting assets, functions, and risk information to justify the TP level to an auditor.

Transfer pricing methods vary in their effects on pricing flexibility, efficiency, and profitability. The no-charge method gives the least incentive to the parent to control efficiency and allows the greatest amount of pricing flexibility and profitability markup at the subsidiary level. On the other hand, the comparable/uncontrolled method gives the most incentive to control efficiency but allows the least amount of pricing flexibility and the least profit markup at the subsidiary level.

The ability to respond to changes in elasticity of demand in the marketplace will depend on the percentage of markup to the ultimate consumer. If the markup is high, the company is more flexible in meeting a price the market will bear—which is of particular concern when demand is volatile.

There is a direct and critical relationship between the TP strategy chosen and the final percentage markup. At one end, when a no-charge TP is chosen between parent and subsidiary, the subsidiary's cost of goods sold is minimal and the percentage markup is maximized relative to other TP strategies. At the other extreme, when a market-based TP is chosen between parent and subsidiary, the latter's cost of goods sold is maximized and the percentage markup is minimized relative to other TP strategies. The more intense the competition, the increased likelihood of an elastic demand in the consumer market. The more elastic the demand in the marketplace, the more sensitive consumers will be to the objective price of the product. When price sensitivity is enhanced by intense competi-

tion, the parent and subsidiary should try to establish a TP policy that will result in the lowest product cost structure. By keeping the cost structure low, the MNC has more flexibility in setting competitive prices while maintaining acceptable profit margins.

It must be emphasized that minimizing effective tax rates is not without risk. A primary danger is a TP audit resulting in assessed penalties. As the MNC departs from the BALS and the criterion used to define it by the tax authority, the risk of a penalty increases. No-charge and cost methods are not BALS-based, so, again, the risk of penalty is substantially higher for these methods.

Transfer Pricing Strategies: The Light at the End of the Tunnel

Research shows that many MNC managers are not aware of the significant penalties of a TP audit. They often make their TP decisions very informally, without legally accurate TP decision guidelines. Figure 1 presents a prescriptive decision-making model designed to help a manager determine whether the TP policies in place are set at a level that protects the MNC from the risk of an intensive TP audit and its substantial penalties. The U.S. Tax Authority, including the Tax Court, has set laws and precedents for transfer pricing. It is firmly established that risk exposure to a TP audit depends on the answers to five key questions:

1. Do comparable/uncontrolled transactions exist?

2. Where is the most value added? Parent, subsidiary, or shared between the two?

3. Are combined profits of parent and subsidiary shared in proportion to contributions?

4. Does the MNC's TP meet the benchmark set by the tax authority?

5. Are the MNC's information reporting requirements able to justify the TP used?

FIGURE 1

A decision-making model for assessing risk of TP strategy

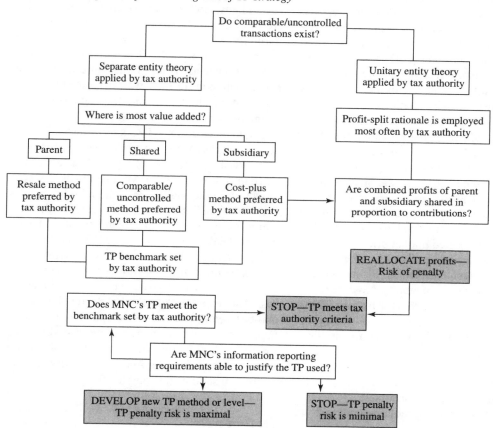

As the prescriptive model shows, the answers to these questions put corporations at critical junctures. For example, if a TP audit occurs, the first question the tax authority asks is, "Do comparable/uncontrollable transactions exist?" If they do, the separate entity theory is applied (that is, the subsidiary is treated as a separate and unique company) and the BALS must be met. Before a reasonable BALS can be calculated, the tax authority must determine if the bulk of the value added is at the parent or subsidiary level. To set what it determines is a "fair" TP benchmark for the BALS, the tax authority has a different "preferred" calculation method, depending on where the most value is added. For example, if the most value added is at the U.S. parent level and the subsidiary is in a lower tax country, the preferred method is the resale method. This ensures that the parent will not be selling to the subsidiary at below or near cost with the result of higher subsidiary profits, and ultimately lower effective tax rates for the MNC as a whole. If the MNC's TP policies in place meet the benchmark calculated by the IRS, the audit is concluded with no penalty. If the benchmark is not met, the MNC's TP records must meet tax authority information reporting requirements for the TP to be justified.

Insufficient TP information reporting leaves the MNC at maximum risk for significant penalties, plus money and time spent on Tax Court appeals, stockholder loss of confidence, supplier and customer skepticism, loss of sales or profitability, and negative publicity. Tax authorities worldwide are forecasting a dramatic increase in the number of audits and the number and size of the penalties as they "crack down" on TP violations.

In the United States, many problems have arisen when a multinational corporation translates Section 482 of the IRS Code into practice because of the perceived ambiguous and vague regulations. Most cases between the IRS and the MNC result in a Tax Court settlement, sometimes after several appeals. Menssen (1988) suggests that a contract price schedule be set for subsidiaries to formalize the TP after (1) projected market prices have been approved by the corporate controller, (2) projected profitability has been established, (3) marketplace constraints on selling/profitability have been assessed, and (4) a legal benchmark for the TP has been met.

Guidelines suggested by the IRS for multinationals are as follows:

1. File with the tax authority.
2. Plan ahead by having justifiable information reporting requirements and APAs.
3. Leave a paper trail.
4. Be consistent, and use comparable/ uncontrolled price or cost-plus pricing.

MNCs must realize that home country tax authorities are not the only threat. Controversies often arise because the tax authority in the host country suspects misuse of transfer pricing. When MNCs review or document TP arrangements with subsidiaries in host countries, tax controversies overseas are minimized, protection against U.S. tax penalties is created, and double taxation is avoided. In addition, the "justified information reporting requirement" criterion can be met.

MNCs can operationalize these guidelines by forming a TP team comprised of departmental product managers, general mangers, management accountants, and sales/marketing managers who are in a position to assess the broad range of opportunity costs and risks of various TP strategies. Team decisions should reflect corporate objectives and coordinate activities of all departments. Members should consult fully with departments on TP, and attention should be paid to its effects on measuring management effectiveness.

Rarely does a single TP strategy meet all needs. This is why an MNC's overall objectives may be best served by a number of legal TPs as defined in all countries of operation. Multinationals will continue to face the challenges of aligning tax regulations with their business objectives. Further research by managers and researchers should look into the TP decision within the MNC itself, examining such internal effects as financial performance measures, motivation incentives for management, and incongruence of goals between functional areas. The external effects—sales, relative sales, ability to competitively price, ability to react to a highly price-sensitive market—are also key areas for research. TP concerns, after all, will not go away or diminish in the future; they will continue to grow in stature and complexity.

References

Jean-Thomas Bernard and Robert J. Weiner, "Transfer Prices and the Excess Cost of Canadian Oil Imports: New Evidence on Bertrand Versus Ragman," *Canadian Journal of Economics, 25,* 1 (1992): 22–40.

Dan R. Bucks, "Will the Emperor Discover He Has No Clothes Before the Empire Is Sold?" *National Tax Journal, 44,* 3 (1991): 311–14.

Lauren Chambliss, "Holier than Thou," *Financial World, 159,* 11 (1990): 20–21.

David C. Donald, "Taxation for a Single Market: European Community Legislation on Mergers, Distributed Profits, and Intracompany Sales," *Law & Policy in International Business, 22,* 1 (1991): 37–73.

John I. Forry and John W. Darcy, "Tax Planning for

U.S. Investment in Japan," *East Asian Executive Reports, 12,* 1 (1990): 9, 12–16.

Jonathan Fox, "European Community Tax Directives," *International Tax Journal,* 17, 2 (1991): 45–50.

Albert Galway, "TP—Choice," *Management Decision, 28,* 3 (1990): 18–21.

Paul Glover, "Taxes: Rationalizing in the Recession," *CMA Magazine, 65,* 6 (1991): 8.

Yoong Neung Kee and Young-Cheol Jeong, "South Korea—TP Rules: Update on Developments," *East Asian Executive Reports, 13,* 1 (1991): 8, 17–18.

John E. Lanman and Tom Anderson, "Japan—Anti-Tax Avoidance: A Survey of Statutory and Nonstatutory Rules (Part 3)," *East Asian Executive Reports, 11,* 11 (1989): 12–14.

M. Menssen, "A Contract Price Policy for Multinationals," *Management Accounting,* October 1988, pp. 27–31.

G. Millman, "The Trauma of TP," *CFO: The Magazine for Senior Financial Executives, 7,* 11 (1991): 30–34.

James R. Mogle, "Intercompany TP in the 1990s: Trading Old Lamps for New Ones," *Taxes,* December 1991, pp. 961–1000.

Michael F. Patton, Michael J. McKee, and Bert J. Hawkins III, "IRS Issues TAM Addressing Currency Risk Under Section 482," *Tax Management International Journal, 21,* 11 (1992): 622–67.

Roger Y. W. Tang, "TP in the 1990s," *Management Accounting, 73,* 8 (1992): 22–26.

Distribution Strategies

The opening paper in this sequence provides a valuable 10-step road map to achieve success in foreign markets. This process begins with an evaluation of a company's readiness to export, combined with an analysis of its strengths and weaknesses, including potential obstacles to exporting. The firm's domestic business plan must be reviewed prior to a global assessment of markets and competition. The next step is the development of a foreign market entry plan, including pricing and budgeting for market entry. Foreign partner selection, compliance with standards and regulations, the development of support services, and market introduction are the remaining steps leading to a physical presence in the foreign marketplace.

A related piece is an exporter's guide for the selection of foreign sales agents and distributors. It is important to remember that intermediaries may be difficult and costly to terminate. The author recommends the use of well-drafted agreements with intermediaries and greater attention to their selection.

The International Franchise Association has defined franchising as "a continuing relationship in which the franchiser provides a licensed privilege to do business, plus assistance in organization, training, merchandising, and management, in return for a consideration from the franchise."[1] From a predominantly U.S. base, franchising has expanded dramatically during the 1990s. The final article in this section well describes the current penetration of American franchisers around the world, and includes predictions about the future of this key international distribution channel for American companies.

---

[1] Andrew Kostecka, *Franchise Opportunities Handbook* (Washington DC: Department of Commerce, 1986), page xxix.

Executive Insights: The 10-Step Road Map to Success in Foreign Markets

Myron M. Miller

Even companies that have been quite successful in the U.S. market can find the process of expanding into foreign markets an intimidating prospect. Assuming that a company has been in business long enough to establish a viable presence in the U.S. market, it has learned how to deal with a variety of complexities of business. The company has learned how to develop and market new products and/or services, deal with logistics and customer services, and successfully handle the financial issues involved in developing a growing, successful company.

When the company faces the prospects of going into foreign markets, its experience in dealing with the complexities of U.S. business is helpful, but that experience doesn't ensure success internationally. Looking at a world of dozens and dozens of countries, all with their own unique characteristics, the prospects of choosing markets and investing in the development of those markets can be awesome.

Seminars and workshops designed to help small and medium-sized business get into international markets provide these companies with some understanding of the principal elements of interna-

tionalizing a business. Some of these are international finance, marketing, letters of credit and banking, freight forwarding and other aspects of logistics, product planning, and the many complexities of getting into international business. Those programs may also provide insights into the peculiarities of various countries. However, there is something missing when all this information is provided to the prospective exporter (or a company seeking some other type of entry into foreign markets).

Sequence of Steps Required to Get into International Markets

When a company gets information on all the various elements of getting into international business, they have very little idea how to put that into some sequence of action steps. Where do I start? In which markets should I begin? What will it cost me to get into international business? How much will it cost to get some help in exporting? A company might get excellent information on all the elements of going international, e.g., marketing, finance, R&D, logistics, etc., yet not be able to see how they are going to put all these elements together into some pathway that will lead them to successful business overseas.

To deal with the lack of sequencing of the steps

needed to move into international markets, the 10-Step Road Map to Success in Foreign Markets was developed.

By putting the activities involved in going international into a sequenced 10-Step Road Map, it becomes much more apparent to a company where it is headed. There is a sense of direction about what it must do to enter foreign markets. No longer is it facing a jumble of activities and functions.

Exhibit 1 shows on the right and left columns a listing of the traditional topics involved in international business. When managers are taught about these traditional elements of international business, they're not told what they must do next Monday morning, nor the next week nor the next month.

The 10-Step Road Map takes all the content of the traditional elements of international business and puts those elements in the order that a company must use in developing international business. Exhibit 1 shows at which steps each of these elements are used. For example, international finance comes into play at steps 4, 5, 8, and 10. Market research is needed at steps 2, 4, 5, 6, and 8. Product planning is involved in the execution of steps 3, 4, 5, 7, and 9.

Overview of the 10-Step Road Map

The following is an overview of the 10-Step Road Map to Success in Foreign Markets, with a brief description of what services are provided at each step. The process is divided into three phases of service:

Assessment Phase

Step 1. Evaluation of a company's readiness to export, or to enter foreign markets by some other method of market entry

Step 2. Company analysis

Planning Phase

Step 3. Reassessment of the domestic business plan

EXHIBIT 1   10-step road map to success in foreign markets©

Traditional International Topics		*Traditional International Topics*
• International finance *Steps 4, 5, 8, 10*	**Assessment:** 1. Company readiness to export 2. Company assessment	• Market research *Steps 2, 4, 5, 6, 8*
• Documentation *Steps 5, 8*		• Pricing *Steps 4, 5, 9*
• Legal *Steps 3, 4, 5, 6, 8, 10*	**Planning:** 3. Domestic business plan 4. Global assessment; global strategic design	• Product planning *Steps 3, 4, 5, 7, 9*
• Strategic planning *Steps 1, 3, 4, 5*	5. Foreign market entry plan	• Research and development *Steps 3, 4, 5, 7*
• Accounting and taxes *Steps 5, 8*	**Implementation:** 6. Foreign partner selection	• Manufacturing *Steps 3, 5, 7, 10*
• Logistics *Steps 4, 5, 8, 9, 10*	7. Compliance with standards and regulations 8. Selection of support services	• Advertising and promotion *Steps 3, 5, 8*
• Value chain analysis *Steps 2, 4, 5, 8*	9. Market introduction 10. Physical presence in foreign market	• Channels of distribution *Steps 5, 6, 10*

Michigan International Business Development Center, Michigan State University, March 1993. Copyright 1990 Myron M. Miller. All rights reserved. Permission granted for use by Michigan State University.

Step 4. Global assessment of markets and competition; global strategic design

Step 5. Development of a foreign market entry plan, including pricing and budgeting for market entry

Implementation Phase

Step 6. Identification and selection of partners in foreign markets

Step 7. Compliance with foreign standards and regulations

Step 8. Selection of service support providers needed in the U.S. and in the foreign market

Step 9. Market introduction of the company's products or services

Step 10. Establish physical presence in foreign market(s)

The Need for a "Coach"— International Business Development Professionals

At each of these 10 steps in the road map, management needs to undertake a series of analyses, strategy development, and actions to enable it to continue the process of getting into international business. Without some guidance in this process, it will be very difficult for any company to use this road map successfully. A company will need a "coach" or advisor to help it progress through this analysis, planning, and implementation process. It will also need quite a variety of other assistance from international trade experts in such areas as market research, finance, logistics, legal, banking, etc. With the right coach, a company can be directed to the most cost-effective assistance available throughout the process of going international.

Would-be exporters may quickly learn about the availability of expertise in banking, freight forwarder, even international market research firms.[1]

What companies are less likely to find is a "coach" that can help them select the best service providers, distributors, franchisees, and others on whom much depends for success. A new category of international trade and investment intermediary is emerging, the international (or "global") business development concern. It is unlikely that a company can find in any directory a designation for international business development professionals, yet that is what is needed to facilitate a company's internationalization. This new category of service, at its best, is capable of helping a company through the internationalization process. The international group managements of multinationals provide this coaching in-house, though they also must turn to outside services for much of the work in developing new country and product markets.

For small to medium-sized companies, some type of outside international business development assistance is vital to their success in going through the sequence of actions described in the 10-Step Road Map. These new international business development intermediaries can be either private sector or public sector, and the range of capabilities and costs of services varies considerably. The importance of defining the services contained in the 10-Step Road Map is that a company can determine whether a prospective "coach" has the experience and abilities to provide all those services. A company needing assistance in going international should choose the international business development organization most capable and experienced in providing the full range of services, and of directing a company to other capable and economical service providers.

While Traveling through the 10-Step Road Map—Side Trips

Before describing the actions that must be taken throughout the 10-Step Road Map, it is important to recognize that this isn't a road map that one follows wearing blinders. It isn't a systematic process that proceeds down a neat path, step by step. In fact, while a company works its way into international markets, it may jump around from step to step and take short-term actions that will enable it to take advantage of opportunities to get sales and get market information whenever it can do so.

One of the best ways to learn about market opportunities is to try to secure some export orders. While the 10-Step Road Map doesn't call for selling internationally until the latter part of the process, most companies will want to undertake some international transactions as soon as possible, if only to begin to learn about some of the challenges of selling internationally. If a company attends a trade show and meets someone who wants to place an order, it is well worth the risks involved to obtain that order to get some revenue and go through that learning experience. That experience will help the company do its planning and develop its strategies throughout the 10-Step process.

It is also valuable to do what the fishermen call "chumming," literally placing cut or ground bait on the water to attract fish. In the sphere of international business, this means letting the world know about your business and products so they can locate you. There are various publications in which you can advertise your products—in particular, publications of the U.S. Department of Commerce. A single advertisement in such a publication may reach thousands of prospective buyers. Advertisements in trade journals can also publicize a company's intention to find distributors or agents overseas.

Attendance at trade fairs is part of the "chumming" process, since such fairs provide a great opportunity to meet companies interested in representing a U.S. company. There are offices representing states of the U.S. in various parts of the world, and they often take products from their states on mini-trade missions throughout their part of the world in search of distributors or other partners for the companies in their state. U.S. Department of Commerce Matchmaker programs are a great way to meet potential partners or distributors in foreign countries.

All of these actions can help enhance the systematic process of building international business, as long as these short-term actions do not prevent the company from taking the correct decisions for the long range. For example, in its haste to get overseas business, a company may choose the first distributor it meets in a foreign market, even before the company has assessed the market and looked carefully for the best distributor in that market. A short-term sale might lock the company out of the best long-term relationship and thereby prevent it from getting the maximum benefits from a particular market.

Finally, most enthusiastic would-be exporters are anxious to see some progress in their attempt to go international, and they like to see some results quickly. By integrating these shorter-term chumming efforts into the more systematic 10-Step process, a company can learn some important lessons in exporting and get some profit contribution from sales to help finance the market studies needed, yet ensure that short-term actions do not conflict with longer-term strategies.

The following will describe the services required at each step in the 10-Step process. This covers not only what a company will need to go international, but also serves as a guide for a company choosing an international business development "coaching" firm. There are organizations that provide some, but not all, of the range of services. Some economic development firms, for example, may be capable of providing the services described under Steps 1 through 3, but may then have to refer their clients to organizations with more experience and capabilities in international management. For companies located far from international business development entities, it may be best to start the process with local intermediaries, then involve the intermediaries with more expertise later.

A Shortcut—Planning, Pricing, and Budgeting for Foreign Market Entry

While we encourage companies to proceed systematically through the 10-Step process, some managers may be anxious to develop a rough plan, to get some idea of the strategies they are likely to pursue, and to get an early idea of the financial implications of their entry into international business. A decision support tool, "Budgeting and Pricing Aids for International Marketers," has been developed at Michigan State University using a computerized spread sheet program, which will be used at Step 5, but can be used earlier if a company wants to develop an earlier vision of the risks and rewards for going international.

This computer-aided program can be used any time after Step 1, the CORE[2] evaluation, which will be explained later in this chapter. It can then be refined at any time throughout the entire 10-Step process. This tool provides for projecting a company's performance *without* the effects of international operations. It then assists a company to prepare a profit and loss statement for the first three or four years of its international activities, and then shows the impact those international operations will have on total company profitability. For a company's officers and directors, this early view provides information on the financial impact of going international. The earlier a company's officers and board of directors understand the risks and rewards, the more committed the company will be.

Financial Management throughout the Internationalization Process

It is strongly recommended that the company's controller be involved throughout the 10-Step process, to ensure that there is a continual awareness of the financial results of the various plans and actions involved. The company's management and owners will want to know what the internationalization process means to the company. Although financial evaluation is not shown explicitly at each of the 10 steps, it is important that the financial officer be involved and aware of the financial impact of the plans at each step. That person should be involved in key meetings and in the planning sessions throughout this process.

The 10-Step Process

Much of the work during the first five steps can be done in the U.S. Much of the data must still be obtained from foreign markets, but it may not be necessary to go overseas for the information, pay overseas services providers to get the local information, or contact foreign companies and potential customers.

After Step 5, when a Foreign Market Entry Plan has been developed, the other steps require considerable input from foreign markets, involvement with research firms overseas, and personal visits to the market. Steps 6 through 10 require a company to invest more heavily in overseas travel and service costs.

Step #1. Company Readiness to Export (CORE) Evaluation. As any company, regardless of its size and experience, decides to go into international markets, it must determine how ready it is to make that move. Fortunately, a computer-aided decision support tool was developed in 1986 by Dr. S. Tamer Cavusgil, now Executive Director, International Business Centers, Michigan State University. That tool is called CORE, COmpany Readiness to Export. Whether a company is considering exporting, or entering foreign markets by some other method of market entry (e.g., franchising, licensing, retailing, joint venture, etc.), this evaluation is a critical beginning point.

CORE is designed to provide an evaluation of internal company strengths and weaknesses in the context of exporting. It is especially useful for small and medium-sized businesses considering exporting for the first time, but it can also be used by larger firms to reassess their strengths and weaknesses regarding their present performance. CORE provides the user company with a reading on the extent of their readiness to export, as well as specific recommendations relating to export-related tasks. This tool can be used by individual companies for self-assessment, but it can also be used by trainers and consultants.

At the end of this session, the user receives an

assessment that includes an indication of what their next steps should be. For some companies, their product and organizational readiness may indicate they are so strong on both attributes that they should proceed into exporting immediately. At the other extreme are the companies that should concentrate on developing their domestic U.S. business and begin the long process of preparing themselves to export some day. In the middle are many companies that are ready to export in some respects, but have some important deficiencies they should correct before proceeding. CORE provides the user with some guidance on what steps they should take before making aggressive commitments.

The end result of the CORE assessment is valuable, but even more valuable is the interaction with a skilled, international business development professional. Possibly 75 percent of the value of the CORE assessment is the definition of issues that arise between the coach and the company.

Step #2. Company Assessment.   While the CORE analysis provides a good beginning in assessing a company's readiness to enter foreign markets, the company cannot proceed without making a much more comprehensive analysis of its present strengths and weaknesses, its structure in terms of its value-added activities, and the areas in which it has distinct competitive advantage and a competitive opening.

When a company goes into international markets, it must earn a niche in new markets. It will do that only if it has some competitive advantages in the new markets. Therefore, the company must take the strengths that have made it viable in the U.S. market and transfer those strengths overseas. If it doesn't know why it has been successful in the U.S. market, it won't know how to penetrate foreign markets successfully.

Therefore, a company must analyze its entire spectrum of activities to determine its strengths and weaknesses, and determine where it has unique competitive strengths, sometimes known as its core competencies. The tool for determining this is a variation of the value chain analysis. An analysis of

the whole spectrum of company activities, from the sourcing of raw materials and components through R&D, manufacturing, marketing, logistics, and after-sales service, provides the basis for determining which activities should be performed in the U.S. and those which must be done by partners or service organizations overseas. Without a thorough understanding of all company activities in the U.S market, it is almost impossible to develop a sound strategy for entering foreign markets.

In the process of assessing the company's activities as it begins its planning to go international, it must:

- Evaluate the product;
- Evaluate markets and competition;
- Evaluate technological and production capabilities;
- Assess financial capabilities;
- Evaluate the company's position in the home market; and
- Prepare situation analysis report, with diagnosis of strengths and weaknesses, condensed into a summary of critical issues.

The company must evaluate the principal obstacles to the company's entering foreign markets. The following are some of the factors that could immediately prevent a company from starting international activities:

- Legal aspects of representation in a market;
- Standards and regulatory issues;
- Export controls;
- Patent and trademark concerns;
- Product adaptations;
- Production capacity and equipment restraints; and
- Financial resources required.

Step #3. Reassessment of the Domestic Business Plan.   With the assessment completed, the company must reassess its domestic business plan before proceeding to address its first steps in moving into international business.

Some companies attempt to move into international markets with no sound foundation of planning in their domestic business. While there may be some exceptions to the rule, in principle, companies that succeed in foreign markets have established a strong, viable position in the U.S. (or home) market. Companies are often impatient to get into foreign markets and want to get started, without having laid the proper foundation for their business at home.

Using much of the analysis described in Steps 1 and 2 above, the company should ensure that they have a business plan for the next three to four years for domestic operations. That plan should address some of the issues described earlier and develop the strategies and action programs that will ensure domestic market success. One particular factor often not addressed specifically in the planning in the United States is the issue of foreign competitors there.

While most competitors in the United States previously were domestic manufacturers or service providers, in recent years there has been a significant increase in both the number and the market share of foreign competitors that have established a presence in the United States. Also, foreign companies may have employed a sales agent or distributor in the United States and have indirectly established a significant presence.

Some employees of U.S. manufacturers have left their previous employers and have established distributorships where almost all of their lines are from foreign manufacturers. These foreign companies, whether represented directly or indirectly, must be identified in the domestic business plan and analyzed carefully.

Step #4. Global Assessment of Markets and Competitors and Development of Initial Strategic Plan.

This step involves a global assessment of the industry to determine the best country or regional markets for the company's products and the assessment of the best strategies for entering those markets. At the same time, an assessment must be made of the principal competitors throughout the world. In Step 3, information was gathered on those global competitors present in the U.S. market, but it is necessary to look elsewhere in the world to determine who else must be dealt with either "defensively," because of the threat of the new company hurting the business in the U.S. market, or in the "offensive" arena when the company goes into foreign markets.

Based on the assessment of potential opportunities or competitive threats in foreign markets, the company must determine its strategy for entering global markets. It must determine which countries to enter, how many at a time, the proper method for entering those markets, and the financial resources required to execute this plan. It may choose to enter Europe first, and start with one or two countries. Or, it may choose a Pan-American strategy, choosing to start by entering the Canadian and Mexican markets.

In many respects, this is the most difficult and complex part of developing a program to go international. Many companies may be able to start in only one or two markets at a time, because they are limited in financial and human resources. Other companies that have the resources, and where the opportunities are imminent, may want to move on a much broader basis, and faster. Each situation must be evaluated on its own merits.

At this step, it isn't necessary to develop a massive, global strategy. What is required is the development of some guiding strategies regarding the means for beginning the development of an international, or global, presence. Henry Mintzberg (1987) of McGill University refers to this process as "crafting" strategy. Gary Hamel and C. K. Prahalad (1989) have also described a process that is worth reviewing when developing this initial thrust into international markets.

Various models of strategic planning are available to guide a company in the development of its initial global strategic plan. Most would include such elements as:

1. Mission statement.
2. Statement of objectives and goals.

3. Situation analysis.
   a. Analysis of strengths and weaknesses.
   b. Analysis of threats and opportunities.
   c. Overview of global markets.
   d. Overview of global competition and their market shares.
   e. Environmental issues that affect the industry.
   f. Significant trends in the industry.
   g. Triggers of change in the architecture of the industry.
   h. Benchmark centers of excellence in the industry.
4. **Product line and pricing analysis.**
   a. Comparison of prices, features, and benefits of the company's product lines against its principal competitors in key markets.
5. **Characteristics of key functional areas.**
6. **Assessment of key factors for success in the industry.**
7. **Critical issues facing the company in its internationalization process.**
8. **Alternative strategies to deal with the critical issues and take advantage of the opportunities; selection of the most favorable strategies.**
   a. Advantages and disadvantages of each alternative.
   b. Financial evaluation of the alternatives.
   c. Reasons for selection of the preferred strategies.
9. **Action programs to implement the strategies.**
   a. Specific action programs developed related to each strategy, with specific responsibilities assigned for each program and each element of the program, and precise beginning and ending dates for each step in the action program.
10. **Projection of human and financial resources required to initiate and implement the plan for the first few years.**

Because there is so much to learn in developing international markets, this initial strategic plan must be continually modified and updated based on daily experiences.

To assist in this step, the company may be put in contact with various agencies that provide information on key markets throughout the world, such as:

a. U.S. Department of Commerce industry sector specialists.
b. Industry specialists in the U.S. International Trade Commission.
c. Department of Commerce market research reports on specific industry sectors (particularly information from the NTDB, National Trade Data Bank).
d. Data from foreign sources (such as trade associations or industry sector groups) that can provide information on markets within their countries.
e. Private sector sources, such as Frost and Sullivan, FIND SVP, etc.
f. Data on exports to key markets from the U.S. Department of Commerce, United Nations, and the European Community.
g. JETRO on Japan.

The company itself may have contacts in the trade, memberships in associations, information from publications, and visits to industry trade shows or symposia that should be tapped. The company should be encouraged, early in its development, to attend overseas trade shows (many of which may be in Germany) as an effective means of developing a global overview of their business in a short time.

Some of this information can be gathered from secondary sources, but invariably it is necessary for a company to do primary research. Some of the information can be gathered at a very low cost, even free. Eventually, however, it's necessary to pay for important information, and the company must budget for this expense or investment.

When the company has made its global assessment and has chosen its means for entering the global market and has selected its initial target markets, it is ready to move to Step 5, where it will develop specific foreign market entry plans.

Step #5. Foreign Market Entry Planning.

Having chosen some initial target markets, the next step is to develop a detailed plan for entering those markets. For each target market, the market entry plan should include such items as:

- The company's objectives for that market, including target market share, sales targets for the first few years, profit objectives, targeted breakeven period, and other quantitative and qualitative objectives.
- Background material on the country relating to the economy, politics, cultural issues, trends in the economy, and other country-related matters that will affect the company's performance in that country. A good starting point for this information is the National Trade Data Bank (NTDB) and a decision support system developed by Michigan State University, *Country Consultant.*
- The opportunities and obstacles in the country for the company in its business sector.
- Strategy for the method of entering the market, whether it be through an agent or distributor relationship, licensing, joint venture, acquisition, or some other method. An important determinant of that strategy will be the company's value-adding chain and its selection of the activities it wants to perform in a country and those it wants to retain in the United States.

Having developed an understanding of all the components of a company's value-adding chain at Step 2, it is now necessary to configure and coordinate those activities. *Configuring* value chain activities basically involves determining where the various activities should be conducted, whether it be in the U.S. market or in other countries. The determination of the company's core competencies in its value chain will help determine how to configure the various activities. When the various activities have been positioned in the appropriate countries, those activities must be properly *coordinated* between the company's home office and the overseas locations.

- Development of principal strategies for the first three to five years in the country.
- Action plans to implement the strategies.

- Projected financial statements for the company's operations in each country.

Other factors may be included in the preparation of the plan, as determined when a plan is being prepared for a particular country.

In all cases, the U.S. Department of Commerce's capabilities provide the logical starting point, particularly with their country desk officers and the U.S. & Foreign and Commercial Service offices in each country. At a point, it will be necessary to use some private sector consultants in particular countries, and the U.S. & FCS offices in each country can help direct a company to those private sector consultants. Those offices also prepare a Country Marketing Plan that provides excellent material on the country in question. Also, those offices can prepare, for a moderate charge, a Comparison Shopping Survey, which provides very specific information on your market in that country. The latter is a particularly invaluable resource.

Step #6. Identification and Selection of Partners.

This step involves the identification, selection, and contracting of the best sales representatives, distributors, licensees, dealers, franchisees, joint venture partners, acquisition candidates, or other types of strategic partners.

To engage in this process, the company must develop a portfolio describing the company, its products, and its services to potential partners in foreign markets and the benefits of association with the U.S. company. Too often a U.S. company just gives its U.S. spec sheets to prospective partners (or to some intermediary to represent the U.S. company), assuming the overseas partner will immediately want to partner with the U.S. company. This is a serious mistake. It is important to prepare first-class material to get a first-class partner, so the U.S. company should assemble first-class visual and printed material to go "courting" for the best possible partners.

From the development of the foreign market entry plan developed at Step 5, information on prospective partners should have been developed.

If further analysis is needed to identify the prospects, one way to identify the potential partners is to use the Agent and Distributor Search (ADS) capabilities of the U.S. Department of Commerce (U.S. DOC).

By providing the U.S. DOC with relevant information about the company and its products and services, along with a profile of an ideal partner, the U.S. & FCS can contact prospects in that country to get a reading on their interest in partnering with the U.S. company. When that short list is developed from the feedback, the U.S. company must still visit those companies personally to determine the best partners.

The selection of the best partner should be made using checklists and other methodologies for evaluating all the considerations in this decision. These methodologies have been captured in several computer-aided decision support systems developed at Michigan State University's International Business Centers—one for the selection of distributors in foreign markets, and the other for choosing partners for various types of international collaborative ventures.

Developing a contract with a distributor or strategic alliance partner is critical to the success of the venture, so good legal advice is very important. There are models of good distributor agreements available to guide the company doing this for the first time. It's important, however, to get good legal assistance. In some cases, it is important to use legal assistance in the target market, because they will be aware of what types of agreements are generally acceptable to partners in those markets. They may also be aware of local or regional issues that must be addressed (such as European Community matters) in a contract.

At this point in the 10-Step Road Map process, it is important for a small to medium-sized company to be working with competent international business development professionals, located either in the United States or in the foreign market, and/or have good contacts in foreign markets to help in the identification and selection of the best distributors, retailers, franchisees, or other types of alliance partners.

Step #7. Compliance with Standards and Regulations.

Often the greatest obstacle to gaining entry into foreign markets is the array of standards and regulations with which it must comply if the company is to market its products or services in that country. One of the first steps in laying the groundwork for doing business in any country is to identify which standards and regulations affect your company, then begin to lay the groundwork for complying with those standards and regulations. These include safety, environment, packaging, labeling, good manufacturing practices, ISO 9000, efficacy (for medical devices, for example), radio frequency interference, electrical standards, patents and trademarks, copyrights, and registrations.

Expert guidance must be selected to help a company identify, then comply with, all the appropriate standards and regulations. There are public sector agencies that can help for moderate fees, and private sector firms that, while more expensive, may have expertise that can ensure a company it will not face legal problems because of failure to comply with some critical regulation.

Step #8. Selection of Service Support Providers.

Even if a company chooses to set up an export department, it will need to rely on a group of service support providers both in the United States and overseas. If the company is just exporting, it will still need the help of freight forwarders, to help get the product to the overseas customers; bankers, to help arrange letters of credit and help the company be paid for what it ships; and some legal assistance, to ensure that the company's patents, trademarks, and copyrights will be protected in the target market.

Therefore, as soon as a company faces its first transaction, it will need to choose freight forwarders, bankers, and attorneys to ensure success. Lists of service providers are available from federal and state departments of commerce, as well as from other providers of international business development services. Selecting those firms in the United States is not too difficult, since a company can always meet a number of firms and choose the best one. Michigan State University's International Business Centers has developed a computer-aided decision support system for selecting a freight forwarder, which is a great aid for a company in choosing the best possible freight forwarder.

Selecting service providers is much more difficult in foreign markets. When a company goes beyond exporting, even to the point of choosing an overseas agent or distributor, it is important to use good local services, like attorneys and bankers. Some of the other service providers needed, particularly as a company becomes closer to having a physical presence in a country, include market research firms, tax and accounting firms, advertising and public relations firms, customs brokers, chambers of commerce, and others as appropriate.

Assistance in locating good service suppliers can be obtained from a company's trade association, the American Chamber of Commerce in the particular country, the commercial counselors at the U.S. & FCS officers in the country, and by contacting other noncompeting companies operating in the country. These service providers in foreign markets can make or break a company in its foreign markets. Often good services are very expensive for a small to medium-sized company, so the company may not be able to afford the services of the U.S. Big 6 accounting firms, for example. However, some of the local firms don't have the capabilities of the larger firms, so a U.S. company could make a false economy by selecting a small local firm that may not adequately serve the U.S. company.

This is a critical step for small to medium-sized companies expanding into foreign markets, and it should rely on the best advisors in the field of international business development, whether it be the governmental or private sector professionals.

Step #9. Market Introduction of the Company's Products and Services.

Many companies choose a distributor in a foreign market, then rely completely on that distributor to do an effective job of introducing the product in the market. That's an unfortunate mistake. The U.S. company should work hand in hand with the distributor

to plan and execute the market introduction. The market introduction in the foreign market should be planned with the same care as any market introduction in a new part of the United States.

The U.S. company should work with the foreign distributor to plan every detail of the product launch in that market. A Pert and Gantt chart (or more sophisticated computer-aided planning tool) should be prepared to show every aspect of the market introduction plan, including:

- Preparation and translation of product literature and videos.
- Sales training.
- Service training.
- Advertising and promotion.
- Product modification.
- Packaging and labeling.
- Inventory planning.
- Logistics.
- Public relations and publicity.
- Government relations.

One of the great benefits of this mutual planning and execution process is that it brings to light issues that might not have been resolved in the relationship to this point, such as:

- Who will take what responsibility in obtaining approvals for standards and regulations?
- Who will do the translations?
- Who will print the product literature and operating manuals?
- Who will prepare the artwork?

Step #10. Establish a Physical Presence in a Foreign Market.

If a company proceeds to the point where it feels confident enough about its progress in getting into foreign markets that it wants a physical presence, it will need to evaluate very carefully the options available. Some presence can be obtained without establishing a legal presence, by using office-sharing facilities available in many countries. A company can have a telephone answering service, some secretarial support, and part-time office space without having a legal presence. The Office of the U.S. & Foreign Commercial Service can help in locating those services.

When a company wants to establish a legal presence as well as some physical presence, the commitment to that market becomes much greater, with concomitant risks and rewards. When taking this step, it's best to get expert assistance from tax and accounting firms, and legal advisors. These firms, while expensive for the small to medium-sized businesses in the United States, are essential if a company's interests are to be protected properly as they become established in the market. The Big 6 accounting firms have capabilities in providing this assistance and have proven track records.

The U.S. & FCS and the American Chamber of Commerce offices in each country can also provide assistance in this process, as well as the offices of the U.S. states in various regions of the world. Also, professional international business development agencies can provide assistance at this critical point in a firm's internationalization.

The long-term consequences involved in entering, with provision for exiting, a market are very important.

Conclusion

The foregoing 10-Step Road Map to Success in Foreign Markets is like any map between two major points—like Brussels, Belgium, to Milan, Italy, for example. It serves as a guide to getting from one point to another, without saying that there is only one precise way to do it. The 10-Step Road Map doesn't provide a set of rules; rather it consists of some principles that seem to work rather

well. A company can undertake some of the steps out of sequence, or do several at a time. It can undertake some export transactions, and it can do some "chumming" to learn where there may be potential customers. All of this can help a company eventually succeed in foreign markets. Properly undertaken, with guidance by international business development professionals, this process can be a great aid to developing a successful exporting or international market presence.

Notes

1. The term *exporter* may be used at times when a company considering going international may decide either to export or to enter foreign markets by one of many other means, such as licensing, R&D partnerships, production-sharing, or establishment of foreign branches or subsidiaries, for example. The issues faced by firms entering foreign markets are similar up to a point, so the term *exporter* can mean any company considering getting into foreign markets.
2. CORE, copyright 1991, S. Tamer Cavusgil. All rights reserved.
3. The U.S. will be referred to as the home market herein, but this process can be used by a company in any country of the world. In the event that a German company is considering expanding into foreign markets, one could substitute Germany for the U.S. throughout this process.

References

Hamel, Gary and C. K. Prahalad. "Strategic Intent." *Harvard Business Review* (May–June 1989): 63–76.

Mintzberg, Henry. "Crafting Strategy," *Harvard Business Review* (July–August 1987): 66–75.

AN EXPORTER'S GUIDE TO SELECTING FOREIGN SALES AGENTS AND DISTRIBUTORS

Thomas F. Clasen

Experts estimate that more than one half of all world trade is handled through agents and distributors. While the use of such sales intermediaries is commonplace, especially for small and medium-sized companies, it is also common for exporters to complain about their foreign agents and distributors. Unsatisfactory sales intermediaries not only cost the exporter sales, but as a result of protective laws in many foreign jurisdictions, they may be difficult and costly to terminate. New Legislation in EC Member States under Directive 86-653, as well as the proposed extension of Article 85 of the Treaty of Rome to "non-integrated" agents, will present additional obstacles to the use of sales intermediaries in Europe.

While exporters can help themselves by using carefully drafted agency and distribution agreements, the best step in minimizing problems is to use more care in selecting the intermediary. It is not uncommon for manufacturing companies to appoint a local agent or distributor without any significant background check at all. This is particularly true where the intermediary appears to be

Reprinted from *The Journal of European Business,* Vol. 3, No. 2, November/December 1991, pp. 28–32. Permission granted by Faulkner & Gray, 11 Penn Plaza, New York, NY 10001.

bringing in a significant amount of business or where the market in the country appears marginal. Since costly disputes frequently arise even in these circumstances, however, it is wise to establish a procedure in selecting foreign agents and distributors and stick to that policy in all cases.

An effective agent-distributor selection procedure normally involves a number of steps. While there are variations depending on the industry, the following core elements will generally be present:

1. Examine the legal and business considerations involved in appointing foreign intermediaries, and establish criteria that reflect the particular geographic market;

2. Assemble a list of potential candidates by using the various directories and consulting other sources of information;

3. Qualify such candidates by applying certain criteria and conducting a preliminary interview; and

4. Make a trip to visit the proposed intermediary to obtain additional information about its resources and facilities, to get a proper feel for the intermediary's compatibility with the organization, and to check the assumptions and objectives of the agent or distributor.

Setting the Criteria

Because the qualifications the intermediary should possess differ from country to country, the starting point for the development of criteria may be an analysis of the peculiar characteristics of the market. Is there sufficient demand for the product in the market to justify its own agent or distributor, or could the market be covered well by an intermediary in an adjacent country? Is the market too large to give exclusively to a single agent or distributor? Is it reasonable to expect an agent or distributor not to handle competing goods in the market? To what extent is the market already familiar with and receptive to the product? Will the establishment of a demand require a long-term strategy that can be pursued only by someone with significant financial resources? Is it desirable to go with a well-established intermediary that can immediately provide access to the market even though this may require more sharing of profits?

A related consideration is the nature of the customers. To the extent that the product will be sold exclusively to governmental agencies, it may be critical for the agent or distributor to have access to officials who influence procurement decisions. If the product is sold primarily as part of a larger construction or turnkey project, access to the project coordinators and the ability to work effectively with the project engineers may be key. Each of these would imply a long-term, focused sales effort for which an agent may be better suited than a distributor. In those instances involving sales to a broader base of ordinary consumers, on the other hand, a distributor with an existing network of sales outlets may be more appropriate. For customers that prefer to purchase "local" products, exporters may want to use a distributor that would sell the goods under its own label.

The nature of the product will obviously have a significant effect on the sales approach. For example, is the product of a highly complex, technical nature so that a sales representative will need to employ advanced engineering and technical personnel to sell it effectively? Is the product comple-

mentary to another line of products, making it desirable to "piggy back" on distributors of such other products? Is it essential for the intermediary to have sufficient resources to provide service and spare parts or can these be obtained elsewhere? Is the product susceptible to copying so that it is critical to saturate the market completely through a broad distribution network before knockoffs begin to appear?

The special characteristics of the market, the customers, and the product determine many of the criteria the exporter should consider in selecting a foreign intermediary. There are, however, some additional characteristics of the relationship that may influence the choice. Many of these will dictate whether the intermediary will be an agent or a distributor. For example, when it is important to exercise a high level of control over the marketing and sales activities of the representative, an exporter may prefer to use an agent rather than a distributor. An exporter's preference to sell directly to the customer in order to build goodwill in the market may also make an agency arrangement more desirable. On the other hand, if the exporter is unwilling to assume the risk of nonpayment by the customer or is opposed to a commission-based compensation structure, a company may find a distributor to be more consistent with its objectives. As mentioned, distributors are also more likely to inventory product and parts and to provide repair and warranty service.

In addition to the basic criteria, there are a number of characteristics that the exporter should look for in the candidate. For example, what kind of track record has the proposed agent or distributor established in promoting comparable products? Is it clear that it was responsible for its past success? Are there adequate explanations for its past failures? What kind of reputation does the prospective intermediary have within the industry? Do potential customers uniformly regard the agent or distributor as a company with whom they wish to do business?

Another important area of consideration is the prospective candidate's financial condition and resources. Does the intermediary have a sufficient net worth or other sources of income to sustain a long-term promotional effort even if sales are not realized immediately? Has it shown a consistent pattern of paying its creditors and employees? Does the proposed distributor have sufficient credit to justify extending terms? Does it have sufficient funds to stock an inventory or meet its other needs? Does the *del credere* agent (one that guarantees the customers' payment to the exporter) have the financial resources to support its guarantee? Who are the owners and creditors of the prospective agent or distributor, and what is the extent of their commitment to the intermediary? Has the intermediary shown a practice of making necessary commitments of funds for advertising and promotional activities, personnel, and office and shop facilities?

Companies should also consider the level of interest and enthusiasm the candidate demonstrates in representing the product in the market. Did the candidate contact the exporter or vice versa? Has it prepared a business plan or otherwise outlined in detail its proposed strategy for market development? To what extent is it willing to put its own money into advertising and promotion? Is it willing to assume the risks associated with minimum sales or other performance criteria? What would be its expectation for an initial term of the agreement and in what circumstances should it be renewable? Are these consistent with the schedule the exporter believes to be appropriate for establishing a foothold in the market? These and other factors should be examined to confirm the level of the candidate's commitment to the promotion of the product.

While business considerations normally predominate in the choice of a foreign intermediary, legal factors can influence significantly the exporter's cost and risks in using agents and distributors abroad. Many legal considerations can be addressed in the contract regardless of the agent or distributor that is ultimately selected. Others are so fundamental, however, that they should be examined at the outset and included in the exporter's criteria for selecting the intermediary.

Perhaps the most important legal consideration relevant to the exporter's choice of a commercial intermediary is the effect of local law on the use of agents and distributors. Local laws limiting the use of certain types of commercial intermediaries, for example, or requiring the agent or distributor to meet certain conditions for qualification, must obviously be considered in establishing the criteria for selection. In countries where local labor laws extend to protect individual agents, the exporter may require the agent to be a corporate entity. In countries whose protective legislation extends only to distributors, the exporter may decide only to consider agents. On the other hand, if the manner in which local tax law defines taxable "permanent establishments" makes it difficult to use agents without becoming subject to local taxation, the exporter may wish to limit possible candidates to distributors. The risk presented by the implied authority that agents are granted under local law may also favor the use of distributors rather than agents.

Identifying Candidates

Having developed the general criteria that will be used in selecting the foreign agent or distributor, the next step is to assemble a list of prospective candidates that appear to meet the criteria. For many manufacturers new to exporting, this may appear to be a somewhat daunting task. To be sure, the means of developing information on foreign firms that may be able and willing to promote a company's products abroad are not the same as those used to identify domestic representatives. There are, however, a number of specialized sources of information on possible candidates, including a number of directories (such as those identified in *Trade Directories of the World* and other publications of Croner, Dun & Bradstreet, and Thomas), assistance from the U.S. Department of Commerce (particularly under its Agent/Distributor Service and World Traders Data Report Service), and information available from trade associations, the commercial section of foreign embassies and consulates in the United States, commercial banks, international carriers, and other private firms.

Exporters should investigate who their competitors and other firms in related businesses are using abroad. The exporter should also consult with its existing and potential customers in the foreign territory about possible candidates. Customers are perhaps in the best position to provide accurate information about agents and distributors that know the industry and the product, can provide adequate service and support, provide prompt service, and in general enjoy a favorable reputation in the market.

Qualifying Candidates

Once the manufacturer or supplier has located a number of candidates that appear to meet its criteria, the next task is to qualify the prospective candidates. While the qualification process will clearly depend on the industry or product involved and will differ from country to country, it normally will consist of three steps: (1) investigating the background of the candidate based on outside sources, (2) contacting the candidate to determine its interest in serving as an agent or distributor, and (3) reviewing additional background information obtained from the candidate itself. The objective of the qualification process is to narrow the list of potential candidates to a small number of firms that are genuinely interested in the arrangement and that appear to meet the basic criteria the exporter establishes. This will eliminate the need to make a trip to a country to visit firms that are either unqualified for or uninterested in the relationship. It will also allow the exporter to concentrate its time on visiting serious candidates in a market where it identified numerous possible agents or distributors.

Conducting a background investigation on a potential candidate involves looking at many issues. What is the firm's reputation in its industry? How is it regarded by its customers? How extensive are its contacts and market position in the territory? How long has it been in this business? Who

are its principals and what are their backgrounds? How strong are its sales and service personnel? Is it qualified to serve the entire market exclusively? Does it have sufficient facilities and personnel? Does it have adequate financial resources? Information on these and similar questions can often be assembled from outside sources. These include trade and other publications, trade associations, foreign and U.S. government agencies and diplomatic posts, banks and consulting firms, and customers in the territory.

The next step is to contact the potential candidates to determine their interest in serving as agents or distributors. For smaller companies with limited resources, this first contact may be made by means of a letter. The letter should describe generally the exporter's plans for appointing an agent or distributor in the territory, provide some background on the exporter, and include complete information on the subject products, including applications and possible sales volume in the territory. The letter may also refer the candidate to existing users of the product in the territory, if any, to give the potential agent or distributor an opportunity to examine the product and discuss it with a customer. The letter should state clearly that it is intended only to determine whether the recipient would have an interest in selling the product, and that the actual appointment of an agent or distributor will be made only following a personal visit and pursuant to a written agreement. It is important to avoid any misunderstanding that the letter itself is an offer to appoint the recipient as the exporter's intermediary.

Before the exporter plans a trip to visit the candidates, it should obtain additional information on any candidates that respond favorably to the initial contact. Like the background investigation, this review is designed to ferret out firms that do not meet the criteria or that are not serious about representing the product line. In this case, the information is secured from the candidate itself. This may include additional information to confirm the accuracy of the information already gleaned from other sources. It should also include more subjective information such as details on how the candidate sees the new product line fitting into its existing business, general information on how the firm would promote the product, and what the firm's requirements might be in terms of compensation. An exporter that has significant bargaining power due to the demand for the product may even require the candidate to prepare a detailed business plan on its proposed marketing and sales strategies.

Meeting with Candidates

Smaller manufacturers and suppliers that have limited financial resources frequently appoint foreign agents and distributors without visiting the intermediary first. They reason that the costs associated with making the trip outweigh the benefit in actually meeting the prospective agent or distributor. They may also feel that they have less to lose than larger companies if the appointment does not work out. In fact, it is probably more important for the exporter with limited resources than for the large multinational to actually meet with the proposed candidates before making a decision—a visit to the candidate's facilities and an opportunity to meet its principals and other personnel is perhaps the best way to confirm that it meets the exporter's criteria. Agents and distributors that meet these criteria are more likely to maximize the exporter's sales in the territory (thus maximizing the exporter's revenue) and less likely to require termination on unfriendly terms (thus minimizing the exporter's costs).

There are at least three separate objectives of meeting with the proposed appointee in person. The first, and most obvious, is to obtain additional information about the candidate's objectives and means of doing business in order to confirm that it is the proper choice. While the exporter should have secured extensive information before the visit, there is normally no substitute for the purely subjective evaluation a supplier can make by actually meeting with the candidate's personnel and spending a reasonable amount of time discussing each other's ideas on how to enter the market and

maximize sales. It is not at all unusual for a supplier to conclude after such a meeting that while the candidate looked great on paper, the chemistry just was not right.

If the supplier finds the candidate acceptable, the meeting can help accomplish a second objective of providing the supplier with additional information useful in negotiating the agency or distribution agreement and improving ongoing communication throughout the term of the appointment. Once again, it is clearly possible to negotiate the agreement without actually sitting down together. Experienced negotiators know, however, that it is very difficult to assess the level of the other side's depth of feeling about a particular issue without sitting across the table from him or her. It is obviously possible simply to show the proposed appointee a printed form and tell it to take it or leave it. Even in these cases, however, it is helpful to spend time discussing the issues to determine the likelihood of the candidate's respect for the terms of the agreement after it is executed. An initial meeting also sets an important tone of mutual communication that can last throughout the term of the agreement. An agent or distributor is much more likely to call and discuss problems with an exporter whose salespeople it knows personally.

But if these were the only purposes for the meeting, then it could just as readily take place at the supplier's facilities or at an airport or trade show someplace in between. This is also undesirable. The third and equally important objective of the face-to-face encounter is to give the exporter an opportunity to personally examine the candidate's facilities and to meet more of its personnel to confirm that they are up to the task. The facilities may be more important in the case of a distributor that will be expected to maintain an inventory and provide service for the products. Both agents and distributors should, however, have acceptable means of communicating efficiently with the exporter and its customers (telex, facsimile, cable, etc.) and a sufficient number of trained personnel to handle the responsibilities of the appointment. This will give the exporter firsthand knowledge of the ability of the candidate to provide effective support for the product.

Finally, the visit to the territory should include calling on potential customers and other sources of information both to develop additional background on the candidate and to obtain additional information on the market.

Maintaining the Relationship

After selecting an agent or distributor, the exporter should take the necessary steps to maintain the intermediary's goodwill. This involves (1) negotiating an agreement that is fair and mutually beneficial, (2) complying in good faith with the terms of the agreement, (3) continuing the communication between the parties, and (4) making occasional adjustments in the relationship in response to changing circumstances.

While there is no sure way to avoid the risks presented by the use of foreign agents and distributors, careful selection of the intermediary by the above steps is the best means of minimizing them.

Franchising Systems Around the Globe: A Status Report

John F. Preble and Richard C. Hoffman

While markets for certain franchised products and services have become saturated in the U.S. (the fast-food sector, for example), international franchising opportunities have been developing at an unprecedented rate due to the growth of global markets. Many developed countries are experiencing similar trends and are turning to franchise strategies for growth. Despite its recent growth, there is relatively little specific information on the current status, challenges, and future prospects of international franchising. The purpose of this article is to provide such an assessment of the status of franchising in world markets.

The Franchising Phenomenon

Franchising has emerged in recent years as a highly significant strategy for business growth, job creation, and economic development both in the U.S. and in world markets (Hoffman and Preble, 1991). Franchisors are classified either as product-tradename or as business format franchisors (Arthur Andersen, 1992). *Product-tradename franchising,* which is prevalent in automobile sales, retail gasoline, and soft-drink distri-

bution, uses franchisees to distribute a product under a franchisor's trademark. *Business format franchising* is designed to have the franchisee replicate, in different locations, the entire franchisor's business concept including the marketing strategy and plan, the operating manuals and standards, and quality control. Restaurants, personal and business services, rental services, and nonfood retailing are examples of the 67 distinct business segments where this "package" concept is currently in use.

Business format franchising is predicted to be the dominant form of franchising internationally in the twenty-first century (Hoffman and Preble, 1993). While business format franchising has been experiencing rapid growth in the U.S. since the 1950s, the 1980s was a period of rapid international expansion during which some 400 U.S. franchisors increased their overseas units by more than 70 percent, to almost 39,000. The majority of these overseas units were located in Canada, Japan, Europe, Australia, and the United Kingdom.

The Diffusion of Franchise Systems

In recent years, international opportunities have been developing at an unprecedented rate for a

This study was partially supported by a Salisbury State University Perdue School of Business summer research grant.

variety of reasons: global economic integration taking place as a result of lowering trade barriers in the European Community (EC); the passage of the North American Free Trade Agreement (Canada, Mexico, and U.S.); and a reduction of entry barriers in many former communist countries (Russia, Central Europe, and Eastern Europe). Deregulation of industries within these nations has also been occurring on an accelerated basis. Furthermore, many developed countries are experiencing trends similar to those that made franchising so successful in the United States (Ayling, 1988; Chan and Justis, 1992). Examples of these developments include a rapidly increasing demand for goods and services, expanding urbanization, increasing mobility, more women in the work force, rising disposable incomes, and a shift to service-dominated economies. The success of non-U.S. franchisors in their home markets, coupled with their often small domestic market, has caused these franchisors to quickly internationalize their operations. The development of international franchising by non-U.S. franchisors has been relatively swift: Benetton, the Italian-based clothing franchise, boasts more than 4,000 licensed outlets worldwide. Canada, France, Italy, and Japan each have several hundred franchised companies, many of which have taken their packaged (format) concepts abroad.

While all this serves to suggest that the franchising concept is rapidly spreading around the globe, actual data on franchising's movement can only be partially gleaned from a patchwork of diverse sources. The above problem is compounded by the fact that the international aspects of franchising have not received much academic or managerial attention. Most of the prior empirical work has either compared international and domestic franchising (Walker, 1989; Huszagh, Huszagh, and McIntyre, 1992) or examined franchising in a specific industry (Preble, 1992), country (Ayling, 1988, Williams, 1994), or region (Chan and Justis, 1990) of the world. No study has adopted a global orientation in investigating the importance and extent of the diffusion of franchising around the

world. The purpose of this research is to provide such a perspective.

Franchising Survey

The basic question that guided this research was: What are the status and general characteristics of franchising outside the United States? In order to assess the development of franchising around the world, a survey instrument was sent by fax to the International Franchising Association's 23 "sister" national franchise associations in North and South America, Asia, and Europe. These organizations comprise the Council of Multinational Franchisors and Distributors (COMFAD), a worldwide network of international franchise executives and resources. Advanced notification of the survey was sent to each association by fax. One week later, the questionnaire with a cover letter was sent by fax to the director of each franchise association. Three weeks later, a follow-up letter and copy of the survey were mailed to all nonrespondents. These procedures yielded a 56.5 percent usable response rate which provided data on franchising in 13 nations located in North and South America (3), Asia (2), Eastern Europe (1), and Western Europe (7).

The survey was designed to collect data to answer three specific research questions. The first question, "What is the extent of development and growth of franchising internationally?" sought information on franchise association membership, the number and type of franchising firms and units, sales levels and movements, and industry growth rates. The second research question, "What are the major international markets for franchised operations in terms of industries and nations?" sought data on the key industries and countries in which franchise operations had developed. The final research question, "What factors are important to franchisors as they consider establishing operations in various countries?" sought information on the legal, cultural, social, and ethical factors that are key to operating in the host country, as well as on product or service opportunities considered attractive there.

Results

What is the extent of development and growth of franchising internationally? At least 24 nations (including the U.S.) have formed franchise associations. This suggests that franchising is sufficiently developed in these countries to warrant a trade association. Despite this, our results indicate that there are sizable differences in the level of franchise development and market penetration by country (see Exhibit 1). Hong Kong, which has potential for rapid growth by extending to the Chinese mainland,

is currently in the early stages of development, with just 31 franchisors and 1,000 franchised units. This is contrasted with Canada, which has about 1,100 franchisors and 25,000 franchised units, and Japan with 703 franchisors and 131,506 units. The median number of franchisors per country was 217, and the majority of the respondents had between 9,000 and 27,000 units operating. Local franchise associations appear to be achieving reasonable membership participation rates, averaging 41 percent of franchisors; about 25 percent of their members are headquartered in foreign countries.

EXHIBIT 1   Franchising Growth and Development: Units and Sales

Region/Country	Association Members % Foreign Membership	Total Franchisors	Franchise Units	Franchise Sales (000,000) % Increase (92–93)
Americas				
Argentina	30 (40%)	70	3,000	N/A
Canada	—	1,100 est.	25,052	C$16,688 12.4%
Mexico	— (40%)	160	9,174	$3,000
Europe				
Austria	95	200	3,000	AS 10,000
France	100 (4%)	500	27,000	$33,600 10%
Hungary	50 (50%)	150–200	3,500	N/A
Italy	40 (10%)	300	17,000	EC 7,000 −10%
Netherlands	—	331	12,640	ECU 6.5
Sweden	38 (2.5%)	200	9,000	SK 47,000 0%
Switzerland	36	150	2,500	N/A 5%
United Kingdom	120	132	18,600	$8,100 10%
Asia				
Hong Kong	27 (56%)	31	1,000	N/A
Japan	N/A (0%)	703	131,506	Y 10,937,000 7.7%

Franchise sales per country surveyed average about $18.8 billion, with Austria reporting just $859 million while Japan had more than $86 billion. Sales growth between 1992 and 1993 was flat in Sweden and slightly negative in Italy, but positive growth was reported in all the other countries in our survey. The recent upturn in the global economy should further boost these sales increases in the near future.

What are the major international markets for franchised operations in terms of industries and nations? Fast food, food retailing, and nonfood retailing were most frequently reported as areas of rapid franchise growth (see Exhibit 2). Additionally, France and the Netherlands reported that the hotel industry was an important growth sector in their countries. These industries parallel those for which franchising has developed in the U.S.

According to Williams (1994), there are two forms of international franchising: (1) franchising by domestic firms abroad; and (2) franchising by foreign firms within a host country. Regarding domestic expansion abroad, five nations in our survey reported the U.S. as an international market into which their franchisors had expanded; four stated their franchisors had expanded into continental Europe; franchisors from two nations participated in the United Kingdom; and Brazil, Australia, and Asia had each been penetrated by franchisors from at least one other country in our survey. As franchisors develop, fine-tune, and become successful with their franchise systems in their home markets, they often look to internationalize their operations (particularly if the domestic market is small). Foreign franchisors operating in the 13 nations of our survey include U.S. franchisors, who were operating in 10 of the countries surveyed. Three of our respondents reported having French franchisors operating in their country, three reported British, and two reported having German franchisors. Also reported were Brazilian franchisors operating in Argentina, Canadian in Mexico, Norwegian in Sweden, Austrian in Switzerland, and both European and Asian in Japan.

Cultural and physical proximity are often two criteria for the selection of international markets (Johanson and Vahlne, 1977). This is particularly important for franchising because of the standardized business format it utilizes (Hopkins, 1993). Our data suggest that these were important factors in the choice of country markets. Regarding physical proximity, Canada and Mexico report the U.S. as its leading international market, and Mexico also lists Canada as a major market for its franchisors. The primary markets for European nations such as Austria, Sweden, and Switzerland are other European nations, while Hungary and Italy are primary markets for franchisors from other European countries. Japan lists other Asian nations as major markets for its franchisors. Cultural proximity as a criterion for selecting an overseas market is evidenced by the existence of both types of international franchising among nations reflecting the following cultures (as identified by Ronen and Shenkar, 1985): Anglo—Australia/New Zealand, Canada, U.K., and U.S.; Germanic—Austria, Germany, and Switzerland; Latin—Argentina, Brazil, France, and Italy; and Nordic—Sweden, Denmark, and Finland. Differing tastes, habits, and preferences were cited by several respondents as important cultural/social factors that international franchising firms would need to consider for adapting their products or services to their country. Franchisors appear to be basing their strategies on country-specific advantages of location and culture. These advantages have been aptly described by the Austrian Franchise Association, which notes that, "[factors of] . . . closeness concerning social, geographic and linguistic competence simplify the chance of an easier expansion toward neighborhood countries" (AFA, 1994, 4).

While proximity and cultural factors are important, what operational factors are considered by franchisors when they assess establishing operations in various countries? The final questions of our survey focused on operational considerations in the countries surveyed. Key legal, tax, cultural, ethical, and economic factors that were most important to our survey respondents are indicated in

---

EXHIBIT 2   International Markets: Industries and Regions

Region/Country	Growth Industries	International Markets	Foreign Franchisors
Americas			
Argentina	Fast food	U.S. (12)[a]	U.S.
	Retail clothing	Europe (30)	Italy
		Brazil (5)	Brazil
Canada	Nonfood retail,	U.S. (13,738)	U.S.
	Recreation/	U.K. (415)	
	entertainment	Australia/	
		New Zealand (712)	
Mexico	Dry cleaning	—	U.S.
	Real estate		Canada
			United Kingdom
Europe			
Austria	Retail	Germany	U.S.
	Restaurants	Central Europe	Germany
France	Services	U.S.	U.S.
	Hotels		
Hungary	Fast food	—	U.S.
	Retail		Germany
Italy	Fashion	—	France
			U.K.
Netherlands	Nonfood retail	—	—
	Retail food		
	Fast food		
	Restaurants		
	Hotels		
Sweden	Service	U.K. (10)	U.S.
	Fast food	Denmark (5)	France
		Finland (5)	Norway
Switzerland	Retail	Germany	France
	Services/restaurants	Austria	Germany
		France	Austria
		Italy	
United Kingdom	Services	Europe	U.S.
	Fast food		
Asia			
Hong Kong	Restaurants	U.S.	U.S.
	Retailing		U.K.
Japan	Convenience stores	Asia	U.S.
	Food service	U.S.	Europe
			Asia

[a] Number of units in each country or region.

Exhibit 3. Language differences were cited, as well as issues of trust and small local market size. The value-added tax and other corporate or property taxes were mentioned as important tax considerations by several nations. Additionally, the trade association in France indicated that potential franchisors should consider France's disclosure requirements while the Japanese Franchise Association indicated a need to consider Japan's antitrust law.

It is important to the franchise relationship that both the franchisor and franchisee discharge their responsibilities appropriately and treat each other fairly. Consequently, franchise associations such as those in Mexico and Argentina require their members to adhere to their codes of ethics. In fact, the British Franchise Association was formed in 1977 by a number of leading companies to ensure that U.K. franchising developed ethically. They followed a U.K. Code of Ethics until 1989, when

EXHIBIT 3   **Local Operational Considerations**

Region/Country	Legal and Tax	Cultural/Ethical	Economic
Americas			
Argentina	6–8% Franchise tax	Code of ethics	Low-cost product
Canada	Goods and Services tax	Dual language	Unique service
			Product with service
Mexico	Registration of Foreign investment	Tastes, habits, preferences	Low-cost product
	Government supports franchising	Code of ethics	Product with service
Europe			
Austria	No well-defined franchise law	EC Code of ethics	Market niches
France	Disclosure law	—	—
	European block exemption		
	VAT 18.1%		
Hungary	VAT	Small size, Tastes	Low-cost service
		European code	
Italy	—	Habits	Product with service
Netherlands	VAT	—	—
	Repatriation of profits allowable		
Sweden	None	Tastes	Unique product or service
		Participate in decision making	
Switzerland	No legal	Committed to contract	Unique product or service
	Few taxes	Honesty and positive attitude	Product with service
United Kingdom	—	EC Code of ethics	Low-cost product
			Unique service
Asia			
Hong Kong	None	Trustworthy franchisor (quality product and support)	Unique product or service
			Product with service
Japan	Antitrust	Japanese Association	Unique product
	Disclosure required	Code of ethics	
	Corporate tax		
	Property tax		

the Europeanwide Code of Ethics was agreed upon among National Franchise Associations in the European community.

Five nations in our survey indicated that a product combined with a service provided the best means for international franchisors to compete in their countries. Several countries indicated that differentiation of product or service or product and service would lead to success in their markets. Nations where disposable incomes are lower, like Argentina and Mexico, indicated that a low-cost product (or in Hungary, a low-cost service) would provide franchisors the best opportunity for success in their countries.

Summary and Implications

This is the first survey on the diffusion of international franchising conducted at the national level. As a result, the survey provides a global perspective to franchising activities beyond that offered by previous firm-level studies. What, then, is the extent of development and growth of international franchising? At least 24 nations (International Franchise Association, 1993) have a sufficiently developed franchising sector to warrant forming a trade association; over half of these countries are represented in this study. All of the countries with such franchising activity are upper- or middle-income countries (World Bank, 1994) where conditions supportive of franchising (such as urbanization, increased disposable income, and growth of a service sector) are increasing. The rate of development of franchising has been uneven; franchising has made the deepest penetration in the markets of Japan and Sweden, where there is one franchised unit for every 950 persons. The least penetration has occurred in Argentina and Mexico, with one unit for every 10,500 persons. In virtually all of these countries, strong future growth is predicted. The implication for franchisors is that the best opportunities for franchising are in the upper- and middle-income countries (the latter seem to have the least saturation), as well as in emerging markets with a substantial middle class. Further-

more, our data suggest that unique products and/or services have the best chance for success in upper-income countries, while low-cost products or services are in demand in middle-income countries.

What are the major markets for international expansion of franchising? The leading sectors of franchising growth in the nations surveyed appear to be the same as those that developed earlier in the U.S.: restaurants, retail, and hotels. This suggests that either these sectors are more suited to franchise strategies, or that first movers in these sectors have developed efficient routines (Huszagh, Huszagh, and McIntyre, 1992) which franchisors from other countries have learned and applied in their markets (Hoffman and Preble, 1993). Regarding country selection for expansion, franchisors appear to move to markets that are either physically or culturally proximate to their own (Johanson and Vahlne, 1977). Furthermore, our survey of nations also reveals that reciprocity might be a factor in country selection. If a foreign franchisor has success in another country's market, firms in the other country are likely to reciprocate and enter that domestic market. This seems to have occurred in 78 percent of the countries for which we have data on both forms of international expansion. The implications of these findings for franchising companies are that companies should target the countries having the greatest growth in their industry, and their initial international expansion should probably be in nations that are nearby or culturally similar. The latter market characteristic is important for minimizing the adaptations needed and, therefore, preserving the core concept of the franchise. Further, there is some evidence that franchises operating in culturally similar markets are more likely to succeed than those where the cultures are dissimilar (Hopkins, 1993).

Finally, our data reveal that operational considerations in various countries differ in terms of taxes and disclosure requirements. For example, France has a disclosure law but Austria does not (Austrian Franchise Association, 1994), and this is not expected to change in the near future. A growing number of countries report that their franchising sector supports codes of conduct and/or ethics. In Europe, the EC has adopted a common code, and even non-EC countries like Austria abide by it. Differences in tastes and habits are reported by most countries as considerations for foreign franchisors operating in their countries. The differences in operational factors in each country underscore the value of expanding using indigenous entrepreneurs as franchisees who can guide the franchise in meeting the necessary legal and tax requirements, and in making the adaptations necessary to ensure customer satisfaction.

The major implication of this study for future research is that there is a great need to study international franchising activities of non-U.S. firms, as more and more countries are expanding the use of this business form. Additional information on the following might be useful to firms considering international franchising: the motivations for international franchise expansion, factors important in country selection, and guides for adapting a standardized business format to meet local needs and tastes.

Conclusions

Substantial franchised activity is prevalent in all of the markets we surveyed and is projected to grow, frequently at double-digit yearly growth rates. Most countries have no special regulations to slow down the growth of franchised activities. Instead, franchise associations are in place that often work with the governmental sector and with banking institutions to promote the interests of franchisors and franchisees and to provide critical information linkages as well as ethical guidance. Numerous international franchisors have been successful in transferring their franchising systems to other markets with only minor adaptations to account for differing tastes, habits, or preferences.

The prospects for franchising on a global basis seem great. Franchising is being increasingly understood as a useful formula for business growth and success. It simultaneously harnesses the energies of individual entrepreneurs, takes advantage of local knowledge and expertise, spreads financial risk among all members of the franchise network, and relies on a proven successful package and set of procedures at each new location. Developed countries use franchising to satisfy the ever-increasing demands of affluent, time-pressured consumers who desire specialized products and services. In emerging economies, franchising can help build a nation's economic base and offer a method of privatization. Existing franchisors act as prototypes for new entrants who subsequently perfect their systems and, as quickly as is feasible, roll out their packages into international markets. The recent improvement in the economic, political, and market environments of numerous countries and regions will only strengthen franchising's ability to play a major role in the global economy of the 21st century.

References

Austrian Franchising Association AFA (1994), "Franchising in Austria," Vienna: Austrian Franchising Association.

Arthur Andersen & Co. (1992), *Franchising in the Economy, 1989–1992.* Washington, D.C.: International Franchise Association Education Foundation, Inc.

Ayling, D. (1988), "Franchising in the U.K.," *Quarterly Review of Marketing* 13 (Summer), 19–24.

Chan, Peng S., and Robert T. Justis (1990), "Franchise Management in East Asia," *Academy of Management Executive* 4 (May), 75–85.

_____ (1992), "Franchising in the E.C.: 1992 and Beyond," *Journal of Small Business Management* 30 (January), 83–88.

Hoffman, Richard C., and John F. Preble (1991), "Franchising: Selecting a Strategy for Rapid Growth," *Long Range Planning* 24 (August), 74–85.

_____ (1993), "Franchising into the Twenty-First Century," *Business Horizons* 36 (November/December), 35–43.

Hopkins, David M. (1993), "International Franchising: Standardization vs. Adaptation to Cultural

Differences," paper presented at the Academy of International Business, Hawaii, October.

Huszagh, Sandra M., F. W. Huszagh, and F. S. McIntyre (1992), "International Franchising in the Context of Competitive Strategy and the Theory of the Firm," *International Marketing Review* 9 (5), 5–18.

International Franchising Association—IFA (1993), "Franchising Around the World," *Franchising World 25* (3) (May–June), 15–18.

Johanson, J., and J. Vahlne (1977), "The Internationalization Process of the Firm: A Model of Knowledge Development and Increasing Foreign Commitments," *Journal of International Business Studies* 8 (Spring), 23–32.

Preble, John F. (1992), "Global Expansion: The Case of U.S. Fast-Food Franchisors," *Journal of Global Marketing* 6 (1/2), 185–205.

Ronen, Simcha, and Oded Shenkar (1985), "Clustering Countries on Attitudinal Dimensions: A Review and Synthesis," *Academy of Management Review* 10 (3), 435–54.

Walker, Bruce J. (1989), *A Comparison of International vs. Domestic Expansion by U.S. Franchised Systems.* Washington, D.C.: International Franchising Association.

Williams, Rhys G. (1994), "The Development of Franchising in Germany," *International Journal of Management* 11 (1), 609–19.

World Bank (1994), *World Tables 1994.* Baltimore, MD.: Johns Hopkins University Press.

V Ethical Issues

The first article in this section provides an excellent overview of the ethical issues American managers face in the global marketplace. It is authored by one of the leading thinkers working in this area. He provides clear directions for managing the most controversial problems of ethics that seem to most often confront marketers (rather than managers in other functional areas) in international companies. He convincingly argues that company policies and managerial attitudes should be established that transcend national boundaries.

The authors of the second paper provide a fascinating account of the similarities and differences in ethical systems in the United States and Russia. They provide a series of recommendations for American companies that are operating in the dynamic Russian business system where laws, regulations, and their enforcement all seem to change on a daily basis.

No book on international marketing would be complete without some mention of the infant formula controversy of the 1970s. It is the classic case about the impact of multinational companies on low-income countries' economies and peoples. The case raises one of the most daunting ethical problems faced and then mismanaged by international marketers during the last 25 years. The article includes a chronology of events regarding the international marketing of infant formula, as well as an analysis of effects of advertising and promotion on the consumption of the product in 79 less-developed countries.

VALUES IN TENSION: ETHICS AWAY FROM HOME

Thomas Donaldson

When we leave home and cross our nation's boundaries, moral clarity often blurs. Without a backdrop of shared attitudes, and without familiar laws and judicial procedures that define standards of ethical conduct, certainty is elusive. Should a company invest in a foreign country where civil and political rights are violated? Should a company go along with a host country's discriminatory employment practices? If companies in developed countries shift facilities to developing nations that lack strict environmental and health regulations, or if those companies choose to fill management and other top-level positions in a host nation with people from the home country, whose standards should prevail?

Even the best-informed, best-intentioned executives must rethink their assumptions about business practice in foreign settings. What works in a company's home country can fail in a country with different standards of ethical conduct. Such difficulties are unavoidable for businesspeople who live and work abroad.

But how can managers resolve the problems? What are the principles that can help them work through the maze of cultural differences and establish codes of conduct for globally ethical business practice? How can companies answer the toughest

question in global business ethics: What happens when a host country's ethical standards seem lower than the home country's?

Competing Answers

One answer is as old as philosophical discourse. According to cultural relativism, no culture's ethics are better than any other's; therefore there are no international rights and wrongs. If the people of Indonesia tolerate the bribery of their public officials, so what? Their attitude is no better or worse than that of people in Denmark or Singapore who refuse to offer or accept bribes. Likewise, if Belgians fail to find insider trading morally repugnant, who cares? Not enforcing insider-trading laws is no more or less ethical than enforcing such laws.

The cultural relativist's creed—When in Rome, do as the Romans do—is tempting, especially when failing to do as the locals do means forfeiting business opportunities. The inadequacy of cultural relativism, however, becomes apparent when the practices in question are more damaging than petty bribery or insider trading.

In the late 1980s, some European tanneries and pharmaceutical companies were looking for cheap waste-dumping sites. They approached virtually every country on Africa's west coast from Morocco

From *Harvard Business Review,* September–October 1996, pp. 48–62.

to the Congo. Nigeria agreed to take highly toxic polychlorinated biphenyls. Unprotected local workers, wearing thongs and shorts, unloaded barrels of PCBs and placed them near a residential area. Neither the residents nor the workers knew that the barrels continued toxic waste.

We may denounce governments that permit such abuses, but many countries are unable to police transnational corporations adequately even if they want to. And in many countries, the combination of ineffective enforcement and inadequate regulations leads to behavior by unscrupulous companies that is clearly wrong. A few years ago, for example, a group of investors became interested in restoring the SS *United States,* once a luxurious ocean liner. Before the actual restoration could begin, the ship had to be stripped of its asbestos lining. A bid from a U.S. company, based on U.S. standards for asbestos removal, priced the job at more than $100 million. A company in the

Ukranian city of Sevastopol offered to do the work for less than $2 million. In October 1993, the ship was towed to Sevastopol.

A cultural relativist would have no problem with that outcome, but I do. A country has the right to establish its own health and safety regulations, but in the case described above, the standards and the terms of the contract could not possibly have protected workers in Sevastopol from known health risks. Even if the contract met Ukranian standards, ethical businesspeople must object. Cultural relativism is morally blind. There are fundamental values that cross cultures, and companies must uphold them. (For an economic argument against cultural relativism, see the Box "The Culture and Ethics of Software Piracy.")

At the other end of the spectrum from cultural relativism is ethical imperialism, which directs people to do everywhere exactly as they do at home. Again, an understandably appealing ap-

---

The Culture and Ethics of Software Piracy

Before jumping on the cultural relativism bandwagon, stop and consider the potential economic consequences of a when-in-Rome attitude toward business ethics. Take a look at the current statistics on software piracy: In the United States, pirated software is estimated to be 35% of the total software market, and industry losses are estimated at $2.3 billion per year. The piracy rate is 57% in Germany and 80% in Italy and Japan; the rates in most Asian countries are estimated to be nearly 100%.

There are similar laws against software piracy in those countries. What, then, accounts for the differences? Although a country's level of economic development plays a large part, culture, including ethical attitudes, may be a more crucial factor. The 1995 annual report of the Software Publishers Association connects software piracy directly to culture and attitude. It describes Italy and Hong Kong as having "'first world' per capita incomes, along with 'third world' rates of piracy." When asked whether one should use software without paying for it, most people, including people in Italy and Hong Kong, say

no. But people in some countries regard the practice as *less* unethical than people in other countries do. Confucian culture, for example, stresses that individuals should share what they create with society. That may be, in part, what prompts the Chinese and other Asians to view the concept of intellectual property as a means for the West to monopolize its technological superiority.

What happens if ethical attitudes around the world permit large-scale software piracy? Software companies won't want to invest as much in developing new products, because they cannot expect any return on their investment in certain parts of the world. When ethics fail to support technological creativity, there are consequences that go beyond statistics—jobs are lost and livelihoods jeopardized.

Companies must do more than lobby foreign governments for tougher enforcement of piracy laws. They must cooperate with other companies and with local organizations to help citizens understand the consequences of piracy and to encourage the evolution of a different ethic toward the practice.

proach but one that is clearly inadequate. Consider the large U.S. computer-products company that in 1993 introduced a course on sexual harassment in its Saudi Arabian facility. Under the banner of global consistency, instructors used the same approach to train Saudi Arabian managers that they had used with U.S. managers: the participants were asked to discuss a case in which a manager makes sexually explicit remarks to a new female employee over drinks in a bar. The instructors failed to consider how the exercise would work in a culture with strict conventions governing relationships between men and women. As a result, the training sessions were ludicrous. They baffled and offended the Saudi participants, and the message to avoid coercion and sexual discrimination was lost.

The theory behind ethical imperialism is absolutism, which is based on three problematic principles. Absolutists believe that there is a single list of truths, that they can be expressed only with one set of concepts, and that they call for exactly the same behavior around the world.

The first claim clashes with many people's belief that different cultural traditions must be respected. In some cultures, loyalty to a community—family, organization, or society—is the foundation of all ethical behavior. The Japanese, for example, define business ethics in terms of loyalty to their companies, their business networks, and their nation. Americans place a higher value on liberty than on loyalty; the U.S. tradition of rights emphasizes equality, fairness, and individual freedom. It is hard to conclude that truth lies on one side or the other, but an absolutist would have us select just one.

The second problem with absolutism is the presumption that people must express moral truth using only one set of concepts. For instance, some absolutists insist that the language of basic rights provides the framework for any discussion of ethics. That means, though, that entire cultural traditions must be ignored. The notion of a right evolved with the rise of democracy in post-Renaissance Europe and the United States, but the term is not found in either Confucian or Buddhist traditions. We all learn ethics in the context of our

particular cultures, and the power in the principles is deeply tied to the way in which they are expressed. Internationally accepted lists of moral principles, such as the United Nations' Universal Declaration of Human Rights, draw on many cultural and religious traditions. As philosopher Michael Walzer has noted, "There is no Esperanto of global ethics."

The third problem with absolutism is the belief in a global standard of ethical behavior. Context must shape ethical practice. Very low wages, for example, may be considered unethical in rich, advanced countries, but developing nations may be acting ethically if they encourage investment and improve living standards by accepting low wages. Likewise, when people are malnourished or starving, a government may be wise to use more fertilizer in order to improve crop yields, even though that means settling for relatively high levels of thermal water pollution.

When cultures have different standards of ethical behavior—and different ways of handling unethical behavior—a company that takes an absolutist approach may find itself making a disastrous mistake. When a manager at a large U.S. specialty-products company in China caught an employee stealing, she followed the company's practice and turned the employee over to the provincial authorities, who executed him. Managers cannot operate in another culture without being aware of that culture's attitudes toward ethics.

If companies can neither adopt a host country's ethics nor extend the home country's standards, what is the answer? Even the traditional litmus test—What would people think of your actions if they were written up on the front page of the newspaper?—is an unreliable guide, for there is no international consensus on standards of business conduct.

Balancing the Extremes: Three Guiding Principles

Companies must help managers distinguish between practices that are merely different and those that are wrong. For relativists, nothing is sacred and nothing is wrong. For absolutists, many things that are different are wrong. Neither extreme illuminates the real world of business decision making. The answer lies somewhere in between.

When it comes to shaping ethical behavior, companies must be guided by three principles.

- Respect for core human values, which determine the absolute moral threshold for all business activities.
- Respect for local traditions.
- The belief that context matters when deciding what is right and what is wrong.

Consider those principles in action. In Japan, people doing business together often exchange gifts—sometimes expensive ones—in keeping with long-standing Japanese tradition. When U.S. and European companies started doing a lot of business in Japan, many Western businesspeople thought that the practice of gift giving might be wrong rather than simply different. To them, accepting a gift felt like accepting a bribe. As Western companies have become more familiar with Japanese traditions, however, most have come to tolerate the practice and to set different limits on gift giving in Japan than they do elsewhere.

Respecting differences is a crucial ethical practice. Research shows that management ethics differ among cultures; respecting those differences means recognizing that some cultures have obvious weaknesses—as well as hidden strengths. Managers in Hong Kong, for example, have a higher tolerance for some forms of bribery than their Western counterparts, but they have a much lower tolerance for the failure to acknowledge a subordinate's work. In some parts of the Far East, stealing credit from a subordinate is nearly an unpardonable sin.

People often equate respect for local traditions with cultural relativism. That is incorrect. Some practices are clearly wrong. Union Carbide's tragic experience in Bhopal, India, provides one example. The company's executives seriously underestimated how much on-site management involvement was needed at the Bhopal plant to compensate for the country's poor infrastructure

and regulatory capabilities. In the aftermath of the disastrous gas leak, the lesson is clear: companies using sophisticated technology in a developing country must evaluate that country's ability to oversee its safe use. Since the incident at Bhopal, Union Carbide has become a leader in advising companies on using hazardous technologies safely in developing countries.

Some activities are wrong no matter where they take place. But some practices that are unethical in one setting may be acceptable in another. For instance, the chemical EDB, a soil fungicide, is banned for use in the United States. In hot climates, however, it quickly becomes harmless through exposure to intense solar radiation and high soil temperatures. As long as the chemical is monitored, companies may be able to use EDB ethically in certain parts of the world.

Defining the Ethical Threshold: Core Values

Few ethical questions are easy for managers to answer. But there are some hard truths that must guide managers' actions, a set of what I call *core human values,* which define minimum ethical standards for all companies.[1] The right to good health and the right to economic advancement and an improved standard of living are two core human values. Another is what Westerners call the Golden Rule, which is recognizable in every major religious and ethical tradition around the world. In Book 15 of his *Analects,* for instance, Confucius counsels people to maintain reciprocity, or not to do to others what they do not want done to themselves.

Although no single list would satisfy every scholar, I believe it is possible to articulate three core values that incorporate the work of scores of theologians and philosophers around the world. To be broadly relevant, these values must include elements found in both Western and non-Western cultural and religious traditions. Consider the examples of values in the Box "What Do These Values Have in Common?"

At first glance, the values expressed in the two lists seem quite different. Nonetheless, in the spirit

What Do These Values Have in Common?

Non-Western	**Western**
Kyosei (Japanese): Living and working together for the common good.	Individual liberty
Dharma (Hindu): The fulfillment of inherited duty.	Egalitarianism
Santutthi (Buddhist): The importance of limited desires.	Political participation
Zakat (Muslim): The duty to give alms to the Muslim poor.	Human rights

of what philosopher John Rawls calls *overlapping consensus,* one can see that the seemingly divergent values converge at key points. Despite important differences between Western and non-Western cultural and religious traditions, both express shared attitudes about what it means to be human. First, individuals must not treat others simply as tools; in other words, they must recognize a person's value as a human being. Next, individuals and communities must treat people in ways that respect people's basic rights. Finally, members of a community must work together to support and improve the institutions on which the community depends. I call those three values *respect for human dignity, respect for basic rights,* and *good citizenship.*

Those values must be the starting point for all companies as they formulate and evaluate standards of ethical conduct at home and abroad. But they are only a starting point. Companies need much more specific guidelines, and the first step to developing those is to translate the core human values into core values for business. What does it mean, for example, for a company to respect human dignity? How can a company be a good citizen?

I believe that companies can respect human dignity by creating and sustaining a corporate culture in which employees, customers, and suppliers are treated not as means to an end but as people

whose intrinsic value must be acknowledged, and by producing safe products and services in a safe workplace. Companies can respect basic rights by acting in ways that support and protect the individual rights of employees, customers, and surrounding communities, and by avoiding relationships that violate human beings' rights to health, education, safety, and an adequate standard of living. And companies can be good citizens by supporting essential social institutions, such as the economic system and the education system, and by working with host governments and other organizations to protect the environment.

The core values establish a moral compass for business practice. They can help companies identify practices that are acceptable and those that are intolerable—even if the practices are compatible with a host country's norms and laws. Dumping pollutants near people's homes and accepting inadequate standards for handling hazardous materials are two examples of actions that violate core values.

Similarly, if employing children prevents them from receiving a basic education, the practice is intolerable. Lying about product specifications in the act of selling may not affect human lives directly, but it too is intolerable because it violates the trust that is needed to sustain a corporate culture in which customers are respected.

Sometimes it is not a company's actions but

those of a supplier or customer that pose problems. Take the case of the Tan family, a large supplier for Levi Strauss. The Tans were allegedly forcing 1,200 Chinese and Filipino women to work 74 hours per week in guarded compounds on the Mariana Islands. In 1992, after repeated warnings to the Tans, Levi Strauss broke off business relations with them.

Creating an Ethical Corporate Culture

The core values for business that I have enumerated can help companies begin to exercise ethical judgment and think about how to operate ethically in foreign cultures, but they are not specific enough to guide managers through actual ethical dilemmas. Levi Strauss relied on a written code of conduct when figuring out how to deal with the Tan family. The company's Global Sourcing and Operating Guidelines, formerly called the Business Partner Terms of Engagement, state that Levi Strauss will "seek to identify and utilize business partners who aspire as individuals and in the conduct of all their businesses to a set of ethical standards not incompatible with our own." Whenever intolerable business situations arise, managers should be guided by precise statements that spell out the behavior and operating practices that the company demands.

Ninety percent of all *Fortune* 500 companies have codes of conduct, and 70 percent have statements of vision and values. In Europe and the Far East, the percentages are lower but are increasing rapidly. Does that mean that most companies have what they need? Hardly. Even though most large U.S. companies have both statements of values and codes of conduct, many might be better off if they didn't. Too many companies don't do anything with the documents; they simply paste them on the wall to impress employees, customers, suppliers, and the public. As a result, the senior managers who drafted the statements lose credibility by proclaiming values and not living up to them. Companies such as Johnson & Johnson, Levi Strauss, Motorola, Texas Instruments, and Lockheed Martin, however, do a great deal to make the words meaningful. Johnson & Johnson, for exam-

ple, has become well known for its Credo Challenge sessions, in which managers discuss ethics in the context of their current business problems and are invited to criticize the company's credo and make suggestions for changes. The participants' ideas are passed on to the company's senior managers. Lockheed Martin has created an innovative site on the World Wide Web and on its local network that gives employees, customers, and suppliers access to the company's ethical code and the chance to voice complaints.

Codes of conduct must provide clear direction about ethical behavior when the temptation to behave unethically is strongest. The pronouncement in a code of conduct that bribery is unacceptable is useless unless accompanied by guidelines for gift

giving, payments to get goods through customs, and "requests" from intermediaries who are hired to ask for bribes.

Motorola's values are stated very simply as "How we will always act: [with] constant respect for people [and] uncompromising integrity." The company's code of conduct, however, is explicit about actual business practice. With respect to bribery, for example, the code states that the "funds and assets of Motorola shall not be used, directly or indirectly, for illegal payments of any kind." It is unambiguous about what sort of payment is illegal: "the payment of a bribe to a public official or the kickback of funds to an employee or a customer . . ." The code goes on to prescribe specific procedures for handling commissions to intermediaries, issuing sales invoices, and disclosing confidential information in a sales transaction—all situations in which employees might have an opportunity to accept or offer bribes.

Codes of conduct must be explicit to be useful, but they must also leave room for a manager to use his or her judgment in situations requiring cultural sensitivity. Host-country employees shouldn't be forced to adopt all home-country values and renounce their own. Again, Motorola's code is exemplary. First, it gives clear direction: "Employees of Motorola will respect the laws, customs, and traditions of each country in which they operate, but will, at the same time, engage in no course of conduct which, even if legal, customary, and accepted in any such country, could be deemed to be in violation of the accepted business ethics of Motorola or the laws of the United States relating to business ethics." After laying down such absolutes, Motorola's code then makes clear when individual judgment will be necessary. For example, employees may sometimes accept certain kinds of small gifts "in rare circumstances, where the refusal to accept a gift" would injure Motorola's "legitimate business interests." Under certain circumstances, such gifts "may be accepted so long as the gift inures to the benefit of Motorola" and not "to the benefit of the Motorola employee."

Striking the appropriate balance between pro-

viding clear direction and leaving room for individual judgment makes crafting corporate values statements and ethics codes one of the hardest tasks that executives confront. The words are only a start. A company's leaders need to refer often to their organization's credo and code and must themselves be credible, committed, and consistent. If senior managers act as though ethics don't matter, the rest of the company's employees won't think they do, either.

Conflicts of Development and Conflicts of Tradition

Managers living and working abroad who are not prepared to grapple with moral ambiguity and tension should pack their bags and come home. The view that all business practices can be categorized as either ethical or unethical is too simple. As Einstein is reported to have said, "Things should be as simple as possible—but no simpler." Many business practices that are considered unethical in one setting may be ethical in another. Such activities are neither black nor white but exist in what Thomas Dunfee and I have called *moral free space.*[2] In this gray zone, there are no tight prescriptions for a company's behavior. Managers must chart their own courses—as long as they do not violate core human values.

Consider the following example. Some successful Indian companies offer employees the opportunity for one of their children to gain a job with the company once the child has completed a certain level in school. The companies honor this commitment even when other applicants are more qualified than an employee's child. The perk is extremely valuable in a country where jobs are hard to find, and it reflects the Indian culture's belief that the West has gone too far in allowing economic opportunities to break up families. Not surprisingly, the perk is among the most cherished by employees, but in most Western countries, it would be branded unacceptable nepotism. In the United States, for example, the ethical principle of equal opportunity holds that jobs should go to the applicants with the best qualifications. If a U.S. company made such promises to its employees, it would violate regulations established by the Equal Employment Opportunity Commission. Given this difference in ethical attitudes, how should U.S. managers react to Indian nepotism? Should they condemn the Indian companies, refusing to accept them as partners or suppliers until they agree to clean up their act?

Despite the obvious tension between nepotism and principles of equal opportunity, I cannot condemn the practice for Indians. In a country, such as India, that emphasizes clan and family relationships and has catastrophic levels of unemployment, the practice must be viewed in moral free space. The decision to allow a special perk for employees and their children is not necessarily wrong—at least for members of that country.

How can managers discover the limits of moral free space? That is, how can they learn to distinguish a value in tension with their own from one that is intolerable? Helping managers develop good ethical judgment requires companies to be clear about their core values and codes of conduct. But even the most explicit set of guidelines cannot always provide answers. That is especially true in the thorniest ethical dilemmas, in which the host country's ethical standards not only are different but also seem lower than the home country's. Managers must recognize that when countries have different ethical standards, there are two types of conflict that commonly arise. Each type requires its own line of reasoning.

In the first type of conflict, which I call a *conflict of relative development*, ethical standards conflict because of the countries' different levels of economic development. As mentioned before, developing countries may accept wage rates that seem inhumane to more advanced countries in order to attract investment. As economic conditions in a developing country improve, the incidence of that sort of conflict usually decreases. The second type of conflict is a *conflict of cultural tradition*. For example, Saudi Arabia, unlike most other countries, does not allow women to serve as corporate managers. Instead, women may work in only a few professions, such as education and health care. The prohibition stems from strongly held religious and cultural beliefs; any increase in the country's level of economic development, which is already quite high, is not likely to change the rules.

To resolve a conflict of relative development, a manager must ask the following question: Would the practice be acceptable at home if my country were in a similar stage of economic development? Consider the difference between wage and safety standards in the United States and in Angola, where citizens accept lower standards on both counts. If a U.S. oil company is hiring Angolans to work on an offshore Angolan oil rig, can the company pay them lower wages than it pays U.S. workers in the Gulf of Mexico? Reasonable people have to answer yes if the alternative for Angola is the loss of both the foreign investment and the jobs.

Consider, too, differences in regulatory environments. In the 1980s, the government of India fought hard to be able to import Ciba-Geigy's Entero Vioform, a drug known to be enormously effective in fighting dysentery but one that had been banned in the United States because some users experienced side effects. Although dysentery was not a big problem in the United States, in India, poor public sanitation was contributing to epidemic levels of the disease. Was it unethical to make the drug available in India after it had been banned in the United States? On the contrary, rational people should consider it unethical not to do so. Apply our test: Would the United States, at an earlier stage of development, have used this drug despite its side effects? The answer is clearly yes.

But there are many instances when the answer to similar questions is no. Sometimes a host country's standards are inadequate at any level of economic development. If a country's pollution standards are so low that working on an oil rig would considerably increase a person's risk of developing cancer, foreign oil companies must refuse to do business there. Likewise, if the dangerous side effects of a drug treatment outweigh its benefits, managers should not accept health standards that ignore the risks.

When relative economic conditions do not drive tensions, there is a more objective test for resolving ethical problems. Managers should deem a practice permissible only if they can answer no to both of the following questions: Is it possible to conduct business successfully in the host country without undertaking the practice? and Is the practice a violation of a core human value? Japanese gift giving is a perfect example of a conflict of cultural tradition. Most experienced businesspeople, Japanese and non-Japanese alike, would agree that

doing business in Japan would be virtually impossible without adopting the practice. Does gift giving violate a core human value? I cannot identify one that it violates. As a result, gift giving may be permissible for foreign companies in Japan even if it conflicts with ethical attitudes at home. In fact, that conclusion is widely accepted, even by companies such as Texas Instruments and IBM, which are outspoken against bribery.

Does it follow that all nonmonetary gifts are acceptable or that bribes are generally acceptable in countries where they are common? Not at all. (See the Box "The Problem with Bribery.") What makes the routine practice of gift giving accept-

---

The Problem with Bribery

Bribery is widespread and insidious. Managers in transnational companies routinely confront bribery even though most countries have laws against it. The fact is that officials in many developing countries wink at the practice, and the salaries of local bureaucrats are so low that many consider bribes a form of remuneration. The U.S. Foreign Corrupt Practices Act defines allowable limits on petty bribery in the form of routine payments required to move goods through customs. But demands for bribes often exceed those limits, and there is seldom a good solution.

Bribery disrupts distribution channels when goods languish on docks until local handlers are paid off, and it destroys incentives to compete on quality and cost when purchasing decisions are based on who pays what under the table. Refusing to acquiesce is often tantamount to giving business to unscrupulous companies.

I believe that even routine bribery is intolerable. Bribery undermines market efficiency and predictability, thus ultimately denying people their right to a minimal standard of living. Some degree of ethical commitment—some sense that everyone will play by the rules—is necessary for a sound economy. Without an ability to predict outcomes, who would

be willing to invest?

There was a U.S. company whose shipping crates were regularly pilfered by handlers on the docks of Rio de Janeiro. The handlers would take about 10% of the contents of the crates, but the company was never sure which 10% it would be. In a partial solution, the company began sending two crates—the first with 90% of the merchandise, the second with 10%. The handlers learned to take the second crate and leave the first untouched. From the company's perspective, at least knowing which goods it would lose was an improvement.

Bribery does more than destroy predictability; it undermines essential social and economic systems. That truth is not lost on businesspeople in countries where the practice is woven into the social fabric. CEOs in India admit that their companies engage constantly in bribery, and they say that they have considerable disgust for the practice. They blame government policies in part, but Indian executives also know that their country's business practices perpetuate corrupt behavior. Anyone walking the streets of Calcutta, where it is clear that even a dramatic redistribution of wealth would still leave most of India's inhabitants in dire poverty, comes face-to-face with the devastating effects of corruption.

able in Japan is the limits in its scope and intention. When gift giving moves outside those limits, it soon collides with core human values. For example, when Carl Kotchian, president of Lockheed in the 1970s, carried suitcases full of cash to Japanese politicians, he went beyond the norms established by Japanese tradition. That incident galvanized opinion in the United States Congress and helped lead to passage of the Foreign Corrupt Practices Act. Likewise, Roh Tae Woo went beyond the norms established by Korean cultural tradition when he accepted $635.4 million in bribes as president of the Republic of Korea between 1988 and 1993.

Guidelines for Ethical Leadership

Learning to spot intolerable practices and to exercise good judgment when ethical conflicts arise requires practice. Creating a company culture that rewards ethical behavior is essential. The following guidelines for developing a global ethical perspective among managers can help.

Treat corporate values and formal standards of conduct as absolutes. Whatever ethical standards a company chooses, it cannot waver on its principles either at home or abroad. Consider what has become part of company lore at Motorola. Around 1950, a senior executive was negotiating with officials of a South American government on a $10 million sale that would have increased the company's annual net profits by nearly 25 percent. As the negotiations neared completion, however, the executive walked away from the deal because the officials were asking for $1 million for "fees." CEO Robert Galvin not only supported the executive's decision but also made it clear that Motorola would neither accept the sale on any terms nor do business with those government officials again. Retold over the decades, this story demonstrating Galvin's resolve has helped cement a culture of ethics for thousands of employees at Motorola.

Design and implement conditions of engagement for suppliers and customers. Will your company do business with any customer or supplier? What if a customer or supplier uses child labor? What if it has strong links with organized crime? What if it pressures your company to break a host country's laws? Such issues are best not left for spur-of-the-moment decisions. Some companies have realized that. Sears, for instance, has developed a policy of not contracting production to companies that use prison labor or infringe on workers' rights to health and safety. And BankAmerica has specified as a condition for many of its loans to developing countries that environmental standards and human rights must be observed.

Allow foreign business units to help formulate ethical standards and interpret ethical issues. The French pharmaceutical company Rhône-Poulenc Rorer has allowed foreign subsidiaries to augment lists of corporate ethical principles with their own suggestions. Texas Instruments has paid special attention to issues of international business ethics by creating the Global Business Practices Council, which is made up of managers from countries in which the company operates. With the overarching intent to create a "global ethics strategy, locally deployed," the council's mandate is to provide ethics education and create local processes that will help managers in the company's foreign business units resolve ethical conflicts.

In host countries, support efforts to decrease institutional corruption. Individual managers will not be able to wipe out corruption in a host country, no matter how many bribes they turn down. When a host country's tax system, import and export procedures, and procurement practices favor unethical players, companies must take action.

Many companies have begun to participate in reforming host-country institutions. General Electric, for example, has taken a strong stand in India, using the media to make repeated condemnations of bribery in business and government. General Electric and others have found, however, that a single company usually cannot drive out entrenched corruption. Transparency International, an organization based in Germany, has been effective in helping coalitions of companies, government officials, and others work to reform bribery-ridden bureaucracies in Russia, Bangladesh, and elsewhere.

Exercise moral imagination. Using moral imagination means resolving tensions responsibly and creatively. Coca-Cola, for instance, has consistently turned down requests for bribes from Egyptian officials but has managed to gain political support and public trust by sponsoring a project to plant fruit trees. And take the example of Levi Strauss, which discovered in the early 1990s that two of its suppliers in Bangladesh were employing children under the age of 14—a practice that violated the company's principles but was tolerated in Bangladesh. Forcing the suppliers to fire the children would not have ensured that the children received an education, and it would have caused serious hardship for the families depending on the children's wages. In a creative arrangement, the suppliers agreed to pay the children's regular wages while they attended school and to offer each child a job at age 14. Levi Strauss, in turn, agreed to pay the children's tuition and provide books and uniforms. That arrangement allowed Levi Strauss

to uphold its principles and provide long-term benefits to its host country.

Many people think of values as soft; to some they are usually unspoken. A South Seas island society uses the word *mokita,* which means, "the truth that everybody knows but nobody speaks." However difficult they are to articulate, values affect how we all behave. In a global business environment, values in tension are the rule rather than the exception. Without a company's commitment, statements of values and codes of ethics end up as empty platitudes that provide managers with no foundation for behaving ethically. Employees need and deserve more, and responsible members of the global business community can set examples for others to follow. The dark consequences of incidents such as Union Carbide's disaster in Bhopal remind us how high the stakes can be.

References

1. In other writings, Thomas W. Dunfee and I have used the term *hypernorm* instead of *core human value.*
2. Thomas Donaldson and Thomas W. Dunfee, "Toward a Unified Conception of Business Ethics: Integrative Social Contracts Theory," *Academy of Management Review,* April 1994; and "Integrative Social Contracts Theory: A Communitarian Conception of Economic Ethics," *Economics and Philosophy,* spring 1995.

FINDING THE COMMON GROUND IN RUSSIAN AND AMERICAN BUSINESS ETHICS

Sheila M. Puffer and Daniel J. McCarthy

In a historic business event in the spring of 1994, the first Presidential Business Development Mission to Russia brought the CEOs of 29 major American firms to negotiate agreements with Russian partners. Among the companies concluding contracts were U.S. West, Westinghouse, McDermott International, and the pharmaceutical firms, Allen & Associates International, and Cytran, Inc.[1] This is a very promising development that holds potential for a new phase in business relations between the two countries. Yet, as managers from both countries know well, there are many obstacles to a successful future. While the many economic and political barriers have been well documented, the ethical issues, although perhaps less prominent, were also highlighted in a Department of Commerce report as a major obstacle to American firms doing business in Russia.[2]

Many in the Western world have heralded Russia's attempts to develop a market-based economy, but have been dismayed at the concurrent unethical and even criminal behavior among segments of Russian business. Among the many publicized problems are mafia connections, bribery, extortion, and even murder.[3] Clearly, such criminal behavior

is unacceptable to Americans and Russians alike. However, beyond these crimes are other less sensational activities which are nevertheless quite questionable from an American perspective. Some American firms doing business in Russia have expressed concern about these less egregious actions which they view as both undesirable and unethical. But much of this behavior might be viewed otherwise by Russians due to the different ethical premises that they hold, as well as the vastly different situational context in which each usually conducts its business activities.

Consider, for instance, the situation faced by the senior American involved in Ben & Jerry's Homemade, Inc.'s ice cream operations in the Karelia region of western Russia. When the senior Russian partner began to "borrow" company materials and equipment for use in his other businesses, the American was dismayed and viewed such behavior as unethical. The Russian manager, however, felt that this was a very reasonable way to utilize the equipment since he was an owner of both companies. This situation illustrates the different views that American and Russian managers have regarding ethical behavior in their businesses. What would you do as the American in this situation?

To help answer such questions, this article compares American and Russian concepts of ethics in

From *California Management Review,* Vol. 37, No. 2 (winter 1996), pp. 29–45.

business. Americans might be surprised to learn that some of their "ethical" practices are seen very differently by Russians. To help prevent such surprises and to prepare Americans to work effectively with Russians, we present a framework that compares ethical and unethical behavior in business as perceived in Russia and in the United States.

Why Is Ethical Behavior Important for the Development of Russian Business?

Attention to ethical behavior may seem premature given the many problems faced by Russian businesses in a highly uncertain environment. In addition to criminal activities, other problems have stemmed from the closed economy of the former USSR. Russian managers have little experience operating in a market economy, Russian businesses have produced notoriously poor-quality products, the former business infrastructure of a planned economy has yet to be replaced, and a legal framework for business has not yet emerged. Given these immediate and pressing concerns, ethics might not seem to be a high priority. But it is precisely these and similar problems that require a fundamental ethical system among Russians if their economy is to advance. If Americans are to participate in and profit from this advancement, they need to contribute to the process.

Russians expecting to do business with one another in some form of free-enterprise system must have a fundamental ethical underpinning to their business dealings. In the absence of a system of business law, clear government policies, established business relationships, and experience with a market economy, what other basis will serve as the common understanding between parties? Also, behavior that is compatible with international standards of business conduct is essential for Russians to engage in business with international parties.

How should the ethics of Russian business be evaluated? Surely less from the Western experience and more from the perspective of Russians trying to build a business culture that they refer to as "civilized business" or "civilized entrepreneurship."[4] This fundamental view of ethical behavior is seen by many thoughtful Russians as necessary to the development of business relationships in a country that has a limited history of entrepreneurship and free association among businesses. A notable exception, of course, has been the shadow economy or black market. For seventy years, managers in Russia have operated in a centrally planned economy and have had little leeway to make decisions requiring judgments about ethical behavior.

When Russians discuss business ethics, they refer to universal values of trust, honesty, and fairness, just as one might hear in the United States and most other societies.[5] Such fundamental values are seen as the only clear basis for business relationships since the Communist regime imposed double standards of ethics that were often at odds with Russians' historical personal ethical values. Specifically, Communist ideology encouraged the use of virtually any means to achieve the desired ends of a Communist society, a terrible exaggeration of what might be termed *utilitarian ethics*. This was true in business as in other facets of life. Recognizing such excesses, a growing cadre of business, academic, and government leaders have been encouraging the development of fundamental business ethics and have sponsored several conferences on the topic in the early 1990s.[6]

American Business Ethics Focused and Directed

Business ethics in the United States has long been an intense topic within business, government, and society in general. An exceedingly high level of ethical behavior is expected, and even demanded, by both government and the populace. This current situation is the result of over a century of development, and values have been systematically codified within the law. Three major factors that have influenced the American conception of business ethics are the Judeo-Christian heritage, belief in individualism, and access to opportunities based on abilities rather than social status.[7] One aspect of the Judeo-Christian heritage, with its emphasis on the Protestant work ethic, is that hard work and the accumulation of wealth were considered virtuous and indicative of a worthwhile life. Second, the belief in individualism as opposed to collectivism instilled the value of personal achievement and accountability. Third, immigrants to America, rejecting oppression in their homelands, sought a society in which their fate was determined by their abilities rather than only by their social status and personal relationships. This orientation resulted in Americans placing a high value on fair play and healthy competition.

All of these influences on the American conception of business ethics have been supported by a comprehensive code of laws stressing individual accountability as well as equal opportunity. The preoccupation with ethics, as well as the passage and strict enforcement of laws upholding ethical standards in the United States, is sometimes viewed by people in other countries as excessive, naive, and unrealistic according to their ethical standards. Europeans, for instance, have gone so far as to call on America to "lighten up."[8] If such politically, culturally, and economically similar societies can differ so much from the United States, shouldn't we expect Russians to view American ethical standards as rather unrealistic?

Russian Business Ethics Pulled in Many Directions

In contrast to the seemingly unequivocal and widely accepted system of ethics that has been reinforced and refined by the legal system in America throughout its history, Russia's situation is markedly different with far fewer certainties and continuing turbulence. Such contrasting situations fit those that led to the integrative social contracts theory of business ethics recently proposed by Donaldson and Dunfee. This theory embraces "the context-specific complexity of business situations," and "the differences between cultures with a traditional acceptance of corporate paternalism and ones with highly individualistic, nonpaternalistic beliefs."[9]

Russia's turbulent history has been characterized by oppressive political regimes that have created confusion about the role and importance of business in Russian society, as well as conflicting standards of ethical behavior. This history, coupled with the recent turmoil created by the move toward a market economy, has created ambiguity among businesspeople about what constitutes ethical behavior. Some unfortunate personal consequences of such ambivalence have been the growing number of businesspeople with psychiatric and addiction problems stemming from moral conflicts.[10]

The important and often conflicting influences contributing to this uncertainty and ambiguity surrounding standards of ethical business behavior include the high value placed on strong authority and collective behavior in traditional Russian culture, and Communist ideology, as well as the country's political and legal structure.

Russian culture, over the centuries, is replete with ruling elites and authority figures who tightly controlled society and suppressed personal freedom. Among these were leaders of the Russian Orthodox Church, tsars, landowners, and the Communist party elite. Regardless of who was in control of the country, the population was subjugated to the values and behaviors of the leaders. The resulting continuous lack of individual freedom, as well as the pervasiveness of social and economic control, strongly shaped Russian values. The Russian Orthodox Church imbued Russians with Christian values such as obeying the golden rule. However, unlike the Protestant Church's work ethic, the Russian Church did not value work as a religious virtue. People who engaged in business were thus often suspected of having selfish and, implicitly, unethical motives.

Instead, the Church emphasized deference and obedience to Church doctrine and religious authority figures, thus reinforcing obedience to authority rather than individual responsibility. Collective values were another fundamental element of religious doctrine, and people were encouraged to subjugate personal interests to the common good. The political environment under the tsars and the economic power of the landowners were grounded in the same autocratic and oppressive philosophies. In summary, the entire environment for centuries was one of central control, oppression, and the lack of individual freedom and opportunity. This climate suppressed personal initiative and achievement as a value in direct contrast to the American value system.

The situation changed little under Communist rule, whose ideology provided a second major influence on Russian ethics. Centralized authority, subjugation of the individual, political and economic oppression, and collectivist values predominated. The Communists, however, tried to instill a work ethic to serve Communist goals, but designed a reward system that recognized collective rather than individual achievements. Thus, individuals had little incentive to work hard or take personal responsibility for their actions. Even the collective rewards were not perceived as equitable to many people who became disillusioned with this, as well as other broken promises offering material and psychic gratification.

The Communist philosophy was distilled in 1962 into a 12-point moral code intended as a guide for ethical behavior for loyal Communists.[11] In some respects the code was similar to the 10 commandments of the Judeo-Christian tradition, but modified to reflect the atheistic Communist philosophy. But as in other areas of Communist ideology, the code failed in its implementation and few took it seriously. The *nomenklatura* (ruling Communist elite) violated it as they saw fit, justifying virtually any means, ethical or unethical, to achieve desired ends. This hypocrisy of the ruling elite created a harsh reality that encouraged people at all economic levels to break rules to survive within the rigid demands of the system. In business, an accepted common practice was to pad production figures to give the appearance of meeting the centrally prescribed plan in order to obtain rewards.

Another Communist goal was the elimination of status differences in society to provide more equal access to opportunities for people from all social levels. For the first time, people of peasant origin were encouraged to pursue higher education and professional and managerial job opportunities.

However, this and other such goals were subverted as the Communist party elite became more entrenched and reserved privileges and positions of influence for themselves. Such actions reinforced the fact that ability and accomplishment were not the determining factors for success. Rather, Communist party membership and loyalty provided the status that became necessary to achieve power and privilege within society. The Communists effectively emerged as the new ruling elite.

A third major influence on the development of Russian business ethics has been the country's political and legal structure and institutions. Much of the political environment under the tsars and Communists has been discussed above, the primary characteristics being centralized dictatorship, oppression of individual expression, and little freedom of opportunity for most of the population. The result was a passive and obedient population with little tolerance for individual accomplishment, business activities, or entrepreneurship. In the legal environment, laws and edicts were dictated by tsarist and Communist authorities with little opportunity for dispute, and trial by jury did not exist. Under Communism, there were so many meaningless, and often contradictory, laws and regulations governing business activity that managers had to become adept at circumventing them in order to meet the unrealistic goals assigned by central authorities.[12] This was a widely accepted practice and even central authorities looked the other way, since it was not considered a serious violation, but simply a pragmatic way of doing business. Nevertheless, flagrantly criminal behavior such as major theft of company property, as well as serious breaches of Communist ethics such as disloyalty to the Party, were severely and publicly punished.

The legalization of private enterprises in the late 1980s became a major source of widespread ethical confusion. Communist philosophy did not recognize the existence of private property or profits, yet both became legalized and even mandated by Soviet and Russian laws. Within the developing free enterprise system, many such laws were passed. They often contradicted one another, were frequently amended or rescinded, and were inconsistently enforced.

This chaotically evolving legal structure gave little direction to people engaged in business. Individuals had to define for themselves the proper conduct in business relationships. They came from different backgrounds and often held different values. Among those who entered into business were managers from state enterprises, former high-ranking Party officials, academics, students, and other professionals, as well as black marketeers. Some were guided by the values and accepted practices of the former Communist system, others by universal values or religious beliefs, and some by criminal and unscrupulous motives. Others, lacking experience in a market economy, simply were ignorant of what constituted ethical behavior in such radically new and uncertain circumstances.

In summary, there is far more uncertainty about what constitutes ethical business behavior in Russia than in the United States. Russia's unique culture, tumultuous history, totalitarian political regimes, and undeveloped system of business laws have led to the current state of ambiguity and ambivalence about business ethics. In contrast, the United States has developed strong traditions and values within society, many of which have been codified in business law.[13] In spite of these differences, both societies recognize the fundamental importance of universal values such as honesty, integrity, trust, and fairness in business relationships.

A Framework for Comparing Ethical Behavior

Although guidelines for ethical behavior are more clearly developed in the United States, most Russians also appreciate the importance of basing their business relationships on universal values. As shown in the four quadrants of Exhibit 1, some business activities are recognized as ethical by businesspeople in both countries (Quadrant I),

EXHIBIT 1   Russian and American Conceptions of Business Ethics

UNITED STATES

	Ethical	Unethical
Ethical	**I** • Keeping one's word • Maintaining trust • Fair competition • Rewards commensurate with performance	**III** • Personal favoritism *(blat)* and grease payments • Price fixing • Manipulating data • Ignoring senseless laws and regulations
Unethical	**IV** • Maximizing profits • Exorbitant salary differentials • Layoffs • Whistleblowing	**II** • Gangsterism, racketeering, and extortion • Black market • Price gouging • Refusing to pay debts

RUSSIA

while other activities are considered to be unethical in both (Quadrant II). Other behaviors, however, may be viewed as ethical by Russians, and yet may appear unethical to Americans (Quadrant III), as well as the opposite situation (Quadrant IV). In proposing this framework of ethical and unethical behaviors as they might be interpreted by businesspeople in both countries, we provide examples illustrating some areas of agreement and disagreement.

The use of this framework serves three objectives. The first objective is to assist business managers from the United States in interpreting the ethics of behaviors they will encounter in dealing with Russian managers. The second objective is to clarify that some behaviors that Americans consider to be ethical or good business practice are often perceived by Russians as unethical or inappropriate. And the third objective is to assist both American and Russian managers in working together toward the development of mutually acceptable ethical standards for doing business together in an international context.

Quadrant I: Ethical to Both.   Russians and Americans agree that it is imperative to keep one's word in a business agreement, and to maintain a trustful relationship. American managers understand from long experience in a competitive market that this fundamental guide to behavior is necessary to maintain relationships with suppliers, customers, employees, and others. Integrity is expected by all parties with whom a businessperson will become involved in the course of business. Engaging in behavior that disregards this fundamental ethical premise is offensive to the other party and discredits the reputation of the person who ignores this guideline. As an ultimate penalty, the dissolution of the business relationship could threaten a firm's survival. Displays of honesty and integrity have become even more important in the context of total quality programs and business alliances among various stakeholders.

Russian managers also recognize the necessity of trust and keeping one's word in business relationships. As in America, honesty and integrity are fundamental guiding principles, since both cultures are grounded in religious traditions that stress these basic human values. These cultural values have endured in Russia even through 70 years of communism. In addition, much like the Japanese and other Asian cultures, Russians place an especially high value on long-term personal relationships in business built on mutual trust and assistance. Such relationships provide greater certainty and dependability than formal bureaucratic and impersonal channels and mechanisms.

As an illustration of the mutual trust in a successful joint venture between American and Russian partners, Gordon Lankton, president of Nypro, Inc., a leading American plastic injection molding company, described an agreement with his Russian partner, Mikromashina:

> Business is a matter of trust. You know, we went into this joint venture with trust, and very little else. I hadn't even read all the documents at the time we went and invested our money into the Soviet Union . . . but we went in because we thought it was the thing to do and we trusted the people.

Lankton also provided an example of how his Russian partners demonstrated their trust:

> I needed to have five of the Russian managers sign documents agreeing to have the Midwestern company become a fourth joint venture partner . . . I spent two or three days discussing these documents and explaining the legal implications to my Russian colleagues. They listened very carefully and ended up not changing a word.[14]

In addition to trust and keeping one's word, other behaviors considered ethical by both Russians and Americans include belief in fair competition, as well as the legitimacy of rewards commensurate with performance. Although these views have been held consistently in America, their acceptance has not always been found in Russian society. The move to a market economy, however, has made them more acceptable within much of the emerging business environment.

Quadrant II: Unethical to Both.

Russians and Americans agree that breaking one's word or violating trust is unethical, as are competing unfairly and rewarding others inequitably. In addition, the criminal acts of gangsterism, racketeering, and extortion, so publicized in Russia today, are clearly unethical in the eyes of both Russians and Americans, as well as illegal. The Communists imposed severe punishments, and the current government's failure to do so is due primarily to a lack of stability and resources rather than to an acceptance of such crimes.

A less clear-cut example of unethical behavior is the black market. Many Russian and American business managers view this activity as unethical because it violates the cultural value of fairness. By exploiting customers with no other alternative to fulfill their needs and sometimes producing goods using stolen materials and equipment, the black market is the epitome of unfair competition. Russians, however, often consider black marketeering an inevitable fact of life in a shortage economy, and therefore, not entirely unacceptable. Americans, in contrast, operating in a well-supplied economic environment, might more readily condemn black marketeering as unethical.

In the more mainstream business environment in both countries, clear instances of price gouging are considered unethical. In Russia, such behavior, specifically that of managers in state enterprises who overcharged customers and kept the excess, was ranked as the most unethical of 30 questionable behaviors in a survey of 1,000 Soviet enterprise executives.[15] The American managers of Polaroid's joint venture understood well this strong aversion to excessively high prices. They priced their popular camera from the start to be within reach of the average Russian citizen rather than charging a higher price. Not only did this action build market share, but it made a statement to the Russian people that Polaroid was a reputable and ethical company.

Another unethical behavior in both countries is refusing to pay one's legitimate debts. In the U.S., such behavior is illegal and subject to appropriate punishment. In Russia today, the refusal of some enterprises to pay their suppliers has brought about hardship and even business failures. Yet this situation is due largely to the government's chaotic monetary policies and hyperinflation, as well as enterprise managers' decision to raise prices of their products, often after mafia pressure to do so. It has been reported that 10 to 20 percent of the sales volume of a large majority of private enterprises and commercial banks is paid in extortion "tax" to the mafia.[16] In such a threatening environment where these payments often exceed enterprise profits, many managers fear for the survival of their own institutions and, at times, resort to withholding payments to their suppliers and even their employees. But regardless of the reason for such behavior, most Russians would still consider withholding payments to be unethical. In summary, even though conditions differ greatly in America and Russia today, a strong consensus exists about the unethical nature of some behaviors, stemming from fundamental universal values shared by both countries.

Quadrant III: Ethical for Russians but Not Americans.

The most frequently encountered questionable behavior in Russia that Americans consider unethical, but Russians view as largely ethical or acceptable, would likely be the occurrence of *blat*. *Blat* involves excessive reliance for favors on personal contacts with people in influential positions. *Blat* is often accompanied by bribes or "grease payments" paid to a network of acquaintances and friends who facilitate the process of reaching the target individual. Such behavior, even though not openly condoned, was considered a necessary fact of life within a centrally controlled, bureaucratic structure in which scarce resources were controlled by a small number of powerful individuals. The practice has continued among Russian managers who either do not see, or refuse to see, alternative methods for accomplishing goals.

Whereas price gouging and keeping the excess is clearly considered unethical behavior in Russia, price fixing is not considered in the same light, as long as it does not result in overt gouging. Given the centrally planned prices under the Communist system and the monopolistic nature of Soviet industry, the idea of setting prices in collaboration with competitors and others seems appropriate to many Russian managers. The danger in such practice in a shortage economy is that it will result in price gouging, since consumers have few alternatives. Although Americans may, at times, set prices to "skim the cream," it is clearly unethical to conspire with others to set prices, and violators have been prosecuted under the law.

Another set of practices generally considered ethical by Russians but not by Americans includes the manipulation of business data in reports to superiors, such as understating material and labor reserves, exaggerating the quality and quantity of goods produced, and covering up mistakes and operating deficiencies.[17] The clear purpose, of course, was to meet externally imposed plans and goals, and to receive the rewards for doing so. To Russian managers this was a completely logical practice since they had limited control over materials, labor, and equipment, and yet were required to meet unrealistic targets. Like so many others, this practice has stemmed from the excesses of the bureaucratic, centrally planned Communist system, and to change behavior and underlying ethics will take time. American managers, even if they were to engage in such practices, would normally recognize them as wrong and unethical. Again, the difference in perceptions of ethicality is based on the vastly different experiences of each group, the Russian managers coping with what they have considered senseless and unfair policies.

In reviewing the behaviors that Russian managers consider ethical, but that American managers would question, a central theme is the disregard or circumvention of what are perceived as senseless laws and policies. These fail to make sense to managers because they do not deal with the reality of the business environment. Rather, they represent the distortions of a bureaucratic system under Soviet Communism, and remain today a chaotic, unenforced, and inconsistently administered set of laws and practices in the transitional business and legal environment of Russia.

A second rationale for disregarding various laws and regulations is that the role of Russian managers is highly paternalistic and substantially broader than that of their American counterparts. Managers traditionally have been much more deeply involved in the personal lives and welfare of employees and their families by providing housing, schooling, recreation, and other amenities. This paternalistic orientation leads Russian managers to place a high value on their employees, as well as the survival of their enterprises. When "senseless" laws and policies appeared to threaten these interests, managers often chose to ignore them. More selfish motives, such as personal career advancement, might also have led to the same behavior, but it would still be considered ethical if the laws and policies were unfair or made no sense.

The response of Russian managers was and continues to be logical and ethical to them. Given their circumstances, they apply what might be considered situational ethics. American managers, experienced in a vastly different environment, might consider such behavior as being undesirable and unethical.

Quadrant IV: Ethical for Americans but Not Russians.   Just as Americans take issue with some business practices that Russians consider to be ethical, so too, Russians do not condone some practices that Americans generally accept as ethical. For instance, whereas American managers seldom question the capitalist view that supports the legitimacy of maximization of profits, this concept is still antithetical to many Russians in doing business. Under Communism, the only exposure to capitalist profit for most Russians was the "dirty" money made by black marketeers and the government's propaganda about the evils of Western capitalism. Recognizing the prevailing ambivalence, one young Russian entrepreneur, who formerly traded goods in the black market, later became engaged in a profitable legitimate real estate business. He explained, "Before they called me a speculator; now they call me a businessman. It's the same thing. The only difference is now I can register as a private company."[18]

The idea of profit-making being ethical is still questionable to some Russians, even those engaged in legitimate business, particularly managers who gained their experience during the Communist era. Many Russian parents are ashamed that making money or profits is the goal of their children who have gone into private business. This feeling is aggravated by the financial dependence of some parents on their enterprising children. The parents are unable to survive on their grossly inadequate state salaries, even though many had been respected professionals. In such situations, it is small wonder that some Russian managers in private business are ambivalent about the legitimacy of profits.

Many Russians would also consider as unethical the exorbitant salary differentials between the work force and top management in the United States. This situation violates the Russian value of fairness and equality, and raises some individuals so far above others as to be incompatible with the collectivist values emphasized by the Communists and prevalent throughout Russian history. Furthermore, in the Russian mindset, it suggests an exploitation of the common worker by still another authoritarian master. It arouses feelings of envy in many Russians who hold the deep-seated belief that the wealth and achievements of others are gained at the expense of those who have less. As a result, many Russians feel resentment rather than admiration for people who earn more, even if material success is obtained through hard work and legitimate means.

Another practice that Russians consider unethical is that of massive layoffs, especially while a company is still fundamentally healthy. For instance, Fleet Bank, a highly profitable organization, laid off thousands of employees in the U.S. in early 1994 in order to reposition itself for the future and further improve its level of profitability. In contrast, while many major Russian enterprises are struggling for their very survival, the Russian government and private individuals resist the prospect of massive layoffs and unemployment, and fear their impact on political and social stability. Under the Communist regime, work was an entitlement as well as an obligation, and even in earlier times the Russian people valued a paternalistic relationship with those in authority. There was an implicit contract that workers would be provided for in exchange for passive compliance with authorities who directed their work. In the current unstable business climate in Russia, the American firm Occidental Petroleum laid off half its Russian labor force in its Western Siberian development project in response to excessive taxation by the Russian government.[19] Such actions, while becoming more common in Russia, are still likely to be perceived as unethical.

Another behavior that Americans consider ethical, but that Russians do not, is whistleblowing on people who commit illegal acts in organizations. Although not always practiced in America, the ethicality of whistleblowing is clear to most, and government legislation protects individuals who come forward with information about illegal or unethical conduct they witness in the workplace. In Russia, however, whistleblowing has connotations of informing, a practice that frequently resulted in harm to innocent people. A flagrant example of such consequences was the incident in the 1930s involving Pavlik Morozov, a child who informed Communist authorities against his parents who were then executed. Although his behavior was glorified by the government, most Russians were horrified by such an act, and saw it instead as a warning of the dangers of informing. Such events contributed to the practice of keeping silent about illegal conduct as a method of mutual protection from possibly arbitrary accusation and punishment.

Toward a More Ethical Business Environment in Russia

These examples illustrate that, in spite of many areas of agreement between Americans and Russians about ethical and unethical behaviors, other actions will be interpreted differently by each group.

The following recommendations will focus not on the areas of ethical agreement, but on disagreements. It is important for American managers, in doing business with Russians, to both anticipate these differences and to understand the reasons why they exist. The following recommendations are offered as a starting point for American managers who want to operate in Russia in an ethical manner and who wish to collaborate with their Russian counterparts in ways that enhance a mutually acceptable ethical environment for decision making.

• *Recognize that the chaotic conditions in Russia—caused by the historic changes in government as well as the dramatic transition to a market-oriented economy—are a major source of ethical confusion.* The lack of certainty about government policy regarding taxation, export rights, and even ownership of property prevents managers from acting consistently and openly. As so often occurred under Communism, managers are virtually forced to disregard senseless and contradictory laws, including those that discourage reasonable business decisions in a competitive market economy. The political and economic environments have created a survival mentality in which strictly construed ethical behavior can hardly be expected. The extreme uncertainty and hardship have led to the widespread practice of situational ethics wherein inconsistent behavior and variable ethical standards are common. The ethical approach of managers might well be described as utilitarian, with the end seen as justifying the means.

Rather than judging Russian managers, Americans should attempt to understand the reasons for such behavior and seek mutually acceptable resolutions within their own ethical limits. One Russian businessman who emigrated to America routinely gives "gifts" such as TVs to facilitate his business dealings with Russian managers. In explaining this practice, he shows an understanding of the Russian situation, stating, "What do you expect from people who manage millions of dollars,

but can't afford a VCR?"[20] American managers will have to decide what to do within the limits of their own ethical beliefs and U.S. law, just as this manager has done.

• *Recognize that the lack of a legal structure for a market economy creates an ethical vacuum for Russian managers leading to ad hoc decisions in a business system in which they have little experience.* Americans doing business with Russian managers must understand that the Russians themselves often do not know the legality of their actions. As they attempt to conduct business under such uncertain conditions, they revert to earlier established values to guide their behavior. In their minds, the situation often dictates the ethicality of the behavior. For instance, a Russian salesman for Baird Corporation's joint venture overstated to customers the product characteristics of the firm's spectrometers. Although he considered this perfectly reasonable behavior, the American manager explained to him that this was an unacceptable business practice. Not only was it basically dishonest, but such misrepresentations could hurt the company's reputation and credibility.[21] In short, Americans should expect situational ethical behavior, explain their own point of view, and seek realistic and acceptable accommodations, rather than simply rendering absolutist judgments.

• *Learn about the foundations of ethical behavior in Russia that originate in its culture, religious heritage, and Communist past.* A brief review of some important influences has been included in this article, but American managers who intend to make a serious commitment to doing business in Russia should develop a deeper knowledge of these forces. By so doing, Americans will better understand the behavior of their Russian counterparts and develop a perspective from which to assess the ethical dimensions from the viewpoint of the Russians. Although there are many areas of agreement between Russians and Americans about what constitutes ethical or unethical behavior, there remain striking differences. The Communist view of profit and promoting oneself above the collective as being immoral and unethical is well known. But even more fundamental is the notion of "Holy Russia" being endowed with "a unique spirituality and mission" that sets it apart from the West as well as Asia.[22] These beliefs led to values that rejected the industriousness of Germans and Japanese as well as the entrepreneurship of Americans.[23] In addition, Russians are often suspicious of what might seem to be obvious solutions to Americans and other non-Russians. The explanation stems, in part, from a history of isolation and near xenophobia encouraged by Russian leaders, as well as the tendency to seek circuitous solutions to problems because of regulations or resource constraints. A senior Russian government official has noted: "There is a peculiar Russian mentality . . . Russian man . . . sees a law and instantly thinks of ways to maneuver around it. This is just a tradition. It will take years for this tradition to be overcome."[24] Patience is required in dealing with Russian counterparts to give them time to build trust and understanding in new relationships.

• *Be aware of the critical attitudes that many Russians hold toward American business practices, some of which are considered to be unethical.* Russians have had a long-term love-hate relationship with America, simultaneously admiring and disparaging it. They admire America's material wealth and achievements, yet disparage the many excesses of capitalism as well as its social and economic inequality. Negative feelings about America have intensified during the 1990s, and the influence of American-type values has been blamed by many for the increasing levels of crime, social inequalities, and economic ills of the people. The Russian media's depiction of the unmitigated selfishness and ostentatious behavior of many Russian nouveaux-riches businessmen as "Cowboy Capitalists" is a direct indictment of American capitalist values and casts them in an unethical light. Furthermore, some Russians are learning about business from unorthodox sources such as American movies where greed and ruthlessness are often depicted as typical of American business practice. One American real estate devel-

oper was shocked by the Russian managers taking his seminar in Moscow when they recommended to "buy a troubled company low, lay off employees, and then sell it in pieces."[25] The source of such advice, he learned, was their exposure to the movie *Wall Street.*

• *Demonstrate the highest standards of ethical behavior.* Keeping in mind the suspicion with which Russians view many practices of American business, American managers should serve as a role model of how to conduct business responsibly in a free market. In so doing, the perceived excesses of capitalism can be avoided and the more positive and ethical practices can be illustrated for Russian managers. Americans, while having no monopoly on standards for business ethics, are practiced in dealing with ethical dilemmas, and America is viewed as the leader in the development of business ethics.[26] Additionally, American managers are held to the highest levels of ethical behavior internationally since they must meet the standards of their American environment, such as complying with the U.S. Foreign Corrupt Practices Act.

Actions and experience speak louder than words in conveying ethical business practices. American managers can recount their experiences and explain how these were important to the ethical conduct of their business. They can also demonstrate their principles through socially responsible actions in the regions in which they conduct business. One American oil company, for instance, cemented goodwill with the local Russian community by donating equipment to start a small factory to produce sausage.[27]

• *Become part of the solution by collaborating with Russian managers in developing sound ethical business practices.* Listening, understanding, and not judging, but helping by acting as a role model will gain respect and create an atmosphere for open dialogue. The development of a trusting relationship and mutually accepted ethical standards should be the objective, and patience will be required to succeed. American managers should be willing to explain to their Russian counterparts their reasons for interpreting practices as questionable, and possibly unethical. In such situations, Russian managers should be encouraged to explain their views and to act according to the highest ethical standards of their culture. At times, such discussions may lead to an impasse based on the different views of ethical behavior by each party. Both American and Russian managers must then decide for themselves what actions to take.

American companies and their managers can motivate Russian managers to act ethically and responsibly by offering assurance that such behavior will be in their own best interests. Like domestic firms in the United States, such positive behavior is best assured when there is clear enlightened self-interest. For instance, 80 percent of Fortune 500 companies have codes of ethics, and many offer training in ethics, but not solely out of altruism.[28] Companies also realize that such practices are in their best interest since they should help prevent lawsuits and enable the firms to be viewed as good corporate citizens. American firms doing business in Russia can assure responsible Russian managers of continued business relationships as long as the two parties continue to discuss and work toward agreement on ethical practices. Russian managers, like Americans, understand the concept of enlightened self-interest.

The Common Ground

Many Americans are attracted by the abundant business opportunities in Russia, yet encounter a high degree of risk. One method for reducing the risk is to understand the ethical environment and build relationships with Russian managers who are committed to ethical behavior. Since major ethical disagreements can end a business relationship, Russian and American managers should at the outset work at developing a mutually acceptable ethical environment.

This mutuality requires that American managers understand the areas of agreement and disagreement on ethical practices between themselves and Russian managers. The ethical standards of Russians have been shaped by different forces than for Americans, and the resulting views on business ethics may lead to practices by both Americans and Russians that the other may view as unethical. These conclusions were presented in the four-part framework contrasting some areas of agreement and disagreement on ethical behavior in Russia and America. The recommendations offered to American managers should assist them in understanding Russian business ethics, and in developing the common ground essential for successful business relationships with their Russian counterparts.

Back to Ben & Jerry's

At this point, it might be clear to you how Ben & Jerry's managers handled the situation they faced. With patience, but firmness, they explained to their Russian partner that the equipment of the joint venture did not belong to the Russian manager, but to the joint venture. As such, it was not to be used in other businesses, but only in the business to which it belonged. Although the Russian manager might not have agreed with the conclusion, he complied with the decision. Ben & Jerry's managers stated their ethical and business beliefs and acted accordingly. In spite of the vastly different business environment, they did not see a legitimate reason to change their standards. In other circumstances, they might well see reason for adapting to the Russian point of view.

References

1. International Trade Administration, U.S. Department of Commerce. "Commerce Secretary Brown Leads Historic Presidential Business Mission to Russia." *Bisnis Bulletin* (April/May 1994).
2. *Obstacles to Trade and Investment in the Republics of the Former USSR: A Review of Impediments as Seen by the U.S. Business Community* (Washington, DC: International Trade Administration, March 1992).

3. Julie Corwin and Douglas Stanglin, "The Looting of Russia," *U.S. News & World Report,* March 7, 1994, pp. 36–41, Fred Kaplan. "In Russia, Capitalism Booms and Busts," *The Boston Sunday Globe,* July 31, 1994, p. 19, Kevin Fedarko, "City on Edge," *Time,* July 4, 1994, pp. 51–53.

4. Iurji I. Ekaterinoslavskii, "Diagnosis, Destruction, and Creation: A New Conception of Training Managers for the Market Economy," in Sheila M. Puffer, ed., *The Russian Management Revolution: Preparing Managers for the Market Economy* (Armonk, NY: M. E. Sharpe, 1992), pp. 149–57, P. Shikhirev, "Ethics, Psychology, and Business in Russia," paper presented at the international conference on business ethics, Academy of the National Economy, Moscow, June 1993.

5. Shikhirev, op. cit.; Robert Anderson and Petr Shikhirev, *"Akuly" i "Del'finy"* [*"Sharks" and "Dolphins"*] (Moscow, Russia: Dolo, 1994).

6. A. A. Lobanov and E. V. Poteeva, eds., *Euka biznesa. Mezhkul'turnye Aspekty* [*Business Ethics: Intercultural Aspects*] (Moscow, Delo, 1992); V. I. Bakshtanovskii and I. V. Sogomonov, *Chestnaia Igra* [*Fair Game*] (Tornsk, Russia: Tornsk University Press, 1992).

7. D. Vogel, "The Globalization of Business Ethics: Why America Remains Distinctive," *California Management Review,* 35/1 (Fall 1992): 30–49.

8. "Hey, America, Lighten Up a Little," *Economist,* July 28, 1990.

9. Thomas Donaldson and Thomas W. Dunfee, "Toward a Unified Conception of Business Ethics: Integrative Social Contracts Theory." *Academy of Management Review,* 19/2 (1994) 255.

10. Shikhirev, op. cit.

11. R. T. DeGeorge, *Soviet Ethics and Morality* (Ann Arbor, MI: University of Michigan Press, 1969).

12. Joseph S. Berliner, *Soviet Industry from Stalin to Gorbachev* (Aldershot, England: Edward Elgar, 1989).

13. Donaldson and Dunfee, op. cit., pp. 252–84.

14. Gordon Lankton and Sheila M. Puffer, "Managing a Plastics Extrusion Operation in Moscow," in Puffer, op. cit., pp. 239–47.

15. John M. Ivancevich, Richard S. DeFrank, and Paul R. Gregory, "The Soviet Enterprise Director: An Important Resource Before and After the Coup." *Academy of Management Executive,* 6/1 (1992): 42–55.

16. Russian Research Center, Harvard University, *Economic Newsletter,* 19/8, April 10, 1994, p. 4.

17. Berliner, op. cit.

18. Fred Kaplan, "Color of Money in Russia: Black." *The Boston Globe,* June 6, 1993, pp. 1, 12.

19. Fred Kaplan, "Russian Taxes Hurting Foreign Firms," *The Boston Globe,* April 25, 1994, pp. 17, 19.

20. Cited in Stanislav v. Shekshnia, "Moral Challenges in the Emerging Russian Market," unpublished manuscript. Northeastern University, Boston, 1992.

21. Jack Medzorian and Sheila M. Puffer, "Manufacturing Spectrometers in St. Petersburg," in Puffer, op. cit., pp. 248–57.

22. Serge Schmemann, "Russia Lurches into Reform, But Old Ways Are Tenacious," *New York Times,* February 20, 1994, pp. 1–14.

23. Ibid.

24. Kaplan (1993), op. cit.

25. Cited in Shekshnia, op. cit.

26. Vogel, op. cit.

27. Vladimir Kvint, "Don't Give Up On Russia," *Harvard Business Review* (March/April 1994), pp. 62–74.

28. Joanne B. Ciulla, "Ethical Business in the USA," *Business Ethics,* 1/1 (1992): 58, 59; Russell Mitchell and Michael Oneal, "Managing by Values: Is Levi Strauss' Approach Visionary—or Flaky?" *Business Week,* August 1, 1994, pp. 46–52.

A MACROECONOMIC STUDY OF THE EFFECTS OF PROMOTION ON THE CONSUMPTION OF INFANT FORMULA IN DEVELOPING COUNTRIES

Mary C. Gilly and John L. Graham

Few issues have stirred more controversy among marketers, governmental organizations, and consumer activists than the Nestlé's infant formula boycott of the late 1970s (see Cateora, 1983; Sethi et al., 1985). The crux of the debate was the causal effect of promotion by manufacturers on the breast-feeding behavior of women in less-developed countries. Nestlé and other infant formula manufacturers strongly argued that their advertising and personal selling efforts did not influence women to stop breast-feeding their children. That is, the only effect of their promotional expenditures was to distribute market share among competitors, *not* to increase the size of the market (Nestlé, 1980). Several critics vehemently disagreed (for example, Schudson, 1984; James, 1983). The purpose of this study is to test these competing hypotheses. Examination of infant for-

mula imports by 79 developing countries during the 1970s provides an answer to this debate.

The remainder of the article is divided into four sections. First, the literature pertinent to the study is briefly described, including a statement of hypotheses. Next, the methods used are discussed. Third, results are presented. The article concludes with an interpretation of the findings and implications for managers and policymakers.

Background Literature

According to Sethi et al. (1986, p. 26), "all market actions have some nonmarket or indirect consequences for societies." In the case of marketing infant formula in developing countries, one consequence was an increased potential for infant malnutrition and mortality. No one has claimed that infant formula is an inherently bad or unsafe product (Pagan, 1986). In fact, physicians consider infant formula superior to other breast-milk substitutes, such as powdered milk (Post, 1978). But while a "mother can safely and adequately breast-

The *Journal of Macromarketing* is published by the Business Research Division of the University of Colorado at Boulder. Reprinted with permission.

feed a child in conditions of poverty and inadequate sanitation . . . . safety and adequacy cannot be guaranteed or achieved with any degree of consistency when bottle-feeding is attempted under the same conditions" (Post 1985, p. 116).

It is useful to discuss the issues surrounding this problem within the framework of marketing's effect on purchase and consumption and the environmental influences on this process. Figure 1 offers such a framework. Promotion is shown as influencing purchase of infant formula, which leads to use (or misuse) of the product. Environmental factors are shown as affecting all three components of the purchase and consumption process: promotion, purchase, and use. This framework serves as the basis for the following discussion of the infant formula problem.

Promotion of Infant Formula. The promotion of infant formula products was "rampant and unchecked before 1970" (Post, 1985, p. 116). Two types of companies produced and marketed formula, depending on the promotion strategy favored. Pharmaceutical firms (typically American) used medical promotion, while the food companies (typically European) preferred consumer advertising (Post, 1978). Several environmental factors influenced the amount and type of promotional ef-

forts. One example is the growing urbanization of the developing countries, which increased the food companies' ability to use consumer advertising efficiently (Post, 1978). Hospitals became more popular birth sites, and newborns typically are fed at the hospital for the first few days. The medical community became a logical focus for the promotion of infant formula by pharmaceutical companies through free samples and other incentives (Sethi and Post, 1979). Thus, the industry norms guiding the two types of marketers of infant formula in developed nations were reinforced by changes occurring there. Most governments of developing nations were cautious and reserved in their regulation of infant formula promotion (Post, 1985), not wishing to alienate business or the medical community. Furthermore, the institutional mechanisms necessary for inspection and regulation generally were lacking (Sethi and Post, 1979).

Purchase of Infant Formula. Consumer advertising and medical promotion contributed to the purchase of infant formula. Critics claimed that most of the advertising was misleading or used "hard sell" techniques to persuade mothers not to breast-feed (Sethi and Post, 1979).

A general criticism of advertising is that it manipulates the minds of consumers so that they buy

FIGURE 1

Commercial and environmental influences on the purchase and consumption of infant formula

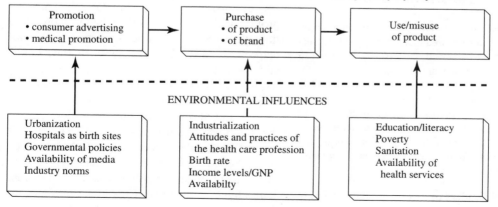

things they do not need or should not have (Schudson, 1984). This has been the reasoning behind the ban on cigarette advertising on television (McGuinness and Cowling, 1975) and the proposed ban on beer and wine advertising (Hume, 1985). The argument that promotion shapes consumers' desires has also been the basis for the censure of marketers of infant formula in developing countries (see James, 1983; Muller, 1975). It was claimed that they were overpromoting their products to poor, uneducated people living in economic and hygienic conditions that made appropriate usage of powdered formula almost impossible (Sethi et al., 1985). According to critics, marketers were contributing to, if not responsible for, women opting for bottle-feeding rather than breast-feeding, resulting in infant sickness and death.

In their defense, marketers maintained that advertising cannot manipulate consumers because it is ineffective or only modestly influential in changing consumption habits. Promotion seeks to change not people's product choices, but their *brand* choices (Schudson, 1984). In a public relations pamphlet, Nestlé (1980) made just such a claim regarding the influence of promotion on breast-feeding and the use of infant formula:

QUESTION: Doesn't the promotion of infant formula in developing countries lead to lower levels of breast-feeding?

ANSWER: The best evidence we have to date shows quite the opposite—the promotion of infant formula is *not* related to less breast-feeding in developing countries.

The WHO Collaborative Breast-feeding Study (1979), which interviewed more than 23,000 mothers in nine nations, showed *no* association between breast-feeding decline and formula promotion. Of fundamental importance is the fact that the WHO Collaborative Study, in reporting reasons why mothers from nine countries did not breast-feed or stopped breast-feeding, listed the main factors as insufficient milk, maternal illness, infant illness, and new pregnancy. *Not once was any commercial factor even mentioned.*

Thus, the defenders of this view would point to other environmental factors that contribute to de-

mand for infant formula and the decline in breast-feeding. For example, the industrialization of the developing countries, which has caused a Westernization of social mores and has increased the need for mobility in employment, has been suggested as a contributing factor. It was a simple matter for mothers to breast-feed in an agricultural setting, but most places of industrial employment do not provide facilities for nursing (Sethi and Post, 1979). The attitudes and practices of the health care profession also have been cited as factors (Benton et al., 1978). Doctors, nurses, and clinicians, as well as the policies of hospitals and clinics, often endorsed the use of infant formula. In many hospitals, newborns were routinely bottle-fed regardless of whether the mother planned to breast-feed (Sethi and Post, 1979). Rising birth rates and income levels also increased potential demand.

A third view of the effects of advertising on purchase is offered by Schudson (1984). He claims that under certain conditions advertising can have a significant effect on sales and, furthermore, may influence cultural life even when it does not do much in the way of selling goods individually. While Schudson feels that advertising is generally ineffective, he believes some groups are particularly vulnerable to advertising. Among these are citizens of developing countries, due to poverty and illiteracy, lack of governmental consumer protection, and lack of personal experience with products. He said this about infant formula: "The powers of marketing here—through the medical professionals as much or probably more than through direct advertising—influence consumer choice" (1984, p. 125). Likewise, Farley, Louis, and Reddy (1980) report consumption of weaning foods in Sri Lanka to be positively influenced by direct mail advertising and free samples.

James (1983) supports this latter view, stating that multinationals use promotional techniques in competing for the mother's initial choice. Once committed to bottle-feeding, mothers then seek reinforcement of the correctness of their decision. James hypothesized that if the infant becomes ill, cognitive dissonance theory predicts that anxiety will be aroused. Because switching to breast-feeding may be impossible at that point, the mother must reduce anxiety by denying the association between infant formula and the baby's illness, thus perpetuating the influence of promotion on consumer choice of infant formula.

In summary, on the one hand, some authors suggest that promotion/advertising is ineffective in increasing product demand and only distributes demand among brands—for our purposes, a null hypothesis. On the other hand, particularly in the case of marketing infant formula in developing countries, other researchers suggest that promotion is effective in increasing product demand. The hypotheses considered in this study are:

H_0: Consumption of infant formula is unrelated to changes in promotional efforts of manufacturers in developing countries. Or, sales of infant formula in developing countries during 1972–1974 were no different from those during 1976–1978.

H_1: Consumption of infant formula is positively related to changes in promotional efforts of manufacturers. Or, sales of infant formula in developing countries were higher during 1972–1974 than during 1976–1978.

The rationale for choosing the specified test periods is delineated in the Methods section.

Product Use/Misuse.

Although not specifically addressed in this study, a brief discussion of the factors causing misuse of infant formula is pertinent. Consumer research typically focuses on product and brand choice, but it is important that marketers consider how consumers *use* products as well as how they purchase them (Nicosia and Mayer, 1976). The infant formula controversy highlights this importance dramatically. The following quotation from Post (1985, pp. 127–28) concisely summarizes the effect of environmental factors on consumers' use of infant formula:

> The reason that children die in developing nations is not because infant formula is a bad product. Rather, there is an environment of poverty, illiteracy, inadequate sanitation, unhealthy water and limited health services that create dangerous conditions for the use

of formula. Marketing did not create these conditions, but marketing was a more *actionable* aspect of the problem than poverty, water or education. Moreover, the manufacturers were placing their products in the stream of commerce without attempting to find out who actually used them, under what circumstances, and with what consequences.

Post went on to say that industry executives admitted at later hearings that their firms had done no research following up the purchase of their products. Thus, poor understanding of product use led to infant death and controversy.

Methods

The Independent Variable.   Measurement of the independent variable in this study, promotional efforts by infant formula manufacturers, is most difficult. Information regarding actual expenditures and/or marketing practices has been closely guarded by the firms because of their involvement in lawsuits associated with the controversy. In 1975, however, the leading companies in the industry agreed to a fundamental curtailment of promotional efforts in developing countries. The events leading up to this crucial change are described below.

As can be seen in Exhibit 1, the controversy regarding promotion of infant formula in developing countries was sparked in 1970 at a conference in Paris sponsored by a United Nations agency, the Protein Advisory Group (PAG). A key recommendation of PAG stated: "It is clearly important to avoid any action which would accelerate the trend away from breast-feeding" (PAG, 1972). Jelliffe (1971), a consultant to PAG at the Paris conference and then director of the Caribbean Food and Nutrition Institute, claimed that the marketing practices of the infant formula manufacturers were the "major factor" contributing to the decline in breast-feeding and the associated increase in consumption of breast-milk substitutes. From these beginnings the controversy grew to be one of the most debated issues of the 1970s, including lawsuits in several countries, international consumer group protests and boycotts, and even U.S. Senate hearings. The history of the controversy is interesting in and of itself and is well documented by others (see Sethi et al., 1985). The focus of this article is not the controversy, however, but the promotional behaviors of the infant formula manufacturers.

Prior to 1970, almost all the manufacturers used a wide variety of promotional techniques in developing countries. Six were considered most objectionable by the several critics (McComas et al., 1983; Nestlé, 1983): advertising to the general public; samples given to new mothers; personal selling through mothercraft workers (that is, women presenting themselves as nutritional experts, often dressed in nursing uniforms); point of sale advertising; the use of commissions/bonuses for sales; and copious samples to physicians.

In response to the criticism of Jelliffe, PAG, and other consumer activists, formula manufacturers began to examine their marketing in developing countries. Nestlé (1983, p. 1), the industry leader (largest market share worldwide), reports beginning "to review its marketing practices on a region-by-region basis" in the early 1970s. In 1974 in the United States, Bristol-Myers was the subject of a shareholder lawsuit demanding information regarding the firm's marketing practices in developing countries (McComas et al., 1983). Post

---

EXHIBIT 1   Important Events in the Infant Formula Controversy

Date(s)	Event	References
1867	Henri Nestlé introduces first commercially produced infant formula.	Post (1978)
1945–1959	Infant formula sales soar in industrialized countries because of post-World War II baby boom.	Post (1978)
1960s	Birth rates in industrialized countries decline, manufacturers begin "rampant and unchecked" promotion of bottle-feeding in developing countries.	Post (1985)
1970	At UN conference in Paris, Jelliffe blames formula manufacturers for infant deaths in less-developed countries.	Sethi et al. (1986)
Early 1970s	Nestlé begins to review marketing practices on a region-by-region basis.	Nestlé (1983)
1972	Abbott/Ross introduces code to control promotions practices.	Beaver and Silvester (1982)
1974	Bristol-Myers in the United States is subject to shareholder lawsuit demanding information regarding formula promotion in developing countries.	McComas et al. (1983)
1974	First public identification of issue with publication of *The New Internationalist* and *The Baby Killer.*	Sethi and Post (1979)
1974–1978	Nestlé phases out all direct promotional practices.	Armstrong (1985)
1975	Nestlé trial in Switzerland and shareholder resolutions filed in the United States.	Sethi and Post (1979)
1975	Formation of International Council of Infant Food Industries (ICIFI) and promulgation of code of marketing ethics.	Sethi and Post (1979)
1976	Borden stops all promotion and sales of infant formula in Hong Kong and Taiwan.	Post (1978)
1977	Boycott against Nestlé begins.	Pagan (1986)
1978	U.S. Senate hearings regarding United States firms' role in controversy.	
1981	First developing-country government (Kenya) takes legislative action to curtail promotion of infant formula.	James (1983)
1981	World Health Organization passes code on marketing breast-milk substitutes.	Pagan (1986)
1982	Nestlé creates Nestlé Infant Formula Audit Commission (NIFAC).	Pagan (1986)
1984	International Nestlé Boycott Committee announces termination of seven-year boycott.	Post (1985)

(1978) reports that Borden stopped all advertising for its infant formula in Hong Kong and Taiwan in 1976. Beaver and Silvester (1982, pp. 2–3) state: "The companies had responded quietly but continuously. Nestlé stopped direct contact between employees and mother and introduced stringent controls over sampling. Abbott/Ross introduced a code in 1972 and by the mid-1970s there was a general tightening up."

At a meeting sponsored by PAG in Singapore in 1974, executives from several formula manufacturing companies first discussed the possibility of forming an industry council to consider marketing practices in developing countries. In 1975, the International Council of Infant Formula Industries was formally organized in Zurich, Switzerland, bringing together eight of the largest U.S., European, and Japanese firms, Nestlé among them. One of their first actions was to develop a code of conduct embodying the principles of the 1970 PAG recommendations. Beaver and Silvester (1982) agree with Armstrong (1985, p. 8): "From 1974 to 1978, Nestlé phased out all direct promotional practices."

Considering the published information summarized in Exhibit 1, 1975 is chosen as the critical year when the industry, based on previous examination of marketing practices, began to curtail its marketing efforts. That is, promotion by the infant formula manufacturers in developing countries was greater immediately before than immediately following 1975. Thus, a dichotomous independent variable is defined—more promotional effort before 1975 versus less promotional effort after 1975.

Imports as an Indicator of Consumption.
Direct measurement of infant formula consumption in low-income countries is not possible using publicly available data. Post (1978, p. 223) explains: "There is no precise information about the world market for infant formula products. Moreover, virtually no individual countries require disclosure of information from manufacturers or sellers by line of business." Post does venture an estimate. Based on extrapolations from bits of in-

formation from three U.S. companies, he speculates sales in less-developed countries in 1978 to be approximately $600 million. Using company data, Cox (1978, p. 243) provides a much lower estimate for the same period. "The prepared infant formula market in the 100 countries generally considered to be Third World is about U.S. $350 million."

Infant formula imports *are* tracked by most countries, and those data are made available through the United Nations. Imports (SITC 048.82) to the 79 low-income countries included in our database amounted to $148.4 million in 1978. Thus, using Cox's lower estimate of the total market, imports appear to account for about 54 percent of infant formula consumption, that is, $148.4 million/($350 million x (79/100)).

Obviously, imports do not take into account local production, but they are directly related to strategies common to several firms. Post (1978) reviewed the operations of formula producers and concludes that in addition to production in the United States and other industrialized countries, a common approach is to produce in a third country or region combined with export distribution. Indeed, Stafford (1978) reports that his firm, Wyeth International, manufactures formula in the United States and 14 foreign countries and markets the product in 90 countries. Since formula production is a high-technology process (Post 1978), requiring the strictest sanitation (Stiegler, 1985), it tends to be concentrated in the industrialized countries. Moreover, when multinationals invest in production facilities, they favor larger markets; for example, American Home Products announced in 1978 that it would be opening a new plant for infant formula production in Indonesia (Post, 1978). Thus, it is reasonable to assume that imports better reflect consumption in smaller, low-income countries.

Dependent Variable.   The dependent variable considered in this study is infant formula imports (IFI) (SITC 048.82) as a percentage of total food imports (TF) (SITC 0). These data were obtained from the *United Nations Trade Statistics Annual*

EXHIBIT 2   Countries Included in the Study

Bolivia[a]	Congo	Tanzania
Brazil	Gabon	Upper Volta
Chile[a]	Algeria	Zaire
Colombia	Angola	Zambia
Ecuador[a]	Egypt[a]	Cyprus[a]
Mexico[a]	Ethiopia	Iran[a]
Peru[a]	Djibouti	Iraq
Uruguay[a]	Gambia	Jordan
Venezuela	Ghana	Lebanon
Belize	Guinea	Oman
French Guyana[a]	Ivory Coast	Syria[a]
Surinam	Kenya[a]	Yemen
Costa Rica[a]	Liberia	D. Yemen
El Salvador[a]	Madagascar	Bangladesh
Guatemala	Mali	Burma
Honduras[a]	Mauritius[a]	Hong Kong[a]
Nicaragua	Morocco	India
Panama[a]	Mozambique	Indonesia
Barbados[a]	Niger	S. Korea
Guyana	Nigeria	Malaysia[a]
Jamaica[a]	Rwanda	Pakistan
Trinidad Tobago	Senegal	Philippines[a]
Dominican Republic	Sierra Leone	Singapore
Haiti	Somalia	Sri Lanka
Cameron	S. Africa[a]	Thailand[a]
Central Africa	Tunisia[a]	

---

[a] Birth rate statistics available (United Nations, 1983).

(1969–1980) for the 79 low-income countries listed in Exhibit 2. The data are summarized in Table 1.

This percentage of food imports measures controls for several potential monetary and economic biases. First, because both import figures (formula and food) are reported in dollars, inflation is controlled by the division. Second, and perhaps more important, economic performance variables in the countries and in the world economy might be expected to influence imports of food and formula in a similar manner. Without this control, then, fluctuations in demand/consumption of infant formula might be attributed to economic conditions, such as overall increases in world trade, changes in GNP, import restrictions, or foreign exchange availability in the individual countries. These issues are further discussed in sections to follow.

Hypothesis Tests.   One-tailed t-tests were used to test the hypotheses. Imports of formula during 1972–1974 and 1976–1978 were calculated for each country, and the pairs of consumption values were compared across the two periods. Three-year periods were selected for two reasons. First, Salvatore (1983), Buzzell and Wiersema (1981), and Weede (1983) all argue for measures of variables averaged over a number of years. Feder (1982, pp. 63–64) adds: "Annual data include substantial random effects that tend to be eliminated by the procedure of averaging. The existence of lagged responses is another element that becomes less severe when averages rather than annual data are used." Second, data for 1971 are not available, thus limiting the test to the three years before 1975 and a comparable period after 1975.

Please note that we considered aggregating the data across the 79 countries and doing a regression analysis over the 10 periods for which we have data (1969 to 1979, less 1971). Then a dummy variable for promotion (0 = pre-1975, 1 = post-1975) might compete with any other possible independent variables to explain the variance in infant formula imports. However, such an approach is precluded by two problems. First, 10 data points give almost no statistical power, particularly with a five-plus-variable regression equation. Second, as mentioned above, the arguments for pooling the data *across time periods* are substantial. Moreover, the pairwise analysis is appropriate for the data, given the *imports 1972–1974* and *imports 1976–1978* for each country are not independent. If they were independent, then analysis of variance or discriminant analysis would have been possible and more appropriate. The method we have chosen takes advantage of all the information in the data, across all 79 countries.

Results

The competing hypotheses are:

H_0: Consumption of infant formula is unrelated to changes in promotional efforts of manufacturers in developing countries. Or, sales of infant

TABLE 1   Imports of Infant Formula and Food

Year	Infant Formula Imports (IFI) (SITC 048.82)[a]	Food Imports (TF) (SITC 0)[b]
1969	21.6	2.38
1970	48.3	2.99
1971	—	—
1972	76.4	3.80
1973	101.0	6.41
1974	99.4	9.72
1975	107.4	10.80
1976	117.5	9.19
1977	125.5	10.64
1978	148.4	12.62
1979	157.5	15.49

Note: See Exhibit 2 for a listing of the countries.

[a] Imports ($ millions) of "diet, infant cereal preps" (SITC 048.82) to 79 countries (*World Trade Annual* 1969–1979).

[b] Imports ($ billions) of "Food all categories" (SITC 0) to 79 countries (*World Trade Annual* 1969–1979).

formula in developing countries during 1972–1974 were no different from those during 1976–1978.

H_1: Consumption of infant formula is positively related to changes in promotional efforts of manufacturers. Or, sales of infant formula in developing countries were higher during 1972–1974 than during 1976–1978.

As indicated in Table 2, Hypothesis 1 is supported by the analysis. That is, imports of infant formula (IFI/TF), controlling for several factors, were lower in 1976–1978 than in 1972–1974. Consumption of infant formula was found to be positively related to changes in industry promotional efforts, and the relationship was statistically significant ($p < 0.05$).

Discussion

Conclusions. The information in Table 2 strongly suggests that infant formula imports (IFI/TF), controlling for several economic factors

in the 79 countries, were reduced by the curtailment of promotion. The empirical evidence in this study supports the views of Jelliffe (1971), Schudson (1984), and James (1983) that promotion affected overall consumption of infant formula and, by implication, breast-feeding behavior.

Indeed the model proposed in Figure 1 is supported by our data and analysis. That is, the infant formula manufacturers aggressively promoted their products, and consumption was thereby increased in environments conducive to misuse. Because the manufacturers took actions to reform and curtail promotion in low-income countries, inappropriate purchase and use of infant formula was also curtailed. The tragedy here is that all the companies did not respond to their critics in an even more prudent and timely manner.

In addition to statistical significance, the results also provided a measure of practical significance. That is, the reduction of infant formula imports between the two three-year periods was 20 percent—calculated (2.10–1.75)/1.75 (see Table 2). In other words, had the manufacturers maintained their much criticized promotional practices through 1978, imports to the 79 countries in 1978 might have been $178 million instead of $148 million, other things being equal.

TABLE 2   Results of T-Tests, Infant Formula Imports (SITC 048.82) as a Percentage of Food Imports (SITC 0)

	All 79 Countries	Sample 31 Countries[a]
Mean (1972 + 1973 + 1974)/3	2.10%	2.16%
Mean (1976 + 1977 + 1978)/3	1.75%	1.68%
t value	2.14	2.40
d.f.	78	30
One-tail probability	.018	.011

[a] 1979 population less than five million.

Alternative Explanations.   Several alternative explanations for the results reported above warrant examination.

1. It might be argued that the activities of the various protest groups influenced consumers or governments to reduce use of infant formula after 1975. Indeed, this was the time when the Nestlé controversy began to gain widespread attention in the popular press. However, the protests and publicity were largely confined to the industrialized countries and did not reach Third World consumers. Indeed, James (1983, p. 165) reports: "Not until April 1981 (with the introduction of a code of ethics in Kenya) was legislative action taken in a developing country against the manufacturers of powdered baby milk. See *The Sunday Times,* London (26th April, 1981)."

2. The decline of imports of infant formula (IFI/TF) reported in the Results section may have been caused by changes in birth rates across the time periods. However, as can be seen in Table 3, the change in IFI/TF was unrelated to changes in birth rates over the test period for the 36 countries for which data were available.

3. Perhaps imports were influenced by changes in individual countries' economic conditions. As can be seen in Table 3, the decline in IFI/TF was found to be unrelated to changes in GDP and/or changes in foreign exchange available during the test period. Apparently, these economic conditions had no systematic influence on infant formula imports.

4. It may be that the decline in imports reflects increased local production. As mentioned previously, the manufacturers favored investments in production facilities in the larger countries. Therefore, we retested the hypotheses using a subset of the smallest countries (1979 population less than five million). As can be seen in Table 2, the decline in formula consumption (IFI/TF) is still statistically significant. Thus, increased local manufacturing does not offer adequate explanation.

5. Other marketing mix decisions, besides promotional practices, may have influenced consumption. However, promotion was the focus of the controversy, the manufacturers' remedial actions, and this study. Indeed, had the firms segmented their markets more carefully and distributed the product more narrowly, or had the product been sold in diluted form (as is done now in the United States), perhaps the negative consequences of formula sale would have been dramatically reduced. Unfortunately, no data are available with which to address such broader questions.

6. One reviewer suggests that infant formula is supplied as part of U.S. foreign aid, which will not show up in import data. Since the government sources we checked provided no information about infant formula as part of foreign aid, this last challenge to the validity of our results remains unanswered.

Indeed, still other challenges may be offered, but our evidence and results must be evaluated in the context of the difficulty of investigating the negative consequences of corporate behavior. Key, even conclusive, information *is* available in company records—promotion expenditures and sales histories—but companies are unwilling to share it (Post, 1978). Until such data are made available for close and objective scrutiny, studies such as this one must suffice. Until companies provide evidence to the contrary, one must conclude that their promotion of infant formula led directly to increased consumption of the product in environments where its misuse led to sickness and death. Post (1978, p. 120) makes a similar comment regarding his research for the U.S. Senate hearings in 1978:

> Data relating to the infant-formula industry is difficult to acquire. Most information on sales volume, profits, market share of manufacturers, and even the manner in which firms do business is regularly denied researchers because of its proprietary nature. Published information is very limited in the United States, and even more scarce in developing nations. This void is frustrating to researchers such as myself; it also frustrates those who want to understand the magnitude of the problems on which these hearings are focused.

TABLE 3   Competing Explanations for the Change in Imports of Infant Formula as Measured by IFI/TF

$$\frac{(1976+1977+1978-1972-1973-1974)}{3}$$

Independent Variables	Pearson Correlation Coefficients
% Change in Birth Rates	
$\dfrac{\text{Births } (1976+1977+1978-1972-1973-1974)}{\text{Births } (1972+1973+1974)}$	.098[a] (N = 36)[b]
Source: *Demographic Yearbook of the United Nations*	
Change in GDP Index	
$\dfrac{\text{GDP index } (1976+1977+1978-1972-1973-1974)}{3}$	.048[a] (N = 59)[b]
Source: *International Financial Statistics*	
% Change in Available Foreign Exchange (deflated)	
$\dfrac{\text{Foreign exchange } (1976+1977+1978-1972-1973-1974)}{\text{Foreign exchange } (1972+1973+1974)}$	.081[a] (N = 66)[b]
Source: *International Financial Statistics*	

[a] Not statistically significant (p < 0.10).
[b] Sample sizes limited by data available.

Implications for Managers and Policymakers.

The results of this study suggest that advertising and promotion can influence consumer behavior in socially undesirable and unintended ways. Despite the good intentions of marketers, advertising can have negative consequences. As suggested in Figure 1, marketing strategies must be evaluated in view of the environment in which they will be executed. In the case of infant formula, promotion strategies designed for *industrialized* countries resulted in sickness and death for infants in *less-developed* countries. The context of promotion, purchase, and product use must be taken into account by producers and distributors.

Managers marketing products with potential usage problems should attempt to anticipate these and do careful research in test markets. Furthermore, marketers should not ignore criticism from responsible sources but instead should thoroughly investigate their own culpability. Finally, as Nicosia and Mayer (1976) advocate, managers must measure and take responsibility for all the effects of their advertising and not just focus on sales.

To the extent that firms fail to recognize their responsibility, policymakers will take action. The World Health Organization's *International Code of Breastmilk Substitutes* (Anderson, 1981) is the most recent example. The ban of cigarette advertising from U.S. television and the Federal Trade Commission's investigation of advertising of sugared cereals (leading to more stringent industry self-regulation) also come to mind. In a similar vein is the present controversy over beer and wine television commercials.

In this last case, the arguments bear a striking resemblance to those that arose in the Nestlé controversy. The critics suggest that TV advertising increases overall consumption of alcoholic beverages and, in turn, alcoholism. Brewers and vintners counter that TV advertising does nothing more than serve to distribute market share (Hume, 1985). Critics maintain that TV advertising influences underage drinking; advertisers argue that the ads are carefully targeted toward adults. Likewise, Nestlé argued that its advertising was aimed at the educated and high-income consumers in developing countries, while their critics suggested that baby formula ads reached other segments. Finally, *60 Minutes* reporters asked teenage drinkers if TV advertising influenced them to drink, and they said no. Similarly, Nestlé cited the World Health Organization study (1979), wherein 23,000 mothers in nine developing countries were asked what induced them to stop breast-feeding. Not once was advertising mentioned. In both situations, one might ask why consumers would be expected to admit to, or even be conscious of, their response to commercial advertising.

Beer and wine advertisers may be operating under the assumption that because one part of the market can use the product safely, all consumers can. A similar assumption was made by the infant formula manufacturers. Just as Figure 1 shows that environmental influences affect purchase and use of infant formula in developing nations, environmental influences may affect the purchase and use of alcoholic beverages by certain groups (for example, teenagers) such that a great potential for misuse (alcoholism, drunk driving) exists.

The similarities in the arguments indicate possible applications of our findings concerning infant formula to the case of beer and wine advertising. The latter may be influencing product consump-

tion rather than simply brand selection, although the study for Anheuser-Busch reported by Hume (1985) concludes the contrary. Further research is needed to learn more about the relationship between promotion, product and brand choice, and product use. This is particularly true in cases where promotion may have undesirable effects on society as well as positive effects on sales.

References

Anderson, K. (1981), "The Battle of the Bottle," *Time* (June 1), p. 26.

Armstrong, J. (1985), "Ethics and the Infant Formula Controversy," a paper presented at the Pan-Pacific Conference: A Business, Economic and Technological Exchange, Seoul, Korea (May).

Beaver, B. and F. Silvester (1982). "The Gall in Mother's Milk: The Infant Formula Controversy and the WHO Marketing Code," *Journal of Advertising,* 1 (January–March), 1–10.

Benton, A., L. Huston, M. J. Janse, and T. D. McCollough (1978), "Infant Malnutrition, Breastfeeding and Infant Formulas in Developing Nations," testimony and supplementary testimony presented to the U.S. Senate Subcommittee on Health and Scientific Research of the Committee on Human Resources, May 23, Washington, DC.

Buzzell, R. D. and F. D. Wiersema (1981), "Modelling Changes in Market Share: A Cross-Sectional Analysis," *Strategic Management Journal,* 2 (January–March), 27–42.

Cateora, P. R. (1983), *International Marketing,* 5th ed. Burr Ridge, IL: Irwin.

Cox, D. O. (1978), "Summary Statement of Abbott Laboratories on the Role of Prepared Infant Formulas in the Third World," and a follow-up letter to Senator Kennedy, both included as testimony and supplementary testimony presented to the U.S. Senate Subcommittee on Health and Scientific Research of the Committee on Human Resources, May 23, Washington, DC.

Farley, J. U., T. D. J. Louis, and S. K. Reddy (1980), "Joint 'Social Marketing' Promotion of a Weaning Food and a Contraceptive in Sri Lanka," *Journal of International Business Studies,* 2 (Winter), 73–80.

Feder, J. L. (1982), "On Exports and Economic

Growth," *Journal of Development Economics,* 12 (February–April), 59–73.

Hume, S. (1985), "Study Snips at Ads' Ties to Beer Demand," *Advertising Age,* 56 (March 4), 18.

International Financial Statistics (1978), International Monetary Fund, Washington, DC.

James, J. (1983). *Consumer Choice in the Third World,* London: Macmillan.

Jelliffe, D. B. (1971): "Commerciogenic Malnutrition? Time for a Dialogue," *Food Technology,* 25 (February), 56.

McComas, M., G. Fookes, and G. Taucher (1983), "The Dilemma of Third World Nutrition," a pamphlet published by Nestlé S.A.

McGuinness, T. and K. Cowling (1975), "Advertising and the Aggregate Demand for Cigarettes," *European Economic Review,* 6 (July), 311–28.

Muller, M. (1975), *The Baby Killer,* 2d ed., London: War on Want.

Nestlé (1983), *The Nestlé Case,* published by the Nestlé Coordination Center for Nutrition, Inc., 1120 Connecticut Avenue, N.W., Suite 301, Washington, DC 20036.

____ (1980), "The Story Behind the Issue: Infant Feeding in Developing Countries," a pamphlet published by the Nestlé Coordination Center for Nutrition, 1900 M Street, N.W., Suite 750, Washington, DC 20036.

Nicosia, M. and N. Mayer (1976). "Toward a Sociology of Consumption," *Journal of Consumer Research,* 3 (September), 65–75.

PAG (1972), "Protein Advisory Group, Statement No. 23 on Rational Promotion of Processed Foods," New York: PAG United Nations (July 18).

Pagan, R. D., Jr. (1986), "The Nestlé Boycott: Implications for Strategic Business Planning," *Journal of Business Strategy,* 6 (Spring), 12–14.

Post, J. E. (1978), "The International Infant Formula Industry," testimony and supplementary testimony presented to the U.S. Senate Subcommittee on Health and Scientific Research of the Committee on Human Resources, May 23, Washington, DC.

____ (1985), "Assessing the Nestlé Boycott: Corporate Accountability and Human Rights," *California*

Management Review, 27 (Winter), 113–31.

Salvatore, D. (1983), "A Simultaneous Equations Model of Trade and Development with Dynamic Policy Simulations," *KYKLOS,* 36 fasc. 1, 66–90.

Schudson, M. (1984), *Advertising, the Uneasy Persuasion,* New York: Basic Books.

Sethi, S. P., H. Etemad, and K. A. N. Luther (1985), "International Social Activism and Its Impact on Corporate Behavior—The Case of the Infant Formula Controversy," a paper presented at the Pan-Pacific Conference: A Business, Economic and Technological Exchange, Seoul, Korea (May).

____ (1986), "New Sociopolitical Forces: The Globalization of Conflict," *Journal of Business Strategy,* 6 (Spring), 25–31.

Sethi, S. P., and J. E. Post (1979), "The Marketing of Infant Formula in Less Developed Countries: Public Consequences of Private Actions," *California Management Review,* 21 (Summer), 35–48.

Stafford, J. R. (1978), "Statement of Wyeth International, A Subsidiary of American Home Products Corporation," testimony and supplementary testimony presented to the U.S. Senate Subcommittee on Health and Scientific Research of the Committee on Human Resources, May 23, Washington, DC.

Stiegler, G. P. (1985), personal interview with Carnation Company Vice President for Asia/Pacific during 1974–1982.

United Nations (1983), *Demographic Yearbook of the United Nations,* New York: Department of Social Affairs, Statistical Office.

Weede, E. (1983), "The Impact of Democracy on Economic Growth: Some Evidence from Cross-National Analysis," *KYKLOS,* 36 fasc. 1, 21–39.

World Health Organization (1979), "Collaborative Study on Breast-feeding: Methods and Main Results of the First Phase of the Study—Preliminary Report, MCH/79.3," Geneva, Switzerland: World Health Organization.

World Trade Annual (1969–1979), *Supplement to the World Trade Annual,* vols. 1–3, New York: Walker and Company.

VI SELECTED CASES AND A DECISION SIMULATION

This section has been expanded in the second edition to nine cases: Nike, Inc. in the 1990s; Budget Hotels Go Global; the SWATCH Project; Parker Pen Company; the McIlhenny Company: Japan; Nestlé—the Infant Formula Incident; Baksheesh; Philip Morris: The Export Warning Labels Issue; and Renault-Volvo: Strategic Alliance.

Most of the cases pertain to firms that course participants will recognize. The final citation is an especially prepared international negotiation simulation, the Siberian Petroleum Production Association. It provides the opportunity for interactive negotiations by participant teams. The cases offer the possibility of team or individual analysis of the problems and opportunities the companies faced.

1 NIKE, INC. IN THE 1990S (A): NEW DIRECTIONS

Robert J. Dolan

For fiscal year 1993 ending May 31, 1993, NIKE's sales were $3.9 billion, a 15 percent increase over 1992. From 1988–93, NIKE's compound annual growth rates were 27 percent and 29 percent in revenues and EPS, respectively (see Exhibit 1). Shortly after the July 1989 appointment of Richard Donahue as President and Chief Operating Officer of NIKE, Phil Knight, CEO, had offered his guide to the 1990s:

> *My own view of the decade ahead goes something like this: we stay primarily in shoes, clothing and accessories, market aggressively around the world, and make a couple acquisitions during the decade that will strengthen us in these three core areas. . . .*
>
> *Our goal is simple: to be the market share leader and the most profitable brand in all 39 footwear, apparel, and accessories lines in which we compete.*

In 1990, 78 percent of NIKE revenues had come from the United States. However, the U.S. athletic footwear market was growing at only 3–5 percent per year—compared to the 25 percent rate of the early 1980s. Thus, Donahue "planned to take a personal interest in expanding NIKE's overseas operations." (NIKE in Transition (C) case, p. 3).

Reebok, NIKE's prime competitor, had similar goals, viz. "to become the number one sports and fitness brand worldwide." In 1990, NIKE and Reebok each had revenues of over $2 billion and were by far the largest athletic shoe manufacturers in the world.

Reebok Initiatives 1990–1993

Like NIKE, Reebok had a strong CEO whose degree of involvement in running the company had varied over time. Paul Fireman, while a single-digit handicap golfer, was not a collegiate track star or Stanford MBA as Knight was. Fireman saw a contrast in styles as

---
EXHIBIT 1   NIKE Financials 1990–1993

| | Fiscal Year Ending May of | | | |
	1990	*1991*	*1992*	*1993*
Revenues	$2,235	$3,003	$3,405	$3,931
Net income	242.9	287.0	329.2	365.0
Net income per share	3.21	3.77	4.30	4.74
Stock price*—May 31	39¼	39¾	58	72½

---

*Adjusted for 2-for-1 stock split of October 5, 1990.
Source: Annual reports.

well: "We're playing a game, okay. I know we're playing a game. I don't think he does." To which Knight, reflecting on laying off 400 people after his return to the NIKE President position in 1984, replied: "It's more than a game. It's much more serious, because it's people's lives."[1]

While NIKE focused on the NIKE brand, Reebok identified itself as a "truly global multibrand consumer products company." Its growth to a $2 billion company was fueled by the success of the Reebok brand "Freestyle" shoe in the women's aerobic market; but, during 1987–88, it acquired AVIA (athletic shoes focused on high performance in sports), Rockport shoes (dress and casual footwear), Ellesse (apparel and footwear), and Boston Whaler (pleasure boats).[2]

Befitting its aerobics origin, Reebok did not follow the market pyramid model associated with NIKE in this case, i.e., the signing of top athletes and the trickle down of the product to the mass market. In 1992, however, Reebok began an assault on NIKE's 50 percent share in basketball shoes (versus Reebok's 15 percent) by signing Shaquille O'Neal to a $15 million, 5-year endorsement contract. O'Neal, the seven-foot, one-inch center from Louisiana State University and number one pick in the collegiate draft in 1992, was widely recognized as likely to be the next true superstar in professional basketball. Reportedly, O'Neal had little interest in competing with Michael Jordan for endorsement dollars at NIKE. He visited NIKE to discuss possible opportunities, but chose Reebok warm-ups as his attire for the day. (NIKE signed Alonzo Mourning from Georgetown, the number two pick in the draft, to a $16 million, 5-year contract). Reebok introduced The Shaq Attack line of basketball shoes in January 1993.

In 1993, Reebok signaled the importance of an integrated global communication strategy by consolidating its advertising agencies. Chiat/Day had held the $80 million U.S. account; Euro RSCG, the $40 million European spending; and Leo Burnett, the Far East $20 million account. Reebok turned over global responsibility to Leo Burnett. Industry observers cited Chiat/Day's lack of an international network as the reason behind its losing the Reebok account.

---

[1] Flerning Meeks, "The Sneaker Game," *Forbes,* October 22, 1990, pp. 114–5.
[2] Ellesse and Boston Whaler would be sold off by 1993.

NIKE 1990–1993

Phil Knight described NIKE's transformation from a production-oriented company to a marketing-oriented one:

> For years, we thought of ourselves as a production-oriented company, meaning we put all our emphasis on designing and manufacturing the product. But now we understand the most important thing we do is market the product. We've come around to saying that NIKE is a marketing-oriented company, and the product is our most important marketing tool. What I mean is marketing knits the whole organization together. The design elements and functional characteristics of the product itself are just part of the overall marketing process.[3]

Industry sources estimated NIKE's 1993 U.S. advertising spending at $281 million—a 22 percent increase over 1992. This $281 million represented 11.5 percent of U.S. sales. NIKE advertising had historically been regarded as path-breaking. The "Bo Knows" campaign featuring football and baseball star Bo Jackson won critical acclaim. Television ads ran the gamut from humorous to deeply emotional to public service advocacy; but consistently featured the famous NIKE exhortation to "Just Do It."

Functions that were previously contracted out were brought "in-house." All sales reps became NIKE employees rather than independent agents. Donahue focused on regaining control of international distribution by buying up distributors in place as distribution agreements with independents came to term. By mid-1993, NIKE regained distribution rights in Australia, New Zealand, Singapore, Hong Kong, Malaysia, and Taiwan. NIKE had established European headquarters in the Netherlands (moving from Germany), Asia/Pacific headquarters in Hong Kong, and Latin American headquarters in Sao Paulo, Brazil. In 1993, the largest non-NIKE-owned distributor was NIKE Japan, a subsidiary of Nissho Iwai Corporation, which sold $200 million of Nikes, including Air Jordans at 21,000 yen (≈$198), and paid royalties to NIKE.

Unlike Reebok, NIKE did not seek out a large advertising agency with an international network of offices to manage its worldwide campaigns. NIKE remained with its longtime Portland, Oregon-based agency, Wieder and Kennedy, who opened an office in Amsterdam to be near NIKE's European headquarters. Tim O'Kennedy, director of marketing for NIKE Europe BV, described building NIKE's European business as "frontier days." O'Kennedy and the ad agency planned to use the same advertising messages that had worked in the United States market explaining it's so "damn hard to do one good ad, any ad, anywhere, that the logistics of doing 16 of them in one targeted culture are impossible . . . The only truly unifying culture in Europe, among its youth, is American culture. American sports are a big part of that."[4] Bertrand Gaillochet, NIKE's Vice President of Operations, expressed a similar view: "France is not Alabama, Germany is not Massachusetts, England is not California. Still, consumers have common interests."[5]

---

[3] "High Performance Marketing: An Interview with NIKE's Phil Knight," *Harvard Business Review*, July–August 1992, pp. 90–103.

[4] Matthew Grimm, "Swoosh over Europe: NIKE Goes Global," *Brandweek*, February 1, 1993, p. 12–3.

[5] Nena Baker, "Successful Marketer of Shoes Has a Simple Goal: To Be #1," *Oregonian*, August 10, 1992.

Women's Fitness

In the early days, Reebok and NIKE had different focuses:

Reebok   —   Fitness for women
NIKE   —   Sports for men

In 1993, NIKE's women's sports and fitness business grew 10 percent to $400 million in sales (principally in the U.S.). This business required a new model of how to market rather than the pyramid model that had been so successful in track and basketball. Early ads to the female market featured Joanne Ernst, a triathlete, in a hard workout with the NIKE mantra "Just Do It, Just Do It" repeated throughout. The ad finished with Ernst turning to the camera and saying: "And it wouldn't hurt to stop eating like a pig, either." The ad was offensive to many in NIKE's new target group, the so-called fringe participants.

Later, the print ad series, Dialogues, featuring mothers and daughters presented women as powerful, capable people. It won critical acclaim and NIKE's share of the aerobics market began to rise. In October 1992, NIKE signed a deal with Jazzercise CEO and founder, Judi Sheppard Missett. Missett would wear Nike apparel and shoes in videos she distributed to Jazzercise's 5,000 instructors who taught 13,000 aerobics classes per week to 500,000 participants around the world. Nike would offer discounts to instructors and be involved in local promotions.

NIKE Town Shops

In November 1990, NIKE opened its first NIKE Town store, a 20,000 square foot operation in downtown Portland. NIKE Town's designer described it as a cross between the Smithsonian, Disney World, and Ralph Lauren. It featured 14 shops, selling NIKE equipment for 25 sports at full price along with life-size renderings of NIKE athletes like Michael Jordan, Bo Jackson, and Andre Agassi.

The second NIKE Town store, a 68,000 square foot operation on Michigan Avenue in Chicago, opened in July 1992. It featured a two-story photo mural of Michael Jordan and a mini basketball court and quickly became the city's busiest tourist attraction, drawing 7,500 people per day compared to the 5,000 at the world renowned Museum of Science and Industry and 4,000 at the Sears Tower Skydeck.

NIKE expected to open 10–12 NIKE Town stores throughout the U.S. designed after the original 20,000 square foot Portland model. The stores were not designed as major sales outlets for the company but rather to showcase the full line, strengthen ties with consumers, and be an extension of advertising building the brand.

New Directions

In 1991, NIKE formed Nike Sports Management (NSM) to help NIKE endorsers develop a coherent portfolio of marketing agreements. NSM helped baseball and football star

Bo Jackson develop a plan for dealing with the flood of endorsement opportunities presented him after the "Bo Knows" NIKE campaign success. Other prominent stars followed, including Deion Sanders (baseball and football) and Ken Griffey, Jr. (baseball). In 1992, NSM expanded from marketing agreement management to career management initially with two collegiate basketball stars, Alonzo Mourning and Harold Miner. Some had referred to Miner as "Mini-Michael," meaning Jordan. Mourning's situation became controversial as NIKE signed him to a $16 million endorsement deal prior to his contract negotiations with his professional team, the Charlotte Hornets. Mourning's negotiations extended into the season and some felt NIKE's agreement interfered with his process.

According to Liz Dolan, V.P. of corporate communications, "We just see this as a natural progression. We are not a shoe company. We are a sports company." Fred Schreyer, head of NSM in early 1993, noted: "We realize this is not something that neatly falls into the way things have been done in this business. But that doesn't make it wrong. In fact, we think we're bringing a much-needed service to the business."[6]

Later in 1993, Terdema Ussery II was appointed to the newly created position of president of NIKE Sports Management. A Princeton graduate with a master's degree from Harvard's Kennedy School and a law degree from Berkeley, Ussery had been commissioner of the Continental Basketball League.[7] In a press release, President Dick Donahue said "with Ussery, we have someone who understands athletes and the importance of planning for a career, not just a game or a season. The goal of NIKE Sports Management is to allow players to concentrate on their on-court or on-field performance, while we help them handle the business of being a professional athlete."

A second new venture for NIKE was with Creative Artists Agency, the Hollywood talent agency. Michael Ovitz, CAA's head, was well known as a celebrity-broker. Ovitz said the NIKE/CAA venture would be aimed at redefining and expanding the world of sports entertainment. Previously, NIKE had purchased the Ben Hogan golf tour for players aspiring to the PGA tour and renamed it the NIKE tour. NIKE had taken a team of NBA stars including NIKE-endorser Charles Barkley to Japan for exhibition games and some felt the next step would be to package such events into programming, sell time to associated sponsors, and then sell the package to a media owner—or even own the media. NIKE Advertising Director Scott Bedbury outlined the potential: "Forget the business NIKE's in for a moment. This is going to boom across the map, and massive amounts of money can be made. Now why does that have to be someone other than NIKE? If we end up spending $300–$400 million on advertising worldwide, some kind of ownership in key media vehicles might not be a bad idea." Reebok's response: "More power to them. We're happy to see them trying to do so many things. It just means they're losing focus and taking their eye off the ball."[8]

---

[6] Charles Brennan, "Shoe Giant NIKE Steps on Sports World Toes," *Washington Post,* May 22, 1993.

[7] The Continental Basketball League or CBA as it was known was a training ground for those players not able to "make it" in the National Basketball Association upon leaving college.

[8] Matthew Grimm, "NIKE Vision," *Brandweek,* March 29, 1993, p. 19ff.

Results through Fiscal Year 1993

In 1993, NIKE revenue reached $3.9 billion. On May 31, 1993, $1,000 invested in NIKE stock on May 31, 1987, was worth $9,024.[9] An equivalent investment in the S&P 500 was worth $1,718. Exhibit 2 gives the breakdown of NIKE revenues by geographic area 1990–93, and Exhibit 3 compares Reebok and NIKE for the same time period. Yet Knight's discussion of these results in the 1993 Annual Report was not without reservation and caveats about the future:

> To our Shareholders: We had our sixth consecutive record year in Fiscal '93 but as we go to press, no one is interested in that. How do you write an annual report when all anyone is interested in is the annum that hasn't occurred yet?
>
> . . . our earnings for '94 are likely to grow at a slower pace than our own target of 15 percent.
>
> . . . we're hitting a series of bumps:
>
> 1. The current economic atmosphere in Western Europe is the worst in 13 years . . .
> 2. Into that environment we install the continent's first real "futures" program . . .
> 3. . . . we hit the "billion dollar management bump," similar to what we had seen in the U.S. in 1986 [when] we succeeded in outgrowing internal systems and support capabilities, and to some extent, management talent . . . Since 1987, our European revenues have grown from $191 million to $1.1. billion, and we find ourselves in a similar position . . .

Knight stated the goals for fiscal year 1994 to be positioning of the international division to grow as economies improve and keeping "growth, albeit single-digit growth, going for the NIKE brand in the U.S."

A key issue in developing the international organization was the development of country nationals who could comprehend the NIKE spirit and message. Spending time at NIKE world headquarters in Beaverton on 74 acres with the Bo Jackson Fitness Center, the Joan Benoit Samuelson Center, the John McEnroe building, and so forth, would help—but that had not prevented one country manager from proposing translations of "Just Do It" into his country's language.

EXHIBIT 2   NIKE Sales by Year

	Geographical Breakdown of Revenues			
	1990	*1991*	*1992*	*1993*
United States	78.5%	71.3%	66.7%	64.3%
Europe	15.0	22.1	27.0	27.6
Latin America, Canada, and Others	1.3	1.9	2.2	4.5
Asia Pacific	5.2	4.7	4.0	3.5

Source: Annual reports.

---

[9] NIKE stock split 2 for 1 in October 1990.

EXHIBIT 3   COMPARISON NIKE AND REEBOK

		Fiscal Year*			
		1990	*1991*	*1992*	*1993*
Revenues (millions)	Reebok	2159.2	2734.5	3022.6	2893.0
	NIKE	2235.0	3003.0	3405.0	3931.0
Net income (millions)	Reebok	176.6	234.7	114.8	223.4
	NIKE	242.9	287.0	329.2	365.0

		Calendar Year			
		1990	*1991*	*1992*	*1993*
Share U.S. athletic	Reebok	21	23	24	21
footwear market	NIKE	29	29	30	32

*Nike's fiscal year ends May 31; Reebok's ends December 31.
Source: Annual reports.

Discussion Issues

1. Summarize the key similarities and differences between NIKE's and Reebok's vision for global dominance in the 1990s.
2. Can NIKE truly be a global marketer—"doing the same things in the same way everywhere"? Why or why not? Explain.

2 BUDGET HOTELS GO GLOBAL

Andrea Alexander and Johny K. Johansson

Rows and rows of hotels dot the shoreline of Kowloon, overlooking the spectacular skyline of Hong Kong Island, a ten-minute ferry ride across the bay. But not all are at the five-star level. Budget and mid-priced hotel chains have moved in on what used to be an enclave of five-star hotels. Only a few blocks away from the Hilton, Sheraton, Westin, Intercontinental, and Four Seasons hotels, the Holiday Inn conducts a brisk business, accommodating middle-class tourists.

Expansion Strategies

In the same manner that first-class hotel chains first swept the globe, second-tier hotels are now expanding globally. Budget and mid-priced hotels now comprise over one third of all hotels in major cosmopolitan centers. Furthermore, these hotels are the fastest-growing segment of the industry. Originally targeting main tourist cities in Europe, current trends show lower-priced hotel construction increasing rapidly in Latin America and Asia. Best Western, the American budget chain, operates hotels in New Delhi and Bombay. The Holiday Inn signboard can be seen in Beijing, China, as well as Temuco, Chile.

Best Western, Holiday Inn, Days Inn, Carlson, and Choice International are examples of American budget and mid-priced hotel chains expanding into Europe, Africa, Asia, and Latin America (see Exhibit 1). Choice Hotels expects to have over 3,000 hotels operating in foreign countries within the next 10 years. Most of the hotel chains expand into foreign markets by franchising their name and, in particular, their electronic reservations network. The company owns very few of the hotels, lessening the need for financing and the risk of foreign exchange exposure.

Source: This case was prepared by Andrea Alexander under the direction of Professor Johny K. Johansson, Georgetown University. It is based on material from: Edwin McDowell, "Midlevel Hotels Look Abroad; Some U.S. Chains Seek to Expand off the Beaten Path," *New York Times,* August 28, 1995, pp. D1, D6 and Jacqueline Simmons, "Budget Hotels Aren't Bargains Abroad," *The Wall Street Journal,* November 17, 1995, pp. B1, B8.

EXHIBIT 1   **Budget Hotels Expand Globally:** *New Hotel Development*

Hotel Chain	Location	Open	Under Construction	Agreement to Open
Best Western	Latin America	34	7	0
	Asia	7	6	0
	Europe, Africa	6	0	0
Carlson (Country Inn)	Latin America	0	1	106
	Asia	0	1	60
	Africa	1	0	0
Choice International	Latin America	20	7	275
(Comfort, Quality,	Asia	23	13	74
Clarion, and Sleep Inn)				
Days Inn	Latin America	8	1	0
	Asia	0	8	0
	Africa	0	0	3
Holiday Inn Express	Latin America	23	24	5
	Asia	29	15	0
	Latin America	28	4	16

While first-class hotels tend to locate one major hotel in a metropolitan or tourist area, the new budget hotels pepper each metropolitan area with several smaller hotels and expand further into the provincial areas. This is similar to the strategy employed by McDonald's and other fast-food chains, which initially opened in core country centers and gradually spread across the countryside.

Industry Factors

The growth of budget hotels abroad can be attributed to a variety of factors. The growth of small but global businesses is a major factor. Not able or willing to afford the five-star hotels, smaller companies house their travelling representatives in cheaper three- and four-star hotels. Tourists also are opting for these cheaper alternatives. Furthermore, in many emerging and newly industrializing countries, these hotels remain the only mid-priced alternatives. And in some of these countries, the fall of communism has created a new and previously untapped market.

Like the growing middle class in these countries, small businessmen and tourists do not necessarily want to pay top dollar for a five-star hotel. They can still demand—and receive—a reasonable level of comfort during their stay. Although these hotels often serve only local cuisine, competitive budget hotels are providing air conditioning, television, wake-up calls, and continental breakfasts.

Technology has also helped to propagate the spread of hotel chains abroad. Even the most remote locations can communicate and make electronic bookings for clients. For example, rather than routing reservations and messages through its central New Delhi location, and then forwarding the message to Phoenix, the Best Western system allows a single hotel manager in Bombay to send requests and messages directly to the Arizona headquarters via speedy and low-cost e-mail.

Competition

These hotels compete not only with local domestic chains and single hotels but with budget hotels from other countries. The globalizing trend can be found among international chains not based in the United States. Accor, for example, a giant French hotel chain, competes directly with the American chains in both Europe and the Pacific. Another competitor is European Novotel, with very strong presence in the United States and elsewhere. Globalizing of competitors is a strong driver of further globalization among existing chains.

Even though most budget chains continue to proliferate, some are standing on the sidelines. For example, giant Marriott has refrained from expanding their mid-level—and very successful—Courtyard hotels internationally. Instead the company plans to build its current hotels in key cities throughout the world, preferring to postpone international budget hotel expansion.

Ironically, the budget hotels abroad are often not as much of a bargain as they might seem. A night at a Quality Inn in the United States will cost approximately $65. The Rome version can cost over $150. A stay at the Beijing Holiday Inn is similarly high-priced. Although high start-up costs and more expensive overhead can account for some of the price disparity, price inflation also gives companies a chance to skim the market. In a transitional period, the new arrival can charge a first-mover premium before competitors move in and put pressure on the prices.

Minor Problems?

In the midst of this optimistic expansion, some problems exist. Many of the newly opened hotels are not yet profitable. Local franchisors can misjudge the market demand, and start-up costs can be high. It is important to create awareness and positive word-of-mouth among customers and taxi-drivers, airport personnel, and so on. Even though the budget hotels tend to refrain from media advertising, in an initial period it is typically necessary to create some awareness of location and amenities in the new market using advertising and various promotions.

Other problems relate to the exchange risks involved. The devaluation of the Mexican peso, for example, made many hotels' Mexican operations a drag on profits.

In spite of these problems, most budget hotel executives contend that the prospects of long-term returns outweigh any current difficulties. The trend toward the expansion of mid-level hotels abroad continues.

Discussion Issues

1. What factors are fueling the rapid demand for mid-level hotels in Latin America and Asia? What market segments are the hotels targeting?

2. Why are mid-level hotels charging such high rates? Can these hotels remain profitable without lowering room prices?

3. Why might Marriott be hesitant to expand their middle-class hotels globally?

3 THE SWATCH PROJECT

Susan W. Nye and Barbara Priovolos

"This watch is the product that will reintroduce Switzerland to the low and middle price market. It is the first step of our campaign to regain dominance of the world watch industry," said Dr. Ernst Thomke, President of ETA SA, a subsidiary of Asuag and Switzerland's largest watch company. Ernst Thomke had made this confident declaration about SWATCH to Franz Sprecher, Project Marketing Consultant, in late spring 1981. Sprecher had accepted a consulting assignment to help ETA launch the watch, which was, at that time, still in the handmade prototype phase and as yet unnamed. This new watch would come in a variety of colored plastic cases and bracelets with an analog face. ETA had designed an entire production process exclusively for SWATCH. This new process was completely automated and built the quartz movement directly into the watch case. Sprecher's key concern was how to determine a viable proposal for moving this remarkable new product from the factory in Grenchen, Switzerland, into the hands of consumers all over the world.

Company Background: ETA, Ebauches and Asuag

SWATCH was only one brand within a large consortium of holding companies and manufacturing units controlled by Allgemeine Schweizer Uhrenindustrie (Asuag, or General Company of Swiss Watchmaking). SWATCH was to be produced by ETA, a movement manufacturer, which was part of Ebauches SA, the subsidiary company overseeing watch movement production within the Asuag organization (Exhibits 1 and 2).

Asuag was founded in 1931 when the Swiss government orchestrated the consolidation of a wide variety of small watchmakers. The major purpose of this consolidation was

Source: This case was prepared by Susan W. Nye and Barbara Priovolos under the direction of Visiting Professor Jean-Pierre Jeannet as a basis for class discussion rather than to illustrate either effective or ineffective handling of an administrative situation. Copyright © 1985 by IMEDE, Lausanne, Switzerland. The International Institute for Management Development (IMD), resulting from the merger between IMEDE, Lausanne, and IMI. Geneva, acquires and retains all rights. Not to be used or reproduced without written permission from IMD, Lausanne, Switzerland.

EXHIBIT 1   Asuag Organization

Subsidiaries	Movements	Components	Industrial Components Equip./Measure Tools/Service
Ebauches SA, Neuchatel (ESA)	x	x	x
ETA, Fabriques d'Ebauches SA, Grenchen	x	x	
Les Fabriques d'Assortiments Reunies SA,			
Le Locle (FAR)		x	x
Nivarox SA, La Chaux-de-Fonds (NIV)		x	x
Pierres Holding SA, Bienne (PH)		x	x
General Watch Co. Ltd., Bienne	x	x	x
Eterna SA, Grenchen			
Eterna	x	x	
Compagnie des Montres Longines,			
Francillon SA, St. Imier			
Longines	x	x	x
Montres Rado SA, Longeau			
Rado	x	x	
Mido, G. Schaeren & Co. SA, Bienne			
Mido	x	x	
Fabrique de Montres Rotary SA,			
La Chaux-de-Fonds			
Rotary		x	
Era Watch Co. Ltd., Bienne			
Edox	x		
Certina, Kurth Frères SA, Grenchen			
Certina	x	x	
Gunzinger SA, Fabrique d'Horlogerie			
Technos, Bienne			
Technos		x	
Endura SA, Bienne			
Microma, Dynasty	x		
Diantus Watch SA, Castel San Pietro			
Dafnis, Diantus	x		
Oris Watch Co. SA, Hölstein			
Oris	x	x	x

Number of employees at the end of December 1980 by subsidiary:

Industries	Switzerland	Abroad	Total
Ebauches SA	6739	719	7458
Fabriques d'Assortiments Reunies SA	1573	39	1612
Nivarox SA	383	—	383
Pierres Holding SA	880	571	1451
Societe du Produit Termine (GWC, ARSA, et ATLANTIC)	2733	435	3168
ASU Components SA/Statek Corp.	194	978	1172
DG Asuag, Asam SA, Asulab SA	330	—	330
Total:	12832	2742	15574

EXHIBIT 2   Summary of Financial Activity for Asuag (In Million Swiss Francs)

Asuag Group/31 December	1972	1973	1974	1975	1976	1977	1978	1979	1980
Consolidated sales	1081	1264	1404	1073	1041	1169	1195	1212	1332
Number of employees	19350	19720	20230	17205	15725	16351	16195	15289	15574
Current assets	696	761	878	786	786	813	782	761	788
Long-term assets	263	272	287	309	319	341	338	324	390
Debt	443	479	589	542	418	483	552	580	680
Equity	1352	1384	1436	1372	1364	1352	1063	998	979

	1980/1981 Francs	1979/1980 Francs
Income Statement		
Dividends from subsidiaries	$ 4,507,001.65	$ 4,938,768.43
Remittances from affiliates	14,225,219.10	10,604,457.95
Interest income	9,910,303.23	10,517,844.92
	28,642,523.98	26,061,071.30
Expenses		
General administrative costs	6,296,053.53	5,404,093.33
Research and development	1,809,858.13	2,050,212.05
Information and promotion	3,550,406.81	3,943,119.75
Taxes	692,994.85	698,932.00
Amortization	2,539,096.00	1,622,761.80
Interest paid	8,985,565.05	7,872,187.46
Profit	4,768,549.61	4,469,764.91
	28,642,523.98	26,061,071.30

Companies or Groups of Companies	Sales 1st Half 1981 (Francs, Millions)	Difference 1st Half 1981–1980	Sales 1980 (Francs, Millions)	Difference 1980–1979
Sales Development of Affiliated Companies				
Ebauches SA	389.2	+ 18.7%	670.7	+ 16.2%
Fabriques d'Assortiments Reunies SA	61.0	+ 4.4	109.8	+ 9.9
Nivarox SA	13.3	− 2.8	25.8	+ 4.1
Pierres Holding SA	38.4	+ 11.1	66.8	+ 4.1
Soc. du Produit Termine (GWC, ARSA, Atlantic)	282.1	+ 23.2	569.9	+ 6.7
ASU Components SA, Statek Corp.	39.8	+ 31.4	62.4	+ 44.4

to begin rationalization of a highly fragmented, but vital, industry suffering the effects of one world war and a global depression. By 1981, Asuag had become the largest Swiss producer of watches and watch components. Asuag was the third-largest watchmaker in the world behind two Japanese firms, Seiko and Citizen. Asuag had a total of 14,499 employees, 83 percent of whom worked within Switzerland. Asuag accounted for about one-third of all Swiss watch exports, which were estimated at Sfr. [Swiss francs] 3.1 billion in 1980.[1] Major activities were movement manufacture and watch assembly. Bracelets, cases, dials, and crystals were sourced from independent suppliers.

Ebauches SA, a wholly owned subsidiary of Asuag, controlled the various movement manufacturers. The Swiss government played an important role in encouraging and funding Ebauches' formation in 1932. An "Ebauche" was the base upon which the movement was built and Ebauches companies produced almost all of the movements used in watches produced by Asuag group companies. Sixty-five percent of Ebauches production was used by Asuag group companies, and the rest was sold to other Swiss watch manufacturers. Ebauches SA recorded sales of Sfr. 675.0 million in 1980, a 3.1 percent increase over the previous year. Ebauches companies employed a total of 6,860 people, 90 percent of them in Switzerland.

ETA SA, the manufacturer of SWATCH, produced a full range of watch movements and was known as the creator of the ultra-thin movements used in expensive watches. The quality of ETA movements was so renowned that some watches were marked with "ETA Swiss Quartz" as well as the name brand. ETA movements were distributed on a virtual quota basis to a select group of watch manufacturers. The demand for its movements had always equaled or exceeded its production capacity. In 1980, ETA employed over 2,000 people and produced more than 14 million watch movements for revenues of approximately Sfr. 362 million and profits of about Sfr. 20 million.

Dr. Ernst Thomke had joined ETA as president in 1978. Early in his career, he had worked as an apprentice in production at ETA. He left the watch industry to pursue university degrees in chemistry and cancer research, earning both a Ph.D. and a medical degree. He then moved on to a career in research at British-owned Beecham Pharmaceutical. Thomke did not stay in the lab for long. He moved into the marketing department where he boosted Beecham sales with ski trips and concerts for physicians and their families. His unorthodox selling techniques led to skyrocketing sales. He looked for a new challenge when faced with a transfer to another country. His colleagues at Asuag and throughout the watch industry described Thomke as a tough negotiator and as iron willed. After joining ETA, he agreed to provide advertising and support allowances to movement customers. However, these agreements stated that ETA only provided aid if it had a role in product planning and strategy formulation.

The Global Watch Industry

To understand the global watch industry, three key variables were considered: watch technology, watch price, and the watch's country of origin.

Watch Movement Technology

Watch design underwent a revolutionary change in the early 1970s, when traditional mechanical movement technology was replaced with electronics. A mechanical watch's

---

[1] US$ = SFR 2.00/1 SFR = US $0.50

energy source came from a tightened mainspring that was wound by the user. As the spring unwound, it drove a series of gears to which the watch hands were attached: the hands moved around the analog (or numerical) face of the watch to indicate the time. Highly skilled workers were required to produce and assemble the movements in accurate mechanical watches and the Swiss were world renowned in this area.

The first electronic watch was built by a Swiss engineer, Max Hetzel, in 1954, but it was U.S. and Japanese companies that first commercialized electronic technology. Bulova, a U.S. company, was the first to bring an electric watch to market in the early 1960s, based upon tuning-fork technology. A vibrating tuning-fork stimulated the gear movements and moved the hands on a traditional analog face. At the end of the decade, quartz crystal technology began to appear in the marketplace. An electric current was passed through a quartz crystal to stimulate high-frequency vibration. This oscillation could be converted to precise time increments with a step motor. Quartz technology was used to drive the hands on traditional analog watches and led to an innovation: digital displays. Digital watches had no moving parts and the conventional face and hands were replaced with digital readouts. Electronic watches revolutionized the industry because for the first time consumers could purchase an inexpensive watch with accuracy within 1 second per day or less.

Ebauches-owned companies had been involved in electronic watch technology since its pioneering stages. In 1962, Ebauches was among a number of Swiss component manufacturers and watch assembly firms that established the "Centre Electronique Horlogère" (CEH). The center's immediate goal had been to develop a movement that could compete with Bulova's tuning-fork movement. CEH was never able to successfully produce a tuning-fork movement that did not violate Bulova's patents. In 1968, Ebauches entered into a licensing agreement with Bulova to manufacture and sell watches using Bulova's tuning-fork technology. In 1969, CEH introduced its first quartz crystal models and Ebauches subsequently took over manufacture and marketing for the new movement, introducing its first quartz line in 1972.

Ebauches also worked with the U.S. electronics firm Texas Instruments and FASEC[2] in the early 1970s to pursue integrated circuit and display technology. By 1973, Ebauches was producing movements or watches for three generations of electronic technology: tuning-fork, quartz analog, and digital. Ebauches did not stay in the assembled watch market for long, and returned to its first mission of producing and supplying watch movements to Asuag companies. Between 1974 and 1980, the Swiss watch industry as a whole spent Sfr. 1 billion toward investment in new technology and Asuag accounted for half the expenditure. Ebauches Electronique on Lake Neuchâtel was a major use of investment funds and was created to produce electronic components.

Price

Price was the traditional means of segmenting the watch market into three categories. "AA" and "A" watches were sold at prices above Sfr. 1200 and accounted for 42 percent

---

[2] FASEC was a laboratory for joint research in semiconductors, integrated circuits, and lasers. It was formed in 1966 by the Swiss Watch Federation (FHS), Brown Boveri, Landis & Gyr, and Philips of the Netherlands.

of the total value of watches sold and 2 percent of total volume. "B" watches priced at Sfr. 120–1200 made up 25 percent of the market in value and 12 percent in units. "C" watches were priced under Sfr. 120 and accounted for 33 percent of the market in value and 86 percent of total units.

Players in the Global Watch Industry

Japan, Hong Kong, and Switzerland together accounted for almost 75 percent of total world watch production. In 1980s, watch producers worldwide were faced with inventory buildups at factory warehouses and retail stores. A worldwide recession had slowed demand for watches and overproduction compounded the problem. 1980 projections were not being met, and factory-based price cutting, particularly by large producers, was becoming common as a substitute for production cuts.

The Swiss Watch Industry

The Swiss watchmakers' position was viewed by many industry observers as being more precarious than others. Since 1970, when the Swiss accounted for 80 percent, their share of the world watch market in units had declined to 25 percent of the world's watch exports. The Swiss ranked third in unit production but remained first in the value of watches sold. Twenty-five percent of all Swiss watch factories were permanently shut down during the 1970s and 30,000 workers lost their jobs.

Despite extensive factory and company shut-downs within the Swiss industry, in 1981 the Swiss still owned the rights to 10,000 registered brand names, although less than 3,000 were actively marketed. Most Swiss watches were priced in the mid- to expensive price ranges, above Sfr. 100 ex-factory and Sfr. 400 retail. In 1981, industry analysis were congratulating the Swiss for their adherence to the upper price segments, as the low-price segments were beginning to turn weak. Industry observers noted that the Swiss seemed to be emerging from a decade of uncertainty and confusion and were focusing on higher quality segments of the watch market. Swiss component manufacturers had been supplying their inexpensive components to Far East assemblers and it was felt that this practice would continue.

Swiss watch manufacturers generally fell into one of three categories. First, there were the well-established, privately owned companies which produced expensive, handmade watches. These firms included Rolex, Patek-Philippe, Vacheron Constantin, Audemars-Piguet, and Piaget. For the most part, these firms were in good health financially. Stressing high quality as the key selling point, these manufacturers maintained tight control through vertical integration of the entire production and marketing processes from movement and component production through assembly and out into the market. The recession had cost them some customers, but these had been replaced by new Middle Eastern clients.

Second, there were a number of relatively small privately owned companies that concentrated on watch components—bracelets, crystals, faces, hands, or movements. This group included an ETA competitor, Ronda SA. The financial health of these companies was mixed.

The third sector of the industry were the largest participants. Asuag and Société Suisse pour l'Industrie Horlogère (SSIH). SSIH was an organization similar to but smaller than Asuag, producing 10 percent of all Swiss watch and movements output. Its most famous brand, Omega, had for years been synonymous with high quality. Omega had recently run into trouble and had been surpassed by the Asuag brand Rado as Switzerland's best selling watch. In June 1981, SSIH announced a loss of Sfr. 142 million for the fiscal year ending March 31, 1981. This loss gave SSIH a negative net worth of Sfr. 27.4 million. A consortium of Swiss banks and the Zurich trading group Siber Hegner & Co., AG, were brought together to save the company.

In the late 1970s, Asuag and SSIH began working in a cooperative effort to cut costs through use of common components. However, this effort did not affect individual brand identities or brand names. Industry analysts did not rule out the eventual possibility of a full merger. Asuag was noted for its strength in production and quality, but was reported to have a weakness in the marketing function. SSIH was noted for strong marketing skills, but had recently been faced with a slippage in product quality. It was believed that both companies would stand to gain from closer ties in research and production.

The watch industry played a significant role in Switzerland's economy. The banks and the government took a serious interest in its operations and the performance of individual companies. Between 1934 and 1971, the Swiss government made it illegal to open, enlarge, transform, or transfer any watch manufacturing plant without government permission. This action was justified as a defensive move to combat potential unemployment due to foreign competition. It was also illegal to export watch components and watch making technology without a government-issued permit. The government essentially froze the industry by dictating both prices and the supplier-manufacturer relationship. These constraints were gradually removed, beginning in 1971, and by 1981 were no longer in effect.

The Japanese Watch Industry

Japan was the world's second-largest watch producer in 1980 with approximately 67.5 million pieces, up from 12.2 million pieces in 1970. The growth of the watch industry in Japan was attributed to the Japanese watchmakers' ability to commercialize the electronic watch. K. Hattori, which marketed the Seiko, Alba, and Pulsar brands, was Japan's largest watchmaker, and responsible for approximately 42 million units. Selling under three different brand names allowed Hattori to compete across a broad price range. Seiko watches fell into the "B" category. Alba and Pulsar competed in the "C" range.

Casio entered the watch market in 1975 selling low-cost digital watches. Philip Thwaites, the U.K. marketing manager, described Casio as follows: "Casio's strategy is simple: we aim to win market share by cutting prices to the bone." Casio's product line was exclusively digital. The company was noted for adding "gadgetry" to its watches, such as timers, stop watches, and calculators. In Casio's view, the watch was no longer just a timepiece but a "wrist instrument."

In contrast to Switzerland, Japan's "big three" watch producers, the Hattori group, Casio and Citizen, had a combined product line of fewer than 12 brands. All three firms were fully integrated: producing movements, most components, assembling and distributing worldwide through wholly owned distribution subsidiaries. These watchmakers made extensive use of automated equipment and assembly-line production techniques.

The Watch Industry in Hong Kong

Hong Kong manufacturers had only entered the market in 1976 but by 1980 unit output had reached 126 million units. Ten major producers accounted for an estimated 70 percent of total volume. Watch design costs were minimized by copying Swiss and Japanese products. As many as 800 "loft workshops" were in operation in the late 1970s. These facilities could be started as low cost and run with minimum overheads. The expanded capacity led to the rapid fall of Hong Kong watch prices; prices of simple watches in the Sfr. 15–20 range in 1978 and dropped to Sfr. 10 the next year with margins of less than Sfr. 1. Hong Kong watches were sold under private label in minimum lot sizes of 1000–2000 units with average ex-factory costs of Sfr. 20 for mechanical watches and Sfr. 50 for quartz analog and Sfr. 10 for electronic digitals. Most watchmaking activity in Hong Kong was concentrated on assembly. The colony had become Switzerland's largest client for watch components and movements. Swiss movement exports to Hong Kong had grown from 13.3 million pieces in 1977 to 38.5 million pieces in 1980.

The "Popularius" Project

The SWATCH project began under the code name "Popularius." Thomke's goal had been to discover what the market wanted and then to supply it. He told his engineers that he wanted a plastic analog watch that could be produced at less than Sfr. 10 and sold ex-factory at Sfr. 15. He also wanted to use the technology that ETA had developed for its high-priced, ultra-thin "Delirium" movements to enter the low-priced watch segment. Thomke was convinced that ETA's long-term viability and profitability depended on increasing the company's volume and integrating downstream into fully assembled watch production and marketing. Thomke had seen the demand for ETA movements dwindle when exports of finished Swiss watches declined from 48 million pieces in 1970 to 28.5 million in 1980. The mass market "C" watch all but disappeared from Swiss production and was replaced by inexpensive Japanese and Hong Kong models. The Swiss manufacturers pushed their products up-market and sales value of exports moved from Sfr. 2,383.7 million in 1970 to Sfr. 3,106.7 million in 1980.

With electronic technology, movements were no longer a major cost factor in the end price of a watch. The average price of an ETA movement was Sfr. 18 and applied whether the watch sold ex-factory at Sfr. 80 or Sfr. 500. Thomke wanted to increase ETA volume output and knew that Asuag transfer pricing policies made this difficult. Asuag was a loose consortium of companies, each operating as an independent profit center. Transfer pricing reflected this fact. At each point of production and sales, movements, components, assembly and through the distribution channels, a profit was taken by the individual unit. Thomke believed that this system weakened the Swiss brands' competitive position for the volume business which his movement business needed to be profitable. Thomke believed that if he wanted to introduce a successful new product, he would need to sell it to

1 percent of the world's population, which amounted to about 10 percent of the "C" market segment. He knew that the Japanese companies were fully integrated and that Hong Kong assemblers, which already operated with low overheads, were moving increasingly toward full integration (Exhibit 3).

Thomke knew he could turn over the "Popularius" project to another Asuag unit, but he did not have a great deal of confidence in the production and marketing capabilities of Asuag branded watch assemblers. ETA was the only company within the Asuag group that had extensive experience in automated manufacturing. If the "Popularius" was to succeed as the latest entry in the low-price market, it would have to be produced in an automated environment. Furthermore, Thomke had watched many of the finished watch companies steadily lose market share to Japanese and Hong Kong competitors over the last decade and he had little confidence in their marketing capabilities. ETA currently sold 65 percent of its output to Asuag companies and Thomke wanted to reduce this dependence. He planned to use the "Popularius" as ETA's own entry into the finished watch market (Exhibit 4).

ETA engineers and technicians, responding to Thomke's specifications, developed the "Popularius." To meet the low unit ex-factory price was no small accomplishment. A cost analysis at that time showed that the required components without assembly would have cost Sfr. 20. Quartz technology provided accuracy within one second per day, and the watch was waterproof, shock resistant, and powered by a readily available and inexpensive three-year battery. The watch weighed 20 grams and was 8 mm thick with an analog face. The face and strap were made of durable mat finished plastic and the strap was at-

EXHIBIT 3   Breakdown of Costs and Margins for Traditional "B" Watches (By Country of Origin)

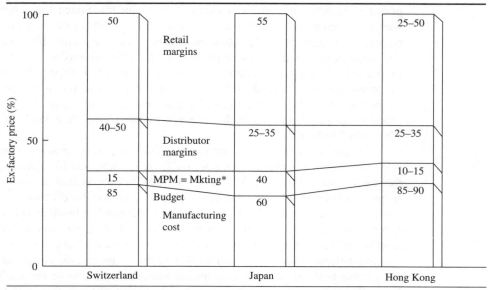

*Manufacturing and profit margins.

EXHIBIT 4   Comparison of Ebauches SA Sales to World Market

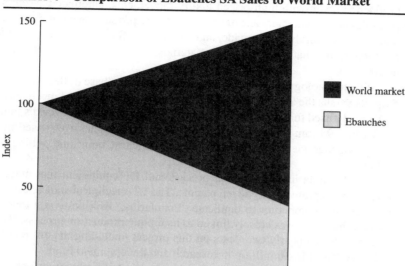

tached with a special hinge that was flush with the face. It was considered stylish and attractive. Further aesthetic enhancements could be made with the careful selection of color and face design. Ultrasonic welding produced a finished product that would not be reopened after it left the assembly line. In the event of failure, designers believed that the watch was essentially unrepairable and would be replaced rather than repaired. Batteries were replaceable by the owner and inserted in the back of the watch.

The product line was, at that time, limited to one size, a large "man's" watch, which could be produced in a number of solid colors with several designs or patterns on the face. Although a 25 percent smaller version for women and children was being considered, no definite introduction plans had as yet been developed. Management believed that the young were a potentially strong secondary market for the new product. A number of ideas were in development for "novelty" watches with special functions, a button watch, and special colors and motifs. A day/date calendar with a quick reset feature was available. The production system was designed for strict quality control conditions to produce highly reliable watches. The movement was designed with a theoretical life of 30 years and "Popularius" would be sold with a one-year guarantee.

Manufacturing Systems for "Popularius"

The ability to produce and sell a watch with the "Popularius" features, for a low price, was largely dependent upon unique production technology developed at ETA. ETA's product development staff was respected throughout the watch industry for its technical abilities in mass production. Its production technology was considered by industry observers to be equal to that of the best Japanese companies. In the early stages of electronic movement production, even with high-priced luxury movements, automated assembly was not only possible but a practical means of production. The production equipment planned for "Popularius" was entirely Swiss made, and would in its final form consist of a fully automated production line that consumed raw materials at one end and delivered complete watches at the other.

ETA technology built the movement right into the base of the watch and required only 51 parts versus the 90 to 150 parts found in most electronic and mechanical watches. ETA had already used this technology to create the "Delirium," the world's thinnest movement measuring .98 mm at its thickest point. These movements were used in high precision, luxury watches measuring 2.4 mm at their thickest point and selling at retail for Sfr. 40,000.

The "Popularius" production process and the equipment that made the technology possible were protected by seven patents. The ETA technical staff felt that it would be impossible for a competitor to duplicate "Popularius," especially at a low ex-factory price, because the watch was closely linked to its unique production process. ETA engineers had already invested nearly two years on this project, including the efforts of 200 employees and more than Sfr. 10 million in research and development funds.

Production was still limited to hand production of prototype watches and watches for test marketing purposes. ETA expected the line to have semi- but not full automation with forecasted production levels of 600,000 men's watches and 150,000 smaller versions for women or children in the first year. Fully automated lines that would produce 2 million units per year were targeted for the second year. Production goals of 3 million units had been set for the third year. Production quotas for later years had not yet been finalized. Management expressed the desire to reach production and sales levels of 5 million units after 3 years.

Initially it was expected that full-unit cost could go as high as Sfr. 16. As volume increased, the per-unit cost would drop and the full-unit cost was expected to be less than Sfr. 10 at production levels of 5 million watches per annum. The project was not considered technically feasible at annual production levels below 5 million, and higher volume was expected to drive the unit price just below Sfr. 7. Asuag pricing and costing policy suggested that individual projects should reach contribution margins of 60 percent for marketing, sales and administrative expenses, fixed costs, and profits. Each size model would require a separate production line. Within each line, economic order runs were 10,000 units for each color and 2,000 units for each face style. Maximum annual production per line was 2 million units and the initial cost of installing a line was Sfr. 5 million, including engineering costs of Sfr. 2 million. Additional assembly lines could be installed at an estimated cost of Sfr. 3 million. Production costs included depreciation of this equipment over four years. The equipment occupied space that was already available and no additional real estate investments were expected.

ETA had applied for special financing packages with local authorities. No response had as yet been received. However, obtaining the necessary financing was not viewed as a problem.

Initial plans suggested a marketing budget of Sfr. 5 per unit. The brand was expected to break even in the third year and begin earning profits for ETA in the fourth year. Per-unit marketing costs were expected to decline as volume increased. Decisions as to how the budgeted marketing funds would be distributed had not been finalized. It was expected that they would be divided between ETA and its distributors, but on what basis and how the "campaigns" would be coordinated could not be decided until distribution agreements had been finalized. Thomke was a firm believer in joint ventures and wanted to develop 50/50 relationships with distributors.

Still to be decided were questions of packaging, advertising, production line composition, and distribution. Packaging alternatives centered around who should do it. ETA needed to decide if the product would leave the factory prepackaged and ready to hang or display, or shipped in bulk and packaged by the distributor or retailer or even sold "as is." Advertising budgets and campaigns had not been finalized. The size of the budgets and the question of whether or not advertising costs would be shared between ETA and the distributors were still open. The advertising agencies had not yet been chosen and no media decisions had been finalized.

Distributing "Popularius"

Sprecher felt that distribution was the most important and problematic of the issues still outstanding. Discussions at ETA on developing an introduction strategy were confined to five industrial markets. Although it was not as yet definitive, the emerging consensus seemed to be that distribution would begin in Switzerland, the U.S., the U.K., France, and West Germany. Distribution in Japan, other industrialized countries, and certain developing countries was also being discussed for a later date.

Market and Country Selection

A major motivation in choosing the target entry markets would be the probability of gaining high-volume sales and meeting Thomke's goal of selling a watch to 1 percent of the world population. The U.S. would be an important market for "Popularius" success. It was the world's single largest watch market and success with a product in the U.S. often signaled global success. Thomke planned to keep the watch priced below $30 in the U.S. Germany and the U.K. were significantly large in terms of population, but could be difficult markets to enter because they were known to be particularly price sensitive. Germany was also noted as being particularly slow in accepting new innovations in consumer goods. Switzerland was chosen because it was the home market. ETA management assumed that their next move would be into Canada and the rest of Europe. If ETA decided to enter Japan and the LCDs, management would have some special considerations. Japan would be a particularly difficult market to crack because almost all "B" and "C" class watches sold in Japan were produced domestically. Furthermore, Sprecher had heard that Seiko was considering plans for introducing a new quartz analog watch which would be priced under Sfr. 50. The LCDs of Africa and Latin America provided ETA with opportunities for volume sales. Sprecher expected that consumers in these markets would use price as the only criterion for choosing a watch. Selling the "Popularius" to LCDs would put ETA in competition with the Hong Kong producers' inexpensive digital watches.

Selecting Distributing Organizations

Within each market there was a range of distribution alternatives. But a fundamental need was a central marketing, sales, and distribution unit within ETA with sole responsibility for "Popularius." However, at that time, there was no marketing or sales department within the ETA organization. ETA's products, watch movements, had always been distributed to a select and consistent group of users. Distribution at ETA had essentially been a question of arranging "best way" shipping, letters of credit, and insurance. The annual cost of establishing a central marketing division within ETA was estimated at Sfr. 1–1.5 million. This figure would cover management and administrative salaries for a marketing manager, regional managers, product managers, service, sales planning, and advertising and promotion planning. Sprecher believed that 8 to 10 people would be required for adequate staffing of the department. Furthermore, he estimated that wholly owned subsidiaries in any of the major target markets could be staffed and run at a similar cost.

Contracting individual, independent marketing organizations in each country and then coordinating the marketing, sales, and distribution from the Grenchen office would, Sprecher believed, allow ETA to retain a much greater degree of control over the product. He felt that this type of organization would allow ETA to enter the market slowly and to learn about it gradually without having to relinquish control.

Following Thomke's suggestion, throughout the summer of 1981 Sprecher took a number of trips to the U.S. to determine possible solutions to this and other marketing problems. Sprecher's agenda included visits to a number of distributors, advertising agencies, and retail stores. Sprecher completed his investigation with visits to some of the multinational advertising agencies' Zurich offices. Sprecher made his rounds with a maquette that he described as an "ugly, little black strap." The "Popularius" prototype still had a number of bugs to iron out and Sprecher could only make promises of the variety of colors and patterns that were planned.

FIGURE 1

Projected marketing costs and profits for SWATCH

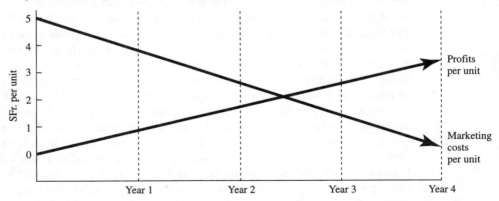

Per unit: Full cost to produce = SFr. 10 (with long range target of less than SFr. 7, including depreciation for production machinery). Ex-factory price = SFr. 15. Contribution margin for marketing costs and profit = SFr.5.

The U.S. would be essential to "Popularius" success because it was the world's largest watch market. Thomke and Sprecher also believed that the U.S. market would be more open to this new idea and felt they would gain the best advice from U.S. distributors and advertising agencies (Exhibits 5A to 5D).

Retailer and Wholesaler Reactions

Sprecher began his first U.S. trip with a visit to Zales Corporation. The Zales organization included both a large jewelry and watch wholesale business and a chain of jewelry stores. Sprecher met with a high-level marketing manager who responded positively to the product, but said that Zales could not seriously consider it at this early stage. He invited Sprecher to return when the project was further along. Zales management did advise Sprecher that if ETA decided to go ahead with the project and start production and sales, then "do it right." Doing it "right" meant heavy spending on advertising, point-of-purchase displays, merchandising, and aggressive pricing.

Sprecher also paid a visit to Gluck and Company. Gluck was a jewelry, watch, and accessory wholesaler operating in the low-price end of the market. An aggressive trader, Gluck operated mainly on price and much of its business involved single lots or short-term arrangements to catalogue and discount houses. Gluck executives told Sprecher that they did not believe in advertising, but relied on low prices to push goods through the distribution chain and into the hands of the customer. If Gluck agreed to take on "Popularius," it would have to be sold with a retail price of under Sfr. 40. Sprecher attempted to discuss the possibility of a long-term relationship between ETA and Gluck, but the wholesaler did not appear particularly interested.

Sprecher's reception at Bulova's New York offices was very different from Gluck. Company President Andrew Tisch's first reaction was that the "Popularius" should be packaged as a fashion watch. Tisch had had substantial experience in consumer

---

EXHIBIT 5A   Retail Watch Purchases in the U.S. (Summary of Market Research)

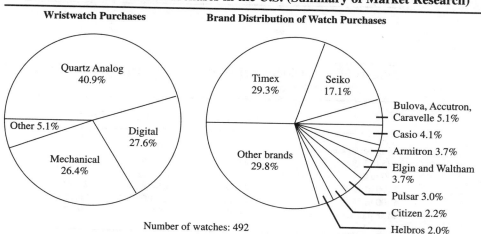

Number of watches: 492

EXHIBIT 5B   Watch Purchases by Retail Price (Sample Size = 465)

	% Quartz Analog	% Digital	% Mechanical
(Number of watches)	(200)	(135)	(130)
Price Categories			
$1,000 or more	.5	.7	1.5
$300 to $999	4.0	.7	1.5
$100 to $299	38.0	8.9	14.6
$50 to $99	33.5	31.9	35.4
$30 to $49	24.0	57.8	47.0

46.6 percent of all watches are purchased on sale or discount.

EXHIBIT 5C   Retail Watch Purchases in the U.S.
(Watch Purchases by Outlet Type [Sample Size = 485])

	% Watches (All)	% Analog Quartz	% Digital
(Number of items)	(485)	(198)	(134)
Jewelry store	27.6	34.3	12.0
Department store	26.2	26.3	27.6
Discount store	16.7	14.7	23.1
Catalog showroom	10.3	14.7	10.4
Mail order	5.4		11.2
Wholesaler	2.1		1.5
Drug store	5.1		6.0
Flea market	0.4		
Other outlets	6.2		7.5

EXHIBIT 5D   Distribution of Watch and Jewelry Purchase Prices by Age of Purchaser

	18–24 Yrs	25–34 Yrs	35–54 Yrs	55 and Over
(Number of customers)	(150)	(419)	(821)	(431)
$25 to $49	39.4%	39.6%	35.7%	32.3%
$50 to $99				
$100 to $299	20.7%	24.8%	25.3%	28.5%
$300 to $999	27.3%	25.3%	26.7%	27.6%
$1,000 or more	11.3%	8.8%	9.0%	10.4%

goods marketing and believed that "Popularius" should be heavily advertised and promoted, suggesting a budget of Sfr. 20 million. He was sufficiently impressed with the project, and voiced some interest in establishing a separate company with ETA to market the watch.

Considering OEM Arrangements

Sprecher was concerned that he might be taking a "hit-or-miss" approach to his investigation and decided to pay a visit to Arthur Young and Company. Arthur Young was among the largest accounting firms in the world, one of the "Big Eight," and was noted for its industry analysis and consulting. Sprecher visited Arthur Young to see if their consultants might have some suggestions on potential partners for ETA. The accounting firm put together a proposal on how to attack the problem of finding a distribution partner. Sprecher was well aware that his investigation was still incomplete, and he returned to Switzerland with the Arthur Young proposal to work out a new agenda of visits.

Included in the Arthur Young proposal was the possibility of turning all marketing responsibilities of "Popularius" over to an independent company. Sprecher investigated this possibility and entered into negotiations with two well-known multinational consumer good companies: Timex and Duracell. Both of these companies had their own extensive and established distribution channels. ETA executives believed that an agreement with either of these two firms might provide "Popularius" with a virtual guarantee of high-volume sales due to the extensive and intensive marketing resources at both.

The Duracell Proposal

Duracell produced and distributed high-quality batteries worldwide and was interested in becoming the exclusive distributor of "Popularius." Contact was initiated with the U.S. battery company's general manager in Zurich and followed up with a visit at Duracell's U.S. headquarters. The company had a distribution system in place that covered the entire globe. Duracell batteries were sold through drug stores, supermarkets, and hardware stores. Duracell made batteries for watches as well and therefore had some contacts in the retail watch trade. The company employed an experienced and well-trained sales force and had a wealth of marketing knowledge. Duracell had unused distribution capacity and its management was looking for extensions to the product line and felt that an electronic watch could be complementary to and a logical extension of Duracell batteries.

Sprecher felt that an agreement with Duracell could be interesting but was concerned that ETA was being relegated to the role of product supplier with little or no impact on marketing decisions. Duracell wanted to establish itself in an original equipment manufacture relationship with ETA. Duracell would buy the watch from ETA and then control the product's marketing strategy. ETA would be supplying the product, the product's name, and some marketing funds, but would be left out of most mass marketing decisions. Furthermore, while Duracell continued to express interest, they were proceeding at what ETA executives considered to be a snail's pace. In late summer, Duracell management informed ETA that they were continuing their evaluation of "Popularius" as a product and that their investigation of its potential market was still incomplete.

The Timex Organization

Timex was known for producing durable, inexpensive watches. The U.S.-based company had become famous in the late 1950s and 1960s for circumventing traditional watch outlets, jewelry stores, and distributing through mass outlets such as drug, department, and hardware stores and even cigar stands. At its peak, Timex had sold watches through an estimated 2.5 million retail outlets. In 1982, Timex had an estimated 100,000 to 150,000 worldwide. Timex and ETA were considering the possibility of ETA production of a limited range of watches under the Timex name. The Timex "Popularius" would be produced in black with a different, but ETA approved, design. The hinge that attached the plastic strap to the watch case would be different and "Swiss Made" would not be stamped on the face. Timex was willing to guarantee a minimum annual order of 600,000 units, at Sfr. 10 ex-factory price.

Sprecher knew that ETA executives considered private-label production as a viable option that could be implemented in either the introductory phase of distribution or later when the brand was well established. However, they felt that the Timex arrangement had some drawbacks. First, they perceived the Timex organization as somewhat stodgy and bureaucratic and ETA executives were unsure as to how close a working relationships they could establish with Timex management. Second, Timex seemed to want "Popularius" for "nothing." Sprecher did not think that they could keep "Popularius" to a Sfr. 50 retail price and gain a profit in the Timex agreement. Sprecher considered the Timex distribution system very costly. Sprecher estimated that Timex watches were distributed with a retail price of 4 to 4.5 times the ex-factory watch price. ETA wanted to maintain a 3 to 3.5 ex-factory ratio. Sprecher believed that the Timex system was costly because it used a direct sales force as well as two middlemen (distributor and broker) to get watches into the retail store. Finally, ETA management was also concerned with Timex's most recent performance. The company had been steadily losing market share.

Positioning Options

Toward the end of his second trip to the States, Sprecher hit upon the "perfect" name for the new product—SWATCH. He had arranged to spend two weeks with the advertising agency Lintas SSC&B to work on developing a possible product and advertising strategy. This arrangement initiated a quasi-partnership between the two firms; Lintas invested its time and talent in the "Popularius" project and would receive payment later if they were to get the advertising account.

Lintas had been influenced by their work with another client, Monet, a producer of costume jewelry. Monet supported its products with heavy point-of-sale promotion activities. Lintas believed that this kind of promotion would be beneficial to "Popularius."

Lintas saw a number of positioning options for the "Popularius," a (new) Swiss watch, a second watch, an activity watch, a fashion watch, or a combination of images. The agency had suggested approaching the "Popularius" positioning with a combination of a fashion and sports image while emphasizing the watch's Swiss origin. The copy staff was excited about stressing the Swiss watch concept and the contraction S'watches was repeated throughout their notes. Sprecher looked at the abbreviation and was struck by the idea of taking it one step further to SWATCH and the "Popularius" finally had a name.

Considering Direct Mail

Back in Switzerland, Sprecher continued interviewing advertising agencies. He visited the Zurich office of McCann-Erickson, a large multinational advertising agency, to discuss advertising strategy and to look into the mail-order market. McCann-Erickson made an investigation of the mail-order market for the SWATCH in West Germany. The purpose of this study was to demonstrate what a mail-order approach might accomplish for SWATCH.

McCann-Erickson's proposal suggested using mail order as an initial entry strategy for SWATCH. This arrangement would later be expanded into a mail-order business through specialized companies with a full range of watches and jewelry. Target group would be young men and women between 20 and 29 years as well as people who "stay young." The target group would be motivated and interested in fashion, pop culture, and modern style.

To achieve sufficient penetration of the large market, which the agency estimated at 12.5 million, advertising support of about Sfr. 1 million would have to be spent. Orders were estimated anywhere from 50,000 units to 190,000. This estimate include volume of 4,500 to 18,000 for a test market, with total advertising costs of about Sfr. 150,000. The effort would be organized in two waves, one in spring and a second in the fall.

Additional costs to be considered were mailing at Sfr. 2.50 per unit sold as well as an unknown amount for coupon handling. Furthermore, experience indicated that about 10 percent of all orders would not be paid.

Considering an Exclusive Distributorship

Zales had suggested that Sprecher contact Ben Hammond, a former Seiko distributor for the southwestern region of U.S. Sprecher was unable to make this contact, but Thomke followed up on this lead on a separate visit to the U.S. in late summer. Ben Hammond, president of Bhamco, was interested in the exclusive distribution rights for North America for SWATCH and a second Asuag brand, Certina. Bhamco was a gemstone firm and Hammond had been in the jewelry and watch business in the southwest for several years. Up until the recent past, he had been the southwest distributor for Seiko. Hammond reported that he and Seiko had had a falling out when the Japanese manufacturer opened a parallel distribution system, selling its watches through new distributors to mass merchandise and discounters in direct competition to its traditional outlets and "exclusive" distributors. He proposed to start a new company, Swiss Watch Distribution Center (SWDC), and wanted an agreement for three years. Hammond was very enthusiastic about the SWATCH and told Thomke that he could "sell it by the ton." Hammond projected first-year sales of 500,000 units growing to 1.2 million and 1.8–2 million in years two and three and then leveling off at 2.5 million.

Hammond felt that the watch should be positioned as a fashion item and sold through jewelry and fine department stores. He believed that a heavy advertising and point-of-sale budget would be important to gaining large volume sales and felt that a Sfr. 5 per watch was a reasonable figure. Furthermore, after his experience at Seiko, he promised a careful monitoring of consumer takeoff and a close relationship with retail buyers to avoid discounting and to give service support. Based in Texas, Hammond had substantial financial backing from a group of wealthy investors. He planned to begin initial efforts in the Southwest and then promised to spread rapidly to all major U.S. cities and Canada.

Next Week's Meeting

Thomke had just returned from the U.S. and briefed Sprecher on his meeting with Ben Hammond. Thomke was anxious to get moving on the project and planned to make a proposal to Pierre Renggli, the president of Asuag, in mid-September, less than three weeks away. At the end of the briefing, they had scheduled a strategy planning session for the next week to evaluate his information and to prepare his proposals for Thomke in preparation for their final presentation to Renggli. Sprecher knew that Thomke expected to receive approval for ETA production and marketing of SWATCH at that presentation. Sprecher knew that his proposals to Thomke needed to be operationally feasible, and with target launch date of 1 January 1982, available implementation time was short. Sprecher knew that they could pursue negotiations with some of the companies that he had visited or "go it alone" with a direct sales force. Sprecher needed to balance the economic restraints which required minimum annual sales volume of 5 million with Thomke's desire to keep strategic control of the product within ETA. Sprecher needed to consider ETA's lack of marketing experience and what that would mean in the international marketplace.

Discussion Issues

1. The case cites a range of possible distributor alternatives. Which should be selected for the SWATCH launch in the United States?
2. Do you prefer another distribution mode in preference to those summarized in the case? If so, explain. If not, why not?

4 PARKER PEN COMPANY

Ilkka A. Ronkainen

Parker Pen Company, the manufacturer of writing instruments based in Janesville, Wisconsin, is one of the world's best-known companies in its field. It sold its products in 154 countries and considered itself number one in "quality writing instruments," a market that consists of pens selling for $3 or more.

In early 1984, the company launched a global marketing campaign in which everything was to have "one look, one voice," and with all planning to take place at headquarters. Everything connected with the selling effort was to be standardized. This was a grand experiment of a widely debated concept. A number of international companies were eager to learn from Parker's experiences.

Results became evident quickly. In February 1985, the globalization experiment was ended, and most of the masterminds of the strategy either left the company or were fired. In January 1986, the writing division of Parker Pen was sold for $100 million to a group of Parker's international mangers and a London venture-capital company.

Globalization

Globalization is a business initiative based on the conviction that the world is becoming more homogeneous and that distinctions between national markets are not only fading but, for some products, they will eventually disappear. Some products, such as Coca-Cola and Levi's, have already proven the existence of universal appeal. Coke's "one sight, one sound, one sell" approach is a legend in the world of global marketers. Other companies have some products that can be "world products," and some that cannot and should not be. For example, if cultural and competitive differences are less important than their similarities, a single advertising approach can exploit these similarities to stimulate sales

Source: This case was prepared by Ilkka A. Ronkainen for discussion purposes and not to exemplify correct or incorrect decision making. The case draws facts from Joseph M. Winski and Laurel Wentz, "Parker Pen: What Went Wrong?" *Advertising Age* (June 2, 1986), 1, 60–61, 71.

everywhere, and at far lower cost than if campaigns were developed for each individual market.

Compared to the multidomestic approach, globalization differs in these three basic ways:

1. The global approach looks for similarities between markets. The multidomestic approach ignores similarities.
2. The global approach actively seeks homogeneity in products, image, marketing, and advertising message. The multidomestic approach produces unnecessary differences from market to market.
3. The global approach asks, "Should this product or process be for world consumption?" The multidomestic approach, relying solely on local autonomy, never asks the question.

Globalization requires many internal modifications as well. Changes in philosophy concerning local autonomy, concern for local operating results rather than corporate performance, local strategies designed for local—rather than global—competitors, are all delicate issues to be solved. By design, globalization calls for centralized decision making; therefore, the "not invented here" syndrome becomes a problem. This can be solved by involving those having to implement the globalization strategy at every possible stage as well as keeping lines of communication open.[1]

Globalization at Parker Pen Company

In January 1982, James R. Peterson became the president and CEO of Parker Pen. At that time, the company was struggling, and global marketing was one of the key measures to be used to revive the company. While at R. J. Reynolds, Peterson had been impressed with the industry's success with globalization. He wanted for Parker Pen nothing less than the writing-instrument equivalent of the Marlboro man.

For most of the 1960s and 1970s, a weak dollar had lulled Parker Pen into a false sense of security. About 80 percent of the company's sales were abroad, which meant that when local-currency profits were translated into dollars, big profits were recorded.

The market was changing, however. The Japanese had started marketing inexpensive disposable pens with considerable success through mass marketers. Brands such as Paper Mate, Bic, Pilot, and Pentel each had greater sales, causing Parker's overall market share to plummet to 6 percent. Parker Pen, meanwhile, stayed with its previous strategy and continued marketing its top-of-the-line pens through department stores and stationery stores. Even in this segment Parker Pen's market share was eroding because of the efforts of A. T. Cross Company.

Subsidiaries enjoyed a high degree of autonomy in marketing operations, which resulted in broad and diverse product lines and 40 different advertising agencies handling the Parker Pen account worldwide.

---

[1] Laurence Farley, "Going Global: Choices and Challenges," presented at the American Management Association Conference, June 10, 1985, Chicago, Illinois.

When the dollar's value skyrocketed in the 1980s, Parker's profits plunged and the loss of market share became painfully evident.

Peterson moved quickly upon his arrival. He trimmed the payroll, chopped the product line to 100 (from 500), consolidated manufacturing operations, and ordered an overhaul of the main plant to make it a state-of-the-art facility. Ogilvy & Mather was hired to take sole control of Parker Pen advertising worldwide. (Among the many agencies terminated was Lowe Howard-Spink in London, which had produced some of the best advertising for Parker Pen's most profitable subsidiary.)

A decision was also made to go aggressively after the low end of the market. The company would sell an upscale line called Premier, mainly as a positioning device. The biggest profits were to come from a roller-ball pen called Vector, selling for $2.98. Plans were drawn to sell an even cheaper pen called Itala—a disposable pen never thought possible at Parker.

Three new managers, to be known as Group Marketing, were brought in. All three had extensive marketing experience, most of it in international markets. Richard Swart, who became marketing vice president for writing instruments, had handled 3M's image advertising worldwide and taught company managers the ins and outs of marketing planning. Jack Marks became head of writing instruments advertising. At Gillette, he had orchestrated the worldwide marketing of Silkience hair-care products. Carlos Del Nero, brought in to be Parker's manager of global-marketing planning, had broad international experience at Fisher-Price. The concept of marketing by *centralized* direction was approved.

The idea of selling pens the same way everywhere did not sit well with many Parker subsidiaries and distributors. Pens were indeed the same, but markets, they believed, were different: France and Italy fancied expensive fountain pens; Scandinavia was a ballpoint market. In some markets, Parker could assume an above-the-fray stance; in others it had to get into the trenches and compete on price. Nonetheless, headquarters communicated to them all:

> *Advertising for Parker Pens (no matter model or mode) will be based on a common creative strategy and positioning. The worldwide advertising theme, "Make Your Mark With Parker," has been adopted. It will utilize similar graphic layout and photography. It will utilize an agreed-upon typeface. It will utilize the approved Parker logo/design. It will be adapted from centrally supplied materials.*

Swart insisted that the directives were to be used only as "starting points," and that they allowed for ample local flexibility. The subsidiaries perceived them differently. The U.K. subsidiary, especially, fought the scheme all the way. Ogilvy & Mather London strongly opposed the "one world, one brand, one advertisement" dictum. Conflict arose, with Swart allegedly shouting at one of the meetings: "Yours is not to reason why; yours is to implement." Local flexibility in advertising was ruled out of the question (see Figure 1).

The London-created "Make Your Mark" campaign was launched in October 1984. Except for language, it was essentially the same: long copy, horizontal layout illustrations in precisely the same place, the Parker logo at the bottom, and the tag line or local equivalent in the lower right-hand corner. Swart once went to the extreme of suggesting that Parker ads avoid long copy and use just one big picture.

FIGURE 1

Ads for Parker's global campaign

Problems arose on the manufacturing side. The new $15 million plant broke down repeatedly. Costs soared and the factory turned out defective products in unacceptable numbers. Conflict was evident internally and the board of directors began to turn against the concept.

In January 1985, Peterson resigned. Del Nero left the company in April; Swart was fired in May; Marks in June.

Discussion Issues

1. Should the merits of global marketing be judged by what happened at Parker Pen Company?

2. Was the globalization strategy sound for writing instruments? If yes, what went wrong in the implementation? If not, why not?

5 MCILHENNY COMPANY: JAPAN

Christopher Gale

In January 1988, Carlos Malespin, Vice-President, International, of the McIlhenny Company, was reviewing all the market and product studies for a new line of Tabasco brand spaghetti sauces to be introduced in Japan later that year. While reassured by the findings, Mr. Malespin realized that this product was an important "first" for this old-line company, and he was anxious that each detail should withstand careful analysis and scrutiny. He was also a firm believer in action, however; as he said, "Any idea can be killed by hypothesizing it to death." Therefore, he was prepared to proceed with the next step, which was to introduce the product at FoodEx (Harumi), a major trade show, in March. Now he needed the go-ahead from his boss, Ned Simmons, a fourth-generation McIlhenny and president of the company.

Company Background[1]

McIlhenny Company was a closely held family business located on Avery Island, Louisiana. Although the company name was relatively unknown, its major product, Tabasco pepper sauce, was marketed in at least 103 countries, with labels in 20 different languages. The brand was over 120 years old, but its recipe had changed little since Edmund McIlhenny first invented and refined it at the close of the Civil War. He had been given the seeds of a pepper (*Capsicum frutescens*) by a friend who had brought them from Mexico; he experimented extensively with both the plants and the sauce he made from the peppers. Finally, because of the product's distinctive flavor and uncompromising quality, his friends and family had recommended that he bottle it for the retail market.

[1] Parts of this section come from the case study, "McIlhenny Company," UVA-OM-0653.

In 1907, McIlhenny Company was formally incorporated with the ownership and rights to all the titles, copyrights, formulas, and trademarks for Tabasco sauce. In 1949, Walter S. McIlhenny was elected president, and under his leadership, McIlhenny Company was launched on an impressive period of growth; in addition, the company introduced the Tabasco brand Bloody Mary mix and Tabasco brand picante sauce. As the demand for Tabasco sauce increased, its quality was never compromised, and continual improvements were made to the growing, bottling, and other aspects of its manufacture.

In 1982, Ned Simmons, great grandson of the founder, assumed the presidency. Mr. Simmons began an aggressive marketing and sales program, and he was also extremely concerned with improving productivity, streamlining operations, and reducing overhead to improve bottom-line profit. As a closely controlled organization, McIlhenny's financial data were not available, but industry experts estimated that 1988 sales would be $50 million, up over 1987. The company's excellent trade relations indicated that the company was well managed and had the resources necessary to finance new-product introductions. U.S. sales of 40 million 2-ounce bottles were growing about 5 percent a year (representing about one-third of the pepper-sauce market), but overseas growth was about 8 percent annually. Mr. Simmons said that the U.S. business, divided about equally between home use and use in restaurants, had the highest market saturation, but that

> the potential even here for added penetration is tremendous. Our penetration is far less in foreign markets, but growth in those areas will require a slow build. We can take advantage of the interest in "international cuisine"—such as, for example, the popularity of western food in Japan—to increase usage.

His goal was to double corporate sales over the next five years.

Tabasco Sauce in Japan

Tabasco was introduced in Japan at the end of World War II by the U.S. occupation forces. By 1988, Japan was McIlhenny's largest international market, followed by West Germany, Canada, and Mexico. The product was handled in Japan by the company's sales agent, PBI Japan, which received a 5 percent sales commission; in return, the agent recommended and worked with the five exclusive importers, formulated an annual sales and marketing plan, searched out new markets, commissioned market research, supervised the work of the advertising agency (Dentsu), kept alert for new opportunities, and in every other respect acted as Mr. Malespin's alter ego in Japan. Recent annual sales growth in Japan was about 8 percent.

Five exclusive importers carried the line; they included some of the largest trading companies in Japan (Sumitomo, Marubeni, Meidi-ya, Toyota, and Nippon Coffee). These importers distributed to "primary wholesalers," who in turn sold to "secondary wholesalers," who then sold to tertiary wholesalers or small neighborhood grocery shops and restaurants. About 80 percent of Tabasco sales were to restaurants and coffee shops, and the little red bottle was a familiar sight to all Japanese. The product was not used on traditional Japanese foods, which were typically mild dishes, but on "Western food," particularly pizza and spaghetti.[2]

Surveys indicated that Tabasco enjoyed 95 percent unaided awareness, that it could be found in about 60 percent of all homes, and that it was on the tables of practically all restaurants serving Western food. Consumer research indicated that it enjoyed a reputation as "a U.S. product of very high quality." The company had worked with local chefs and cooking schools to develop new recipes using Tabasco sauce that would appeal to the new "hot taste"; these recipes were promulgated via package inserts, quarterly newsletters distributed through the Cajun Cooking Club, and at the company's booth at FoodEx, which annually attracted over 100,000 distributors, retailers, and sales agents. There was no direct competitor to Tabasco.

Japan: The Spaghetti-Sauce Opportunity

Mr. Malespin was the company's first manager for international marketing. Prior to his arrival, the company used a New York-based export-management company for sales overseas and had licensing agreements with a few foreign firms for manufacturing and/or marketing Tabasco. Mr. Malespin had obtained an MA in economics and an MA in international trade from the Catholic University of Louvain in Belgium. After graduation, he spent eight years in various international assignments, including working on tariff and trade matters in the Nicaraguan Central Bank and as an export sales manager for a trading company in New Orleans.

Upon joining McIlhenny in 1985, Mr. Malespin spent a great deal of time studying the company's various international markets and preparing a handbook on "how to do business abroad." He took a long tour of the company's major international markets to meet licensees, importers, and major retail accounts.[3] From these studies, he concluded that the Tabasco name had built up as much equity abroad as it had in the United States and that attractive opportunities existed to offer other products under this ample umbrella.

He decided to make his first move in Japan, where the size of the market, the trend toward Western foods, and the rapid growth of U.S. fast-food chains (especially Kentucky Fried Chicken and McDonald's) seemed to offer McIlhenny a platform for new growth. For example, a growing interest in Cajun food was a felicitous opportunity to popularize jambalaya and gumbo (Cajun specialties based on rice, vegetables, and seafood), because these dishes used basic Japanese culinary ingredients and cooking systems. Through the services of Paul Prudhomme (a gifted U.S. chef specializing in Cajun delights), these recipes were introduced at the 1986 Matsuo Food Fair; they received national attention, and over time, jambalaya became part of the repertoire of modern Japanese cooks and housewives.

By 1987, however, Mr. Malespin could not envision any further accelerated growth

---

[2] More information on Japan and its people is given in Appendix A.

[3] "Too long!" he said. "I spent five weeks on that trip, and increasingly found that my clients were far more refreshed than I was! Most practitioners would say that 15–18 days abroad is max, before you lose your acuity in cutting deals."

for Tabasco through recipe programs. He therefore explored other avenues by asking such questions as, "What is Tabasco sauce? What does it mean to Japanese consumers? How do they use it?" In the process of answering these questions, he and the managers of PBI Japan concluded that the spaghetti-sauce market offered a promising opportunity. PBI agreed to undertake research on this market and on consumer attitudes toward and use of spaghetti sauce.

Market Research

PBI's research indicated that wholesale canned spaghetti sauce accounted for $86 million of the total estimated market of $110 million (the balance of sales was in retort pouches). The meat-sauce portion had sales of $73 million.[4] Of the approximately 35 brands of canned sauce currently on the market, none was dominant. The top four brands controlled 62 percent of market share; they were Kewpi ($15 million), Mama ($13.5 million), Kagome ($12.5 million), and Oh-My ($11.8). Five other brands had sales of $30 million altogether, and the remaining brands controlled $2.5 million. All were Japanese companies with the exception of a Heinz joint venture ($6.8 million).

The industry spent $4.2 million annually in 1986 for advertising (based on data for five of the top seven brands). Mr. Malespin observed that 10 feet of gondola space was devoted to this product in grocery stores ("a tremendous amount of shelf space!") and that spaghetti was perceived in Japan to be a Western dish.

Mr. Malespin believed that the market was ready for a new entry that (1) built on the excellent reputation and distribution of the Tabasco name, especially given its powerful association in Japan with spaghetti and pizza products and (2) offered a better product but priced the same as competition. The new product was to offer more beef, yet be formulated to appeal to Japanese tastes.

For the past 20 years, the company had retained a food consultant, Ms. Ichikawa, to create recipes using Tabasco sauce. Now she was asked to develop a new spaghetti-sauce recipe using not only Tabasco sauce but other ingredients that she believed would improve on the major brands and still appeal to Japanese palates. At this point, the decision on sourcing the product was deliberately held open.

In her lab, Ms. Ichikawa analyzed the current brands with respect to flavors, size of cans, texture, appearance, etc., based on both taste tests and ingredient analysis. From this analysis, she elicited complaints ranging from "thin, color drab" and "smells too spicy, bad can smell" to "good but doesn't go with spaghetti well," and so on.

Ms. Ichikawa then experimented with different ingredients, including red wines, beef, pork and mutton, cheeses, olive and sunflower oils, and such different vegetables as carrots, onions, potatoes, celery, and many more. These recipes were tested among small consumer groups and, once refined, were subjected to production in larger quantities in order to see if the "homemade" characteristics were preserved.

By December 1987, the product formulation was complete: compared with U.S.

---

[4] At this time, the exchange rate was $1 = ¥128.

brands, the product was darker (a "meaty-brown"), thicker, and sweeter. Containing 12 percent meat solids, it could be imported into Japan under current beef tariff restrictions (20 percent maximum) yet still be called "meat sauce" under U.S. standards. (By now the company had determined that the high price of beef in Japan made production in the United States more profitable than in Japan.) Ms. Ichikawa reported that, based on the taste tests, "Texture, aroma, freshness, and can smell all got highest marks."

Based on an assumed first-year level of 1 percent of the market, Mr. Malespin estimated the production and marketing costs (see Exhibit 1). The proposed retail price of ¥300 for a 300-gram can would yield a factory price of $1.09 and a unit profit of $0.24.

For the typical three layers of distribution between the retailer and the factory, the margins (over the buyer's cost) were as follows: importer, 12 percent; primary wholesaler, 6 percent; secondary wholesaler, 6 percent; and the retailer, 38 percent. For companies importing into Japan, the sales agent received a fixed commission, usually 5 percent. In addition, promotional allowances were frequently given to the importer, which were in turn passed down the chain in the form of price discounts; these allowances could include "1 free case in 10" or discounts off invoice. Thus, a 300-gram can of spaghetti sauce with a list price of ¥300 normally sold for ¥220 to ¥240. (See Exhibit 2 for a projection of distribution costs and trade pricing.)

EXHIBIT 1 McIlhenny Company: Japan
Spaghetti-Sauce Estimated Product and Selling Costs, 1988
(300-gram can)

	$	¥	%
Gross sales[a]	$1.09	¥139.5	100.0%
Cost of goods sold	.64	81.9	58.7
Gross profit	.45	57.6	41.3%
Selling Expenses			
Advertising and promotion	.07	9.0	7.8
Returns and allowances	.025	3.2	3.3
Interest	.005	0.6	0.5
Containerization[b]	.02	2.5	1.8
Freight to Japan	.024	3.1	2.2
Commission	.06	7.7	5.5
Miscellaneous	.01	1.3	0.9
Total selling expenses	.21	26.9	19.3
Net profit	$0.24	¥ 30.7	22.0%

[a] C&F Japan. That is, all McIlhenny prices were quoted in U.S. dollars.
[b] Including inland cartage (U.S.)
Source: Company records

EXHIBIT 2   McIlhenny Company: Japan
Distribution Costs and Trade Pricing
(300-gram can)

A. Importer's Cost

McIlhenny price	¥139.5[a]
Insurance	0.5
Duty charges	13.5
Landed cost	¥153.5
Customs	2.5
Warehouse (90 days)	5.0
Delivery	5.0
Interest (150 days)	5.4
Total cost	¥171.4

B. Typical Trade Selling Prices

	¥	Percentage of Retail Price	Profit Margin[b]
Retail price	300	100.0	38%
Secondary wholesaler price	216	72.0	6%
Primary wholesaler price	204	68.0	6%
Importer selling price	192	64.0	12%

[a] Based on $1.00 = ¥128.

[b] The gross margin is based on the buyer's cost.

Source: Company records

Consumer Surveys

In July 1987, the sales agent, PBI, had conducted an initial written survey involving 110 respondents (basic conclusions are in Exhibit 3). In October, PBI commissioned two focus groups (selected results from this research are in Appendix B). Two more focus-group sessions were conducted in December to test the actual Tabasco formulation, packages, and "catch phrases"; selected results from these sessions are found in Appendix C.

The Proposal

In its review of the situation, PBI stated,

> There is currently no clear, overall leader in the canned meat-sauce market. Tabasco brand spaghetti sauces will interface well with the Tabasco pepper sauce principal market position as the pasta/pizza condiment. Tabasco spaghetti sauce offers an opportunity to capitalize on consumer brand awareness. The sauce will expand McIlhenny's product base and its distribution

EXHIBIT 3   **McIlhenny Company: Japan**
Findings from Initial Written Questionnaire, July 1987
(N = 110 respondents)

- 64 percent were between 25–40 years old; 40 percent had children, mostly ages 1–17; dinner meals were probably eaten at home.
- 72 percent prepared spaghetti at least every 2 weeks; 65 percent prepared it for family consumption, 22 percent for themselves; 74 percent prepared 2–4 servings.
- 66 percent bought spaghetti in a supermarket; the frequency of purchase was at least every 2 months.
- 62 percent prepared meat sauce or Japanese-style sauce—could be soy-based, sukiyaki type, fermented soy bean sauce, fish egg, ground white radish and barbecue meat slices, Japanese mushrooms, or even seaweed.
- Spice was the most popular additive (38 percent), then meat (30 percent), mushrooms (14 percent), tomato or onion (11 percent), and Tabasco (7–11 percent).
- 65 percent had no regular brand; those who were loyal cited "taste" and "price" as the reason for their loyalty.
- 76 percent would try new brands.

Source: Company records

channels can carry the product along with the pepper sauce. Tabasco-brand spaghetti-sauce products would increase tabasco pepper sauce sales by (1) creating more Tabasco-brand merchandising space at the retail level, (2) standardizing Tabasco-brand merchandising locations in retail outlets, (3) creating Tabasco pepper sauce impulse-buy opportunities, and (4) broadening the entire Tabasco-brand base of consumers in Japan.

Mr. Malespin proposed offering the spaghetti sauce in Japan in three 300-gram versions: a mild version (suitable for children), a regular, and a "spicy" version. Because even the spicy version was relatively mild by American standards, there was still opportunity for consumers to use Tabasco on the product. In order to offer a fuller product line, McIlhenny would also produce a chile con carne sauce (in mild and regular flavors), which was similar to spaghetti sauce but had pinto beans. This product had been as thoroughly tested by Ms. Ichikawa as had the spaghetti sauce.

By this time, about ¥6.5 million had been spent on the consumer research, product development, and product/consumer tests. The next step was to introduce the product to the trade in the company's booth at the March FoodEx show. In addition to this chance for the 100,000 distributor/retailer representatives to taste the product, Mr. Malespin planned a private showing to the five trading companies that imported Tabasco pepper sauce into Japan.

Mr. Malespin believed there was no point in conducting a regional test market, because Japan was so concentrated: a regional test would be tantamount to a national introduction. As he pointed out, 45 percent of the country's population lived within 100 miles of Tokyo.

Thus, given no surprises at the show, Mr. Malespin anticipated a national introduction in November 1988. He would give one of the usual trade allowances to spur trial, which in this case would be "one case free with 10." Advertising for the product would be piggybacked by taking the top third of the one-page newspaper and magazine ads normally used for advertising Tabasco sauce; two ads were scheduled for November and two for December in the three major national Japanese newspapers. The copy points were:

> Tabasco made it—it must be delicious! There are a number of sauces with meat, but Tabasco has made a real meat sauce as it should be: (1) high volume of meat; (2) only high-quality, 100% beef; and (3) best-quality ingredients carefully selected to complement nutrition and taste.
>
> These production criteria have guided Tabasco's recipe development. We hope that you and your family will enjoy this sauce soon.

Mr. Malespin's target was to get the product on the shelves by November 20 and to attain a 1 percent share by the end of the first year. While he believed that the Tabasco brand could be the market leader in five years, he knew the project had some risks. The greatest was the possible loss of good will among the many levels of distribution should the product fail. Mr. Malespin was aware that few of the 80,000 new products introduced into the market each year survived. A major contributor to this worry was the fact that the Japanese government could ban the product if it did not live up to the inspectors' very high quality standards, including the prohibition of food additives. So far, only samples of the imported Tabasco sauce had been submitted for government inspection, and any question about the company's standards could lead to more rigorous inspection of that product as well. Not only would such an eventuality cloud the company's name, it could substantially increase the difficulty and costs of working in this most important market.

APPENDIX A

McIlhenny Company: Japan

Selected Facts on Japan and the Japanese

Part I—Selected Data from Student Report, December 1987

Population.   Japan was one of the most densely populated nations in the world. The total Japanese population approximated 120 million densely settled, highly literate, and homogeneous inhabitants. The total population was estimated to peak at 130 million soon after the coming century, at that time reaching a zero population growth rate. The land area of Japan was about 146,000 square miles (378,000 square kilometers), approximately the size of the state of Montana. Over half of the population was concentrated within the Tokyo/Osaka urban belt. The population continued to grow at a .6 percent rate annually, but the average age was increasing. It was estimated that, by the year 2000, the elderly (those over age 65) would account for over 15 percent of the total population. Japan currently had the highest life expectancy in the world for both males and females, at 72.2 and 77.4 years, respectively. The total labor force was over 60 million. Japanese women were becoming increasingly significant in Japanese industry. Currently, women were over one-third of the total work force.

Source: Part I of the material in this appendix was taken from parts of "Tabasco in Japan," a study performed by students at the American Graduate School of International Management in the fall of 1987. Part II is taken from a presentation made by PBI in its yearly presentation to McIlhenny executives at Avery Island.

Language and education.   Japanese was the language of Japan and was understood throughout the land. There were regional dialects, but on the whole the language was the same. The writing system consisted of the three alphabets of Hiragana, Katakana, and Kanji (Chinese characters). Japan had a literacy rate of 99.7 percent, which was one of the highest in the world. There was compulsory and free education up to the age of 15. English was a required subject from junior high through college. About 41 percent of men and 33 percent of women went on to higher education.

Religion.   The basic religions of Japan were Buddhism and the Japanese religion of Shinto. However, some Japanese (0.8 percent) practiced Christianity and other religions. Most Japanese actively practiced Buddhism only when honoring the dead. Shintoism, on the other hand, was associated with happy occasions such as weddings, purification of buildings, ground-breaking ceremonies, etc. Many national holidays were closely related to significant religious events.

Psychographics.   Traditionally, housewives held the purse strings in the Japanese family. Except for very large purchases, the housewife made most shopping decisions. Typically, the Japanese housewife made several trips a week to the neighborhood grocery store.

The Japanese consumer was one of the most demanding the world. She was brand conscious and expected high quality regardless of price. Because of the immeasurable number of consumer goods available (both foreign and domestic), the Japanese consumer placed great emphasis on the reputation of the producer. When it came to consumer goods, the Japanese were obsessed not only with product quality, but also with the way the product was packaged. The market almost seemed to require "overpackaging."

The *Shinjinrui* (new humankind) was a new breed of image-conscious Japanese consumer who was the driving force behind the current restructuring of the Japanese retail industry. The young adults' affluence and changing personal value system had forced mom-and-pop corner store retailers to specialize or be left behind. Specialty stores carrying a single line of merchandise continued to gain share in the Japanese market. In many cases, their success was a result of their ability to market a slice of American life. The young Japanese generation was very attuned to American culture.

Fish, vegetables, rice, or noodles were the main fare of most Japanese, but such food as pizza, hamburgers, steak, etc., had been receiving attention among younger Japanese consumers. The Japanese tended to distinguish types of food depending on the occasion and location. For example, pizza, hamburgers, or fried chicken could replace Chinese or Japanese food for lunch. These types of food were usually consumed for lunch or a snack rather than as a main dish at dinner. Traditional Japanese cooking was often time-consuming and required the preparation of many kinds of food; as many as 30 dishes might be served at one meal.

The Japanese did not invite guests into their homes as frequently as Americans did. This was partially because Japanese homes were not large enough to accommodate guests. Seventy-six percent of the population were urban dwellers, and Japanese urbanites often lived in very small apartments, or "rabbit hutches," as some foreigners called them.

Legal environment.   By far the most common problem experienced by exporters of food to Japan was the prohibition of food additives. There were several hundred inadvertent violations per year. Consumer co-ops existed that viewed additives as one of the key trade issues, ranking them more important than market access or pricing and distribution of goods. Japan allowed 347 synthetic chemical compounds to be used as food additives, fewer than in many Western countries.

Japan's customs tariff was administered by the Ministry of Finance through its Customs Bureau. All imported food products had to be labeled in Japanese. Any artificial coloring or preservatives, the name and address of the importer, and the date of manufacture had to be stated on the outside label.

There were few legal restrictions on advertising in Japan. Commercials for liquor and cigarettes flourished, and sexy images were not uncommon. One of the few restraints placed on advertising concerned the amount of time allotted to commercials during each broadcasting hour: the limit was set at six minutes. However, networks had colluded with advertisers in finding a loophole: by rearranging program scheduling, they stretched hourly advertising to eight minutes.

Income distribution and expenditure. Japan's gross national product was the second largest in the Free World, amounting to approximately half of U.S. GNP. The average family income was between ¥4 and ¥6 million, which at an exchange rate of ¥142.41 to the dollar (as of September 11, 1987) equaled $28,000 to $42,000. Japan had one of the highest savings rates in the world, at slightly under 20 percent of total net income. Real disposable income had stagnated since 1978, resulting in more women entering or remaining in the work force. Because of the contribution of working women to the family budget, two-income families were able to save and consume more.

Communication. Japan was ideally suited for much mass-media advertising because of its literate, highly concentrated, and homogeneous population. There were over 4,000 advertising agencies servicing the country through newspapers, television, magazines, radio, and outdoor advertising. Traditionally, Japanese advertising agencies had assumed the role of "space broker," buying media space or time and reselling it to clients. The top 5 advertising agencies in Japan did over 50 percent of the total business, with the largest, Dentsu, accounting for 26.5 percent of the total. There were 102 commercial television broadcasters across Japan, 5 in the Greater Tokyo area alone. The largest national daily newspapers were the *Yomiuri* and the *Asahi*. Each printed roughly 13 million copies (morning and evening editions) and carried 37 percent of all newspaper advertising.

Distribution. For a foreign company looking to establish a presence in Japan, the most common approach to market entry was the use of the existing distribution channels of the large trading companies (*sogo shosha*). They could handle up to 25,000 different products and provide a range of services that included financing, warehousing, transporting, wholesaling, and servicing. However, many foreign companies believed that the *sogo shoshas* were too large and would not aggressively market their products. Of the 2,300 U.S. companies operating in Japan, the majority chose subsidiaries or joint ventures.

The traditional distribution system was changing, albeit gradually, to the advantage of the foreign manufacturer. This was partially a result of the formation and growth of specialty, chain, and convenience stores. Recently, supermarkets and department stores had been moving toward selling their own brands.

Part II—Excerpts from a PBI Presentation to McIlhenny, 1988

A. Macroenvironment Overview

1. Japan's population is about 122 million. Its GNP is the second largest in the Free World at $2.5 trillion. In consumer spending and capital investment, Japan's domestic market is the world's second largest.

2. The typical Japanese household consists of 4 persons living on an average monthly income of about $3,600, nearly 85 percent of which is disposable. Purchasing power in dollars has doubled since 1981.

3. Japanese consumers can afford to be selective and choose products that meet strict standards of quality. Ownership of consumer durables is high, with over 98 percent of

households owning refrigerators, washing machines, and color televisions. Central heating is uncommon, and space heaters remain the most prevalent way to heat residences.

4. Standards of education are high—compulsory through 9th grade, but 95 percent of all students go on to senior high school and 35 percent on to higher education. The five leading newspapers have a combined morning circulation of more than 25 million.

5. Medical and health facilities are good, with life expectancy among the highest in the world, and nearly the entire population is covered by national or company health insurance provided at a cost that varies according to income.

6. Crime-related injury is low. In 1985, there were 15 murders per million population in Japan (compared with 79 in the U.S. and 37 in the U.K.). Property crime is low, while arrest and conviction rates are very high.

7. Housing standards are lower than Western industrialized countries, since both land and construction are expensive in Japan. About 60 percent of Japanese households own their homes.

8. Japanese consumers spend less time at home than people in other industrialized countries. The number of workers having only a five-day workweek is increasing but is still far lower than in the U.S. The number of national holidays is greater than in the U.S. or Germany, but companies give fewer individual paid holidays to employees. The working year in Japan in recent years has been 253 days (compared with 233 in the U.S. and 230 in the U.K.). The Japanese take 10 days paid vacation yearly (compared with 19 in the U.S. and 31 in Germany).

B. Japanese Consumers

1. Consumer spending in Japan is highly influenced by the compensation used by most companies. Although changing, the features of the current system show that wages are tied to seniority and that lifetime employment provides security for significant portions of the population and their families. Also, the practice of paying semiannual bonuses coincides with the two gift-giving seasons. The bonuses are paid in mid-summer and in December, the best times for purchases of high-quality foods, accessories, and other gifts as well as for major consumer durables such as color televisions, VCRs, etc. These bonus seasons are prime marketing targets for both domestic producers and imported goods manufacturers.

2. The largest expenditures in the typical family's budget are for food, transportation, communication, reading and recreation, and apparel. The Japanese have a reputation for demanding quality at reasonable cost and place emphasis on product appearance and packaging as well as superior functions.

3. The Japanese sense of taste for color is affected by a long heritage and differs from that of most other nations. For consumer items other than clothing, there has been a trend toward individuality, leading to a wider variety of colors in appliances and interior furnishings.

4. The Japanese diet has become greatly influenced by other cuisines, and families eat a wide range of foods.

5. The Japanese market is highly segmentable by income, region, age, sex, and lifestyle. Mass media and compulsory education have had substantial influence on growing homogeneity, but climate, food, and consumer preferences nevertheless vary from region to region.

6. Different age groups in Japan have very different tastes and lifestyles. While a majority of men go on to university, more women attend shorter programs at junior colleges. Single working women have high discretionary incomes. After marriage, women leave their jobs

to take care of the household and budget, while men concentrate on career advancement within the company.

C. Dietary Habits and Trends

1. The Japanese diet has been strongly influenced by other countries' cuisines over the past 15 years and has become more Westernized and diversified. It is characterized by a high consumption of cereals and fish, and by a low consumption of dairy products.

2. As a proportion of food expenditures, rice has declined since 1970, and bread has taken up the slack. Fish and meat expenditures have increased, while spending on diary products has declined slightly.

3. The proportion of frozen foods consumed has risen with the increase in ownership of home freezers, and a rise in the ownership of microwave ovens has laid the groundwork for an increasing use of prepared frozen foods and oven-cooked foods:

Annual Household Expenditures—Major Food Items

Year	Rice	Bread	Fish	Meat	Vegetables	Dairy	Prepared Foods
1970	¥41,890	5,814	44,670	33,189	44,830	24,791	12,044
	(20.2)	(2.8)	(21.6)	(16.0)	(21.6)	(12.0)	(5.8)
1986	¥74,397	24,059	130,191	96,567	112,663	42,657	61,972
	(13.7)	(4.4)	(24.0)	(17.8)	(20.8)	(7.9)	(11.4)

* Figures in parentheses indicate percentage of food expenditures.

4. The predominant flavors in Japan tend to remain the traditional ones, such as soy sauce and miso, but the Japanese diet has diversified to a great extent. Many products in the growing category of prepared foods are sauces and bases for Chinese and other types of cuisine.

5. Although the Japanese welcome an increasing variety of foods, they still generally tend to prefer the milder flavors. In addition, foods are presented in a pleasing manner—attractive to the eye with subtle combinations of color and design.

6. Salt intake, most of which comes from the traditional flavorings, has been high in the past but has dropped as consumers have become more concerned with salt-related health problems. Growing concern with health has also created a growing demand for low-calorie foods.

D. Summaries of Market Research Surveys

1. Sumitomo Bank: Eating Habits in the Gourmet Age. 800 wives of salaried workers in Tokyo and Osaka (multiple answers).
   - 73 percent often watch TV programs featuring eating and cooking.
   - 64 percent try to choose foods without additives.
   - 59 percent like to read books and articles on dining out.
   - 22 percent think they are "gourmet"; 44 percent definitely do not.
   - 55 percent of families dine out once a month or more.

2. Ministry of Health and Welfare: National Nutrition Survey. 7,000 households throughout the country.
   - Intake of animal fat continues to decrease.
   - Intake of salt continues to decrease.
   - Levels of calcium considered inadequate by Ministry of Health.
   - Intake of green vegetables continues to increase.
3. Ajinomoto: Food Preferences. 5,000 men and women aged 12 and up in 16 cities around the country.
   - Those below the age of 30 prefer a variety of Western foods.
   - Those aged 50 and up prefer traditional Japanese foods.
   - Those in their 30s and 40s have no strong likes or dislikes.
   - Men generally tend to prefer protein foods.
   - Women seem to prefer carbohydrates.

Source: Company records

APPENDIX B

MCILHENNY COMPANY: JAPAN

Selected Findings from Focus-Group Study
(conducted October 12, 1987)

I. Objective:

To evaluate the concept of a Tabasco-brand canned spaghetti meat sauce and to estimate future potential for this product in Japan.

II. Research Scheme:

1. Focus Group Participants—Users of canned spaghetti meat sauce. Half of the participants use it 2–3 times per month, and the rest use it less often (no habitual usage).
2. Region—Tokyo and suburban areas.
3. Sampling—Two groups of eight participants.
   Group No. 1—Housewives from 23–46 years old with annual income of ¥4 million or more.
   Group No. 2—Single women 21–30 years old with annual income of ¥2.5 million or more.

III. Findings:

Conditions of Usage and Purchase

Housewives' group. Demographics of participants' family members are widely dispersed. The largest family is seven members of three generations. Children vary from kindergarten to adult ages. Eating habits include Japanese, Western, and Chinese dishes, but there is an inclination toward

Western-style foods. Spaghetti is one dish favored by children and appears on the family's dinner menu frequently.

Although participants make small efforts at consuming lots of vegetables and maintaining a low-sodium diet, they are not very strict about it, and the desire for tasty foods seems to be somewhat stronger.

Dining-out frequency is two to three times per month, and spaghetti is one of the meals ordered most often. On these occasions, they tend to order Tarako (cod eggs), Natto (soy beans), Wafu (soy sauce), and other flavors that they don't usually prepare at home.

Single women's group.   All but one live with their parents and all but one bring their lunch to work. All claim their cooking repertoire is very limited. They eat out two or three times per week and often frequent spaghetti restaurants, where they order sauces not usually home prepared such as Tarako (cod eggs), white sauce, etc.

Household usage.   About 70 percent of the participants use canned spaghetti meat sauce 1–3 times per month, and the other 30 percent, most of whom are housewives, use it once per week. Usage by housewives varies from normal meals to lunch with children, late-night snacks, sudden visitors, and Sunday lunch. When they have time, they add meat or vegetables that are on hand such as green peppers, carrots, onions, tomatoes, and mushrooms. Spices added are usually oregano, cinnamon, black pepper, Tabasco, basil, or flavorings such as broth, Worcestershire sauce, and wine according to taste. If time does not allow for additional ingredients, they use it as is.

Compared with the housewives, single women tend to use canned spaghetti meat sauce for breakfast or lunch on days when the mothers are away, or when supper has not been made for them. Most of them simply heat the sauce and put Tabasco on it.

In most cases, usage of the sauce is for two or more people—especially housewives who eat with their children.

Utilization of canned meat sauce varies from such dishes as gratin and lasagna to potato casseroles and stews for housewives. Single women say they use it for cheese casseroles with noodles or broccoli and often simply use it as stuffing for hot-dog buns.

The majority of housewives use two to three 300-gram cans at once, whereas single women use only one can.

Reasons for usage.   The major attraction for canned spaghetti meat sauce is that it is "very handy and easy to use," and some participants think the flavor is close to sauce in restaurants. Also, it's difficult to make from scratch.

The reasons housewives add things to canned meat sauce are to: (1) eliminate the can smell, (2) increase the meat content, and (3) insure enough flavoring to suit everyone's taste. A psychological element is that they don't want to appear lazy by using sauce "as is." Historically, most housewives started using canned sauce when they got married, while single women began usage five to six years ago in high-school home economics classes.

The most common reason for use is "Mother used it." Other reasons given include TV commercials, noted products on store shelves, and heard about it from others.

Although retort pouch and packaged sauces from hotels or restaurants are sometimes used by participants, canned meat sauce is by far the main vehicle. Single women think the retort pouch is convenient because of its one-serving size, but housewives say the pouch is uneconomical and show little intent to purchase.

Canned-sauce and retort-pouch comparisons.   Advantages of the can include long storage time, easy to store, restaurant flavor, and easy to prepare. Advantages of the retort pouch are convenient for one, easy to prepare, no can smell; disadvantages are insufficient amount and hands get dirty.

Purchasing conditions.   Within the single-women's group, two claim they buy the product themselves, while others eat the brand their mothers buy. Hardly any participants recognize any taste difference between one brand and another.

Housewives claim they buy canned meat sauce when supermarkets are having a sale or when they don't have much other shopping to do. They buy from two to four cans at each purchase.

Most participants show no brand loyalty and are only concerned that the brand name is a well-known one or that they have seen the product advertised on TV. Taste is thought to be standard among most brands.

Brands Purchased

Kewpi 9
Heinz 5
Kagome 5
Mama 3
Oh-My 2
Meidi-Ya 1

- Kewpi is purchased by both groups, but housewives buy mostly Heinz.
- Reasons for purchasing Kewpi are: commercials, packaging (red and white), used to taste, and usage of other Kewpi products.
- Reasons for purchasing Heinz are: used to taste, safe product, and children seem to like it. No real brand loyalty noted among participants.

Other brand images and reasons are: Mama: often discounted and same brand as spaghetti noodles. Meidi-Ya: high quality, reliable, can be used as a gift. Kagome: same brand as famous ketchup.

Housewives said that average prices for the 300-gram can were ¥250, but they said it could be bought for ¥200 on sale. Single women had very little idea on prices but thought that ¥300 sounded reasonable.

Flavor Evaluations

Canned meat sauce.   General complaints about flavor and contents of canned meat sauce are made concerning its sweetness and lack of spices, but are for the most part focused on the scarcity of meat. Both housewives and single women, however, think that's all they can expect from canned sauces and seem to value convenience above any other factors.

Housewives.   Flavor suits everyone, but too sweet/not enough spice; too thin/watery; insufficient amount; tomato too strong; flavor unsatisfying; strong can smell; gets lumpy. Therefore, add Tabasco and more spices, more base ingredients, and more parmesan cheese.

Single women.   School lunch flavor, children like it, but not enough meat; too sour or too sweet; too much for single serving; too rich, can't finish. Therefore, add sugar, put Tabasco for more flavor, add spices for distinct taste.

Evaluation of Overall Concept

Brand not shown to participants.   Housewives' group said the concept photo had "lots of ingredients and seems thick enough not to soak through the noodles . . . actually looks very tasty." On the other hand, single women showed very little interest in the photo, saying "all products look alike."

Both groups, nevertheless, felt a difference between the concept brand and the ordinary types. Housewives felt the concept brand is one that can be served to family or visitors without having to add anything. All of them wanted to try it and thought it was a "real meat sauce." The single women split into two factions: One saying they had no interest in it, since "all canned meat sauces taste the same," and if they want a special dish, they could go to a restaurant. The other half of single women wanted to try the concept brand because they could make it and "it really looks thick and complete."

Standard and mild types.   Single women thought the brand was aimed at those who were unsatisfied with conventional products and those who like spicy and hot tastes. The housewives think the concept is attractive because it seems to have an adult taste and uses many spices. Both groups felt the concept sauce would be difficult to make at home by themselves with any success.

Pricing of ¥500.   Housewives accept this price if the product is tasty, since it would still be cheaper than going out to eat. Also, most said the price should be in accord with the taste.

Some of the single women felt it would be acceptable if tasty and if ¥500 is for two servings, but others said it was expensive for a canned meat sauce and showed surprise and hesitation. Most said they would go to a special restaurant if the price difference was trivial.

100 percent lean beef.   Participants felt that the secret in making an ideal sauce is to use 100 percent beef. Many do not know what kind of meat is in the canned sauces they currently use, a fact especially true with the single women's group. It was pointed out that it would be better to use ground beef than shredded beef or chunks of beef.

Some felt that the phrase "Beef—40 percent of the contents" was somewhat ambiguous and desired a clearer, easily understood explanation of all ingredients in the product.

Tabasco brand shown to participants.   The initial response from both groups upon hearing the brand "Tabasco" was similar: "It sounds hot and spicy." The housewives said they welcomed the concept of a Tabasco brand as a flavor for adults, while the single women showed surprise, having a strong image of "Tabasco" as a spice manufacturer.

Although all the participants thought about a spicy type for adults and a mild type, it was a common opinion that the "Tabasco" name gives a direct impression that it is too hot and spicy for children, regardless of the two different types. Therefore, it was felt that a phrase that emphasizes its mild flavor be used to convey the idea that it would suit anyone's taste.

Some housewives thought Tabasco originated from the U.S. or Mexico. Most, however, thought it came from Italy, where pasta has its origins, since Tabasco is used on pizza and spaghetti in Japan. Single women had an impression that Tabasco came from some area in Latin America.

Even after the brand name "Tabasco" was opened to the participants, there was no change in response to the ¥500 price inquiry put to them earlier regarding the 300-gram can. The housewives were still positive, and the single women were split into two groups.

Evaluation of Current Packaging

Both groups showed amazingly similar tastes in packaging. Favorable responses came forth on all the existing brands except for extremely negative comments on Mama and Showa.

Type of packaging.   About half the participants prefer litho cans, claiming paper labels (1) are easily torn, (2) fade quickly, and (3) get dirty if stored a long time. Some showed a strong rejection of paper labels and said they project an "image of pineapple cans." The other half say they receive a high-class image from paper labeling.

Colors.   Both groups shared the common opinion that a combination of red, white, and green colors give an Italian image. However, nearly every manufacturer uses them in some way, and group participants suggested a unique design and color pattern to create a high-class image.

Tabasco logo.   Housewives think the Tabasco logo is quite fashionable and feel it should be on the label, using its quality image to assist in advertising and promotions. The single women split again, half saying the logo should be used, and half insisting it will confuse the consumer by implying the product is a type of spicy flavoring and not a meat sauce.

Source: Company records

APPENDIX C

McIlhenny Company: Japan

Second Focus Group, Conducted with Actual Product

Participant Profiles

Housewives

Twelve housewives aged between 25 and 45 who reside in the suburbs of Tokyo. Four participants have no children. The others all have two children each from kindergarten to high-school ages. In terms of eating habits, most of them make home meals where children's tastes get first consideration since husbands arrive home late. The trend, therefore, is to light and sweet flavors. Those with no children cook easy-to-prepare foods when husbands come home late and tend to favor hot and spicy tastes.

Single Working Women

Four single working women participated. Two of them work full time, and the two others work part time. One lives with her parents, two live by themselves, and one lives with a grandfather. All but the one who lives with her parents prepare meals regularly. Most of them claim they dine out almost half of the time. The three who cook regularly make simple meals at home.

Eating and Purchasing Habits

Almost half the participants claim they eat spaghetti two or three times a month, and the other half claim they eat it at least once a week. Housewives with children use it largely for lunch or snacks on holidays, when schools do not serve lunches, or when the husband comes home late. Housewives with no children and single women don't specify times of use.

Housewives with children normally add some ingredients like onions, carrots, mushrooms, and meat for nutritional purposes, and tend to adjust flavors by adding spices and some condiments such as ketchup or tomato puree. Housewives with no children and single women use salt, pepper, Tabasco, and often spices and Worcestershire sauce or soy sauce. They take more advantage of convenience factors.

Housewives with children also tend to make other dishes—such as eggplant gratin, omelets, and lasagna—with canned spaghetti meat sauce.

Taste Testing

Mild Meat Sauce

Close to conventional meat sauce; weak tomato taste, seems thin, lacks spices, lacks richness.

Regular Meat Sauce

Plus points: conventional flavor, flexible usage; minus points: instant taste, ordinary. Because of its light flavor and admitted flexibility, nearly half felt that it would be suitable for children. [Note: The focus group moderator cautions that panel members feel a psychological need to be critical of the product.]

Spicy Meat Sauce

Nearly all of the participants in this, the second, focus group felt that the spicy variation of sauce offers a unique alternative to what is currently on the market in Japan. The level of spiciness is judged to be stimulating and with a flavor that differs from other products.

Those who prefer a spicy product (about one-third of the group participants) are usually in their 20s and feel the spicy product has both flavor and character. The rest of the participants feel it is too spicy and kills the flavor of the meat sauce itself, leaving a lingering taste that is unsuitable to them.

Most housewives feel it is too strong and spicy for children to eat, and the overall impression is that the product is one for young adults and grown men.

The smell of red peppers in the sauce is believed to be attractive to men, and it was felt that the sauce would go well with beer in the evening.

Plus points: elaborate taste, good overall aroma; minus points: too spicy for children.

Relative Evaluation

Almost 40 percent of the participants picked the mild meat sauce as the best among the flavors, and if we consider the number of second-place votes mild meat sauce received, that flavor gets a 60 percent vote of confidence.

Family considerations: Housewives with younger children chose the mild meat sauce and the regular meat sauce because of their relatively sweeter flavors. The choices by single women were spread across the mild, regular, and spicy meat sauces in near-equal sectors. The spicy meat sauce was least popular due to its high spice level.

Catch-Phrase Evaluation

[Ten "catch phrases" were shown to respondents: (1) Beefy sauce made by Tabasco, the spaghetti specialists; (2) A supreme sauce with supreme beef—dedicated to spaghetti lovers; (3) Pasta luxury—supreme beef and secret flavors; (4) Ungrudging amount of supreme beef—ungrudgingly real; (5) Thick and profound—finished with supreme beef and ripe spices; (6) Starting today, learn the taste of a real sauce full of selected beef; (7) Real sauce with simmered beef—the epitome of a luxurious pasta; (8) Supreme beef meets supreme spices; (9) Full of the tasty flavor of excellent beef. The true sauce of luxury; (10) Finally—a sauce that's too tasty for words.]

General comments: Participants in this focus group chose each of the 10 proposed catch phrases except "Starting today, learn the taste of a real sauce full of selected beef."

Fully 40 percent of the participants liked the last copy best of all. Reasons for this particular selection were: simple and unpretentious; concise and clear; sounds nice; easy to imagine.

The phrase that was thought to be second by the group was: "Supreme beef meets supreme spices." Reasons given were: easy to understand; simple and clean.

The third-place phrase was: "A supreme sauce with supreme beef—dedicated to spaghetti lovers." This phrase was chosen based on the idea that it sounds as though people would like to hear it in commercials on TV or read it in magazine and newspaper advertisements.

Purchasing Intentions

(Prior to being told the price): Judging from the average existing price of canned sauces, which is felt to be between ¥250–¥260 at most supermarkets, housewives showed an intent to purchase if it is below ¥350. They claim they would definitely buy if it were ¥300 or less.

On the other hand, single women showed intent to purchase if the price is ¥340–¥350 or up to ¥400 at most, reflecting a wider range than housewives.

(After being told the price): When a target price of ¥350 was shown, most participants showed intent to purchase once on a trial basis, and if it doesn't taste any different from the others, they will go back to their old brands.

The image of canned meat sauces is that they all taste about the same, and the focus-group participants felt the ¥300 price will be lowered to the mid-¥200 range on sale eventually.

A couple of participants admit that their decision on purchasing is affected greatly by the image they get from packaging.

Source: Company records

Discussion Issues

1. What are the major risks associated with introducing a new spaghetti sauce in Japan?
2. What are the key points of information derivable from the focus groups?
3. If the Japan introduction proves successful, will McIlhenny be able to introduce the same product in other countries?

6 NESTLÉ—THE INFANT FORMULA INCIDENT

J. Alex Murray, Gregory M. Gazda, and Mary J. Molenaar

Nestlé Alimentana of Vevey, Switzerland, one of the world's largest food-processing companies with worldwide sales of over $8 billion, has been the subject of an international boycott. For over 10 years, beginning with a Pan American Health Organization allegation, Nestlé has been directly or indirectly charged with involvement in the death of Third World infants. The charges revolve around the sale of infant feeding formula that allegedly is the cause of mass deaths of babies in the Third World.

In 1974, a British journalist published a report that suggested that powdered-formula manufacturers contributed to the death of Third World infants by hard-selling their products to people incapable of using them properly. The 28-page report accused the industry of encouraging mothers to give up breast-feeding and use powdered milk formulas. The report was later published by the Third World Working Group, a lobby in support of less-developed countries. The pamphlet was entitled, "Nestlé Kills Babies," and accused Nestlé of unethical and immoral behavior.

Although there are several companies who market infant baby formula internationally, Nestlé received most of the attention. This incident raises several issues important to all multinational companies. Before addressing these issues, let's look more closely at the charges by the Infant Formula Action Coalition (INFACT) and others and the defense by Nestlé.

The Charges

Most of the charges against infant formulas focus on the issue of whether advertising and marketing of such products have discouraged breast-feeding among Third World mothers and have led to misuse of the products, thus contributing to infant malnutrition and death. Following are some of the charges made:

Source: This case is an update of "Nestlé in LDCs," case written by J. Alex Murray, University of Windsor, Ontario, Canada, and Gregory M. Gazda and Mary J. Molenaar, University of San Diego. Originally appeared in P. R. Cateora, *International Marketing,* 8th ed., Richard D. Irwin, © 1993.

• A Peruvian nurse reported that formula had found its way to Amazon tribes deep in the jungles of northern Peru. There, where the only water comes from a highly contaminated river—that also serves as the local laundry and toilet—formula-fed babies came down with recurring attacks of diarrhea and vomiting.

• Throughout the Third World, many parents dilute the formula to stretch their supply. Some even believe the bottle itself has nutrient qualities and merely fill it with water. The result is extreme malnutrition.

• One doctor reported that in a rural area, one newborn male weighed 7 pounds. At four months of age, he weighed 5 pounds. His sister, aged 18 months, weighed 12 pounds, the weight one would expect a 4-month-old baby to weigh. The children had never been breast-fed, and since birth, their diets were basically bottle feeding. For a four-month baby, one tin of formula should have lasted just under 3 days. The mother said that one tin lasted two weeks to feed both children.

• In rural Mexico, the Philippines, Central America, and the whole of Africa, there has been a dramatic decrease in the incidence of breast-feeding. Critics blame the decline largely on the intensive advertising and promotion of infant formula. Clever radio jingles extoll the wonders of the "white man's powder that will make baby grow and glow." "Milk nurses" visit nursing mothers in hospitals and their homes and provide samples of formula. These activities encourage mothers to give up breast-feeding and resort to bottle-feeding because it is "the fashionable thing to do or because people are putting it to them that this is the thing to do."

The Defense

The following points are made in defense of the marketing of baby formula in Third World countries:

• First, Nestlé argues that the company has never advocated bottle-feeding instead of breast-feeding. All its products carry a statement that breast-feeding is best. The company states that it "believes that breast milk is the best food for infants and encourages breast-feeding around the world as it has done for decades." The company offers as support of this statement one of Nestlé's oldest educational booklets on "Infant Feeding and Hygiene," which dates from 1913 and encourages breast-feeding.

• However, the company does believe that infant formula has a vital role in proper infant nutrition as (1) a supplement, when the infant needs nutritionally adequate and appropriate foods in addition to breast milk and (2) a substitute for breast milk when a mother cannot or chooses not to breast-feed.

• One doctor reports, "Economically deprived and thus dietarily deprived mothers who give their children only breast milk are raising infants whose growth rates begin to slow noticeably at about the age of three months. These mothers then turn to supplemental feedings that are often harmful to children. These include herbal teas, and concoctions of rice water or corn water and sweetened, condensed milk. These feedings can also be prepared with contaminated water and are served in unsanitary conditions."

• Mothers in developing nations often have dietary deficiencies. In the Philippines, a mother in a poor family who is nursing a child produces about a pint of milk daily. Mothers in the United States usually produce about a quart of milk each day. For both the Philippine and U.S. mothers, the milk produced is equally nutritious. The problem is that there is less of it for the Philippine baby. If the Philippine mother doesn't augment the child's diet, malnutrition develops.

• Many poor women in the Third World bottle feed because their work schedules in fields or factories will not permit breast-feeding.

• The infant feeding controversy has largely to do with the gradual introduction of weaning foods during the period between three months and two years. The average well-nourished Western woman, weighing 20 to 30 pounds more than most women in less-developed countries, cannot feed only breast milk beyond five or six months. The claim that Third World women can breast-feed exclusively for one or two years and have healthy, well-developed children is outrageous. Thus, all children beyond the ages of five to six months require supplemental feeding.

• Weaning foods can be classified as either native cereal gruels of millet or rice, or commercial manufactured milk formula. Traditional native weaning foods are usually made by mixing maize, rice, or millet flours with water and then cooking the mixture. Other weaning foods found in use are crushed crackers, sugar and water, and mashed bananas.

There are two basic dangers to the use of native weaning foods. First, the nutritional quality of the native gruels is low. Second, microbiological contamination of the traditional weaning foods is a certainty in many Third World settings. The millet or the flour is likely to be contaminated, the water used in cooking will most certainly be contaminated, the cooking containers will be contaminated, and therefore, the native gruel, even after it is cooked, is frequently contaminated with colon bacilli, staph, and other dangerous bacteria. Moreover, large batches of gruel are often made and allowed to sit, inviting further contamination.

• Scientists recently compared the microbiological contamination of a local native gruel with ordinary reconstituted milk formula prepared under primitive conditions. They found both were contaminated to similar dangerous levels.

• The real nutritional problem in the Third World is not whether to give infants breast milk or formula; it is how to supplement mothers' milk with nutritionally adequate foods when they are needed. Finding adequate locally produced, nutritionally sound supplements to mothers' milk and teaching people how to prepare and use them safely is the issue. Only effective nutrition education along with improved sanitation and good food that people can afford will win the fight against dietary deficiencies in the Third World.

The Resolution

In 1974, Nestlé, aware of changing social patterns in the developing world and the increased access to radio and television there, reviewed its marketing practices on a region-by-region basis. As a result, mass media advertising of infant formula began to be phased out immediately in certain markets and, by 1978, was banned worldwide by the company. Nestlé then undertook to carry out more comprehensive health education programs to ensure an understanding of the proper use of their products reached mothers, particularly in rural areas.

"Nestlé fully supports the WHO (World Health Organization) Code. Nestlé will continue to promote breast-feeding and ensure that its marketing practices do not discourage breast-feeding anywhere. Our company intends to maintain a constructive dialogue with governments and health professionals in all the countries it serves with the sole purpose of servicing mothers and the health of babies." This quote is from *Nestlé Discusses the Recommended WHO Infant Formula Code.*

In 1977, the Interfaith Center on Corporate Responsibility in New York compiled a case against formula-feeding in developing nations and the Third World Institute launched a boycott against many Nestlé products. Its aim was to halt promotion of infant formulas in the Third World. The Infant Formula Action Coalition (INFACT, successor to the Third World Institute) along with several other world organizations successfully lobbied the World Health Organization (WHO) to draft a code to regulate the advertising and marketing of infant formula in the Third World. In 1981 by a vote of 114–1 (three countries abstained and the United States was the only dissenting vote), 118 member nations of WHO endorsed a voluntary code. The eight-page code urged a worldwide ban on promotion and advertising of baby formula and called for a halt to distribution of free product samples and/or gifts to physicians who promoted the use of the formula as a substitute for breast milk.

In May 1981, Nestlé announced it would support the code and waited for individual countries to pass national codes that would then be put into effect. Unfortunately, very few such codes were forthcoming. By the end of 1983, only 25 of the 157 member nations of the WHO had established national codes.

Accordingly, Nestlé management determined it would have to apply the code in the absence of national legislation and in February 1982 issued instructions to marketing personnel, delineating the company's best understanding of the code and what would have to be done to follow it.

In addition, in May 1982, Nestlé formed the Nestlé Infant Formula Audit Commission (NIFAC), chaired by former Senator Edmund J. Muskie, and asked the commission to review the company's instructions to field personnel to determine if they could be improved to better implement the code. At the same time, Nestlé continued its meetings with WHO and UNICEF to try to obtain the most accurate interpretation of the code.

NIFAC recommended several clarifications for the instructions that it believed would better interpret ambiguous areas of the code; in October 1982, Nestlé accepted those recommendations and issued revised instructions to field personnel.

Other issues within the code, such as the question of a warning statement, were still open to debate. Nestlé consulted extensively with WHO before issuing its label warning statement in October 1983, but there was still not universal agreement with it. Acting on WHO recommendations, Nestlé consulted with firms experienced and expert in developing and field-testing educational materials, so that it could ensure that those materials met the code.

When the International Nestlé Boycott Committee (INBC) listed its four points of difference with Nestlé, it again became a matter of interpretation of the requirements of the code. Here, meetings held by UNICEF proved invaluable, in that UNICEF agreed to define areas of differing interpretation—in some cases providing definitions contrary to both Nestlé's and INBC's interpretations.

It was the meetings with UNICEF in early 1984 that finally led to a joint statement by Nestlé and INBC on January 25. At that time, INBC announced its suspension of boycott activities, and Nestlé pledged its continued support of the WHO code.

Nestlé Supports WHO Code

The company has a strong record of progress and support in implementing the WHO Code, including:

- Immediate support for the WHO Code, May 1981; and testimony to this effect before the U.S. Congress, June 1981.
- Issuance of instructions to all employees, agents, and distributors in February 1982 to implement the code in all Third World countries where Nestlé markets infant formula.
- Establishment of an audit commission, in accordance with Article 11.3 of the WHO Code, to ensure the company's compliance with the code. The commission, headed by Edmund J. Muskie, was composed of eminent clergy and scientists.
- Willingness to meet with concerned church leaders, international bodies, and organization leaders seriously concerned with Nestlé's application of the code.
- Issuance of revised instructions to Nestlé personnel, October 1982, as recommended by the Muskie committee to clarify and give further effect to the code.
- Consultation with WHO, UNICEF, and NIFAC on how to interpret the code and how best to implement specific provisions, including clarification by WHO/UNICEF of the definition of children who need to be fed breast milk substitutes, to aid in determining the need for supplies in hospitals.

Nestlé Policies

In the early 1970s, Nestlé began to review its infant formula marketing practices on a region-by-region basis. By 1978, the company had stopped all consumer advertising and direct sampling to mothers. Instructions to the field issued in February 1982 and clarified in the revised instructions of October 1982 adopt articles of the WHO Code as Nestlé policy and include:

- No advertising to the general public.
- No sampling to mothers.
- No mothercraft workers.
- No use of commission/bonus for sales.
- No use of infant pictures on labels.
- No point-of-sale advertising.
- No financial or material inducements to promote products.

- No samples to physicians except in three specific situations: a new product, a new product formulation, or a new graduate physician; limited to one or two cans of product.
- Limitation of supplies to those requested in writing and fulfilling genuine needs for breast milk substitutes.
- A statement of the superiority of breast feeding on all labels/materials.
- Labels and educational materials clearly stating the hazards involved in incorrect usage of infant formula, developed in consultation with WHO/UNICEF.

Even though Nestlé stopped consumer advertising, they were able to maintain their share of the Third World infant formula market. By 1988, a call to resume the seven-year boycott was called for by a group of consumer activist members of the Action for Corporate Accountability. The group claimed that Nestlé was distributing free formula through maternity wards as a promotional tactic that undermines the practice of breast-feeding. The group claims that Nestlé and others have continued to dump formula in hospitals and maternity wards and that as a result "babies are dying as the companies are violating the WHO resolution."[1]

The boycott focus is Taster's Choice Instant Coffee, Coffeemate Nondairy Coffee Creamer, Anacin aspirin, and Advil.

Representatives of Nestlé and American Home Products rejected the accusations and said they were complying with World Health Organization and individual national codes on the subject.

The Issues

Many issues are raised by this incident. Such questions as: How can a company deal with a worldwide boycott of its products? Why did the United States decide not to support the WHO Code? Who is correct, WHO or Nestlé? But a more important issue concerns the responsibility of an MNC marketing in developing nations. Setting aside the issues for a moment, consider the notion that, whether intentional or not, Nestlé's marketing activities have had an impact on the behavior of many people, that is, Nestlé is a cultural-change agent. And, when it or any other company successfully introduces new ideas into a culture, the culture changes and those changes can be functional or dysfunctional to established patterns of behavior. The key issue is—what responsibility does the MNC have to the culture when, as a result of its marketing activities, it causes change in that culture?[2]

Discussion Issues

1. What could Nestlé have done to avoid the accusations of "killing Third World babies" and still market its products?
2. After Nestlé's experience, how do you suggest that it or any other company protect itself in the future?

Endnotes

1. "Boycotts: Activists' Group Resumes Fight against Nestlé, Adds American Home Products," Associated Press, October 5, 1988.
2. This case draws from the following: "International Code of Marketing of Breastmilk Substitutes," World Health Organization, Geneva, 1981; INFACT Newsletter, Minneapolis, Minn., February 1979; John A. Sparks, "The Nestlé Controversy—Anatomy of a Boycott," Grove City, Pa.. Public Policy Education Fund, Inc.; "Who Drafts a Marketing Code," *World Business Weekly,* January 19, 1981, p. 8; "A Boycott over Infant Formula," *Business Week,* April 23, 1979, p. 137; "The Battle over Bottlefeeding," *World Press Review,* January 1980, p. 54; "Nestlé and the Role of Infant Formula in Developing Countries: The Resolution of a Conflict" (Nestlé Company, 1985); "The Dilemma of Third World Nutrition" (Nestlé S.A., 1985), 20 pp.; Thomas V. Greer, "The Future of the International Code of Marketing of Breastmilk Substitutes: The Socio-Legal Context," *International Marketing Review,* Spring 1984, pp. 33–41; James C. Baker, "The International Infant Formula Controversy: A Dilemma in Corporate Social Responsibility," *Journal of Business Ethics,* no. 4, 1985, pp. 181–90; Shawn Tully, "Nestlé Shows How to Gobble Markets," *Fortune,* January 16, 1989, p. 75.

7 BAKSHEESH

Tom Delay and Susan Schneider

It was the middle of the night. My legs and neck ached as I stood up in the aircraft, but, as a young man about to start his first expatriate assignment, I was thrilled to be in East Africa. Outside the air was hot. The terminal building was floodlit against the night sky. A small crowd of people moved out toward the aircraft, eager to meet relatives who had been to Europe on business or expats back for another tour of duty, and to receive supplies of fresh food, newspapers, and other goods from Europe.

The general manager of the local company, Mr. Lagarde, stood there on the tarmac to welcome me. He was French, in his early 50s, and had spent the last 15 years as an expatriate in Africa moving from country to country every three or four years. He seemed friendly enough and spoke to me in fatherly tones. I was far younger than he and had only worked one year for the company. I thought that he might resent my university background and early promotion to line responsibility overseas, but I also realized that he desperately needed a willing subordinate to manage an investment program to rebuild the company's facilities, which had fallen into disrepair.

The local company marketed oil products in the country and used its storage facilities in the port for transshipment to neighboring countries as well. The oil storage tanks, which sat between the small two-story office block and the Red Sea, had been built in 1936, but since the closure of the Suez Canal they had been little used. The company had run down its operations and was only just profitable. It was wholly owned by one of the oil majors but was fully autonomous in day-to-day operations. With about 100 local staff and three expatriates, it was too small to receive much attention from the parent company other than an annual review of the business plan. In 1983, an unexpected upturn in business had put new demands on the facilities, which no longer met the appropriate safety standards. I was sent out for 18 months or so with a mission to patch up the damage and update the facilities where necessary.

Source: This case was written by Tom Delay, M.B.A., under the supervision of Susan Schneider, Associate Professor at INSEAD. It is intended to be used as a basis for class discussion rather than to illustrate either effective or ineffective handling of an administrative situation. Copyright © 1988 INSEAD, Fontainebleau, France. Revised 1992.

To meet my objectives, storage tanks, pumps, and pipework would need to be replaced section by section in order to keep the depot operational. The work would have to be done by local contractors, as the company only employed a small maintenance crew of semiskilled workers. I would depend on these contractors to do their work properly and finish on time. I was pleased when, in the first couple of weeks, a number of them came to see me in my office. As they had no offices and ran their business from their cars, they would turn up at any time and sit outside waiting for me to arrive. They would come in, usually alone, introduce themselves, and sit down. I explained to them that each section of the work would need to be bid for and that I would contact them soon.

Saïd Guedi must have been the fifth such contractor to come and see me. He told me that his firm had worked for my company for many years and hoped that we would have a long and fruitful relationship. He reached into his pocket and pulled out a gold chain which he held out to me as a "gift for my lady."

I was shocked. I had imagined this scene many times but felt unable to respond. This was "baksheesh," not a bribe relating to a particular job or contract but a token offering which, he hoped, would win him my favor. Eventually, I thanked him but explained that I could not accept his gift, which, in any case, was not necessary. He replied, "But your predecessor took my gifts."

Suddenly I felt quite alone. I had assumed that my colleagues would turn down baksheesh but now I wasn't sure. I said no again, led him out of my office, then sat back and thought about my position. I was flattered that my position justified such treatment but upset that he thought I might accept his gift. I realized that I would have to establish a position of principle in order to avoid this problem in the future.

I felt unsure that I could trust anyone within the company. Guedi had made me realize that my expatriate colleagues could possibly be taking bribes. A couple of days later, the general manager came into my office and asked me to consider a particular contractor for a forthcoming job, explaining that he had been "recommended by a Minister." He was probably quite honest and his story was probably true, but I had a lingering doubt in my mind. I never told him what had happened with Guedi and, more generally, we never discussed the subject of bribery.

Two months or so later I had settled down in both the country and the company. I had moved into a small apartment in town away from my colleagues but close to a number of other expatriates. I had a small jeep to get me around and had built up an active social life. I did have some problems when the Port Police began to stop and search the jeep on my way into work every day, but I had learned to be patient and they gave up after a week. I later found that Guedi had arranged this "stop and search" to put me in my place. Other contractors had apparently heard that I was "clean" and I got no more offers of baksheesh.

At work, things were going well and I had established a good rapport with the clerical staff and the manual labor out in the depot. Some of them, in fact, seemed more able and enthusiastic than the local managers. These able young men were being managed by four local managers who could barely read and write. Among the four was a man called Ismail Farah. He was the ringleader and had ambitions of being promoted to the post of operations manager, a job that had always been done by an expatriate. Previous general managers had considered him for the post but none had recommended him, despite the company's declared policy of promotion for nationals wherever possible. I wondered why.

Before leaving for Africa, I had been told that two of the last three general managers had had nervous breakdowns which had caused them to be repatriated, but I was also told that these were caused by "age" in one case and "marital problems" in the other. The standard of living of the expats in the country was not high, but there was no particular hardship to explain why two previously successful managers should crack up in that way. I had been told that one of them would come to the office at night and work through the company's accounts. On one occasion, he was found sitting on the floor in tears by his secretary when she arrived in the morning. If life outside the company was not responsible, what within it could cause this level of anxiety?

Late one night, I stood on the quay in the Port, watching our men couple up hoses to a tanker that had to discharge oil into the storage tanks. As I looked down the quay, I could see someone walking up toward me. It was Ismail. He came up and we chatted for a few minutes before he started to tell me about his career and how he had been overlooked for promotion. I pointed out that I had not discussed his position with the general manager, but that the company would promote nationals whenever possible. It was a weak reply but it was honest.

Ismail was reportedly the most talented of the four local managers, but I didn't know him well enough to form any other opinion. He seemed pleased that I would discuss the matter with him and hoped that we would "be good friends." He started to talk about the past, about how the country had broken away from colonial rule, and about the company's development through that time. Eventually, he started to talk about the first of the general managers who had had a nervous breakdown. He smiled and appeared to mock the man's misfortune. "That man was trouble to me. He was a racist and he was weak. He treated us like children so we behaved like children. We would make mistakes in our work that he could never find and it drove him crazy."

I was stunned. I must have looked quite shocked because he went on to say, "Don't worry, you'll be all right; you are my friend." This time I went to see the general manager. We talked about Ismail and his past, which, it transpired, had been well documented in appraisal reports. He had the support of a minister within the government, which prevented us from firing him. There was nothing we could do.

Eventually, I had come to terms with both internal and external threats and had learned to be cautious in my dealings. I had good working relationships with a number of contractors and no problems dealing with the local authorities. When the Chief of Port Police came to see me in my office, I assumed that his visit was a courtesy call.

He sat down and, after a few minutes' discussion, started to explain that his mother was ill and needed medical care which he could not pay for until he received his pay at the end of the month. "Could you, as a personal favor, lend me the money until the end of the month?" I had had similar requests before and knew that the story was almost certainly a fabrication. "I'm sorry, I would help you if I could, but I have no money in this country." He leaned across the desk and beckoned me forward so that he could whisper in my ear: "But I know that you have money here; I have seen your account file in the bank." I felt quick sick. I had lied and he knew it.

Although his request was clearly extortion, I felt guilty. I stood up, told him that he must have made a mistake, and led him out of my office. Later that day I went to see the bank manager. As upset about the leak in confidential information as I was, he gave me an overdraft so that from that day on I never did have any money in the bank.

As work in the Port depot progressed, we decided to invest in a small office block out at the airport to house the aviation manager and the 15 staff responsible for fueling European Airlines as they stopped over en route to and from the Indian Ocean. It would be a small, single-story, Arab-style building designed by a young French architect, a resident in the country, who reckoned that it would cost about $200,000 to build. Five contractors had bid for the construction work and I had awarded the contract to the lowest bidder, subject to planning approval being granted. To get the approval, the architect had completed the necessary forms and submitted them in the company's name to the Ministry of Public Work, six weeks beforehand. We hadn't received any reply in writing when Abdi Issa, officer in charge of planning at the Ministry, called me on the phone. "I have a few queries about the drawings you submitted with the planning application forms for your new airport office. Nothing serious, the sort of thing we should discuss around the table. Could you come in and see me tomorrow morning in my office?" Now what? I wondered.

Discussion Issues

1. Do the provisions of the Foreign Corrupt Practices Act provide guidance in helping to resolve the ethical issues in this case?
2. Should the expatriate in this case have been provided with a corporate code of ethics before being sent abroad? If so, delineate the key elements in such a code.

8 PHILIP MORRIS

The Export Warning Labels Issue

W. Kent Moore and Phyllis G. Holland

In 1992, the management of Philip Morris Companies faced a potentially major problem. One of Philip Morris's shareholders, the Midwest Province of the Capuchin Order, planned to present a resolution at the next annual shareholders' meeting. The resolution would require that the company print warnings about the dangers of cigarette smoking on every package of cigarettes produced, including exported cigarettes.

While a similar measure had been defeated by stockholders at the 1991 annual meeting, the introduction and discussion of the resolution by the religious order would provide antismoking activists with a highly visible forum for airing their views. The negative publicity could be damaging to the company. Publicity on this issue was particularly unwelcome because there were indications that Congress was turning its attention to warning labels for exported cigarettes.

There were several alternatives for dealing with the situation. The company could take a proactive stance by placing the warning labels on all cigarettes before the motion could be made. Other possible responses included seeking procedural methods to inhibit the motion, distributing a position paper describing the views of the company, or simply doing nothing. In any case, a decision was needed prior to the upcoming meeting.

Background

Philip Morris Companies, Inc., is a diversified, multinational firm that obtains revenues from the manufacture and distribution of tobacco, food, and beer products, from financial services and from real estate operations. In 1991 Philip Morris had net earnings of $3.9 billion on revenues of $56.4 billion. The company's operating revenues from inter-

Source: This case was prepared by W. Kent Moore and Phyllis G. Holland of Valdosta State University. Copyright © 1993 by the *Business Case Journal* and W. Kent Moore and Phyllis G. Holland.

national tobacco operation ($12.2 billion) had topped operating revenues from U.S. operations ($11.5 billion) for the second consecutive year. Earnings for domestic tobacco operations were $4.7 billion compared to earnings of $1.6 billion for international tobacco. Philip Morris International, Inc. (PMI), is the subsidiary that manufactures and exports cigarettes to a growing number of countries worldwide. During 1991, PMI increased export volume nearly 10 percent over 1990 and contributed $3.6 billion to the U.S. balance of payments.

From 1987 to 1991, unit sales of cigarettes in the United States declined while world sales increased. Differences in performance in the domestic and international cigarette businesses may be attributed to a number of factors, not the least of which is antismoking activism. The U.S. Surgeon General, American Cancer Society, and the Heart Association are just a few of the individuals and groups who have sought to reduce, if not ban, smoking from American life. A measure of their effectiveness is found in the diminishing percentage of Americans who smoke. Antismoking groups have begun to turn their attention to the export of cigarettes. Former Surgeon General C. Everett Koop has stated:

> At a time when we are pleading with foreign governments to stop the export of cocaine, it is the height of hypocrisy for the United States to export tobacco. Consider these figures. Last year in the United States, 2,000 people died from cocaine. In that same year, cigarettes killed 390,000.[1]

Antismoking activism was not limited to the United States. The Asian Pacific Association for Control of Tobacco was formed in 1989 with a goal of a smokeless Asia by the year 2000. Another group, the Asian Consultancy on Tobacco Control, representing 14 nations, met in Hong Kong in January 1991, to devise a four-year plan to combat smoking in the region. The essence of their plan was to train antismoking activists and persuade Asian countries to adopt uniform tobacco control regulations. In 1990, Philip Morris shareholders voted down a shareholder proposal that would have required exported cigarettes to carry the same labels in the appropriate language as those marketed domestically.

The U.S. Cigarette Industry

With sales in excess of $35 billion in 1990, the United States cigarette industry continues to be a huge enterprise. According to a 1990 survey, 32 percent of American men and 27 percent of American women were smokers. In 1989, U.S. cigarette production was 685 billion, and worldwide, sales of cigarettes ran into the trillions. This sales volume has been achieved with a product that has been linked to cancer and heart disease since the landmark Surgeon General's report in 1964, that has carried health warnings on packs since 1966, and that has been banned from television and radio advertising since 1971. Although Americans have typically started smoking before age 21, by industry agreement, advertisements have not appeared in youth-oriented media or used illustrations or themes aimed at young people.

Smoking Trends in the United States

Trends in domestic consumption of cigarettes and percentages of smokers have been of great concern to tobacco companies. Figure 1 shows domestic consumption of cigarettes in the 1980s; Figures 2 and 3 show percentages of smokers by gender and educational level. If these trends continue, the Centers for Disease Control estimated that by the year 2000, only 22 percent of the adult population in the United States will be smokers. The percentage of female smokers (23 percent) was projected to be slightly higher than the percentage of male smokers (20 percent). By 1987, there were more teenage girl smokers than teenage boy smokers. Also, smoking in the United States is more and more becoming primarily a behavior of the less educated and the socioeconomically disadvantaged.

Almost half of all adults who ever smoked have quit. Each year, about 2 million American cigarette customers have been lost, either through death or quitting smoking. A 1991 Gallup pole revealed that 70 percent of smokers would like to quit and 80 percent wished they had never started smoking. For 16 consecutive years, the per capita consumption of cigarettes had decreased, and during the last 5 years, the total national consumption has decreased also.

Exhibit 1 shows the impact of these trends on the major U.S. tobacco companies. From the peak in 1981, cigarette production for the domestic market had dropped by almost 15 percent in 1980. Annual profits were still increasing in 1989, but at modest

FIGURE 1

Domestic consumption of cigarettes

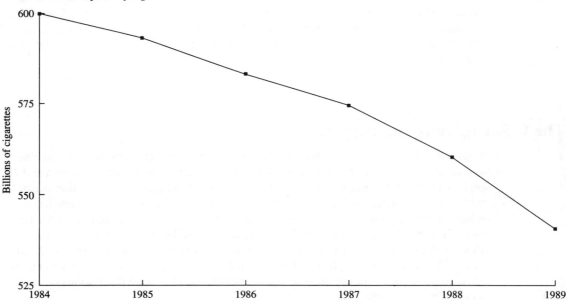

Source: *Farmline*, March 1990, p. 20.

FIGURE 2

Smoking prevalences for men and women with projections to year 2000

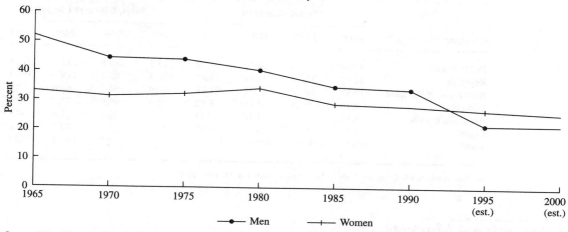

Source: *Editorial Research Reports,* Mar. 24, 1989, p. 153; *Statistical Abstract of the United States,* 1990, p. 123; *The Atlanta Journal and Constitution,* June 27, 1990; *Journal of the American Medical Association,* Jan. 6, 1989, p. 63.

FIGURE 3

Smoking prevalences by education level with projections to the year 2000

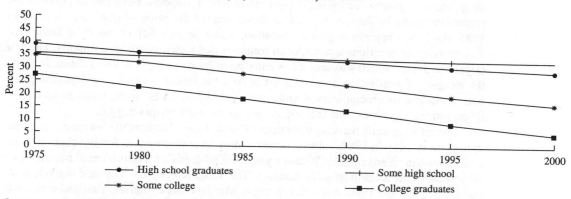

Source: *Journal of the American Medical Association,* Jan. 6, 1989, p. 64.

levels in the 10 percent range rather than at the dramatic rates of previous decades. The industry had been involved in an increasing number of legal and political battles and smoking had been banned from domestic airline flights, many public buildings, portions of restaurants, and some workplaces.

TABLE 1   **Rankings of Cigarette Manufacturers, 1985 to 1988**

Company	Market Shares (%)				Sales, Billion of Cigarettes			
	1988	*1987*	*1986*	*1985*	*1988*	*1987*	*1986*	*1985*
Philip Morris	39.38	37.83	36.77	35.89	218.7	215.5	214.2	213.6
Reynolds	31.78	32.53	32.33	31.61	176.4	185.3	188.3	188.1
Brown and Williamson	10.95	10.97	11.67	11.88	60.9	62.5	68.0	70.7
Lorillard	8.26	8.23	8.15	8.12	45.9	46.9	47.5	48.3
American Brands	6.85	6.88	7.18	7.53	38.1	39.2	41.8	44.8
Liggett	2.88	3.56	3.90	4.97	16.0	20.3	22.7	29.6
Total	100.0	100.0	100.0	100.0	556.0	569.7	582.5	595.1

Sources: *Business Week,* Jan. 23, 1989, p. 59; *Business Week,* Jan. 18, 1988, p. 89.

International Markets

To offset declining sales at home, American cigarette manufacturers, led by Philip Morris, had begun to devote more attention to international markets, with special focus on the Pacific Rim. Figure 4 shows the percentages of men and women in various countries in 1990 who smoked and the total population of those countries at the time. Until the mid-1980s, most Asian countries protected their state-run tobacco monopolies either by banning foreign cigarettes or by imposing high tariffs on imports. For example, quotas and protective tariffs in Taiwan and Korea almost tripled the price of imported tobacco. In 1985, the U.S. Cigarette Export Association, under Section 301 of the 1974 Trade Act, threatened trade sanctions against Asian countries that restricted tobacco imports. The first target was Japan, which was seen as an entry point for the rest of the Pacific Rim. In 1986, the Reagan administration drew up a list of possible retaliatory tariffs on Japanese products, including supercomputers, textiles, and automobile parts. Soon, Japan lifted its tariff on foreign cigarettes, and U.S. cigarette exports to Japan quadrupled.

Taiwan's cigarette markets were opened next. Again, Section 301 was used, and lobbying was intense. In 1987, Taiwan agreed to drop its restrictions on foreign cigarettes, including its ban on advertising. Within a year, Philip Morris's Marlboro brand had captured 30 percent of the sales in its price category. The South Korean and Thailand markets were opened in 1988 and 1990, respectively, but unlike the other countries, Thailand continued its ban on advertising.

The U.S. government played a crucial role in opening these markets, largely because of its desire to reduce balance of trade deficits. Figure 5 shows U.S. merchandise trade balances for 1973 to 1991. Tobacco was one of only four major categories of goods that produced a positive trade balance.

The response of Asian markets is reflected in the export data shown in Exhibit 2. U.S. cigarette exports to Japan increased by 56 percent in 1987 and exports to Asia increased by 75 percent in 1988. Total U.S. cigarette exports increased 17 percent in 1989 and 7 percent in 1990. In 1990, cigarette consumption increased by 5.5 percent in Asia, and the smoking rate in these countries was increasing by 2 percent annually while the smoking rate was decreasing by 1.5 percent annually in industrialized countries.

FIGURE 4

Percentages of smokers in selected countries (1980–1985)

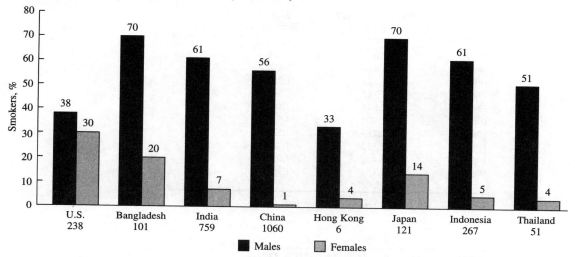

Note: The numbers below the country names refer to population, in millions.

Source: *Journal of the American Medical Association,* June 27, 1990, pp. 3315–16.

FIGURE 5

Merchandise trade balances.

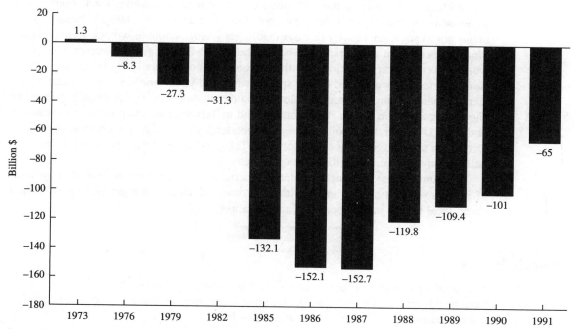

Source: *Statistical Abstract of the United States: 1990; Federal Reserve Bulletin,* 1991, 1992.

Exhibit 2   Domestic Exports of Tobacco, 1970 to 1988

	Total Tobacco and Manufacturers	Leaf Tobacco	Cigarettes
1970	679	481	159
1980	2,426	1,334	1,055
1981	2,723	1,457	1,229
1982	2,845	1,547	1,235
1983	2,647	1,462	1,126
1984	2,704	1,511	1,120
1985	2,789	1,521	1,180
1986	2,732	1,209	1,298
1987	3,400	1,090	2,047
1988	4,153	1,252	2,645

Source: *Statistical Abstract of the United States: 1990*, p. 881.

Marketing Cigarettes in the Pacific Rim

The presence of U.S. firms in the Asian market has been manifested in both an increase in the number of cigarette ads and a change in the type of ads and promotion used by all cigarette manufacturers. In Japan from 1986 to 1988, advertising time devoted to cigarettes on prime-time television rose from a rank of fortieth to a rank of second. Before the entry of American firms, Japan had planned to ban cigarette ads on television.

With the assistance of the U.S. government, tobacco companies used sophisticated advertisements that included techniques not allowed in the United States. Voluntary agreements not to advertise heavily in ways that target young people or women were dropped. Since 90 percent of smokers began before the age of 21 and a low percentage of Asian women were smokers, promotion to these groups was considered very important. Television commercials were aired during sports events and youth-oriented movies, and American companies sponsored motorcycle races and rock concerts. Young women gave away cigarette samples on Tokyo street corners, and in Taiwan, free samples were handed out at discos. Domestic tobacco companies responded by intensifying their promotional efforts at the same targets. For example, Japan Tobacco introduced a new brand, Dean, capitalizing on the young, rebellious image of actor James Dean.

In countries less affluent than Japan, American cigarettes were promoted as symbols of success, sophistication, and wealth. This was reflected in the practice of disguising cheap local brands in Marlboro or Camel wrappers.

Health Issues

The primary concerns about smoking, and consequently about cigarette exports, have been health-related. The Advisory Committee to the Surgeon General of the United States concluded that there are causal relationships between smoking and many diseases, including emphysema, cancer of the esophagus, and lung cancer. Exposure to smoke in the environment has been related to lung cancer in nonsmokers. Women who smoke while pregnant are more likely to deliver low-birth-weight babies. Deaths attributable to smoking include 30 percent of cancer deaths, 21 percent of coronary heart disease deaths, 18 percent of stroke deaths, and 82 percent of deaths from chronic obstructive pulmonary disease. Each year in industrialized countries, 1.8 million deaths are linked to smoking; this number exceeds "the combined total of all deaths due to any form of violence, be it accident, homicide, or suicide."[2] Smoking two or more packs of cigarettes a day decreases life expectancy more than eight years, and one pack a day shortens life expectancy six years. Smoking has been costing an estimated $23 billion annually in the United States for medical expenses, and another $30 billion has been lost to society each year because of illness and premature death.

On the basis of health issues, various spokespersons within the United States have strongly and persistently criticized cigarette sales overseas. A U.S. Congressman said, "For the past 100 years, America has been the world's foremost exporter of public health. . . . Now the U.S. Trade Representative wants to add a new chapter to that legacy . . . a chapter entitled: America, the world's greatest exporter of lung cancer, heart disease, emphysema, and death."[3] Koop states:

> It's reprehensible for industrial nations to export disease, death, and disability in the way of cigarette smoke to developing countries, putting on their backs a health burden that they will never be able to pay for 20 or 30 years from now.[4]

One observer described U.S. policy as "trading the lungs of people who wear ties for those who wear kimonos."[5]

In recent years, foreign groups have also become vocal about the perceived evils of cigarettes from the U.S. The Asia-Pacific Association for the Control of Tobacco sent a letter to President George Bush in 1989 stating:

> The cigarette issue is not an issue of trade or trade imbalances. It is an issue of human health, and Asian health is as important as American health. Asians want to purchase good American products, not harmful ones.[6]
>
> The Executive Director of the Hong Kong Council on Smoking and Health has noted that smoking-related illnesses, like cancer and heart disease, have overtaken communicable diseases as the leading cause of death in parts of Asia. Health warnings have not been required and have not appeared on cigarette advertisements in Asian countries, and the general level of awareness of the health hazards of smoking has been much lower than in the United States. In the mid-1980s, 95 percent of developed nations had laws pertaining to cigarette marketing and health warnings, but only 24 percent of underdeveloped nations had such regulations. This disparity has continued to exist.

Other Concerns about Exports

Beyond the health issue has been the concern that the Office of the U.S. Trade Representative's "full-throttle pursuit of profit is fueling an anti-American backlash that could translate into hostility toward other American exports."[7] Many people feel that exporting cigarettes puts the United States in the position of pushing drugs. In 1989 one critic of the industry said: "In a government purportedly concerned with drug abuse, this [exportation and aggressive marketing of American cigarettes] is hypocrisy of the first order."[8]

Tobacco and the Economy

Tobacco, the sixth-largest cash crop, is one of the most profitable crops a farmer can grow. It is an important source of cash income for America's family farmers.

Tobacco grown on the nation's farms is dried and sold at auction, then transported to manufacturers who make all different types of tobacco products.

Finally, the finished tobacco products are delivered to American consumers by wholesalers and retailers.

All of these businesses that make up the tobacco industry create jobs for over 414,000 people. These same businesses pay their employees more than $6.72 billion.

These jobs and wages are not limited to tobacco-growing states. Although industry employment averages 100,000 people in the major tobacco growing states—Kentucky, North Carolina, Tennessee, South Carolina, Virginia, and Georgia—more than 314,000 additional workers are employed by the industry elsewhere around the nation.

At a time when the United States is buying more goods from overseas than it is selling, it is important to note that the world loves America's tobacco and tobacco products. In 1987, the tobacco industry exported $3.4 billion worth of products and only imported $730 million. The result? A $2.7 billion trade surplus in tobacco products.

Jobs, wages, and a positive trade surplus are only a part of the contribution the tobacco industry makes to our economy (see Exhibit 3).

Tobacco Supplier Industries

The tobacco industry buys many goods and services from other industries that can be referred to as tobacco supplier industries.

Tobacco farmers purchase farm machinery and fertilizer. Tobacco manufacturers buy equipment and paper. Tobacco retailers buy vending machines and advertising. Examples of the goods and services provided by the tobacco supplier industries could go on and on.

The main point is clear: Tobacco supplier industries produce more than $35 billion worth of goods and services to meet the requirements of the tobacco industry. These same supplier industries employ 296,000 workers and pay out almost $7.4 billion in compensation.

Add the tobacco industry and tobacco supplier industries together and what do you get? Jobs for 710,000 people and a $31.5 billion contribution to the Gross National Product (the value of all goods and services) of the United States.

But the story doesn't end here.

The Full Impact

Workers in the tobacco industry and in the tobacco supplier industries are also consumers. They take vacations and buy houses, cars, groceries, appliances, gas and so on. They also buy services, such as day care, legal help, medical care, and insurance.

When you add up all the money these employees spend on goods and services, the total is surprising. The value of all these goods and services totals $50.6 billion, which is a tremendous contribution to the country's Gross National Product. To meet the demand for goods and services generated by tobacco industry and tobacco supplier industry employees, more than 1.59 million people are employed by all sorts of companies.

The Tobacco Industry and Taxes

The big spenders in government who oppose the tobacco industry are biting the hand that feeds them. Why? Because tobacco excise taxes and sales taxes by federal, state, and local governments added up to more than $10 billion in 1987.

The industry's tax liability doesn't end there, however. If you add individual and corporate income taxes paid by the tobacco industry to the more than $10 billion already mentioned, the total tax payment exceeds $13 billion. In fact, tobacco companies are among the largest taxpayers in the world.

In short, government red ink would be a lot redder without the tobacco industry.

Millions of jobs, billions of dollars spent on products and services, a boost to America's family farmers, a trade surplus, and billion of tax dollars—these are the contributions of the tobacco industry to our economy. Keep these contributions in mind as you read the rest of *The Great American Smoker's Manual*.

Source: Philip Morris, *The Great American Smoker's Manual*, pp. 1–3.

EXHIBIT 3   **The Tobacco Industry—Employment and Compensation**

Sector	Average Annual Employment	Annual Compensation $ Millions
Tobacco growing	100,000	$ 610,700
Auctions	9,240	90,800
Manufacturing	76,900	2,837,000
Wholesale trade	35,357	883,900
Retail trade	192,720	2,303,100
Total	414,217	$ 6,725,500

Still another concern has arisen in countries where per capita income is low. There has been some evidence that cigarettes divert spending from food purchases. In Bangladesh, studies revealed that higher cigarette consumptios by adults resulted in reduced caloric intake among children and decreased survival among children.

The Effect of Tobacco Products on the Economy

Philip Morris's view is quite different from the view of the antismoking activists. The box on page 420, "Tobacco and the Economy," is taken from the Philip Morris publication *The Great American Smoker's Manual.*

A Brief History of Cigarette Warning Labels

In 1957, 20 years after the first study of smoking and lung cancer appeared, Senator Wallace Bennett (R—Utah) introduced a bill that would require the following warning label on cigarettes: "Warning: Prolonged use of this product may result in cancer, in lung, heart, and circulatory ailments and in other diseases."

When the first warning labels appeared in 1966, they read: "Warning: The Surgeon General has determined that cigarette smoking is hazardous to your health." In 1971, the label was changed to read "Warning: The Surgeon General has determined that cigarette smoking is dangerous to your health."

Beginning in 1986, a new labeling system was mandated. Four labels were required to appear an equal number of times annually on each brand. The labels read:

Surgeon General's Warning: Cigarette Smoke Contains Carbon Monoxide.

Surgeon General's Warning: Smoking by Pregnant Women May Result in Fetal Injury, Premature Birth, and Low Birthweight.

> Surgeon General's Warning: Quitting Smoking Now Greatly
> Reduces Serious Risks to Your Health.

> Surgeon General's Warning: Smoking Causes Lung Cancer,
> Heart Disease, Emphysema and May Complicate Pregnancy.

Although the tobacco industry resisted these labeling requirements, it has been suggested that the industry also benefited. Specifically, agreeing to label cigarettes in 1966 was part of a deal that won the industry exemption from the normal federal, state, and local regulatory processes and also made the consumer responsible for the legal risk of cigarette usage. When cigarette ads were banned from radio and television as part of the antismoking campaign in 1971, free air time for antismoking ads also ended. Subsequently, the print media was saturated with cigarette ads, and antitobacco stories began to appear less frequently in magazines, which were the recipient of the advertising revenue bonanza. Finally, the original version of the new warnings in 1986 contained the words "death" and "addiction." Neither appears in the final version of the warnings.

While the United States and Scandinavian countries had the harshest cigarette warnings in 1992, some type of warning labels were mandated in about 100 countries. Philip Morris estimated that only 10 percent of its exported cigarettes were not labeled for health risks. Countries not requiring labels included Thailand, the Philippines, the Dominican Republic, Morocco, and the former Yugoslavia.

The competitive situation for Philip Morris was clouded by the presence of former government tobacco monopolies in many of their overseas markets. Members of Asian Consultancy on Tobacco Control admitted that a strong anti-American sentiment fueled antismoking efforts. Richard L. Snyder, Executive Vice President of PMI, was more blunt: "It's just covert protectionism."[9] American tobacco interests pointed out that most Asian governments controlled tobacco monopolies and stood to lose from American competition. China's revenues from the state-owned monopoly were approximately $5.2 billion annually, 10 percent of the Korean government's revenues came from the sale of tobacco products, and Japan's government monopoly had an 84 percent share of a market in which 60 percent of all males were smokers. The cigarette warning label mandated by the Japanese government may be translated "For your health, don't smoke too much."

It was difficult for Philip Morris to assess the effects of a unilateral labeling of export cigarettes. The effect could be to hurt Philip Morris's market share but not necessarily reduce overall smoking. That is, Asian customers might conclude that Marlboro (a Philip Morris brand) was hazardous to their health but that other American or domestic brands were not dangerous. In some countries, such an unmandated warning label was actually misleading. In Taiwan, for example, the brand with 90 percent market share was the government brand, Long Life. This cigarette had 24 milligrams of tar compared to Marlboro's 16 milligrams. Similarly, Thailand's top brand, marketed by the government, had 25 milligrams of tar, while the Thai government also sold a filterless brand for about 16 cents a pack.

Those familiar with the process of marketing cigarettes in underdeveloped countries questioned whether the cigarette warnings would do the good hoped by the antismoking activists or simply cause the competitive problems feared by PMI. Where illiteracy was high, a warning label would have little impact. In some areas, cigarettes were sold individually by street vendors, and the smoker never saw the warning-labeled package. Others pointed out that where per capita cigarette consumption was low, there was less likelihood that the majority of smokers would smoke enough to develop smoking-related health problems.[10]

A decision to change the warning label policy for exported cigarettes had a number of implications. Politically, a change might be preferable to a policy and wording mandated by Congress. In the United States, 30 members of the House of Representatives sponsored a bill that would require exported cigarettes to meet all domestic standards including warning labels and nicotine and tar labels. This legislation also would make cigarette ads abroad subject to the same restrictions as the United States. Competitively, a change might put Philip Morris at a disadvantage in foreign markets. Philip Morris has been in the forefront of the attacks on studies linking smoking and health. To add a warning label without being required to do so might be viewed as an admission of the health hazards of smoking. On the other hand, a full-blown discussion of the ethics of exporting unlabeled cigarettes was not an attractive agenda item for a stockholders' meeting either.

References

1. Cockburn, Alexander. "Getting Opium to the Masses: The Political Economy of Addiction." *The Nation,* 30 October 1989: 482.
2. Gehorsam, Jan, and Rebecca Perl. "Smoking Is the No. 1 Killer, World Health Survey Shows." *Atlanta Journal and Constitution,* 26 April 1991: E3.
3. Chen, Ted T. L., and Alvin E. Winder. "The Opium Wars Revisited as U.S. Forces Tobacco Exports in Asia," *The American Journal of Public Health,* 80(6), June 1990: 661.
4. Chen and Winder, p. 659.
5. Glazer, Sarah. "Who Smokes, Who Starts—And Why." *Editorial Research Reports,* 1(11) 1989: 150–63.
6. Chen and Winder, p. 661.
7. Schmeisser, Peter. "Pushing Cigarettes Overseas." *The New York Times Magazine,* 10 July 1988: 20.
8. Warner, Kenneth E. "Smoking and Health: A 25-Year Perspective." *The American Journal of Public Health,* 79(2) 1989: 143.
9. "Asia: A New Front in the War on Smoking," *Business Week,* February 1991: 66.
10. "Should the Activities of the Tobacco Industry in Third World Countries Be Restricted?" In Lisa H. Newton and Maureen M. Ford (eds.). *Taking Sides: Clashing Views on Controversial Issues in Business Ethics and Society.* Guilford, Conn.: The Dushkin Publishing Group, Inc., 1990, p. 310.

Discussion Issues

1. Summarize the ethical, economic, and social issues in this case.
2. Should the United States government require warning labels on American cigarettes that are destined for export? Explain.

9 RENAULT-VOLVO STRATEGIC ALLIANCE: MARCH 1993

Robert F. Bruner and Robert Spekman

In March 1993, the French elections turned the privatization of Régie Nationale des Usines Renault (Renault) from a hypothetical possibility into a likelihood. Louis Schweitzer, Renault's CEO, regarded this exciting development as a challenge and opportunity. The French government had a legacy of being fairly interventionist—would it give up control in Renault in one transaction or, instead, would it choose to relinquish control more slowly? More important, how would the privatization of Renault affect the strategic alliance between Renault and AB Volvo, which had been in force since 1991? The alliance had been based on the exchange of shares, the formation of an elaborate structure of coordinating committees, and the initiation of several strategic projects, including a jointly designed executive car targeted for sale by the year 2000. The long-run vision had been that the strategic alliance might one day culminate in a merger of the two automotive manufacturers. Whether the firms should combine would depend importantly on considerations of timing, the health of the strategic alliance, a careful assessment of the benefits to be gained and the lessons Volvo and Renault had learned through the alliance thus far. Volvo and Renault had discussed the possibility of merger for years—as recently as 1992. Should the two firms aim to consummate a merger before privatization, or after?

Similar questions preoccupied Pehr Gyllenhammar, Volvo's CEO. The answers, however, seemed less problematic. As a small automobile manufacturer, Volvo would find it increasingly difficult to keep pace with the new-model development and manufacturing initiatives of its competitors. Indeed, 1992 had been a disastrous year for Volvo's financial performance, and lent strength to the industrial logic of combining with another automotive manufacturer. It seemed to Gyllenhammar that the alliance with Renault was working well. While Swedes might be reluctant to dilute their control over Scandinavia's largest industrial group, Gyllenhammar had argued for years that fuller integration of Sweden—and Volvo—into the European community was the best path to national prosperity. The strategic alliance with Renault embodied that vision.

In short, Gyllenhammar and Schweitzer would need to develop a plan of action to respond to Renault's changing circumstances. One possibility would be to do nothing and simply continue as strategic allies indefinitely. Alternatively, the two firms could aim to merge, assuming this was even more beneficial than an alliance. If this were the preferred course, then questions of speed, timing, and form would need to be resolved.

Renault S.A.

Renault had produced automobiles since 1898 and was, by 1993, the largest business enterprise in France based on the number of employees (61,000 in France, 147,000 worldwide) and total revenues (170 billion French francs (FF) for the group). In 1993, the company sold 1,761,306 vehicles worldwide, ranking ninth in unit output in the industry. Over 80 percent of Renault's unit sales were in Europe, where it commanded 10.3 percent of the car and light-commercial-vehicle market.[1] The company had been nationalized in 1945 by General Charles de Gaulle on charges that it collaborated with the enemy during the German occupation of France in the Second World War. The firm's "régie" status indicated that it was not simply a company, but a "state body" wholly owned by the government of France. The firm was headquartered in Boulogne Billancourt, a suburb of Paris.

Renault's financial performance had varied considerably in the postwar period—it nearly entered bankruptcy in the early 1980s. Renault recovered by the mid-1980s (see Exhibit 1) and, in 1992, reported an operating margin of 4.4 percent, ranking it among the most profitable automotive manufacturers in the world.[2] The engine of profitability was Renault's passenger-car segment; the truck-and-bus segment (Renault Véhicules Industriels S.A.) lost FF1.59 billion in operating income in 1992 as a result of declining demand for heavy trucks in Europe.

The turnaround in overall performance stemmed largely from the accession to power of a cadre of business-oriented enterprise managers led by Raymond H. Lévy, a widely respected CEO who joined the firm in 1986. Lévy's management team implemented a broad-ranging restructuring of the firm, including substantial work-force reductions, changes in work rules, implementation of a total-quality management program, introduction of a successful line of new products (including Clio [an inexpensive subcompact], Safrane [an expensive executive luxury car], and Espace [a van-style family car]), and a refocusing of the firm's activities toward Europe. Renault had entered North America in 1980 with a purchase of 46 percent of American Motors Corporation (AMC). In 1983, the AMC Alliance (designed in collaboration with Renault) won the Motor Trend Car of the

---

[1] Other leading competitors in the European new-car market in 1993 were Opel (12.5 percent share of market), Ford (11.3 percent), Volkswagen (10.8 percent), Fiat (8.3 percent), Peugeot (7.4 percent) and Citroen (4.9 percent).

[2] Only Saab-Scania reported a higher operating margin (4.6 percent). Next highest were Suzuki (4.1 percent) and PSA (3.8 percent). By contrast, the largest manufacturers were substantially lower: GM (–2.5 percent), Ford (–2.1 percent), Volkswagen (–0.2 percent), Toyota (2.1 percent), Nissan (–0.1 percent), and Honda (–2.6 percent).

EXHIBIT 1   Renault-Volvo Strategic Alliance (A)

Highlights of Renault's Financial History
(in millions of French francs for fiscal years ending 31 December)

	1985	1986	1987	1988	1989	1990	1991	1992
Turnover (revenues)	111,382	134,935	147,510	161,438	174,480	163,620	165,794	179,449
Operating profit (loss)	(4,398)	3,549	9,204	14,385	12,940	6,299	4,663	7,920
Pretax profit (loss)	(12,255)	(5,210)	3,562	8,975	9,730	1,380	4,109	6,549
Tax expense (tax credit)	(1,330)	648	(127)	62	910	516	963	(869)
Minority interests	28	176	433	79	48	(346)	68	236
Net profit (loss)	(10,953)	(6,034)	3,256	8,834	9,300	1,210	3,078	5,680
Total assets	42,003	45,988	43,489	46,648	49,780	119,451	127,098	132,081
Net debt	61,962	55,627	46,377	23,786	17,590	81,854	72,733	71,727
Capital expenditures	8,269	5,551	7,021	7,295	10,360	10,669	9,434	11,200
Total equity	(9,450)	(11,433)	(7,811)	14,012	16,770	20,513	31,331	33,965

Source: Renault annual reports. Note that Renault changed accounting policies in the early 1990s, and restated results only back to 1990. Thus, the figures for 1985–89 may not be directly comparable with those for 1990–92.

year Award. Yet AMC never attained the desired market position or profitability, so Renault sold its interest in 1987 to Chrysler and exited from the North American market. The refocus on Europe had paid off with increases in market share and unit sales. A Renault executive told an interviewer.

> Even though Renault is a state-owned enterprise, we could not have recovered and achieved high profitability unless we had been run as if we were a private company. Renault is no longer the showcase for new social experiments by the French government. We cut the work force dramatically in the past seven years. The government accepts that Renault must become competitive.

The demand for new cars in Europe was relatively stable from 1989 to 1992, varying between 13.2 and 13.5 million per year. But in 1993, as recession swept Europe, new-car sales fell 15 percent; and in France, demand for heavy trucks plummeted 21 percent.

AB Volvo

In 1993, Volvo was Scandinavia's largest industrial group, with headquarters in Gothenburg, Sweden. As a global competitor in several industries, AB Volvo was an object of Swedish national pride. Total sales in 1992 were 83 billion Swedish kronor (Skr) on which the firm lost SKr3.3 billion in earnings. Volvo's assets amounted to SKr117 billion. Exhibit 2 presents a graph of the Volvo price per share since 1971. Exhibit 3 gives selected financial data for AB Volvo over recent years. (For comparative purposes, the exchange rate of Swedish krona to French franc was about 1.3:1.)

Volvo's business portfolio in 1993 could be broken down into four main segments: (1) automobiles, (2) trucks and buses, (3) engines and aerospace, and (4) consumer prod-

---

EXHIBIT 2   Renault-Volvo Strategic Alliance (A)
Price of Volvo "B" Shares, 1971 to 1993

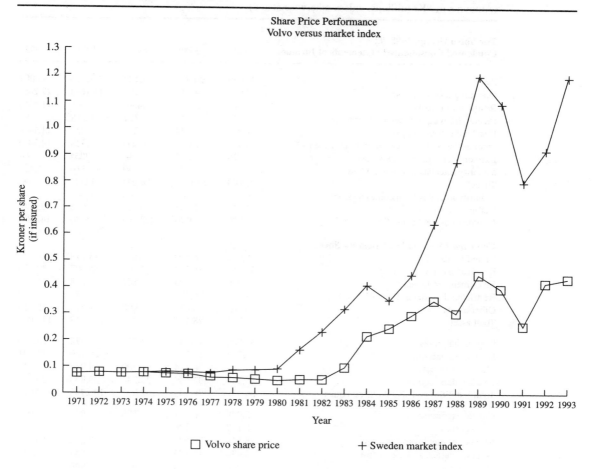

Share Price Performance
Volvo versus market index

□ Volvo share price   + Sweden market index

ucts. Car production accounted for 54 percent of total revenues in 1992. The company held a 1.1 percent share of the world auto market, producing 311,000 cars in 1993. Over 90 percent of Volvo's auto sales were outside Sweden, principally to North America and the United Kingdom. Volvo also owned 20 percent of Renault, as part of the strategic alliance formed in 1990. Volvo was second in world sales of heavy trucks and buses, with 51,300 units commanding a 10 percent share of market. Production of trucks and buses accounted for 37 percent of Volvo's total revenues in 1992. Over 95 percent of truck and bus sales were outside Sweden. As part of the Renault alliance, Volvo owned 45 percent of Renault Véhicules Industriels, the truck-and-bus manufacturing operation.

Volvo (which is Latin for "I roll") began operations in 1927 as a manufacturer of cars. Diversifying gradually into trucks, buses, and marine engines, the company grew steadily.

EXHIBIT 3   Renault-Volvo Strategic Alliance (A)
Volvo's Recent Financial History
(Amounts in SKr millions, unless otherwise stated)

The Volvo Group, 1988–92 Condensed Consolidated Statements of Income	1988	1989	1990	1991	1992
Sales	96,639	90,972	83,185	77,223	83,002
Operating income (loss)	7,028	4,817	567	(1,168)	(2,249)
Restructuring costs	—	—	(2,450)	—	(1,450)
Income from equity-method investments	—	1,015	1,322	1,218	96
Financial income (expense)	1,039	822	234	1,478	(1,146)
Income (loss) after financial income (expense)	8,067	6,654	(327)	1,528	(4,749)
Extraordinary income (expense)	176	313	—	(725)	—
Minority interests in (income) loss	—	(56)	40	310	1,437
Taxes	(3,200)	(2,124)	(733)	(431)	(8)
Minority interests in (income) loss	(103)	—	—	—	—
Net income (loss)	4,940	4,787	(1,020)	682	(3,320)
Income (loss) per share, SKr	63.70	61.70	(13.10)	8.80	(42.80)
Condensed Consolidated Balance Sheets					
Liquid funds	15,632	18,470	17,585	18,779	21,760
Receivables and inventories	33,346	35,248	35,604	35,087	39,979
Investments in bonds	3,956	3,455	2,854	928	—
Restricted deposits in Bank of Sweden	4,034	5,293	2,072	41	2
Other assets	29,963	35,677	43,982	51,913	55,266
Total assets	86,951	98,143	102,097	106,748	117,007
Current liabilities	34,500	42,846	48,712	47,778	59,386
Long-term liabilities	18,727	17,244	17,794	20,120	23,981
Minority interests	484	414	300	4,986	3,919
Shareholders' equity	33,240	37,639	35,291	33,864	29,721
Total liabilities and shareholders' equity	86,951	98,143	102,097	106,748	117,007
Capital expenditures	3,948	6,281	4,598	2,874	2,915
R&D costs	5,139	6,176	7,061	6,414	6,178
Number of employees, year-end	78,614	78,690	68,797	63,582	60,115
Wages, salaries, and social costs	15,434	16,875	17,865	17,654	16,857
Share capital	1,940	1,940	1,940	1,940	1,940
Dividends to shareholders	1,086	1,203	1,203	1,203	601
Dividend per share, SKr	14.00	15.50	15.50	15.50	7.75
Return on capital employed, percentage	17.2	13.8	4.4	6.8	0.7
Return on shareholders' equity, percentage	15.8	13.3	neg	2.0	neg
Shareholders' equity and minority interests to total assets, percentage	38.8	38.8	34.9	36.4	28.8

Source: AB Volvo annual reports.

Plants were established in Belgium, Peru, and Canada. In 1966, Volvo introduced its model 144, which was acclaimed as the "Car of the Year"; thereafter, sales grew rapidly, especially in North America. In 1971, Volvo's CEO, Gunnar Engellau, designated Pehr G. Gyllenhammar (his 36-year-old son-in-law) as the new CEO, and Volvo entered a new phase of its history. Gyllenhammar's rise to power coincided with a shift in strategy toward reducing the firm's dependence on cars. Sweden itself offered little room for sales growth; so any car-based stretegy would need to be export oriented. But to compete in the export market meant regular style changes, which raised significant challenges from the high cost of product development. Accordingly, Gyllenhammar undertook a series of investments and merger attempts aimed at diversifying Volvo's business base and/or attaining greater economies of scale and scope for Volvo cars. These moves included eight major transactions.[3]

Gyllenhammar retained the CEO title until 1990, when he appointed Christer Zetterberg to be CEO and himself "Executive Chairman"—a realignment that would allow Gyllenhammar to focus on larger strategic issues, especially those pertaining to the alliance. Zetterberg resigned in 1992 following disagreements with Gyllenhammar and in the midst of Volvo's cyclical decline. Gyllenhammar then appointed Soren Gyll CEO, and gave him the mandate to turn the company around. Gyll had been president and CEO of Procordia, a large Swedish state-owned pharmaceuticals and consumer-products company, and had proved to be a tough-minded and effective general manager. Before the year had ended, Gyll announced a profit-improvement program for Volvo called Volvo 95. Under this plan, Volvo closed two car plants, reduced the cost basis of the firm by SKr 4.5 million, reduced working capital by 25 percent, increased capital turnover by 25 percent, and reduced product-development lead times by 50 percent throughout the organization. The program had an enormous financial impact, helping to deliver a rebound in profitability beginning in early 1993.

Volvo's financial outlook for 1993 was positive: the demand for automobiles in North America, Japan, and Southeast Asia was increasing. The 850 car model was very well received. The Volvo 95 cost-reduction program would deliver larger profit margins. Despite these positive trends, Volvo's financial report for the first quarter (ended March 31) included these results:

---

[3] The transactions included:

• Attempted merger with Saab-Scania, Sweden's other major car manufacturer. Plans for merger were announced in May 1977, but abandoned in August when opposition to the merger developed.

• Attempted investment in the Norwegian oil industry. In August 1977, Gyllenhammar initiated discussions with Norway's prime minister to exchange Volvo shares for a 40 percent interest in Norway's North Seal oil fields. The proposal was abandoned in January 1978 after a majority of Volvo shareholders opposed the plan.

• Acquisition of Beijerinvest Group in late 1981. Gyllenhammar was attracted by Beijerinvest's oil-trading firm, though the firm also operated food, engineering, and other businesses.

• In 1980, sale of a 9.9 percent share interest in Volvo to Renault. This took place in combination with a public share offering. Other issues of stock took place in 1981 and 1982.

• In the early 1980s, Volvo acquired a number of minority interests in consumer-foods manufacturers.

• In 1986, Gyllenhammar negotiated the sale of Volvo's pharmaceuticals business to Fermenta AB, and the acquisition of 20 percent of Fermenta's shares. This deal broke down when it appeared that Fermenta's CEO had engaged in fraud.

• In 1986, Volvo acquired a 25 percent interest in a pharmaceuticals company, Pharmacia.

• In 1991, Volvo organized NedCar B.V. as a joint venture with Volvo, Mitsubishi, and the Dutch government. The objective of this joint venture was to manufacture car models in the medium-sized segment for sale under the Volvo and Mitsubishi names.

(in SKr millions, except per-share figures)	First Three Months, 1993	First Three Months, 1992
Volvo Group sales	22,946	20,023
Operating loss	(189)	(347)
Income (loss) per share, most recent 12-month period	(44.10)	2.10
Return on capital employed during most recent 12-month period	0.9%	6.2%

As the company explained,

> The business climate remained weak in nearly all of Volvo's markets. Sales of cars in Western Europe are estimated to decline slightly more than 10 percent during 1993. The fall in the European truck market is expected to be 25–30 percent during the year. Low domestic consumption is foreseen in Sweden, and car sales during the first months of the year were the lowest in over 30 years.[4]

Strategic Alliance between Volvo and Renault

In 1990, Volvo and Renault agreed to establish a strategic alliance through a complicated scheme of cross-shareholdings, joint production and R&D agreements, and supervisory boards. The alliance was the culmination of almost 20 years of industrial cooperation between the two firms. A components-exchange agreement began in 1971. Renault invested in Volvo shares in 1980 (and sold them in 1985). Gyllenhammar and Raymond Lévy (CEO of Renault at the time) believed that closer cooperation was necessary to exploit opportunities that faced both companies. The European automotive industry had witnessed a number of combinations in recent years, including Ford/Jaguar, GM/Saab, and Peugeot/Citroen. Volvo estimated that the undiscounted value of economies available through the alliance would amount to SKr14 billion between the years 1991 and 2000. The alliance was consummated in January 1991 with an exchange of minority share interests in each company; the structure of the resulting alliance is shown in Exhibit 4. The network of cross-shareholdings was accompanied by a "poison pill," which made unwinding the alliance difficult and costly. The official language of the alliance was to be English. The alliance would be headquartered in both Paris and Gothenburg.

The two companies began their alliance by targeting economies in several areas: purchasing, quality, components, and the introduction of a new range of executive cars in 1997 on the basis of a jointly developed platform known as the P4 Project. By early 1993, Volvo and Renault had created 21 coordinating committees. These committees were staffed equally from each firm. The understanding was that the two firms would share equally in decision making (i.e., the power would be divided 50–50). By early 1993, Renault was the larger partner in the alliance, almost five times larger in sales revenue and

---

[4] AB Volvo, *Volvo Interim Report: Three Months Ended March 31, 1993.*

Exhibit 4   Renault-Volvo Strategic Alliance (A)

Structure of the Strategic Alliance and Cross-Shareholdings
(established January 1, 1991)

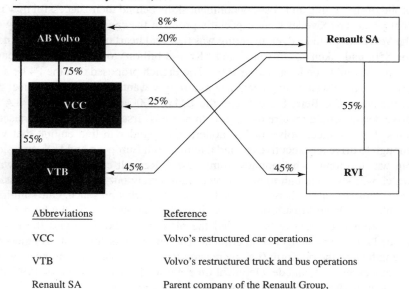

Abbreviations	Reference
VCC	Volvo's restructured car operations
VTB	Volvo's restructured truck and bus operations
Renault SA	Parent company of the Renault Group, following conversion to a capital stock company
RVI	Renault Véhicules Industriels SA

*Renault had acquired 8.24% of Volvo shares, and 10% of the votes.

Source of Information: AB Volvo, *"Information Prior to Extraordinary General Meeting of Shareholders in AB Volvo, November 9, 1993,"* p. 40.

employees, six times larger in car units sold, and seven times larger in operating profit. Only in truck and bus units sold was Volvo slightly larger.

By most accounts, both partners perceived the alliance to be healthy as could be expected. Components exchange had worked well. Purchasing had begun to realize economies, but would take more time to achieve full potential. Quality efforts had made some headway. The two firms could look to such successes as the development of a new family of rear-axle drives and the establishment of a joint venture for manufacturing buses in France. The language difference was still a concern, although the French had made strides in mastering English for the alliance. Some newspaper accounts, however, reported that Renault engineers had reverted to speaking French and that some Swedes perceived that as a means of excluding them. Many observers believed that, by 1993, the alliance had exploited the easy gains and that more difficult challenges lay ahead. Two projects exemplified these challenges:

• **P4 Project:** The effort to develop a new common platform for a high-end executive car occupied 200 to 300 engineers. For the French and the Swedes, the design of the flagship-model car summoned forth the strongest skills and feelings. The French were proud of the styling and cost-containment skills behind their successful new models of recent years. The Swedes were especially proud of the engineering and safety embedded in the Volvo cars—indeed, engineering was the "real heart of Volvo." Volvo's newest model, the 850, had taken seven years[5] and SKr 7–8 billion[6] to launch. Models built on the P4 platform were to be launched in 1997. The French proposed that the P4 be a front-wheel-drive car; the Swedish engineers just as strongly wanted it to be rear-wheel drive, similar to the Mercedes-Benz S class, and the BMW 500- and 700-series cars. A front-wheel-drive design would require the engine to be transverse mounted, which raised other problems. For instance, Volvo had a modern six-cylinder in-line engine that was powerful enough to drive an executive car and that met both European and U.S. emission standards, but was too long to be mounted transversely. Renault could supply its own V6 engine, which was short enough to be mounted transversely but did not meet emission standards in the United States where Volvo had a material market presence. One solution was to buy a V6 engine from Mitsubishi, but this idea was unpopular with the French. Finally, computer-simulated crash tests revealed the platform to be too light: the engine could be pushed into the passenger compartment. The safety-conscious Volvo engineers insisted on strengthening the platform (i.e., increasing its weight); Renault engineers were concerned about weight, cost, and development time. With a launch planned for 1997, the final commitment on the platform would be needed in six months.

• **Truck Production:** Questions about truck production illustrated the need for making hard decision to rationalize the efforts of the two firms. Should Volvo supply engines for sale in Renault trucks? Truck buyers were much more sophisticated than car buyers and perceived Volvo engines as being of higher quality than Renault engines. Because the price of Volvo trucks was higher than comparable Renault trucks, might it not be possible to acquire a Volvo engine for less money by buying a Renault truck? Volvo's solution was to propose that Volvo assume responsibility for all production of heavy trucks—where Volvo was a major, if not dominant, producer—and that Renault assume responsibility for production of medium and light trucks, where it had good volume. Renault resisted, pointing out that it had a strong heavy-truck position in France. Observers sensed that Renault Véhicules Industriels was afraid of being swallowed by Volvo, and that Volvo feared losing or diluting part of its brand identity with the customer.

With a 50–50 control arrangement, both companies had the power to veto decisions. Many of these decisions were delicate. On the industrial side, they could affect the allocation of production—and jobs—between Sweden and France. Renault, a state-owned enterprise, was sensitive to the loss of jobs. In the area of new-model development, the two firms were protective of their respective brand identities. But real cost savings lay with

---

[5] The launch cycle for the 850 line took longer than normal because the designers changed the specifications two years into the project.

[6] The development cost of SKr 7–8 billion excludes the cost of a new engine plant built to produce gasoline engines for the 850 line. If the investment in the engine plant were included, the total launch cost would be SKr 15 billion.

replacing a product completely; it would be difficult to obtain large savings with old products in the system. Compromises on product design would tend to erode savings. Volvo had a decentralized management structure; it was relatively easy to obtain and share information. Renault had a more centralized structure.

Gyllenhammar and Schweitzer believed that the two years of working together had proved the wisdom of the alliance, but they were impatient with the pace of joint work and integration. As Louis Schweitzer said, "If you want to win, you must go faster. Speed is of the essence. We must go beyond the limits of cooperation to date." He and Gyllenhammar viewed merger as one obvious solution. Schweitzer added, "The advantage of a complete merger is simplicity and speed. Agreement between the two companies does not go as fast as managing a single group."

Louis Schweitzer

Renault's chief executive officer in 1993 was Louis Schweitzer, grandson of Nobel Laureate Albert Schweitzer. Born in 1942, Louis Schweitzer was educated at École Nationale d'Administration, one of the elite French *grandes écoles*. He began his career as a civil servant and rose to the position of chief of staff to French Prime Minister Michal Rocard. In 1988, Schweitzer was recruited by Renault's CEO Raymond H. Lévy, to become a vice president at Renault. One of Schweitzer's prime assignments was to negotiate the terms of the strategic alliance with Volvo. In 1992, Schweitzer rose to become Lévy's successor as CEO of Renault. In 1993, he was a director of Renault, Institute Pasteur, Pechiney, Banque Nationale de Paris, and Union des Assurances de Paris.

Pehr G. Gyllenhammar

After 22 years at the helm of Volvo, Pehr Gyllenhammar was one of the most prominent businessmen in Scandinavia. Born in 1935, he had studied law in Sweden and other countries, after which he practiced briefly with a specialty in admiralty law. He joined Skandia Insurance Company (Sweden's largest insurer) in 1965 as an assistant manager, and by 1970 had risen to president and CEO, having been appointed by his father, who had headed the insurer. In late 1970, he joined AB Volvo and was appointed managing director and CEO in 1971. He was prominently associated with the series of investment and merger transactions proposed by Volvo over the next 22 years, playing a personal role in their design and proposal. From 1983 to 1990, he served as chairman of the board and CEO; after 1990, his title was executive chairman of the board. He served on numerous boards of directors,[7] and had received a number of honors.[8]

Gyllenhammar found time to cast his management ideas into numerous articles and

---

[7] Gyllenhammar's board memberships included Skandinaviska Enskilda Banken (Sweden's largest bank), United Technologies Corporation, Kissinger Associates, Pearson PLC, Reuters Holdings PLC, NV Philips Gloeilampenfabrieken, and Renault.

[8] His honors included four honorary doctorates and the Legion d'Honneur (France), King's Medal (Sweden), Lion of Finland (Finland), and Order of Merit (Italy).

four books: *Towards the Turn of the Century at Random* (1970), *I Believe in Sweden* (1973), People at Work (1977), and *Industrial Policy for Human Beings* (1979). This body of writing conveyed a humanistic orientation toward factory work, emphasizing a concern for worker safety, dignity, and fulfillment. Two prominent innovations associated with his early years as CEO were the construction of a revolutionary car-assembly plant at Kalmar, Sweden (in which Volvo developed the team-based manufacturing techniques for which it became famous), and the invention of individual industrial carriers to move cars through the plant rather than using an assembly line—this technology innovation permitted the firm to experiment with team-based manufacturing techniques.

Up to 1993, the business press used such words as "outspoken," "visionary," "ambitious," "industrial statesman," and "strong advocate of Sweden's need to move closer to the rest of Europe" to describe Gyllenhammar. He was perceived as a charismatic and popular leader. But the tone of his press treatment changed when Aktiespararna (the Swedish Small Shareholders' Association) petitioned the board of directors to disclose his salary. At the April 1993 Annual Meeting, Gyllenhammar revealed that he was paid SKr9.5 million, the highest individual compensation package in Scandinavia. Aktiespararna charged that Gyllenhammar had taken advantage of a board that had no compensation committee to pay himself an "excessive" salary at a time when the company was closing plants, cutting the dividend, and losing money. Former business associates regarded Gyllenhammar as distant and even arrogant in his regard for the views of other senior managers at Volvo. One publication wrote that he was "a charming, gregarious autocrat whose nickname at the company is 'the emperor.' His critics say of him that he has used Volvo as a platform for his personal ambitions."[9] A Francophile, he could speak French fluently, sometimes reverting to French in his negotiations with Renault, to the consternation of his Volvo associates, who felt excluded.

Conclusion and Discussion Issues

Following the French elections in March 1993, the CEOs of Volvo and Renault needed to consider what modifications to their strategic alliance might be suggested by Renault's impending privatization. Was this the time to merge? What benefits would merger bring that were not already embodied in the alliance? How might merger transform the alliance? If merger were appropriate, then when should it be implemented? What controlling interests should the French and Swedish sides have?

---

[9] Phyllis Berman, "Stretching the Platform," *Forbes,* December 19, 1994, 198.

10 SIBERIAN PETROLEUM PRODUCTION ASSOCIATION: A NEGOTIATION SIMULATION

John L. Graham

Recently Harland Smith, vice president of marketing for Bolter Turbines International (BTI), attended a two-day conference in Houston sponsored by the U.S. Commerce Department. The purpose of the conference was to stimulate trade between American companies in the oil and gas industry and potential Russian customers. Details regarding the conference and associated programs were reported in a recent article in *Business America.*[1]

A 40-member Russian delegation of oil and gas government officials and industry experts, led by Deputy Minister of Fuel and Energy Audry Konoplyanik, visited Houston, Texas, April 28–May 7. The mission, hosted by the U.S. government and organized by the Department of Commerce, was sponsored by the U.S. Agency for International Development through the U.S. Energy Association.

The trip was the result of an agreement by both the U.S. and Russian governments during the first meeting of the U.S.–Russia Oil and Gas working group, which decided to hold a conference and meeting in conjunction with the Houston Offshore Technology Conference, the largest annual trade show covering oil and gas equipment. (The oil and gas working group is one of seven industrial-sector working groups established under the auspices of the Business Development Committee, an organization co-chaired by Commerce Secretary Ronald H. Brown and Russian Deputy Prime Minister Alexander Shokhin.)

The delegation's program was organized by the Commerce Department's Basic Industries division, which was assisted by the Greater Houston Partnership and other federal agencies. The agenda consisted of a conference on "Opportunities in Russia for U.S. Oil and Gas Firms," attended by more than 200 U.S. oil and gas industry representatives (April 29–30); the second U.S.–Russia Oil and Gas working group meeting, May 1–2; and visits to the Offshore Technology Conference, May 3–6. In addition, the delegation participated in private meetings with American firms, special briefings, and social events hosted by U.S. companies. The conference on opportunities in Russia for U.S. oil and gas firms was presented by Russian officials representing Russian federation ministries, regional administrations, and state/commercial enterprises. It was structured to provide a variety of settings within which American companies could interact with the entire Russian delegation. The conference consisted of a general session in the morning, followed by concurrent roundtable discussions and private meetings in the afternoon. Presentations at the general sessions covered the main direction of Russian energy policy, particularly concepts for attracting foreign investors, access to resources and licensing, state enterprise transformation to stock holding companies, and privatization. Methods of cooperation in the main business activities of the oil and gas subsectors, specifically exploration, production, refining, supply of oil products, and gas services, were also addressed.

The roundtable discussions elaborated on the subjects presented in the plenary sessions. During the private meetings conducted concurrently with the roundtables in the afternoon, a number of U.S. companies were able to discuss specific projects with members of the Russian delegation and establish contacts for future contracts or business collaboration.

American businesses participating in the conference and those involved in hosting the delegation appeared to have benefited from the interchange. "The great value of this conference," said Richard Hildahl of Ernst & Young, "was that key Russian government and industry representatives met with their counterparts in the United State to discuss the challenges and possible solutions to the complexity of doing business in Russia."

William Gottfried, an American petroleum consultant, said, "The conference format allowed the American participants to work directly with the key decision makers from the Russian oil and gas industry. This conference served as a real catalyst for American investment and cooperation in the Russian oil and gas sector."

Rod A. Johnson, president of OptiMarket, a U.S. firm promoting investment projects in the Russian Federations Krasnoyarsk region, offered this view, saying, "The Department of Commerce has created a milestone in world energy affairs. Every major issue of cooperation between the United States and Russia had been identified and addressed by the countries' governments and industry representatives at one forum in two days. A generation of errors and mistakes will be avoided. In an international energy market marked by embargoes and energy cartels and energy price escalation, we are seeing two great world energy powers bring their industry leaders together to maximize and facilitate their countries' energy resources and energy technologies. We are seeking not just solutions, but the format for future solutions. This conference sets the precedence, procedure, and pace for future Russian/American business and government cooperation, which will stimulate the economies and futures of the United States and Russia."

The Russian delegation appeared to be equally satisfied with the results of the conference. The leader of the Russian delegation, Audrey Konoplyanik, commented, "The value of the conference was in the discussion of key issues characterizing the situation in the oil and gas sector of Russia. This allowed the American participants to understand better possible ways of interacting with Russian federal and regional bodies, as well as with commercial entities."

Aladimir Filanovsky, president of the Kamneft Joint Venture, who moderated the roundtable on priorities of the subsectors, expressed his views on the conference: "The discussions showed the necessity for the development of an effective mechanism for the financing of joint ventures with American companies for the manufacturing of oil extraction equipment based on conversion of Russian defense enterprises. These discussions also showed the need for providing U.S. companies with detailed information clarifying the procedures for involvement in the Russian oil market."

At the second U.S.–Russia Oil and Gas working group meeting, the results of the conference were discussed in detail. Both the U.S. and Russian sides agreed that important joint government actions needed to be taken to realize the full potential of U.S. commercial capabilities in assisting Russia to modernize its oil and gas sector. It became clear to the group that financing of trade and investment is clearly one of the major constraints for U.S. firms seeking to do commercial business in Russia in the oil and gas sector.

The working group also discussed its work plan for the next 12 months, tentatively agreeing to four priority projects to be completed over the next six months, including:

- Preparing and publishing proceedings for the "Opportunities in Russia for U.S. Oil and Gas Firms" conference.
- Assisting Russian officials in preparing an information directory on the Russian oil and gas sector.
- Jointly organizing a series of expert workshops on Western approaches to financing, accounting, taxes, and selected legal issues, and
- Distributing to the American business community information on the 19 defense conversion projects selected by the Russians as priority projects and assisting U.S. firms in structuring business ventures.

During the last four days of their visit to Houston, the Russian delegation attended the Offshore Technology Conference. The Russian delegation members were able to view in person and discuss advanced oil and gas field products, services, and systems with more than 1,200 petroleum equipment exhibitors.

In addition to organized briefings given by major U.S. equipment manufacturers, there were a number of one-on-one meetings that enabled smaller U.S. firms to gauge the potential interest for their products in Russia.

The Russian delegation attended a number of social events hosted by U.S. companies. Among the firms involved were McDermott Marketing Services, Dresser Industries, Butler Taper Joint, Inc., CIS American Chamber of Commerce, Enron Corporation, Gulf Publishing Company, Petroleum Advisory Forum, Smith Meter Inc., Wheatley TXT Corporation, and Bolter Turbines International.

At the conference Harland Smith met Leonid Vihansky, the director of the newly formed Siberian Petroleum Production Association (SPPA). SPPA is a quasigovernment-owned oil and gas production company with operations in northwestern Siberia and offices in Moscow. SPPA, like many other former Soviet industrial concerns, is now being privatized as part of the most recent economic reforms in Russia.

Vihansky's job is to increase the production of oil and gas of his production unit *at a profit*. The last stipulation, at a profit, is a new one to Vihansky, and he and his associates are still learning the ropes of Western-style free enterprise. But they are learning quite fast.

Vihansky is interested in buying equipment from BTI. In the months following the conference in Houston, SPPA and BTI representatives met several times in both Moscow and Los Angeles to discuss equipment needs of SPPA. These meetings resulted in an initial price quotation for the first of what SPPA describes as a series of orders to revitalize the production capacity of its Siberian fields.

You have been assigned by Smith to participate in the final negotiations for this initial order from SPPA. Your team consists of three people: your Europe regional sales manager, a sales representative, and an applications engineer. You are to meet with three representatives of SPPA: Vihansky, his chief production engineer, and a trade representative. The last, Oleg Evenko, is very experienced in dealings with Western companies. He formerly worked for the Soviet Foreign Trade Organization involved in purchasing oil field equipment. Your team will be meeting with the SPPA people in Nice, France, to close the deal.

A price quotation and a schematic of the JR2000 are attached. More details about your assignment will soon be provided by Smith. Good Luck!

Bolter Turbines, Inc.

Price Quotation

For Siberian Petroleum Product Association
  Arbotov 687
  Moscow, Russia
	Installation: Timon
	Perchora Field.
	Northwest Siberia

Model JR2000 Natural Gas Compressor Set (the standard package includes an XJ1 compressor)	$2,500,000
Product options	
Custom-built Cold Weather Shelter	400,000
XJ3 compressor (replacement for XJ1)	800,000
Service contract (2 years normal maintenance, parts, and labor)	150,000
Total Price	$3,850,000

Standard Terms and Conditions

Delivery	6 months
Penalty for late delivery	$10,000/month
Cancellation charges (if client cancels order)	10% of contract price
Warranty (for defective machinery)	Parts, one year
Terms of payment	COD
Inflation escalator	10% per year

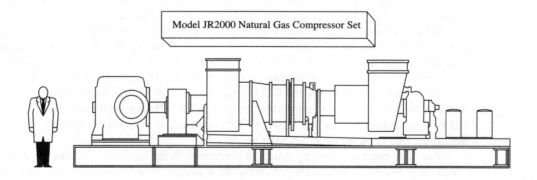

Model JR2000 Natural Gas Compressor Set

Endnotes

1. Joseph Yanick (Office of Energy) and Marianne Vanatta (Basic Industries, U.S. Department of Commerce), "U.S.–Russian Oil and Gas Officials Establish Close Links for Future," *Business America,* May 31, 1993.

Discussion Issues

1. Is Nice, France, the best place to hold the final negotiations? Why?
2. Generally, how important are service contracts in such transactions?
3. What is the potential range of terms of payment in such a contract?